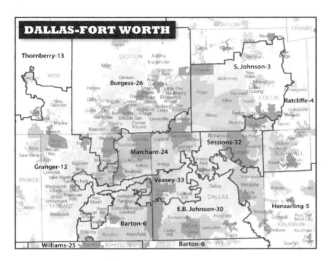

DALLAS-FORT WORTH

Thornberry-13

S. Johnson-3

Burgess-26

Ratcliffe-4

Granger-12

Marchant-24

Sessions-32

Veasey-33

Barton-6

E.B. Johnson-30

Hensarling 5

Williams-25

Barton-6

AUSTIN

Carter-31

Williams-25

Flores-17

Smith-21

McCaul-10

Cloud-27

Smith-21

Doggett-35

SAN ANTONIO

Smith-21

Gonzalez-15

Castro-20

Hurd-23

Doggett-35

Cuellar-28

HOUSTON

Brady-8

Poe-2

McCaul-10

Jackson Lee-18

Babin-36

Culberson-7

G. Green-29

A. Green-9

Olson-22

Weber-14

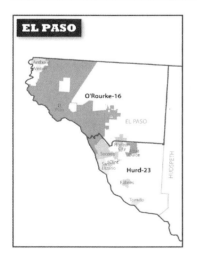

EL PASO

O'Rourke-16

Hurd-23

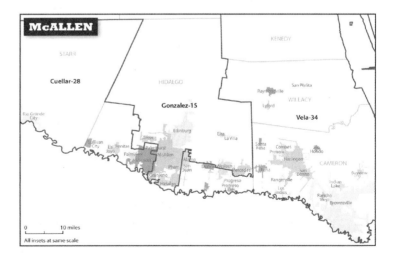

McALLEN

Cuellar-28

Gonzalez-15

Vela-34

0   10 miles

All insets at same scale

Students:
Looking to improve your grades?

SAGE
Premium Video

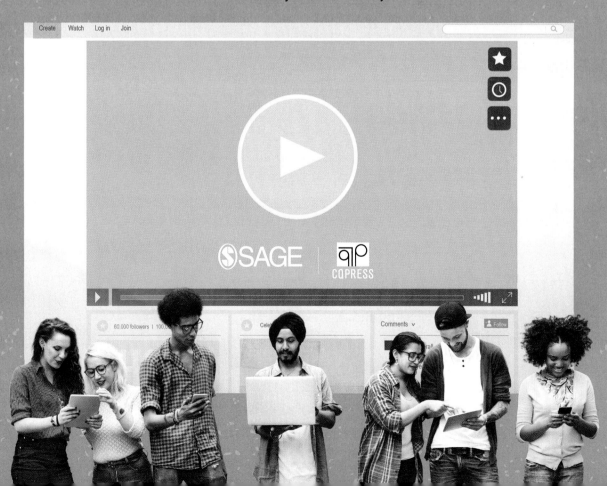

The
Hallmark
Features

Learning tools throughout the text help your students make sense of the dynamics and complexities of Texas politics. Learning objectives set clear expectations, core assessment and Chapter Review questions keep students on track, and features prompt critical thinking and deeper learning.

- **"TEXAS VS." BOXES** are an extension of the book's comparative method, incorporating a data literacy approach that encourages students to think about how Texas differs compared to other states.

- **"FEDERALISM IN ACTION" BOXES** appear in nearly every chapter and highlight city and state issues, such as fracking in Denton, campus carry, voter I.D. laws, and transgender bathrooms.

- **"TEXAS LEGENDS" BOXES** showcase figures and events that have shaped—and continue to influence—Texas politics. Examples include Sam Houston, Barbara C. Jordan, the League of United Latin American Citizens, and Texas Supreme Court justice Raul A. Gonzalez Jr.

- **CORE ASSESSMENT QUESTIONS** aligned with the Texas Higher Education Coordinating Board's (THECB) *Academic Course Guide Manual* (ACGM) reinforce chapter content and ensure that learning outcomes are achieved.

Sara Miller McCune founded SAGE Publishing in 1965 to support the dissemination of usable knowledge and educate a global community. SAGE publishes more than 1000 journals and over 800 new books each year, spanning a wide range of subject areas. Our growing selection of library products includes archives, data, case studies and video. SAGE remains majority owned by our founder and after her lifetime will become owned by a charitable trust that secures the company's continued independence.

Los Angeles | London | New Delhi | Singapore | Washington DC | Melbourne

LONE STAR POLITICS

6TH EDITION

To some of the women who have
given back to the state of Texas:

Barbara Bush
Kay Bailey Hutchison
Barbara Jordan
Ann Richards

LONE STAR POLITICS

TRADITION AND TRANSFORMATION IN TEXAS

6TH EDITION

KEN COLLIER
Stephen F. Austin State University

STEVEN GALATAS
Stephen F. Austin State University

JULIE HARRELSON-STEPHENS
Stephen F. Austin State University

FOR INFORMATION:

CQ Press
An Imprint of SAGE Publications, Inc.
2455 Teller Road
Thousand Oaks, California 91320
E-mail: order@sagepub.com

SAGE Publications Ltd.
1 Oliver's Yard
55 City Road
London EC1Y 1SP
United Kingdom

SAGE Publications India Pvt. Ltd.
B 1/I 1 Mohan Cooperative Industrial Area
Mathura Road, New Delhi 110 044
India

SAGE Publications Asia-Pacific Pte Ltd
18 Cross Street #10-10/11/12
China Square Central
Singapore 048423

Library of Congress Cataloging-in-Publication Data

Names: Collier, Kenneth E., author. | Galatas, Steven, author. | Harrelson-Stephens, Julie, author.

Title: Lone star politics : tradition and transformation in Texas / Ken Collier, Steven Galatas, Julie Harrelson-Stephens.

Description: 6th edition. | Washington, D.C. : Sage ; CQ Press, [2020] | Includes bibliographical references and index.

Identifiers: LCCN 2018047186 | ISBN 978-1-5443-1626-0 (pbk. : alk. paper)

Subjects: LCSH: Texas—Politics and government.

Classification: LCC JK4816 .C65 2020 | DDC 320.4764—dc23
LC record available at https://lccn.loc.gov/2018047186

This book is printed on acid-free paper.

SFI label applies to text stock

19 20 21 22 23 10 9 8 7 6 5 4 3 2 1

Executive Publisher: Monica Eckman
Content Development Editor: Scott Harris
Editorial Assistant: Sam Rosenberg
Production Editor: David C. Felts
Copy Editor: Rachel Keith
Typesetter: C&M Digitals (P) Ltd
Proofreader: Theresa Kay
Indexer: Laurie Andriot
Cover Designer: Gail Buschman
Marketing Manager: Erica DeLuca

BRIEF CONTENTS

CONTENTS

Texas Tribune, © Bob
Daemmrich Photography.

Rodolfo Gonzalez/Austin
American-Statesman via AP

AP Photo/Eric Gay

Robert Daemmrich Photography Inc/Corbis via Getty Images

CHAPTER 7   220
TEXAS-SIZED JUSTICE

Nikki Kahn/The Washington
Post via Getty Images

CHAPTER 8   246
CAMPAIGNS AND ELECTIONS, TEXAS STYLE

Marjorie Kamys Cotera/Bob
Daemmrich Photography /
Alamy Stock Photo

AP Photo/Eric Gay

© 2015 The Dallas Morning News, Inc.

Marcus Yam/Los Angeles Times

Courtesy of the Office of the Texas Governor

Matt Turner/Flickr

Bob Daemmrich/Alamy
Stock Photo

SOCIAL POLICY: EDUCATION, HEALTH, AND IMMIGRATION

PREFACE

As has often been said, there is no State in the Union whose history presents such varied and romantic scenes as does that of Texas. This alone would recommend it to the general reader and the earnest student. But there is in addition to its interest a weighty reason why every school in the State should give Texas History a place in its course of study. No one who learns well the lessons taught can fail to become a better and wiser citizen.[1]

—Anna J. Hardwicke Pennybacker,
A New History of Texas for Schools (1888)

Mrs. Pennybacker's "new" history of Texas presents a traditional view of the state's history. The copy we used when writing this book originally belonged to Earl B. Persons, the great-uncle of one of the authors. In the century since young Earl Persons first read this quotation in his schoolbook, Texans have written some new history and revised some old. Mr. Persons served in World War I before taking part in the rise of the oil business in East Texas—a period during which he saw his pastures become more valuable for the oil under them than the cattle that grazed on them. The next generation of Texans saw America through World War II, the Cold War, and the space race directed from NASA in Houston. That generation grew up on *Texas History Movies,* a comic version of Texas history sponsored by an oil company. Another generation saw the high-tech boom take root in the state. Texans born today may never own a printed book on the state's politics and history, and thus they will be unlikely to leave their names scrawled in a textbook to remind descendants of the Texas their ancestors knew. (However, today's students can still preserve the Texas they know by buying copies of this text and setting them aside so that their children and grandchildren can share the fun of Texas circa 2019—please contact CQ Press for inquiries regarding bulk sales.)

The economic, demographic, and political changes in the state continually introduce new ways of life to its citizens. Over the past century, as Texans moved from the ranches and farms of the countryside into more urban areas, these cities, suburbs, and exurbs became the natural habitat of Texans. As small towns gave way to cities, Texans found themselves living closer and closer together, meaning that they had to cooperate more with neighbors and fellow citizens. The farmer's lonely but simple commute from farmhouse to field has been replaced by long treks to work on crowded superhighways. For Texans of an earlier time, commerce meant the weekly trip into town to sell goods, buy supplies, and check the mail at the post office. Social networking meant gathering at the local coffee shop to swap stories over breakfast. Today, many Texans remain in constant contact with other Texans, other Americans, and other people from around the world. Many Texans have trouble working when their Internet connection goes down even briefly.

Clearly, we Texans aren't what we used to be. However, our image of ourselves has not changed quite as much as the circumstances of our lives. During the century since Mrs. Pennybacker wrote those words that appear at the beginning of this chapter, most Texans have looked again at our history and found a much more nuanced view of our conflicts with the Mexican government during the revolution and with the U.S. government during and after the U.S. Civil War. Although scholars have reviewed and revised the stories of Texas, Texans have often clung to the more romantic version of our history. At the same time, Texans effortlessly blend together many of the traditions and cultural traits that find their way into the state. One can't help to think about the blending of cultures when revising chapters over a breakfast of jalapeño cheddar biscuits, which combine the state's southern and Mexican heritages, in the familiar confines of Whataburger, a chain restaurant with roots in Corpus Christi that has become a Texas tradition of its own. In Texas, we often take the blending of cultures for granted. Such a meal is neither Mexican nor southern—it's Texan.

Our state's government is in the unenviable position of having to keep pace with all the changes in the state while still remaining true to our traditions and legends. Texas government needs to be both lean and modern, capable of managing the affairs of more than 28 million Texans while retaining a small-town feel and the frontier spirit. Texas leaders must be both engaged and rooted, nimble enough to respond to global competition and regional hurricane devastation but still able to ride a horse and swap stories with fellow Texans, whether over the counter of the local diner or over the Internet on Reddit, Facebook, Twitter, or Instagram.

One of the most remarkable things about teaching Texas politics is that, although many Texas students only take the course because it's required, and so many instructors have trepidations about teaching it, the subject is actually pretty enjoyable. As Molly Ivins said, "I believe politics is the finest form of entertainment in the state of Texas: better than the zoo, better than the circus, rougher than football, and more aesthetically satisfying than baseball."[2] Generations of textbooks have stepped into the breach between these reluctant participants, often with mixed results. Textbooks about Texas politics tend to be rather dry, but the topic can be spicy, as our state's history is full of legends, criminals, preachers, hucksters, and even comedians. Somehow, when all is said and done, the life is too often taken out of Texas politics, and we think that's a true Texas tragedy.

We've tried to breathe a little of that life back into the study of Texas politics. We can't engage in storytelling for storytelling's sake. However, any effort to put together a dry, story-free (i.e., "serious") textbook on Texas politics would lead us to forget the role that the state's legends and myths play in shaping how Texans think and how our politicians behave. You can't tell the story of Texas without revisiting a few tall tales, debunking some persistent myths in the state, and captivating the readers with the true stories that are often more interesting than the legends.

READING BETWEEN THE LINES OF LONE STAR POLITICS

he plan for the book is relatively simple. We open with an introduction to the state and its history in Chapter 1. While much of this story will be familiar to many readers, we feel it bears repeating to bring focus to the political history of the state and to refresh the memories of Texas students who haven't read much about their state's history since middle school. Building on the state's history, Chapter 2 examines the birth and rebirth of the state through its constitutions. That chapter emphasizes that while the Texas Constitution continues to evolve, it has not been able to keep pace with a rapidly changing state. Chapter 3 looks at how the Texas Legislature is elected and how it functions, and also looks at the legislative process. The legislature, which is at the heart of Texas democracy, is a fine example of how changes have been slow to come. Next, Chapter 4 visits the Texas governor's mansion to see if the governor's office is ready to keep up with the dynamic state. Chapter 5 examines many of the organizations that make up the Texas bureaucracy. Chapter 6 considers the court system of Texas, and Chapter 7 looks at the process of dispensing justice in Texas. Chapter 8 examines how Texans elect their officials, including discussion of how candidates campaign for those offices. Chapter 9 looks at how Texans work together (sometimes) through parties, and Chapter 10 explores the impact of organized interests in the state. Chapter 11 considers local government in Texas (including those pesky homeowners associations [HOAs]). Chapter 12 begins our discussion of what government produces: policy. That chapter focuses on our fiscal policy—how and why we tax citizens and how that money is spent. Chapter 13 investigates what Texas is doing in the areas of transportation, natural resources, the environment, and trade. Finally, Chapter 14 focuses on the public education system (K–12), higher education, the state's role in health care, and immigration. It also concludes the book and revisits a few themes.

FEATURING OUR FEATURES

his text is designed to draw readers into the key issues of politics in Texas. Several features of the text are designed to bring the reader's attention to an issue, often helping the reader to see it in a new light.

Texas Legends

John Steinbeck observed after his first visit to Texas, "Like most passionate nations Texas has its own history based on, but not limited by, facts."[3] We have made a discussion of Texas legends a recurring feature of this text. When we look at the characters and stories that fill Texas politics, we often find that Texas's legends differ from reality. These legends play a role in shaping Texans' self-image whether or not they can be proven true. One historian, who suggested that the real Davy Crockett surrendered rather than died fighting—unlike Fess Parker's heroic portrayal of Crockett in Disney's movie version of the battle of the Alamo—was told by an angry reader that the "Fess Parker image has done more for children than your book can."[4] Discussing what has been termed the "Texas creation myth," one writer concluded, "The mythic Alamo of the American collective imagination has become far more important than the Alamo of tedious historical fact."[5] It is odd that Texans have allowed Davy Crockett, Jim Bowie, and other legends of the Alamo to be recast (especially by Walt Disney). Many of the men who defended the Alamo were brave, but their lives were not necessarily family fare. For example, Bowie partnered in a slave-smuggling ring with pirate Jean Lafitte before arriving in Texas,[6] and William Travis abandoned a young son and a pregnant wife before he came to the state.

That these men and women lived hard lives and made serious errors is not the point of retelling their stories. Texas is a place where people come to start over and find a new identity. The celebrated Baron de Bastrop was really a Dutchman named Philip Hendrik Nering Bögel who invented the title when he arrived in San Antonio with very little money. When Moses Austin came to Texas in 1820 to win the right to form colonies in Texas, only to be sent packing by a Spanish governor who distrusted foreigners, it was the baron who persuaded the governor to forward Austin's proposal to the Spanish government. As one author put it, "He was among the first, but certainly not the last, loser to come to Texas to reinvent himself and emerge in prominence."[7] The flaws in Texas's leaders remain evident today. George W. Bush was honest—if not always specific—about the mistakes in his past. Despite those flaws, Texans twice chose him as their governor before recommending him to a nation that then twice elected him as president.

Even as the legends of our history reinvented themselves, we Texans have reinvented our own history. Our recollection of history is less fixed than we care to admit. After the Texans won the Battle of San Jacinto with the battle cry "Remember the Alamo," the Alamo itself would lie in neglect for half a century, a forgotten monument that was used to store onions and potatoes before being restored and elevated as the "Shrine of Texas Liberty."

Our explorations of Texas legends are not an attempt to resolve the debate between views of "Disneyland Davy" and other versions of Texas history. Texans need not be sidetracked by the debate about whether their state's heroes were perfect. They were not. Neither were the founders of the United States. What we need to understand is how important these images are to the people of Texas. Describing the "passionate nation" that is Texas, John Steinbeck noted that "rich, poor, Panhandle, Gulf, city, county, Texas is the obsession, the proper study and the passionate possession of all Texans."[8] The aspirations embedded in our myths play a role in how the state approaches change. Because our legends are about who we once were, retelling these stories now reminds us who we are today and keeps us from drifting too far from our values. At the same time, these legends can tell us a great deal about who we want to be and where our hopes come from. As Steinbeck wrote, "I have said that Texas is a state of mind, but I think it is more than that. It is a mystique closely approximating a religion."[9]

Winners and Losers

Politics involves the distribution of goods and by its nature produces winners and losers. While Texas's history, culture, and predilections may seem vague and distant to students today, the politics that spring from them have ramifications that are very real for the citizens of the state. This text is intended to encourage students to think critically about Texas politics, identify problems, and look ahead to solutions. We will frequently pause and look at who gets what from government by looking at winners and losers in Texas politics and featuring questions that encourage critical thinking. This is especially valuable in studying Texas political history because the victories won by a group in one era most often lay the groundwork for the next battles. Texas is in a constant state of change, and citizens need to consider what issues need to be addressed to deal with these changes and how their fellow Texans might be affected by them.

Texas versus . . .

We will occasionally pause to compare Texas to other states, often focusing on those states that provide the most dramatic or interesting contrasts to Texas. We want to illustrate how Texas is different and why that difference is significant. Because most citizens of a state seldom consider their options, we felt it was important to illustrate the possibilities of state government and to illustrate the consequences of choices that people face. Comparisons were selected to provide examples from potentially familiar settings, such as Louisiana or California, as well as settings that Texans may have little exposure to, such as Vermont or North Dakota. It is our hope that students will come to appreciate why Texas is just a little bit different. Our comparison of Texas to other states is a good place to highlight critical thinking. We pose questions alongside each comparison to encourage students to look at options and ponder what would best serve the state.

Federalism in Action

Chapter 2 introduces the topic of federalism, but it's nearly impossible to leave behind the relationship between the state and federal governments. Federalism permeates a diverse set of issues covered throughout the book, and students can get to know that relationship more intimately. This box feature explores how Texas and the federal government—and Texas local governments—relate on topics including abortion; redistricting; voting rights; lesbian, gay, bisexual, and transgender (LGBT) rights; and campus carry. These are important contemporary issues that deserve greater scrutiny. Questions that go with each box encourage students to think actively about what they've just read and engage in debate or draw their own conclusions.

How Texas Government Works

With every edition, we try to ensure a good representation of visual material because we know that some people simply process information better that way. We also understand that sometimes a picture really is worth a thousand words. We haven't taken those words out of the book, because not everyone gets what the picture is saying, but we have included full-page infographics in this edition—roughly one for each chapter. They focus on processes and structures that convey how Texas government works, and they provide big-picture perspective in showing how Texas compares to the rest of the United States or even internationally. Students will come away with a better understanding of not only how Texas government functions but also how it fits into this wider world in which we live.

NEW TO THE SIXTH EDITION

Texas politics in the twenty-first century spends a lot of time talking about the federal government and the state increasingly finding itself in conflict with local government. We've continued to expand upon our coverage of federalism, especially our feature called Federalism in Action, to cover more of those issues that the different levels of government clash over. This feature appears throughout the book and has been carefully developed to compare the local, state, and federal approaches on a topic. These discussions also encourage students to think critically about the state and federal relationship and probe beyond what they may hear with half an ear on the news or read in a tweet.

At the request of several of our adopters, we have streamlined the discussion of the Texas legislature and combined that material into one chapter (Chapter 3). We have tried to retain the essential elements of the legislative process while trying to make sure that students do not get bogged down in the detail of the process. In addition, we have tried to streamline several other chapters to make the text as efficient and readable as possible. Finally, readers will notice that the impact of Hurricane Harvey can be found throughout the text as recovery from the storm and the lessons we learned (or should have learned) from that storm continue to present challenges to Texas government.

In this sixth edition, we continue to give attention to diversity in the book—from its main narrative and feature boxes to the data it conveys and the photos it displays. We want all students in Texas to find themselves represented within *Lone Star*'s pages, and we welcome your suggestions on how we can improve our coverage.

Like everyone else who teaches in core curriculum at the state's universities, we're very aware of the impact of the Texas Higher Education Coordinating Board (THECB) curriculum standards and have tried to make the connections between the text and coordinating board's assessment goals as clear as possible. The book's chapter objectives and the inclusion of questions on critical thinking, quantitative reasoning, personal responsibility, and social responsibility throughout each chapter are designed to make the instructor's assessment tasks as easy as possible. *Lone Star*'s comparative approach provides a wealth of opportunities to get students thinking from a variety of angles, and many questions are crafted with THECB standards in mind to ensure that students develop these skills. The end of each chapter includes Active Learning assignments that address the standards of communication and teamwork. Further, a set of multiple-choice review questions is now included at the end of each chapter. These questions give students the opportunity to check understanding and ensure they are in command of the key concepts presented in the book. We realize, though, that instructors will want something more, and we've arranged for that in the expanded offerings in our instructor resources, available from SAGE edge for CQ Press.

DIGITAL RESOURCES

Our content tailored to your LMS
sagepub.com/coursepacks

SAGE COURSEPACKS FOR INSTRUCTORS makes it easy to import our quality content into your school's LMS.

For use in: Blackboard, Canvas, Brightspace by Desire2Learn (D2L), and Moodle

Don't use an LMS platform? No problem, you can still access many of the online resources for your text via SAGE edge.

SAGE coursepacks include:
- Our content delivered directly into your LMS
- Intuitive, simple format that makes it easy to integrate the material into your course with minimal effort
- Pedagogically robust assessment tools foster review, practice, and critical thinking, and offer a more complete way to measure student engagement, including:

- o Diagnostic chapter **pretests and posttests** identify opportunities for improvement, track student progress, and ensure mastery of key learning objectives
- o **Test banks** built on Bloom's Taxonomy provide a diverse range of test items with ExamView test generation
- o **Data exercises,** powered by SAGE Stats, promote data literacy and allow students to visualize data through interactive graphics tied to assessment questions
- o **Activity and quiz options** allow you to choose only the assignments and tests you want
- o **Instructions** on how to use and integrate the comprehensive assessments and resources provided
- **Chapter-specific discussion questions** help launch engaging classroom interaction while reinforcing important content
- **SAGE original video with corresponding multimedia assessment tools** bring concepts to life, increase student engagement, and appeal to different learning styles, featuring select Topics in American Government videos discussing foundational concepts in the text
- **Video and multimedia resources** bring concepts to life, are tied to learning objectives, and make learning easier
- Editable, chapter-specific **PowerPoint® slides** offer flexibility when creating multimedia lectures so you don't have to start from scratch but you can customize to your exact needs
- **Integrated links to the interactive eBook** make it easy for your students to maximize their study time with this "anywhere, anytime" mobile-friendly version of the text. It also offers access to more digital tools and resources, including SAGE Premium Video
- **All tables and figures** from the textbook

SAGE EDGE FOR STUDENTS

edge.sagepub.com/collier6e
SAGE edge enhances learning in an easy-to-use environment that offers:

- Mobile-friendly **flashcards** that strengthen understanding of key terms and concepts, and make it easy to maximize your study time, anywhere, anytime
- Mobile-friendly **practice quizzes** that allow you to assess how much you've learned and where you need to focus your attention
- **Chapter summaries** with learning objectives that reinforce the most important material
- **Video and multimedia resources** that bring concepts to life, are tied to learning objectives, and make learning easier

ACKNOWLEDGMENTS

Obviously, we didn't do this by ourselves. We did make all the mistakes. Against all odds, a small band of dedicated people tried their best to detect these mistakes and set us right.

While the book's heart came from Texas, we got some help from friends in Washington, D.C. As parts of this book were being written at a small-town Whataburger, the good people at CQ Press, located far from Texas, labored to keep us on schedule and under control. Despite the fact that they still haven't found the pictures we wanted of the "Los Conquistadors Coronado Burro Ride" at the Six Flags Over Texas amusement park (or hid them from us if they did), we would like to thank executive publisher Monica Eckman, senior content development editor Scott Harris, editorial assistant Sam Rosenberg, copy editor Rachel Keith, and production editor David Felts for their benevolence, patience, and diligence. We'd also like to thank Theron Waddell and the other reviewers who offered up a valuable balance of criticism and encouragement:

Alicia Andreatta, Cisco College

Gabriel Bach, North Lake College

Leda Barnett, Our Lady of the Lake University

Deborah Beange, Tyler Junior College

Annie Benifield, Lone Star College–Tomball

Jeffrey Berry, South Texas College

Dina Castillo, San Jacinto College

Mark A. Cichock, University of Texas at Arlington

Brian Cravens, Blinn College

Richard Daly, St. Edward's University

Kevin Davis, North Central Texas College

Joseph Denman, Blinn College

Cecil Dorsey, San Jacinto College–South

Henry Esparza, Del Mar College

Michael J. Faber, Texas State University

Robert Findley, Odessa College

Bonnie Ford, Collin College

Paul Gottemoller, Del Mar College

Richard Hoefer, University of Texas at Arlington

Floyd W. Holder IV, Western Texas College

Rebecca Jackson McElyea, University of Texas at Tyler

Brian Johnson, Tarrant County College–Northeast Campus

Richelle N. Jones, Texas Southern University

Heidi M. Lange, Houston Community College–SWC

Mary Linder, Grayson County College

Hamed Madani, Tarrant County College–Southeast Campus

Maurice Mangum, Texas Southern University

Thomas Miles, University of North Texas

Eric Miller, Blinn College

Patrick Moore, Dallas County Community College

Brian Naples, Panola College

Sharon A. Navarro, University of Texas at San Antonio

Jalal Nejad, Northwest Vista College

William Parent, San Jacinto College

Lisa Perez-Nichols, Austin Community College

Paul J. Pope, Montana State University Billings

Tim Reynolds, San Jacinto College

Celeste Rios, Austin Community College

Jo Marie Rios, Texas A&M University–Corpus Christi

Robert Rodriguez, Texas A&M University–Commerce

Debra St. John, Collin County Community College

Raymond Sandoval, Richland College

John Seymour, El Paso Community College

Gino Tozzi Jr., University of Houston–Victoria

Christopher L. Turner, Laredo Community College

Joel Turner, Western Kentucky University

Glenn Utter, Lamar University

M. Theron Waddell, Galveston College

NOTES

1   Mrs. Anna J. Hardwicke Pennybacker, *A New History of Texas for Schools* (Tyler, Tex.: Author, 1888), v.

2   Molly Ivins, *Nothin' But Good Times Ahead* (New York: Random House, 1993), 55–56.

3   John Steinbeck, *Travels with Charley: In Search of America* (New York: Bantam Books, 1961), 226.

4   James E. Crisp, *Sleuthing the Alamo: Davy Crockett's Last Stand and Other Mysteries of the Texas Revolution* (New York: Oxford University Press, 2004), 142.
5   Ibid., 144.
6   Ibid., 17.
7   James L. Haley, *Passionate Nation: The Epic History of Texas* (New York: Free Press, 2006), 70.
8   Steinbeck, *Travels with Charley*, 226.
9   Ibid., 227.

ABOUT THE AUTHORS

Ken Collier is a professor at Stephen F. Austin State University, with a PhD from the University of Texas at Austin. He is the author of *Between the Branches: The White House Office of Legislative Affairs* and *Speechwriting in the Institutionalized Presidency: Whose Line Is It?* He has published articles in such journals as *Journal of Politics, White House Studies, Presidential Studies Quarterly, Public Choice,* and *Social Science Quarterly.* His research and teaching currently focus on presidential speechwriting and Texas politics.

Steven Galatas is an associate professor at Stephen F. Austin State University, with a PhD from the University of Missouri. He has published articles in *Journal of Politics, Public Choice, Party Politics, Politics and Policy,* and *PS: Political Science and Politics.* His research and teaching concern comparative elections, voting behavior, and Texas judicial and legislative elections.

Julie Harrelson-Stephens is an associate professor at Stephen F. Austin State University, with a PhD from the University of North Texas. She has co-edited, with Rhonda L. Callaway, *Exploring International Human Rights: Essential Readings* and has been published in *Conflict and Terrorism, PS: Political Science and Politics, Human Rights Review,* and *International Interactions.* Her primary research interests include human rights, regime theory, and the Texas governor.

INTRODUCTION

CHAPTER 1

Chapter Objectives

★ Describe how the state's geography and demographics shape its politics.
★ Discuss the role of tradition and legend in Texas politics.
★ Describe the political culture of Texas and its impact on Texas government.
★ Explain the context of Texas's increasingly diverse population.

After watching immigrants stream across the border into Texas year after year, government officials on the Texas side began to worry that their state was being transformed into a part-Mexican, part-Anglo society that would prove unmanageable and ungovernable as the growing number of immigrants asserted their political power. Some immigrants entered lawfully, patiently working through the government's cumbersome process; others came without regard for the laws, exploiting a border that was too long and too remote to be effectively monitored. Most of the new immigrants proved to be both hardworking and enterprising additions to Texas's society and economy. Many brought their families for a chance at a better life or planned to bring family along as soon as they earned enough money to do so. A few crossed the border to escape legal and financial problems back home and contributed to criminal enterprises or squandered their wages on alcohol and vice, eventually abandoning their families. Established residents worried that they would become foreigners in their own country or doubted that their new neighbors would ever prove anything but a challenge, since many newcomers refused to assimilate or adopt the politics and culture of their new home. Many of the new arrivals stubbornly clung to their native tongue; some even began to demand that official business be conducted in it.

The government felt that much of the problem lay on the other side of the border. Some of these immigrants seemed to be entering the state to foment change, and many had strong ties to political leaders back home. Sam Houston, the former governor of Tennessee, was a close political and personal friend of U.S. president Andrew Jackson. Davy Crockett, also a product of Jackson's Democratic Party in Tennessee, had served in the U.S. Congress and was one of the more dynamic political figures of the day. It seemed likely that his political ambitions had followed him to Texas.

Many of the early Texans who fought for independence from Mexico came to Texas against the expressed wishes of the Mexican government. Whereas early American colonists along the Eastern Seaboard settled among, and then pushed aside, the more loosely organized Native American populations, some early Texans violated a border officially recognized by the American government as they brushed aside Mexican law. The immigration issue—today as then—represents the challenge of governing a rapidly changing state. While immigrants today generate a great deal of revenue for the state through sales and income taxes, they also cost the counties and local governments a great deal in services. Immigrants contribute greatly to the economic success of the state by meeting the demand for inexpensive labor, but they sometimes do so at the expense of native-born labor.

Immigration, then and now, shows us that Texas's placement at the crossroads between new and old has been one of the few constants in the politics of the state. Texas has relished its growth but has often been uncomfortable with the new arrivals who have fueled it. Texans have enjoyed the prosperity that growth brings but have only reluctantly accepted the new Texans and the changes they have triggered.

The 55-foot Big Tex, which presides over the Texas State Fair, is an icon to all Texans, no matter their origin. The 2010 census found that about 61 percent of Texans were born in Texas, 23 percent were born elsewhere in the United States, and 16 percent were foreign born.

While change may be inevitable, a society is rooted by the stories citizens share and hand down from generation to generation. We Texans are especially attached to our state's history and its legends of larger-than-life people and events. Stories from Texas history are more than dramatic scenes we retell and re-create for entertainment; these stories define who we are and remind us of our values. Texas's unique relationship with its history is reflected in a favorite theme park, Six Flags Over Texas, an amusement park originally constructed around Texas history themes and that at one time featured rides such as "La Salle's River Boat Adventure" in the French section and "Los Conquistadores Mule Pack Coronado Trek" in the Spanish section.[1] Like the state it represents, the theme park has undergone constant change since its inception. Today, the legends portrayed at Six Flags Over Texas are decidedly modern, and tourists are more likely to pose for pictures with Batman and Bugs Bunny in front of gleaming metal roller coasters than with the costumed deputies who duel horse thieves in front of the replica county courthouse.

Legends are stories passed down for generations—but stories that are often presented as history. While not always entirely true, legends play an important role in politics. Legends reveal a desire to be culturally connected to our fellow citizens and to a larger entity, and they also tell us a great deal about who we want to be.

So where, between legend and reality, is the true Texas? Even as it takes care to project a rustic frontier image, Texas today is home to many of the most innovative businesses in the global marketplace. Greg Abbott launched his campaign for governor in La Villita near the Alamo in San Antonio, but he did so in front of a large video screen that flashed his message digitally to the crowd. Thus, even as they remember the Alamo and the rest of Texas's past, the leaders of Texas today embrace new technology as well as the state's oldest traditions.

In this chapter, we will chart the contours of this gap. We will start by looking at Texas history and geography, casting an eye toward the traditions and transformations that have shaped the state's politics. We will examine some of the legends behind Texas politics and highlight the differences between Texas and another one-time independent U.S. state. We will conclude the chapter by focusing on the state of Texas today—its people, economy, and culture.

TEXAS GEOGRAPHY

The landmass of Texas defines the state's image as much as it has determined the course of its history. With a land area totaling 263,513 square miles, it is the second largest of the U.S. states, behind Alaska's 663,276 square miles. From east to west, the state spans 773 miles and from north to south 801 miles. The 785-mile drive from Marshall to El Paso takes a traveler from the Piney Woods of East Texas to the sparse landscape of the West Texas desert. Driving the 900 miles north from Brownsville to Texline takes the traveler from the border of Mexico and the Gulf of Mexico to the borders of Oklahoma and New Mexico. The Texas Gulf Coast consists of shoreline and marshy areas, while the Trans-Pecos region includes the arid desert of Big Bend and Guadalupe Peak, the highest point in Texas at 8,749 feet.

Texas runs the full gamut from urban to rural. The state's most populous county, Harris County, which contains Houston, had 4,652,980 residents in 2017, making it more populous than half the states in the United States. All told, the state is home to five counties with populations over one million. Texas also has some of the nation's least populated counties, with Loving County's 677 square miles in the Panhandle occupied by only 134 residents. The state has eight counties with populations under 1,000, and about one-third (eighty-six) of Texas's 254 counties have populations under 10,000.

Texas's size encourages more than bragging rights. V. O. Key, a native Texan and one of the founders of modern political science, pointed out that the geographic size of the state has limited the face-to-face interactions needed to develop closely knit political organizations. While this helped inoculate Texas from the large party machines that corrupted politics in many other states during the nineteenth century, it has also inhibited the formation of beneficial groups that would bring together more benevolent forces from across the state.

The state's size makes campaigning expensive for candidates trying to win votes statewide and has left the state's politicians more dependent on those capable of financing a statewide campaign. The sheer size of the state has also rewarded a dramatic style. As Key observed after surveying the electoral history of his home state, "attention-getting antics substituted for organized politics."[2] In the absence of closely knit state political networks, and given Texans' fondness for independence, the path to power for the political outsider may be a little bit easier. The ability to quickly grab the imagination of voters has given Texas politics a colorful cast of characters rivaled by few other places. Texas's political candidates are often larger than life, and while change has been a constant in Texas politics, subtlety is often lacking. These colorful characters often make for good storytelling, but they do not always make for good government. As former lieutenant governor Ben Barnes once mused as he looked out at the Texas Senate, "there were more eccentric, unpredictable, and flat crazy characters than you'd find in any novel."[3]

Size has contributed to the state's mentality in other ways. With its seemingly endless frontier, Texas represents limitless potential to many. At the same time, its spaciousness offers an escape that reinforces Texans' sense of independence and freedom. With Texans dispersed across such an extensive landscape, history and legends become even more important as a shared culture. The vast geographic distances and the differences in human geography leave many wondering exactly what it is that binds so tightly all these people from all these places and makes them into such fiercely loyal Texans. The answer, of course, is Texas's unique history. As John Steinbeck wrote, "there is no physical or geographical unity in Texas. Its unity lies in the mind."[4]

While Texas's history unites its citizens, it also represents a long string of transitions that brought with them conflict between old and new. As we will see, the Texas political system has often resisted the needs and wishes of new arrivals because those that preceded them were reluctant to give up the power for which they had fought. While this pattern is not unique to Texas, Texas's history offers a vivid tableau of upheaval along the hard road of change.

HISTORY: THE BIRTH OF TEXAS TRADITIONS

The first wave of change began about 12,000 years ago when humans who had drifted into North America some 20,000 years ago eventually found their way into Texas. These earliest Texans hunted mammoths before those large animals became extinct. Later, bison served as a primary food source on the grassy plains that covered present-day West Texas. As changes in the climate began to warm the plains, the land could no longer support the large mammals the hunting tribes depended on, and as a result, hunter-gatherer tribes became more prevalent.

As with native people from other parts of the continent, the Native American tribes of Texas were diverse. About 1,500 years ago, the Caddo people developed agricultural tools and practices that gave them a more stable food supply, which meant less need to roam and more time to form a society with social classes and to establish trading relations with other tribes. By 1500, an estimated 200,000 Caddos inhabited a society that was extensive enough to lead some historians to call the Caddos the "Romans of Texas."[5] Along the Gulf Coast, the Karankawa tribe relied on fish and shellfish for much of their diet. Dubbed cannibals by some, the Karankawas ate only their enemies and were in fact so shocked to learn that the Spanish survivors of the Narváez expedition had cannibalized each other that some Karankawas expressed regret at not having killed the Spanish explorers when they first came ashore.[6] Coahuiltecan tribes roamed the area southwest of the Karankawas, surviving on a diverse diet of whatever they could gather or catch. Because subsistence needs forced them to move about the prairies, these small hunter-gatherer bands lacked the cohesive society that developed among tribes such as the Caddos. The Apaches, who inhabited areas of what would become the Texas Panhandle, lived in large, extended families in a peaceful and well-ordered society.

Christopher Columbus's first voyage brought great change to the Texas region as the Spanish Empire in America began to take root in the Caribbean, Central America, and the Southwest. As would many others after them, the conquistadores Álvar Núñez Cabeza de Vaca and Hernán Cortés visited the region seeking wealth. One of the most significant instruments of change the Spanish brought with them was the horse. Even though the Spanish forces were never a large enough presence to transform the region, the horses they brought changed American Indian society by giving some tribes the means to move their camps more quickly and become more effective hunters and warriors.

The French, led by René-Robert Cavelier, Sieur de La Salle, managed only a brief presence in Texas. La Salle, who, in the view of one historian, had the sort of personality and exhibited the kind of behavior that "led many to question his mental stability,"[7] had an ambitious plan to build a series of posts down the Mississippi River to the Gulf of Mexico, claim all the land drained by the Mississippi, and name it Louisiana in honor of the French king Louis XIV. La Salle's venture into Texas failed, and La Salle himself was killed in an ambush. However, La Salle's incursions spurred the Spanish to increase their settlement of East Texas to counter any future French arrivals.

Although relative newcomers themselves, the Spanish, like the American Indian tribes before them, were suspicious of the motives of new arrivals and sought to bar outsiders; they attempted to strengthen their hold on the area by encouraging their own people to establish or expand settlements in the area. Over the course of the eighteenth century, the Spanish gradually established themselves in Texas through a system of missions and presidios (forts). The missions were designed to bring American Indians closer to God while pushing the French away from the area. Native Americans in the area showed little interest in converting to Catholicism, however, and the Spanish had to supplement their religious outposts with presidios. Given the high costs of maintaining these forts, Spanish investments in the area ultimately proved inadequate, and by the 1790s, there were fewer than 3,200 Spanish-speaking people in Texas.

Building a border wall to keep American immigrants out of Spanish territory was out of the question, but Spanish officials declared in 1795 that local officials should take "the utmost care to prevent the passage to this kingdom of persons from the United States of America."[8] In one of the first recorded verbal assaults on immigrants, one Spanish official colorfully warned that the American immigrants "are not and will not be anything but crows to pick out our eyes."[9]

Despite the efforts of Spanish officials, the tides of change proved too strong to resist, and eventually the Spanish government resorted to giving citizens of the United States land grants to settle in Louisiana (before that territory was acquired by France in 1800). While recruiting Anglo settlers from the United States to serve as a buffer against intrusion by the U.S. government seems self-defeating, the Spanish

MAP 1.1 Independent Texas

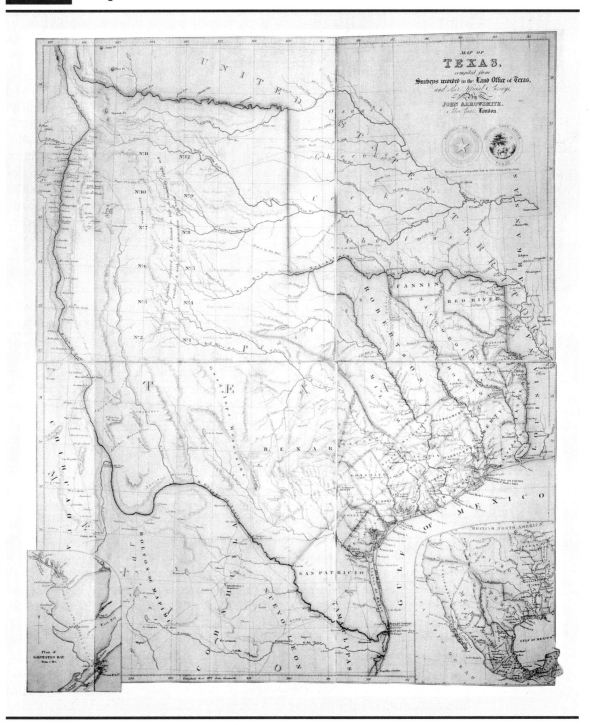

The Granger Collection, New York

The Alamo, the most famous historic site in Texas, was originally part of the network of missions that the Spanish hoped would establish their presence in Texas.

government had little choice. Many in Spain realized that closing off Texas was futile. Spanish officials hoped that by abandoning Florida and negotiating the Adams-Onís Treaty of 1819, which established clear boundaries between Spanish and U.S. claims, American interest would be diverted away from Texas long enough for Spain to build a stronger presence there.

The Spanish legacy in Texas can be seen on any Texas map, as every major river except the Red River bears a Spanish name. Spanish rule also left a different, but particularly Texan, kind of mark: a 1778 Spanish proclamation stated that all unbranded cattle were property of the king, which led to the practice of cattle branding to identify ownership.[10]

The roots of the organized Anglo settlement of Texas in the early nineteenth century can be traced to the last years of Spanish rule in Texas. A Missouri resident, Moses Austin, visited Texas in 1820 in hopes of winning the legal right to form colonies in the area. Unfortunately, the return trip took its toll on Austin after his horses were stolen, and he died soon after returning to Missouri, though not before expressing the hope that his son Stephen would carry on the endeavor. In fact, Stephen F. Austin had little interest in serving as an **empresario** (an entrepreneur who made money colonizing areas), and Texas was initially a somewhat unwanted inheritance. However, Austin, a canny businessman, came to see the potential of the land and ultimately warmed to his task.

empresario
an entrepreneur who made money colonizing areas of the Mexican territories

Mexican Independence

The next round of change began on September 16 (still celebrated by many Tejanos— Texans of Mexican origin—as Diez y Seis de Septiembre) when Father Miguel Hidalgo y Costilla launched the Mexican War of Independence against Spain through his revolutionary "Call of Hidalgo" (also known as the "Grito de Dolores"), which demanded that those born in the New World be endowed with the same rights as those born in Europe. Mexican independence ended Spanish control of Texas, but it did not end the desire of local authorities to stop the growing trickle of immigrants from the United States. The fledgling Mexican government eventually approved Austin's colonization plan in the hope that legal settlers brought by authorized empresarios like Austin would become loyal to the Mexican government rather than their U.S. roots.

By 1824, Austin had assembled the 300 families allowed under his initial contract and begun to settle in Texas. While these colonists suffered more than their share of hardships, Austin's colonies prospered so much that he received four additional contracts to bring settlers to the area over the next seven years. In what would become a familiar problem in Texas, the same opportunities that drew legal settlers and other empresarios to the colonies of Austin also drew illegal immigrants unwilling to deal with the encumbrance of law. Soon Austin and other empresarios found themselves laboring to protect their legal colonies from a flood of illegal squatters.

By the 1830s, there were about 10,000 Anglo settlers in Texas. Some came to Texas hoping to make money quickly in land speculation, but most were subsistence farmers looking for a chance to own land and control their own destiny. Some were fleeing financial ruin brought on by the Panic of 1819; others came to Texas to escape legal problems in American states. Tensions between the Anglos and the Mexican government developed as a result of differences in political culture and the Mexican government's insistence on Spanish as the official language. In addition, many Anglo settlers were Protestants who resented the Mexican government's requirement that they become Catholics. Finally, some wanted to use their land to produce cotton, a cash crop that depended heavily on the labor of the approximately 1,000 slaves they brought with them. This, too, created conflict, as the Mexican government was opposed to slavery. In fact, the risk of losing their slaves kept many wealthy southern plantation owners from moving into Texas.

The Texas Revolution

The tension between the Mexican government and the Anglo settlers eventually turned into that most dramatic political transformation—revolution. Initially, Anglo settlers were divided on the issues of revolution and independence. Stephen F. Austin and many of the established settlers advocated a moderate course, asking for separate statehood within the Mexican nation. The Mexico Constitution required that Texas have a population of 80,000 before becoming a state, a number far greater than the 30,000 inhabiting the area at the time. During the early 1830s, the Mexican government granted some of the Anglos' other requests: the right to trial by jury and the official use of the English language. Despite these concessions, many Anglos remained unhappy and began to openly defy the Mexican government. When Texans in Gonzales fired on Mexican troops who came to take away the cannon the town used for its defense, the Texas Revolution began.

Tejanos were in a difficult position. In the 1820s, about 4,000 Tejanos inhabited the region, including many former soldiers who had been stationed in the area and remained after leaving military service. Many had become community leaders and owned large ranches. While Anglo settlers were unhappy about life under the Mexican government, Tejanos were uneasy about the possibility of living under the rule of Anglo settlers, many of whom considered Mexicans and their culture inferior. At the same time, Tejanos shared the concerns of Anglo settlers who did not want a central government in Mexico City controlling their fate and hampering their economic development.

The politics of the independence movement was often chaotic. When Mexican president Antonio López de Santa Anna became less tolerant toward the Texans' aspirations and sent troops to enforce his laws, the Texans began to mobilize politically, calling for a meeting to organize their response. They termed the meeting the "Consultation" of the people of Texas to avoid drawing the ire of Mexican officials with the label "convention," which implied the authority to rewrite the constitution. The Consultation assembled on November 1, 1835, and on November 13 passed the Organic Law. This law created a government with a governor, lieutenant governor, and the General Council, which comprised representatives from each geographic district. Henry Smith, the leader of the more radical group favoring immediate independence, was elected governor by a 30–22 vote, beating out Stephen F. Austin, who clung to a more moderate course. Perhaps Texans should have worried more about their choice. Smith had been married to—and quickly widowed by—two sisters in succession, only to marry a third sister, the twin of his second wife. Smith's political relationships died even more quickly than his romantic relationships. Smith resisted compromise and suspended the General Council. Meanwhile, the council impeached him after less than four months in office. The effect of all this was a government paralyzed.

The revolution was further hamstrung when the council created a regular army under the command of Sam Houston without formally bringing the volunteers already in the field under Houston's command. The volunteers were notorious for their autonomy and lack of discipline, as Austin would find out on November 23 when he ordered them to attack Mexican troops in Bexar, only to have his order refused.

Voters on February 1, 1836, elected representatives to serve as delegates to a new convention that began deliberations on March 1. Shunning most of the more cautious men who had served in the earlier Consultation and in the General Council, Texans chose younger men, many of whom were newcomers—nearly half of the fifty-nine delegates had lived in Texas fewer than two years. They met in the town of Washington (on the Brazos River) in part because local business owners provided a building without charge. There the delegates adopted, without debate, a declaration of independence drafted by George C. Childress, who had been in Texas for fewer than eight months. The convention continued meeting until it completed the Constitution of the Republic of Texas on March 17. The constitution protected slavery and permitted a freed slave to live in Texas only with the permission of the Texas Legislature. A government ad interim, made up of the members of the constitutional convention, was empowered to run the affairs of the state. One of the first orders of business was the election of David G. Burnet as Texas's first president. For vice president, the convention selected Lorenzo de Zavala, who had served as Mexican minister to Paris under Santa Anna but left his post when Santa Anna claimed dictatorial powers in 1835.

While united by their struggle against the Mexican government, the revolutionary leaders of Texas often fought among themselves even after independence was won. After Houston's ankle was shattered in the Battle of San Jacinto on

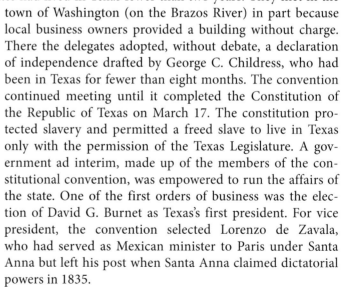

An 1836 flyer offers free transportation and land to new settlers in hopes of reinforcing the Anglo presence in Texas.

April 21, 1836, President Burnet denied the victorious general permission to leave for New Orleans to seek medical treatment. Burnet eventually relented when the captain of the boat Houston was set to embark on refused to take anyone at all if he was not allowed to take Houston.

The Republic of Texas

On September 5, 1836, Sam Houston was elected president of the Republic of Texas by a landslide, receiving 5,119 votes compared to 743 for Henry Smith and only 586 for Stephen F. Austin. The Constitution of the Republic of Texas also won approval from voters, as did a referendum on pursuing annexation to the United States. With over 3,000 citizens voting to seek annexation and fewer than 100 objecting, Texas's interest in joining the United States was clear from its first day of independence.

The government was temporarily located in Columbia but soon moved to a new town located on Buffalo Bayou that backers, much to the new president's delight, suggested be named Houston. The new capital city, like much of the republic, was improvised; the legislature met in an unfinished capitol building with tree branches forming the roof.

While the period of Texas independence was relatively brief, it was neither simple nor quiet. The population of Texas doubled. Just after the revolution in 1836, Texas had about 30,000 Anglos; 5,000 black slaves; 3,470 Tejanos; and 14,500 American Indians. By 1847, its "white" population (including 12,000–14,000 persons of Mexican descent) had soared to 102,961 and its black population had climbed to 39,048 (38,753 slaves and 295 freed blacks).

Change was not limited to population. While the republic's second president, Mirabeau B. Lamar, helped develop the Texas education system, his administration proved disastrous for the American Indian tribes living in Texas. Houston had worked to build friendships with Texas's tribes, but Lamar sought to eradicate them. During the three years of the Lamar administration, the Republic of Texas's debt skyrocketed from $2 million to $7 million and the value of its currency plummeted. Lamar opposed annexation by the United States at a time when the United States was expressing doubts of its own. Sam Houston returned to the presidency only after a bruising political battle. Once back in office, Houston helped make peace with the American Indians and brought fiscal discipline back to government, spending one-tenth of what Lamar had spent.

The path to statehood would not be as simple as Houston hoped. In the United States, northern interests in the U.S. Congress, led by John Quincy Adams, balked at bringing another slave state into the nation. Houston managed to stir U.S. interest by making overtures to European powers—a course of action designed to pique the jealousy of the United States and make it wary of foreign intervention along its borders. As threats from Mexico continued into the 1840s, Texas turned to England and France for help in obtaining the release of Texas soldiers imprisoned in Mexican jails. Houston also positioned Texas for future bargaining by claiming for the republic disputed land reaching west and north as far as Wyoming, including portions of the Santa Fe Trail used for trade between the United States and Mexico. The Texas Congress went even further and passed (over Houston's veto) a bill that claimed all the land south of the forty-second parallel and west of Texas to the Pacific, as well as portions of Mexico—a claim that would have made Texas larger than the United States at the time.

TEXAS STATEHOOD

The issue of the annexation of Texas eventually became central to the 1844 U.S. presidential election when James K. Polk, the candidate backed by Andrew Jackson, campaigned for the acquisition of Texas. Texas's expansive claim to territory was resolved when Henry Clay crafted a compromise whereby Texas accepted its present borders in return for a payment of $10 million. While the joint resolution inviting Texas to join the United States passed the U.S. House easily, it barely squeaked through the Senate, 27–25. John Quincy Adams and Texas's opponents made one final, last-ditch effort to stop Texas statehood by asserting that the admission of Texas through a joint resolution was unconstitutional because that method of admission was not spelled out in the U.S. Constitution.

Texas called a convention for July 4, 1845, to approve annexation and draft a constitution to accommodate Texas's new role as a U.S. state. The only vote in the Texas Legislature against entering the United States came from Richard Bache, who allegedly voted against annexation because he had come to Texas to escape his ex-wife and did not care to live in the same country with her again.[11] Texas was able to retain ownership of its public lands, a term of annexation that other new states did not enjoy. The U.S. Congress accepted the state's new constitution in December, and President James K. Polk signed the bill on December 29, 1845. Texas formally entered statehood on February 19, 1846.

A telling part of the residual folklore of Texas's admission is the notion that Texas retains the right to secede—and if it so chooses, to reenter the United States as five separate states. The origins of this idea come from a compromise designed to overcome objections in the U.S. Congress to the original admission of Texas. The joint resolution that admitted Texas to the Union provided that Texas could be divided into as many as five states. New states north or west of the Missouri Compromise lines would be free; in states south of the compromise lines, a popular vote would determine the legality of slavery. However, the power to create new states ultimately rests with the U.S. Congress, and the right to divide was not reserved to Texas.

J. Pinckney Henderson earned the honor of serving as Texas's first governor after winning the election by a large margin. Texas sent Sam Houston and Thomas Jefferson Rusk to serve as the state's first two U.S. senators. Texas's only Jewish member of Congress for 130 years was among its first: David Kaufman of Nacogdoches, a Philadelphia-born Jew who had worked as a lawyer in Mississippi before arriving in Texas, distinguishing himself as an Indian fighter, and then serving two terms as the Speaker of the Republic of Texas's legislature. Kaufman was only the second Jewish member of the U.S. House, taking office the year after Lewis C. Levin became the nation's first Jewish representative in 1845. Passed over in the selection of Texas's first congressional delegation was Anson Jones, who had been sworn in as president of Texas on December 9, 1844. Jones was embittered by this perceived slight and set about putting together his own volume of the history of the republic, published post-humously a year after Jones shot himself on the steps of the old capitol in Houston.

Americans who had resisted the admission of Texas for fear of provoking war with Mexico soon saw those fears realized when fighting broke out in 1846. Many historians believe that U.S. president Polk orchestrated the Mexican-American War by ordering General Zachary Taylor into territory near the mouth of the Rio Grande that Mexican officials had claimed was part of Mexico. Mexico responded by declaring a defensive war on April 23, with the United States responding with its own declaration of war on May 13. The Mexican-American War ended after troops under the command of U.S. general Winfield Scott moved into Mexico City. The **Treaty of Guadalupe Hidalgo** was signed on February 2, 1848, recognizing the Rio Grande as the official boundary between Texas and Mexico. While the treaty offered assurances that the rights of erstwhile Mexican citizens who suddenly found themselves citizens of the United States would be protected, this promise proved fragile.

The rapid population growth following Texas's annexation further transformed the state. However, not every group grew at an equal rate. Despite the general population surge, the Tejano population declined, and by the 1847 census, the 8,000 Germans in Texas were one of the largest ethnic minorities in a state with a total population of around 142,000, including 40,000 slaves and only 295 free people of color. Even though the Tejanos had fought for independence, many were forced to move to Mexico as the clash of Mexican and Anglo cultures intensified, marking one of just a few times in its history that Texas saw people moving away.

Treaty of Guadalupe Hidalgo
signed February 2, 1848; this agreement between the United States and Mexico ended the Mexican-American War and recognized the Rio Grande as the boundary between Texas, now part of the United States, and Mexico

Texas in the Confederacy

The rise of cotton farming in Texas increased the importance of slavery to the Texas economy as production of cotton grew from 40,000 bales in 1848 to 420,000 bales in 1860.[12] By 1860, Texans held 182,566 slaves, compared to a total population of 604,215.[13] While much of Texas was becoming dependent on slave labor, Sam Houston battled slavery and in 1855 became one of the few southern members of Congress to publicly oppose it. Once again, Houston's personal popularity was undone by an unpopular stand on the burning issue of the day. In 1857, two years before his term expired, the Texas Legislature voted to not return Houston to the Senate for another term, leaving Houston to serve the remainder of his term as a lame duck. Houston responded to the insult by running for governor in 1857. Over the course of this campaign, he traveled over 1,500 miles, visited forty-two cities, and gave endless speeches, many lasting as long as four hours. Despite his efforts, Houston lost the election to Hardin R. Runnels by a vote of 32,552 to 28,678. Houston's loss came in part from his association with the anti-immigrant Know-Nothing Party, which proved unpopular among voters of Mexican and German ancestry who might otherwise have sympathized with Houston's antislavery stance.

After serving out the remainder of his term, Houston left the U.S. Senate in 1859 to run once again for governor, hoping that when the South seceded from the Union he could lead Texas back to independence. This time, Houston was successful,

North Wind Picture Archives/Alamy

Sam Houston

By the time he became a Texan and led Texas to independence, Sam Houston had gone through two wives and lots of alcohol and was, in the words of Texas historian James L. Haley, "considered in respectable circles as unsavory as he was colorful."[i] However, no one better reflects the reality that the greatness of Texas's legends can be found in less-than-perfect people, as Houston guided Texas through some of its most dramatic transitions.

In his youth, Houston generally preferred sneaking away to live among the American Indians to working in the family business. Houston distinguished himself during the War of 1812, serving bravely and winning the admiration of General Andrew Jackson. Houston followed Jackson, his new mentor, into politics and was sometimes mentioned as a successor to President Jackson. However, Houston's first marriage abruptly ended in 1827 in the middle of his term as governor of Tennessee and just two months after his wedding. His marriage over and his political career in ruins, Houston went to live again among the Cherokees. During this time, he took a Cherokee wife without entering into a formal Christian marriage. Over time, Houston's state of mind deteriorated and his hosts eventually stripped him of his original American Indian name ("The Raven") and began to call him Oo-tse-tee Ar-deet-ah-skee ("The Big Drunk").[ii] After abandoning his second wife and returning to public life in America, Houston narrowly avoided jail after assaulting a member of Congress who had insulted his integrity. Brought before Congress to face charges, Houston delivered an impassioned defense on his own behalf, allegedly because his lawyer, Francis Scott Key, was too hungover to speak.

During the Texas Revolution, gossips frequently attributed Houston's disappearances to drinking binges rather than military missions. Some questioned his bravery and military leadership during the war. Many Texans wanted Houston to turn and fight the Mexican Army sooner, despite Houston's protest that his troops were undertrained and outnumbered. While most Texans sided with Houston after his victory at San Jacinto, criticisms of his conduct of the war reappeared in political campaigns for the rest of his career.

After leading Texas through the revolution, Houston continued to play a major role in the changes in the state while serving as Texas's first president during its years as an independent nation. Houston struggled in the years after the Texas Revolution to protect the Tejanos who had served alongside him during the war. Similarly, his years among the Cherokees and his continued fondness for them left him at odds with many Anglos who preferred to see Native Americans driven off or killed.

After playing a central role in winning Texas's entry into the United States, Houston's final political act was the struggle to keep Texas from seceding and joining the Confederacy. Houston disliked slavery and defied state law by freeing his own slaves. He had been one of few southern senators to speak out against slavery, a sentiment that led the Texas Legislature to vote against his return to the Senate. His final departure from politics came when he refused to support the secession of Texas in the American Civil War and, as a result, was forced by the legislature to resign his governorship. If Texans had followed Houston's leadership, the lives of many Texas soldiers would have been saved and the state spared postwar Reconstruction.

Houston finally settled down after marrying his third wife and finding redemption, but he never denied his faults. When asked if his sins had been washed away at his river baptism, Houston joked and said, "I hope so. But if they were all washed away, the Lord help the fish down below."[iii]

However numerous his sins, Houston's principles make him a much more heroic historical figure than many of his more sober peers. From the moment Houston arrived in Texas, he became a central figure in the transformation of the state, and for thirty years he guided Texas through its most turbulent times. While Houston might not be able to be elected today, he did more to shape modern Texas than any other person.

> **How should Sam Houston's contribution to Texas shape how voters think about elected officials?**

 PERSONAL RESPONSIBILITY

> **How do people's personal lives shape how they can serve the public?**

 CRITICAL THINKING

---

i. James L. Haley, *Passionate Nation: The Epic History of Texas* (New York: Free Press, 2006), 107.

ii. James E. Crisp, *Sleuthing the Alamo: Davy Crockett's Last Stand and Other Mysteries of the Texas Revolution* (New York: Oxford University Press, 2004), 29.

iii. Haley, *Passionate Nation*, 277.

defeating Runnels 33,375 to 27,500. Nonetheless, over the objections of Governor Houston, the Secession Convention was subsequently convened, and on February 1, 1861, it voted overwhelmingly in favor of secession. A few weeks later, voters statewide approved a secession ordinance by a three-to-one margin. The Secession Convention approved a requirement that all state officers swear an oath of loyalty to the Confederacy. After Houston refused to take the oath, the governor's office was declared vacant.

The Confederate regime in Texas was a disaster for many. Not only were free blacks victimized, but Germans were targeted for harassment because of their opposition to slavery. Tejanos saw their land seized, and many Tejanos chose to align themselves with the Union. Some enlisted, becoming the heart of the Union's Second Cavalry, while others fought as pro-Union guerrillas. Many pro-Union Anglos were forced to flee the state. William Marsh Rice, whose wealth would one day endow Rice University, had to leave Houston and move his businesses to Matamoros in Mexico.

Reconstruction in Texas

Northern rule arrived with the end of the Civil War on June 19, 1865, when Union forces under General Gordon Granger arrived in Galveston, bringing with them a proclamation ending slavery in Texas. That date, known as "Juneteenth" in Texas, was the day on which the slaves in Texas were actually freed, despite President Abraham Lincoln having signed the Emancipation Proclamation in January 1863. While many transformations in Texas history involved the arrival of new citizens from outside the state, the end of slavery meant that former slaves were now new citizens in their old state. Joining with a small number of Anglo Republicans, African Americans helped elect Republicans to statewide offices and constitutional conventions.

Freedom proved a mixed blessing for the "freedmen." While legally they were free, in practical terms freedmen endured horrendous intimidation and exploitation. State law would not recognize any marriage involving African American Texans until 1869. Although the Freedmen's Bureau was created to help former slaves, the bureau's efforts were sometimes limited by administrators who, while supporting the end of slavery, doubted the goal of racial equality. Texas, like other southern states, passed so-called Black Codes that were designed to limit the rights of the former slaves. In Texas, any person with one-eighth or more of Negro blood could not serve on a jury or vote. With local law enforcement often in the hands of Confederate sympathizers, African Americans relied on Union troops for protection. As elsewhere in the former Confederate states, the Ku Klux Klan became a vehicle for terrorizing former slaves and those sympathetic to their cause, as well as "carpetbaggers" (people from the North who came south to assist or cash in on Reconstruction) and "scalawags" (Republicans of local origin).

In January 1866, Texans elected delegates to a convention to draft a new state constitution aimed at winning the state readmission into the United States. However, the Texas Legislature seemed to have missed the news that the South had lost the war: the legislature refused to ratify the Thirteenth Amendment (ending slavery) and Fourteenth Amendment (guaranteeing equal rights) and instead drafted a framework of laws limiting the rights of freed slaves. The Constitution of 1866 failed to meet the demands of the Radical Republicans, who had won control of the U.S. Congress in the 1866 election. While much has been made of the influx of carpetbaggers during this time, in fact the political transition to Republican control of Texas government during Reconstruction resulted less from an influx of outsiders from the northeast and more from freed slaves gaining the right to vote at the same time that supporters of the Confederacy lost their right to vote or hold office after Congress passed the Second Reconstruction Act. With most white Democrats purged both from office and from voting lists, the next constitutional convention was dominated by Republicans, who accounted for seventy-eight of the ninety delegates. The resulting Constitution of 1869 won for Texas readmission to the United States by including many provisions granting rights to freed slaves: the rights to vote, run for office, serve on juries, testify in court against whites, and attend public schools.

The End of Reconstruction and Rise of the "Redeemers"

Texas politics was transformed again when Reconstruction ended and more Confederate sympathizers were allowed to vote. The Democrats (the party of the white Confederate sympathizers) won control of the legislature in the election of 1872. Like the emancipation of the slaves, this transformation of Texas politics did not arise from an influx of new Texans but rather resulted from the renewal of citizenship of old citizens. Republican E. J. Davis was widely despised by Democrats, who considered him at best a symbol of northern oppression and at worst incredibly corrupt. Once in control of Texas government, the Democrats proclaimed themselves "Redeemers" and removed the last remnants of Republican rule. On August 2, 1875, the Texas Legislature authorized a new constitutional convention and elected three delegates each from the state's thirty senatorial districts. None of the ninety members of the 1875 convention had been members of the convention that drafted the Constitution of 1869, and the partisan composition was dramatically different. Seventy-five members were Democrats while only fifteen were Republicans. At least forty were members of the Patrons of Husbandry, also called the Grange, an economic and political organization of farmers. Voters ratified the constitution on February 15, 1876, by a vote of 136,606 to 56,652.

The rise of the Redeemers and the impact of the Grange are especially important transitions in Texas politics because the constitution of this era remained in force long after the politics and politicians responsible for it had vanished. Texas has continued to change and grow, but the Texas Constitution has not been replaced since, only amended—piecemeal changes resulting in minor alterations to the basic design of 1876. The twenty-five years that followed the Civil War spawned the cowboy imagery that Texans still relish. It was during this brief period that the frontier truly existed, when Texas was in fact home to the quintessential rugged cowboy who tended large ranches and oversaw herds of cattle—a stereotype that has remained rooted in the Texan persona ever since. And even then, the image of Texas as the "Old West" was based on the lives of only a small number of Texans. Although Texans hold the legend of the cowboy in high esteem, the cowboy's life was anything but glamorous. Most were young. About one-third were Hispanic or African American. The ranch owners generally regarded them as common laborers on horseback, and the men who rode the range and drove the cattle were paid less than the trail cooks.[14] By the 1890s, the fabled trail drives had come to an end, finished by drought, quarantines, barbed-wire fencing across the open range, and competition from the railroads.

The state government encouraged immigration in the last half of the nineteenth century to help settle and populate the western part of the state and drive off Native American tribes. Some state officials saw the immigration of white settlers and farmers as a means of counteracting the increase in former slaves, many of whom had become sharecroppers. Germans flooded into Texas, their numbers surging from 41,000 in 1870 to 125,262 in 1890; at this time, Texans of Mexican ancestry numbered only 105,193. While Texas west of Austin may have resembled the Wild West, most Texans resided in the eastern portion of the state, which resembled the "New South" that was emerging elsewhere out of the former Confederacy and was characterized by railroad networks and urbanized cities, such as Dallas.

Although glamorized in movies and television shows, cowboys, or vaqueros, led a hard life and were often shunned by civilized society.

The Era of Reform

As Texas transitioned from the farming and ranching of the nineteenth century to the industrial and oil economy of the twentieth century, the state began to struggle with the limits of the Constitution of 1876. In 1890, Attorney General James Stephen Hogg decided that his office lacked the resources to adequately enforce regulations on the state's railroads. Hogg's call for the creation of a railroad commission became a centerpiece of his campaign for governor. The railroads labeled Hogg "communistic," but his economic and political reforms proved popular, and his election represented the first stirrings of the reform movement in Texas. While the creation of the Texas Railroad Commission was heralded as a means to achieve fair competition, in practice it was often used to restrict out-of-state railroads and protect Texas-based businesses from international competitors.

Frustrated by the lack of responsiveness from the Democrats to their needs, farmers organized the People's Party, more commonly known as the Populist Party. While the populists were short-lived, their call for radical reforms, including public ownership of the railroads, and their willingness to reach out to black voters rattled the political order. After the populists were absorbed into the Democratic Party, the progressives took up the role of reform party. In contrast to the populists' narrow base in agricultural communities, the progressives emerged in the 1890s as a broader reform movement attacking both the railroads that bedeviled the farmers and the big industries that challenged urban labor.

While progressive candidates for governor won elections, their legislative victories were limited. Thomas Campbell won the governorship in the election of 1906 only to see much of his progressive agenda hijacked or sidetracked by the legislature. Most crucially, Campbell was unable to win approval of statewide referenda and recall. Legislation requiring that insurance companies invest 75 percent of their premiums in Texas did change the way insurance companies operated, but this mainly benefited Texas businesses and drove foreign insurers from the state.

The progressive movement in Texas became consumed by the alcohol prohibition issue, in part because Texas politics lacked the large corporations and big-city political machines that energized the efforts of progressives in the North. Much of the prohibitionists' efforts took place at the local level; they were especially successful at winning local option elections that outlawed drinking. In 1891, the Texas Legislature put a prohibitionist constitutional amendment before the state's voters. The campaign was intense, and voters turned out at more than twice the rate they had in the previous gubernatorial election to narrowly reject the amendment by a 237,393 to 231,096 vote.

While the emergence of a new Texas economy early in the twentieth century and the reforms of the progressive movement captured the attention of many voters, others remained fixated on the old issues of race and the Civil War. In a struggle that foreshadows today's battle over the history that is taught in Texas's classrooms, Governor Oscar Branch Colquitt struggled in his 1912 reelection bid because he had criticized the state textbook board for rejecting a history book because it contained a photograph of Abraham Lincoln. Meanwhile, voters flocked to see Colquitt's opponent, William Ramsay, who played upon southern sentiments in his speeches and had bands play "Dixie" during campaign events. Prohibition was a hotly contested issue on its own and reflected old racial hatreds as alcohol was portrayed as a vice of the Germans and Mexicans.

No one better personifies the failures of Texas progressives to produce reform in the state than James E. "Pa" Ferguson. While the rest of the Texas political system obsessed over prohibition, "Farmer Jim" shunned the issue and instead won office with promises of capping how much rent tenant farmers could be charged by their landlords. Ferguson's tenant farmer law was ultimately ruled unconstitutional, but he remained a hero to the state's small farmers. Ferguson could be charming, but his politics were often petty. For example, he used appointments to the board of Prairie View State Normal and Industrial College to remove Principal Edward Blackshear, who had had the temerity to support a political rival. Ferguson also took his personal political fight to the University of Texas (UT), demanding the removal of William J. Battle, the president of the university. When asked his reason for wanting Battle's removal, Ferguson proclaimed, "I don't have to give any reason. I am Governor of the State of Texas."[15] Later, Ferguson vetoed appropriations for the university. After Ferguson was elected to a second term in 1916, his battle with the university and its allies ultimately brought him down. On July 23, 1917, the Speaker of the Texas House called for a special session to consider impeachment, and in August the Texas House voted on twenty-one articles of impeachment, including charges dealing with Ferguson's personal finances, especially bank loans. The Senate found him guilty on ten charges, primarily those dealing with his finances. While impeachment removed Ferguson from the governor's office and disqualified him from holding other public office, Texas was not so easily rid of his influence.

Ferguson's departure made passage of statewide prohibition easier. The presence of military training camps in Texas led prohibitionists to argue that patriotism required that the state protect young recruits from liquor. Initially, the Texas Legislature simply made it illegal to sell alcohol within ten miles of a military base. The next year, in May 1919, Texas voters approved an amendment to the Texas Constitution that brought prohibition to Texas a year before it went into effect nationwide.

As in other states, prohibition in Texas proved unworkable, as many Texans refused to give up alcohol. The legislature contributed to the failure of the initiative by providing very little funding for the enforcement necessary to make prohibition a success. Organized crime thrived on the revenue that illegal alcohol distribution and sales brought and allegedly worked with prohibitionists to keep alcohol illegal. During prohibition, over 20 percent of all arrests in the state were related to prohibition.[16] Galveston became a major center for liquor smuggling as foreign ships anchored along "Rum Row," a line just beyond U.S. territorial waters where boats dropped anchor to distribute alcohol just out of the reach of American law.

While voters were approving prohibition, they also rejected an amendment that would have embraced another item on the progressives' list of reforms: the right of women to vote in all elections. Some of the resistance was based solely on gender discrimination, but some southern voters believed that granting equal rights to women would open the door to "Negro rule" and socialism.

The economic changes that came with the new century resulted from a flood of oil, not of new citizens. While oil's presence in Texas had been noted since Spanish explorers used natural tar seeps to patch their boats, its impact on the state was not realized until the early twentieth century. A few wells were drilled in Texas in the 1890s, but the state lacked the refinery capacity to make use of the oil. After the first refinery was built in Texas, interest in oil exploration increased, but the state remained a minor producer. That changed in 1901 when the Spindletop oil rig near Beaumont hit oil and gas, eventually producing 100,000 barrels of oil a day. Investors began streaming into the state in search of oil; by 1928, Texas was leading the nation in oil production, providing 20 percent of the world's supply. By 1929, oil had replaced "King Cotton" as the largest part of the Texas economy.

Just as oil investors transformed much of the Texas countryside and economy, oil revenues had a huge impact on Texas government, contributing almost $6 million to state accounts by 1929 and reducing the need for other state taxes. Texas's other major business was lumber, which grew dramatically early in the twentieth century, eventually topping 2.25 billion board feet in 1907 before overcutting slowed production. Highway construction boomed in Texas, and by the end of the 1920s, Texas had almost 19,000 miles of highway. Fruit trees were introduced into southern Texas, providing a new segment of the economy and planting the seeds for future immigration, as seasonal, migratory labor was needed to harvest these fruits. By the 1920s, Texas seemed well on its way to establishing a strong and diverse economy—a trend that would be undone by the Great Depression.

The Great Depression and the New Deal in Texas

By the late 1920s, Texans were beginning to show a little independence from the Democratic Party. The state went for a Republican presidential candidate for the first

TEXAS *Legends*

Bob Bullock

When Texas governor George W. Bush delivered the eulogy for Bob Bullock in June 1999, he honored him as "the largest Texan of our time." Although the state's historical museum in Austin now bears his name, Bullock's path to legendary status was neither steady nor straight. Bullock began his political career aligned with segregationists, transformed himself into a liberal Democrat, and then metamorphosed into one of Republican George W. Bush's most important political allies. Bullock was very much like Sam Houston, a Texan who transcended personal failing to rise to greatness and become a state icon. As Bullock quipped when Hill Junior College put his name on a building, "I'm so happy that they named a gym after me instead of a prison."[i]

Bullock grew up in Hillsboro, Texas, where it seemed to many that he was more likely to end up inside the walls of one of the state's penal institutions than atop its political institutions. Some in Hillsboro attribute to a young Bob Bullock a prank right out of *American Graffiti*. One night someone wrapped a chain around the rear axle of a police cruiser, tied it to a telephone pole, and then called the police to tell the officer on duty that evening about a big fight at a local

café. When the officer leaped into his car, the car lurched as far as the end of the chain before its rear end was yanked clear off.

Bullock battled his way through Texas government as legislator, lobbyist, staffer for Governor Preston Smith, and secretary of state. Even as he worked his way up in Texas politics, he chain-smoked and drank a fifth of whiskey daily. In 1974, Bullock won statewide election to the position of comptroller of public accounts, and he modernized the office's accounting practices by replacing paper-and-pencil account ledgers and mechanical adding machines with computers. Bullock won an expanded budget for his office by promising legislators that, with a few more million dollars provided for auditors and enforcers, he would find a few hundred million more in revenue that the legislature could appropriate. Bullock used these resources to stage dramatic, highly visible seizure raids at some businesses. The raids encouraged other delinquent businesses to settle their accounts. Bullock never shied from a battle, once forcing the Texas Council of Campfire Girls to pay $13,284 for sales taxes on their fund-raising candy sales. He also used the comptroller's ability to generate tax revenue estimates that effectively served as a cap on legislative spending as a tool for influencing state policy.

As much as Bullock mastered political office, he was unable to master his appetites. Bullock occasionally showed up at work drunk and traveled around the state on business accompanied by a companion selected from the secretarial pool. Once, after being caught using a state airplane for personal use, Bullock proclaimed, "Yeah, I'm a crook, but I'm the best comptroller the state ever had."[ii] While he could be blunt in his politics, he wasn't interested in having too much truth reported. When pressed too insistently by reporters at a press conference, Bullock warned, "I keep files on

reporters, too. I could name your girlfriends and where they live and what flowers you buy them . . . if I wanted to tell that to your wives."[iii] When the paper began reporting on his use of public funds for a new truck, Bullock mailed boxes of cow manure to the *Dallas Morning News*, a move his spokesman later defended by saying, "He did it on his own time, on his own money."[iv]

By the time he was elected lieutenant governor in 1990, Bullock had put most of his troubled past behind him, telling one person, "There is nothing left for me to do but what's good for Texas." When George W. Bush became governor, he immediately realized that Bullock's years of experience, fund-raising skills, and legislative connections made him an indispensable partner, especially for a governor new to state government. Working closely with Bullock, Bush built the record of bipartisan legislative success that helped propel him to the White House. The endorsement of Bullock, a longtime Democrat, gave Bush an important boost. Known for closing his remarks with "God bless Texas," Bullock found a way to move beyond the personal controversy that often swirled around him and help Texas forge ahead.

How did Bullock survive political scandal?

 CRITICAL THINKING

Would a candidate like Bob Bullock be electable today?

 PERSONAL RESPONSIBILITY

i. Dave McNeely and Jim Henderson, *Bob Bullock: God Bless Texas* (Austin: University of Texas Press, 2008), 16.

ii. Ibid., 7

iii. Ibid., 114.

iv. Ibid., 141.

time in 1928 when Texans shunned Democrat Al Smith, a Catholic New Yorker who drank. However, many Texans regretted their vote for Republican Herbert Hoover, as Texas was hit hard by the depression that many blamed on him. As many as one-third of farmers in some areas were driven from their farms by the depression, and the Texas oil boom did little to spare the state. Overproduction of oil caused prices to fall to as low as three cents a barrel. When the Railroad Commission refused to act to reduce overproduction, Governor Ross S. Sterling declared martial law and used members of the National Guard to shut down the East Texas oil fields. The desperation of the times brought about the repeal of national prohibition, with "wets" arguing that repeal would aid recovery.

Burdened with a depressed economy and the overproduction of oil and cotton, Governor Sterling ran for reelection against "Pa" Ferguson's legacy, his wife, Miriam "Ma" Ferguson, who trounced Sterling at the ballot box. While the Fergusons finally departed the governor's office for good in 1935, it wasn't long before another character, Wilbert Lee "Pappy" O'Daniel, ushered in a new brand of populist politics. O'Daniel, a former sales manager for a flour mill, became known statewide as the host of a radio show that featured the music of the Light Crust Doughboys mixed with inspirational stories. Purportedly encouraged by listeners' letters urging him to run—although some suggested that wealthy business interests and a public relations expert had done the urging—O'Daniel declared his candidacy, proclaiming the Ten Commandments as his platform and the Golden Rule as his motto. He won the Democratic nomination without a runoff and, facing no real opposition, won the general election with 97 percent of the vote.

Although a colorful personality on the campaign trail, O'Daniel accomplished little of importance once in office, as he lacked the skill to work with legislators and tended to appoint less-than-qualified people to office. After winning reelection to the governorship in 1940, O'Daniel shifted his sights to Washington, DC, when the death of Senator Morris Sheppard created a vacancy in 1941. O'Daniel won the special election to replace Sheppard, narrowly edging out a young ex-congressman named Lyndon Johnson in a disputed election.

TRANSITIONS TO THE TWENTY-FIRST CENTURY

Texas spent the rest of the twentieth century in transition, shedding some old habits. Even with the landmark *Brown v. Board of Education* Supreme Court decision in 1954, Texas managed to resist desegregation, despite the court's mandate of instituting it with "all deliberate speed." Many Texas schools remained segregated well into the early 1970s, when federal courts ordered them to desegregate. In 1954, Texas women belatedly won the right to serve on juries, but further progress toward equality was slow. In the 1960s, only six women served in the Texas Legislature, and the state failed to ratify the national equal rights amendment (ERA). However, in 1972, voters approved an equal rights amendment to the state constitution, and the legislature voted to ratify the ERA (although it would fail to get the required three-quarters of states nationally). In 1975, Liz Cockrell was elected mayor of San Antonio, making her the first woman mayor of a major Texas city.

By the 1960s, the partisan legacy of the Civil War was finally beginning to wear off. In 1961, John Tower was elected to the U.S. Senate, becoming the first Republican to win statewide office since Reconstruction. With the Republican Party showing signs of viability, many conservative Democrats shifted their allegiance to the Republican Party in state elections. This followed years of dividing their loyalty by voting for Republicans in national elections while supporting Democrats for state and local offices, a practice labeled presidential republicanism. The career of Texas governor John Connally is a case in point. Connally, although friendly with Lyndon Johnson and elected governor as a Democrat, served in the cabinet of Republican president Richard Nixon before eventually seeking the presidency himself as a Republican candidate. Texas did not seat its first Republican governor until 1978 when William P. Clements won an upset victory. His narrow victory proved a significant first step, as Texas Republicans thereafter began to score more and more successes. Once conservatives saw that they could win elections under the Republican banner, they began to shift their party affiliation. By the 1996 elections, Republicans dominated, winning every statewide office on the ballot.

Texas Today

Texas can be viewed through a variety of lenses. In a political science course, it is natural to look at the boundaries that define Texas politically. Such boundaries create the most obvious sketch of the state, but this is not the only way of looking at Texas and its citizens. If Texas is, as John Steinbeck suggested, as much a state of mind as a geographic state, then we may need to look at who we are and where we come from.

For generations, waves of people have come to Texas to make new lives for themselves; in the process they have brought with them new ideas and new customs. Texas has always been a meeting ground for different ambitions and cultures. These cultures have clashed, blended, and evolved into a complicated modern state that can be a challenge to govern.

In a classic study of political life in America, Daniel Elazar focused on political culture. Political culture is the shared values and beliefs about the nature of the political world that give us a common language that we can use to discuss and debate ideas.[17] The individualistic political culture that many observers attribute to Texans holds that individuals are best left largely free of the intervention of community forces such as government, which should attempt only those things demanded by the people it is created to serve.[18] Government operates in a marketplace; its goal is to encourage private initiative but not particularly create "good society."[19] The individualistic subculture is most dominant in western parts of the state where vast amounts of land created opportunities for individual success. Texans, initially attracted to the state by the promise of land, were often forced to develop and protect that land without help from the government. According to Elazar, the individualistic subculture is present where people seek to improve their lot and want the government to stay out of their lives. From these roots, a preference for as little government as possible and a general distrust of government persists today across much of the state.

In contrast, the traditionalistic political culture sees government as having a limited role concerned with the preservation of the existing social order. The traditionalistic culture can be seen in areas such as East Texas that were more heavily influenced

HOW TEXAS GOVERNMENT WORKS

Who It Serves

Population by Race and Ethnicity

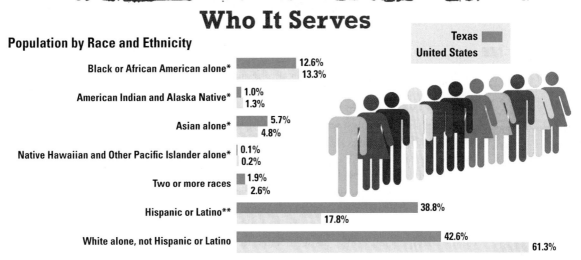

Texas ▮
United States ▯

	Texas	United States
Black or African American alone*	12.6%	13.3%
American Indian and Alaska Native*	1.0%	1.3%
Asian alone*	5.7%	4.8%
Native Hawaiian and Other Pacific Islander alone*	0.1%	0.2%
Two or more races	1.9%	2.6%
Hispanic or Latino**	38.8%	17.8%
White alone, not Hispanic or Latino	42.6%	61.3%

Source: U.S. Census Bureau, "QuickFacts Texas; United States," July 1, 2017, https://www.census.gov/quickfacts/fact/table/tx,US/PST045217, accessed August 25, 2018
* Includes persons reporting only one race.   ** Hispanics may be of any race, so also are included in applicable race categories.

Percent Hispanic Population by State

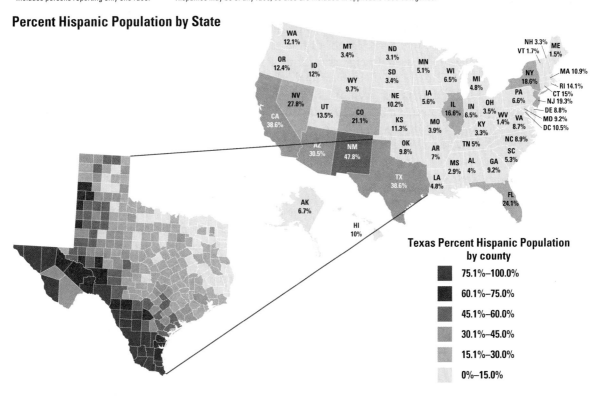

WA 12.1%
MT 3.4%
ND 3.1%
MN 5.1%
NH 3.3%
VT 1.7%
ME 1.5%
OR 12.4%
ID 12%
WY 9.7%
SD 3.4%
WI 6.5%
MI 4.8%
NY 18.6%
MA 10.9%
NV 27.8%
UT 13.5%
CO 21.1%
NE 10.2%
IA 5.6%
IL 16.6%
IN 6.5%
OH 3.5%
PA 6.6%
RI 14.1%
CT 15%
NJ 19.3%
CA 38.6%
KS 11.3%
MO 3.9%
KY 3.3%
WV 1.4%
VA 8.7%
DE 8.8%
MD 9.2%
DC 10.5%
AZ 30.5%
NM 47.8%
OK 9.8%
AR 7%
TN 5%
NC 8.9%
SC 5.3%
TX 38.6%
MS 2.9%
AL 4%
GA 9.2%
LA 4.8%
AK 6.7%
HI 10%
FL 24.1%

Texas Percent Hispanic Population by county

- ▮ 75.1%–100.0%
- ▮ 60.1%–75.0%
- ▮ 45.1%–60.0%
- ▯ 30.1%–45.0%
- ▯ 15.1%–30.0%
- ▯ 0%–15.0%

Source: U.S. Census Bureau, American Community Survey (ACS), 2016. https://factfinder.census.gov/faces/tableservices/jsf/pages/productview.xhtml?pid=ACS_16_5YR_DP05&prodType=table

Sources: Anna Brown and Mark Hugo Lopez, "II. Ranking Latino Populations in the States," Pew Research Center, Hispanic Trends, August 20, 2013, http://www.pewhispanic.org/2013/08/29/ii-ranking-latino-populations-in-the-states/; U.S. Census Bureau, American Community Survey, 2016, https://factfinder.census.gov/faces/tableservices/jsf/pages/productview.xhtml?pid=ACS_16_5YR_DP05&prodType=table; U.S. Census Bureau, "QuickFacts Texas; United States," July 1, 2017, https://www.census.gov/quickfacts/fact/table/tx,US/PST045217.

moralistic political culture
rare in Texas, the view that the exercise of community pressure is sometimes necessary to advance the public good; it also holds that government can be a positive force and citizens have a duty to participate

How does the state's ethnic diversity differ from that of the U.S.?

★ EMPIRICAL AND QUANTITATIVE

How will the growing Hispanic population change Texas politics?

★ CRITICAL THINKING

by the traditions of the Old South. Finally, the moralistic political culture sees the exercise of community forces as sometimes necessary to advance the public good. In this view, government can be a positive force and citizens have a duty to participate. While this view can be found in many places in New England and other parts of the United States, it is rare in Texas.

Elazar's division, based on immigration patterns, is useful in distinguishing political cultures between states overall. However, its applicability to a large and complex state like Texas is limited. Texas continues to be significantly characterized by its long-standing frontier. For most of its existence, Texas had a vast and significant frontier that hampered the ability of Spain and later Mexico to govern the state. Political culture in Texas, as in other frontier states, would develop peculiar preferences and institutions quite distinct from those of states far from the frontier. Life on the frontier was more difficult and more uncertain than life in Massachusetts or Virginia. Moving to Texas meant that in exchange for inexpensive land, settlers had to build their homes, cultivate the land, and defend their home. Law enforcement, for example, was sparse in Texas, with the Texas Rangers traveling around the state. If the average Texan preferred small government and few social services, as Elazar contended, they also came to prize their guns and their right to defend their home. Justice needed to be swift and harsh to deter criminals. This created a punitive understanding of justice rather than a preference for rehabilitation. We see the influence of the frontier continue today in our preferences for little gun control, a permissive castle doctrine (the right to defend your castle), a greater amount of behavior criminalized, and a punitive justice system including the death penalty.

While the discussion of distinct cultures or nations within Texas or the United States might seem foreign at first, it reflects an ongoing discussion in political science about distinguishing *nations* from *states*. A nation is "groups of people who share—or believe they share—a common culture, ethnic origin, language, historical experience, artifacts and symbols."[20] On the other hand, a state represents a sovereign political entity with defined political boundaries.

Colin Woodard has argued that the United States includes eleven such nations, four of which can be found in Texas: the Deep South, Greater Appalachia, the Midlands, and El Norte. (See Map 1.2.) El Norte is actually part of the oldest area of civilization on the continent. It took root when Columbus arrived in the New World and witnessed the Spanish expeditions that had viewed the Smoky Mountains of Tennessee and the Grand Canyon by the time the English arrived in Jamestown. This nation, which includes parts of northern Mexico as well as southern Texas, shares a language, cuisine, and societal norms that are distinct both from other parts of Texas and from the interior of Mexico. While the political divisions created by the Texas Revolution may have tried to divide El Norte, like the *norteños* of northern Mexico, Tejanos value a reputation for being more independent, self-sufficient, adaptable, and work centered than residents of the interior of Mexico.

Parts of Texas are also included in the Deep South nation, a tradition where the remnants of aristocratic privilege and classical republicanism can still be seen in the notion that democracy is a privilege of the few. The Deep South is internally polarized on racial grounds and deeply at odds with other nations over the direction of the state and the country. Greater Appalachia runs through much of the northern part of the state and shares some of the Deep South's resistance to the intrusion of northern nations via the Civil War, Reconstruction, and subsequent social and economic reforms. Greater

MAP 1.2 Texas within Colin Woodard's American Nations

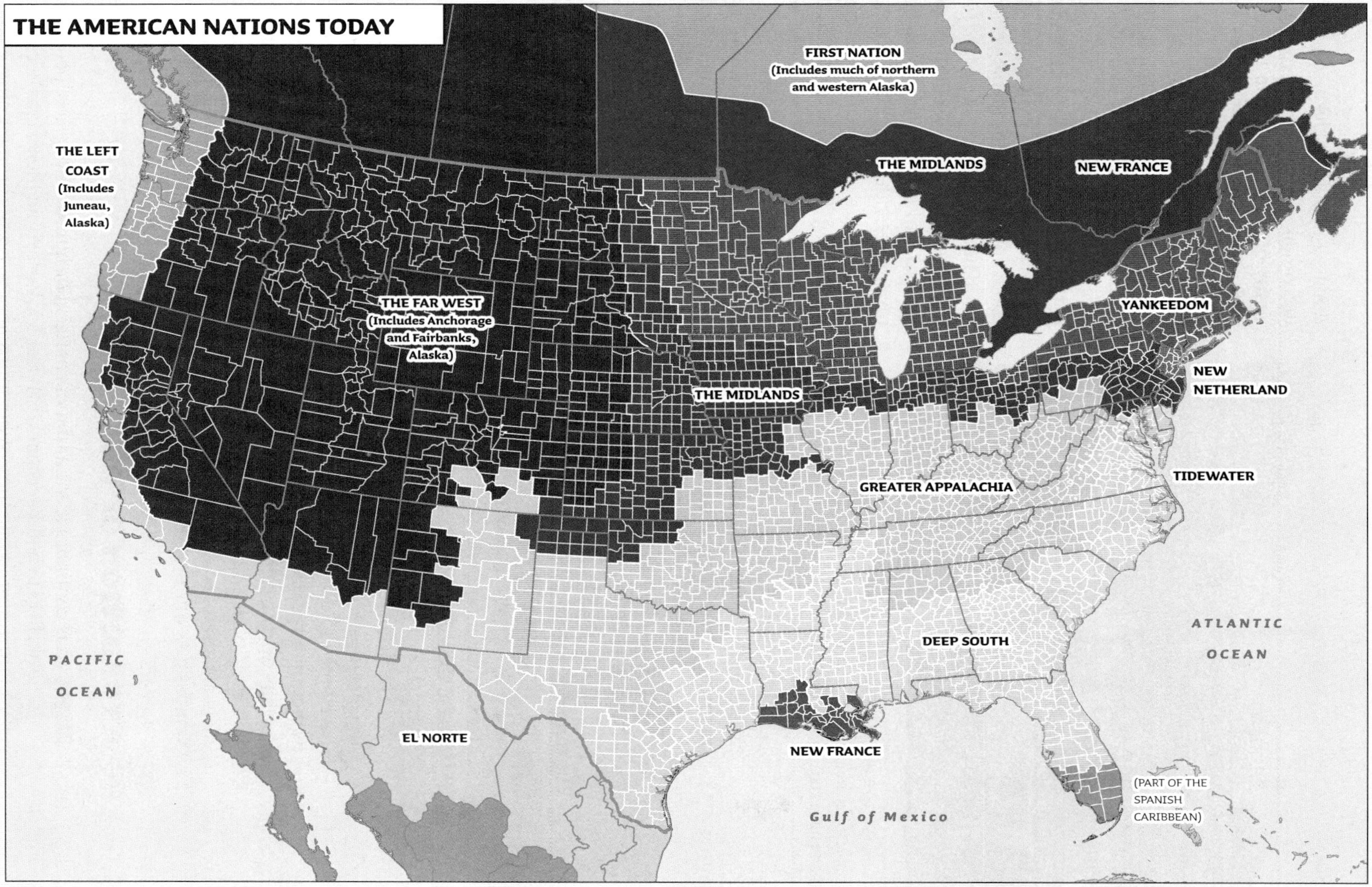

THE AMERICAN NATIONS TODAY

THE LEFT COAST (Includes Juneau, Alaska)

FIRST NATION (Includes much of northern and western Alaska)

THE FAR WEST (Includes Anchorage and Fairbanks, Alaska)

NEW FRANCE

THE MIDLANDS

YANKEEDOM

NEW NETHERLAND

TIDEWATER

GREATER APPALACHIA

THE MIDLANDS

DEEP SOUTH

EL NORTE

NEW FRANCE

(PART OF THE SPANISH CARIBBEAN)

ATLANTIC OCEAN

Gulf of Mexico

PACIFIC OCEAN

Source: *From American Nations: A History of the Eleven Rival Regional Cultures of North America by Colin Woodard, copyright © 2011 by Colin Woodard. Used by permission of Viking Books, an imprint of Penguin Publishing Group, a division of Penguin Random House LLC. All rights reserved.

Residents of Laredo watch the 2017 Washington's Birthday Parade from a rooftop. The parade is part of an annual celebration of George Washington's birthday that reflects the blending of cultures and traditions found in Texas.

Appalachia holds a deep commitment to individual liberty and personal sovereignty but is as adverse to the aristocrats of the Deep South as it is to social reformers from the northeast. The Midlands, which comprises only the northernmost counties of the state, is skeptical of government but subscribes to the idea that it should benefit ordinary people. Residents of the Midlands are moderate and at times even apathetic about politics and care little about either ethnic or ideological purity.

The mixing of cultures in Texas has produced entirely new cultures unique to the state. In no place is this unique mixture more evident than in Laredo's annual Washington's Birthday Celebration, a monthlong festival to celebrate George Washington's birthday. Created in 1898, it takes an American-style celebration and unites it with the city's diverse roots. Today, Mexican food, colonial gowns, and fireworks all star in this celebration of the city's multicultural roots, and Laredoans and their guests move easily from an International Bridge ceremony to jalapeño-eating contests to formal colonial pageants and a Princess Pocahontas pageant. In this sense, Laredo perfectly embraces the tradition of change that defines Texas as very different cultures find their place in the Texas spirit.

Much was made of Texans' independent streak after Governor Rick Perry tossed around language about secession. However, a 2009 Rasmussen Poll taken after Perry's comments revealed that 75 percent of Texans wanted to remain part of the United States and only 18 percent would support secession.[21] The issue arose again in 2016 when Texas Republicans rejected the effort of some members to put Texas secession up for a vote at the state Republican convention. Clearly, most Texans love being Americans just as much as they love being Texans.

The diverse range of legends underlying modern Texas has given Texans a choice of legends from which to draw on. According to historian Randolph B. Campbell, Texans have opted to draw upon the rugged individualism of the cowboys of the cattle drive rather than the slavery, secession, and defeat of the Old South.[22] Even then, the lonely cowboy driving cattle across the open plains is an uncertain guide for Texans trying to find their place in the state today. Texans' identity and expectations of their government are grounded in images of the past that may not be entirely true. Thus, we have to wonder how our understandings of our past are shaping the state's future.

A TRADITION OF CHANGE

Texas continues its tradition of change. For hundreds of years, people left their old lives to build new ones in Texas, leaving behind them signs declaring "Gone to Texas." While these generations of new Texans brought different languages and cultures, all consistently brought one thing—change. Such transformations have defined Texas since the 1500s when newly arrived Spanish explorers turned the Caddo word for *friend* (*techas*) into *Tejas*, a term describing the Caddo tribe.[23] In the centuries since, waves of people have come to Texas seeking opportunity and bringing change.

The changes have not always been welcome by established Texans. When explorer Francisco Vázquez de Coronado's expedition arrived and proudly proclaimed to the Zuni Indians who lived in Texas that the tribe now enjoyed protection as subjects of the Spanish king, the Zunis answered with a volley of arrows.[24] The arrows bounced off the Spanish armor, and today immigrants arriving from across the nation and around the world generally receive a better reception. Still, new arrivals have often been seen by many Texans as competitors rather than partners in the state's future.

New arrivals remain a constant in Texas. The state's population has increased about a hundredfold since joining the United States, growing at an average of just over 40 percent each decade (see Figure 1.1). The U.S. Census Bureau estimated that there were 28,304,596 Texans in 2017, up 12.6 percent since 2010. Viewed differently, the 3.1-million-person growth that Texas saw from 2010 to 2017 is larger than the population of twenty states. Seven counties in Texas grew more than 50 percent in the ten years between the 2000 and 2010 censuses: Rockwall (81 percent), Williamson (69 percent), Fort Bend (65 percent), Hays (61 percent), Collin (59 percent), Montgomery (55 percent), and Denton (53 percent). Of the ten counties nationwide with the biggest population growth from 2015 to 2016, four were in Texas: Harris, Tarrant, Bear, and Dallas.[25]

FIGURE 1.1 Population and Percentage of Growth in Texas since 1850

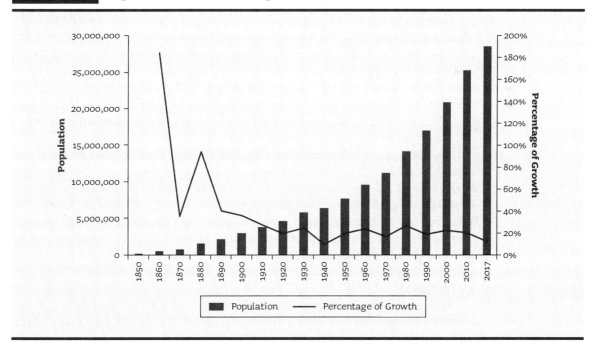

Source: Data from U.S. Census Bureau, "QuickFacts: Texas," accessed August 23, 2018, http://www.census.gov/quickfacts/table/PST045215/48.

According to the Office of the Texas State Demographer, Texas will do a lot more growing. Changes in immigration and birth rates make predictions difficult, but the state could have as many as 31.2 million citizens in 2050, even if there is zero migration into the state. If migration into the state continues at the pace seen from 2000 to 2010, then 2050 could see over 54.4 million Texans.[26] How today's Texans make room for the millions of new residents expected over the next two decades will be an important part of the state's politics.

While we often focus on the arrival of new Texans and the state's growing population, part of the change that defines Texans is that we have people both coming and going. In 2013, Texas had an estimated 545,715 "in-migrants" and 411,966 "out-migrants."[27] We sometimes focus on the number of "net migrants" (the increase in the number of residents) while forgetting that some years see almost 1 million people move to or move out of the state.

What do the different measures of population tell us about changes to Texas?

★ CRITICAL THINKING

How do the state's recent changes in population compare to early Texas history?

★ EMPIRICAL AND QUANTITATIVE

Change is especially difficult for a political system that must meet the needs of a large, diverse, and ever-shifting population. Political systems tend to represent the status quo, and established groups are inherently threatened by changes to the government's base of power. Because politics is, in the words of a classic definition, about who gets what, newcomers compete against established residents, leaving the government to resolve the conflict and determine who wins and who loses. Politics becomes a battle between the old and the new, and this battle is often repeated in Texas. The Texas Revolution, which came about when Mexican officials refused to meet the needs of Anglo settlers, is probably the most dramatic—and ultimately literal—example of politics as a battle.

A snapshot of Texas reveals increasing population diversity as the state grows. In 2005, Texas became a majority-minority state, joining Hawaii, New Mexico, and California as states in which the nation's majority (Anglos) make up less than half of the state's population. In Texas today, Anglos account for 42.6 percent of the state's population. While about 77 percent of Texas residents describe themselves as white, this category includes both Anglos and Hispanics (see the "How Texas Government Works: Who It Serves" infographic). About 16.7 percent of Texans (compared to 13.2 percent of Americans) are foreign born, and just over one in three Texans speaks a language other than English at home (compared to one in five Americans).[28]

The state's future will be even more diverse. The state demographer estimates that from 2010 to 2050, Texas's Hispanic population will grow from just under 10 million to just over 30 million. During that same time, the Anglo population is expected to stay relatively unchanged at 11 to 12 million.[29] While some of the rise of Hispanics in Texas may result from immigration, the number will rise even if immigration ends because the state's Hispanic population is much younger than its Anglo population. In 2017, Hispanics in Texas under age thirty-seven outnumbered Anglos in the same age group. Thus, the Texans most likely to make baby Texans in the immediate future are Hispanic.

While much has been made of the emergence of a Latino majority in Texas, we have to remember how broad these racial categories are and how many differences exist within such groups. The term *Hispanic* includes many recent immigrants who may share a language but have origins that go beyond those of the Mexican Americans usually considered Hispanics in Texas. In fact, Texas has seen immigration from both Central and South America. While Hispanics who come from countries in these regions may share a language, the nations are very different. At the same time, some Hispanics in Texas trace their lineage to Spain's control over the region before the United States, Texas, or even Mexico existed. These Texan families represent some of the state's oldest, and including them in the same category with the state's newest arrivals illustrates the problems of relying on such broad categories.

At the start of the twentieth century, German Americans were considered distinct and foreign enough to generate fear among some that they would align themselves with Germany during World War I. Many of 2050's Hispanics will be the product of several generations of living in America and all of the socialization inherent in the public school system, media, and broader culture.

Some observers believe that the rising number of Hispanics will lead inevitably to a Democratic electoral majority in Texas. In 2016, Hispanics nationally favored Hillary Clinton over Donald Trump 66 percent to 28 percent, but in Texas the margin was slimmer at 61 percent to 34 percent.[30] Of course, the popularity of the two parties among Hispanics will turn on a variety of policy issues. Hispanics, like German Americans and other groups, will continue to evolve and eventually become a natural part of political life in Texas. Further, while segregation remains a reality in the United States, that barrier is often not enough to stop the cause of true love; as one study found, 26 percent of Hispanics had married someone of another race or ethnicity.[31] By 2050, several generations will have married Texans from other demographic groups and have produced Texans who do not fit the demographic labels we attach so much meaning to today. Today's great-grandchildren of the German and Irish immigrants likely put little stock in the distinctions between these groups.

Also overlooked in the debate over immigration today is the rising number of immigrants coming from Asia. A recent analysis by the state demographer's office found that while 44.1 percent of noncitizen immigrants came to Texas from Latin America, 35.8 percent came from Asia and another 13.1 percent from Africa and other regions.[32] Thus, new Texans are more increasingly diverse, a reflection in part of the state's continued involvement in an increasingly complex global economy.

The state's rural nature has been transformed, and today about 80 percent of Texans live in 1,210 cities or suburbs. In fact, Texas has four of the country's fifteen largest cities: Houston (#4), San Antonio (#7), Dallas (#9), and Austin (#11).[33] Texas's suburbs have seen even higher rates of growth. In fact, the U.S. Census Bureau found that five Texas cities were among the ten fastest-growing cities in the United States, with Conroe (#1), Frisco (#2), McKinney (#3), Georgetown (#5), and New Braunfels (#9) having growth rates of 4.7 percent or higher from 2015 to 2016.[34]

Texans often quip that they are "the buckle in the Bible Belt," reflecting a strong Christian presence in the state. A 2016 study found that Texas rated as the eleventh most religious state, with 63 percent of Texans saying religion is very important in

FIGURE 1.2 Religious Traditions in Texas

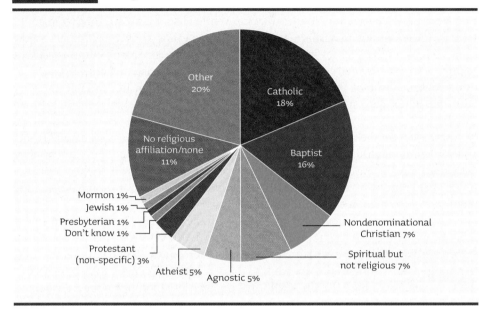

Source: Data from University of Texas and *Texas Tribune*, "Texas Statewide Survey," October 15–21, 2018, https://static
.texastribune.org/media/files/9ec7041712e3c2c2d7e23f79ba5d2387/ut-tt-201810-summary-3.pdf.

their lives and 69 percent reporting that they believe in God with absolute certainty (Alabama led the nation with 77 percent saying religion is very important in their lives and 82 percent saying they believe in God with absolute certainty).[35] While most Texans might generally fall under the label "Christian," the more specific practices that fall under that broad category are quite diverse. For example, one recent poll found that the percentage of Catholics (18 percent) and Baptists (16 percent) was roughly equal in Texas.[36] (See Figure 1.2.)

The state's economy is as diverse as its people. The state still has more farms and ranches (241,500 averaging 537 acres) than any other state,[37] but Texans today are engaged in providing virtually every kind of product and service (see Table 1.1). Educational services and health care are the biggest industries, while agriculture, despite the image, is one of the smallest, with fewer people working in agriculture than in public administration.

The Texas economy is massive and still growing. In 2016, the state's economy was estimated to have produced almost $1.6 trillion in gross state product (GSP). If Texas were a country, its economy would be one of the largest in the world, just behind Brazil and ahead of Canada. (See Table 1.2.)

Texas is a state on the move, sometimes more than others. While Texas is often defined by its open spaces, many Texans spend much of their day stuck in traffic. According to the Census Bureau, the average working Texan spends 25.9 minutes every day getting to and from work. As more people move to Texas, the demand for roads

How much religious diversity does Texas have?

★ EMPIRICAL AND QUANTITATIVE

What is the best way of summarizing the religious views of Texans?

★ CRITICAL THINKING

and mass transit systems will only increase, presenting new challenges for local governments as well as the state.

Even as Texas grapples with challenges within its borders arising from its diverse, growing population and expansive economy, it also must deal with competition from overseas. While Texans have always relished their independence, the state today must work to ensure its place in a growing global economy. Even farmers must look overseas as they attempt to cultivate foreign markets for their products while warding off foreign competitors.

While the wealthy Texas oil baron or cattle rancher is a familiar image in movies and television, Texans fall below the national average on many measures of wealth. Compared to the national average, Texans have a lower per capita income ($27,828 versus $29,929 in 2017), a higher poverty rate (15.6 percent versus 12.7 percent of all Americans), and a lower rate of home ownership (61.9 percent versus 63.6 percent). While Texas may be a land of great wealth, it is also a land of great need.[38] One study found that Texas ranked seventh in income inequality.[39]

What does the number of Texans working in an industry tell us about the politics of the state?

⭐ CRITICAL THINKING

How accurately do the job categories reflect the differences in jobs in Texas?

⭐ EMPIRICAL AND QUANTITATIVE

TABLE 1.1 Texas Civilian-Employed Population, Sixteen Years and Older

Employment	Number Employed	Percentage of Employed
Agriculture, forestry, fishing and hunting, and mining	354,801	2.7%
Construction	1,121,391	8.7%
Manufacturing	1,082,507	8.4%
Wholesale trade	380,131	2.9%
Retail trade	1,479,675	11.4%
Transportation and warehousing, and utilities	714,666	5.5%
Information	230,634	1.8%
Finance and insurance, and real estate and rental and leasing	870,728	6.7%
Professional, scientific, and management, and administrative and waste management services	1,471,877	11.4%
Educational services, and health care and social assistance	2,826,330	21.9%
Arts, entertainment, and recreation, and accommodation and food services	1,204,191	9.3%
Other services, except public administration	682,935	5.3%
Public administration	507,590	3.9%
Total	**12,927,456**	**100.0%**

Source: U.S. Census Bureau, "2016 American Community Survey 1-Year Estimates," accessed March 13, 2018, https://factfinder.census.gov/faces/tableservices/jsf/pages/productview.xhtml?pid=ACS_12_1YR_DP03&prodType=table.

TABLE 1.2	Gross Domestic Product, 2016	
Rank	**Nation**	**Millions of Dollars**
1	United States*	$18,624,475
2	China	$11,199,145
3	Japan	$4,940,159
4	Germany	$3,477,796
5	United Kingdom	$2,647,899
6	California**	$2,622,731
7	France	$2,465,454
8	India	$2,263,792
9	Italy	$1,858,913
10	Brazil	$1,796,187
11	Texas**	$1,599,283
12	Canada	$1,529,760
13	New York**	$1,500,055
14	South Korea	$1,283,163
15	Spain	$1,237,255
16	Australia	$1,204,616
17	Mexico	$1,046,923

Source: Compiled from data from the Bureau of Economic Analysis and World Bank.

* Includes all states.

** Calculated as if an independent country.

Thus, the state with a constitution that was authored in the nineteenth century by isolated farmers who formed the Grange to connect with other farmers has become a booming high-tech center with citizens connected to each other and to the wider world through Facebook, Twitter, Instagram, and Snapchat. Visitors arriving in the Texas capital will not find lonely cowboys astride horses on the open plains; instead, they will encounter computer engineers and game programmers checking social networks on their smartphones while stuck in traffic.

WINNERS AND LOSERS

Certainly one of the most significant forces of change that has shaped Texas's past, present, and future is immigration. Texas is a state defined by its ever-changing and constant immigrant population. In understanding Texas's past and trying to prepare Texas for the future, no immigrant population is more integral to the state than the Hispanic population. As the historical overview in this chapter makes clear, Tejanos in early Texas were central to its development. As Anglos came to dominate the state, historical revisionists overlooked early cooperation between Anglos and Tejanos, emphasizing and often exaggerating the tensions between the two groups. Just as many Tejanos were driven out of Texas after the revolution against Mexico, their contributions to the war on both sides of the conflict were driven from the pages of Texas history. At some point the Mexican flag failed to appear in the Alamo's "Hall of Honor" that commemorates the country of birth of the Alamo's defenders, allowing Texans to forget that nine of the eleven defenders of the Alamo born in the Mexican territory of Texas had Hispanic origins. Juan Nepomuceno Seguín, who neither wrote nor spoke English, was a close friend of Stephen F. Austin and helped drive Mexican forces from San Antonio before slipping out of the Alamo to seek reinforcements. Later, Seguín joined Sam Houston's army at the decisive battle of San Jacinto. As one historian put it, "'Remember the Alamo' became a formula for forgetfulness."[40] A rapidly anglicizing Texas replaced the legend of heroic Tejanos with a legend that emphasized dictatorial Mexican rulers seeking the expulsion of the Anglos.

The Tejano population of Texas declined from the time of the revolution until a repressive regime in Mexico, coupled with decades of revolution within that country, created a new wave of immigrants. This tripled the Mexican population in Texas from 1900 to 1920. While these immigrants played an important role in cotton production, they were often not welcome and took their place somewhere between Anglos and African Americans, unaccepted in either community. Techniques such as "white primaries," which were used to exclude African Americans from voting, were eventually also employed against Tejanos. As the state continued to change and immigrants continued to move into Texas, Hispanics were marginalized in the political process as well as in the history books.

TEXAS VERMONT

A comparison of Texas and Vermont illustrates the diversity of states within the United States. Vermont, a northeastern state, got its start when Ethan Allen and the Green Mountain Boys rebelled against attempts by New York and New Hampshire to exert control over the region after the American Revolution. On January 15, 1777, the independent Republic of New Connecticut was declared; later, the name was changed to the Republic of Vermont. Vermont sent ambassadors to France, the Netherlands, and the United States. In 1791, Vermont entered the United States as the fourteenth state to balance the admission of slaveholding Kentucky as the fifteenth state.

While both Texas and Vermont share a history of independence before joining the United States, the similarity ends there. Geographically, Vermont is quite small, at 9,250 square miles. Vermont's size is smaller than the combined area of the largest two Texas counties (Brewster and Pecos counties in West Texas, together totaling 10,957 square miles). Vermont's landscape is dominated by the Green Mountains, abundant forests, and plentiful rivers and streams. As the second-largest state by area, Texas covers a vast territory that varies tremendously in land formations, water resources, and natural resources.

The demographics of the two states are also strikingly different. Settled by the English and some French colonists from nearby Quebec, Vermont remains among the most homogeneous states in the United States. In 2017, Vermont held the distinction of being one of the "whitest" states in the United States, with over 94 percent of its residents describing themselves as white and not of Hispanic origin; Texas, in contrast, was among the most racially and ethnically diverse states, with the largest group, Anglos, constituting only 42.6 percent of the population.

Vermont also consistently ranks as one of the smallest states in population. In 1850, the first census in which Texas participated, Vermont had a slightly larger population than Texas. Immigration over the following decade saw Texas surpass Vermont in population by the 1860 census, at which point Texas already had over 600,000 residents. It would take Vermont 140 years to reach that level of population. By the time it did, in 2000, Texas recorded over 22 million residents.

Large cities are found throughout Texas; three of the nation's ten largest cities are located in Texas. Vermont's largest city, Burlington (42,239 in 2017), is so small that it would rank seventy-fifth in city size in Texas. Even the images of the two states generate contrasts. Texas is the land of open plains, oil wells, cattle, gunslinging cowboys, and big-time football. Vermont is the land of maple syrup, ice cream, fall foliage, and quaint towns.

Texas versus Vermont: Ethnic Makeup

Population Group	Texas	Vermont
White alone, not of Hispanic origin	42.6%	94.6%
Hispanic/Latino	39.1%	1.9%
African American	12.6%	1.3%
Asian American	4.8%	1.8%

Sources: U.S. Census Bureau, "Quick Facts: Texas," 2017, https://www.census.gov/quickfacts/fact/table/tx/PST045217; U.S. Census Bureau, "Quick Facts: Vermont," 2017, https://www.census.gov/quickfacts/fact/table/vt/PST045217.

Obviously, to govern a diverse population spread over a vast geographic area with extensive mineral wealth, Texas requires a fundamentally different approach than Vermont. In many instances, Texas politics is vastly different in practice than Vermont's political system. However, these differences may not be exactly what we expect.

Is your community more like typical Texas or Vermont?

⭐ **CRITICAL THINKING**

What are the advantages and disadvantages of a diverse state like Texas?

⭐ **SOCIAL RESPONSIBILITY**

What does the size of the state's economy tell us about its politics?

CRITICAL THINKING

What are other ways of looking at the size and scope of the Texas economy?

EMPIRICAL AND QUANTITATIVE

How accurate should our Texas legends be?

CRITICAL THINKING

How will changes to the population and economy shape Texas state government in the future?

CRITICAL THINKING

One of the enduring legends of early Texas history is how Anglo order and hard work saved the state from Mexican chaos. According to this view, it was immigrants from the United States who, in the words of one public school textbook from the 1880s, "changed Texas from a wilderness into a civilized state: Mexico had nothing but fear and hatred."[41] Like other legacies, this historical "truth" ignores some aspects of history and exaggerates others. So far, Hispanics have been the losers in the formation of historical legend.

By 1930, the Tejano population of Texas had begun to rise with the rest of the population, reaching almost 684,000. Reflecting the return of Tejanos to Texas politics, the League of United Latin American Citizens (LULAC) was formed in Corpus Christi in 1929. LULAC quickly became a major factor in Texas politics. In 1956, Henry B. González became the first Tejano in over half a century to hold a seat in the Texas Senate. During the 1957 legislative session, González set the record for a filibuster in the Texas Senate as he fought laws backing segregation in Texas public schools. In 1961, González broke ground again by winning a seat in the U.S. House of Representatives. By that time, half a dozen Tejanos were serving in the Texas Legislature and a Tejano was serving as mayor of El Paso. Tejanos won their first statewide office when Dan Morales was elected attorney general in 1992. Hispanics are both the largest and fastest-growing group in the state and today hold a variety of offices. In 2009, Eva Guzman became the first Hispanic woman to serve on the Texas Supreme Court when Governor Perry appointed her to fill a vacancy on the court. Tejanos are increasingly successful in organizing and exerting political pressure in Texas. As the Hispanic population continues to increase and organize its interests within the state, Hispanics are in a position to be the winners in a future Texas.

Today, Texas is again dealing with immigrants whose numbers are increasing so rapidly that they form a majority in some parts of the state. The struggle to deal with this change is part of what defines Texas as a state. As we will see throughout this text, legends tend to be static and are often at odds with the changing nature of the state. The myth that Texas's story is a primarily Anglo one ignores others' contributions. What's more, the myth of Anglo primacy remains the dominant legend in Texas's history books. Throughout the rest of the book, we will continue to explore this tension between legend and change.

CONCLUSION

In August 2017, a major hurricane approached the Gulf Coast of Texas. Although the storm, dubbed Harvey, had temporarily weakened, it roared back to life and eventually swelled to Category 4 status. Its center made landfall at about 10 PM on August 25 near Rockport. With winds as high as 102 miles per hour, Harvey battered the coast there and in nearby Corpus Christi. After moving inland, it turned back out over the warm Gulf of Mexico waters, where it regained strength before heading toward Houston. Harvey crept slowly along southeast Texas and Louisiana from August 26 through 30, dropping massive amounts of rainfall that created catastrophic flooding in and around Harris County. While Houston would not see the hurricane-force winds that pounded areas including Port Aransas, historic levels of rainfall overwhelmed drainage systems. Nederland endured the largest rainfall total of 60.58 inches between August 24 and September 1, with Groves close behind at 60.54 inches during that same period. Texans who thought their homes would never be flooded found their entire neighborhoods underwater. The National Hurricane Center declared that Harvey was "the most significant tropical cyclone rainfall event in United States history, both in scope and peak rainfall amounts, since reliable rainfall records began around the 1880s."[42]

The response of the flooded neighborhoods highlighted some of the best aspects of the state's identity and culture. Whatever political differences had divided Texans during the 2016 election evaporated as Texans found ways to help each other. Hundreds of people from Texas and Louisiana came together in a small makeshift navy of flat-bottomed fishing boats that proved perfect for rescuing stranded residents along submerged streets. Stranded for two days by floodwaters inside El Bolillo's bakery, four bakers spent that time turning the 4,400 pounds of flour they had on hand into almost 4,000 pieces of bread that would be distributed to those in need.[43] Houston's football star J.J. Watt turned his millions of social media followers into an army of contributors that gave more than $37 million in private donations.[44] In a remarkable number of ways, private citizens found ways to come together to help the community that is Texas.

While some of the damage could be mended by everyday Texans, Harvey presented challenges that went beyond the ability of individuals to solve. Despite our individualistic nature and our historical roots in the frontier, Texans sometimes need government to prevent future floods. Fixing drainage systems in the areas hit by Harvey is as expensive as it is complex, and asking local residents to plan and pay for the changes as so many struggle to recover is impossible. This leaves cities and the state with the daunting challenge of protecting Texans against similar floods in the future.

An effect of Houston's growth and prosperity has been that its rapid development has put thousands of homes in the path of flooding. The Federal Emergency Management Agency (FEMA) inspected about 575,000 homes affected by the storm and estimated the total damages wrought by Harvey to be $125 billion.[45] As more people move to Texas, they find themselves living in areas like floodplains—areas for which Mother Nature may have other plans. Protecting residents from threats—both natural and man-made—will remain a challenge that state leaders must face.

The story of Harvey reflects both the resilience of individual Texans and the challenges of governing a rapidly growing state. While Texas's traditions, built upon the history of the Alamo and years as the western frontier, created a hardy community whose spirit will continue to overcome ordeals, the twenty-first century demands a Texas government ready and able to face the challenges that come from being a rapidly transforming state.

Volunteers maneuver boats along a flooded street at the east Sam Houston Tollway in Houston, Texas, as rescues continue from the flooding following Hurricane Harvey.

SAGE edge™
for CQ Press

Want a better grade?

Get the tools you need to sharpen your study skills. Access practice quizzes, eFlashcards, video, and multimedia at **edge.sagepub.com/collier6e**.

KEY TERMS

empresario (p. 8)
individualistic political culture (p. 22)
moralistic political culture (p. 24)
political culture (p. 22)

presidential republicanism (p. 22)
traditionalistic political culture (p. 22)
Treaty of Guadalupe Hidalgo (p. 13)

ACTIVE LEARNING

- Create a short brochure that introduces someone who's never been to Texas to the cultural and historical ideas that define the state. Think of the brochure as something that might be distributed at a visitors center at the state border. **Communication**

- Either as an entire class or in smaller groups, generate a list of characteristics that define Texas and that also distinguish Texans from other Americans. **Teamwork**

CHAPTER REVIEW

1. The state's geographic size has _____.

   a. helped protect it from the kinds of party machines that corrupted politics in some cities and states

   b. made it easier to govern the state by making it more diverse

   c. made it harder for charismatic politicians to win statewide office

   d. made the state's history less important

2. During the period when the Republic of Texas was an independent nation, _____.

   a. the U.S. Congress vigorously pursued Texas's admission to the United States

   b. Texans resisted aligning with the United States or any other nation

   c. most Texans favored joining the United States

   d. Texas remained at peace with the American Indian tribes in the area

3. "Juneteenth" is the celebration of _____.

   a. the end of the Texas Revolution

   b. Texas's formal admission to the United States

   c. Texas's joining the Confederacy

   d. the day slaves in Texas were freed

4. Sam Houston _____.

   a. led an exemplary life without controversy

   b. spoke out against slavery and opposed joining the Confederacy

   c. led Texas forces during the Civil War

   d. led Texas forces in raids against American Indian tribes

5. The "Redeemers" were a political force in the 1870s as they led a movement to _____.

   a. end Reconstruction and Republican rule in the state

   b. bring Christianity to farmers in remote parts of the state

   c. push civil rights laws that would remove the last remnants of slavery

   d. reduce the influence of the Democratic party in Texas cities

6. The _____ political culture asserts that individuals are best left free of government interference and that government should take on only those functions demanded by the people.

   a. traditionalistic

   b. individualistic

   c. moralistic

7. The _____ political culture holds that government has a limited role related to preservation of the existing social order.

   a. traditionalistic

   b. individualistic

   c. moralistic

8. Over its history, Texas has seen _____ population growth.

   a. rapid

   b. slow

   c. virtually no

9. Today, Texas is a "majority-minority" state, meaning that _____.

   a. the state's demographics have stopped changing

   b. Anglos still make up over half of the Texas population

   c. no one racial group makes up a majority of the state

10. The Texas economy today is _____.

    a. dominated by oil and gas

    b. dominated by farming and ranching

    c. a diverse mixture of different types of businesses

    d. dominated by transportation companies

CHAPTER 2

TEXAS CONSTITUTIONS

Chapter Objectives

★ Explain the purpose of a constitution.

★ Define federalism and discuss the difficulties in sharing power between the state and national government.

★ Describe the evolution of Texas's previous constitutions and the historical events that influenced them.

★ Explain how Texas's current constitution reflects the preferences of Texans today.

★ Identify problems with the current Texas Constitution.

When Texas joined the Union in 1845, its residents wanted a federal government that could help them control their remote frontier, but they did not particularly want much else. A few years later, the election of President Abraham Lincoln, who Texans feared would threaten the institution of slavery, pushed the state toward secession. Texans were concerned that the federal government would come and take their slaves, and most Texans at the time preferred to leave the Union rather than remain on what they viewed as such unjust grounds. The rhetoric in Texas leading up to the Civil War was filled with speeches about states' rights and federal intrusion. The Texas Ordinance of Secession drafted by Texans at the 1861 Secession Convention indicated the general mood in the state:

> The recent developments in Federal affairs, make it evident that the power of the Federal Government is sought to be made a weapon with which to strike down the interests and prosperity of the people of Texas and her Sister slaveholding States, instead of permitting it to be, as was intended, our shield against outrage and aggression.

Frontier Texans lived a hard life but one in which they largely made their own destiny and provided for their own defense. Today's Texans continue to want the federal government to control their border but otherwise stay out of their lives. In the past few years, Texas politicians have once again focused on federal policies they view as too intrusive and as a threat to state sovereignty. Texans don't want the federal government to tell them how to conduct their business, whether that business involves elections, guns, clean air, or health care. Texans would rather have policies that represent their

Citizens of Denton organized a rally on the Denton City Hall lawn to protest the passage of a 2015 bill overturning a City of Denton vote to ban fracking. The bill was passed by Texas governor Greg Abbott.

preference; Washington politics seem too distant from the everyday life of a Texan. Texans have long been individualistic, espousing a "pull yourself up by your bootstraps" approach to life and holding individuals responsible for their own welfare. Texans had only themselves to depend on, and that was just fine with them.

Texas politicians continue to espouse this deep-seated individualism that defines the Texas identity. Railing against the national government remains a popular way to connect with Texans. Texans have long distrusted governments, both national and state, and preferred that those governments stay out of their lives. Texas frontier life created a preference for as little government as possible. If we have to have government, the government that is closest to the people is the best. Former governor Rick Perry, who was the poster boy for federalism during Obama's administration, argued he is fed up with the national government's arrogance in telling Texans how to live their lives. Perry often referenced the need for local control, claiming that "the very essence of America stems from a limited, decentralized government. When we empower Washington at the expense of local control, we rip apart the concept of civic virtue by removing the ability of the citizens to govern themselves."[1] At the same time, in the last few years Texas politicians have fundamentally redefined their approach to federalism. State officials have been walking the precarious tightrope of telling the national government to stay out of Texans' lives while simultaneously becoming more willing to override local decisions. This fundamental change has occurred quietly, and swiftly, in almost all areas of policy. The Texas Legislature has begun to centralize a wide range of policies that once were left to local governments. In recent legislative sessions, the state government has overturned local laws on everything from tree removal to ride sharing to minimum wage. Lieutenant Governor Dan Patrick spent most of the 85th legislative session trying to pass a bill that would override local school board policies on transgender bathrooms.

In one of the most jarring examples, when Denton citizens voted to ban fracking within city limits, the state legislature passed a law to overturn the citizens' decisions. Governor Abbott appears particularly poised to centralize control even further, arguing that this is not "the United States of Municipalities."

The move to centralize power at the state level has drawn criticism from local officials and longtime Republicans. Then–Texas House Speaker Joe Straus once noted, "I don't think a blanket policy on exerting power from Austin over locals is a particularly attractive idea."[2] A more pointed objection was made by the Texas Municipal League, who pointed out that "seventy-four percent of Texans live in our 1,215 towns and cities and the decisions they have made at the local level have put Texas cities at the top of the nation in success. Stifling their voices through an all-powerful, overreaching state government is a recipe for disaster."[3]

Texans continue to oppose national government encroachment into their lives. It remains to be seen whether Texans will accept the move to centralize power at the state level or if they want decisions made closer to home. This chapter explores the constitutional arrangement of federalism and the development of the Texas Constitution more generally. We will first outline the federalist structure of the national government and how Texas fits into that structure. We will then survey how the Texas Constitution has evolved over time, reflecting our rich history and culture. Finally, we discuss the problems of the current constitution and examine the prospects for constitutional reform.

CONSTITUTIONAL GOVERNMENT

The founders created a government based on a written **constitution** that outlines the powers of government and limitations on those powers to protect the rights of citizens. Ideally, a constitution should be a brief, flexible document that broadly defines what the government can and cannot do. The government, in turn, works within the boundaries of the constitution as it goes about day-to-day operations. The legislature, for example, passes laws that do not violate the basic principles outlined in the constitution. The more fundamental the constitution's provisions, the less likely the need for it to be updated over time. The U.S. Constitution, for instance, has lasted over 200 years, with Congress passing and repealing more specific laws to reflect the changing times. Ideally, a constitution should protect individual rights while being flexible enough to remain relevant as society changes.

Our country's founders believed that a constitutional government was necessary to prevent tyranny. James Madison wrote in *Federalist* No. 51 the following:

> If men were angels, no government would be necessary. If angels were to govern men, neither external nor internal controls on government would be necessary. In framing a government which is to be administered by men over men, the great difficulty lies in this: you must first enable the government to control the governed; and in the next place oblige it to control itself.

The U.S. founders, concerned with tyranny often displayed by the monarchs at the expense of the people, set out to create a new form of government. The U.S. Constitution checked potential tyranny in several ways: by creating different levels of government (federalism), by separating power among different branches of government (separation of powers), and by empowering the people to check the government (popular

Do Texans still prefer local control?

★ CRITICAL THINKING

constitution
a written document that outlines the powers of government and the limitations on those powers

sovereignty). While the U.S. Constitution was revolutionary in the eighteenth century, today written constitutions are the norm. Since independence, Texas has followed the U.S. model and created government based on a written constitution.

The idea of popular sovereignty, or creating a government in which the power to govern is derived from the will of the people, is a critical aspect in limiting tyranny. This idea stands in sharp contrast to rule by divine right, where the right to rule is derived from the will of God. The founders, rebelling against the unchecked power created by divine right, instead created a government where power comes from the people. The U.S. Constitution explicitly references popular sovereignty in the preamble, which begins "We the people." The founders of Texas invoked similar principles in the Texas Revolution; Texas had to free itself from tyranny imposed by Mexico's rule under Santa Anna. The Texas Constitution explicitly invokes the idea of popular sovereignty in the preamble, which affirms that the people of Texas establish the constitution. Popular sovereignty is pervasive throughout Texas government: Texas voters elect almost all state officials, including members of the legislative, executive, and judicial branches, as well as approve amendments to the state's constitution.

The United States invented modern constitutional government, and the U.S. Constitution is a model of brevity and flexible language. It is a relatively short document, with only twenty-seven amendments. The Constitution outlines the fundamental functions and limits of government while leaving the legislature to pass more specific legislation.

Rather than creating a brief and flexible document that outlines the fundamentals of government, Texas has a constitution that is extremely long and specific. This means that specific changes in Texas law often require constitutional amendment rather than legislation. The result is a state constitution that undergoes constant amendment as the government tries to keep up with a rapidly growing and changing state. The current Texas Constitution, Texas's sixth since its independence from Mexico, reflects Texas's historical experiences under Mexico and Spain, its reaction to the Civil War and Reconstruction, and its experiences as a frontier state. The current constitution also represents the federal nature of the U.S. government.

THE FEDERAL SYSTEM OF THE UNITED STATES

Federalism—the sharing of powers between two levels of government—is a uniquely American creation. The North American colonies had relatively little influence in decisions made by the central government back in London. The founders were frustrated over lack of representation in the British government, and they believed that governmental tyranny could be checked by separating the powers of government. In an attempt to limit the potential for tyranny, the framers divided powers among the branches of government as well as between the levels of government. The federalist concept specifies a division of powers between the central, or national, government and the lower levels, or state governments.

In creating a federal system, the U.S. framers compromised between two alternative ideal systems: unitary and confederal. A confederal system is a governmental arrangement where the lower units of government retain decision-making authority. The United States experienced a confederacy twice: first under the Articles of Confederation and later in the short-lived Confederacy created by southern states during the Civil War. In both cases, the states retained decision-making authority, creating a relatively weak

> **popular sovereignty**
> a government in which the power to govern is derived from the will of the people

> What is the purpose of a constitution?
>
> ★ CRITICAL THINKING

> **confederal system**
> a type of government in which the lower units of government retain decision-making authority

unitary system
a type of government in which a central government holds all the power

federalism
a form of government based on the sharing of powers between the levels of government; in the United States, between the national and state governments

enumerated powers
the powers such as those listed in Article 1, Section 8 of the U.S. Constitution that are expressly granted to the national government

implied powers
powers beyond those enumerated in the Constitution; implied powers are powers deemed "necessary and proper" to execute the enumerated powers of the national government

concurrent powers
powers that are shared by the national government and the state governments

Should the national government intervene to protect minority rights?

 SOCIAL RESPONSIBILITY

national government. A modern-day example of a confederacy is the United Nations, where member countries can participate in various treaties, choose to opt out of other treaties, and withdraw from the UN at any time. The UN has only the powers that are expressly granted to it by its member countries.

A **unitary system**, by contrast, vests power in a central government; lower units of government have only the power that is granted to them by the central government. For the most part, the North American colonies had only the powers granted to them by the British government. Today, about 75 percent of governments are unitary, making this the most prevalent type of government in the world. An example of a unitary government close to home is the relationship between Texas and its local governments. Cities and counties in Texas are granted only limited lawmaking authority by the state constitution and the state legislature.

The founders, having experienced both a unitary and confederal government, created an alternative form of government known as federalism. **Federalism** is a system of government where power is shared between the national and state governments, and it represents a compromise between a unitary and confederal system. The U.S. Constitution created a federal system by vesting certain powers in the national government while reserving other powers for the states. Theoretically, dividing power among levels of government prevents the national government from imposing one-size-fits-all standards that may not make sense for a particular state or region. On the one hand, federalism allows states to experiment with new policies and permits flexibility as states pass laws that represent their distinct political culture and preferences. On the other hand, federalism imposes significant costs on the United States, since different levels of government create policy for the same issue areas—at taxpayers' expense. The founders believed that the prevention of tyranny was more important than the inefficiency that different levels of government create. Moreover, federal intervention is often necessary to prevent majority rule from overwhelming minority rights. As Madison explained in *Federalist* No. 10, larger governments are more likely to respect minority rights, a fact we learned during the fight against slavery and the subsequent civil rights movement.

The U.S. Constitution specifically grants the national government exclusive authority over coining money, establishing a navy, declaring war, and regulating interstate commerce, among other things. Many of those **enumerated powers** are listed in Article 1, Section 8 of the U.S. Constitution. In 1819, the Supreme Court ruled in *McCulloch v. Maryland* that the "necessary and proper clause" of the U.S. Constitution created **implied powers**. Thus, in addition to those powers specified in the Constitution, the national government was given broad discretionary powers to enact any law necessary and proper to carry out its enumerated powers. Implied powers refer to a group of powers that are unspecified and thus constantly expand our understanding of the role of the national government. The U.S. Constitution also outlines explicit roles for the states about the conduct of elections, the selection of electors to the Electoral College, the establishment of voter qualifications, and the approval of constitutional amendments. Moreover, Article 1, Section 10 of the U.S. Constitution explicitly prohibits states from entering into treaties, coining money, or granting letters of marque or titles of nobility, among other things. Other powers, such as the power to tax and spend, to establish courts, or to charter banks, are **concurrent powers** shared by the national and state governments.

Vertical Federalism

Although the founders generally believed that dividing powers among levels of government would be beneficial, the exact division of power within our federal system is unclear. Vertical federalism, or the distribution of power between the national government and the state governments, has been highly contested for much of our history. The difficulty in describing the federal nature of the U.S. government is best exemplified by juxtaposing the supremacy clause and the reserved powers clause of the U.S. Constitution. The supremacy clause guarantees that the national government is the supreme law of the land. Thus, the U.S. Constitution and laws created by the national Congress supersede state laws and state constitutions. States can make laws within their territory so long as those laws do not conflict with national laws or the U.S. Constitution. The Tenth Amendment, or reserved powers clause, however, declares that "the powers not delegated to the United States by the Constitution, nor prohibited by it to the States, are reserved to the States respectively, or to the people." This provision creates a class of powers called reserved powers, although the Supreme Court has interpreted these powers narrowly in recent times. These two constitutional clauses have generated opposing views of the division of powers between the national government and the state governments. The reserved powers clause seems to indicate a federal system in which states have most of the power, whereas the supremacy clause points to a government where most of the power rests with the national government.

Horizontal Federalism

The U.S. Constitution also includes provisions designed to regulate the relations among states. Horizontal federalism refers to the relationship between states. The founders specified certain state obligations to other states, in part to create a sense of national unity among them. For instance, states are required to grant the same privileges and immunities to citizens of other states as they grant to their own citizens. This provision means that states may not fundamentally treat citizens of other states differently than their own citizens. The privileges and immunities clause makes travel between states easier and discourages discrimination against citizens of other states. However, exceptions to the privileges and immunities clause have been recognized in two cases.[4] First, states may deny the right to vote to nonresidents. Thus, the laws of one state cannot be unduly influenced by citizens from neighboring states. In addition, states may distinguish between residents and nonresidents in the distribution of certain state-subsidized benefits, such as in-state tuition rates or welfare payments. This exception has been deemed reasonable since otherwise "individuals could benefit from subsidies without being subject to the taxes that pay the subsidies."[5] The full faith and credit clause creates an additional obligation between states. States are required to recognize the acts, records, and judicial decisions of other states. This means that court judgments or legal contracts from one state will be honored by all other states. Thus, debt or child support payments cannot be avoided by moving to another state. Finally, the U.S. Constitution requires that states deliver someone suspected or convicted of a crime in another state back to the state where the crime is alleged to have occurred so the accused can face trial and sentencing. This process, known as extradition, was designed to keep criminals from escaping justice by moving from state to state.

---

vertical federalism
the distribution of power between the national government and state governments

supremacy clause
the section in the U.S. Constitution that guarantees that the national government is the supreme law of the land and that national laws and the national constitution supersede state laws and state constitutions

reserved powers
the Tenth Amendment provision that all powers not delegated to the national government belong to the states

horizontal federalism
refers to the relationship between the states

privileges and immunities
the constitutional requirement that states may not fundamentally treat citizens of other states differently than their own citizens

full faith and credit clause
the constitutional requirement that court judgments or legal contracts entered into in one state will be honored by all other states

extradition
the constitutional requirement that a state deliver someone suspected or convicted of a crime in another state back to the state where the crime allegedly occurred so the accused can face trial or sentencing

The Evolving Idea of Federalism

Creating a new type of government generated a significant amount of uncertainty. It is clear that America's founders sought to produce a system of government in which powers are shared between two levels of government. It is considerably less clear exactly what that distribution of power was supposed to look like. From its inception, the idea of federalism has engendered a good deal of controversy, culminating, in part, in a civil war less than a century after the republic was founded. Very few policy areas have escaped this tension.

The idea of sharing power between the national government and the states was an ambiguous one from the beginning. The tension of trying to reconcile the supremacy clause and the Tenth Amendment continues to create different outlooks on how big the national government should be and exactly what it should do. Not surprisingly, those who focus on the supremacy clause view the national government as more powerful, whereas those who focus on the Tenth Amendment view the national government's power as exceedingly limited. In the past, this tension led to a theory of **dual federalism**, in which state powers and federal powers were separate and distinct. However, after the New Deal, those policy distinctions began to erode as the federal government developed policies in areas traditionally left to state governments, such as civil rights. As the strict separation between levels of government gave way to both levels of government sharing authority over the same policy areas, dual federalism gradually transformed into **cooperative federalism**. This moniker suggests that the national government and the states cooperate in various policy areas. In reality, the national government is often leading the policy change and state governments often engage in active resistance to federal policy.

Today, the United States continues to grapple with exactly which powers belong to the national government and which should be reserved for the states. Sentimental attachment to the idea of federalism is often usurped by a preference for efficiency and uniformity. The result is that, over time, the power of the states has eroded significantly. Most notably, states have historically enjoyed policy control over issues such as police power, marriage, education, and election laws. Yet in the last half century, the national government has begun to encroach on policy areas traditionally reserved for the states. Proponents of a federal system that vests more power in the national government point to issues such as slavery and civil rights that did not improve without national intervention. On the other hand, Texans prefer to be masters of their own destiny, which has historically meant a preference for more local control. Proponents of state power support **devolution**, or the idea that power should be returned to the states. Negotiating these competing views continues to be a source of conflict within the United States, one that is not easily resolved. There remains a very real trade-off between respect for minority rights, which historically required national intervention, and respect for cultural preferences that might create a wide variance among state laws.

Perhaps the most effective tool the national government uses to gain control of state policy areas is money. With the creation of a national income tax in 1913, the national government enjoyed a significant increase in revenues. Since that time, Congress has used its financial advantage to influence issues that were traditionally

dual federalism
the theory of federalism that suggests that state governments and the national government have separate spheres of policy influence and restrict their involvement to policies in their areas

cooperative federalism
the theory of federalism that suggests that both levels of government cooperate within specific policy areas rather than maintaining distinct policy arenas

devolution
returning power to state governments

HOW TEXAS GOVERNMENT WORKS

The Federal System

	Legislature	Executive	Judiciary
National Government			
	U. S. Senate U.S. House of Representatives	President	U.S. Supreme Court Federal Circuit Courts Federal District Courts
State Government			
	Texas Senate Texas House of Representatives	Governor Lieutenant Governor Agriculture Commissioner Attorney General Comptroller Land Commissioner Secretary of State	Supreme Court of Texas Texas Court of Criminal Appeals Texas Appellate Courts Texas District Courts
County Government			
	County Commissioner's Court		Constitutional County Courts Statutory County Courts Statutory Probate Courts Justice of the Peace Courts
City or Municipality Government			
	City Council	Mayor City Manager	Municipal Courts

considered state policy areas. Use of financial incentives to encourage policies at the state or local level is referred to as fiscal federalism. The national government has awarded two types of grants to state and local governments. The categorical grant is money given to state and local governments that must be spent for specific activities. When the national government specifies how the money is to be spent, it can then set national policy goals in traditionally state-controlled policy areas. In response to this, Republican administrations favored the block grant as a way to return policy control to the states. A block grant is given to state and local governments for a broader purpose and imposes fewer restrictions on how the states can spend the grant money. In the 1970s, President Richard Nixon reorganized existing categorical grants into block grants to continue the flow of money from the national government to the states while allowing the states to exert more discretion on how the money was spent.

A current example of a categorical grant is Medicaid. Medicaid was established to provide health care to the children of low-income families, the elderly, and individuals with disabilities, among others. As long as states meet the guidelines set by the national government, they receive national funds that supplement state funds to cover the cost of the program. Currently, Texas receives about $58 in federal matching funds for every $42 it spends on Medicaid in the state.[6] Many in the GOP have pushed for the national government to convert Medicaid into a block grant. This would continue the flow of money from the national government to the state without the current federal requirements. Proponents of changing Medicaid to a block grant argue that it would give states more flexibility as to how to spend the money and that the state and the national government would save money. Opponents worry that removing the requirements attached to Medicaid dollars would allow states to discontinue covering certain groups or medical services. While block grants are a popular means of reviving state power, they have been politically difficult to achieve. Members of Congress prefer to allocate money attached to specific policies, making it easier for them to take credit for the resulting goods provided to their home states. One example of fiscal federalism occurred in the 1980s when Congress wanted to establish a national drinking age. Congress, faced with increasing pressure from the organization Mothers Against Drunk Driving, and absent clear constitutional authority to establish a national drinking age, passed legislation that would take away 10 percent of a state's federal highway funds if the state did not raise its drinking age to twenty-one within two years. South Dakota sued the national government, arguing that the policy amounted to coercion and was a blatant intrusion on states' rights. In *South Dakota v. Dole*, the U.S. Supreme Court ruled that the national government could reasonably attach conditions to national grants. In a dissenting opinion, Justice Sandra Day O'Connor concurred with South Dakota that the law violated the spirit of federalism, arguing that "the immense size and power of the Government of the United States ought not obscure its fundamental character."[7] Nonetheless, Texas, along with most states, raised its drinking age to twenty-one as a result of the law. This case illustrates how the national government has used its substantial tax base to considerably increase its policy authority beyond its delegated powers.

Congress sometimes passes a law that requires state or local governments to implement policy without providing funding. An unfunded mandate occurs when the national government passes legislation that imposes requirements on state and local governments that then bear the cost of meeting those requirements. Examples include

FEDERALISM IN *Action*

Abortion

In 1973, the U.S. Supreme Court ruled in *Roe v. Wade* that state laws prohibiting abortion violated a woman's right to privacy. Since then, pro-life advocates have searched for ways to undo *Roe*. At the heart of the issue for pro-life supporters is the argument that all life is sacred. A secondary issue is whether the national government or the state governments have the power to decide whether or not to allow abortions. Pro-choice advocates argue that women should have control over their own bodies. Moreover, they contend that privacy rights must be protected at the national level to protect individuals who may face discrimination locally. Indeed, James Madison argued in *Federalist* No. 10 that minority rights are more likely to be protected when a government covers an expanded sphere. Yet critics argue that abortion is a states' rights issue. From this point of view, issues such as abortion that are not directly addressed in the U.S. Constitution are left to state governments, which should adopt policies that reflect their state's cultural preferences.

Supporters of states' rights realized a significant victory when the U.S. Supreme Court ruled in *Webster v. Reproductive Health Services* (1989) that states could place restrictions on abortion. Since then, numerous states have attempted to limit or deny abortions by passing onerous legal requirements on facilities that provide abortions. In 2011, Texas passed a law that required a sonogram at least twenty-four hours before an abortion. In 2013, the Texas Legislature passed House Bill (HB) 2, which, among other things, required that doctors who provide abortions have admitting privileges at nearby hospitals and that clinics that provide abortions meet the same standards as ambulatory surgical centers, which would require multimillion-dollar renovations for almost all providers. The effect of the law was immediate—nearly half the abortion providers in the state closed or stopped providing abortions once the requirement that doctors have nearby hospital privileges went into effect. The affected clinics were also key providers of contraception, sexually transmitted disease (STD) testing, and cancer screening. The closure of these clinics disproportionately affected rural and poor Texans. Texans who lived in the south and the west were hit particularly hard, as it could now take them more than five hours to drive to a clinic. The constitutionality of HB 2 was challenged in the courts, and eventually the Supreme Court weighed in. In 2016's *Whole Woman's Health v. Hellerstedt*, the Supreme Court ruled that the law created an undue burden on a woman's right to an abortion. The Supreme Court specifically struck down the provisions of the law that required abortion providers to meet the same standards as hospitals and the requirement that doctors have nearby hospital admitting privileges.

Abbott criticized the Supreme Court ruling, stating that it "erodes states' lawmaking authority to safeguard the health and safety of women." The effect on abortions in Texas, however, has already been significant. Even as the number of abortions nationally has decreased, Texas's abortions have fallen at an even greater rate. Abortions in Texas are down about 25 percent since the 2011 law went into effect.[i] Yet there is also preliminary evidence of a rise in sales of misoprostol, a drug sold over the counter in Mexico that is sometimes used to self-induce an abortion.[ii] It is also difficult to estimate the number of Texans who are seeking abortions in other states. One doctor at a clinic in New Mexico estimates that more than half of her patients come from Texas.[iii] Even after the Supreme Court ruled the law unconstitutional, nearly all the clinics that had closed in Texas remain closed. In addition, since so many clinics have closed, the wait time for abortions is much longer, which has resulted in an increase in second-trimester abortions.[iv] The 85th Texas legislature then passed a law that banned the most common type of second-trimester abortion. However, the Fifth Circuit Court of Appeals struck down that law, saying it posed an undue burden on women. Although the national government has ruled abortion legal, it is clear that state officials are going to continue to attempt to limit abortions with state laws.

> In drafting its restrictions against abortion, does the Texas Legislature have a responsibility to consider the impact of the legislation on women's access to other services offered at these facilities?
>
> **SOCIAL RESPONSIBILITY**

> How does the issue of abortion illustrate the tension between the power of the national government and the power of states?
>
> **CRITICAL THINKING**

i. "Vital Statistics Annual Report" for 2011, 2012, 2013, 2014 and 2015, Texas Department of State Health Services, https://www.dshs.texas.gov/chs/vstat/annrpts.shtm.

ii. Erica Hellerstein, "The Rise of the DIY Abortion in Texas: A Pill That Revolutionized Reproductive Rights in Latin America Is Now Gaining Ground on the Black Market in South Texas," *Atlantic*, June 27, 2014, www.theatlantic.com/health/archive/2014/06/the-rise-of-the-diy-abortion-in-texas/373240.

iii. Abby Goodnough, "Texas Abortion Law Has Women Waiting Longer, and Paying More," *New York Times*, March 18, 2016, https://www.nytimes.com/2016/03/20/us/women-cite-longer-wait-and-higher-costs-for-abortions-in-texas.html.

iv. Ibid.

Abortion rights activists dressed as characters from *The Handmaid's Tale* gathered in the rotunda of the Texas State Capitol to protest antiabortion bills in Austin, Texas, in May 2017.

requirements that all states, including Texas, ensure equal access to public facilities for disabled persons, guarantee civil rights, provide public assistance for single parents, and enforce clean air standards.[8] In each of these cases, the states and local governments must pay for a significant portion of these regulations that are imposed on them by the national government.

The debate over the appropriate division of power between the national government and state governments has intensified in the last decade. The expansion of the national government, first with the wars in Afghanistan and Iraq and later with the bailouts of American financial and automobile industries, renewed America's interest in the proper role and size of the national government. The subsequent stimulus package, followed by the divisive passage of the Affordable Care Act (ACA), once again put the issue of federalism at the forefront of the political debate in America. Other issues, such as gay marriage, education policy, and responses to natural disasters such as Hurricane Katrina and, more recently, Hurricanes Harvey and Maria, serve to highlight the differing views of Americans concerning the responsibilities of government.

One of the most contentious debates over federalism currently involves the states' customary authority over marriage. Traditionally, states have enjoyed almost complete control over rules governing marriage, including defining licensing requirements, establishing an age of consent, providing for common-law marriages, and determining general guidelines for divorce. While states defined the specific requirements for marriage, the full faith and credit clause required all states to recognize marriages performed in other states. So when Vermont approved civil unions and Massachusetts became the first state to allow same-sex marriage, other states worried that they would have to recognize same-sex marriages. The national government responded by passing the 1996 Defense of Marriage Act, which defined marriage as between a man and a woman for the purposes of federal laws and also allowed each state to adopt its own definition of marriage. With this act, the national government explicitly attempted to relieve the states of their obligation to grant full faith and credit to public acts in other states. At the state level, many states began to pass laws explicitly denying the validity of same-sex marriages within their state. Thirty-one states, including Texas, amended their state constitutions to allow marriage between only a man and a woman. In 2015, the Supreme Court ruled that all states must recognize same-sex marriages. The same-sex marriage controversy illustrates the inherent struggle with federalism, which is the fundamental question of who gets to decide who can get married: the national government, the state governments, or local governments? In addition to the question of which government has the power to decide the question, governments have the responsibility to protect civil rights of various minority groups who might hold different values than the majority. The preferences of a community must be weighed against the civil rights of the gay community. In the case of same-sex marriage in Texas, the political culture is slowly changing. A 2017 University of Texas (UT)/*Texas Tribune* poll indicates that a majority of Texans, 55 percent, support same-sex marriage and 32 percent oppose it, indicating that Texas's attitudes toward same-sex marriage have slowly shifted. That same poll indicates that a majority of Texans oppose exempting people from antidiscrimination laws even for a sincerely held religious belief. Nonetheless, when the national government extends civil rights to any minority group, there is some portion of the population that fervently resists that extension.

While the battle over same-sex marriage has been contentious, the battle over the passage of a national health care policy has taken the conflict over federalism to a whole new level. A national health care system has been a goal of the Democratic Party since President Harry Truman proposed a national health insurance plan in 1945. Indeed, health care reform was the hallmark of Massachusetts senator Ted Kennedy's nearly five decades in Congress. Hillary Clinton made national health care central to her 2008 presidential campaign after championing a similar proposal as first lady. When Barack Obama campaigned for president in 2008, he promised to make health care reform a priority. While national health care has been popular among Democrats for some time, it has been equally unpopular among Republicans. Even as President Obama signed the ACA into law on March 23, 2010, Republican opposition to the bill was still growing. Though many provisions of the ACA are quite popular, the most controversial provision required all citizens to either purchase insurance or pay a penalty. Ironically, this provision originated among conservatives as a way to prevent free riders in health care. Nonetheless, Texans, who tend to distrust government in general, by and large don't want anything approaching universal health care. Only a few hours after the bill passed, Governor Rick Perry released a statement suggesting that "Texas leaders will continue to do everything in our power to fight this federal excess and find ways to protect our families, taxpayers and medical providers from this gross federal overreach."[9] From the beginning of the battle over the ACA, Perry described the bill as an encroachment on states' rights and "the largest unfunded mandate in American history."[10] In that spirit, Perry championed a bill reaffirming Texas's commitment to the Tenth Amendment. The so-called Tenthers contend that policies such as national health care reform, Social Security, and Medicare are an unconstitutional violation of the Tenth Amendment. According to a statement posted on his website when he was attorney general, Greg Abbott joined other states in suing the federal government "to protect all Texans' constitutional rights, preserve the constitutional framework intended by our nation's founders, and defend our state from further infringement by the federal government."[11] When the Supreme Court upheld the ACA in 2012 as a constitutional tax, Governor Perry responded that "freedom was frontally attacked by passage of this monstrosity—and the court utterly failed in its duty to uphold the Constitutional limits placed on Washington."[12] As of 2017, a majority of Texans, 52 percent, support repeal of the ACA, but 68 percent of Texans want the government to have a replacement ready before repealing the law.[13] Texans continue to oppose the ACA overall, although they support many of its individual provisions. A 2013 University of Texas (UT)/*Texas Tribune* poll showed that a majority of Texans support providing tax credits to small businesses, providing financial assistance to low- and

MAP 2.1 The United States, 1837

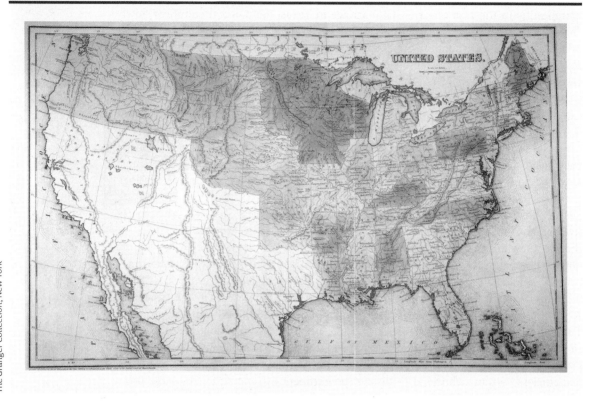

The Granger Collection, New York

The northern part of Mexico in 1837 extended across most of what is today the American Southwest and most of California.

moderate-income Americans to help purchase insurance, allowing children to stay on their parents' insurance until they are twenty-six, and increasing Medicare payroll tax for upper-income Americans as well as the creation of health insurance marketplaces. As we can see, after 200 years, federalism in the United States continues to evolve. How much power the national government should have and how much power should be retained by the states remains an issue as contentious today as it was at our nation's founding. Nevertheless, state constitutions vary greatly in their length and specificity, the amount of power they confer to each branch of government, and the structure of their state judiciary, among other things.

TEXAS CONSTITUTIONS

Texas's constitutions, including the current document, reflect its experiences as a province of Spain and later Mexico. For almost three centuries, Texas was part of the Spanish Empire, its population was relatively sparse, and no written constitution existed. This period of Spanish rule left an indelible mark on Texas law. Under Spanish law, in contrast to English common law, property rights for women were well defined and included the right to hold property, the right to half of all property accumulated during a marriage, and the right to manage their own financial affairs.[14] In addition, Spanish law traditionally protected a debtor's home and farming equipment from seizure for repayment of debt, and this protection has persisted throughout Texas's constitutions under the homestead provisions.

Under Mexican rule, Texas, as part of the state of Coahuila y Tejas, experienced its first federal constitution when the 1827 Constitution of Coahuila y Tejas divided the state into three districts and created a unicameral legislature. Texans were always somewhat frustrated with their limited voice within the Mexican government, and most felt underrepresented in the state. Although they largely comprised the district of Bexar, Texans held only two of the state's twelve legislative seats. Anglo-Texans also resented certain aspects of Mexican rule, in particular the use of Spanish language for official state business and the establishment of Catholicism as a state religion. Officially, Texans were required to join the Catholic Church. In general, Texans favored local control of government and distrusted centralized government, a preference that endures today. As more Anglos moved to Texas for access to cheap land, Mexico became increasingly worried about its ability to control the region. The Mexican government responded to this concern by attempting to bar further immigration from the United States. While the central Mexican government saw further Anglo immigration as a threat to its control over the region, Anglo-Texans saw attempts to stop such immigration as a threat to their continued existence. Texans began to favor the creation of a separate Texas state. The central government, which had long looked the other way as Texans brought slaves into the region, also moved to outlaw all forms of slavery.[15] However, it was a change in tactics by Mexican president Antonio López de Santa Anna that made independence from Mexico inevitable. President Santa Anna, originally popular in Texas because of his commitment to federalism, abolished the Mexican Constitution and moved to centralize power.[16] When the Mexican Army arrived in the town of Gonzales in the fall of 1835 to collect a cannon they had loaned the town, Texans attached a flag with the words "Come and Take It" to the cannon. The clash in Gonzales marked the point of no return.[17] Texans, Anglos and Tejanos alike, moved to fight for independence from Mexico. After several months of fighting, including the ill-fated battle of the Alamo, Texans finally turned the tides of the revolution at San Jacinto. On April 21, 1836, Texans defeated Santa Anna at the Battle of San Jacinto, and both sides signed the Treaties of Velasco, which granted Texas its independence.

Immigration Rights

When Texans declared independence from Mexico, they brought up a lengthy list of complaints, including unfairness in the judiciary, a lack of adequate political representation, and the imposition of a state religion. Anglo-Texans were frustrated with Mexican laws that seemed to ignore their preferences. Texas was given only two seats in the legislature, and the Mexican judicial system often seemed to disregard the struggles of the new settlers. But much of Texans' frustration with Mexico was that Mexico simply didn't represent the cultural preferences of its Anglo settlers. Immigration issues were high among the grievances that fueled Texans' impetus to separate from Mexico. Ironically, much the way today's Texas economy benefits from immigrant labor, Texas under Mexico depended on immigration for the security of the sparsely populated state and initially encouraged immigration from both America and Europe. Under Spain and during the early years of Mexican rule, immigration laws were quite liberal. However, as Anglos began to outnumber Tejanos in the eastern part of the state, Mexican authorities became increasingly concerned about the growing influence of Anglos in Texas. Eventually, Mexico outlawed immigration from the United States with the Law of April 6, 1830, although a significant number of Americans continued to enter Texas illegally.[18]

Anglo immigrants to Texas under Mexico faced a variety of difficulties arising from their inability to speak or write Spanish. Indeed, Anglo immigrants complained about their inability to understand the laws or Spanish law books. Stephen F. Austin, in an attempt to avoid revolution, wrote to the Mexican government in 1833 that "with only two measures Texas would be satisfied, judges who understand English . . . and trial by jury."[19] The basic difficulties of English-speaking immigrants living under a Spanish-speaking government were a primary concern of Anglos in Texas. One of the demands Texans made at the Consultation of 1832 was that the Mexican government create bilingual primary schools with instruction in both English and Spanish. In 1834, Santa Anna, responding to the unrest in Texas, passed several reforms, including making English the official language of the state of Coahuila y Tejas.[20] Nevertheless, Santa Anna soon abolished the constitution and concentrated power in the central government in Mexico, precipitating a war of secession. Once independent, Texans would not forget their experiences under Mexico, and they resolved to have their new constitution and subsequent laws passed printed in multiple languages.

Anglo-Texans' experiences as an immigrant minority were manifest in the Constitution of 1836, which established extraordinarily liberal immigration policies. It declared that "all persons, (Africans, the descendants of Africans, and Indians excepted,) who were residing in Texas on the day of the Declaration of Independence, shall be considered citizens of the Republic."[21] Furthermore, the constitution made the following provision for future immigrants: "After a residence of six months, [if the immigrant] make oath before some competent authority that he intends to reside permanently in the same, and shall swear to support this Constitution, and that he will bear true allegiance to the Republic of Texas, [the immigrant] shall be entitled to all the privileges of citizenship."[22]

Before Texas declared its independence from Mexico, Anglo-Texans complained that they were inadequately represented in Mexico. The framers of the new Texas Constitution sought to grant immigrants the right to vote, regardless of citizenship. That right has persisted to the current constitution of Texas, which authorized "male persons of foreign birth" to vote in the state so long as they had "resided in this State one year next preceding an election, and the last six months within the district or county in which he offers to vote" and had declared their "intention to become a citizen of the United States."[23] Originally, Texas constitutions were designed to ensure that future immigrants could easily and reasonably attain both citizenship and the right to participate in the government. This provision remained in force until 1921, when Texans, by a slim majority (52 percent in favor; 48 percent opposed), passed a constitutional amendment allowing only citizens to vote.

Hispanics in Texas today fight for many of the same rights that Anglos demanded under Mexican rule more than a century ago. Immigrants in modern-day Texas make similar demands for easing citizenship requirements and for language rights.

Anglo-Texans today, sufficiently distanced from their own experience as an immigrant population, have, in many cases, forgotten the difficulties they faced as the immigrant minority. Nevertheless, the immigration issue was as critical in the independence movement of Texas as it is in Texas politics today.

The Republic of Texas: The Constitution of 1836

No episode has contributed to the mythology of Texas more than its brief period as an independent country. Delegates from across the state met at Washington-on-the-Brazos to write a constitution for the future Republic of Texas. Of the fifty-nine delegates, almost half had been in Texas less than two years, and most of them had emigrated from southern American states. The constitutional convention occurred in the midst of the revolution, and delegates hurriedly wrote the new constitution, well aware that the conflict was in danger of arriving at their doorstep at any moment.[24] The resulting document was largely influenced by the U.S. Constitution in that it was relatively brief and flexible, provided for three branches of government, and established a system of checks and balances. The president was elected to a three-year term, prohibited from serving consecutive terms, and appointed commander in chief of the Texas military. A bicameral legislature was established, with one-year terms in the House and three-year terms in the Senate. The short legislative terms and the nonconsecutive presidential term reflected Texans' distrust of government in general, an attitude that continues to dominate state politics today. At the end of the constitution was a declaration of rights, which enumerated individual rights similar to those found in the national Bill of Rights, such as freedoms of speech, the press, and religion. While Anglo and Hispanic males were given a broad range of freedoms, free persons of African descent were prohibited from residing in the state without the consent of the Texas Legislature.

There were, however, some notable differences between the U.S. Constitution and the Republic of Texas Constitution. For instance, the Texas Constitution was distinctly unitary rather than federal in nature, since the Republic of Texas did not create lower units of government with any independent power. In a reaction to the establishment of Catholicism as the state religion under Mexico, the republic's constitution prohibited priests from holding office. Perhaps the most important feature of the new constitution was its legalization of slavery, a provision that had irreversible consequences for both Texas and the United States. Immigrants moving to Texas were permitted to bring their slaves with them, and Texas slave owners were prohibited from freeing their slaves without the consent of the legislature. However, the constitution stopped short of allowing the slave trade in Texas. When Texas was a part of Mexico, its slave population was relatively small. Once Texas left Mexico, and with annexation into the United States seen as inevitable by many, the slave population exploded in Texas, rising from an estimated 5,000 slaves (12 percent of the population) in 1836 to 58,161 (27 percent of the population) by the 1850 census and 182,566 (30 percent of the population) by 1860.[25] The rapid growth of slavery in the state following independence would solidify Texas as a slave state.

Texas voters overwhelmingly supported the new constitution; Texans also supported immediate annexation by the United States. While Texans wanted to join the Union, annexation was not immediate. There were two significant obstacles to Texas joining the United States. First, Texas's claim of independence was precarious. Upon his return

A flag from the Republic of Texas, representing Texas's time as an independent country.

Manifest Destiny
the belief that U.S.
expansion across the
North American continent
was inevitable

to Mexico, Santa Anna renounced the Treaties of Velasco and reiterated Mexico's claims to Texas. Any attempt by the United States to annex Texas could potentially provoke a war with Mexico. Second, Texas's constitutional protection of slavery made annexation controversial within the United States. Abolitionists objected to the addition of another slave state; at the same time, existing slave states saw the admission of Texas into the United States as a guarantee of the future of slavery. Initially at least, the annexation of Texas was unpopular in the United States, particularly outside the South. Thus, a first annexation treaty failed to receive Senate ratification. Eventually, though, the idea of **Manifest Destiny**, or the inevitability of the expansion of the United States across the continent, won out. James K. Polk campaigned for the presidency based on expanding the United States through immediate annexation of Texas and expansion into Oregon. In 1845, Texas was finally admitted into the United States. According to the annexation agreement, Texas retained responsibility for its debt as well as the rights to its public land. In addition, Texas could divide itself into as many as five states as the population continued to expand and then be admitted to the United States under the provisions of the national constitution.

Some of the greatest legends in Texas are built on this brief period of independence. Today Texans speak fondly of a time when they were masters of their own domain. According to popular imagery, Texas's time as an independent country makes it exceptional among the states. In truth, the Republic of Texas, though unique, was also relatively short-lived, poor, and unproductive. Much of Sam Houston's presidency was spent trying to convince the United States to annex Texas while simultaneously attempting to secure international recognition of Texas's independence by the United States, Great Britain, and France, as well as trying to procure financial aid from these governments.[26] While the United States hesitated to bring Texas into the Union, Britain wanted an independent Texas to counter growing American power. President Houston played British preferences against American distrust of British intentions to help increase support for Texas annexation. The Texas legend of a proud independent state often fails to mention that Texas was saddled with debt; devastated by a war that had seen towns destroyed, crops devastated, and much of the population displaced; and under constant threat of attack from Mexico. Offshoots of this legend continue to prevail throughout the state. For instance, many Texans believe that Texas is the only state permitted to fly its flag at the same height as the U.S. flag as an indication of its unique status. In truth, U.S. flag code permits all states to fly their flags at a height equal to that of the U.S. flag.

Statehood: The Constitution of 1845

Once Texas was admitted into the United States, a new constitution was necessary. The statehood constitution continued to specify separation of powers and a system of checks and balances while recognizing the federal nature of the United States. The terms for legislators were lengthened to two years for the Texas House and four years for the Texas Senate, although the legislature would now meet biennially, or every other year. The governor's term was shortened to two years, and the governor was prohibited from serving more than four years in any six. The governor's appointment power was expanded to include the attorney general, the Supreme Court of Texas judges, and district court judges, in addition to the secretary of state. Texans' experiences under both Spain and Mexico were evident in the guarantees of property rights for women and homestead provisions in the new constitution.

The new constitution reflected the experience of Texans in other ways as well. Most Texans were in debt and highly distrustful of creditors, and indeed, many individuals, including Stephen F. Austin, came to Texas to try to get out of debt. Thus, the statehood constitution specified guarantees against imprisonment for debt. The bill of rights was moved to the beginning of the constitution, an indication of the importance Texans placed on individual freedom and limited government. Most of the republic's constitutional guarantees, such as freedoms of speech and the press and protections for the accused, were continued. At the same time, the provisions protecting slavery remained, and the Texas Legislature was prohibited from emancipating slaves without compensation. Voting rights for African Americans and women were not considered in the deliberations, although there was a vigorous debate over enfranchising all free "white" men. Historically, the category of white had included both Native Americans and native Mexicans, though some of the delegates expressed concern that the term might now be used to exclude those populations.[27] In the end, the right to vote was conferred on "every free male person who shall have attained the age of twenty-one years . . . (Indians not taxed, Africans and descendants of Africans excepted)."[28] In addition, the constitution mandated that one-tenth of the state's annual revenue be set aside to create a permanent school fund. Overall, the statehood constitution was relatively brief and flexible. Daniel Webster, a U.S. senator at the time, referred to the framers of this constitution as the "ablest political body assembled in Texas," producing the best constitution of the day.[29]

With the election of Abraham Lincoln as U.S. president, however, secessionist movements erupted in many southern states, including Texas. According to Texas's *Declaration of Causes*, Texas joined the United States with the promise of "holding, maintaining and protecting the institution know as negro slavery"; when nonslaveholding states aligned to "demand the abolition of negro slavery throughout the confederacy, the recognition of political equality between the white and negro races, and avow their determination to press on their crusade against us, so long as a negro slave remains in these States," Texas dissolved their affiliation with the United States.[30] When Texas voted to secede, Angelina County in East Texas was opposed, but in the rest of East Texas, where cotton farming dominated the economy, there was almost

MAP 2.2 Texas Secession Vote, 1861

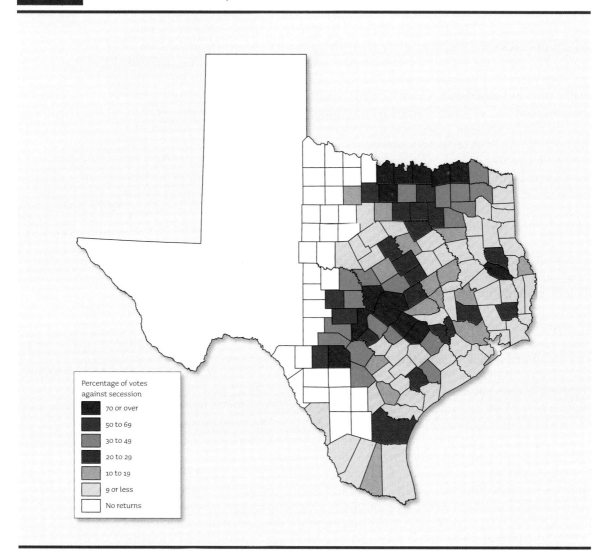

Percentage of votes
against secession

- 70 or over
- 50 to 69
- 30 to 49
- 20 to 29
- 10 to 19
- 9 or less
- No returns

Source: Annals of the Association of American Geographers, "Vote on Secession, 1861," accessed September 25, 2012, www.lib.utexas.edu/maps/atlas_texas/texas_vote_secession_1861.jpg.

universal support for secession (see Map 2.2). Although the movement to secede was strong in Texas, Governor Sam Houston led a substantial opposition. Houston believed joining the confederacy would involve Texas in a war it could not afford and would not win. Several counties in Central Texas and North Texas voted against secession. The Central Texas frontier relied on protection from the U.S. Army, and the ethnic German population there opposed slavery, making secession less popular.

Secession was also unpopular in North Texas, where slavery was virtually absent.[31] Nonetheless, on February 23, 1861, Texas voted to secede and joined the Confederate States of America.

Secession and the Confederacy: The Constitution of 1861

Joining the Confederacy meant that a new constitution was needed. However, the 1861 Confederate constitution was primarily a revised version of the 1845 statehood constitution, replacing references to the United States with references to the Confederate States of America. One notable difference was that under the Confederate constitution, slavery received even stronger protection. In the statehood constitution, the legislature was prohibited from emancipating slaves without compensating their owners, and owners were prohibited from emancipating slaves without permission of the legislature. In the 1861 constitution, both slave owners and the state legislature were prohibited from emancipating slaves under any circumstance. Otherwise, the Confederate constitution kept the same general governmental structures as the 1845 statehood constitution.

The First Reconstruction: The Constitution of 1866

With the end of the Civil War, Texas needed a new constitution that recognized the new political reality of the defeated Confederacy and reconstituted Union. Lincoln assigned a provisional governor, A. J. Hamilton, who immediately called for a constitutional convention. Adult white males who swore an oath of allegiance to the United States of America could participate in electing delegates to the convention. Once again, the approach of the drafters at the 1866 constitutional convention was to revise the 1845 statehood constitution rather than write an entirely new constitution. The United States required Texas and other seceding states to include certain provisions in their constitution. The 1866 constitution specifically renounced secession, repudiated the debts associated with fighting the Civil War on the side of the Confederacy, and acknowledged that slavery was "terminated by this State, by the Government of the United States, by force of arms."[32]

Although slavery was ended, African Americans were not granted voting rights in the 1866 constitution, and other provisions expressly prohibited them from holding office. In addition, the scope of the governorship was altered. Positions that had been previously appointed by the governor, such as the attorney general and state-level judges, would now be elected. The governor's term was extended to four years, with the stipulation that the governor serve no more than eight years in any twelve-year period. In addition, the governor was granted a line-item veto for appropriations bills. Perhaps the most significant contribution of the 1866 constitution was a clause that made it legal for individuals to acquire the mineral rights of their property.[33] In the end, though, this constitution was short-lived, as Radical Republicans, frustrated with the lack of any substantive change in the South, gained control of the national Congress and passed the Reconstruction Acts designed to punish southern states.

The Second Reconstruction: The Constitution of 1869

The Reconstruction Acts passed by Congress divided the South into military districts and assigned military leaders. Texans were required by Congress to write a new constitution in which African Americans realized full political rights, and were further required to ratify the Thirteenth and Fourteenth Amendments to end military rule in the state. Moreover, the Radical Republicans who gained control of Congress prevented ex-Confederates, including anyone who had held a political office during the Confederacy, from either participating as delegates at this convention or voting on the resulting constitution. The result was that only six of the ninety delegates at the 1866 constitutional convention attended the 1869 convention.[34] The delegates then, most of whom were unionist Republicans, were viewed with suspicion and resentment by the majority of Texans. Thus, the 1869 constitution is perhaps best viewed as an anomaly in Texas's constitutional development, as many of its provisions were out of step with the preferences of most Texans. For instance, the office of the governor was again given broad appointment powers, including the power to appoint Texas's Supreme Court justices, district court justices, the attorney general, and the secretary of state. The governor's salary was increased, and the line-item veto was retained. The 1869 constitution also created a plural executive that consisted of eight offices, including the governor. The Republican authors of the 1869 constitution also adopted a broader range of social services and corresponding tax policies that most Texans, who overwhelmingly identified as Democrats, opposed. For example, the new constitution created a road tax that funded bridge building and road improvements in Texas. In addition, this constitution made elementary education compulsory and funded it with one-fourth of the state's annual tax revenues, along with a poll tax and monies from the state's public lands. Adult males were guaranteed the right to vote, regardless of race, color, or previous condition, and both slavery and systems of peonage were outlawed. The convention delegates also proposed the creation of a new state of West Texas, although this was ultimately defeated.[35]

To protest the exclusion of ex-Confederates while including African Americans in the creation of the 1869 constitution, many Democrats boycotted the election to ratify the constitution. Nonetheless, in November 1869, the participating voters approved the new constitution, and Republican E. J. Davis was elected governor of Texas. The climate in which the 1869 constitution was written had lasting effects. After all, the U.S. Congress had mandated many of the provisions of the new constitution, and many Texans had not participated in the election of the convention members, the vote to ratify the constitution, or the subsequent election of Governor Davis. Davis would be the last Republican elected as governor in the state for a hundred years. Because the events surrounding the 1869 constitution occurred during a period of military administration of the state, most Texans doubted the legitimacy of both the new constitution and the new governor from the outset.

E. J. Davis would prove to be one of the most controversial governors in the state's history. The taint of illegitimacy was impossible for Davis—and, for the next century, the Republican Party—to overcome. After Reconstruction ended and former Confederates were again eligible to vote, Democrats won back control of the state legislature and the governorship, ousting Davis and replacing him with Democrat Richard Coke in the 1873 gubernatorial election. With a Democrat safely in office, Texans immediately set

TEXAS *Legends*

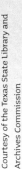

E. J. Davis

According to Texas legend, Texas needed the "Redeemer" constitution of 1876 to cleanse the state of the despotism endured under Republican governor E. J. Davis. Davis represented the more extreme branch of the Republican Party and narrowly won the gubernatorial election in 1869 with the backing of black voters. This connection to both ex-slaves and the Republican Party no doubt helped to alienate most Texans. In the eyes of many, Davis ballooned the debt, declared martial law in much of the state with his control of the state militia and state police, and sold out the state's farmers to big business, including railroads, at the expense of the mainly agrarian population. And, to add insult to injury, when it became clear that Republicans would likely lose the next election, Davis postponed the legislative election and initially refused to leave office after losing the governor's race. This version of events allowed Texans, still stinging from their loss of the recent "War of Northern Aggression," to blame the North for the economic decline of the state and diminish the Confederates' recent military defeat. It also gave birth to the legend of Democrats as redeemers who saved the state from a corrupt "foreign" invader.

It is true that Davis increased the debt of the state, but this is only part of the story. The state of Texas had been financially devastated by the Civil War and would have faced a lack of revenue regardless of who occupied the governor's office. Davis advocated an expansion of social services favored by the Republican Party, which necessarily translated into higher state taxes. The Republican policies were no doubt more progressive than Texas Democrats preferred. That does not necessarily indicate wastefulness or dishonesty, though. For example, Davis advocated a compulsory education system that was viewed as exorbitant by many Texans. Moreover, both taxes and state debt were actually higher under the succeeding Democratic administrations.[i]

Davis also used the state police and the state militia to deal aggressively with lawless areas in Texas. Texas still had large expanses of frontier to protect. There was also a good deal of resistance remaining from the Civil War. For instance, Davis declared martial law in Hill County in January 1871, following the arrest of a state police officer. The police officer had offended locals when he attempted to arrest the son of the county's largest landowner for killing a freedman and his wife.[ii] Similarly, racially motivated attacks and murders in Limestone County, along with a mob threatening the state police, led Davis to declare martial law there in 1871. So, while it is true that Davis used expanded police powers to maintain order in the state, often the disorder was the result of whites attempting to repress the newly freed African American minority and reject the authority of the Republican-dominated state government and police.

Given that many Democrats were disenfranchised during punitive Reconstruction, Davis knew that Republican control of both the governorship and the legislature would be short-lived. Although Davis postponed the legislative and congressional elections, when they finally did take place, the Democrats won decisively. The new Democratic-controlled legislature passed a law calling for the election of state and local offices, including the governor, to be held on December 2, 1873. In that election, Davis was overwhelmingly defeated by Democrat Richard Coke. However, the validity of the election was challenged by Republicans in the *Ex parte Rodriguez* case in the Supreme Court of Texas. The 1869 constitution stated that "all elections for State, district and county officers shall be held at the county seats of the several counties, until otherwise provided by law; and the polls shall be opened for four days, from 8 o'clock, a.m., until 4 o'clock, p.m., of each day."[iii] Democrats argued that the constitution allowed the legislature to change either the allotted time or the place of the election. Republicans argued that the semicolon after the phrase "provided by law" created two independent clauses, and that though the legislature could change the location of the polls, it could not change the time allotted for the elections. The Supreme Court of Texas sided with the Republicans, thus earning the nickname "the Semicolon Court." Although the Supreme Court of Texas ruled that Coke's election was invalid, Democrats ignored the ruling and inaugurated Coke. Davis, unwilling to resort to force to protect his position, vacated the office.

In many ways, vilifying the Davis administration extended the tensions of the Civil War, as Democrats blamed Republicans for all of the state's problems. That we still see many textbooks repeat the one-sided view of the Davis administration even today is a testament to the pervasiveness of the anti-Republican and anti-northern myth.

---

i. Janice C. May, *The Texas State Constitution: A Reference Guide* (Westport, CT: Greenwood Press, 1996); see also Randolph B. Campbell, *Gone to Texas* (New York: Oxford University Press, 2004).

ii. For more details of this incident, see "Hill County Rebellion," *Handbook of Texas Online*, accessed September 3, 2014, www.tshaonline.org/handbook/online/articles/jchka.

iii. Texas Constitution (1869), art. 3, sec. 6.

out to write a new constitution. Some sought to prevent a "tyrant" such as Davis from ever again gaining so much power in Texas. Others leaped at the opportunity to replace the constitution that the national government and the Republican Party had imposed on them. Either way, Texans were once again writing a constitution.

THE CURRENT SYSTEM: THE CONSTITUTION OF 1876

The current constitution of Texas emerged from the tangled mess left by the demise of Radical Republican rule and the return to power of the Democrats. The 1876 constitution created three branches of government, with separation of power between the branches and a system of checks and balances. Texas's constitution is based on the idea of popular sovereignty, evidenced in the preamble: "Humbly invoking the blessings of Almighty God, the people of the State of Texas do ordain and establish this Constitution." The constitution also embodies the principle of federalism in recognizing that Texas is free, "subject only to the Constitution of the United States."[36]

Several clashes created the context for the current Texas Constitution. First, the Civil War and the subsequent Reconstruction fostered considerable resentment toward northern Republican interests throughout the South. The Reconstruction era in Texas saw a Republican-dominated government exclude the majority of Texans from participating in the creation of the constitution and in the state's political processes in general. Thus, the Republican Party spent the next 100 years almost completely shut out of the state's political arena. Second, a preference for independence and individual freedom, along with a deep-seated distrust of government, has always characterized the state's political culture. Texas has consistently sought to restrict the powers of government. While the current constitution represents the most extreme attempt at restricting Texas government, all of the constitutions, with the exception of the 1869 constitution, sought to create a government that would generally stay out of the lives of most Texans. The 1869 constitution was objectionable both because it represented the frustrations of losing the Civil War and because it consolidated power at the state level, away from local governments. The constitution drawn up in 1876, in reaction to its comparatively progressive predecessor, went further than any previous constitution in specifying exactly what the government could and could not do. Delegates who authored the current constitution were overwhelmingly Democrats who distrusted government, favored local control, preferred fiscal restraint, and wanted to fix the perceived injustices of the Republican-created 1869 constitution. Third, the delegates who wrote the current constitution were primarily concerned with protecting agrarian interests, as most Texans in 1876 were farmers. Indeed, close to half of the delegates were members of the Grange, an organization created to protect the interests of farmers. These farmers sought to limit the power of the railroads, which they relied on to deliver their crops and livestock to market. The Davis administration's policies aided the expansion of the railroads in Texas, which led to increased rail rates that frustrated the farmers in the state. In fact, the founders of the Texas Constitution distrusted big business and sought to protect individual rights at the expense of businesses. Thus, the constitution includes a wide range of limits to big business in the state, including explicit restrictions designed to keep railroads, banks, and oil companies small. The resulting constitution is one of specific limitations on governmental power rather than a fundamental set of laws.

Individual Freedom

Texans have always placed a high value on individual freedoms. Since 1845, a bill of rights has been the first article in each Texas constitution, demonstrating the importance Texans place on individual freedom (see Table 2.1). The Texas Constitution carries over rights from the previous constitution, such as freedoms of speech, the press, and assembly, along with the right to bear arms. It also includes protections against unreasonable search and seizure and cruel and unusual punishment and guarantees a trial by jury.

Texans' experiences during the Civil War also influenced the writers of the current constitution. Because President Lincoln had suspended habeas corpus during the war so that people who were suspected of disloyalty could be arrested and held indefinitely without being charged, the framers of the current Texas Constitution specified that the right to habeas corpus shall never be suspended. The authors kept the provisions for freedom of religion while adding a requirement that state officeholders "acknowledge the existence of a Supreme Being." Moreover, the current constitution prohibits public money from being used for the benefit of "any sect, or religious society, theological or religious seminary." Long-standing prohibitions against imprisonment for debt, provisions for community property, and protections for family homesteads were retained in the new constitution.

Distrust of Government

The most prominent feature of the current Texas Constitution is the general distrust of government. Article 1 underscores the attitudes of most Texans that "all political power is inherent in the people, and all free governments are founded on their authority . . . they have at all times the inalienable right to alter, reform or abolish their government in such manner as they may think expedient." We see evidence of Texans' distaste for government throughout the document. For example, the circumstances under which the government can tax and incur debt are spelled out in the Texas Constitution. To keep the government small, the powers, terms, and salaries of the executive and legislature are strictly limited. The framers of the Texas Constitution created a system in which political power is retained by the people. The result of attempting to keep all political power with the people in Texas is the long ballot, a system in which almost all positions in the state are elected rather than appointed. This distrust of government continues to pervade Texans' attitudes today and is one of the main reasons why a complete constitutional revision has failed to get support in the state.

long ballot
the result of a system in which almost all the positions in a state are elected rather than appointed

The Legislative Branch

Consistent with Texans' preference for small government and their distrust of politicians, the current constitution was designed to create a part-time citizen legislature. The constitution restricts the legislature to biennial sessions for only 140 days. The idea was that, rather than having professional politicians, any citizen could participate in a legislature that met so infrequently. To discourage professional politicians further, the constitution originally spelled out only a modest salary for state legislators, a salary that required a constitutional amendment to change. This persisted until 1991, when the constitution was amended to create the Texas Ethics Commission (TEC) to set legislative salaries, subject to voter approval. Today legislative salaries remain limited to only $7,200 a year plus a per diem for days the legislature is in session. The legislative branch is composed of a Texas House of Representatives with 150 members and a Texas Senate with thirty-one members. Members of the House continue to be elected every two years, while the terms of the senators have been shortened to four years. While the legislature is limited to a relatively short session, thirty-day special sessions can be called by the governor, who sets the agenda for those sessions.

Much of the Texas Constitution is a list of things that the legislature is specifically prohibited from doing. For instance, the constitution spells out the types of taxes the legislature can and cannot levy. It explicitly prohibits the state from passing a property tax and sets ceilings on the amount of property taxes that local governments can collect. The constitution further forbids the government from imposing a state income tax without approval by a majority of voters. The legislature is required to place the subject of the bill in the title, and each bill can only have one subject. A reading of the current constitution makes clear that the main goal of the framers was to expressly limit the government rather than to create a broad governing mandate.

The Executive Branch

Under Reconstruction, supporters of the Confederacy were banned from voting and participating in the creation of the constitution. In the resulting government, the Republican governor centralized power, often to deal with Texans who resisted extending rights to newly freed slaves. As soon as all Texans were once again permitted to participate in elections and write a constitution, the reaction was swift. The authors of the current constitution wasted no time writing a new constitution that severely stripped the powers of the governor and distributed traditional executive powers into several offices. According to Article 4, the executive branch is divided among a governor, lieutenant governor, secretary of state, comptroller land commissioner, and attorney general.[37] Thus, in contrast to the U.S. executive, the Texas Constitution created a plural executive, an institutional arrangement where traditional functions of the executive branch are divided among several officeholders rather than vested in a single person. To further limit the power of the governor, offices that had previously been appointed by the governor would now be elected. In fact, the only significant state-level appointment left to the governor is the secretary of state. The delegates of the constitutional convention also shortened the term of office for the governor to two years, decreased the governor's salary, and limited the governor to two terms in office. Later amendments increased the governor's term to four years and removed the term limits.

Clearly, though, one of the main goals of the delegates creating the current constitution was to create an institutionally weak governor.

The Texas Judiciary

Article 5 of the Texas Constitution created a judicial branch with county courts, commissioners courts, justice of the peace (JP) courts, district courts, and appellate courts, as well as "such other courts as may be provided by law." It also specifies the creation of two high courts, the Supreme Court of Texas to hear final civil appeals and the Court of Criminal Appeals to hear final criminal appeals.[38] Moreover, the constitution specified the election of all state judges, although judicial vacancies are filled by gubernatorial appointment. Thus, all state judges in Texas are constantly raising campaign funds in order to get reelected. This is in sharp contrast to the federal judiciary, which is appointed for the purpose of creating an independent judiciary.

Civil Rights in Texas

As soon as slavery was abolished, Texas created new ways to deny civil rights to minorities. Immediately following the Civil War, African Americans were allowed to own property and enter into contracts, but black codes were enacted to attempt to control virtually every other aspect of life, prohibiting blacks from marrying whites, gaining public lands, or sharing in the public school fund. Railroad companies were required by law to segregate. Although black codes were written to target the black population, in practice they were often applied to Hispanics as well. Texas also passed a law that required laborers to enter binding contracts when they worked for an employer for more than thirty days. The contract prohibited the laborer from leaving the employment, required laborers to be polite, fined laborers for work missed for "feigned sickness," and required them to promptly answer calls and obey commands on all days and at all hours. Many Texans devised new ways to continue slavery across the state. Apprenticeship laws provided a means for black and Hispanic children under twenty-one to be contracted to employers for unpaid work. Parents could enter their children into such contracts, children could enter into apprenticeship contracts themselves, or county judges could create a contract without the parents' consent, so long as they placed a notice in the county newspaper. In some cases, local law enforcement would cite youths for vagrancy and the court would order an apprenticeship.[39] More common was the use of sharecropping and peonage to keep unpaid labor in service. Peonage

TABLE 2.1	Articles of the Current Texas Constitution
Preamble	
Article 1	Bill of Rights
Article 2	The Power of Government
Article 3	Legislative Department
Article 4	Executive Department
Article 5	Judicial Department
Article 6	Suffrage
Article 7	Education
Article 8	Taxation and Revenue
Article 9	Counties
Article 10	Railroads
Article 11	Municipal Corporations
Article 12	Private Corporations
Article 13	Spanish and Mexican Land (repealed August 5, 1969)
Article 14	Public Lands and Land Office
Article 15	Impeachment
Article 16	General Provisions
Article 17	Mode of Amending the Constitutions of This State

TEXAS (VS) CONNECTICUT

The constitutions of Texas and Connecticut date from very different eras in the country's history. The Texas Constitution, the state's sixth, was written in 1876 and reflects the agrarian, rural nature of the state at the time. The Connecticut Constitution is one of the country's newer state constitutions, having been written and adopted in 1965. It is the state's third, following the Fundamental Orders of Connecticut (1638) and the Connecticut Constitution (1818).

The Connecticut Constitution reflects in many ways the world of the 1960s. Its language is less formal and archaic than that of either the Texas Constitution or the U.S. Constitution. An extensive list of civil rights and liberties takes center stage in the Connecticut Constitution. We might expect issues surrounding the free exercise of religion and separation of church and state to be reflective of the time and to therefore be more pronounced in the Connecticut Constitution than in the Texas Constitution. After all, Connecticut wrote and adopted its constitution after the U.S. Supreme Court eliminated mandatory prayer and mandatory religious instruction in public schools.

In fact, the Texas Constitution and Connecticut Constitution share a number of characteristics regarding religious liberty. For example, both guarantee freedom of worship, prohibit compulsory attendance at religious services, and prohibit any requirement that individuals give money to build places of worship. The constitutions of both states also contain a number of prohibitions on their respective state governments. Yet the two documents differ in many respects, too. The Connecticut Constitution features specific language that guarantees the right of ministers and religious teachers to pursue their professions. Texas lacks such language in its constitution. In Texas, public lands cannot be given to religious organizations; a similar provision does not appear in the Connecticut Constitution.

The table in this box lists key provisions of the Texas Constitution and Connecticut Constitution in the area of religious liberty.

Which state imposes a greater degree of separation between church and state?

⭐ EMPIRICAL AND QUANTITATIVE

Which state provides the most guarantees of religious liberty?

⭐ EMPIRICAL AND QUANTITATIVE

Religious Liberty: Texas Constitution (1876) and Connecticut Constitution (1965)

Issue/Topic	Texas Constitution	Connecticut Constitution
Freedom of worship is guaranteed	✓	✓
Attendance at services cannot be compelled	✓	✓
Contributions to build places of worship cannot be required	✓	✓
Preference for any religious society cannot be conferred	✓	✓
Equality of denominations is guaranteed	✓	✓
Equal protection of the law cannot be denied based on religion	✗	✓
Alternative voting is permissible where religion forbids action on Election Day	✗	✓
The right of ministers and religious teachers to pursue their profession is guaranteed	✗	✓
Religious tests as a prerequisite to holding office are not permitted	✓	✗
Disqualification as a witness in court based on religion is not permitted	✓	✓ *
State funds cannot be given to religious organizations	✓	✗
Public lands cannot be given to religious organizations	✓	✗

* In equal protection clause.

allowed debts to be paid with labor. In South Texas, debts, real or merely alleged, could result in young African American or Hispanic men being taken to a farm to work without pay. One example that made national news was the Willacy County peonage case, in which the local sheriff, the justice of the peace, and local cotton farmers cooperated to force young men into unpaid labor. When young men were arrested for vagrancy, the sheriff assessed fines and then forced the men to work in the cotton fields under armed guards to pay their fines. To prevent laborers from leaving the county, a "pass system" was utilized, which required laborers to have a pass signed by a local farmer in order to leave the area.[40]

When the current constitution was written, Texans wanted to erase the memory of Reconstruction. However, some elements of Reconstruction, most notably the Fourteenth Amendment's guarantee of equal protection and the Fifteenth Amendment's extension of suffrage to African Americans in Texas, could not be undone. There were those at the 1875 Constitutional Convention, however, who favored a poll tax in order to vote, ostensibly in an attempt to disenfranchise African Americans in Texas. However, the Grange and other poor farmers objected to the poll tax, which would also disenfranchise poor whites in Texas. In the end, the convention delegates defeated the poll tax. The 1876 legislature promptly adopted a poll tax as a means to generate revenue, but it was not until 1902 that the Texas Constitution was amended to make payment of a poll tax a requirement for voting.[41] The poll tax remained in place until it was abolished by the Twenty-Fourth Amendment to the U.S. Constitution. A second official means of disenfranchising African Americans included the Democratic Party's use of a whites-only primary (see full discussion of voting rights in Chapter 8), which the Texas Legislature formalized with a 1923 law explicitly banning blacks from voting in the Democratic primary. The white primary was particularly effective because the Democrats held a virtual monopoly of state offices for about 100 years. Unofficially, local groups, often including law enforcement, would use intimidation and violence to discourage participation. Hispanics in Texas were similarly disenfranchised in many parts of the state. In other parts of the state, local political bosses organized the local Hispanic vote to deliver large blocs of votes to a particular candidate.[42] The framers of the current Texas Constitution also refused to grant women's suffrage. Interestingly, the current constitution protects voters from arrest on their way to and from the polls on Election Day, a provision intended to protect minority voters from intimidation by local law enforcement.

Perhaps an even more controversial topic than voting rights was the educational system, which was originally mandated in the 1869 constitution. During the Reconstruction period, education was compulsory, regardless of race, and was paid for with tax revenue. At a time when the Texas economy had been devastated by the Civil War, a majority of Texans saw a universal educational system as excessive. Opposition to this system was widespread, as white landowners objected to paying for the education of African American children, and farmers in general favored local control of education, which could be tailored to the needs of particular communities while corresponding to crop cycles.[43] Thus, the 1876 constitution ended compulsory education. The 1876 constitution did mandate the "Legislature of the State to establish and make suitable provision for the support and maintenance of an

black codes
laws passed by southern states to limit the freedom of African Americans after the Civil War; these laws affected every part of the lives of African Americans, regulating everything from whom they could marry to the conditions under which they could work, attend school, and even vote

apprenticeship laws
laws that allowed minors to be forced into contracts with unpaid labor

peonage
laws that allowed debts to be paid with labor; debts were often "created" by arresting individuals for vagrancy

efficient system of public free schools"[44] but specified that "[s]eparate schools shall be provided for the white and colored children."[45] Texas would not reinstate compulsory education until 1915.

In response to attempts by southern states to legalize discrimination, the National Association for the Advancement of Colored People (NAACP) was formed to fight discrimination in the courts. The NAACP was created nationally in 1909, and the first NAACP branch in Texas was established in El Paso in 1914. The early NAACP in Texas concentrated on voting rights and segregation laws. Segregation laws in Texas were subject to the standard set by the U.S. Supreme Court in *Plessy v. Ferguson* (1896). According to this case, laws segregating the races did not violate the Fourteenth Amendment of the U.S. Constitution so long as the facilities were equal. In Texas, the first significant limit to segregation was *Sweatt v. Painter* (1950), in which the U.S. Supreme Court ordered the University of Texas at Austin (UT Austin) to admit black students. The NAACP successfully argued that the establishment of a blacks-only law school in Houston was not equal, in facilities or opportunities, to UT Austin. Desegregating primary and secondary schools would be more difficult. In 1954, the U.S. Supreme Court overturned the *Plessy* decision with *Brown v. The Board of Education of Topeka*. The Supreme Court ruled that segregation was inherently unequal and ordered schools to desegregate with all deliberate speed. In 1956, the Mansfield school district was continuing to bus its black students to Fort Worth. The NAACP sued on behalf of three black children, and federal courts ordered the school district to comply with the *Brown* decision and desegregate. That fall when the black students showed up for school, they were met with a large and angry mob determined not to allow the children to enter the school. The governor of the state sent the Texas Rangers to ensure the school remained segregated, and the three black students were once again sent to Fort Worth. The governor successfully prevented desegregation of Mansfield Independent School District (ISD) and no doubt inspired the governor of Arkansas, who would try a similar approach the following year in Little Rock. Although some school districts in the state quietly desegregated, others engaged in long-term, massive resistance,

AP Photo

A crowd prevents seventeen-year-old Steve Poster from entering Texarkana Junior College in 1956. During this period, southern states resisted federal mandates to desegregate schools.

TEXAS *Legends*

Mansfield High

Before the desegregation of Little Rock High School became the turning point in the desegregation of public schools in America, a similar battle was fought in Texas. Mansfield, a small town southeast of Fort Worth, had 1,450 residents in the 1950s, about 350 of them African American. As in most southern communities, Mansfield's restaurants, churches, schools, and social functions were segregated. And, as in many southern communities, African Americans realized that the path to full citizenship and equality led through quality schools.

In an effort spawned by the Bethlehem Baptist Church and organized by the National Association for the Advancement of Colored People (NAACP), black residents began to look for ways to get the *Brown v. Board of Education* decision declaring segregated schools unconstitutional applied to Mansfield. Black parents were not interested in seeing their children receive the kind of second-rate education that would virtually assure them a life as a second-class citizen. While some advocates of continuing

segregation asked that the state be able to set its own timeline for ending segregation, many hard-liners saw the separation of the races as a traditional value that should not be tinkered with. Governor Shivers demonstrated the uncompromising view of many segregationists when he proclaimed, "We are going to keep the system that we know is best. No law, no court, can wreck what God has made."[i]

As was often the case in Texas, opposition to desegregation was passionate and carried implied or explicit threats to students crossing the separation between the races. While Mansfield High was technically open to black students, they knew attending put their lives at risk. Large crowds gathered in front of the school when it opened for registration in the fall of 1956. For several days, an effigy of a black figure hung from the flagpole in front of Mansfield High School instead of the American flag, and black students who were thinking about enrolling likely understood that the local law enforcement officers who would not remove the black figure would also not protect black

Bettmann Collection via Getty Images

students attempting to enroll at the campus beneath it. State and local officials refused to ensure the safety of black students, and those students decided that making the long bus ride into schools in Fort Worth was safer than risking their lives at Mansfield High School.

---

i. Robyn Duff Ladino, *Desegregating Texas Schools: Eisenhower, Shivers, and the Crisis at Mansfield High* (Austin: University of Texas Press, 1996), 38.

---

typically involving busing students to alternative school districts to maintain separate schools. Eventually, the federal government intervened to implement integration in the holdouts. In *United States v. Texas* (1971), the U.S. District Court in Tyler was granted the authority to oversee and implement desegregation of the remaining segregated schools.

Ironically, today, many schools in the state are more segregated than they were under legal segregation. As whites have moved to the suburbs, many urban school districts are predominantly black and Hispanic. According to the Texas Education Agency, "fifteen years ago, about one out of every five Texas public schools had a student population that was 90 percent or more minority . . . Now it's one in

How should government weigh the predominant political culture against minority rights?

⭐ SOCIAL RESPONSIBILITY

three."[46] Other persistent effects of segregation are less obvious. In 2016, a woman in Normanna was told she could not bury her husband in the "whites only" cemetery because he was Hispanic. Although Anglos and Tejanos fought side by side for Texas's independence, the segregated South saw increased racial discrimination against Hispanics across the state. The League of United Latin American Citizens (LULAC) was founded in Corpus Christi in 1929 to fight discrimination and segregation targeting Hispanic populations. An early and significant success for LULAC was *Hernandez v. State of Texas* (1954), which ruled that Hispanics and other racial groups had equal protection under the Fourteenth Amendment. Hernandez's lawyers argued that Hispanics were systematically excluded from juries, which violated their constitutional rights. Hispanics and other non-English-speakers achieved a victory of another sort in 1973, when the state legislature passed the bilingual education act. This act required every school district with a population of twenty students in any language classification to implement a bilingual education program. While Hispanics in Texas have faced a wide range of difficulties, they are the largest minority in the state and have continued to contribute to the political landscape across the state.

Women in Texas fared somewhat better than women in other parts of the United States. This is in part due to Texas's roots in Spanish law, which recognized women's property rights and established community property. Texas also granted women the right to vote in state elections in 1918, just ahead of the national government granting women the right to vote in national elections in 1920. Women would not get the right to serve on juries in Texas until 1954. *Roe v. Wade* (1972) granted women the right to an abortion, although recent Texas legislation has attempted to restrict that right (see the "Federalism in Action: Abortion" section in this chapter). The Texas Constitution does include a provision to prevent discrimination based on sex; in 1972, it was amended to guarantee equality under the law regardless of "sex, race, color, creed or national origin"—the so-called Texas equal rights amendment. A similar amendment failed to pass at the national level.

The civil rights issue currently dominating the attention of the Texas Legislature revolves around lesbian, gay, bisexual, transgender, and queer (LGBTQ) rights. Many Texans continue to oppose criminalizing discrimination against the LGBTQ community. Legal widespread discrimination against the LGBTQ community has been fairly common until recently. The first significant victory for the LGBTQ community was the 2003 U.S. Supreme Court case *Lawrence v. Texas*. Prior to this case, Texas had outlawed "deviant sexual intercourse," which was a class C misdemeanor. The Supreme Court ruled that outlawing homosexual sex violated the right to privacy. The second momentous victory focused on the right to marry. After the national Congress passed the Defense of Marriage Act, which allowed each state to define marriage, Texans voted in 2005 to amend the state's constitution to define marriage as "the union of one man and one woman." However, political culture was changing rapidly across the country, and in 2009, Texas elected its first openly gay mayor, Annise Parker, in Houston. Still, gays could not openly serve in the military until 2012 and could not legally get married in many states, including Texas, until 2015. In 2015, in *Obergefell v. Hodges*, the U.S. Supreme Court ruled that states must recognized same-sex marriages, reasoning that choice in marriage is fundamental to individual rights and that the right to marry provides safeguards to families and children. In addition, a 2016 U.S. Supreme Court ruling made it legal for gay couples to adopt children in all fifty states.

There are still no state laws prohibiting discrimination based on sexual orientation and gender identity. In 2014, the Houston City Council passed legislation that would prevent discrimination in housing, public places, and employment based on a wide range of criteria, including race, gender, sexual orientation, age, disability, and military status. The Houston Equal Rights Ordinance, or so-called HERO law, eventually went before the voters, who overwhelmingly defeated the legislation. Nonetheless, there are twelve Texas cities with populations of more than 100,000 that have some rules in place to protect city employees or residents based on sexual orientation or gender identity.[47] Political leaders continue to push for a transgender bathroom law.

Photo from the first League of United Latin American Citizens (LULAC) meeting, 1929.

CRITICISMS OF THE TEXAS CONSTITUTION

The state's current constitution was written in the era of cowboys and cattle drives. Today's Texas is one of computers and commuters. The population in the 1880s was slightly over 1.5 million people, whereas in 2017 the U.S. Census Bureau estimated Texas's population at 28.3 million. Hispanic and African American populations comprised the two largest minorities in Texas in the 1880s. The Hispanic population has increased significantly since then, but the African American population has declined, and other minorities, such as Asian immigrants, have a greater presence in the state today. Economically, Texas in 1876 was agrarian, with small farms and ranches dominating the state. Today, the state's economy is one of the most diverse in the United States and continues to diversify. Texas has a substantial aerospace and defense industry as well as a significant telecommunications and computer sector and is an important center of finance, shipping, energy, and other big business. It is not surprising, then, that the current constitution is considered outdated and inadequate for such a large and diverse state.

The current constitution reflects the desire of the framers to eliminate the last vestiges of Reconstruction rather than to write a long-lasting constitution. One of the most frequently cited criticisms is the amount of detail in the document. The Texas Constitution is a long list of specific rules rather than a set of fundamental principles for state law. For instance, in 2003, Texans approved twenty-two constitutional amendments, including one permitting cities to donate their surplus firefighting

Should Texas cities be allowed to pass ordinances against discrimination? Or should state law preempt city ordinances?

⭐ CRITICAL THINKING

FIGURE 2.1 Texas Constitution of 1876: Amendments Proposed and Adopted, 1879–2017

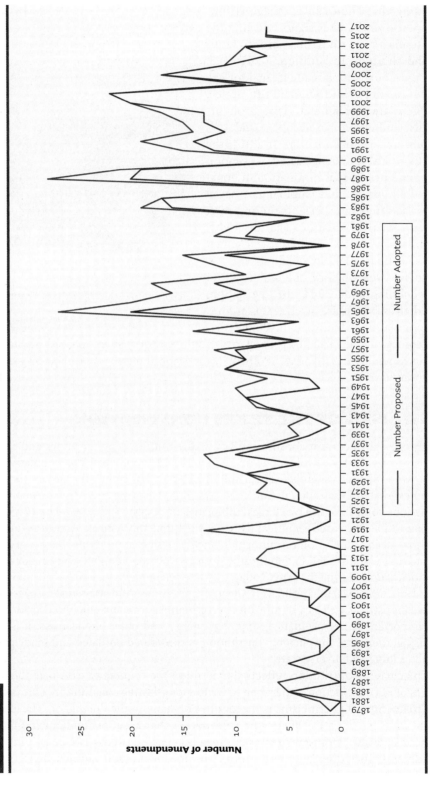

Source: Texas Legislative Council, www.tlc.state.tx.us.

equipment to volunteer fire departments. Similarly, in 2017, the constitution was amended to expand the definition of *professional sports team* for fund-raising purposes. While both of these amendments may be commendable, they are the sort of specific policymaking ideally originating in the state legislature rather than being embedded in a constitution.

Including such detail in the state's constitution leaves Texas with the second-longest constitution in the United States, one that is both disorganized and unwieldy. The problem is compounded because the more detailed the constitution is, the more likely it is that enactment of new statutes will require constitutional amendment rather than passage in the legislature. The result is a constitution that continues to grow; it is now approximately 87,000 words.

In addition, the constitution severely limits the government. The legislature's session is limited to 140 days every other year. While that may have been desirable in 1876 agrarian Texas, today's Texas is the second-largest state in the United States and has an increasingly diverse population and economy. Extremely low legislative pay means that average Texans cannot afford to take the job. Instead of being a citizen legislature, the Texas Legislature is dominated by wealthy individuals and big business. Finally, judges in Texas constantly have to raise money for reelection, which creates a climate of mistrust in the Texas judiciary. The result is a judiciary that most Texans believe is overly influenced by money.

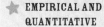

How has the number of amendments adopted changed over time?

★ EMPIRICAL AND QUANTITATIVE

Has Texas become more likely to adopt proposed amendments?

★ EMPIRICAL AND QUANTITATIVE

Amending the Constitution

The current Texas Constitution outlines the process by which it can be amended. Both houses of the Texas Legislature must approve any proposed amendments by a two-thirds vote. Once approved, the amendment must be published twice in major newspapers and posted in each county courthouse thirty days prior to Election Day. Finally, the amendment must be approved by a simple majority of voters. The Texas Constitution has been amended 498 times, making it one of the most frequently amended constitutions among the states.[48] Alabama's state constitution has been amended the most, passing 926 amendments, while Rhode Island's constitution has been amended the least, with a mere twelve amendments. (See Table 2.2 for comparison of other facts about the constitutions of the fifty states.)

As Figure 2.1 illustrates, the overwhelming majority of proposed constitutional amendments in Texas are approved by electors; 88 percent of all proposed amendments have been adopted since 1985. Almost all constitutional amendments are put on the ballot in odd years or in special elections. Unfortunately, the voter turnout during special elections is significantly lower than during general elections (see Figure 2.2). Since 1985, the average turnout in elections with constitutional amendments has been 9.1 percent of the entire voting-age population.[49] Voter turnout remains alarmingly low even when the proposed amendment is relatively popular or controversial. For example, in 2007, when 88 percent of voters approved school tax relief for the elderly and disabled in Texas, less than 7 percent of potential voters actually participated in that election. In 2003, voters approved twenty-two constitutional amendments, including a controversial limit on medical malpractice lawsuits, with a mere 9.3 percent turnout rate. In 2005, 76 percent of voters approved a constitutional amendment

TEXAS MASSACHUSETTS

The Massachusetts Constitution of 1780, which predates the U.S. Constitution by nearly ten years, is the oldest written constitution still in use not only in the United States but also anywhere in the world. The framers of the Massachusetts Constitution included three heroes of the American Revolution: John Adams, Samuel Adams, and James Bowdoin. These larger-than-life heroes established a pattern that many states now follow for state constitutions: a preamble, a declaration of the rights of citizens, a framework for government, and amendments to the constitution. The virtues of the relatively broad language of the Massachusetts Constitution have served the state well, as opposed to the highly specific and technical language of the Texas Constitution. Fewer constitutional amendments (120 total) have been passed in Massachusetts than in almost half the states—certainly fewer than Texas's 498 amendments. Also unlike Texas, Massachusetts still uses its original document, while Texas is on its fifth constitution since statehood (and its sixth if you add the short-lived Constitution of the Republic of Texas).

The original Texas Constitution (1845) after Texas joined the United States reflected many characteristics of state constitutions of the time, including that of Massachusetts. Some thirty-one years later, in 1876, the framers of the current constitution of Texas created a very different document. The 1876 document is informed by experiences in the Civil War and Reconstruction eras of U.S. history.

> Why do you think the Massachusetts Constitution is a model for other states?

 CRITICAL THINKING

> How is the Texas Constitution (1845) similar to that of Massachusetts and to the current state constitution? How is it different?

 EMPIRICAL AND QUANTITATIVE

A Constitutional Comparison of Massachusetts and Texas

Feature	Massachusetts	Texas (1845)	Texas (1876)
Year adopted	1780	1845	1876
Word length	45,000	11,600	87,000
Amendments	120	1	498
Feature	**Massachusetts**	**Texas (1845)**	**Texas (1876)**
Major sections	4	13	17
Executive offices elected			
Governor	✓	✓	✓
Lieutenant governor	✓	✓	✓
Secretary of state	✓	✗	✗
Attorney general	✓	✗	✓
Treasurer/comptroller	✓	✗	✓
Other	✓ (1)	✗	✓ (2)
Legislature	General Court	Texas Legislature	Texas Legislature
Senate			
Size	40	At least 19 but no more than 33	31
Length of term	2 years	4 years	4 years
House			
Size	160	At least 45 but no more than 90	150
Length of term	2 years	2 years	2 years
Judiciary	Appointed	Appointed	Elected

Feature	Massachusetts	Texas (1845)	Texas (1876)
Statewide referendum to amend constitution	✓	✓	✓
Statewide referendum to make general laws	✓	✗	✗
Initiative petition to amend constitution	✓	✗	✗
Initiative petition to make general laws	✓	✗	✗

TABLE 2.2 Comparison of State Constitutions

State	Number of Constitutions	Date of Current Constitution	Approximate Word Length	State	Number of Constitutions	Date of Current Constitution	Approximate Word Length
Alabama	6	1901	388,882	Montana	2	1973	12,790
Alaska	1	1959	13,479	Nebraska	2	1875	34,934
Arizona	1	1912	47,306	Nevada	1	1864	37,418
Arkansas	5	1874	59,120	New Hampshire	2	1784	13,060
California	2	1879	67,048	New Jersey	3	1948	26,360
Colorado	1	1876	66,140	New Mexico	1	1912	33,198
Connecticut	2	1965	16,401	New York	4	1895	44,397
Delaware	4	1897	25,445	North Carolina	3	1971	17,177
Florida	6	1969	56,705	North Dakota	1	1889	18,746
Georgia	10	1983	41,684	Ohio	2	1851	53,239
Hawaii	1	1959	21,498	Oklahoma	1	1907	81,666
Idaho	1	1890	24,626	Oregon	1	1859	49,016
Illinois	4	1971	16,401	Pennsylvania	5	1968	26,078
Indiana	2	1851	11,476	Rhode Island	2	1986	11,407
Iowa	2	1857	11,089	South Carolina	7	1896	27,421
Kansas	1	1861	14,097	South Dakota	1	1889	27,774
Kentucky	4	1891	27,234	Tennessee	3	1870	13,960
Louisiana	11	1975	69,876	**Texas**	**5**	**1876**	**87,000**
Maine	1	1820	16,313	Utah	1	1896	17,849
Maryland	4	1867	43,198	Vermont	3	1793	8,565
Massachusetts	1	1780	45,283	Virginia	6	1971	21,899
Michigan	4	1964	31,164	Washington	1	1889	32,578
Minnesota	1	1858	11,734	West Virginia	2	1872	33,324
Mississippi	4	1890	26,229	Wisconsin	1	1848	15,102
Missouri	4	1945	69,394	Wyoming	1	1890	26,349

Source: Data from *The Book of the States*, vol. 49 (Lexington, KY: Council of State Governments, 2017), Table 1.1.

defining marriage as a union between a man and a woman. An amendment this controversial was based on a 14 percent voter turnout. Amending the fundamental state law with such low turnout rates raises serious questions about the nature of popular sovereignty in Texas.

Constitutional Revision

Distrust of government has generally translated to suspicion of change in Texas. The current constitution has been criticized since its inception. Demands for constitutional revision have been almost continuous in Texas, with early calls for constitutional conventions occurring in 1913, 1917, 1949, 1957, and 1967.[50] As early as 1922, Governor Pat Neff urged the legislature to write a new state constitution, arguing that the 1876 constitution had become a "patchwork"—this after only thirty-nine amendments.[51] However, it wasn't until the early 1970s, in reaction to the Sharpstown scandal, a banking and stock fraud scandal involving officials at the highest levels of government, that Texas came close to substantial constitutional revision. The legislature created a constitutional revision commission that proposed sweeping changes to the current Texas Constitution. The proposal included providing annual sessions for the legislature, increasing the power of the governor, creating a single high court, and changing the selection process of the judiciary. The proposed document would have contained only 14,000 words and would have reduced the number of articles from seventeen to eleven. The final proposal was considered a well-drafted constitution and contained many of the changes constitutional experts continue to propose today. In the end, though, a joint meeting of both houses of the legislature failed by three votes to get the two-thirds vote necessary to pass it. In its next regular session, the legislature revived most of those proposals in the form of eight amendments to the constitution, but Texas voters overwhelmingly rejected each of the amendments.

Another serious attempt at significant constitutional revision came in 1998, spearheaded by Senator Bill Ratliff and Representative Rob Junell. The Ratliff-Junell proposal also reduced the document to about 18,000 words, granted expanded appointment power to the governor, increased the length of legislators' terms while imposing term limits, created a salary commission appointed by the governor to set compensation for legislators (without voter approval), and reorganized the judiciary with a single high court and gubernatorial appointment of judges followed by a retention election. Ratliff and Junell argued that the current constitution is clearly broken and imposes an intolerable cost on the state. Ratliff suggested that "[voters know] that any document you have to try to amend 20 times every other year is broke. It's sort of a Texas tragedy, actually, that we can't seem to come to grips with the fact that we need a new, basic document going into the next century and the next millennium."[52] Moreover, the cost of the frequent elections necessary to amend the constitution is considerable, manifesting itself in the forms of "voter fatigue and the temptation for special-interest groups to push amendments that aren't in the public interest."[53] Unfortunately, the Ratliff-Junell proposal unceremoniously died from neglect in the legislature. As with previous attempts at constitutional revision, Texans resisted change and chose to continue to patch up the old constitution. The constitution thus remains mired in legislative detail, and Texas politicians remain unwilling or unable to create a constitution designed for the diversity and complexities of our state.

Absent a constitutional convention, constitutional revision can occur in a variety of other ways. In Texas, constitutional revision has been accomplished primarily through amending the constitution. This incremental change in Texas, while not ideal, has been necessary since many Texans resist more sweeping changes, such as wholesale revision through constitutional conventions. Theoretically, change could also be accomplished with the voter-led initiative and referendum. An **initiative** occurs when voters gather signatures on a petition in order to place either statutes or constitutional amendments on a ballot. A **referendum** allows voters to cast a popular vote on statutes passed by the legislature. These two voter-led mechanisms are consistent with Texans' legendary preference for limited government and popular control. So it is particularly surprising that the Texas Constitution does not have provisions for either procedure. While Texans' preference for limited government may be notorious, in this case it is apparently trumped by their equally entrenched resistance to change. In the end, prospects for constitutional change seem limited. Most Texans, even as they acknowledge the problems with the current constitution, still distrust the potential problems of a new one more.

initiative
a mechanism that allows voters to gather signatures on a petition in order to place statutes or constitutional amendments on a ballot

referendum
a mechanism that allows voters to cast a popular vote on statutes passed by the state legislature; the legislature can place measures on the ballot for voter consideration

WINNERS AND LOSERS

In Texas, the general distrust of government and resulting resistance to change has created an environment in which the fundamental law is unyielding—a difficult situation for one of the nation's most rapidly changing states. The authors of the current Texas Constitution distrusted the Reconstruction government, which they viewed as the government of an occupying army. Their reaction was to create a constitution intended to limit the power of government, curb the potential for abuse by business, and preserve the power of citizens in the state. Ironically, the constitution entails such a high democratic cost to Texas citizens that the goals of the framers were guaranteed to fail. In an effort to safeguard the power of individuals, voters in Texas routinely face a long ballot and are literally overwhelmed by the number of offices and constitutional amendments put before them at each election. Instead of ensuring popular control of government, such a burden on citizens ensures voter fatigue and apathy. When citizens don't play their role to keep government in check, professional politicians and special interests fill the gap.

The winners of the current constitutional rules tend to be big-business interests. Business in Texas can dominate both the elections of officials and the approval or defeat of constitutional amendments, as overwhelmed voters simply opt out. The voters comprise the losers of the stagnant Texas Constitution. The voters, who continue to distrust government and therefore resist change, face a political system in which business and political interests often override popular concerns. Moreover, the short biennial legislative sessions stipulated in the constitution create a government that has not kept up with the increasing complexities of the state. The goal of the framers was to create a citizen legislature. By keeping the legislative sessions fixed and biennial and the salary

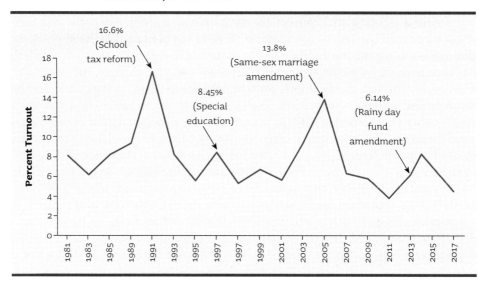

FIGURE 2.2 Voter Turnout during Special Elections and Off-Year Elections, 1981–2017

Source: Texas Secretary of State, www.sos.state.tx.us/elections/historical/70-92.shtml.

small, the framers hoped to preclude the creation of a professional legislature. In fact, in the twenty-first century, these constitutional impediments guarantee that the legislature is dominated by people who depend on business corporations or legal firms for their salary, entities that often have business before the state legislature. The constitution has created a legislature that is indebted to big business and special interests rather than one concerned with representing the people.

The election of judges in Texas, when most citizens are already overwhelmed by the number of officials on the ballot, adds to an environment in which citizens' interests may be marginalized in favor of big-business interests. Judges must raise significant amounts of money to be elected in the state, even as most citizens are simply not paying attention to judicial elections. Big business and other special interests are willing to fill that gap. In general, the Texas Constitution as it currently stands does not effectively empower the people in the state, and the general distrust of government means the people do not favor changing the constitution.

CONCLUSION

Texans continue to cling to a constitution written well over 100 years ago at a time when the state was largely dominated by agriculture. Texas has undergone constant and dramatic change since the constitution was written, and there is no sign that this change is slowing down. Gone are the days of the rugged

How does Texas's mistrust of government and resistance to change manifest itself in the current constitution? How does this conflict with the political preference for limited government?

★ CRITICAL THINKING

To what extent does the Texas Constitution create a citizen legislature?

★ CRITICAL THINKING

frontier. In today's Texas, you are more likely to see a computer chip than a longhorn. Yet even as the state continues to change, Texans adhere to the myth that the constitution continues to serve them. Mistrust of government overrides concerns over an unresponsive governmental structure. Texas continues to face increasingly complex issues, but Texans' tradition of mistrust undermines the ability of the government to respond to the state's transformations. Reliance on its outdated constitution will not serve Texas in the future.

Want a better grade?

Get the tools you need to sharpen your study skills. Access practice quizzes, eFlashcards, video, and multimedia at **edge.sagepub.com/collier6e**.

KEY TERMS

apprenticeship laws (p. 63)

black codes (p. 63)

block grant (p. 46)

categorical grant (p. 46)

concurrent powers (p. 42)

confederal system (p. 41)

constitution (p. 40)

cooperative federalism (p. 44)

devolution (p. 44)

dual federalism (p. 44)

enumerated powers (p. 42)

extradition (p. 43)

federalism (p. 42)

fiscal federalism (p. 46)

full faith and credit clause (p. 43)

horizontal federalism (p. 43)

implied powers (p. 42)

initiative (p. 75)

long ballot (p. 61)

Manifest Destiny (p. 54)

peonage (p. 63)

popular sovereignty (p. 41)

privileges and immunities (p. 43)

referendum (p. 75)

reserved powers (p. 43)

supremacy clause (p. 43)

unfunded mandate (p. 46)

unitary system (p. 42)

vertical federalism (p. 43)

ACTIVE LEARNING

- Break into groups of five. In each group, identify the arguments for giving more power to the state governments and the arguments for giving more power to the national government. **Teamwork**

- Draw a cartoon that illustrates a problem or problems with the current Texas Constitution. **Communication**

CHAPTER REVIEW

1. The type of constitutional arrangement where power is shared between two levels of government is called ____.
   a. unitary
   b. confederal
   c. federalism
   d. constitutional

2. A categorical grant is money given by the national government to state and local governments and is spent ____.
   a. however the state wants to spend the money
   b. according to the guidelines outlined by the national government
   c. according to the vote of the people

3. Which constitution made it legal for Texans to acquire mineral rights of their property?
   a. The Republic Constitution
   b. The statehood Constitution
   c. The Confederate Constitution
   d. The first Reconstruction Constitution

4. Which Texas constitution had the strongest provisions to protect slavery?
   a. The Republic Constitution
   b. The statehood Constitution
   c. The Confederate Constitution
   d. The first Reconstruction Constitution

5. The first Reconstruction Constitution was written to ____.
   a. satisfy the requirements of the national government
   b. guarantee African Americans the right to vote
   c. guarantee African Americans equal protection
   d. guarantee women the right to vote

6. The men who wrote the current Texas Constitution preferred ____.
   a. fiscal restraint
   b. local control
   c. limiting the power of big businesses
   d. all of these

7. The current Texas Constitution requires ____.

   a. thirty days' notice to suspend habeas corpus

   b. all state officeholders to have law degrees

   c. all state officeholders to acknowledge the existence of a Supreme Being

   d. all of these

8. In the Willacy County peonage case, if you were passing through town, you could be arrested and ____.

   a. sent back to where you came from

   b. put in jail indefinitely without bond

   c. forced to work in the cotton fields to pay your fine

   d. have your land sold to pay your debts

9. When a federal court ordered Mansfield ISD to desegregate in 1956, it ____.

   a. refused to desegregate after the governor sent Rangers to Mansfield

   b. desegregated only after the president sent troops to Mansfield

   c. desegregated after a local vote

   d. quietly desegregated

10. The League of United Latin American Citizens (LULAC) was founded in Corpus Christi in 1929 to fight discrimination targeting ____.

    a. women

    b. Hispanics

    c. African Americans

    d. LGBTQ persons

TEXAS LEGISLATURE

Chapter Objectives

★ Describe the form and function of the Texas Legislature.

★ Identify the different types of state legislatures and their advantages.

★ Discuss how legislative districts are drawn and how the Texas Legislature is elected.

★ Describe the leadership roles in Texas's legislative organization.

★ Explain the process for a bill becoming law in the Texas Legislature.

★ Assess who wins and who loses in how Texas's Legislature functions.

Generations of Texas students have been taught about bicameralism—the division of the legislature into two equal chambers—and wondered why their teacher was burdening them with such an obscure term. In 2017, legislators did their best to demonstrate the impact of bicameralism as the Texas House and Senate battled enthusiastically over a range of issues. While Americans have been told that the stark differences between Republicans and Democrats are responsible for much of the gridlock in Washington today, there was plenty of conflict and deadlock between the Texas House and Senate, even while both were dominated by Republicans.

At times, the Texas House and Senate seemed to share little except a building. The architecture of the capitol places the Senate in the east wing and the House in the west wing, with the rotunda in the middle keeping them at a safe distance from each other. However, while the Texas Constitution divides the legislature into two different chambers, it also requires that legislation pass both the House and Senate in exactly the same form before becoming law. Put another way, what bicameralism separates must come together for a bill to become law.

One of the issues dividing the two chambers in 2017 was education. The Texas Senate quickly embraced the idea of school vouchers—a system of allowing families to use state dollars to pay for tuition if they want to change schools. Vouchers had long been a favorite issue of some conservative "school choice" advocates. In the House, such plans were not always popular because some Republicans in the 150-member

Lieutenant Governor Dan Patrick, House Speaker Joe Straus, and Governor Greg Abbott meet to work out differences on legislation on May 27, 2017.

House represented districts dominated by small towns and rural areas where vouchers are less attractive. These districts do not always have enough students to support the number of schools that voucher plans require to give parents choices if they want to move their students from a public school. The Senate, with only thirty-one members, had few districts dominated by rural areas and leaned toward a reform favored by the more heavily populated cities and suburbs.

The way in which each chamber selects its presiding officer contributed to the conflict between the House and Senate. The Senate was led by Lieutenant Governor Dan Patrick, an elected official who needed support to win the votes of Republicans statewide in the primary. The House had begun the session by reelecting Joe Straus from their own membership. Given the ability to choose for themselves, the House selected a moderate leader more closely connected to business interests than the social conservatives in the party. A tug-of-war began early when Patrick made as one of his highest priorities the so-called "bathroom bill," which required that people use the bathroom based on their assigned gender at birth. The Texas House, under the leadership of Straus, showed less interest in the controversial subject of transgender people's use of restrooms, given that a similar North Carolina law had led to a number of entities boycotting that state. Eventually, the House approved a compromise that would have required school districts to provide single-occupancy bathrooms or changing rooms for students who do not want to use the rooms associated with their biological sex. However, this compromise version was not enough to satisfy the Senate, and the bill died at the end of regular session because the two chambers could not agree.

The significance of the basic structure of the legislature is subtle and more important than many Texans realize. The design and rules of the Texas Legislature determine much of what will happen every session. Texas government was designed to be inherently deliberate and slow moving, and conflicts like those between Dan Patrick and Joe Straus were predestined when the authors of the 1876 constitution opted to keep the bicameral legislature. The structures the authors of the Texas Constitution put in place almost 150 years ago guarantee that legislation will face extensive scrutiny from a wide variety of perspectives before it become law. James Madison, writing in *Federalist* No. 10, argued that one of the ways to keep the powers of government in check is to pit "ambition against ambition." In that regard, the conflict between the House and Senate in 2017 may be considered a testament to Madison's vision, as the ambitions of the state's political leaders often clashed and held each other in check.

In this chapter, we'll look at bicameralism and other features of the Texas Legislature to explore how these features shape who wins and who loses in Texas politics. We also will examine the organizational structure of the Texas Legislature, including an overview of the various types of committees as well as their function and structures. We will also consider the role of presiding officers and the impact of political parties in the Legislature. Finally, we will examine the legislative process, comparing the Texas Senate and House of Representatives across different areas that shape legislation, such as calendars, blocking bills, and filibusters.

THE TEXAS LEGISLATURE IN CONTEXT

The legislative branch in Texas is usually referred to as the Texas Legislature, or in Texas as simply *the* legislature. Like most states, Texas has chosen to have a legislative branch that resembles the U.S. Congress. (See Table 3.1 for a comparison of some of the characteristics of the U.S. Congress and the Texas Legislature.) The Texas Legislature is bicameral, meaning that it is divided into two separate chambers. Of the fifty states, only Nebraska has a single-chamber, or unicameral, state legislature. The lower house in Texas is called the House of Representatives, and the upper house is called the Senate. References to "upper" and "lower" houses developed from the British Parliament, in which the House of Lords represented the nobility of the "upper" class and the House of Commons represented the ordinary citizens of the "lower" class. Despite the revolution against England, these terms somehow carried over into the American experience. Some members of the Texas House and their staff will tell you that the Texas Senate still considers itself the "upper" house—this only feeds the rivalry between the two chambers. Some states use different names for these chambers. For example, in Virginia, the lower house is called the House of Delegates.

The decision to have a dual-chambered state legislature reflects more than just a simple desire to mirror the U.S. Congress. James Madison suggested in *The Federalist Papers* that the protection of liberty from passionate majorities rests in part with dividing the power of the legislature.[1] Requiring any new law to pass in two chambers makes it more difficult for a majority to abuse its power and take away the rights of a minority.

While all federal systems in the world have bicameral national legislatures, many have unicameral state or regional legislatures. For example, all of the ten provincial legislative assemblies in Canada are unicameral, while the national parliament

bicameral
a legislature that consists of two separate chambers or houses

TABLE 3.1 U.S. Congress and the Texas Legislature: A Comparison

	U.S. Congress		Texas Legislature	
Characteristic	U.S. Senate	U.S. House	Texas Senate	Texas House
Size of chamber	100	435	31	150
Term in office	6 years	2 years	4 years	2 years
Minimum age for election	30	25	26	21
Resident of state	Yes	Yes	5 years	2 years
Resident of district	N/A	No	1 year	1 year

is bicameral. Mexico uses a similar system, where each state has a unicameral state legislature even though Mexico's national Congress is bicameral. Outside North America, unicameral state legislatures are found in Austria, Brazil, Germany, and Malaysia. In Germany, state governments are directly represented in the upper house of the national parliament (the *Bundesrat*), which consists of members of each state's executive branch.

In the past, some U.S. states mirrored the relationship between the two houses in the U.S. Congress by making counties the basis of representation in the upper house of the state legislature in the same way states are the basis for representation in the U.S. Senate. However, with 254 counties in Texas, giving each county their own senator was never practical. The Texas Constitution of 1876 specified that no county could have more than one state senator. In 1962, the U.S. Supreme Court rejected counties and other local governments as a basis for representation in state legislatures in the *Baker v. Carr* (1962) ruling. The court found that the equal protection clause of the Fourteenth Amendment asserts the principle of "one person, one vote," meaning that the population of state legislative districts must be roughly (give or take 5 percent) equal.[2]

Size of the Legislature

Each of the forty-nine states in the United States with a bicameral state legislature has an upper house that is smaller than the lower house. The smaller size of the upper house again mirrors the U.S. Congress; the U.S. Senate, with 100 members, is much smaller than the 435-member U.S. House of Representatives.

The sizes of state legislatures vary because each state determines the best fit for its needs. For example, the Texas Constitution sets the size of the Texas Senate at thirty-one members and the Texas House at 150. As the population of Texas has grown, the legislature has increased the size of the Texas House of Representatives over time to its current 150, a size approved by voters in 1999 when they agreed to amend the state constitution. The size of the membership of a state's legislature is not proportional to the population of the state. Large-population states such as Texas, Florida, and California do not always have the largest state legislatures. New

Hampshire, one of the smallest states, has the largest legislature, with 400 members representing about 1.3 million people.

One of the most interesting differences is the relationship between the number of citizens and the number of legislators. In states where there are more legislators relative to the population, each legislator represents fewer people and, in some sense, the legislator is closer to the people. In Texas, with the eleventh-largest legislature and the second-largest population, each member represents an average of almost 156,000 people. The Texas Senate's thirty-one members each represent about 913,000 people, but in the Texas House of Representatives the ratio is about 189,000 per member. When comparing the ratios of representation to population, Texas ranks forty-ninth in the United States. Thus, Texans are less represented in their own state legislature than citizens of almost every other state. Only California has fewer state representatives per person than Texas.

A practical limitation on the ratio of legislators to population is the fact that extremely large legislatures are difficult to organize. If Texas used the same ratio as New Hampshire, where each member of the state legislature represents over 3,200 people, the Texas Legislature would have to find space for over 8,900 members, a group too large to be managed effectively.

Legislative Sessions

The Texas Legislature is one of four state legislatures that do not meet yearly for a regular session, instead convening every two years. Texas joins Montana, Nevada, and North Dakota in having legislatures that meet biennially.[3]

Regular Session

regular session
meetings of a legislature that are required by a constitution or law; the Texas Legislature meets every other year for 140 days

When in **regular session**, the Texas Legislature meets for 140 days, making the length of its session one of the longest in the country. However, eleven states, including large-population states such as California, Michigan, New York, North Carolina, Ohio, and Pennsylvania, do not limit the length of state legislative sessions.[4]

The length and frequency of legislative sessions shapes how legislatures go about their work. Legislatures that meet annually are able to review the budget each year and make adjustments. The Texas Legislature faces a tremendous amount of work when it meets for its biennial session. As the regular session opens, the legislature faces a backlog of interim appointments made by the governor since the end of the last legislature session as well as budget problems caused by fluctuations in the economy since the last session. Every session the Texas Legislature has to pass a budget and laws that will address the needs of a rapidly growing and changing state for the next two years. One textbook decreed way back in 1966 that the biennial session was "sound enough when it was written into the constitution in 1876, but in the second half of the 20th Century it is unquestionably obsolete."[5] Critics of the current system argue that annual sessions would allow the legislature to more effectively oversee the executive branch and help the state to respond more quickly to changes—including mandates from the federal government and changes to the economy. Advocates of biennial session believe that limiting the legislature's sessions limits their ability to interfere in the lives of citizens and forces legislators to spend more time living and working under the laws they write.

Special Sessions

Often, state legislatures find it necessary to have the legislature meet beyond regular sessions. These special sessions of the legislature may occur after an unexpected event or to complete work on important legislation that did not pass during the regular session. Texas and fourteen other states have rules that allow only the governor to call a special session. In the other thirty-five states, either the governor or the legislature can call for a special session. In some states, such as Alaska and Florida, a supermajority of legislators (usually, two-thirds or three-fifths of the members of each chamber) must agree to hold the special session by filing a petition. Some states, such as Delaware, allow the presiding officers of each chamber to call the legislature into special session. Moreover, a majority of states do not limit the number of days the legislature meets in special session, and there are no limits on the number of special sessions that can be called.

> When the Texas Legislature is called into special sessions, each of these sessions is limited to thirty days. The governor summons the legislature into special session by issuing an official proclamation referred to as "the call." This document gives governors a great deal of power to lead the legislature because it states when the legislature will begin meeting for the special session and the subjects it can consider. If the governor is not satisfied with the work of the Texas Legislature during a special session, the governor may call the legislature back into session as often as he or she wishes. The governor may also add new issues to the call during the session. For example, in 2013, then-governor Rick Perry called legislators to Austin for a special session from May 27 to June 25. He asked for laws to place restrictions on when and where abortions may be performed, to prioritize and fund transportation projects, and to pass a final redistricting plan for the state legislature and Texas's seats in the U.S. House of Representatives. When a filibuster by Texas senator Wendy Davis blocked action on abortion at the end of the first special session, Perry called the legislature back into session again a few days later, and this time it passed abortion legislation.

special session
meetings of a legislature that occur outside the regular legislative session; in Texas, special sessions are called by the governor and last up to thirty days

supermajority
a majority that is larger than a simple majority of 50 percent plus one; supermajorities include requirements of 60 percent, two-thirds, three-fourths, or 80 percent to make a decision

Rights and Privileges

When the legislature is in session, its members enjoy certain rights and privileges. Article 2, Section 14 of the Texas Constitution provides that "Senators and Representatives shall, except in cases of treason, felony, or breach of the peace, be privileged from arrest during the session of the legislature, and in going to and returning from the same." In addition, Article 2, Section 21 protects members' right to speak freely while debating legislation: "No member shall be questioned in any other place for words spoken in debate in either House." Such protections, known as legislative immunity, originated with parliamentary immunity that emerged from the struggle between parliament and the monarchy. Protecting legislators from arrest ensures that state and local officials cannot interfere with a legislator's efforts to represent his or her constituents. Similarly, protecting what legislators say during debates ensures that they remain free to say everything they need to as they represent their constituents.

legislative immunity
the protection from arrest that legislators receive to ensure that state and local officials cannot interfere with a legislator's efforts to represent their constituents

TYPOLOGIES OF STATE LEGISLATURES: FULL-TIME AND PART-TIME

Based on factors such as length of legislative session, compensation for legislators, and professional resources, state legislatures may be classified as one of three types: citizen, professional, or hybrid. A citizen legislature seeks to limit the role of a state legislator to a part-time task so that many or most citizens can perform it. Typically, citizen legislatures meet every other year or for only a few weeks each year. The duties of a legislator in these states are about as time-consuming as a part-time job, taking up just over twenty hours a week. Compensation is minimal for citizen legislators (averaging $18,449 a year) and in some cases amounts to no more than reimbursement for travel and other expenses associated with attending legislative sessions. Staffing and other professional resources are minimal. Montana, North Dakota, South Dakota, and Wyoming are states that have citizen legislatures. Another ten states (Idaho, Kansas, Maine, Mississippi, New Hampshire, New Mexico, Rhode Island, Utah, Vermont, and West Virginia) have "lite" versions of part-time legislatures that demand more of a legislator's time and have more extensive staff support than a traditional part-time legislature.[6]

In contrast, a professional legislature meets annually, often for as many as nine months of the year. In these states, being a member of the state legislature is a full-time occupation and legislators are paid accordingly, since such service effectively precludes holding a job outside. Members of professional legislatures are well compensated, averaging $82,358 among the eleven state legislatures classified as professional.[7] More generous office allowances allow members of the legislature to hire and maintain extensive staffs that typically include secretarial support and researchers. Only California, Michigan, New York, and Pennsylvania have professional legislatures. Another six states (Alaska, Hawaii, Illinois, Massachusetts, Ohio, and Wisconsin) have "lite" versions of professional legislatures where the workload is lighter because sessions are shorter and their districts are smaller.

Texas and most other states fall in between these two extremes and have hybrid legislatures. In Texas and twenty-five other states, the legislature spends less time in session and has a staff budget that is less than half of those of professional legislatures. Members of the legislature receive some compensation. Average compensation in states with this type of legislature is $41,110.[8] In 1991, Texas voters approved a constitutional amendment raising the base pay for Texas legislators to $7,200 a year and creating the Texas Ethics Commission (TEC), which was empowered to recommend future pay raises, subject to approval by the voters. The TEC also establishes "per diem" allowances for members ($190 per day in 2017) to compensate legislators for personal expenses while the legislature is in session, meaning that Texas legislators earned a total of $33,800 for 2017 because they were in session 140 days.[9] Legislators can also receive reimbursement for travel from their home district to Austin and receive coverage under the state health insurance plan offered to all state employees. Legislators who do not ordinarily reside in Austin may use political contributions to pay "reasonable household expenses in Austin."

In terms of staffing resources, members of the Texas Senate receive an allowance of $38,000 per month to pay for the costs of maintaining offices in Austin and in their district. These funds are used to purchase office equipment and supplies, pay for office space, and provide salaries and other compensation for office workers. On average, members of the Texas Senate keep six staffers employed year-round. Members of the Texas House of Representatives receive $13,250 per month for staff support, enough to provide each

citizen legislature
a legislature that attempts to keep the role of a state legislator to a part-time function so that many or most citizens can perform it; normally, a citizen legislator is provided minimal compensation, offered few staffing resources, and has short or infrequent legislative sessions

professional legislature
a legislature that meets annually, often for nine months of the year or more; a professional legislator is provided a professional-level salary and generous allowances to hire and keep support and research staffs

representative an average staff size of three persons. Legislators may use campaign contributions to supplement staff salaries, and some legislators supplement their regular paid staff with student interns and volunteers.

Although the framers of the Texas Constitution sought to establish a citizen legislature, the Texas Legislature today is classified as a hybrid legislature for several reasons. While salaries in the Texas Legislature may be low, legislators receive one of the most generous retirement plans among the fifty state legislatures. Legislators who have served eight years in the legislature can start receiving benefits at age sixty (or age fifty if they have served twelve years) if they have left the legislature. In 1975, the legislature tied the retirement benefits of elected officials to the salary of state district judges. Their annual retirement income is 2.3 percent of the base compensation of the judges' salary times their years of service. When the legislature raised the salary of the district judge to $140,000, this made the annual minimum benefit for legislators $25,760 per year after eight years of service in the legislature. Former Speaker Tom Craddick, one of the longest-serving members in the history of the Texas Legislature, qualified for the maximum pension of $140,000 at the end of the legislative session in 2017.

The Texas State Capitol is surrounded by a sea of constituents during the Women's March on January 21, 2017.

While some members may have generous benefits awaiting them when they retire, the low level of pay does ensure that most legislators will need to make money during their legislative careers. This reflects the principle that government should be in the hands of citizens who must earn a living under the laws they write. However, most Texans simply cannot leave their job for 140 days every other year to serve in the legislature. Many ordinary Texas citizens simply cannot afford to be a legislator while the conditions for other professions are more favorable.

QUALIFICATIONS FOR OFFICE AND LENGTH OF TERMS

The state constitution requires that members of the Texas House of Representatives be at least twenty-one years of age and have been a resident of Texas for two years and a resident of the district for at least one year prior to the election. Election to the Texas Senate requires that a citizen be at least twenty-six years of age and have been a resident of Texas for five years and a resident of the district for at least one year before the election. While the constitution may allow for younger members, the people elected are older. In 2017, no members of the legislature were under thirty. In fact, the youngest senator was forty-five and the average age of a Texas senator was 58.5.[10]

Like other legislatures, the Texas Legislature has the right to refuse to seat a winning candidate and has the power to decide whether an election is valid. According to the state constitution, "[e]ach House shall be the judge of the qualifications and election of its own members; but contested elections shall be determined in such manner as prescribed by law."[11] Such refusals are extremely rare. However, several decades ago, a representative from Gillespie County was elected as a write-in candidate. The losing candidate appealed to the Texas House, requesting that it not seat the winner because he had not competed in the primary, had never announced his candidacy, and had never paid a filing fee. The House refused to consider the appeal.[12]

The term of office for members of the Texas House of Representatives is two years. Texas senators are elected every four years, but the elections are staggered so that one-half of the Texas Senate is chosen every two years. An exception to this rule occurs when new senate districts are created by **redistricting**. After the U.S. Census data are released and the redistricting process to adjust election districts for the legislature is completed, the entire Texas Senate is elected at the next election. Thus, the entire Texas Senate was elected in 2012. Then, by lottery, one-half of the Texas Senate comes up for reelection after just two years—2014 in this case. The other half of the Texas Senate began a four-year term in 2012 and was up for reelection in 2016.

The timing of elections to the state legislature also varies by state. While Texas holds elections in even-numbered years, coinciding with U.S. presidential elections and midterm elections to the U.S. Congress, a few states, including Louisiana, conduct elections to the state legislature in odd-numbered years to separate state politics from national politics.

In the 1990s, some states began imposing term limits on their elected representatives. A **term limit** legally limits legislators to a specific number of terms after which they are no longer eligible for reelection. Currently, fifteen states have term limits. Some states limit the amount of time an individual may serve in a specific chamber of the legislature. Other states place a limit on the total number of years a person may serve in either chamber of a state legislature. Michigan has the most restrictive limits on the amount of time someone may serve in the state legislature: six years for the lower house of the state legislature and eight years for the upper house. California and Oklahoma limit an individual to serving only twelve years in either chamber.

Texas, along with thirty-five other states, does not have term limits.[13] Proponents of term limits argue that these limits encourage **turnover** to prevent politicians from making their elected office their primary occupation and thereby losing touch with the needs and concerns of the average citizen. Opponents argue that voters should have the ability to retain quality legislators and can vote bad members out at any point.

As Figure 3.1 reflects, the rates of incumbency in the Texas Legislature have dropped in recent years. The 2012 election saw the lowest rate of incumbency in the recent history of the Texas House of Representatives. This rate of incumbency reflects the impact of the 2011 redistricting of the legislature, with many members running in redrawn districts where voters did not know them. Another bad year for incumbents occurred during the November 2002 elections that saw Republicans win control over both houses for the first time in more than 100 years. Usually Texas senators are equally or more likely to be reelected than their counterparts in the Texas House. This trend held despite redistricting for the 2012 election. These rates of incumbency are quite different from the U.S. Congress, where the U.S. Senate has a lower rate of incumbency than the U.S. House.

redistricting
the periodic adjustment of the lines of electoral district boundaries

term limit
a legal limitation on the number of terms an elected official may serve in office

turnover
when current officeholders step down from office and are replaced by new officeholders; turnover may result from retirement, defeat in an election, or term limits

REPRESENTATION: THEORIES AND DEMOGRAPHICS

One of the key functions of a legislature is **representation**, or the relationship between the people and their representatives. There are three views on what constitutes an appropriate relationship between a representative and the electorate. According to the **delegate** approach, the people elect a representative to follow the views of the district.[14] The legislator as delegate is expected to carry out specific tasks and vote as instructed by voters, regardless of his or her own personal beliefs, and should not exercise independent judgment. In contrast, the **trustee** approach begins by assuming that elected officials have access to information that voters do not. As a result, the representative understands issues from the broader perspective of the best interests of the entire district, state, or country. In this view, the people trust their representative to make the best choices for them. Therefore, the representative, who is better educated about the issue, may go against the wishes of the majority. Finally, the **politico** approach asserts that a representative follows the wishes of the voting majority on the most important issues while on other issues he or she has more leeway.[15] In the latter case, the representative's personal beliefs may conflict with those of the majority, and the representative then must choose between conscience and constituency.

Representation Based on Geography

In the United States, representation is based on geography that emphasizes representation of citizens based on where they live. The advantage of geographic representation is that geographic districts provide a direct connection between the representative and the voters. Voters are assumed to share political values and economic interests based on where they live.

representation
the relationship between an elected official and the electorate

delegate
an elected official who acts as an agent of the majority that elected her or him to office and carries out, to the extent possible, the wishes of that majority

trustee
an elected official who is entrusted to act in the best interests of the electorate based on his or her knowledge; he or she is understood to be generally better informed than the broader electorate

politico
an elected official who is expected to follow the wishes of the electorate on some issues but on others is permitted more decision-making leeway; a hybrid of the trustee and delegate

FIGURE 3.1 Rates of Incumbency for the Texas Legislature, 1995–2017

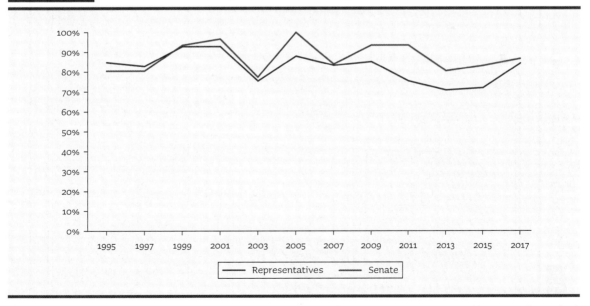

Source: Adapted from Legislative Reference Library of Texas, "Membership Statistics for the 83rd Legislature," 2013, www.lrl.state.tx.us/legeLeaders/members/memberStatistics.cfm (accessed June 21, 2018).

MAP 3.1 State Senate Districts in Texas for the November 2018 Elections

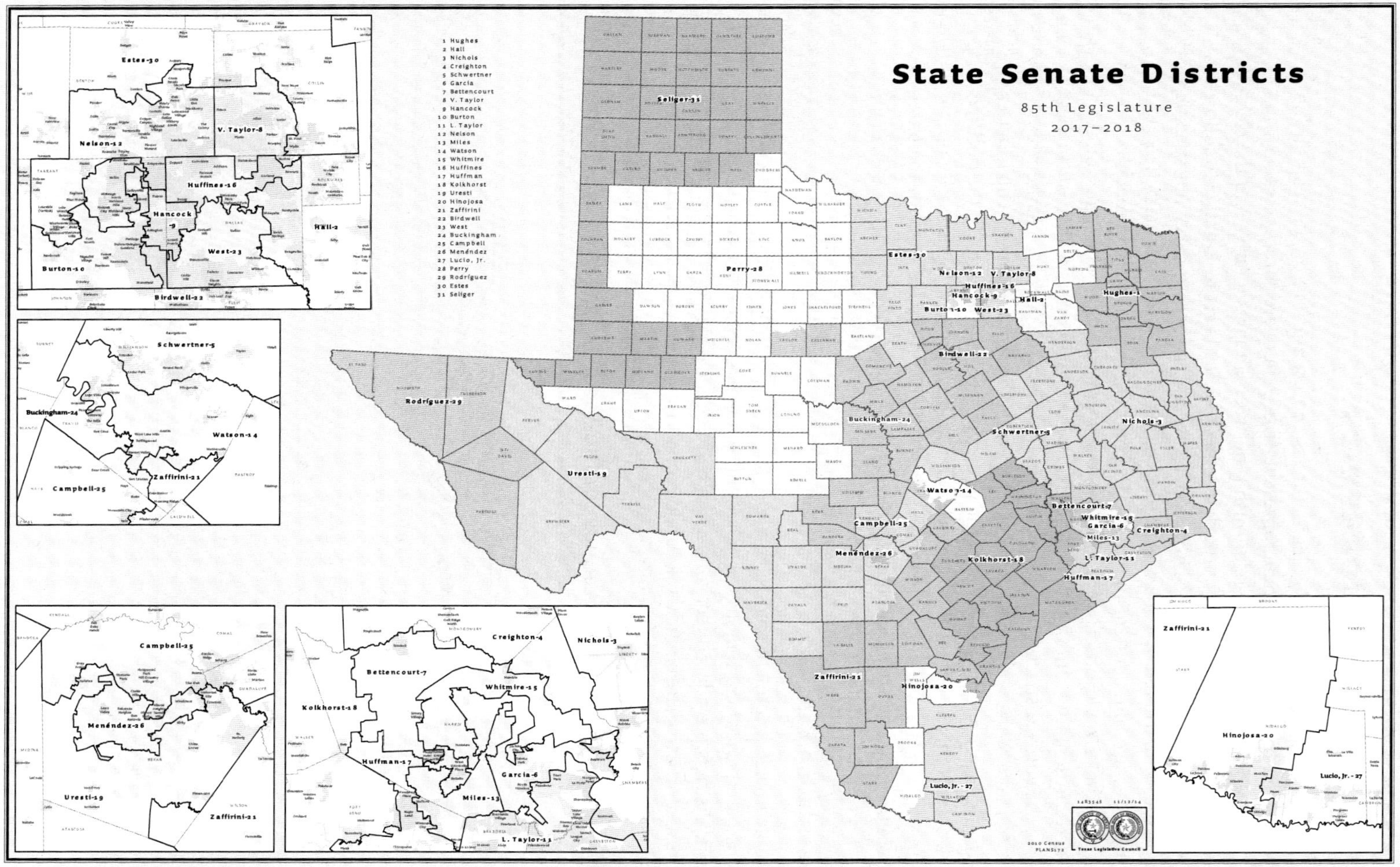

Source: Texas Legislative Council, "State Senate Districts, 85th Legislature, 2017–2018," http://www.tlc.state.tx.us/redist/pdf/senate/map.pdf (accessed September 27, 2018). Reproduced with permission from the Texas Legislative Council, http://www.tlc.state.tx.us.

MAP 3.2 State House Districts in Texas for the November 2018 Elections

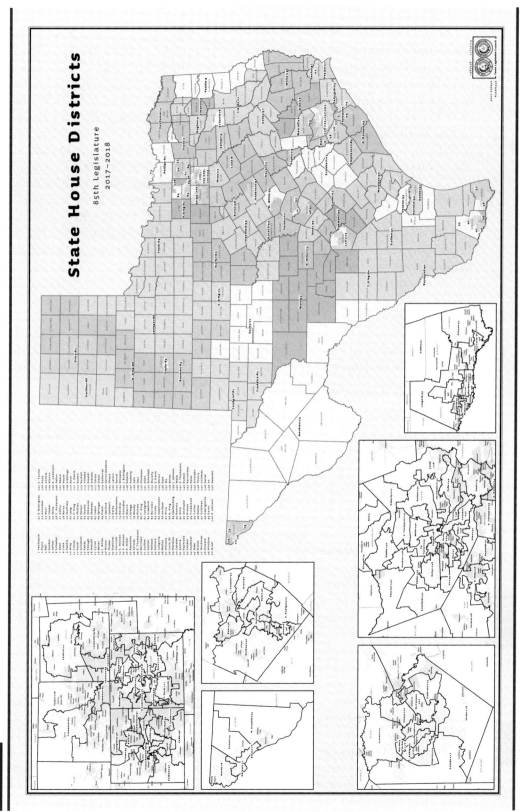

Source: Texas Legislative Council, "State House Districts, 85th Legislature, 2017–2018," http://www.tlc.state.tx.us/redist/pdf/house/map.pdf (accessed September 27, 2018). Reproduced with permission from the Texas Legislative Council, http://www.tlc.state.tx.us.

Microcosm Theory and Demographics

One perspective on representation is microcosm theory. John Adams, the second president of the United States and an early proponent of the theory, believed that a legislature should look like the larger society.[16] The aim is to have the legislature be as close to a perfect representative sample as possible.[17] Microcosm theory holds that, while each individual member cannot truly represent the public at large, collectively the legislature should represent the whole population. In microcosm theory, the assumption is that people with the same ethnic, racial, socioeconomic, or sex/gender background share political values and beliefs, regardless of where they live. The Texas Legislature, then, should "look like" Texas in, among other things, its gender, racial, and educational makeup. If we assume that a legislator's income, education, race, religion, and gender all shape the decisions that he or she makes, then microcosm theory offers one way of looking at whether the legislature reflects the population. If the legislature looks like the larger society, citizens may accept its legitimacy and decisions more readily. If the legislature does not seem to mirror the larger society, then its legitimacy may be questioned.

In fact, the Texas legislature does not mirror the population. Some of this may be the result of deliberate choices by voters. For example, over 90 percent of the members of both houses of the Texas Legislature in 2017 had completed at least a four-year college degree. This stands in sharp contrast to the 17 percent of Texans overall who hold a degree from a four-year institution of higher learning. In this instance, Texans might have deliberately decided that college-educated Texans are better advocates for their causes.

Gender and Racial/Ethnic Gaps in the Legislature

After women won the right to vote, some politicians argued that women should find influence by electing "the right man."[18] Microcosm theory suggests that the best way to take measure of the representation of women is by looking at the gender of who is elected, and looking at the representation of women in state legislatures is especially easy because, while racial and other characteristics may vary widely from state to state, every state has close to half males and half females. When the Texas legislature convened in January 2017, only 20.4 percent of the members were female. As Figure 3.3 reflects, Texas is not alone in the underrepresentation of woman, and women rarely comprise more than one-third of a state's legislature. This is not surprising because women have historically been underrepresented in both Texas and national politics. In 2018, 25.4 percent of state legislators and 20 percent of members of Congress in the United States were women. As Figure 3.2 indicates, while that number may be low, it represents a dramatic rise from 1971, when 4.5 percent of legislators were female.[19] Compounding the underrepresentation of women was their treatment once in office. After Edith Williams became the first woman elected to the Texas Legislature in 1922, she found that she had to fight to be treated professionally. In 1926, Margie Neal became the second woman elected to the legislature and the state's first female senator. She would go on to serve eight years without any other female senators, and the Texas Senate would not have more than one female member until 1987. Even when women were elected to the legislature, they were often marginalized. For example, when Frances Farenthold was the only woman in the Texas House in 1969, capitol guards sometimes assumed she was not a legislator and tried to prevent her from entering the floor of the House.[20]

The demographic makeup of the Texas Legislature is not reflective of the wider population. The legislature is significantly whiter/more Caucasian than the general population. Asian Americans and African Americans in particular have been underrepresented. African

How has the representation of women in politics changed over the last forty years?

⭐ EMPIRICAL AND QUANTITATIVE

How important is it to the representation of Texans that women are elected?

⭐ SOCIAL RESPONSIBILITY

FIGURE 3.2 Women in Office

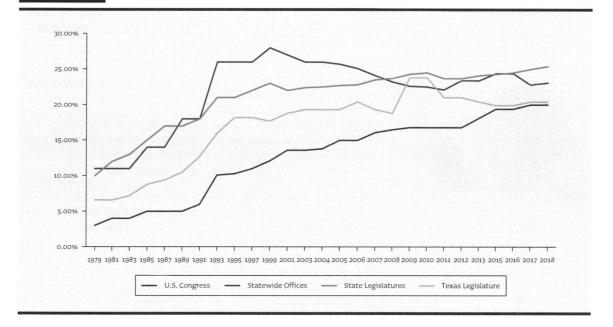

Americans initially enjoyed some representation in the Texas Legislature in the years after the Civil War. In 1869, Texas had two black state senators and twelve black members of the Texas House. However, once Reconstruction ended, disenfranchisement of black voters took hold. African Americans would not serve again in the legislature until the 1966 election brought Barbara Jordan, Curtis Graves, and Joe Lockridge into the Texas House.

In a similar fashion, Tejanos initially held some political power after the Texas Revolution (1835–1836), but these positions soon waned. Despite gains in the overall population, Hispanic representation in the Texas Legislature continues to lag behind that in the wider society. In 2015, about 38.8 percent of Texans identified as Hispanic, while the legislature that convened in Austin was about 22.7 percent Hispanic.

Proponents of microcosm theory might point toward distrust of the state government as a result of the gap between the makeup of the legislature and the population of Texas. As Laredo senator Judith Zaffirini put it, "cumulatively, women comprise half of the population, and cumulatively, we are the mothers of the other half . . . We need a population in the legislature that reflects the population of the state."[21] Yet critics of microcosm theory point out that representation is not just about social and demographic characteristics of constituents and legislators. Representation is about sharing a wide variety of values and beliefs. Just because a representative differs from the wider population in his or her age, educational background, ethnicity, or religion does not mean that that representative does not share relevant values and beliefs of voters. Even if the state legislature matched its citizens in terms of gender, race, and religion, there may be other aspects of our lives that are more important to how Texans want to be represented in Austin. Certain professions (teachers), interests (hunting), and issues (abortion) might be much more relevant to the laws written in Austin than race, gender, or religion. An evangelical farmer might feel better served by a Buddhist who farms for a living than by a fellow evangelical who works in an office all day.

TEXAS Legends

Barbara C. Jordan

Barbara Jordan's career in Texas politics represents both personal and institutional victories. Jordan graduated from Boston University Law School. Her first two efforts at winning a seat in the Texas House of Representatives were foiled by a system that chose the twelve members of the House from Harris County at large through a countywide vote that diluted the political strength of minorities. Under this system, even though about 20 percent of Houstonians were African American, none of Harris County's representatives were black. However, the *Baker v. Carr* (1962) and *Reynolds v.*

Sims (1964) U.S. Supreme Court decisions required that members of the state legislature be elected from districts that were roughly equal in population, thus putting an end to the at-large system. Helped by the newly drawn single-member districts (SMDs) mandated by the court's decisions and by the removal of the poll tax as a barrier to voting, Jordan was elected to the Texas Senate in 1966, the first African American to serve since 1881.

Initially, Jordan faced insults from some legislators, who called her "Mammy" or "the washerwoman" behind her back.[i] However, Jordan's intelligence and political skills won over many of her fellow legislators, and the Texas Senate unanimously elected her as president pro tempore in 1972. Later that same year, Jordan became the first black woman from the South to win election to the U.S. House of Representatives.

While in the U.S. Congress, Jordan became an important player in the impeachment of President Richard Nixon,

delivering a speech in which she declared, "My faith in the Constitution is whole; it is complete; it is total. And I am not going to sit here and be an idle spectator to the diminution, the subversion, the destruction, of the Constitution." In 1976, she became the first African American woman to deliver the keynote address at the Democratic National Convention, delivering what many observers consider one of the best speeches given at a party convention.

While much of what Barbara Jordan accomplished resulted from her character and intelligence, her political career would not have been possible without the Supreme Court opening the door to more representative legislative bodies through its redistricting decisions that protected the representation of minorities.

---

i. James L. Haley, *Passionate Nation: The Epic History of Texas* (New York: Free Press, 2006), 545.

WINNERS AND LOSERS

The Texas Legislature was designed to be the heart of representative democracy in Texas. In theory, a citizen legislature protects citizen interests over those of the organized interest groups that so frequently dominate legislatures. In Texas there are several institutional constraints that preclude the establishment of a true citizen legislature. The low level of financial compensation forces most legislators to maintain outside sources of income, and individuals with higher levels of education, higher incomes, and more flexible work schedules can more easily serve in the Texas Legislature. Very few professions have the flexibility that allows you to take 140 days off work every two years (and be ready to take off work for the occasional special session). Given the high cost of modern campaigns, legislators also need to be able to set aside time for fund-raising as they seek reelection. The average citizen generally can't afford to take the job of a state legislator. Thus, the effort to maintain a "citizen" legislature often falls short and may result in a legislature that does not "look like" Texas. In this regard, the average citizen may end up an accidental loser in the attempt to have a citizen legislature.

At left, Representative Frances Farenthold stands at the podium in the state House of Representatives around 1970. At right, after his election in 1966, Curtis Graves became the first African American to serve in the Texas House since 1899. The demographic makeup of elected officials in the Texas Legislature—then and now—is not representative of the state's population as a whole.

Sources: (L) Frances Tarlton Farenthold Papers, e_sf_0140, The Dolph Briscoe Center for American History, The University of Texas at Austin; (R) The State Preservation Board, Austin, Texas.

ELECTING THE STATE LEGISLATURE

Most state legislatures and the U.S. House of Representatives employ some type of **single-member district (SMD)** system where the state is divided into a number of districts equal to the number of members of the chamber. Thus, for elections to the Texas Senate, the state of Texas is divided into thirty-one districts, with each district electing one person to the chamber. For the Texas House of Representatives, the state is divided into 150 districts, with each district electing one representative.

Single-Member District versus Multimember District

Currently, ten states use some form of a **multimember district (MMD)** system to elect their state legislature. These states are divided into election districts, but some districts elect more than one person to the state legislature. Arizona, Idaho, New Jersey, North Dakota, South Dakota, and Washington have two-member house districts, while Maryland, New Hampshire, Vermont, and West Virginia use a mixture of SMDs and MMDs. Voters normally cast a single vote for their most preferred candidate on the ballot. After the votes are counted, the candidates with the highest vote totals equal to the number of seats in the district are elected. The advantage of the MMD system is that candidates from more than one political party (or faction of a political party) are able to win a seat from the district. Theoretically, this logic applies to racial and ethnic minorities as well. In practice, at least in the American South (including Texas), MMDs have diluted minority representation and allowed whites to overwhelm the state legislature with their candidates.

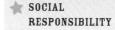

What assumptions underlie microcosm theory? How fair are those assumptions?

⭐ **SOCIAL RESPONSIBILITY**

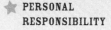

What changes would help bring more typical Texans into the legislature?

⭐ **PERSONAL RESPONSIBILITY**

single-member district (SMD)
an election system in which the state is divided into many election districts and each district elects just one person to the state legislature

The Texas House of Representatives originally elected representatives based on counties, with large counties having more than one member of the Texas House of Representatives. Instead of creating separate districts within the county, two or more representatives would represent the entire county. The impact of these MMDs became an important one during the civil rights era of the 1960s. While the U.S. Supreme Court held that the equal protection clause of the Fourteenth Amendment of the U.S. Constitution did not require the use of SMD election systems,[22] the courts found that the MMD system used for the Texas Legislature appeared to depress representation of African Americans and Hispanics.[23]

The Redistricting Process

One of the challenges facing the legislature of a changing state is the regular need to redraw district lines. If election district lines for the state legislature did not change as the population grew, then over time some areas will have many more people per representative than other areas. Between 1921 and 1951, the Texas Legislature did not redistrict, despite rapid population growth in some parts of the state. For example, over those thirty years, Harris County's population grew from 186,667 to 806,701. In *Baker v. Carr* (1962), the U.S. Supreme Court ruled that representation in the state

FIGURE 3.3 Women in State Legislatures, 2018

Source: Center for American Women and Politics, "Women in States Legislatures 2018," accessed August 25, 2018, www.cawp.rutgers.edu/women-state-legislature-2018.

legislatures was subject to judicial review if it violated the equal protection clause of the Fourteenth Amendment.[24] In *Reynolds v. Sims* (1964), the U.S. Supreme Court extended this logic by requiring that both houses of state legislatures represent the population of a state on a one-person, one-vote basis.[25] The principle of one person, one vote requires that the vote of any one person carry the equivalent weight of the vote of any other person.

Today, redistricting in Texas normally occurs every ten years, after the results of the U.S. Census are provided to the states. Redistricting occurs through one of three methods. The simplest is that the legislature itself draws up the new districts. The Texas Legislature is responsible for drawing the lines for its own election districts as well as those for the state's board of education and the state's seats in the U.S. House of Representatives. The Texas Constitution requires that Texas legislature districts be contiguous, meaning that all the parts must be connected and a person should be able to travel from one part of the district to another without leaving the district. In addition, districts must respect county boundaries as much as possible. Obviously, allowing members of the state legislature to define their own election districts encourages incumbents to draw district lines to their political advantage, a process referred to as gerrymandering.

If the Texas legislature is unable to pass a redistricting plan for its own districts, the process is handed over to the Legislative Redistricting Board (LRB). This system, and similar ones in states such as Connecticut, Mississippi, and Oklahoma, are called hybrid systems because the redistricting occurs through a combination of the legislature and some other body that includes membership from outside the legislature. The LRB in Texas, which was created by a 1948 amendment to the state constitution, is composed of the lieutenant governor, the Speaker of the Texas House of Representatives, the attorney general, the comptroller of accounts, and the commissioner of the Texas General Land Office. The LRB is only an advisory board that develops a plan for redistricting that must be submitted to the state legislature for approval. The board also becomes involved in redistricting the state legislature when a state or federal court invalidates a plan approved by the state legislature. However, the LRB redistricts only the state legislature. The task of drawing election districts for the members of the U.S. House of Representatives from Texas remains the exclusive domain of the state legislature.

In some states, a commission separate from the legislature has primary responsibility for developing a redistricting plan that the legislature must approve with little or no change to the plan. These states hope to remove partisan politics from the process as much as possible and keep the members of the state legislature from drawing district lines to protect their reelection. Several types of commissions exist. Alaska, Colorado, and Vermont establish a commission from nominations made by the governor, state supreme court justices, and/or members of the legislature. In Arkansas and Ohio, members of the state executive branch, such as the governor and attorney general, make up the commission that develops the redistricting plan. Other states, including Idaho, New Jersey, and Pennsylvania, have commissions appointed by the legislature itself. Finally, a few states rely on a nonpartisan or bipartisan independent commission. These states, which include California and Arizona, remove direct political control from the process even more extensively by having unelected

one person, one vote
shorthand term for the requirement of the U.S. Supreme Court that election districts be roughly equal in population

gerrymandering
the practice of politicians creating oddly shaped electoral districts to maximize their political advantage in an upcoming election

Legislative Redistricting Board (LRB)
created by a 1948 amendment to the Texas Constitution, this group steps in if the state legislature is unable to pass a redistricting plan or when a state or federal court invalidates a plan submitted by the legislature; the LRB is active only with respect to redistricting of the state legislature

nonpartisan or bipartisan independent commission
a system of drawing electoral district lines that attempts to remove politics from the process of redistricting

Lydia Camarillo, cochair of the Texas Latino Redistricting Task Force, addresses the media following a hearing in federal court on Wednesday, February 15, 2012, in San Antonio. The task force was one of several civil rights groups that raised concerns about the redistricting process used by the Texas Legislature during the 2011 regular session.

government officials appoint the redistricting commission. In all of these cases, the commission must develop the redistricting plan for the legislature to approve.

Redistricting Games

Efforts at redistricting in the past decade illustrate the politics behind the redistricting process and the state's conflict with the federal government (see the "Federalism in Action: Texas Redistricting and Federal Law" box). In 2001, Texas faced the unusual situation of divided control of the state legislature, with Republicans controlling the Texas Senate and Democrats controlling the Texas House of Representatives. When two chambers were unable to agree on a redistricting, the LRB developed a proposal that could be voted on by the Texas Legislature. This plan was authored by Attorney General John Cornyn, a Republican, and helped Republicans increase their majority in the Texas House of Representatives.[26]

Redistricting for U.S. House of Representatives seats also proved contentious. With the Texas Legislature unable to arrive at a consensus, the federal courts stepped in and drew the lines. Following the 2002 elections, Republicans gained control of the Texas House of Representatives and retained control over the Texas Senate. With Republicans now in charge of both houses of the state legislature and the governorship, U.S. House of Representatives majority leader Tom DeLay (R–Sugar Land) proposed to Republican leaders in the state legislature a plan to redistrict Texas that would increase the number of Texas seats controlled by Republicans. After intense debate in the state legislature during the regular session, Governor Rick Perry called the Texas Legislature into special session three times in order to complete redistricting. In the middle of this political drama, Democratic members of the Texas House fled to Oklahoma and later to New Mexico in attempts to prevent the quorum necessary to conduct business. However, the state legislature did eventually pass a mid-decade redistricting plan. In the 2004 elections, the new district lines yielded Texas Republicans a net gain of six seats in the U.S. House of Representatives.

This mid-decade redistricting plan was challenged in federal courts by civil rights groups in Texas who identified three issues. First, the mid-decade redistricting violated the U.S. Constitution. Second, the new districts disenfranchised minority voters by diluting their votes and downplaying their growing strength in violation of the Voting Rights Act of 1965. Third, the district lines were drawn in such a partisan manner as to violate earlier U.S. Supreme Court rulings. In 2006, the U.S. Supreme Court issued a decision in *League of United Latin American Citizens v. Perry* (2006), or *LULAC v.*

FEDERALISM IN Action

Texas Redistricting and Federal Law

According to Article 1, Section 4 of the U.S. Constitution, "[t]he Times, Places and Manner of holding Elections for Senators and Representatives, shall be prescribed in each State by the Legislature thereof; but the Congress may at any time by Law make or alter such Regulations, except as to the Places of chusing [sic] Senators." In practice this has meant that states take the lead in election laws. Still, over the years the federal government has provided some restrictions on drawing election districts.

For example, when Texas gained four seats in the U.S. House of Representatives after the 2010 census, the state drew new districting maps. The U.S. Department of Justice objected to the maps, arguing that they did not create enough **majority-minority districts**, or districts in which the majority of voters are minorities. Some Texans contended that since much of population gain was in minority populations, at least half of the new districts should be drawn as majority-minority districts. The U.S. Supreme Court, federal courts, state politicians, and civil rights groups all entered the fight to draw new district lines. The Republican Party wanted to protect its advantage in any new district map, and Texas politicians objected to federal oversight of the state's election laws.

Until 2013, Texas was subject to a provision of the Voting Rights Act of 1965 that required states that had discriminated against minorities in the past to get changes in election laws approved in advance by the Department of Justice. In the summer of 2013, Texas won a major victory when the U.S. Supreme Court eliminated this "preclearance" requirement.[i] The U.S. Department of Justice or citizen groups can still bring court cases against states for redistricting if the state engages in discrimination, but such cases must occur after the fact. In addition, the burden of proof shifts from states with a history of discrimination proving that they are not engaged in discrimination to the national government proving that a state continues to engage in discrimination.

Federal courts continued to rule that the drawing of district lines for partisan advantage remains acceptable as long as the principle of one person, one vote established by the U.S. Supreme Court in *Baker v. Carr* is followed.

A lot is at stake in the battle over redistricting. Whichever party controls the state legislature can significantly alter the power distribution in the state. Texas no longer has to have changes in its election laws precleared, but the federal government can step in later if those laws are found to disenfranchise a minority. If our recent redistricting battles tell us anything, the next census is likely to bring another round of legislative battles and legal challenges.

> **How long should states remain under suspicion due to past discrimination?**
>
> ⭐ **SOCIAL RESPONSIBILITY**

> **How much gerrymandering should states be allowed to engage in?**
>
> ⭐ **CRITICAL THINKING**

i. *Shelby County, Alabama v. Holder* (2013), 570 U.S. __.

Perry.[27] The court ruled that the mid-decade redistricting was permissible and held that the Texas districts were not drawn in an excessively partisan manner so as to completely dilute Democratic voters. However, the court did find that some of the district lines violated the Voting Rights Act of 1965, primarily by reducing the strength of Hispanic voters in at least one district. These unacceptable district lines were redrawn to solve the problem identified by the U.S. Supreme Court. Thus, redistricting battles shifted from the tradition of defending the reelection chances of incumbents of both parties to securing partisan control for the majority party.

While the legislature passed bills in the 2011 session that redrew the districts for both houses of the Texas Legislature, the attempt to redistrict Texas's seats in the U.S.

majority-minority district an election district in which the majority of the population comes from a racial or ethnic minority

House of Representatives failed during the 2011 special session in June as the legislature struggled to pass a redistricting plan that both houses could agree upon. The federal courts were pulled into the fray when the Mexican American Legislative Caucus (MALC), consisting of Mexican Americans in the Texas Legislature, filed challenges to the maps that the legislature approved for itself. The challenge from the MALC and other Hispanic civil rights groups was that the districts were designed to dilute Hispanic votes and decrease Hispanic representation, violating the Voting Rights Act of 1965 and the equal protection clause of the Fourteenth Amendment. The federal district court in San Antonio threw out the districts drawn by the Texas Legislature and drew new lines for the Texas Senate, Texas House of Representatives, and Texas's seats in the U.S. House of Representatives. However, the U.S. Supreme Court blocked use of the districts drawn by the court in San Antonio in order to hear arguments from the

TEXAS ARIZONA

Redistricting in Texas leaves the process in the hands of the Texas Legislature and the Legislative Redistricting Board (LRB), all elected officials with a vested interest in engineering district lines. For members of the legislature, protecting incumbents of both parties or securing gains for their party in the legislature can be important. For members of the LRB, assisting their party in gaining or retaining control of the legislature also matters. However, the implications for wider issues, such as partisan control over state delegations to the U.S. House of Representatives, are apparent from the recent battles in Texas.

Arizona voters in 2000 approved Proposition 106, which amended the Arizona Constitution to create an independent commission to oversee redistricting for the state legislature and U.S. House of Representatives. The Arizona Independent Redistricting Commission consists of five persons.[i] By law, two members are Democrats, two members are Republicans, and one member is independent. All five must have maintained the same party affiliation, or no affiliation in the case of the independent, for at least the previous three years. In addition, all five members cannot have served as public officials, lobbyists, campaign workers, or political party officials in the three years prior to their appointment. Nominees are compiled by another independent commission charged with making nominations to Arizona appellate courts and are presented to the leadership of the Arizona Legislature for final appointment.

Proposition 106 contains explicit language to specify how the commission carries out the redistricting process.[ii]

For example, the initial mapping of electoral districts cannot consider party affiliations of voters or the history of voting in existing districts. The commission must follow the guidelines of the Voting Rights Act of 1965, other legislation passed by Congress, and relevant rulings by the courts. District lines are to be compact and to respect the boundaries of existing communities, counties, and cities. Also, districts are expected to be competitive between Democratic and Republican candidates. This provision is tested only after the initial plan is developed. Thus, highly gerrymandered districts that clearly favor one party or another are not possible in Arizona.

How does the system of the Arizona Independent Redistricting Commission attempt to depoliticize the redistricting process?

 CRITICAL THINKING

Does Arizona's system provide better representation of citizens?

 SOCIAL RESPONSIBILITY

i. Arizona Independent Redistricting Commission, "Frequently Asked Questions," accessed August 28, 2014, www.azredistricting.org/?page=faq.

ii. Arizona Independent Redistricting Commission, "Proposition 106," accessed August 28, 2014, http://azredistricting.org/2001/Prop-106.asp.

state of Texas, represented by Texas attorney general Greg Abbott, on the intent of the legislature during the redistricting process.[28] In the end, the MALC reached agreement with Abbott, who was tasked with representing the state government and legislature before the courts, but the NAACP did not.[29] The spring 2012 primary elections for the political parties to nominate their candidates for the Texas Legislature and U.S. Congress were placed in jeopardy, since elections could not be planned for districts that did not exist. Agreement was reached on new maps in late February, and the primaries were pushed to May 29 to meet the timetables for nominating candidates, voter registration, and ballot preparation.

LEGISLATIVE ORGANIZATION

Legislatures are typically organized around the presiding officers, committees, and party organizations. These institutional features can shape legislation in profound ways by offering legislators a variety of means of manipulating the process. The impact is most evident in the working of the committee system, but chamber leadership positions offer another opportunity for a handful of members to exercise strong influence over bills. While the Texas legislature has historically operated in a relatively bipartisan manner, party organization has become increasingly important in recent years. In the end, institutional "rules" or "organizations" determine what becomes law and who wins and who loses in the legislature itself.

Presiding Officers

The presiding officer of a legislative body is the person most responsible for organizing its work. In Texas these are the Speaker of the Texas House of Representatives and the president of the Texas Senate. Individuals holding these positions possess important powers they can use to shape the agendas of the chambers. This ability to control the agenda influences the likelihood that a bill will become a law.

Lieutenant Governor

The presiding officer of the Texas Senate is the **lieutenant governor**. This is the most common arrangement in U.S. state legislatures, used in twenty-six of the fifty states. In these states, the lieutenant governor is elected by voters across the state; thus, senators work with a presiding officer chosen for them by voters. Most states with this arrangement give the lieutenant governor limited power over the chamber. Exceptions to these limits are found in the South, including in Texas, where the lieutenant governor is unusually powerful. Twenty-four states allow the membership of the state's upper house to select one of its members as the presiding officer.

If the lieutenant governor's position is vacant, as when Lieutenant Governor Rick Perry became the governor after George W. Bush was elected president of the United States, then the Texas Senate can elect a senator to perform the duties of lieutenant governor until the next general election. When the lieutenant governor is unable to attend sessions, the **president pro tempore** takes over as the presiding officer. The president pro tempore is elected by the membership of the Texas Senate.

The rules of the Texas Senate give the lieutenant governor tremendous power. The lieutenant governor assigns each bill introduced in the Senate to one of the committees.

lieutenant governor
the presiding officer of the Texas Senate, elected directly by the voters; also serves as a member of the Texas executive branch and assumes the duties of the governor when the governor is out of state, dies in office, resigns from office, or is impeached

president pro tempore
a presiding officer elected by the members of the Texas Senate; takes over when the lieutenant governor is unavailable

As the presiding officer, he or she recognizes speakers during debates on the floor of the Texas Senate and also interprets the rules of debate in the Texas Senate. The lieutenant governor appoints, without limitation, members of the committees of the Texas Senate and selects the chairs of those committees. Finally, the lieutenant governor enjoys the right that most presiding officers have to cast a vote in the Texas Senate to break a tie. The lieutenant governor also serves on the Legislative Redistricting Board (LRB) and the Legislative Budget Board (LBB). As discussed elsewhere in this text, these boards play important roles in Texas politics.

The lieutenant governor's election by the voters of Texas in a statewide election gives the position tremendous political clout beyond the power granted by Senate rules. Unlike individual senators, the lieutenant governor may point to a statewide electoral mandate like the one enjoyed by the governor. Legislation that the lieutenant governor supports will be assumed to reflect the will of the people of Texas because all Texas elected him or her. Thus, the lieutenant governor can claim that senators opposed to him or her in the Texas Legislature are defending the narrow interests of only their district, not the broad interests of all Texans.

Speaker of the House

Once a largely honorary role that rotated between members, the Speaker of the Texas House of Representatives has become one of the most important elected officials in Texas.[30] The Speaker of the House presides over sessions of the Texas House of Representatives. The Texas Constitution requires that the Texas House elect a Speaker from among its members as the first order of business at the beginning of the legislative session. For decades, the election of the Texas Speaker has been bipartisan, with potential Speakers seeking the support of members of both parties. Shortly after the 2018 election, Republican Dennis Bonnen became the presumptive speaker when he revealed that that 81 Republicans and 28 Democrats in the House had declared their support for him as Speaker. While some Republicans wanted to monopolize the leadership of House committees, Bonnen announced that he intended to continue the tradition of naming both Republicans and Democrats to serve as committee chairs.

The powers of the Speaker include presiding over debates on the floor of the House, including deciding whether to recognize a member to speak or introduce a motion. The Speaker's power also extends to interpretation of the rules of the House—a power that often proves critical late in the session when legislative maneuvering is required. In addition, the Speaker appoints half of the standing committee members, the chairs of standing committees, and members of conference committees from the Texas House. The Speaker may also create select committees. Unlike the lieutenant governor in the Texas Senate, the Speaker's power to appoint committee members to House committees is somewhat limited, since one-half of the makeup of some standing committees is determined by seniority. The Speaker also assigns bills to the committees. Thus, the Speaker has a great deal of control over committee structure and which bills those committees receive. The ability to appoint interim committees while the legislature is not in session further strengthens the power of the Speaker by letting him or her focus committee work on issues between sessions.

The Speaker also serves on the LRB and appoints some of the members of the LBB, which he or she also cochairs with the lieutenant governor. The Speaker also serves on the

Legislative Budget Board (LBB)
the group that develops a proposed state budget for legislative consideration

Speaker of the House
the presiding officer of the Texas House of Representatives

Legislative Council, the legislative agency that assists legislators with bill drafting, computer resources, and policy research. The powers of the Texas Speaker provide members of the House plenty of reasons to work with the Speaker. However, the Texas Speaker has less power in regard to control over standing committees than other Speakers in the Southern states.[31]

Political Parties in the Texas Legislature

Political parties can provide a basis for organizing legislatures because they bring together people with similar political beliefs; the parties are a natural way of lining up support for or opposition to bills. They can also play an important role in the selection of committees and the organization of the work of committees, and they now control the election of the Speaker of the Texas House.

The **party legislative caucus** (usually referred to as *party caucus*) is the organization of members of the political party in each house of the Texas Legislature. Members of the caucus must pay dues to join to pay for operating expenses and staff.

Democratic Party Organization in the Texas House

Party caucuses were slow to organize in Texas, just as were the rest of the single-party states in the South where the Democratic Party dominated politics for about a century after Reconstruction. In the Texas House, the creation of the Democratic Party caucus in 1981 signaled a shift in the role of party within the Texas Legislature. The growing number of Republicans spurred Democratic members to organize and discipline party members.[32] From 1981 until 1993, many Democratic members did not join the party caucus, and conservative Democrats preferred working on bills with Republicans. By 1993, most Democratic members had found that working on a common position on bills within their own party helped to get legislation passed and served as a counterbalance to the growing influence of Republicans in the chamber. The transition to a more competitive two-party legislature led the Texas Democratic Party, at that time still in the majority, to institutionalize, or formalize, its party organization in the legislature to meet a growing Republican challenge. Democrats hoped that passing bills more effectively might prevent the loss of additional seats to the Republican Party.

Republican Party Organization in the Texas House

Republicans did not formally create a party caucus in the Texas House until 1989. Even then, Republicans resisted forming party caucuses in the legislature, in part because they feared focusing on party differences would isolate Republicans and limit their influence.[33] Many were still receiving good committee assignments, and some were appointed chairs of committees by Democratic Speakers.

The continued bipartisanship that remained also reflected the power of the Speaker of the Texas House and the lieutenant governor. Both presiding officers continued to

Robert Daemmrich Photography Inc/Corbis via Getty Images

Lieutenant Governor Dan Patrick presents his inaugural address as Greg Abbott formally becomes the forty-eighth governor of Texas. The lieutenant governor wields significant clout in the Texas Senate.

party legislative caucus the organization of the members of a specific legislative chamber who belong to the same political party; normally shortened to *party caucus*

wield tremendous power and remained able to reward Republicans who were loyal to their presiding officer, even when that officer was a Democrat. Thus, Republicans had an incentive to maintain a degree of bipartisan support for the presiding officers in each chamber of the legislature.

Beginning in 2003, Republicans, winning control over the legislature, launched a series of debates and fights within the party over just how much power they should share with the now-minority Democratic members. While power-sharing with Democrats was appealing in some regards, Republicans had pledged to reduce the size of government and cut taxes. Bipartisanship meant compromising on these key issues.

Party Organization in the Texas Senate

Formation of party caucuses in the Texas Senate occurred much later than in the Texas House of Representatives, in part because the Texas Senate is so much smaller and creating formal organizations less necessary. In addition, the Texas Senate had historically been more informal, less structured, and more consensus oriented than the Texas House. Following the creation of party legislative caucuses in the Texas House, the Republicans in 1999 created the first party caucus in the Texas Senate, with Democrats following suit in 2001.[34]

Party Caucus Organization and Functions

Today, both parties have party caucuses in both houses of the Texas Legislature to facilitate communication among caucus members in discussing bills and amendments and to raise money for campaigns.[35] Each party caucus also elects a **party caucus chair**. The party caucus chair is elected by the caucus to oversee the day-to-day operation of the party. The party caucuses in the Texas House of Representatives also have a **floor leader** elected by the caucus membership. Deputy floor leaders assist the floor leader. The job of the floor leaders and deputy floor leaders is to encourage members of the party caucus to vote with the party's position on procedural motion, amendments, and bills. The party caucuses are increasingly using technology to carry out their activities. For example, the Texas House Democratic Caucus uses text messaging to remind members about upcoming votes. Both parties use social media to promote issues with the general public. Thus, party caucuses organize the work of members of the legislature and promote candidates and issues to the general public.

The party caucuses in the Texas House of Representatives conduct research on pending legislation and help draft amendments to bills. When it is time to debate a bill, the caucuses help find members to give speeches on bills or ask specific questions during floor debates. The party caucuses also maintain professional staff who help prepare bills and amendments, develop press releases, and provide logistical support. To fund their activities, the party caucuses may charge dues from their members.[36] Because the Texas House of Representatives is larger than the Texas Senate, party organization there is more developed and more relevant.

Special Legislative Caucuses

While party legislative caucuses are organized on party lines, a special legislative caucus is a group of legislators brought together by a common interest and may include

party caucus chair
a party leader whose main job is to organize party members to vote for legislation on the floor

floor leader
a party member who reminds legislators of the party's position on a bill and encourages members to vote with the rest of the party caucus; the floor leader is assisted by one or more deputy floor leaders

special legislative caucus
an organization of members of the state legislature who share a common interest or have constituencies with a common interest

TEXAS VS NEBRASKA

Nebraska possesses the only unicameral state legislature in the United States. All other state legislatures, including Texas, are bicameral. The history of Nebraska's unicameral legislature dates back to the time of the 1930s and the Great Depression. U.S. senator George William Norris (R–Nebraska) suggested that Nebraska change its state legislature from a bicameral to a unicameral one. According to Norris, bicameralism was a result of the British system, in which the House of Commons and House of Lords represented different citizens' social classes (aristocracy and commoner), but Nebraska lacked such classes, so there was no reason to have a bicameral state legislature.[i] Norris campaigned all over the state advocating a single-chambered legislature. Voters apparently agreed, and they amended the state's constitution in 1934 to abolish the lower house, retaining only the upper house. Almost 60 percent of voters approved the change.[ii] As a result, the costs of operating the legislature fell in half when the newly unicameral legislature met for the first time in 1937.[iii]

In addition, the Nebraska Legislature sits as a nonpartisan legislature. Unlike in Texas, where legislative candidates run with clear party affiliations, candidates in Nebraska do not refer to political party affiliation. The top two candidates in the primary election compete in the general election, with the candidate with the most votes winning the election to the state legislature.[iv] Once elected to the Nebraska Legislature, the legislators sit according to geographic location in the state, not by party affiliation as they do in the Texas Legislature and in all other state legislatures. It is important to note that the Republican Party at various levels of government in Nebraska does list candidates running for the Nebraska Legislature who have Republican support.[v] Democratic Party organizations within the state do the same thing.[vi]

The nonpartisan nature of the Nebraska Legislature is also a result of the efforts of Norris, the "Father of Unicameralism." He believed the lack of partisanship allowed the legislators to focus on their own beliefs, not the wishes of party leaders. Norris also believed the nonpartisan approach resulted in legislators paying attention to the needs of their districts, which would better serve the people of Nebraska.[vii] This nonpartisan approach was consistent with the Progressive Era belief that political parties were controlled by party leaders, who in turn were assumed to be dominated by big business, labor unions, and organized interests, not the broader body of citizens.

Since the Nebraska Legislature is unicameral and nonpartisan, its legislative process differs as well. For example, a nonpartisan legislature does not need to worry about the balance between Democratic and Republican members on standing committees, as the Texas Legislature does. In addition, the issue of which party controls the chair of each standing committee does not exist. Finally, there is no need to reconcile bills using a conference committee, as in all other states, including Texas. This approach also reflects Norris's approach to politics. Norris noted that in Nebraska during the days of bicameralism, conference committees consisted of six members who met in secret without any public record of their decisions and produced a bill that legislators could not amend. This suggested to Norris that the political parties were able to hide their agendas and not be accountable to voters. As a result, he believed that conference committees increased the power of interest groups.[viii]

Does a partisan or nonpartisan system do a better job of representing citizens?

 SOCIAL RESPONSIBILITY

What advantages and disadvantages exist in a unicameral state legislature?

 CRITICAL THINKING

---

i. Nebraska Legislature, "History of the Nebraska Unicameral," accessed September 18, 2014, http://nebraskalegislature.gov/about/history_unicameral.php.

ii. Ibid.

iii. Nebraska Legislature, "On Unicameralism," accessed September 18, 2014, http://nebraskalegislature.gov/about/ou_experience.php.

iv. Nebraska Legislature, "History of the Nebraska Unicameral."

v. Lancaster County Nebraska Republican Party, "Primary Elections," accessed August 9, 2012, www.lcgop.com/news/primary-elections.

vi. Nebraska Democratic Party, "Candidates," accessed October 10, 2012, www.nebraskademocrats.org/candidates.

vii. Nebraska Legislature, "History of the Nebraska Unicameral."

viii. Ibid.

members of both parties and both chambers of the Texas Legislature. Members meet to discuss topics of mutual interest. The roughly thirty caucuses operating in the Texas Legislature today fall into three types. The oldest caucuses are minority and women's caucuses. These caucuses exist to represent the unique concerns and beliefs of women and ethnic groups across a broad spectrum of policy areas and political issues. They include the Texas Legislative Black Caucus (TLBC), the Texas Women's Political Caucus, and the Mexican American Legislative Caucus (MALC). These caucuses bring together members of the Texas Legislature who share a bipartisan desire to discuss issues affecting women, African Americans, and Hispanics. Often the groups assist in developing new bills or building support for bills that the caucus members believe to be important. The Texas Women's Political Caucus became inactive in recent sessions of the legislature because the more conservative members and the more liberal members were heavily divided over the issues of abortion and public funding for birth control. As a result, several liberal Democratic members of the legislature formed the Women's Health Caucus to promote their positions on these issues and others.[37]

A second type of special legislative caucus is an ideological caucus, which is designed to promote a broad ideological agenda. In 1985, when the Democratic Party held the majority, conservative members of the Texas Legislature created the Texas Conservative Coalition. The Legislative Study Group was created in 1993 and works to promote liberal policies. The Texas Progressive Caucus met during the 2011 session to promote issues important to liberals. In 2017, the Texas Freedom Caucus, a new coalition of some of the House's most conservative members, helped kill off more than 100 bills from the usually noncontroversial local and consent calendar in what some called the "Mother's Day Massacre." This was done in retaliation for what they called "petty personal politics."

The final type of special legislative caucus is the issue caucus. An issue caucus exists to promote bipartisan and cross-chamber support for policies and bills that advocate positions in a relatively narrow range of policy areas or political issues that are important to key constituents. One example is the Rural Caucus, which advocates health care, transportation, and education policies favorable to rural Texas. The Sportsmen's Caucus promotes and protects hunting and fishing rights, and the Texas Farm-to-Table Caucus supports the production and consumption of Texas-made food and beverage products. Some caucuses, such as the Interstate 14 Legislative Caucus, focus on a very narrow issue.

In contrast to political party caucuses, the special legislative caucuses lack a formal role in the legislative process. They do not control appointments of members to committees nor form the organizational basis of choosing chamber leadership. In addition, special legislative caucuses lack the ability to discipline members for voting against the caucus position. Thus, they are often left with secondary strategies, such as giving speeches and lobbying other members of the legislature, to get what they want. The influence of a special caucus varies tremendously by the type of special caucus, degree of organization, and issues addressed by the caucus. The influence and significance vary widely over time as well, depending on the dynamics of a session and the individual issues addressed in a session.

Committees

Like the U.S. Congress, the Texas Legislature utilizes a committee system to assist the legislature in managing its workload. A legislative committee is a subgroup of legislators who handle specific, specialized legislative topics. The presence of committees allows a division of labor so that bills may be reviewed in detail before being considered by the entire chamber. Three broad types of committees exist in the Texas Legislature: standing committees, statutory committees, and special committees.

Standing Committees

The standing committee is the most important type of committee in the Texas Legislature. The Texas Constitution requires that every bill introduced into the legislature must pass through at least one of the standing committees before it can be passed. The standing committees of the Texas Legislature are created through the rules of each chamber. Although standing committees are officially re-created at the beginning of each session when each chamber votes to approve its rules, they are considered permanent committees because they are specifically written into the rules and typically exist across legislative sessions. Standing committees are chamber exclusive—that is, each standing committee is associated with a specific chamber of the legislature and is made up of members from only that chamber. In the Texas Senate, the fourteen standing committees in the 85th legislature had an average of nearly nine members, with committees ranging from seven senators to fifteen. The thirty-eight Texas House standing committees during that session averaged 9.5 members, with committees ranging from seven to twenty-seven members of the House.

A standing committee is considered a substantive standing committee if it is authorized to review and revise policy bills and resolutions before the legislature. Thus, the substantive standing committees influence the substance of what the legislature passes into law. These committees are functionally divided, meaning each committee handles bills in a specific area of government's function, such as transportation or higher education. Some substantive standing committees will play a role in bills from a variety of areas. For example, every bill in the Texas House of Representatives that authorizes spending money, regardless of the specific policy area, must pass through the Appropriations Committee. The importance of appropriations is reflected in the fact that it has twenty-seven members. The House Ways and Means Committee has jurisdiction over every bill involving tax law.

Another type of standing committee is the procedural standing committee. These committees focus on how the Texas Legislature operates. One procedural standing committee in the House is the Committee on Calendars that determines when a bill will be debated. Others handle rules, or the terms of debate, associated with a bill. Some procedural committees review House organization and administration. Thus, a bill on higher education finance would pass through the two substantive standing committees just named plus the Committee on Calendars and possibly the Rules and Resolutions Committee for a total of four standing committees. Procedural committees also include General Investigation and Ethics, House Administration, Redistricting, and the Local and Consent Calendars.

---

committee
a formally organized group of legislators that assists the legislature in accomplishing its work, allowing a division of labor and an in-depth review of an issue or a bill before review by the entire chamber

standing committee
a permanent, chamber-specific formal work group that typically exists across sessions and across elections

substantive standing committee
a type of standing committee that is authorized to review and revise proposed policy bills and resolutions before action by the legislature

procedural standing committee
a type of standing committee that controls how the legislature functions

Given the importance of committees in the legislative process, legislators are very concerned about the committees they are assigned to. Every member of the Texas House of Representatives sits on two or three standing committees, and Texas Senate members sit on at least four. The appointment process for members of the standing committees varies between the Texas House and Texas Senate. The lieutenant governor appoints the members of the standing committees in the Texas Senate.

In the Texas House, the process is a bit more complicated. All members of procedural standing committees in the Texas House are appointed by the Speaker. However, only half the seats on standing substantive committees are appointed by the Speaker, with the rest being assigned based on seniority. Prior to the start of each session of the legislature, members of the Texas House provide the Speaker a list of the committee assignments they prefer. A member is entitled to become a member of the committee of his or her highest preference on which there is an open seniority position.

For much of the legislature's history, committee appointments were made with little regard for party. Beginning in the 1990s, committee assignments began to gradually shift in the Texas House toward the more party-centered model found in the U.S. Congress. After the Republicans became the majority party in 2003, the practice of allowing the minority party to be a majority on some committees continued. Several committees during the 81st Texas Legislature, which met in 2009, contained a majority of Democratic members, despite Republican control over the legislature. Criticism of Speaker Joe Straus's leadership of the Texas House led to changes, and Republicans would have a majority of the seats on all standing committees in the Texas House during the 2011 session. However, in 2013, Straus allowed three standing committees to have Democratic majorities, and fourteen committees were chaired by Democrats.

Despite growing partisanship, some power-sharing remains in the Texas Legislature. In 2017, Speaker Straus picked twenty-six Republicans and twelve Democrats to chair the House's thirty-eight standing committees. This included choosing Democrats to chair important committees, such as Rules and Resolutions and Human Services. In the Senate, Republican lieutenant governor Dan Patrick gave Democrats two of the Senate's fourteen committees, with Democrat John Whitmire chairing the Criminal Justice Committee and Eddie Lucio Jr. leading Intergovernmental Affairs.

Standing Committee Organization and Functions

This power-sharing is significant because committee chairs in Texas can be quite powerful. Presiding over the committee includes the power to determine the order in which bills sent to the committee are considered. As a result, the committee chair may schedule bills that he or she supports early in the legislative session to ensure that they are considered first by the committee. Likewise, the committee chair may move bills that she or he does not support to the end of the committee's calendar, effectively ensuring that the committee runs out of time before those bills are considered. The chair also establishes the length of debate and the amendment process for each bill. The

TABLE 3.2   Standing House Committees in the 85th Texas Legislature

Texas House of Representatives	
Agriculture and Livestock	Insurance
Appropriations	International Trade and Intergovernmental Affairs
Business and Industry	Investment and Financial Services
Calendars (procedural)	Judiciary and Civil Jurisprudence
Corrections	Juvenile Justice & Family Issues
County Affairs	Land and Resource Management
Criminal Jurisprudence	Licensing & Administrative Procedures
Culture, Recreation, and Tourism	Local & Consent Calendars (procedural)
Defense and Veterans' Affairs	Natural Resources
Economic and Small Business Development	Pensions
Elections	Public Education
Energy Resources	Public Health
Environmental Regulation	Redistricting (procedural)
General Investigating & Ethics (procedural)	Rules and Resolutions (procedural)
Government Transparency & Operation	Special Purpose Districts (procedural)
Higher Education	State Affairs
Homeland Security & Public Safety	Transportation
House Administration (procedural)	Urban Affairs
Human Services	Ways and Means

Note: Committees not marked *procedural* are substantive committees.

Source: Texas House of Representatives, "House Committees," accessed July 12, 2018, http://www.capitol.state.tx.us/Committees/CommitteesMbrs.aspx?Chamber=H.

committee chair decides how much time is devoted to hearings and oversight of the executive branch and its agencies. This power over the agenda and the flow of legislation in and out of the committee gives the chair of a standing committee tremendous control over the legislative process.

Standing committees perform several important functions for the legislature, including marking up and amending bills. An **amendment** is a formal change to a bill made during the committee process. **Markup** is the process by which a committee

amendment
a formal change to a bill made during the committee process or during floor debate in front of the whole chamber

markup
process whereby a committee goes line by line through a bill to make changes without formal amendments

TABLE 3.3 Standing Senate Committees in the 85th Texas Legislature

Texas Senate
Administration (procedural)
Agriculture, Water & Rural Affairs
Business & Commerce
Criminal Justice
Education
Finance
Health and Human Services
Higher Education
Intergovernmental Relations
Natural Resources & Economic Development
Nominations (procedural)
State Affairs
Transportation
Veteran Affairs and Military Installations

Note: Committees not marked *procedural* are substantive committees.

Source: Senate of Texas, "Senate Committees," accessed July 12, 2018, http://www.capitol.state.tx.us/Committees/CommitteesMbrs.aspx?Chamber=S.

oversight
the process whereby the legislature reviews policies and decisions of the executive branch to make sure the executive branch is following the intentions of the legislature

goes line by line through a bill to make changes without formal amendments.

Because a committee is not required to report every bill to the whole chamber, committees often kill a bill through inaction. By not sending a bill to the whole chamber, the standing committee in effect ensures that the bill will not become a law. There are two ways in which a standing committee can kill a bill. First, a majority of the members on the committee can vote against it. As a result, the bill dies in committee and does not return to the whole chamber. In addition, a bill may be placed toward the end of the committee's schedule for the legislative session. If the committee runs out of time for the legislative session and fails to act on the bill before the session ends, the bill dies in committee. This ability to kill a bill makes standing committees very powerful. While this power in the standing committees of the Texas Legislature is consistent with that in the U.S. Congress and other state legislatures, it is fairly unique among non-American legislatures. For example, this ability to kill a bill in committee is not typically found in France, Britain, Japan, or Canada, regardless of the level of government, national or regional.

An important function of standing committees in Texas is to conduct **oversight** of the executive branch agencies. Oversight occurs when the legislature reviews functioning and decisions of offices in the executive branch to make sure that the executive branch is following the intentions of the legislature. Because some laws passed by the legislature provide only general guidelines to the executive branch, the specific agency that carries out the law often has discretion to determine exactly how to implement the law.

New administrative regulations are also subject to review by standing committees. For example, if the Texas Parks and Wildlife Department decides to impose a user fee of $5 on everyone who goes fishing at a state park, it is up to the legislature, if it so chooses, to review this decision the next time it meets in regular session. However, the standing committees lack the power to effect changes in new regulations and can only issue advisory opinions, which executive agencies take seriously. Keeping the legislature that writes your agency's budget satisfied is always a good idea, and being consistent with the legislature's intention avoids having the committee, or the legislature, develop new laws to replace administrative regulations.

Committees hold hearings to evaluate legislation and oversee the executive. In these meetings, experts, invited guests, organized interests, officials from other parts of government, and private citizens offer their perspectives on the effectiveness of legislation or executive agencies.

The work of standing committees is enhanced by the research and writing of the committees' professional staffs. Each standing committee retains a permanent staff of up to six people in the Texas House and up to fifteen people in the Texas Senate. A committee's staff helps with research on bills, evaluation of the performance of state agencies, organization of committee meetings, and other tasks essential to the smooth operation of the committee.

There are also staff organizations available to all members of the legislature. Members of the Texas House may use the services of the House Research Organization, while senators can turn to the Senate Research Center. These offices help research issues, draft legislation, and provide information to members of the legislature. The Legislative Reference Library also provides reference and research resources for members of the legislature, committees, and committee staff to use when researching and writing bills.

Members of the tax-writing House Appropriations Committee gather on the floor of the Texas House of Representatives for an impromptu discussion.

Standing committees can create subcommittees in order to provide greater efficiency and division of labor. The Appropriations Committee in the Texas House contained five subcommittees during the 2017 session. Four of these subcommittees handled bills associated with particular parts of the state budget, and one subcommittee focused on issues of budget transparency and reform. Likewise, the Higher Education Committee created a subcommittee on students' readiness for the workplace and postsecondary education.

The standing committees sometimes get homework between sessions. After the 2015 regular session, Speaker Straus issued more than 150 interim charges that filled sixty-four pages with directions for thirty-five House committees to look into a broad range of issues before the next legislative session.[38] Speaker Straus and Lieutenant Governor Patrick directed committees in their respective chambers to monitor the implementation of the state's new campus carry laws passed during the 2015 session. After the death of Sandra Bland and others in Texas jails, Lieutenant Governor Patrick created an interim jail safety study committee to look into the safety and mental health of inmates.

Statutory Committees

Statutory committees are those mandated by state law. The LBB and the Legislative Audit Committee are both statutory committees. As discussed in more detail in Chapter 12, the LBB plays an import role in shaping state government because it develops the initial state budget for the Texas Legislature to consider. The board consists of the lieutenant governor, the Speaker of the Texas House, four senators, and four representatives. Senators and representatives must include the chairs of finance and budget committees in each chamber. Since 1973, the board has also been charged with estimating the fiscal impact of every resolution being considered by the Texas Legislature that has a budgetary impact. Between legislative sessions, the LBB works with the governor to monitor implementation of the state budget and make recommendations to state agencies about their spending.

The Legislative Audit Committee consists of the lieutenant governor, the Speaker of the Texas House, the chairs of the budget and finance standing committees from each chamber, and at least one other senator. The committee oversees the Texas State Auditor's Office and hires the auditor. The primary function of the committee is to review state agency compliance with state laws and policies. For example, the committee investigates if contracts for outside services, such as office equipment purchases, are correctly conducted or if reimbursement expenses for official state travel are correctly handled.

Conference Committees

Conference committees are necessary because the Texas Legislature contains two chambers. Bills may be passed in different versions in each chamber. When a bill passes both houses in different versions as a result of these actions, a single version must be agreed to by both houses before the bill goes to the governor. If the bill begins in the House of Representatives and the Senate amends the House version of the bill, then the bill returns to the House as amended by the Senate. If the House agrees to the Senate's amendments, then the bill goes to the governor to be signed into law. If the House rejects one or more of the Senate's amendments, the bill goes to a conference committee. If the bill begins in the Senate, the process is reversed.

A **conference committee** is a special committee created to reconcile the differences in the Texas Senate and Texas House versions of one bill. These committees are formed when both chambers agree to form the committee. Conference committees contain ten members, five from the Texas House and five from the Texas Senate. Normally, some of the members of the standing committees who played important roles on the legislation serve on the conference committee that reconciles the different versions. After the conference committee meets to reconcile the differences on a bill, at least three members of the conference committee from the Texas Senate and at least three members from the Texas House must agree to the reconciled version of the bill. After producing a single, reconciled version of the bill, the committee disbands. The bill is then reintroduced to both chambers for consideration. Each chamber must then vote on the reconciled version of the bill without additional amendments and changes. If the reconciled version passes both houses of the legislature, the bill is sent to the governor to sign.

While the conference committee process used by the Texas Legislature mirrors the process of the U.S. Congress, other bicameral legislatures in the world do not use such a process. For example, in Canada, when the Canadian House of Commons and Canadian Senate pass a bill in different forms, the bill is shuttled back and forth between the chambers until the two houses reach agreement. This process was adopted in Canada based on the British Parliament, where a bill is shuttled back and forth between the British House of Commons and British House of Lords.

conference committee
an official legislative work group that meets on a limited basis to reconcile the different versions of a bill that has passed in the Texas House and Senate

However, Canada's constitution allows for another option unavailable in Britain. If the Canadian House of Commons and Canadian Senate are deadlocked and unable to come to a complete reconciliation on the bill, the prime minister of Canada may temporarily add up to eight members of the Canadian Senate to break the deadlock. In France, U.S.-style conference committees may be used, or a bill may shuttle back and forth between the National Assembly and French Senate, as in Canada and Great Britain. Also, the president of France has a third option. He or she may seize the bill, rewrite the bill to his or her liking, and reintroduce the bill to the National Assembly. The National Assembly may simply vote for or against the bill. If the bill passes the National Assembly, the president signs the bill into law. The French Senate is left out of the process.

Select or Special Committees

The rules of the Texas Legislature allow for the creation of temporary committees other than conference committees. The House rules label these "select" committees and the Senate rules use the term "special" committees; a **select or special committee** is a temporary committee that the presiding officer can use for a narrow, specific purpose. For example, in 2017, Lieutenant Governor Dan Patrick formed a select committee to "address the school violence and school security" in the wake of the school shooting at Santa Fe High School. The rules give these special committees the same kind of powers given a standing committee except as limited by the charge of the presiding officer that created them, and these committees function only for the period of time specified by the presiding officer. If the lieutenant governor and Speaker create a select committee containing members of both the Texas Senate and Texas House, then the committee is called a joint committee. Regardless of the makeup of the membership, these committees exist for a special purpose.

Some of the work of both standing and select or special committees is done between legislative sessions. Such "interim" committee work is especially important on complicated issues that cannot be adequately researched and resolved during the 140-day session. Interim work may also be needed to address crises that appear between sessions. For example, in 2017, Speaker Joe Straus issued forty pages of "Interim Committee Charges" that directed House committees to address a range of issues; the impact of Hurricane Harvey was included in the interim charges of thirty-one of the House's thirty-eight standing committees.

select or special committee
a legislative work group created by the lieutenant governor or Speaker of the Texas House of Representatives for a specific purpose; called a joint committee when the lieutenant governor and Speaker create a select committee with members from both chambers

WINNERS AND LOSERS

Party caucuses, special legislative caucuses, and committee organizations have an important impact on the Texas Legislature. Committee organizations, especially the standing committees, have historically proved to be a place for individual legislators to influence bills by offering amendments, changing the language of bills, and even killing bills in committee. Likewise, interim committee work allows legislators to influence state policy and politics while the legislature is not in session, and conference committees offer legislators an opportunity to develop a final version of a bill that most likely will pass into law. Because both the lieutenant governor and the

Speaker of the Texas House have power over these committees through appointment of members, referring bills to standing committees, issuing charges to the interim committees, and the like, the committee structure and organization reinforce the powers of the presiding officers of each chamber.

Party caucuses and special legislative caucuses may offer an alternative to the power of the presiding officers. Party caucuses are becoming increasingly important to the legislature. For the majority party, the party caucus offers a mechanism to more directly control the content of bills and amendments. For the minority party, the party caucus works as a mechanism to get its message to the public through public relations and awareness campaigns.

The transformation of the Texas Legislature associated with the strengthening of party caucuses is making the majority party, the Republicans, the winners as long as the party remains cohesive within each chamber. That the Democrats are reduced to public relations and awareness campaigns reflects their limited power within the legislative process. Democrats are clearly the losers in the new arrangement of Texas politics. The leadership of party caucuses and the leadership style of the lieutenant governor and Speaker influence the role and function of the political parties and the extent of bipartisanship. As a result, winners and losers depend on this factor and will vary over time.

Special legislative caucuses are also important in the legislative process. Because they provide opportunities for members of the legislature to network on common interests, these caucuses offer a chance to work outside the normal committee system and away from the presiding officers of both chambers of the legislature. Special legislative caucuses also provide a springboard for amendments and other changes to legislation. As a result, these caucuses may work against the presiding officers and may offer an alternative to the rising power and influence of the party caucus system. However, their likelihood to be winners or losers depends on the degree of party cohesion and the style of chamber leadership.

Why are the Speaker of the Texas House and lieutenant governor such powerful figures in Texas politics?

★ CRITICAL THINKING

How significant a role should the party caucus play in the legislative process?

★ SOCIAL RESPONSIBILITY

LEGISLATIVE PROCESS

A primary function of the Texas Legislature is making new laws and updating existing ones. While this process is often considered relatively mundane and ordinary, understanding these rules means understanding who wins and who loses in the legislative process. It's not just *who* you know in the Texas Legislature; it's often *what* you know about rules that contributes to success. The complicated set of rules and organizations outlined in this chapter presents a path to success that is foreign and inhospitable to newcomers. As Ross Ramsey observed, "votes count, of course. But at the end, rules can count more."[39] As Ramsey and others have pointed out, the complicated legislative process in Texas combined with the limits of a 140-day session make efficient navigation through the legislative labyrinth essential to a representative trying to serve the needs of their district. The procedural hurdles and the time limits of the process provide opponents of legislation plenty of opportunity to bury reforms. And, as we will see in Chapter 10, the "revolving door" that leads many former legislators directly into professional lobbying ensures that organized interest lobbyists are well trained in the legislative arts. A part-time legislature is especially receptive to full-time lobbyists and presiding officers that can help legislators find a safe route out of the maze of rules and procedures that make up the legislative process.

A **bill** can be the product of a number of sources. Some legislators are policy experts who enjoy researching and writing bills to solve problems or address issues of concern to them and their constituents. The Texas Legislative Council, a professionally staffed arm of the legislature, helps legislators without a legal background convert their ideas into the correct legal form. Interest groups or other organized interests often develop model legislation that some legislators rely on when they propose legislation. Agencies of Texas government, such as the Texas Department of Transportation (TxDOT) or Texas Coordinating Board for Higher Education, suggest possible bills to the legislature. Finally, the creation of the Republican policy chair in the Texas House of Representatives reflects a new, party-centered source for bills.

bill
a proposed new law or change to existing law brought before a legislative chamber by a legislative member

Introducing Bills in the Legislature

While anyone can suggest the idea for a new law, before a bill can be considered by the House or Senate, it must be introduced by a member of that chamber. The member who introduces the bill is known as the author or sponsor of the bill. Other members may add their name to support of the bill and be considered coauthors or cosponsors. Because a bill must pass both chambers of the Texas Legislature, the author of a bill will often seek out members of both chambers to help cosponsor it. If the bill originates outside the legislature itself, the organized interest or government agency seeks out a member of the legislature to **introduce** the bill. Sponsoring or cosponsoring a bill allows a member of the legislature to take credit for helping the bill to become a law, if it does become a law. Such credit claiming helps reinforce the idea that the legislator is hard at work promoting the interests of his or her district by pointing to a list of bills that he or she helped to become law.

introduce (a bill)
to officially bring a bill before a legislative chamber for the first time; this first official step in the formal legislative process is reserved for members of the legislature

Bills may be prefiled before the start of each legislative session, meaning that the bill is introduced prior to the start of the legislative session. Many members prefile legislation to demonstrate their commitment to the issue. Most states allow prefiling of bills, with the notable exceptions of Michigan, North Carolina, and Wisconsin.

In Texas, a bill may be introduced up to sixty calendar days after the start of the legislative session. To introduce a bill after the sixtieth day requires the agreement of 80 percent of the members of the chamber present.

Any bill dealing with the state budget must be considered by the Texas House of Representatives first. Budget bills must be introduced by the thirtieth day after the legislative session opens. Any bill that impacts the state budget must be sent to the LBB for preparation of a "**fiscal note**," which includes an analysis of the costs incurred by the government if the bill is passed. Texas also requires statements about the impact of the bill on the equalized public education funding formula and on criminal justice policy. These last two provisions are unique to Texas.

fiscal note
a required document outlining the probable costs of the legislation

resolution
a legislative act that expresses the opinion of the legislature on an issue or changes the organizational structure of the legislature

Introducing Resolutions in the Legislature

In addition to bills, members of the legislature may introduce resolutions. A **resolution** expresses the opinion of the legislature on an issue or changes the organizational structure of the legislature. For example, the legislature may pass a resolution asking the U.S. Congress to change a policy. A resolution may also cover seemingly trivial matters, such as commending the University of Texas (UT) football team for winning the Cotton Bowl or the Texas A&M women's golf team for winning a conference championship. Three types of resolutions exist: a simple resolution, a concurrent resolution, and a joint resolution. A simple resolution addresses organizational issues, such as changing the number of standing committees or altering the powers of committee chairs. These resolutions may be limited to a single house of the legislature. A concurrent resolution expresses the opinion of the legislature and requires passage in both houses. A joint resolution is particularly important because this legislative act, when passed by both chambers, proposes amendments to the Texas Constitution. Those amendments are then sent to the voters for approval at the next election.

When a bill or resolution is introduced into a chamber, it is assigned a code by the secretary of the Texas Senate or the chief clerk of the Texas House. This combination of letters and numbers indicates the chamber in which the legislation originated and the order that it was introduced. For example, HR 10 indicates the tenth resolution introduced into the Texas House, while SB 351 is the 351st bill introduced into the Texas Senate.

Legislation in Committee

After legislation has been formally introduced, the presiding officer of the chamber assigns the bill to a committee (see "How Texas Government Works: Lawmaking" on pp. 118–119). In the Texas Senate, bills are referred to committee by the president of the Senate, the lieutenant governor. Bills in the Texas House are referred to committee by the Speaker of the House. Normally, bills are referred to the committee with jurisdiction over the policy area. Yet the Speaker and lieutenant governor have the power to send a bill to any standing committee in their respective chambers that they choose.

The rules of the legislature require that committee meetings be open to the public. While basic transparency may seem like a mundane requirement, making sure that the public—as well as the legislators—has access to the process is fundamental to representation. In the 1960s, one female member of the Constitutional Amendments Committee was denied entry to a committee meeting because it was being held at the all-male Citadel Club.[40] To assist in their work, a handful of standing committees in both chambers of the Texas Legislature contain subcommittees. A subcommittee may conduct a detailed examination of the bill or resolution and report to the whole committee before the final committee vote is taken. Subcommittees have the same powers as their related standing committee to amend or kill a bill.

Calendars in the Texas House

After a committee votes to report a bill favorably, the bill is ready for review by the entire membership of the chamber. Bills with statewide implications go to the Committee on Calendars, which is charged with managing all the bills trying to find their way onto the floor of the House. The committee places each bill that it receives on one of several different calendars and proposes rules for consideration

simple resolution
a legislative act that addresses organizational issues; may be limited to a single house

concurrent resolution
a legislative act that expresses an opinion of the legislature; must pass in both houses

joint resolution
a legislative act whose approval by both chambers results in amendment to the Texas Constitution; an amendment must be approved by voters at the next election

calendar
list of bills and resolutions that are eligible for consideration by the chamber

of the bills. The Texas House maintains seven different calendars for bills approved by its committees and separate calendars for bills and resolutions already passed by the Senate. Bills on more important calendars are considered first, whereas bills on less important calendars are handled if time remains during the legislative session. However, a bill or resolution may be shifted to a faster calendar by a two-thirds vote of the entire House.

Bills affecting only a specific county, city, or other local government and other bills unlikely to face opposition can be sent by the originating committee to the Local and Consent Calendar. This calendar is overseen by the Committee on Local and Consent Calendars rather than the Calendars Committee. This standing committee determines when local and consent bills are considered by the whole Texas House and how long a bill is to be debated. The Rules and Resolutions Committee performs a similar function for memorials and other resolutions.

Calendars in the Texas Senate

In the Texas Senate, there is no special calendar committee and only one calendar exists, with bills being listed in the order they were formally introduced. However, the Texas Senate almost never considers bills in this order. Instead, it has developed a trick that allows senators to change the order of consideration. The first bill introduced each session is known as a blocking bill, or stopper—a bill that is introduced not to be passed but merely to hold a place at the top of the Texas Senate calendar. Because the usual process is that bills are taken up in the order in which they are put on the calendar, this bill prevents bills below it on the calendar from being considered. Like the Texas House of Representatives, the Texas Senate may move a bill up on the calendar by a three-fifths vote of the chamber. Thus, a bill down the list on the calendar may be bumped ahead of the blocking bill to the top of the calendar by a three-fifths vote.

blocking bill
a bill regularly introduced in the Texas Senate to serve as a placeholder at the top of the Senate calendar; sometimes called a stopper

The three-fifths requirement for moving a bill to the top of the calendar enhances the minority party's ability to block any bill, since it allows twelve senators to prevent a bill from even being considered. While the three-fifths rule does create a high hurdle for consideration of a bill, there was a time when the standard was higher. In January 2015, the Senate, under the leadership of new lieutenant governor Dan Patrick, changed the Senate rules to reduce the vote needed to move a bill up on the calendar from two-thirds to three-fifths. The two-thirds rule had been a target of Patrick since his earliest days in the Senate in 2007 because it made it more difficult for the Senate to move ahead on legislation favored by a majority of senators. On the other hand, fans of the two-thirds rule point to a seventy-year-old tradition of building broad-based consensus for new laws and respect for minority rights.

Floor Debate in the Legislature

When a bill or resolution comes up for consideration by the whole chamber, the entire membership engages in a floor debate. The sponsors of the bill arrange for members to speak on its behalf, and opponents recruit members to speak against it. The trick in both cases is gaining recognition from the presiding officer of the chamber for the purpose of addressing the chamber. Amendments to the bill can also be offered to

floor debate
period during which a bill is brought up before the entire chamber for debate

HOW TEXAS GOVERNMENT WORKS

Lawmaking

Idea for bill from:

A person

A state legislator

An interim committee

An organized interest

Legislation Introduced

Legislation may be introduced as early as 60 days prior to session.

First Reading
Referral to committee

Committee Work

 Bills can originate in either the House or the Senate

First Reading
Referral to committee

An approved House bill with amendments is printed and sent to the Senate for consideration

Tagging

Public Hearings

Debate and Amend

Committee Report

Committee Work

House Bill on Senate Floor

House Bill Sent to the Senate

STOP A majority vote of committee membership is required

A senator may filibuster and hold the floor for an unlimited debate

Senate amendments to House bills go to the House for approval

House concurs with amendments

Reconciled in conference committee

Placed on Senate Calendar

STOP

Third Reading

Debate and Amend

Vote

Vote

Enrollment

Second Reading

STOP Tie vote or failure to gain a simple majority **STOP**

Legend

House **Senate** **Governor** **STOP** Chance for the bill to fail   Additional information

 Fiscal impact statement is prepared and distributed to committee

Committee Chair **Bill Analysis** **Public Hearings** **Debate and Amend** **Committee Report**

 STOP The chair can refuse to schedule a bill for a committee hearing

A majority vote of committee membership is required **STOP**

Sent to Calendar Committees

A majority vote is needed to send to the House floor **STOP**

Tie vote, chubbing, or failure to gain a simple majority

STOP **Vote** **Third Reading** **STOP** **Vote** **Debate and Amend** **Second Reading** **House Floor**

Failure to concur with Senate amendments

Each conference committee must report to its respective chambers. Both the House and Senate must pass the bill before it goes to enrollment.

Conference Committee

The governor may veto a bill, which the legislature may override by a 2/3 vote

Failure to reconcile differences or gain a majority in either chamber

STOP *Signing in Presence of House* **Governor**

STOP Vetoed Bill

Signed Bill

Unsigned Bill

Law
Goes into effect after 90 days unless otherwise stipulated

change them. Sometimes opponents of a bill propose a "poison pill" or killer amendment, an amendment that would add language to a bill designed to make the bill unacceptable to a majority of the legislature or draw a veto from the governor. For example, in 2017, attempts to fix the funding system for the state's public schools fell apart after senators inserted a "private school choice" program that included subsidies for private school tuition.[41]

Another legislative trick is to attach a rider to a bill. A rider is an amendment to the bill that deals with an unrelated subject. A rider often calls for the spending of money or creates programs in a specific member's district. During the 2015 session, Senate Republicans attempted to attach a budget rider that would have stopped any state support for the proposed bullet train project connecting Dallas and Houston.[42]

Like the U.S. Senate, the Texas Senate has a tradition of allowing unlimited debate. Sometimes a member of the Senate engages in a filibuster, which is an effort to kill a bill by engaging in speaking continuously on the floor of the Senate and refusing to yield the floor to another member. This stalling tactic serves to prevent a vote from being taken. While filibustering, a senator must keep her or his discussion relevant to the legislation being discussed and cannot sit down or even lean on the desk. While Wendy Davis's 2013 filibuster attempting to stop restrictions on abortions is the most recent example of a major filibuster in the Texas Senate, her filibuster fell short of the state (and national) record set by Texas state senator Bill Meier in 1977 when he filibustered for forty-three hours.

Because a member's speaking time is limited to ten minutes by the rules of the Texas House, a filibuster cannot occur there. However, members of the House deliberately engage in lengthy debate over bills that are not controversial. This action is generally employed late in the legislative session and is used to prevent the Texas House from beginning debate on a more controversial issue or bill. This technique of delaying action on a bill to prevent the consideration of another bill is called chubbing. Representatives engaged in chubbing may or may not be in favor of the current bill but are trying to block consideration of bills later on the Texas House calendar. The filibuster in the Texas Senate and chubbing in the Texas House are important tools for slowing down the legislative process and preventing the majority from getting everything it wants.

Another tool employed by the minority party to influence voting is the quorum. Texas Senate rules require that two-thirds of the membership be present to take a vote. This means that any eleven senators (one-third of the Senate) may prevent business from being conducted if they absent themselves from the chamber. The need for a quorum is another example of how the Senate's rules compel it to consider the opinion of the minority party.

Voting

In general, voting processes are similar in both houses of the legislature. Votes may be either a voice vote or a roll call vote. A voice vote occurs when the presiding officer asks verbally for those members in favor of the bill or amendment to call out "aye," then asks for those members opposed to call out "nay." For these voice votes, the presiding officer simply announces whether the bill or amendment passes. If the presiding officer is uncertain of the result, the officer calls for a roll call vote. A member of the chamber who questions the outcome of the voice vote may call for a roll call vote. Normally, the presiding officer agrees to allow the roll call vote to occur. Typically, any important vote will be conducted as a **roll call vote** in which the vote of each member is recorded. In the Texas House, roll call votes are recorded electronically, with each member being able to vote using a set of buttons on his or her desk. In the Texas Senate, roll call votes are recorded as each senator's name is called and the senator answers out loud.

Once a bill has passed one chamber of the legislature, it goes to the other chamber for consideration. While the Texas Constitution requires that bills dealing with taxation must start out in the Texas House of Representatives before going to the Texas Senate, legislation on other matters may start out in either. If the House and Senate have passed different versions of the same bill, then the bill first goes to a conference committee for reconciliation. The conference committee may amend or may rewrite the bill before sending their recommendation back to both chambers of the Texas Legislature. Each chamber may accept the changes to the bill, reject the changes to the bill, or send the bill back to the conference committee. If both chambers accept the changes, the bill has passed. If the bill fails to pass either chamber or if the conference committee cannot reconcile the differences, the bill dies. Twenty-four states allow some legislation to carry over from one session to another,[43] but a bill that has not passed by the end of legislative session dies. The same idea can be introduced in the next session, but it begins again with a new number and must start the legislative process at the beginning.

The Governor's Veto Power

If both chambers have passed a bill in identical form, the bill goes to the governor for signing. After a bill is sent to the governor, he or she must sign the bill into law or veto it. If the governor does not sign the bill into law and the legislature is still in session, after ten days it automatically becomes law. While the governor possesses the power to veto legislation, this power is limited. For all bills but those dealing with spending, the governor must veto or accept the entire bill. The governor may use a **line-item veto**, or a selective veto of some parts of a bill, on spending bills only. An override of the governor's veto is possible only by a two-thirds vote of each house of the state legislature. If the legislature ends its session, the governor has twenty days to veto the bill; otherwise, the bill becomes law. Ninety days after the legislature ends its session, any law enacted becomes effective unless the bill contains an **emergency clause**, which makes a bill effective immediately upon being signed into law.

Trends in Legislative Activity

Given the relatively short session for the Texas Legislature to complete its business, just 140 calendar days every two years, the

roll call vote
a form of voting for which a permanent record of each member's vote is created; used for more important votes

line-item veto
the ability of the executive to selectively veto only some parts of a bill; in Texas, available only on spending bills

Representative Scott Sanford is congratulated by Representative Patricia Harless in the Texas House chamber after Sanford's sponsored SB 2065, a bill for religious opposition to gay marriages, was heavily supported by Democrats and Republicans for its protection of religion. The large board in the background displays every representative's name and vote.

emergency clause
language that makes a
bill effective immediately
upon being signed into
law rather than subject to
the customary ninety-day
waiting period

legislature's time is at a premium. The brevity of the legislative session is compounded by the Texas Constitution's requirement limiting legislative activity in the first sixty days of the regular session. The constitution limits action in the first thirty days of the session to the introduction of legislation, dealing with emergency appropriations, confirmation of the recess appointees of the governor, and any emergency issues designated by the governor. The second thirty days is reserved for action by committees and such emergency matters as may be submitted by the governor. As a result of these provisions, the more serious work of the legislature begins after the sixtieth day of the legislative session.

It is clear that as the state continues to grow, the Texas Legislature must assemble a larger budget and oversee a complicated government that deals with more people and more issues every year. Whether you want to create new government programs or cut old, outdated programs, you need the legislature to pass legislation to bring change.

WINNERS AND LOSERS

Historically, legislative organization and process have produced clear winners and losers in the game of Texas politics. The relatively weak position of parties produced a system that concentrated power in the hands of the presiding officers of the state legislature. Thus, the two most powerful positions in Texas are the Speaker of the House and the lieutenant governor in the Senate. The amount of power in these two offices, which is often unchecked by an institutionally weak legislature and governor, resembles the concentrated power the framers of the Texas Constitution were trying to avoid. The lieutenant governor is in a unique position, able to dominate the Texas Senate through his or her control over debate, the appointment of committee chairs, and the appointment of members of committees. Yet his or her power is not unlimited. Much of the lieutenant governor's powers derive from internal rules that the Senate approves or from personal leadership style. Rules may be changed by the Texas Senate at any time, and leadership style varies from person to person. Techniques such as the blocking bill and filibuster place limits on the lieutenant governor and the majority party as well. However, these limits are traditions, and the Senate's decision in 2015 to change the two-thirds rule proves that tradition can quickly give way to other considerations. As the Texas legislature continues to evolve into a more partisan organization, these limits may be observed less frequently when the lieutenant governor is from the same political party as the majority party. These changes in legislative process, if they occur, will clearly benefit the majority party and harm the minority party.

For decades, people who wanted to serve as the Speaker of the Texas House courted support from individual legislators regardless of party affiliation and rewarded supporters with favorable consideration of legislation and committee assignments. However, the Speaker's power is limited by possible revolts when the Speaker attempts to be too autocratic or runs afoul of his or her own political party caucus members. To the extent that the Texas model creates a system in which power is concentrated in the hands of the presiding officers of the state legislature, a vigorous system of checks and balances often seems absent. The ability to shape and control debate in the chamber makes the Speaker a clear winner in Texas.

Recent attempts to organize the party caucuses and raise the level of partisanship within the Texas Legislature may have detrimental effects. The traditional bipartisan system that allows the minority party significant influence in the Texas Senate and Texas House is eroding. The emergence of a Republican majority in the legislature, coupled with stronger cohesion, organization, and political pressure within the Republican caucuses in both chambers, has made the Republicans the clear winners in the battle to influence legislation. Legislation favored by the majority may be more easily passed, even when ill considered, while bills and amendments with support from the minority party may be killed quickly, either in committee or on the floor of the chamber. Here the legislative process rewards the majority party.

Much of the legislative process remains essentially the same in terms of the formal steps for a bill to become a law. The committee structure of the Texas Legislature remains consistent with the past. However, Texas is seeing a transition in who gets to chair these committees as partisanship rises.

Service in the Texas Legislature in Austin is sometimes a precursor to later service in the U.S. House of Representatives in Washington, DC; thus, the tradition of bipartisan cooperation in the state legislature has historically translated into a bipartisan congressional delegation from Texas in the U.S. Congress. One group of scholars has suggested that Texas's domination of leadership positions in the U.S. Congress during the twentieth century (e.g., the speakerships of Sam Rayburn and Jim Wright in the U.S. House of Representatives and the Senate leadership of Lyndon Johnson) reflects the ability of the Texas delegation to build coalitions and work with various factions within both parties.[44] The Texas federal delegation has long had a reputation for putting party concerns aside to cooperate in the best interests of the state. As a result, Texas has enjoyed outsized influence in the U.S. Congress and received more than its share of favorable national legislation and program funding. That Texas is home to NASA and so many military bases suggests that Texas politicians have found a way to put the state at the heart of some of the nation's more important goals.

If rising partisan politics in the Texas Legislature continues to interfere with the ability to work together, the recent increase in partisan divisions at the state and national level may undermine legislators' abilities to get things done. Concentration of power in the hands of the presiding officers of the Texas Legislature, and the bipartisan support that results, has historically created a different set of incentives and outcomes in Austin than in Washington, DC. In Austin, the current trajectory increasingly leaves the Democratic Party with a strategy of communication and public awareness campaigns as the primary means to get its message across. The majority party may be the winner in the short term, but status as a majority party is not guaranteed in the long term. The losers may ultimately be Texans as a whole. However, the influence of the political party is dependent on the leadership style of the presiding officer of each chamber, the cohesion in the majority party (currently the Republicans), and the style of leadership of the majority caucus leaders. Winners and losers are determined in part by these factors as well.

Is following the bipartisan tradition of the Texas legislature wise in the current political climate? How important should parties be in the legislature?

★ SOCIAL RESPONSIBILITY

What are the consequences of the Texas Senate reforming practices such as the filibuster and the three-fifth rule? What is the best balance between allowing deliberation and getting bills passed?

★ SOCIAL RESPONSIBILITY

CONCLUSION

The Texas Legislature is in a period of transition in terms of the role and function of political parties in legislative organization. The parties shape legislative process through control over committees, committee chairs, and floor debate. As the party caucuses in each chamber continue to organize, their ability to structure votes and communicate objectives is enhanced. Social media tools are beginning to assist both parties in their tasks within the Texas Legislature. The days of bipartisanship may be ending as the realities of a more partisan legislature emerge.

However, certain traditions may still have value. The basic legislative process itself remains largely the same as it was in the twentieth century. Both chambers retain unique processes that profoundly shape how a bill becomes a law. The Texas Senate continues to use blocking bills, quorum calls, and filibusters, while the Texas House maintains its multiple calendars, utilizes chubbing, and has a more elaborate committee structure. Despite the rise of party caucuses and partisanship in the Texas Legislature, both chambers continue to accept granting extensive powers to their respective presiding officers. In some sense, Texas is reflecting the changes in the national political scene as well. The U.S. Congress is more partisan than in the past, and politics has become more contentious in Washington, DC. Additionally, other southern states have also seen a shift from Democratic dominance over the executive and legislative branches to Republican dominance. Ultimately, changes in legislatures are often slow to occur, and many decades may be required to shift key aspects of the legislature. Texas is certainly no exception to this.

for CQ Press

Want a better grade?

Get the tools you need to sharpen your study skills. Access practice quizzes, eFlashcards, video, and multimedia at **edge.sagepub.com/collier6e**.

KEY TERMS

amendment (p. 109)

bicameral (p. 82)

bill (p. 115)

blocking bill (p. 117)

calendar (p. 116)

chubbing (p. 120)

citizen legislature (p. 86)

committee (p. 107)

concurrent resolution (p. 116)

conference committee (p. 112)

delegate (p. 89)

emergency clause (p. 121)

filibuster (p. 120)

fiscal note (p. 115)

floor debate (p. 117)

floor leader (p. 104)

gerrymandering (p. 97)

ideological caucus (p. 106)

KEY TERMS (CONTINUED)

introduce (a bill) (p. 115)
issue caucus (p. 106)
joint resolution (p. 116)
killer amendment (p. 120)
Legislative Budget Board (LBB) (p. 102)
legislative immunity (p. 85)
Legislative Redistricting Board (LRB) (p. 97)
lieutenant governor (p. 101)
line-item veto (p. 121)
majority-minority district (p. 99)
markup (p. 109)
minority and women's caucuses (p. 106)
multimember district (MMD) (p. 95)
nonpartisan or bipartisan independent
    commission (p. 97)
one person, one vote (p. 97)
oversight (p. 110)
party caucus chair (p. 104)
party legislative caucus (p. 103)
politico (p. 89)
president pro tempore (p. 101)

procedural standing committee (p. 107)
professional legislature (p. 86)
quorum (p. 120)
redistricting (p. 88)
regular session (p. 84)
representation (p. 89)
resolution (p. 115)
rider (p. 120)
roll call vote (p. 121)
select or special committee (p. 113)
simple resolution (p. 116)
single-member district (SMD) (p. 95)
Speaker of the House (p. 102)
special legislative caucus (p. 104)
special session (p. 85)
standing committee (p. 107)
substantive standing committee (p. 107)
supermajority (p. 85)
term limit (p. 88)
trustee (p. 89)
turnover (p. 88)

ACTIVE LEARNING

- Prepare a short memo or presentation that you would use to persuade a legislator to support a change to higher education in Texas. **Communication**

- Break into groups, with each group representing a committee. As a committee, draft a change to current law and then present it to the entire class for approval. **Teamwork**

CHAPTER REVIEW

1. Drawing district boundaries to deliberately benefit a candidate or party is an example of _____.

   a. realignment
   b. gerrymandering
   c. chubbing
   d. reallocation

(Continued)

2. The view of representation that elected officials should use their own judgment in casting votes in the legislature is known as the _____ view.
   a. delegate
   b. trustee
   c. politico
   d. constituency

3. The Texas Legislature meets in regular session every _____.
   a. six months
   b. year
   c. two years
   d. four years

4. The division of the legislative branch into two chambers is known as _____.
   a. gerrymandering
   b. bilateralism
   c. duopoly
   d. bicameralism

5. The primary responsibility for drawing the boundaries of elections is held by the _____.
   a. U.S. Census Bureau
   b. U.S. House
   c. U.S. Senate
   d. Texas Legislature

6. The Texas legislature is an example of a _____ legislature.
   a. citizen
   b. professional
   c. hybrid
   d. quasi

7. A _____ is the minimum number of legislative members required for the legislative body to conduct business.
   a. quorum
   b. filibuster
   c. supermajority
   d. totality

8. A _____ is an addition to a bill that deals with an unrelated subject.
   a. point of order
   b. quorum
   c. rider
   d. poison pill

9. The House calendar is a _____.
   a. schedule for the 140 days of the legislative session
   b. schedule for the day's votes in the Texas House
   c. list of bills in the order in which they'll be taken up
   d. list of approved days for committee meetings

10. A standing committee is a _____.
   a. permanent committee of the House or Senate
   b. committee created to deal with a specific bill or crisis
   c. committee responsible for resolving who speaks for and against bills during debate
   d. committee charged with writing the standing rules of the House or Senate

TEXAS GOVERNORS

The ability of past Texas governors to influence policy often relied on their powers of persuasion. Governor Greg Abbott, though, possesses more tools for exerting influence than past governors. Assessing the governor's impact on the legislative session can be a murky business, since much of it happens behind closed doors. What we can observe reveals a governor that directs the state's lawmakers in multiple ways. The most visible attempt to influence the legislature is the governor's state of the state address, which occurs just as the legislative session gets underway. In 2017, Abbott's state of the state address identified twenty items he wanted lawmakers to pass, including four emergency items. The legislature eventually passed all but two of Abbott's policy goals, including all four emergency items. That is an impressive session, but Abbott's policy goals did not stop at the twenty he mentioned in his speech. As the session came to a close, it looked as if the legislature might not pass a voter identification law, something Abbott had not mentioned in his address. At that point, Abbott declared voter ID an emergency, which prompted the legislature to pass a last-minute bill. The governor not only had some visible policy wins; he also made sure his projects received full funding. When the legislature was poised to pass a budget that allocated less money than Abbott had requested for his Texas Enterprise Fund and Governors University Research Initiative, the governor threatened a last-minute veto. The legislature stayed late reworking the budget to add another $100 million for his programs. Abbott would go on to veto fifty bills and use his line-item veto, a selective veto of some parts of a bill, to reject $120 million from the legislature's budget.

Rodolfo Gonzalez/Austin American-Statesman via AP

After citizens in Denton voted to ban fracking within city limits, Governor Abbott signed legislation that prevents Texas cities from curtailing or prohibiting oil companies from fracking.

Before the legislature adjourned, it was clear that the governor would have to call a special session. The lieutenant governor forced the issue. Lieutenant Governor Dan Patrick held back legislation that would prevent sunset closures on several Texas agencies in order to force Governor Abbott to call a special session (see Chapter 5 for a discussion of the sunset review process). Patrick wanted to pass a transgender bathroom bill; forcing a special session gave his bathroom bill a second chance. Unlike the regular session, where the legislature can choose to ignore the governor's policy goals, the special session gives the governor exclusive control over the agenda. Governor Abbott called a special session with only one agenda item, the sunset legislation necessary to keep several agencies open. Abbott promised that, once the sunset legislation was passed, he would add nineteen other agenda items to the session, including the lieutenant governor's bathroom bill. At the end of this political showdown, about half of Abbott's special session agenda passed, but Patrick's bathroom bill did not. The governor demonstrated substantial influence on the legislative process and got the lion's share of what he asked for.

Abbott exerted considerable weight in the legislative session. But he did not stop there. During the session, three Republican House members pushed for stronger ethics reform legislation, including limits on how the governor raises campaign contributions. The next year when those Republicans came up for reelection, Abbott actively campaigned against them. A governor working to unseat three sitting members of his own party is unprecedented in Texas politics. It appears the governor is sending a message to legislators who don't agree with his policy agenda. Governor Abbott's subtle style is very different from the bipartisan cooperation of Governor Bush or the swagger of Governor Perry. But make no mistake, he is exerting influence throughout the legislative process. In this chapter, we will review the formal and informal qualifications of the office. We will then explore the governor's various roles. We will conclude with a discussion of the emergence of a strong Texas governor.

THE OFFICE OF THE GOVERNOR

Texans have long distrusted executive authority, going all the way back to the American colonists' experiences under the British king and the vast powers exercised by colonial governors. The result was that early on in America, most states created relatively weak executives and preferred to vest power in the legislative branch. Texas was no exception. Distrust of governors in Texas was reinforced by Texans' experience under Mexican president Antonio López de Santa Anna. Indeed, throughout the state's history, Texans have distrusted government in general and governors in particular—as governors are the most visible manifestation of state authority. Early Texans built their life from scratch in a harsh frontier environment, in which the government was viewed more as an impediment to survival than a facilitator of the public good. This attitude was amplified by what occurred in Texas after the Civil War, when the Reconstruction era featured a relatively strong governor and a perceived "illegitimate" government. The subsequent Texas Constitution of 1876 deliberately weakened the executive, granting the governor little formal power, shortening the governor's term to two years, allowing the governor to make relatively few appointments, and instituting other elected executives that rivaled the governor's power. Absent formal constitutional powers, Texas governors through history have become astute at employing informal powers. The power of the Texas governor has grown both formally and informally, even as Texans' preference for limited government remains entrenched.

The governor of Texas tends to be a national political figure simply by virtue of governing such a large state. A governorship is highly visible and can serve as a stepping-stone to appointments to state and federal posts and election to national office, including the presidency itself. For example, former governor Preston Smith served as chair of what is now the Higher Education Coordinating Board, and after his term as governor, Price Daniel was selected by President Lyndon B. Johnson to head the Office of Emergency Preparedness and was later appointed to the Supreme Court of Texas. Daniel, who had already served the state in a variety of elected and appointed offices, has held more high offices than anyone else in Texas history.[1] After serving as governor of the state, John Connally, who famously survived bullet wounds received when John F. Kennedy was assassinated in Dallas, became secretary of the treasury during Richard Nixon's administration. Pappy O'Daniel resigned the governorship to become a U.S. senator. Most notable, of course, is George W. Bush, who left the governor's office to assume the presidency of the United States. Other governors, such as Bill Clements and Ann Richards, chose not to seek further elected office after vacating the governor's mansion.

Qualifications

The Texas Constitution specifies three requirements to be governor in the state. The governor must be at least thirty years of age, have resided at least five years in the state of Texas, and be a U.S. citizen. (Table 4.1 compares these requirements against those for

TABLE 4.1 Terms and Qualifications of Elected Chief Executives

Constitutional Provisions	Texas Governor	U.S. President	Other States
Age	30 years	35 years	34 states set the minimum age at 30; 6 states set the age at 18; 6 states set a 25-year age limit; one state sets the age limit at 31; and another 3 states set no age limit
Residence	5 years	14 years	13 states require more than 5 years, 34 states require 5 years or less, 3 states have no residency requirement
Terms	4 years	4 years (limited to 2 terms of office or 10 years)	48 states establish 4-year term, but 36 states limit the number of consecutive terms

Source: Audrey S. Wall, ed., *The Book of the States*, vol. 49 (Lexington, KY: Council of State Governments, 2017), tables 4.1 and 4.2.

the U.S. presidency and for governors in other states.) The governor of the state is further restricted from holding any other job or receiving outside compensation, a restriction notably absent from the state's legislature. Specifically, the Texas Constitution specifies that the governor:

> shall hold his office for the term of four years, or until his successor shall be duly installed. He shall be at least thirty years of age, a citizen of the United States, and shall have resided in this State at least five years immediately preceding his election. [Amended Nov. 7, 1972.][2] During the time he holds the office of Governor, he shall not hold any other office: civil, military or corporate; nor shall he practice any profession, and receive compensation, reward, fee, or the promise thereof for the same; nor receive any salary, reward or compensation or the promise thereof from any person or corporation, for any service rendered or performed during the time he is Governor, or to be thereafter rendered or performed.[3]

Beyond the constitutional requirements, Texas governors have tended to share other common characteristics. Since 1876, most governors in Texas have been white, Protestant, wealthy men. Texas has had two Roman Catholic governors, Francis Lubbock and Greg Abbott. Nearly all modern governors had some higher education—mostly in law—and nearly half of Texas governors also had some military experience, ranging from service in the U.S. Army or U.S. Navy to service in the Texas National Guard or Texas Air Guard. Although the myth of the Texas rancher or Texas oilman is often used to tap into the Texas legend during gubernatorial campaigns, few modern governors actually have such experience. Notable exceptions include Dolph Briscoe, who was a wealthy cattleman and horse trader, and Clements and Bush, who owned oil companies.

Modern governors of Texas have also, by and large, had previous political experience. Many of the state's governors have risen from the ranks of other Texas offices, including the Texas Legislature, the Railroad Commission of Texas, and often the lieutenant governor's office. Others held national offices prior to becoming governor of the Lone Star State. Notable examples include Bill Clements, who had been deputy U.S. secretary of defense, and

How long do governors typically hold office in Texas and how has that changed over time?

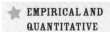 **EMPIRICAL AND QUANTITATIVE**

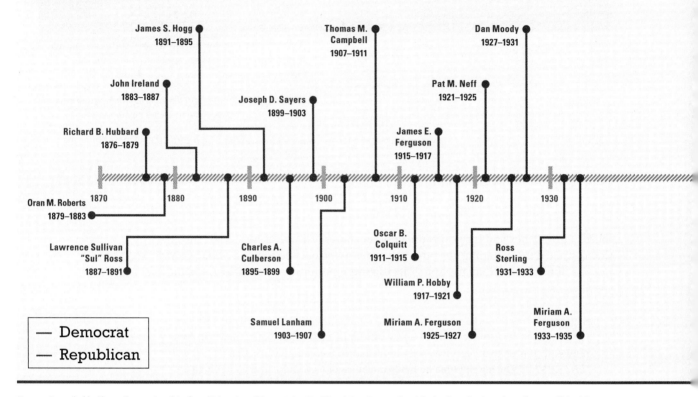

FIGURE 4.1 Texas Governors since 1876

- James S. Hogg 1891–1895
- John Ireland 1883–1887
- Joseph D. Sayers 1899–1903
- Richard B. Hubbard 1876–1879
- Thomas M. Campbell 1907–1911
- Dan Moody 1927–1931
- Pat M. Neff 1921–1925
- James E. Ferguson 1915–1917
- Oran M. Roberts 1879–1883
- Lawrence Sullivan "Sul" Ross 1887–1891
- Charles A. Culberson 1895–1899
- Oscar B. Colquitt 1911–1915
- Ross Sterling 1931–1933
- William P. Hobby 1917–1921
- Samuel Lanham 1903–1907
- Miriam A. Ferguson 1925–1927
- Miriam A. Ferguson 1933–1935

— Democrat
— Republican

Source: Compiled by the authors using data from University of Texas at Austin, Liberal Arts Instructional Technology Services, http://texaspolitics.laits .utexas.edu/html/exec/governors/index.html (accessed August 30, 2014); Legislative Reference Library of Texas.

John Connally, who ascended to the governorship after serving as the secretary of the Navy in the Kennedy administration.

Although Texas governors often have other political experience, many view the Texas governorship as the pinnacle of their career. In fact, research suggests that the governor's job is the best job in politics, even during times of economic hardship.[4] Alan Rosenthal argues that governors, unlike other officeholders, are singular decision makers who can lay claim to accomplishments and who are more likely to be listened to. After serving as U.S. senator, Price Daniel famously declared he would "rather be governor of Texas than the president of the United States"[5] and returned to Texas to run for governor. President George W. Bush called Governor Perry from the White House to let him know that governing Texas was the best job in the world.[6]

Texans have occasionally displayed a willingness to elect governors with no political experience. While inexperienced gubernatorial candidates can tap into Texans' distrust of government, it is a larger-than-life personality that helps make up for lack of experience in public service. James "Pa" Ferguson, for example, had no political experience when he was

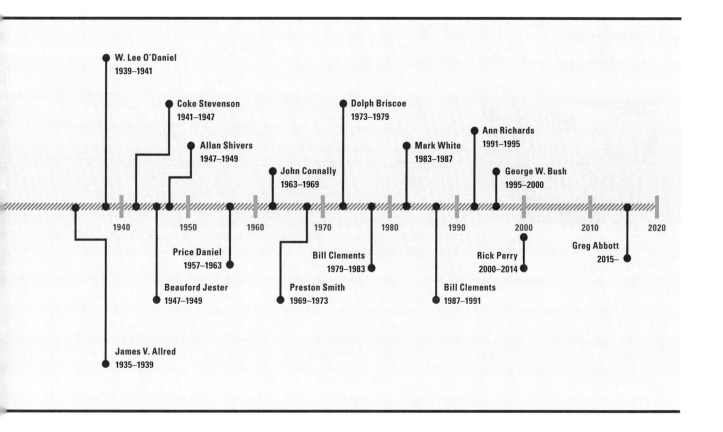

elected governor in 1914. His popularity was based less on political skill and more on his self-styled image as "Farmer Jim," who represented tenant farmers and poor workers across the state. He also impressed audiences by quoting Shakespeare, Jefferson, or Hamilton whenever the opportunity presented itself.[7]

Equally colorful—and perhaps equally ineffectual—was Governor Wilbert Lee "Pappy" O'Daniel. O'Daniel worked at a flour mill and hosted a weekly radio show during which he sold flour; featured his band, the Light Crust Doughboys; and expressed his opinions. O'Daniel's platform promised to block a state sales tax, end capital punishment, and institute a state pension for elderly Texans. Despite his lack of experience, his popularity on the radio helped him win the governor's office—twice—and afterward a U.S. congressional seat. O'Daniel was highly popular as a radio personality; he inspired a character in the Coen brothers' movie *O Brother, Where Art Thou?* As governor, however, he proved unproductive, delivering none of his campaign promises.

Inexperience does not always equate with ineffectiveness, however. In 1994, George W. Bush ran for governor with no prior experience in office. Bush did have

TEXAS Legends

Ann Richards

As governor of Texas, Ann Richards reflected both new and old Texas, embracing the transformation of the state while remaining rooted in its traditions. She challenged the historical male dominance of state offices as Texas's "good ol' boys" loosened their generations-old grip on state governance. Although she changed the way things were done, Richards proved equally fluent in the language and symbols of traditional Texas.

Richards moved up quickly in the ranks of state politics. After teaching junior high school social studies while raising her family, she entered government in 1976, winning a seat on the Travis County Commissioners Court. Richards fit easily into the small-town image revered in Texas, often proclaiming proudly that her father had come from a town called Bugtussle and her mother from one called Hogjaw. In 1982, she won election as state treasurer and became the first woman elected to statewide office in Texas in fifty years.

She campaigned for the governor's office in 1990, calling for a "new" Texas that would offer opportunities to more residents. In the end, she won a hard-fought battle, besting West Texas rancher Clayton Williams. While in office, Richards worked aggressively to bring more women and minorities into state government. She made clear that women could find a place in Texas politics, advising them in patently Texas style, "Let me tell you, sisters,

seeing dried egg on a plate in the morning is a lot dirtier than anything I've had to deal with in politics."[i] She appointed the first black regent to the University of Texas (UT) Board of Regents and brought more black, Hispanic, and female officers into the ranks of the legendary Texas Rangers.

Richards proved to be just as colorful as her predecessors. She once quipped, "Let me tell you that I am the only child of a very rough-talking father. So don't be embarrassed about your language. I've either heard it or I can top it."[ii] Like many of the men who came before her, Richards also had flaws, including a battle with alcoholism that ended in rehab and a strained marriage that ended in divorce.

She demonstrated repeatedly that women could be tough on crime, dramatically increasing the size of the Texas prison system and limiting the number of prisoners granted parole. She also championed education and environmental causes. Richards looked to modernize the way in which departments were administered and led the state in insurance reform and ethics reform.

While her tongue was sharp, her language was folksy. Richards's style won her a national following when she delivered the keynote address at the 1988 Democratic National Convention. Complaining about George H. W. Bush, the Republican Party's presidential candidate, Richards suggested the Democrats would expose his shortcomings, or, as she put it, "We're going to tell how the cow ate the cabbage."

Richards championed political activism, saying, "Sometimes it's serendipitous. Good things happen accidentally. But they're not going to happen unless well-meaning people give of their time and their lives to do that."[iii] One of her legacies is the Ann Richards School for Young Women Leaders, a school focused on

giving girls the education and confidence necessary to serve as leaders in their communities. Richards preached feminism, informing the audience at the 1988 Democratic National Convention that "if you give us the chance, we can perform. After all, Ginger Rogers did everything that Fred Astaire did. She just did it backwards and in high heels."

Beaten by George W. Bush in her bid for reelection, Richards remained in the spotlight, making frequent media appearances and working as a political consultant. Asked what she would have done if she had known she would serve only one term, Richards remarked, "Oh, I probably would have raised more hell."[iv] Richards died of esophageal cancer on September 13, 2006. Governor Rick Perry's eulogy summed up her already legendary status. "Ann Richards," he said, "was the epitome of Texas politics: a figure larger than life who had a gift for captivating the public with her great wit."[v] Richards embodied change in a state that has held fast to tradition. She embraced the traditions of the state more than many of the good ol' boys, all the while challenging the state's limited role for women and minorities.

i. Mimi Swartz, "Ann Richards: How Perfection Led to Failure," *Texas Monthly*, October 1990, 60.

ii. Ann Richards with Peter Knobler, *Straight from the Heart: My Life in Politics and Other Places* (New York: Simon & Schuster, 1989), 165.

iii. "Political People and Their Moves," *Texas Weekly*, accessed August 30, 2014, www .texastribune.org/texas-weekly/vol-23/ no-12/people.

iv. "Former Texas Governor Ann Richards Dies," *USA Today*, September 14, 2006, http://usatoday30.usatoday.com/news/ nation/2006–09-13-richards-obit_x.htm.

v. "Political People and Their Moves."

the benefit of name recognition from his father's presidency and enjoyed a conservative reputation in an overwhelmingly conservative state. As governor, Bush was known for his ability to forge bipartisan coalitions. He successfully supported several education initiatives and state tax cuts and was a relatively popular governor.

One of the most consistent traits of Texas governors throughout the state's history is their conservative bent—and their Democratic Party affiliation. Nothing is more ingrained in Texas legend than the Democrats' hold on the state, which, until recently, was nearly absolute. Since Reconstruction, Texas has elected four Republican governors, beginning with Bill Clements, who finally broke the Democrats' century-long winning streak in 1978. The dissolution of the Democratic Party monopoly is one of the most significant changes experienced by the state in recent years. The change is particularly noteworthy because it brought with it an almost complete reversal in party affiliation. Democratic Party dominance has given way to Republican Party control, and the recent trend of electing Republican governors will likely continue for the near future. Although party identification in Texas has changed, Texans have long displayed a preference for conservative governments and limited social policy, regardless of party affiliation.

Relatively few early Texas governors were born in the state. Since statehood, just twenty-three out of forty-eight governors, or 48 percent, were born in Texas. Texas's first native-born governor was the state's twentieth, James Stephen "Jim" Hogg, elected in 1890. Hogg was a Democrat who brought progressivism to the state. Texans

appreciated him for protecting the interests of ordinary people rather than those of big business. Hogg was best known for creating the railroad commission, passing antitrust legislation, and attempting to limit the influence of lobbyists in the state. Hogg also earned his place in Texas folklore by famously naming his only daughter "Ima." The myth that he named a second daughter "Ura" persists today, though in fact no such person existed. Modern governors have been much more likely to have been born in Texas, although Pappy O'Daniel and George W. Bush are both notable exceptions.

Although nearly all the state's governors have been white men, twice Texas has elected women to its highest office. In 1924, Miriam A. "Ma" Ferguson became the first female governor of Texas and the second female governor in the country, being sworn in just two weeks after Wyoming's Nellie T. Ross. After Pa Ferguson was impeached and prevented from holding office in the state, Ma Ferguson ran as a proxy for her husband, using the campaign slogan "Two governors for the price of one." Ironically, Pa Ferguson rejected women's suffrage, arguing that a woman's place was in the home. Pa promised he would do the actual governing if Ma won. Thus, the women's suffrage movement opposed Ma Ferguson's election, though she went on to appoint Texas's first female secretary of state, Emma C. Meharg. Ma Ferguson's administration confronted the Ku Klux Klan (she passed an antimask

Miriam "Ma" Ferguson served as the first female governor of Texas and was the second woman in the country to assume a governorship.

> Why does minority representation in the governor's office matter?
>
> ★ SOCIAL RESPONSIBILITY

law that the courts subsequently overturned), contested prohibition laws, and called for fiscally conservative economic policy. It was accusations of corruption, though, that Ma Ferguson's administration became known for. During her administration, more than 2,000 pardons were granted, leaving the impression that pardons were for sale under the Fergusons. Ma claimed that most of the pardons were given to liquor law violators who were not really criminals, but in fact hundreds of pardons were granted to violent felons as well.[8] Ma lost her bid for reelection in the next two gubernatorial races but was elected governor again in 1932, becoming the first governor in Texas to serve two nonconsecutive terms.

In 1990, Ann Richards became the second woman elected governor of Texas. Richards personified the iconic Texas image: cowboy boots, straight talk, and a reputation for being tough. She had previous experience on the Travis County Commissioners Court and as the Texas state treasurer. A former teacher, Governor Richards decentralized education policy, encouraged economic growth, and promoted women and minorities during her administration. In contrast to Ma Ferguson, Richards became a symbol of women's progress in the state, famously displaying a T-shirt of the state capitol with the caption "A woman's place is in the dome."

Although Hispanics have increasingly added their voices to the state's dialogue and are both the largest and fastest-growing minority in Texas, the state has yet to elect a Hispanic governor. In 2002, wealthy oil tycoon Tony Sanchez made an unsuccessful bid for the governor's office, spending a reported $59 million of his own money.[9] Although Sanchez lost to Rick Perry, many observers saw Sanchez's campaign as a test of whether the Democratic Party could tap Hispanic voters to loosen the grip of the Republican Party on the state.[10]

Terms

What are the arguments for and against term limits?

⭐ CRITICAL THINKING

The Texas Constitution of 1876 originally established a relatively short term of just two years for the governor. A preference for short terms, usually one or two years, was common in early American politics, reflecting a distrust of executive power carried over from the colonial era. Most governors in Texas were elected to two terms, serving a total of four years. In 1972, the Texas Constitution was amended to increase the governor's term to four years. Despite the fact that Texas has no term limits, few governors have been elected to two terms since that time. Dolph Briscoe served six years after he was initially elected to a two-year term, which began in 1973, before the amendment took effect, and was reelected to a second term under the new rules. Governors elected after Briscoe won only a single four-year term until George W. Bush. Bush was the first governor to be elected to a second four-year term, although he resigned in 2000 to become president after having been governor for only six years. While Texans have shown a consistent preference for regular turnover of their governors, everything changed with Rick Perry. Then–lieutenant governor Rick Perry finished out Bush's term and then ran successful bids for reelection in 2002 and 2006. In 2010, Governor Perry, already the longest-serving governor in Texas, won a third term, serving as governor for an unprecedented fourteen years. Today, Texas is one of fourteen states that have no limits on the number of terms their governors can serve.

Obviously, the longer a governor serves, the more likely it is that governor will successfully pass his or her own political agenda. The absence of term limits and four-year terms create a potential source of power for Texas's governors. The constitutional design of the governorship attempts to limit the power of a single governor by staggering gubernatorial appointments across multiple terms. Since Perry was in office for so long, he was able to appoint every appointive office in the state; this afforded his administration a broad base of loyalty.

What are the arguments for paying the governor more? Less?

★ CRITICAL THINKING

Succession

If a governor is unable to fulfill his or her term, the Texas Constitution outlines an explicit line of succession. If the governor resigns, is impeached and convicted, or dies while in office, the lieutenant governor succeeds to the governorship. After the lieutenant governor, the line of succession goes next to the president pro tempore of the Texas Senate, then to the Speaker of the Texas House, then to the attorney general. Thus, after the 2000 presidential election, when George W. Bush resigned the governorship to assume the presidency, Lieutenant Governor Rick Perry assumed the office, and the Texas Senate elected Bill Ratliff as the new lieutenant governor. Ratliff became the first lieutenant governor in the history of the state to be selected by the Texas Senate rather than by winning the position in a statewide election.

succession
a set order, usually spelled out in the constitution, denoting which officeholder takes over when the sitting governor resigns, dies, or is impeached

When the governor is out of the state, the lieutenant governor is acting governor. Thus, when George W. Bush was campaigning for president, Rick Perry gained considerable hands-on experience in the governor's office. Similarly, Perry's unsuccessful 2012 presidential bid resulted in then–lieutenant governor David Dewhurst acting as governor for 126 days and cost Texans an additional $32,000 in pay to Dewhurst. By custom, both the governor and the lieutenant governor arrange to be out of the state at least one day during their terms, allowing the president pro tempore of the Senate to act as governor for the day.

Compensation

Originally, the Constitution of 1876 specified the governor's salary, which meant that a pay raise required a constitutional amendment approved by a majority of voters. In 1954, however, the constitution was amended to allow the Texas Legislature to set the governor's salary. Currently, the Texas governor is paid $153,750, which puts the state above the average of $138,625 for all governors.[11] Tennessee and Florida governors do not accept a salary, and Illinois and Michigan governors collect only $1.00 of their salary.[12] Ironically, governors are paid well below the average $2.4 million annual salary of football coaches at public universities.[13] In 2017, Texas's highest-paid state employees were the head football coaches for Texas A&M and the University of Texas, who, at $7.5 million and $5.5 million respectively, are paid considerably more than the governor. Pennsylvania has the highest-paid governor, with a salary of $193,304; Maine's governor receives the lowest salary, at $70,000. In January 2012, then-governor Perry drew criticism when he officially "retired" and began to draw on his state pension, which amounted to $92,000 a year in addition to his $150,000 governor's salary.[14] Perry was able to collect retirement his last four years in office under the state's rule of eighty, which allows individuals to begin collecting their state retirement when their age and years of service collectively total eighty years.

Compensation for the Texas governor includes several perks in addition to salary. He or she is allocated a travel allowance and use of a state limousine, state helicopter, and state airplane. All fifty states provide an automobile for their governor; another thirty-eight provide a state airplane and twenty-one provide a state helicopter.[15] Texas is one of forty-four states that also provides a governor's residence. The governor employs a staff to help coordinate the office, as well as drivers, pilots, chefs, housekeepers, and stewards. Depending on the governor, the staff can number anywhere from 200 to over 300 people. Governor Abbott's staff is just under 300 people, the largest of the fifty states. The average staff size for American governors is around fifty-four staff members.[16] In addition, Texas maintains a governor's mansion around the corner from the capitol. The governor of Texas is also given a security detail for his or her protection, which provides security when the governor travels, whether or not the travel is related to state business. For example, Texas paid nearly $4 million each for both George W. Bush's and Rick Perry's bids for the presidency.[17] Governor Abbott spent $1 million in security expenses in his first term; his costliest trip was to Hawaii, which included a $71,000 security detail. In recent sessions, the legislature considered, but failed to pass, legislation that would require officeholders to reimburse the state for out-of-state travel that is not state business.

Impeachment

impeachment
formal procedure to indict and remove an elected official from office for misdeeds

The Texas Constitution vests the power of impeachment in the Texas Legislature. According to the constitution, the legislature can impeach the governor, lieutenant governor, attorney general, commissioner of the General Land Office, and comptroller as well as the judges of the Supreme Court of Texas, court of appeals, and district court. To impeach the governor, the Texas House of Representatives must approve the articles of impeachment (similar to a grand jury indictment) by a simple majority. Impeachment by the Texas House indicates that there is enough evidence to proceed with a trial. Impeachments are then tried in the Texas Senate, where conviction requires a two-thirds vote. While the Texas Constitution outlines a clear procedure for impeaching the governor, it is silent on what constitutes an impeachable offense.

Pa Ferguson remains the only governor in the state's history to have been impeached and removed from office. Ferguson balked when the UT Board of Regents refused to let him handpick university presidents or fire university professors who opposed his governorship. When asked why he wanted to fire the professors, Governor Ferguson famously quipped, "I am governor of Texas, I don't have to give any reasons."[18] To indicate his disapproval with the board, Ferguson vetoed the university's appropriations. Up to this point, only six American governors had been impeached, and five of those were Reconstruction-era governors in the South.[19] Nonetheless, the Texas Legislature voted to impeach and remove Ferguson for misappropriation of public funds, and he was subsequently barred from holding a state office again. In spite of that, Ferguson continued to exert significant influence on politics in the state. The day before the impeachment verdict was announced, Ferguson resigned as governor. He would later claim that this made the impeachment verdict obsolete. Amazingly, in 1924, despite his conviction, Ferguson again ran for governor of the state, although an appellate court upheld his prohibition from holding state office. Even this was not enough to prevent Ferguson's influence, as he subsequently convinced his wife Miriam to run for governor in his place.

POWERS OF THE GOVERNOR

How should the Texas governor fill appointments?

★ SOCIAL RESPONSIBILITY

The Constitution of 1876 originally created a formally weak governor, which relied on the officeholder's ability to generate support informally for a policy agenda. In general, strong governors are granted significant appointment power, exert considerable control over the state's budget, and exercise substantial power to veto legislation. The Texas governor's limited enumerated powers in the Constitution of 1876 can be traced to the governorship of E. J. Davis and, in particular, to the belief that Davis's Reconstruction government did not represent most Texans' preferences. Thus, originally, the Texas governor's appointment power, veto power, and budget power were relatively limited. Over time, though, each of these powers has expanded, sometimes a reflection of a natural drift of executive power, sometimes a formal expansion. As we shall see, today, the power of the governor has substantially increased.

Executive Roles

The governor's executive roles involve directing the state bureaucracy to administer the laws passed by the state legislature. According to the Texas Constitution, the governor of the state "shall cause the laws to be faithfully executed and shall conduct, in person, or in such manner as shall be prescribed by law, all intercourse and business of the State with other States and with the United States."[20] In 2018, Governor Abbott, pointing to "the success of regulatory review at the federal level," directed all state agencies to submit any proposed rule changes to the governor before posting them in the Texas Register.[21] This sort of gubernatorial intervention in bureaucratic rulemaking represents a significant increase in the role the governor plays. The success of the governor in guiding the bureaucracy is also directly tied to his or her appointment power, or ability to determine who will occupy key posts. Gubernatorial appointees will be much more responsive to the governor's policy goals than officials who are elected independently of the governor and with their own policy agendas. The current Texas constitution originally gave the governor almost no appointment power. The governor was originally empowered to appoint the secretary of state and notaries public. Most of the governor's early appointment power arose from filling vacancies that occurred between elections. The design of the Constitution of 1876 was to severely limit the power of the governor. Thus, Texas has a plural executive, where administrative powers are shared with other officials who are elected independent of the governor's office. Since they serve based on popular election rather than gubernatorial appointment, members of the plural executive often pursue their own policy goals, which may or may not complement the governor's goals. The plural executive can even represent opposing parties, making the executive more fragmented and less unified than one in which the governor appoints other executive members.

appointment power the ability to determine who will occupy key positions within the bureaucracy

plural executive an executive branch in which the functions have been divided among several, mostly elected, officeholders rather than residing in a single person, the governor

On the other hand, while the governor has limited influence over many statewide officials, as the legislature has created new boards and agencies, it has often granted the governor new appointment powers. The result has been a slow drift toward greater appointment power over time. Governors can appoint based on a wide range of criteria. Nearly all Texas governors have disproportionately appointed white males, though Governor Ann Richards remains a notable exception; she appointed Hispanics and African Americans at rates that mirrored their population numbers, and forty-five percent of her appointees were female.[22] Moreover, gubernatorial appointees usually share the governor's basic political philosophies and tend to be loyal to the governor. Governors also make appointments based on patronage.

Should the governor be allowed to fire appointees who do not support him or her in the next election?

★ CRITICAL THINKING

The Powers of the Governor

Executive Role

Appointment power: As one part of the plural executive, the Texas governor has limited appointment powers; many posts are independently elected; the longer a governor is in office, the more impact this power has.

Executive orders: An order issued by the governor directing agencies to address a particular policy.

Budget power: Twenty-seven states give the governor sole responsibility for drafting a budget; in Texas, the Legislative Budget Board dominates the process.

Legislative Role

Agenda setting: The state of the state address provides the governor with an opportunity to influence the legislative agenda.

Call a special session: Thirty-six states allow only legislators or the legislature's presiding officers to call a special session; Texas governors can use special sessions to force the legislature to address their proposals.

Veto power: The governor must sign or veto a bill within 10 days and has line-item veto authority; the legislature rarely musters the two-thirds vote needed to overturn a veto.

Judicial Role

Pardons: A 1936 constitutional amendment took pardon power away from the governor, who must now have the majority support from the Board of Pardons and Parole before granting clemency.

Military Role

Commander in chief of the Texas National Guard and Texas State Guard

Other Roles

Ceremonial duties: As head of state, the governor represents Texas in various functions.

Crisis manager: The governor acts as a point person and handles resources during a disaster.

Patronage is the act of giving preferential treatment to political supporters when choosing appointments or awarding government contracts. Governor Perry was very generous with his use of patronage to reward supporters to his campaign. Approximately one-third of Perry's appointees had made campaign donations, contributing on average $3,769; Perry had received an additional $3 million from his appointees' employers.[23] As governor, Perry earned a reputation for appointing big donors to university regent positions. The *Texas Tribune* reports that about half the regents appointed by Perry donated money to his campaign, with the average contribution being $64,000.[24] In addition, Perry's appointees alleged that their appointments were contingent on continued support. In 2010, two Texas Tech regents alleged that Perry's office pressured them to resign once they announced they were supporting Kay Bailey Hutchison in her failed attempt to win the Republican primary.[25] Perry was not unique in his use of patronage, as previous Texas governors have also used high-level appointments to reward supporters. Former governor George W. Bush also appointed some of his most generous contributors to the UT Board of Regents.[26] Among Governor Abbott's first 900 appointments, nearly a third have gone to individuals who made campaign contributions.[27] The use of political jobs to reward supporters is one of the most visible and effective tools the governor employs to increase the odds of realizing his or her political agenda.

The governor's single most significant appointment is that of secretary of state, although the governor also appoints other important positions, including the adjutant general, the health and human services commissioner, and the state education commissioner. The governor will make approximately 3,000 appointments over a four-year term. The governor's appointment of board members typically occurs where the legislature has specifically granted the governor that power. The legislature has also, at times, limited the governor's appointment power. The members of two boards, the Railroad Commission of Texas and the Texas State Board of Education, were originally appointed by the governor but today are elected. The governor can also appoint members to fill elected positions that are vacated before the holder's term has expired.

The constitution further limited the governor's appointment power by staggering the terms of appointees. Typically, members of Texas boards or commissions serve staggered, six-year terms that overlap the governor's term. This means that a governor will not appoint a majority of any board or commission until the end of his or her first term. Only governors who can successfully obtain a second term will eventually appoint all the members of the boards and commissions in the state. Thus, the longer the tenure of the governor, the more effective the governor is likely to be at wielding appointment power as a tool to achieve his or her goals. The unprecedented tenure of Perry meant that he was the first governor in Texas history to go through the entire appointment cycle two times during his time in office.

The Texas Constitution mandates that all gubernatorial appointments be approved by a two-thirds vote in the Texas Senate. This is a stricter requirement than that of presidential appointments, which are approved with only a simple majority vote in the U.S. Senate. Since the Texas Legislature is in session only 140 days biennially, often it is necessary to fill a position while the Texas Senate is not in session. In such cases, the governor can make a provisional appointment, but such **recess appointments** require Texas Senate approval within ten days of the next session. An informal limit to the governor's appointment power stems from a custom called **senatorial courtesy**. Any appointee must have the approval of his or her own state senator in order to obtain the support of the Senate. If the appointee's senator does not support the appointment, then the Texas Senate will not consent to it. A governor must consider the preferences of state senators to make successful appointments.

patronage
when an elected official rewards supporters with public jobs, appointments, and government contracts

recess appointment
a gubernatorial appointment made while the Texas Senate is not in session; requires Texas Senate approval within ten days of the next legislative session

senatorial courtesy
the informal requirement that a gubernatorial appointee have approval of her or his own state senator in order to obtain support within the Texas Senate

removal power
the power of the governor,
with consent of the
Texas Senate, to remove
appointees

executive order
an order issued by the
governor to direct existing
agencies or create new
committees or task forces
in order to address a
particular policy area

Finally, with appointment power comes removal power. A governor's appointees are able to exercise much greater autonomy if the governor lacks the power to remove them from their posts subsequent to their appointment. In 1980, the state's constitution was amended to allow the governor to remove his or her own appointees as long as he or she obtains two-thirds support of the Texas Senate.

In addition to appointment and removal power, governors can attempt to direct the bureaucracy by issuing executive orders. The power to issue executive orders is not enumerated in the state constitution, and early Texas governors did not issue any. It wasn't until 1950 that Governor Allan Shivers issued the first executive order. Since that time, Texas governors have issued an average of three executive orders per year. Modern governors utilize executive orders to address a particular policy by issuing a directive to a state agency or creating a specific task force. For instance, as governor, George W. Bush issued executive orders to create a committee to promote adoption, a task force on illegal gambling, and a citizens' committee on tax relief.

There is also a temptation to use executive orders to accomplish policy goals the governor has been unable to convince the legislature to implement. Governor Perry was often criticized for using executive orders to circumvent the state's legislature. In one instance, he issued an executive order to shorten the time required for coal power permits. A state district judge later ruled that Perry lacked the authority to shorten the hearing time.[28] Perry's most controversial executive order required that all sixth-grade girls in Texas public schools receive the human papillomavirus (HPV) vaccine. Both liberal and conservative Texans across the state opposed what they viewed as the governor's power grab. Eventually, the legislature passed a bill that prevented the vaccine from being required for school enrollment.

budget power
the executive's ability to
exert influence on the
state's budget process

The budget power can be viewed as both an executive and a legislative power. A governor's ability to steer the bureaucracy is significantly influenced by the gubernatorial budget power. Governors can also attempt to influence the legislative process by exerting pressure on the budgetary process. In a strong executive model, like that of the national government, the executive exerts considerable influence on the budget by initially proposing the budget that the legislature will consider. Twenty-seven states give their governors sole responsibility for drafting the state's budget.[29] However, in Texas, the governor's budgetary powers are notably weak. In 1949, the Texas Legislature created the Legislative Budget Board (LBB) to seize budgetary power from the executive branch. Since then, the LBB, cochaired by the lieutenant governor and the Speaker of the House, has dominated the budgeting process. The legislature works from the budget prepared by the LBB and ignores the governor's budget, causing some governors to skip preparing a budget altogether. In 2011, Perry attempted to reassert gubernatorial influence on the budgeting process by asking members of the Texas Legislature to sign a budget compact. At a time when the Texas budget shortfall was estimated at $27 billion and the previous legislature had already made deep cuts in education and social services, Perry's budget compact was a declaration of fiscal conservative values and thus largely supported by Texas Republicans. The compact called on legislators to oppose tax increases, limit the use of Texas's Rainy Day Fund, and balance the budget with spending cuts. Although Texas Democrats felt the budget cuts were too deep, Perry's ability to successfully shape the state's budget was a significant legislative success.

line-item veto
the ability of the executive
to selectively veto only
some parts of a bill; in
Texas, available only on
spending bills

The Texas governor can also exert significant influence on the budget process utilizing the line-item veto. The line-item veto allows the governor to reject a specific line or lines out of an appropriations bill without vetoing the entire bill. Governor Abbott increased the power of the line-item veto, using it to strike out both appropriation items and the descriptive riders attached to them, a practice that the Texas Supreme Court had previously ruled unconstitutional. This use of the line-item veto allows the governor to exert much more control in how money is actually spent and can form a much sharper weapon if used to strike out a legislator's pet project. The Texas Legislature essentially did not challenge Abbott's expanded veto, de facto increasing the governor's veto power. Abbott used the line-item veto in the 85th legislative session to veto $120 million in appropriations, mostly cutting funding for environmental initiatives. The Texas governor is one of thirty-four governors in the country given this power over appropriations bills. Another nine governors are given the power to line-item veto any bill.[30]

Legislative Roles

Although the governor's primary job is chief executive, the governor can exert significant influence in the legislation that passes the state. The governor's legislative power comes from the power to direct the legislative agenda and to veto legislation, in addition to the power to shape the budget. **Agenda setting** refers to the power of the governor to persuade the legislature to focus on particular policy priorities. The governor's authority to address the legislature, declare emergency legislation, and call special sessions each enable the governor to shape the legislature's agenda. The governor can directly influence the state's legislative agenda through the **state of the state address**. According to the Texas Constitution, the governor will inform the legislature of the condition of the state at the beginning of each legislative session and at the end of his or her term. A few weeks into the 85th legislative session, Governor Abbott delivered his state of the state address, which outlined twenty policy goals he wanted the legislature to address. For example, he urged lawmakers to pass measures funding his pre-K program, the National Guard, the university research initiative, and the Texas Enterprise Fund. In addition, Abbott's address mandated that state agencies freeze hiring for eight months. Although there is no constitutional authority for the governor to unilaterally restrict spending, state agencies quietly acquiesced to the governor's edict. The state of the state address can make the governor's priorities a focal point for the legislative session, thereby increasing the governor's influence on the state legislature's agenda.

Governors can substantially increase the chances of their legislative agenda passing by declaring their legislative priorities emergency legislation. Generally, the Texas Legislature can introduce new legislation in the first sixty days but cannot vote on that legislation until after sixty days. However, the Texas Constitution (Article 3, Section 5) provides an exception for "such emergency matters as may

agenda setting
the ability of the governor to prioritize the problems facing the state, and thereby influence which policies the legislature will address

state of the state address
the constitutional requirement that the governor address the state legislature about the condition of the state; the state of the state address occurs at the beginning of each legislative session and at the end of the governor's term

AP Photo/David J. Phillip, File

In 2014, Attorney General Greg Abbott became the first new governor of Texas in fourteen years, succeeding Rick Perry. After a victory speech in Austin, Abbott acknowledges his crowd of supporters.

be submitted by the Governor in special messages to the Legislature." **Emergency legislation** can be introduced in the first thirty days and voted on immediately after that. The constitution is silent on what constitutes an emergency, which has meant that, in practical terms, an emergency is anything the governor declares it to be. Since Texas has relatively short legislative sessions, the timing of the introduction of legislation is critical to its success or failure. The ability to declare proposed legislation an emergency and therefore move it up on the legislature's agenda significantly increases the likelihood that the legislation will become law. At the start of the 85th legislature, Abbott declared four emergency priorities, including endorsing a convention of states to amend the U.S. Constitution, each of which passed the Texas Legislature. Governor Abbott used this power again in the last week of the 85th session, declaring a stalled voter identification law an emergency. The last-minute pressure appeared to work, as the legislature managed to eke out a voter ID bill in the last days of the session.

The governor's power to call the legislature into **special session** "on extraordinary occasions" represents another powerful tool to shape the legislature's policy agenda. According to the constitution, the governor may convene a special session for thirty days and determine the agenda for the session. This process stands in contrast to thirty-six states that allow the members of the legislature or the legislature and its presiding officers to call a special session. The Texas Legislature is prohibited from considering anything not put on the agenda by the governor, compared with thirty-nine states that allow the legislature to determine the topic of the session. Thirty-three states place no limit on the length of special sessions.

Because the governor has sole discretion over the agenda of a special session, Texas's governors can use these sessions to force the legislature to address the governor's legislative proposals. Most modern governors use special sessions, although Bush was a notable exception. In his five years in office, Bush did not call a special session. Perry used special sessions frequently to prioritize legislation. The special session remains an effective source of power for a governor although one that comes with a hefty price. Texans pay well over $1 million in tax dollars for each thirty-day session, and governors who use this too often risk angering voters.

One of the most important tools the governor wields to influence legislation is the **veto power**. Legislation passed by the legislature can be signed or vetoed by the governor within ten days. Signing the legislation is largely ceremonial, since the legislation will automatically become law if it is not vetoed. If the governor chooses to veto legislation, the Texas Legislature needs a two-thirds vote in both houses in order to override the veto. Vetoes rarely achieve the two-thirds support necessary to be overridden. The last time the legislature successfully overrode a governor's veto in Texas was in 1979. In Texas, the governor's veto power is buttressed by the short legislative session, in which most bills are passed toward the end of the 140 days. Passing bills late in the legislative session increases the likelihood that the legislature will no longer be in session when the veto occurs. After the legislative session is adjourned, the governor gets an additional twenty days to act on all bills still under consideration. A **post-adjournment veto**, or a veto that occurs after the legislature has adjourned, is absolute, as there is no way for the legislature to overturn it.

The veto is one of the most important sources of legislative influence for the Texas governor. To avoid a veto, the governor's position on any proposed legislation theoretically would be taken into account during the writing of the bill. This makes the true impact of the veto power difficult to assess. For example, as governor, George W. Bush actively worked with the legislature during the session rather than relying on the

What should the criteria be for calling a special session?

★ **SOCIAL RESPONSIBILITY**

emergency legislation
a designation by the governor that allows the governor to prioritize legislation; legislation designated as an emergency can be voted on during the first sixty days of the session

special session
meetings of a legislature that occur outside the regular legislative session; in Texas, special sessions are called by the governor and last for up to thirty days

veto power
the formal power of the executive to reject bills that have been passed by the legislature; in Texas, a veto can be overridden only by a two-thirds vote in both houses

post-adjournment veto
a veto that occurs after the legislature has adjourned, leaving the legislature unable to overturn it

veto to exert his influence on the state's policy. A governor who vetoes a considerable amount of legislation runs the risk of being perceived as weak; a large number of vetoes indicates that a governor did not exert sufficient influence on proposed legislation earlier in the legislative process.[31] A governor who successfully used the threat of a veto to gain legislative compromise without actually having to veto legislation is doubtless more powerful than a governor who had to resort to the veto.

Since 1876, Texas governors vetoed an average of twenty-six bills per session. As governor, Perry vetoed more legislation than previous governors, averaging forty-three bills a session. Perry also holds the record for most vetoes in a single session, vetoing a record eighty bills in 2001 in what has been dubbed the "Father's Day massacre." In his first two legislative sessions, Abbott vetoed an average of forty-seven bills per session. In the 85th legislature, Abbott reportedly threatened to veto the budget if the legislature did not add more money for some of the governor's pet projects, including the Texas Enterprise Fund and the Governor's University Research Initiative. The legislature scrambled to add an additional $100 million to meet Abbott's demands.[32]

Should the legislature be allowed to meet to overturn vetoes that happen after the session is over?

⭐ **CRITICAL THINKING**

Judicial Roles

The framers of the Texas Constitution of 1876 sought to limit the power of the governor by making all state- and county-level judges elected rather than appointed posts. In spite of this, the governor of Texas often makes a significant number of judicial appointments to fill vacancies in between elections, subject to senatorial approval. These appointments can be a significant source of gubernatorial influence over the judiciary, since the vast majority of incumbent judges in Texas win reelection.

In addition, the Constitution of 1876 originally granted the governor the authority to "grant reprieves, commutations of punishment and pardons."[33] This power was curbed after Ma and Pa Ferguson were accused of selling pardons. In 1936, a constitutional amendment created the Board of Pardons and Paroles, which was authorized to recommend **pardons** in the state. Today, the governor can grant clemency or mercy only with a majority recommendation from the board. The governor exercises some influence over the board, as its members are appointed by the governor with senatorial approval. While the governor is not bound to follow the board's recommendations and grant clemency, he or she can grant no clemency absent the board's recommendation. The governor can also independently grant a one-time, thirty-day stay of execution in death penalty cases.

pardon
an executive grant of release from a sentence or punishment in a criminal case; in Texas, the governor can grant a pardon only upon the recommendation of the state's Board of Pardons and Paroles

ceremonial duties
appearances made by the governor as the most visible state officeholder that can function as a source of power; includes appearances at events and the participation in formal functions

Other Roles

The Texas governor fulfills many formal and informal roles. The governor performs a variety of what might otherwise be viewed as **ceremonial duties**. Often the ceremonies involve a ribbon cutting at a new facility or delivering a graduation speech. Since the September 11, 2001, attacks, the

One of the governor's roles is that of crisis manager. Greg Abbott coordinated the state's response to Hurricane Harvey in 2017.

Drew Anthony Smith/Stringer

FEDERALISM IN *Action*

Abbott's Texas Plan to Reassert States' Rights

Recent Texas governors have charged the federal government with overreaching, and current governor Greg Abbott is no exception. When running for the state's highest office, Abbott famously quipped, "I go to the office, sue the national government, and go home." Now Abbott is trying to increase the stakes. His book, *Broken but Unbowed: The Fight to Fix a Broken America*, calls for a constitutional convention to rein in the national government and reassert states' rights. If thirty-four state legislatures call for a constitutional convention, then Abbott will get his way.

The Texas Plan proposes nine new amendments to the U.S. Constitution. The amendments would do the following:

1. prohibit Congress from regulating activity that occurs within a state

2. require Congress to balance its budget

3. forbid federal agencies from creating federal law

4. forbid federal agencies from preempting state law

5. allow states to override U.S. Supreme Court decisions with a two-thirds majority vote

6. require a seven-justice supermajority for U.S. Supreme Court decisions that invalidate a democratically enacted law

7. limit the national government to powers expressly delegated to it in the U.S. Constitution

8. allow state officials to sue in federal court when federal officials overstep their bounds

9. allow a two-thirds majority of states to override a national law or regulation[i]

Other southern states (Florida, Georgia, Tennessee, and Alabama) have also called for a constitutional convention. The Texas legislature became the eleventh state to call for a convention in 2017. Proponents of a new convention would like to see significant power devolved back to the states. If implemented as Abbott's plan suggests, the surviving national government would be weak.

Critics argue that, once called, a new convention would have the power to create any type of government it wanted and could result in a runaway convention. In many ways, those who support a constitutional convention want to revisit federalist arguments lost by their predecessors. It is unclear, however, just what a convention could produce. A new constitutional convention might result in the removal of environmental regulations, as Abbott prefers. Or it might lead to the abolishment of the Second Amendment, as others might want.

> **If we held a convention of states today, which changes do you think we would adopt?**
>
> ⭐ **CRITICAL THINKING**

> **What effect, if any, might the Texas Plan have on minority rights?**
>
> ⭐ **SOCIAL RESPONSIBILITY**

i. Greg Abbott, "2016 Press Release: Governor Abbott Unveils Texas Plan, Offers Constitutional Amendments to Restore the Rule of Law," accessed July 1, 2016, http://gov.texas.gov/news/press-release/21829.

---

crisis manager
the responsibility to act as a policymaker, coordinator of resources, and point person in the wake of natural and man-made disaster

governor's role as **crisis manager** has also become increasingly important.[34] How a governor handles crises increasingly corresponds with his or her degree of constituent support. In the aftermath of Hurricane Harvey, Governor Abbott was front and center to both manage state resources and press the national government for more federal aid. Although these highly visible ceremonial and crisis manager roles can be critical sources of power, particularly for a charismatic governor, traditional sources of power for the governor continue to revolve around his or her executive and legislative roles.

Military Roles

Finally, the governor of Texas is commander in chief of the Texas National Guard and the Texas State Guard. The governor appoints the adjutant general to command these units. The Texas National Guard, which has an army and an air force division, remains under the governor's control unless it is being used for national service. In 2014, Perry called up Texas National Guard troops to control the influx of undocumented children at the Texas border, at an estimated cost of $12 billion a month. More recently, at the request of President Trump, Governor Abbott increased the state's National Guard presence at the border to assist border patrol agents. If the Texas National Guard is unavailable, the Texas State Guard can be called into action for state emergencies. However, the Texas State Guard can be activated only by the governor. Governor Abbott mobilized both the Texas National Guard and the Texas State Guard in response to Hurricane Harvey.

In 2006, the U.S. Congress restricted a governor's power over National Guard troops during natural disasters. During the chaos following Hurricane Katrina, President George W. Bush sought federal control over guardsmen in Louisiana, but Louisiana governor Kathleen Blanco refused to hand over power.[35] Prior to 2006, governors had sole control of the National Guard during a crisis within their state, though the president could take command of the guard for national service and domestically in times of insurrection. After Hurricane Katrina, Congress expanded the president's domestic power and now allows the president to take control of troops during "natural disaster, epidemic, or other serious public health emergency, terrorist attack or incident" if the president determines that state authorities "are incapable of maintaining public order."[36] Not surprisingly, all fifty state governors objected to this expansion of federal power.

Texas Governor: Weak or Strong?

Texans have historically preferred a weak executive, and Texas's mythos is replete with tales of Texans fighting tyranny. The Texas frontier didn't rely on government; individuals tended to solve their own problems and saw little need for government. When the current state constitution was written in 1876, its framers went to great lengths to create an institutionally weak executive. However, the days of the weak executive are over.

Measures of institutional power focus on the length of tenure, appointment power, budget powers, and veto powers. The state's constitution originally established two-year terms, relatively few appointments, a limited salary, and modest budgeting power. The power of the governor was explicitly restrained by staggering the governor's appointments over six years to limit the ability of any one governor to appoint many officials. Texas also vested traditional gubernatorial power among several elected offices to dilute the executive power of a single individual. Since then, several institutional changes have facilitated the rise of a powerful governor. The salary was increased to be relatively competitive nationally. The terms were increased from two years to four, giving the governor more time to amass power in general, while diluting the effect of staggering the appointments. Although the governor does not have term limits, for over 100 years Texans preferred regular turnover of their governors. That norm was broken with Rick Perry's unprecedented fourteen-year reign.

In addition, only a handful of appointments were granted in the original constitution. As the legislature created new boards and commissions, it often granted the governor the power to appoint their members.

The long tenure of Governor Perry created not only a powerful governorship for him but established new norms of deference to the governor's office for future occupants. Under Perry, the bureaucracy that was designed to be run by commissions and boards independently "has evolved into a cabinet form of government, more or less, with the governor in complete control of every state agency. Government in Texas

Should we care about the power of the governor, so long as we are happy about the job he or she is doing?

★ PERSONAL RESPONSIBILITY

informal powers
powers based on factors other than those enumerated in the constitution

popular mandate
the claim that an elected official's legislative agenda is the will of the people based on a high margin of victory in a general election

political ambition ladder
the manner in which a political figure has come up through the ranks, working through various levels of state governmental offices and positions on the way to the top position; climbing several levels on the ladder can increase a politician's contacts, allies, and political savvy

has become a Monopoly board on which every square is controlled by the governor's office."[37] Moreover, most of the legislators that Abbott had to work with had experience only under Governor Perry and Republican control. The institutional memory of the current legislature is unfamiliar with long-held norms of bipartisan cooperation and acting as a check on gubernatorial power.[38] The state's legislature failed to check the governor, for example, when he expanded gubernatorial veto power. Governor Abbott inherited a bureaucracy and a legislature hesitant to challenge the governor's office. Finally, the governor's power and role in the budget expanded under the current governor, suggesting that we might expect future governors to play a much larger role than previous governors. Gone are the days of dismissing the Texas governor as institutionally weak. Today's Texas governor is stronger than ever.

INFORMAL POWERS

In Texas, it is often the case that "personality transcends policy."[39] Thus, Texas governors often augment their institutional powers through informal powers such as visibility or charisma. Research on gubernatorial power focuses on four attributes of informal power, such as a governor's electoral mandate, political ambition ladder, personal future as governor, and performance ratings.[40]

A governor that wins an election by a significant margin can claim a popular mandate, making the legislature less willing to challenge him or her. In contrast, governors who win by small margins have less political capital when dealing with the legislature and other administrators in the state. Perry won a second term as governor with support from only 39 percent of voters. After this, his relationship with the Texas Legislature was divisive, and Perry sought to veto or circumvent the legislature rather than work toward consensus building. Abbott won his second term handily, indicating broad popular support across the state. Similarly, a governor whose public approves of his or her performance will have greater political capital—and thus a greater ability to influence others in the political process.[41]

In addition, a governor who has worked his or her way up the political ambition ladder to the state executive position via other state or local offices will have more allies and political savvy than an individual whose first state office is the governorship and who is learning on the job.[42] Finally, a governor at the beginning of his or her term can exercise greater influence on other offices than those governors who are approaching the end of their gubernatorial career.[43]

Personal power in Texas has always been somewhat different than that in other states. As noted in Chapter 1, V. O. Key argues that the size of Texas means personal politics frequently gives way to legendary personalities. Texas governors in particular have often been elected for their larger-than-life personalities rather than their ability to lead. Those larger-than-life personas can be aided by the size, location, and economic might of the state. For example, Abbott travelled as far afield as Switzerland and India to drum up business for the state. In addition, the highly visible role Texas played in the aftermaths of Hurricanes Harvey, Katrina, and Ike garnered national media attention. Texas's international border with Mexico can also be used to increase visibility. Savvy governors can use national policy negotiations on trade or discussions of immigration policy to garner national media attention and place the governor front and center on the national political stage.

How important are the informal sources of power for the governor?

★ CRITICAL THINKING

In what ways has the power of the governor transformed since the state constitution was written?

★ CRITICAL THINKING

How have Texans' views of government changed over time? Do you think Texans still prefer limited executive power?

★ CRITICAL THINKING

TEXAS  LOUISIANA

Strong, interesting personalities have often dominated the governor's office in Texas. Sam Houston, Ma and Pa Ferguson, Pappy O'Daniel, and Ann Richards all left their mark on Texas politics. A neighbor to the east, Louisiana, is not without its own brand of larger-than-life politicians. Louisiana's first governor, William C. C. Claiborne (1812–1816), was known for his attempts to arrest the notorious pirate Jean Lafitte, a popular figure who attained Robin Hood status in the state. Claiborne went so far as to offer his own money as a bounty for Lafitte's capture, an act that allegedly prompted Lafitte to place a bounty on the governor's head. The twentieth century also saw its share of colorful figures who dominated the Louisiana state capitol building in Baton Rouge. Jimmy Davis ran for governor in the 1940s and again in the 1960s. He was known for taking out his guitar at campaign stops and singing his song "You Are My Sunshine." Edwin Edwards, who served several terms in the 1970s through the early 1990s, was noted for piling up various indictments in federal court on racketeering charges, some related to his frequent visits to Las Vegas and other world-famous gambling locations. Probably the best-known Louisiana politician is Huey Long, the populist governor and "share the wealth" advocate who was assassinated in the state capitol building in 1935.

Lesser known both inside and outside Louisiana is Oscar K. Allen, also known as "O. K. Allen." Allen was a schoolteacher from rural Winn Parish who served in several local elected offices and the Louisiana Senate. In the Senate, Governor Huey Long picked Allen to be the Democratic Party floor leader. Long also appointed Allen chair of the State Highway Commission. In these capacities, Allen served in both the executive and legislative branches of government simultaneously. When Long was elected to the U.S. Senate, he handpicked Allen as his successor. The subsequent election of Allen as governor surprised no one in Louisiana. More startling was Allen's own willingness to acknowledge Long as the source of his power. Long openly directed Allen's agenda as governor, making almost daily telephone calls to instruct Allen on what to do.[i] Even the special session of the Louisiana Legislature in 1935 that Long was observing when he was assassinated had been formally called by Governor Allen per Long's instructions.

Why does Louisiana produce personality-driven politics in the same way as Texas? While the outcome may be the same, the sources are actually different. Texas's geography and weak party system contribute to its personality-driven style of governance. Noted scholar V. O. Key suggested that Louisiana's brand of governance is based on the tight control of elites over the political system, which serves to produce populist backlash.[ii] Key suggested that Louisiana voters have long been faced with a choice of "outsiders," who use charismatic appeals to the masses to court their votes and then amass political power, versus "insiders," who offer a reform agenda to undo the agenda of the populists.

> Do you feel more connected to interesting personalities? Or are you more interested in campaign issues?

⭐ **CRITICAL THINKING**

i. Office of the Secretary of the State, "Louisiana Governors: 1877–Present: Oscar K. Allen," accessed August, 30, 2014, www.sos.la.gov/HistoricalResources/AboutLouisiana/LouisianaGovernors1877-Present/Pages/OscarKAllen.aspx.

ii. V. O. Key, *Southern Politics in State and Nation* (New York: Knopf, 1949), 156–82.

WINNERS AND LOSERS

Madison's vision for American government centered on the idea that the best government is one that is based on the branches keeping each other in check. In other words, rather than creating a government and hoping that those who hold power use it for good, Madison advocated a governmental design in which the legislature and the executive are each powerful enough to keep the other in check. The framers of the Texas Constitution of 1876, by contrast, consciously created a weak executive and gave more power to the legislature. Most of Texas history has been characterized by this institutional design. Today, Texas government appears to be moving toward a stronger executive model. If this trend continues, the winner of that model will be governors of the state. To the extent that today's Texans continue to distrust government and prefer diffused power over concentrated power, Texans lose. Thus far, the legislature has put up very little fight in response to the governor's power grab. If the state legislature makes no attempt to check the growth in gubernatorial power, then the Madisonian model of government will also lose. If the state legislature vigorously defends its traditional powers and acts to hold the governor's power in check, then Texas may well move to a stronger Madisonian model of government.

CONCLUSION

For over a hundred years, the Texas governor was one of the weakest in the country. Institutional changes, single-party dominance, the unprecedented tenure of Governor Perry, and Governor Abbott's expansion of veto powers have all contributed to a new political reality in Texas politics: a strong governor. The power of the Texas governor was on full display during the 85th legislative session, where Abbott exerted continued influence on both the agenda and budgeting process. In Texas, the people have continued to resist an overall change in the formal powers granted to the governor even as the state has continued to change and face increasingly complex problems. Texans remain content to allow their political institutions to evolve rather than addressing a wholesale change in institutional design.

KEY TERMS

agenda setting (p. 143)

appointment power (p. 139)

budget power (p. 142)

ceremonial duties (p. 145)

crisis manager (p. 146)

emergency legislation (p. 144)

executive order (p. 142)

impeachment (p. 138)

informal powers (p. 148)

line-item veto (p. 142)

pardon (p. 145)

patronage (p. 141)

plural executive (p. 139)

political ambition ladder (p. 148)

popular mandate (p. 148)

post-adjournment veto (p. 144)

recess appointment (p. 141)

removal power (p. 142)

senatorial courtesy (p. 141)

special session (p. 144)

state of the state address (p. 143)

succession (p. 137)

veto power (p. 144)

ACTIVE LEARNING

- Break into groups of five. In each group, identify which institutional changes we should make to the Texas executive. **Teamwork**

- Write a short poem, song, or love letter that supports or opposes term limits for the Texas executive. **Communication**

CHAPTER REVIEW

1. Early Texans preferred a ____.
   a. strong governor to challenge presidential power
   b. strong president to keep the governor in line
   c. weak governor
   d. governor with the power to override the legislature

2. Since Reconstruction, Texas has not elected a(n) ____.
   a. Hispanic governor
   b. Roman Catholic governor
   c. female governor
   d. governor without previous political experience

3. The Texas Constitution created a weak governor by ____.
   a. creating an elected judiciary
   b. creating two-year terms
   c. staggering gubernatorial appointments
   d. all of these

4. Today's Texas governor can serve ____.
   a. a single four-year term
   b. unlimited four-year terms
   c. no more than three two-year terms
   d. unlimited two-year terms

5. Dividing traditional executive powers into multiple positions is called ____.
   a. a plural executive
   b. a divided executive
   c. divided government
   d. patronage

6. The governor can make a recess appointment, but such appointments must ____.
   a. hold a bachelor's degree in a relevant field
   b. be approved by voters in the next election
   c. be approved by the Senate within ten days of the next legislative session
   d. be approved by the president within ten days

(Continued)

7. In Texas, the budget is prepared by the _____.

   a. governor

   b. Texas Senate

   c. Legislative Budget Board

   d. Texas Supreme Court

8. If the governor calls a special session, the _____.

   a. governor has complete control over the agenda

   b. legislature and the governor must agree on the agenda

   c. legislature can consider any laws once it has completed the governor's agenda items

   d. legislature has sole control over the agenda

9. A post-adjournment veto, which occurs after the legislative session is over, _____.

   a. is not allowed in Texas

   b. is absolute, since the legislature cannot override the veto

   c. can be overridden by the legislature with two-thirds of both houses

   d. requires the governor to call the legislature into a special session

10. Strong governors tend to have _____.

    a. significant appointment power

    b. strong budget power

    c. veto power

    d. all of these

CHAPTER 5

THE PLURAL EXECUTIVE AND BUREAUCRACY IN TEXAS

Chapter Objectives

★ Explain the structure of the Texas plural executive.

★ Identify the roles of key members of the Texas plural executive.

★ Identify the roles of Texas boards and commissions.

★ Explain the measures in place for bureaucratic accountability.

★ Assess who wins and who loses under Texas's plural executive structure.

"Remember the Alamo," that iconic emblem of Texas independence. The Alamo took center stage during the Republican primary elections in the spring of 2018—specifically, a controversy over the management of the Alamo and the land around it. Since 1905, the Alamo has been owned by the state of Texas, which purchased the site from the Roman Catholic Church and handed over management to the Daughters of the Republic of Texas (DRT). In 2012, a review of the management of the Alamo issued by the Texas attorney general's office found the DRT misappropriated state funds and mishandled ownership of historic artifacts.[1] George P. Bush announced on March 12, 2015, that management of the Alamo was being shifted to the General Land Office (GLO). In April, an agreement was reached with the city of San Antonio to transform the area around the Alamo, with the state purchasing several buildings in an attempt to remove the more touristy venues and eventually replace them with more historically appropriate attractions. In July, the Alamo was declared to be a United Nations Educational, Scientific, and Cultural Organization (UNESCO) World Heritage Site,[2] which in typical Texas fashion also sparked a controversy. Protestors and demonstrators gathered outside the Alamo to protest the UNESCO designation as an infringement on Texas sovereignty and feared that Texas was handing the Alamo over to ownership by the United Nations.[3] While the process to get the UNESCO designation had begun as early as 2006, misinformation about the UN designation had led to wild rumors of UN control of the area in downtown San Antonio. Concerns over the ownership of the Alamo site had prompted Texas senator Donna Campbell of New Braunfels to introduce legislation in the 2015 session of the Texas Legislature to prohibit

Texas Land Commissioner George P. Bush (left) talks with San Antonio mayor Ivy Taylor in September 2015. Both Bush and Taylor were participating in a news conference to celebrate funding from the General Land Office to preserve and develop the Alamo.

foreign ownership of the Alamo and its surrounding environs.[4] Her bill never made it out of committee. To counter these claims, the General Land Office set up a website, AlamoTruth. com, to disseminate information about the GLO's work on the Alamo.[5]

As part of the work of the GLO regarding the Alamo, the land office commissioned a master plan to add a visitor's center and develop a museum associated with the monument and its current displays. Critics of the plan focused on the $450 million price tag and their perception that the plan deemphasizes the battle at the Alamo. The state allocated $75 million to the project in 2017, with Bush attempting to raise much of the remaining funds from nonprofit groups.[6] However, during the interim, the Senate Finance Committee became critical of the funding arrangements, including fund-raising by nonprofit groups in support of the Alamo project and Bush's role as chair of the board of directors for the Alamo Trust, a private, not-for-profit entity created to oversee the master plan. Criticism also focused on the seventy staffers that Alamo Trust hired.[7]

During the election campaign for the Republican primary in 2018, George P. Bush's administration of the Alamo came under scrutiny by his opponent Jerry Patterson, ironically as a result of an internal audit within the GLO. Patterson claimed the audit pointed toward Bush's own mismanagement of the landmark. Patterson, who served as commissioner of the GLO prior to Bush, seized on the audit to decry Bush as incompetent. Although Bush won the Republican nomination in March 2018, his Democratic opponent in the general election, Miguel Suazo, also hammered Bush on this issue.[8] Ultimately, Jerry Patterson endorsed Suazo, not fellow Republican Bush. Bush continued his efforts to redevelop and to overhaul the area around the Alamo.

While students of Texas politics, and political science in general, may tend to think of the state's executive agencies as rather boring and static, true to Texas's tradition, the executive branch contains some colorful figures. As the story above illustrates, a seemingly simple act, ensuring the future of a key Texas landmark, can erupt in controversy quite quickly. The ability to navigate the myriad state rules, regulations, and aspects of legislative oversight requires a skilled, often seasoned leader. Relative newcomers like George P. Bush find that stepping into a new role often results in unexpected controversies and restraints that one might not find in the private sector. The balance between tradition and transformation, therefore, is often difficult.

In this chapter, we will review the makeup of the Texas executive branch, including five of the six statewide, directly elected offices. We will also examine an important appointed official, the Texas secretary of state. We examine the organization, roles, and functions of important state agencies, including the Texas Department of Transportation (TxDOT), the Texas Department of State Health Services (DSHS), the Railroad Commission of Texas, the State Board of Education (SBOE), and the Public Utility Commission of Texas. The chapter concludes with a review of the administrative operation of Texas state agencies and an examination of the accountability of the bureaucracy to the wider public.

THE PLURAL EXECUTIVE

The Texas executive branch consists of six offices that are chosen directly by the voters of the state. While the governor is the most recognized and familiar of these offices, the other five exert significant political and administrative power over the state government. These other five are the lieutenant governor, the attorney general, the comptroller of public accounts, the commissioner of agriculture, and the commissioner of the General Land Office. In addition, the secretary of state is an important, but unelected, officer in the Texas executive branch.

Because Texas has six statewide-elected offices, the Texas executive branch is typically called a plural executive. Each of these offices is elected independently of the governor, meaning that each elected member of the executive branch is chosen separately from the others. In other words, the election of these officials is not on a single slate. The voter casts separate votes for each office. This approach contrasts to the U.S. executive branch, in which the U.S. president and U.S. vice president are chosen jointly as one selection or vote. Only eight states in the United States, including Florida and Ohio, elect the governor and lieutenant governor jointly.

Each member of the Texas executive is directly accountable to the voters of Texas, not to the governor or to each other. An advantage to the plural executive is that Texans have more direct control over each of the six members of the plural executive. This approach is widely used in other states, though those states vary in the number of directly elected offices in the state executive branch. For example, Maryland and New Jersey elect only two statewide offices: the governor and the lieutenant governor. In contrast, North Carolina and North Dakota elect ten offices, including positions such as the state auditor, secretary of state, head of the labor department, and head of the insurance department. The election of multiple offices increases the democratic accountability of each executive to the voters directly. While electing a large number of the executive branch may seem a bit overwhelming, a distinct disadvantage occurs in a plural executive system such as Texas's. Because each office is independently elected,

plural executive
an executive branch in which the functions have been divided among several, mostly elected, officeholders rather than residing in a single person, the governor

each may legitimately claim a direct mandate from the people for their political agenda. After all, the people chose them directly. Thus, the plural executive carries the disadvantage of the lack of accountability to a single head executive, such as the governor. As a result, various parts of the executive branch may engage in contradictory activities. For example, a controversy developed in 2011 regarding whether or not Amazon.com was supposed to charge sales tax on its sales in Texas. Governor Perry initially opposed such taxes, while comptroller of public accounts Susan Combs vocalized her support for them.[9] The governor's claim to a mandate to set a political and policy agenda in Texas is often rebuffed by other members of the Texas plural executive. Moreover, the governor may sometimes be blamed by the voters of Texas for actions of other members of the executive who are beyond the governor's control. In short, the governor of Texas is not simply an elected CEO for the state government.

In the U.S. government, the president meets with his cabinet, which consists of the heads of the key government departments and the vice president. While their frequency of meetings and topics of discussion vary, cabinet meetings allow the president to discuss issues and policies with key leaders in the U.S. executive branch and to coordinate policies. At the state level, despite the use of plural executive systems that lack accountability to the governor, many states also maintain some form of a cabinet. In those states that formally and constitutionally require a cabinet to meet, the governor may have the power to decide when and how often this occurs. In other states, the cabinet is required to meet weekly, monthly, or at least once a quarter based on the state's constitution or statutory law. To some extent, the cabinet approach attempts to act as a board of directors for the state executive branch.

Texas is one of only five states without a formal executive cabinet.[10] Nevada allows the governor to assemble a cabinet if the governor desires. This approach by Nevada is unique among the states. Thus, in Texas, not only are the other executive offices not accountable to the governor, but the other leaders of the executive branch do not even have to meet with the governor individually or collectively, nor do they have to meet with each other. This approach significantly limits the power of the governor over the executive branch.

Lieutenant Governor

The office of the **lieutenant governor** is often considered one of the three most powerful positions in Texas. The lieutenant governor is elected by voters statewide every four years, with no term limits. Most states, including Texas, elect the governor and the lieutenant governor in the same year. Despite this, the governor and lieutenant governor are elected as separate and distinct offices. If the position of lieutenant governor becomes vacant, the Texas Senate elects from its membership a person to serve as the lieutenant governor until the next election. The lieutenant governor is the presiding officer of the Texas Senate, and he or she exerts great influence on both the debates and the bills that reach the floor in that chamber. Although this position is mainly legislative in nature (as discussed in Chapter 3), it is also constitutionally granted some executive authority. The primary executive function of the lieutenant governor is to assume the governorship temporarily when the governor is out of the state or permanently if the governor is impeached, resigns, or dies in office. In terms of executive powers, the lieutenant governor exerts considerable influence on the

What are the advantages to the Texas plural executive, and what are the disadvantages?

★ CRITICAL THINKING

lieutenant governor
the presiding officer of the Texas Senate, elected directly by the voters; also serves as a member of the Texas executive branch and assumes the duties of the governor when the governor is out of state, dies in office, resigns from office, or is impeached

state's budget. The lieutenant governor cochairs the Legislative Budget Board (LBB) with the Speaker of the Texas House and appoints the senatorial members of that board. Unlike the governor and other members of the Texas executive, the lieutenant governor is not well compensated, receiving a salary of $9,612 per year.[11]

To be lieutenant governor in Texas, a person must be at least thirty years of age, a U.S. citizen, and a resident of Texas for at least five years. While the lieutenant governor possesses a few constitutional powers, the position is relatively weak constitutionally, as discussed in Chapter 3. The real power of the lieutenant governor comes from his or her leadership style and persuasive abilities as the presiding officer of the Texas Senate. Texas's current lieutenant governor is Republican Dan Patrick. Prior to being elected as the lieutenant governor, Patrick had spent two terms in the Texas Senate representing part of suburban Harris County and greater Houston. A native of Maryland, Dan Patrick graduated from the University of Maryland, Baltimore, campus with a degree in English. He worked in television in Scranton, Pennsylvania, and Washington, DC, before joining KHOU Channel 11, the CBS affiliate in Houston, as a sportscaster. After attempting co-ownership of a sports bar, a venture that eventually failed and caused Patrick to file for personal bankruptcy, Patrick eventually bought a radio station, now KCVE. Patrick hosts a program, *Dan Patrick and Friends*, on the radio station.

In 2014, Dan Patrick, a Tea Party–style Republican, defeated fellow Texas state senator Leticia Van de Putte, a Democrat from San Antonio, for the lieutenant governor position. Van de Putte's campaign broke new ground in Texas as the first Hispanic woman to run for the office. However, true to recent tradition in Texas, Patrick—a Republican—won easily.

While in office, Patrick quickly set his priorities. His efforts focused on tax reform, including significant reductions of property taxes levied by counties, cities, school districts, and other local governments and new requirements that property tax increases by local governments be passed by the local government by a 60 percent vote. In addition, he promoted a bill to reduce the franchise tax paid by many businesses in Texas. In the area of gun rights, Patrick pushed for open carry legislation, allowing individuals with a concealed gun permit to now carry their gun openly, and for campus carry, allowing individuals to carry guns onto public university and community college campuses. Long a critic of several internal rules and procedures of the Texas Senate, Patrick oversaw the reduction of the number of standing committees in the Texas Senate from eighteen to fourteen and moved from a two-thirds majority (twenty-one members) to a three-fifths majority (nineteen members) to move bills to the floor for consideration. Finally, in social policy, Patrick authored a bill that changed the conditions under which abortions are performed in Texas, including requirements that abortion providers have admitting privileges at a local hospital and that abortions be performed in buildings that are accessible to emergency services vehicle medical beds. After becoming law in the 2015 legislative session, this law ultimately was struck down by the U.S. Supreme Court.

During the 2017 session of the Texas Legislature, Patrick promoted giving parents of children who attend private schools a state subsidy. He endorsed legislation requiring transgender persons to use the bathroom of their biological sex and reforming the state's property tax system. His attempt to pass legislation that would make it more difficult for individuals to file claims on their insurance for weather-related damages ran into difficulty. In addition, Patrick locked horns regularly with his Republican counterpart from the Texas House of Representatives, Joe Straus. When the legislature failed to

TEXAS (VS) NEVADA

We often think of state governments as miniature versions of the U.S. national government, assuming the structure and function of state governments are the same as their national counterparts. Of course, this thinking is not without foundation: Most state legislatures are bicameral like the U.S. Congress. All state governments feature separation of powers between legislative, executive, and judicial branches. All state governments have checks and balances across the three branches. Most state legislatures are elected by the single-member district (SMD) system. However, as you have already discovered, state governments vary significantly from the U.S national government, and through boxes like these, you have discovered that Texas differs from other state governments as well.

One important area of difference is the role and function of state cabinets. Some states require state governments to have the governor preside over a cabinet, regular meetings of the governor and the heads of key state-level bureaucratic departments and agencies to coordinate policymaking, policy implementation, and policy development. These cabinets work to keep the executive branch running smoothly and efficiently, minimizing conflict within the executive branch. This approach to state executive branches is a mirror of the U.S. president and their cabinet, in which the president meets periodically with the heads of major executive departments such as State, Treasury, Education, Energy, and Defense. Each of the cabinet officers holds the title of department secretary, and they are appointed by the president and confirmed by the U.S. Senate.

Nevada is an interesting model of the executive cabinet. Unlike all other states with a cabinet, Nevada's state constitution does not mention a cabinet, nor does state law require a cabinet to exist. Instead, Nevada allows the governor to create a cabinet at their will, to determine the makeup of the cabinet, and to decide how often the cabinet meets. While some governors have served without a cabinet, others have relied heavily on a cabinet to help the governor accomplish his or her political goals and policy objectives.

The current Nevada governor, Brian Sandoval, followed the precedent of many governors by creating a cabinet. His cabinet consists of twenty-one members. While the governor has complete freedom to decide who serves and who does not serve in the cabinet, the method of selection to the respective offices varies. Some members were appointed to their office directly by the governor. They are not approved or confirmed by anyone else and may be removed from their office by the governor at any time. These members answer solely to the governor for their actions in office and include the heads of the Governor's Office of Economic Development and the Nevada Department of Health and Human Services. Some members are nominated by the governor and confirmed by a board or commission of state government including the director of the state tourism and cultural affairs department. In an unusual twist, the head of the state's agriculture department is nominated by the state agriculture board and then confirmed by the governor. The head of the state's transportation department is selected by their respective board. This arrangement gives the governor no direct control over this member of his cabinet.

The lieutenant governor is directly and independently elected by the voters of Nevada, leaving the governor no control or influence over that office as well. However, the lieutenant governor is currently serving in the cabinet. Should the governor so decide, the lieutenant governor could be removed from the cabinet.

This approach to coordination in the executive branch stands in sharp contrast to the state of Texas, in which no executive cabinet exists. Instead, the governor either directly interacts with heads of various state agencies, often individuals he does not appoint or must serve more than one term to completely influence, in the case of some board and commissions. No regular meetings occur across with the governor and key state agency leaders like higher education, health, and transportation. In addition, the governor shares power with several directly elected executive branch agencies. While the governor in Nevada may face this situation in the case of the lieutenant governor or attorney general, Nevada's currently does attempt to include his direct appointees and other key agencies, but noticeably absent are individuals like the attorney general.

What are the advantages of a cabinet that is structured like that of Nevada?

⭐ **CRITICAL THINKING**

Would a cabinet make Texas's executive branch more efficient? Why or why not?

⭐ **CRITICAL THINKING**

FEDERALISM IN Action

Transgender Bathrooms

The battle of the bathrooms first came to Texas in 2015 in the 84th legislative session when four different bills were introduced that would regulate which restrooms transgender students could use. None of those bills, including one that attached a $2,000 fine for using the wrong restroom, made it out of committee. Far from dying, the issue reemerged in 2017, particularly as Lieutenant Governor Dan Patrick has called it a "come and take it" moment. The issue produced several bills during the 2017 session of the Legislature. When these bills failed during the regular session of 2017, mostly resulting from opposition of Speaker Joe Straus, the transgender bathroom battle continued into the special session in July 2018. The question is whether or not to allow people to use restrooms based on their gender identity. Who gets to decide—the local government, the state government, or the national government—is a question of federalism.

Until recently, local governments had been deciding this question in Texas. Several school districts across the state had already quietly adopted policies to accommodate gender identity. However, when the Fort Worth superintendent announced in late April 2016 new guidelines calling for its district to allow students to use the bathroom consistent with their gender identity, state officials

objected. Ironically, the new policy was merely formalizing what the Fort Worth Independent School District (ISD) had been doing for the past sixteen years.[i] In practice, transgender students in Fort Worth would be allowed to use single stall restrooms, access private restrooms (in the nurse's office), or access restrooms when other students are not around. Fort Worth mayor Betsy Price supported the Fort Worth ISD policy, stating, "While I respect the passion on this particular issue and drastically differing opinions, I strongly believe this is a local issue that needs to be focused on the safety, inclusion and education of all 86,000 FWISD students."[ii]

As the fight between the state government and local school boards heated up, the national government joined the fray. In early May 2016, the U.S. Departments of Justice and Education issued a joint letter outlining new guidelines for schools across America. According to the new guideline, gender identity should be treated as a student's sex for the purpose of Title IX Educational Amendments of 1972 adherence, which prohibits discrimination based on sex for programs receiving federal funds. This approach reinterpreted the term "sex" to mean "gender identity" and occurred without legislative input from Congress or an executive order from the president. This is an example of fiscal federalism because Texas receives approximately $6 billion a year from the U.S. government for education programs.

The redefinition provoked predictable opposition from state officials.[iii] Attorney General Ken Paxton announced that Texas will join other states to sue the national government over the new directive. Meanwhile, Lieutenant Governor Patrick sent a letter to all school districts in the state, calling on them to defy the new national guidelines, declaring "Now that's a violation of local control—when the president of the United States of America decides

to get into every schoolhouse in the United States of America."[iv] However, the election of President Donald Trump changed the position of the U.S. government; DOJ and DOE quickly reversed the position of the U.S. government, withdrawing the letter and suggested guidelines. This issue illustrates the ambiguity created by the plural executive, as the lieutenant governor made this issue his rallying cry even as the attorney general is charged with legally representing the state. The result of this push and pull is local school boards who have long been dealing with the practical issues once again find themselves at the mercy of a looming battle between the state officials and the national government.

> **What responsibility does government have to protect the rights of transgender persons?**
>
> **SOCIAL RESPONSIBLITY**
>
> **Which level of government should get to create transgender policies for schools?**
>
> **CRITICAL THINKING**

i. Marjorie Owens and Jim Douglas, "Former Fort Worth Council Member Calls Lt. Gov. Patrick a 'Bully,'" WFAA.com, May 10, 2016, http://www.wfaa.com/news/politics/fw-council-member-calls-lt-patrick-a-bully/184693217.

ii. Frank Heinz, "Texas, Fort Worth ISD Transgender Bathroom Debate Could Put Billions in School Funding at Risk," NBCDFW.com, May 11, 2016, http://www.nbcdfw.com/news/local/Texas-Fort-Worth-ISD-Transgender-Bathroom-Debate-Could-Put-Billions-in-School-Funding-at-Risk-378892281.html.

iii. Ibid.

iv. Patrick Svitek, "Patrick Suggests Legislature Might Step In on Bathroom Guidelines," Texas Tribune, May 31, 2016, https://www.texastribune.org/2016/05/31/patrick-escalates-battle-against-transgender-guide.

pass key items on Patrick's agenda, he promoted them during the special session called by Governor Abbott in July 2017. Although most of Patrick's items passed the Texas Senate, The Texas House of Representatives failed to approve. In the aftermath, Patrick, with Governor Abbott, placed much of the blame on Speaker Straus.[12]

Following the 2017 session, Patrick focused on Hurricane Harvey–related issues like reducing government regulation related to rebuilding the Gulf Coast, the impact on school financing, and the use of federal and state funds to rebuild affected areas. He supported efforts to allow churches to create voluntary security teams and to eliminate any perceived restrictions preventing congregants from bringing guns to church. He also asked a Senate interim committee to examine possible bias against conservative speech on Texas's public university campuses.

Patrick, running for reelection in the spring of 2018, easily defeated his opponent Scott Milder, with 76.1 percent of the vote. In the general election, Patrick faced Mike Collier, who won the Democratic nomination in a tightly contested primary. Collier, a 2014 former candidate for Texas comptroller of public accounts, worked as an auditor with PricewaterhouseCoopers and as the founder and chief financial officer of the Texas-based oil company Layline Petroleum.

While Collier, a former punk rocker who skateboarded outside a Whataburger restaurant as a campaign stunt, tried to paint Patrick as an enemy of public education, Patrick's significant campaign finances and conservative base of support led Dan Patrick to an easy re-election with 51.1 percent of the vote, compared to Collier's 46.9 percent.

Attorney General

The Texas constitution requires the **attorney general** to "represent the State in all suits and pleas in the Supreme Court of the State in which the State may be a party."[13] This means that the main function of the attorney general is to serve as legal representation for the state in court. Texas's first constitution provided for the appointment of the attorney general, but subsequent constitutions, including the current one, stipulated that the attorney general be elected. Today, the attorney general in Texas is elected in off-year elections to a four-year term, with no term limits. Like Texas, most states elect their attorney general, with only twelve states continuing to appoint the office. The salary of the attorney general in Texas is $153,750 per year.[14]

The attorney general's office is involved in a wide range of issues, including pursuing deadbeat dads for unpaid child support, protecting the elderly population of Texas from false consumer and insurance schemes, collecting delinquent state taxes (as it did from Enron in 2005), and recovering fraudulent Medicare and Medicaid payments, to name just a few. The attorney general is also charged with ensuring that corporations in Texas comply with state and federal laws. Thus, in 1894, the attorney general sued John D. Rockefeller's Standard Oil Company and its subsidiary, Waters-Pierce, for antitrust violations. The attorney general successfully made his case, and these companies were barred from doing business in Texas.[15]

One of the most important functions of the attorney general is to issue advisory opinions to the governor's office, the legislature, and other state agencies. These opinions offer a legal interpretation of the Texas Constitution, a state law passed by the Texas Legislature, or an executive order from the governor. For example, in 2007, Governor Perry issued an executive order requiring that all girls receive the human papillomavirus (HPV) immunization before entering the sixth grade. State senator Jane Nelson

attorney general
chief legal adviser for the state who represents the state in courts and issues advisory opinions on legal matters to the governor, legislature, and other state agencies

AP Photo/Eric Gay

Ken Paxton began his first term as Texas attorney general in 2015. Despite a number of ethical and legal issues in his private and professional life, Paxton was reelected in November 2018 to a second term.

What role should public schools play in promoting the right to vote?

⭐ **SOCIAL RESPONSIBILITY**

disagreed with the governor's mandate and met with Greg Abbott, then the attorney general, who issued an opinion that the governor's HPV order was merely a suggestion and not legally binding. This opinion meant that the medical community was not bound to follow the executive order. Another important task of the attorney general is to appoint the solicitor general. The solicitor general and his or her staff are the key lawyers for Texas who actually argue appellate cases before state and U.S. courts.

Once a request for a legal opinion has been received, the attorney general's office conducts extensive research into the issue, relevant laws, and constitutional provisions. Much of this work is conducted by a group of assistant attorneys general and their staff as the Opinion Committee. The committee may also ask individuals and groups that might be affected by the opinion to offer their perspectives, and the public may comment on these issues by submitting briefs. Most opinions are completed within 180 days of the initial request.[16] Once issued, the opinions of the attorney general are rarely challenged and typically carry the weight of law. For example, in early 2018, a request by Republican state senator Paul Bettencourt asked whether school districts could provide free transportation using school district funds to bus students to polling locations on election day. While ostensibly aimed at promoting civic literacy and awareness among new, young voters, Bettencourt became suspicious that such activities were occurring primarily in urban, heavily Democratic-voting schools and school districts. The attorney general's office issued an opinion ruling that the practice violated provisions of the Texas Education Code that prohibits Texas public schools and funds from being used to elect candidates for office.

In November 2014, voters of Texas elected Ken Paxton to the position of attorney general. Paxton is a graduate of Baylor University and the University of Virginia School of Law. In 2002, he was elected to the Texas House of Representatives where he served for ten years. Paxton then served briefly in the Texas Senate from 2013 to 2014, representing parts of Collin County, including Frisco, Allen, and McKinney. After his election, Paxton become involved in a number of personal scandals. One issue was the gifting of shares in Servergy, a technology corporation, by its CEO William Mapp, while Paxton served in the Texas House of Representatives and whether the gift violated federal civil law.[17] While this case eventually went away, Paxton later faced criminal charges in state court over this same issue. Moreover, the state criminal case spawned another case, with allegations that Paxton withheld state funding for public prosecuting attorneys' offices in the Metroplex linked to investigating and prosecuting Paxton's alleged violations of the law. Paxton faced accusations that he was party to an improper land sale in McKinney, north of Dallas, that included exerting undue influence on local government officials to change zoning laws boosting the property value of land to which Paxton was connected. This investigation was eventually terminated.

However, the mounting legal issues surrounding Paxton's personal actions prior to and during his first election campaign raised other issues about his personal financing of the legal fees to defend himself. In such situations, it is not unusual for the defendant to set up a legal defense fund to raise money from other sources to help pay court costs. Complicating this issue was the fact that the Texas attorney general's office provides legal advice to the Texas Ethics Commission (TEC), the state agency that among other issues rules on the ethics of government officials' actions such as how and when they may raise money for their own personal legal battles while holding public office. In addition, the Texas State Securities Board conducts oversight of securities cases under investigation by the state and receives legal advice from the attorney general as well. Paxton recused himself from involvement in any cases brought to the attorney general's office that dealt with securities or ethics.[18] Ultimately, the TEC ruled that Paxton could not receive donations for his legal defense fund.

Yet, Paxton's legal issues were not limited to his private behavior. The attorney general became the center of a controversy surrounding the termination of several key employees in his office. One individual, Allison Castle, senior communications director for the attorney general, had been appointed by Governor Rick Perry in 2015, just before Perry left office. Castle was given a prewritten resignation letter and sixty-four-day paid leave.[19] Such packages were not unusual, including payouts for unused vacation time and unused compensation time. Castle, however, was placed on "emergency" administrative leave. Emergency administrative leave is normally granted to state employees when there is a death in the immediate family or for those called to military duty. Revelations emerged of other individuals in the attorney general's office as well as other executive branch agencies being placed on "emergency leave" as a form of severance, extending for months past the normal termination period. Governor Greg Abbott and Comptroller Glenn Hegar announced in June 2016 the end of this practice by state agencies via executive order.[20]

As attorney general, Paxton continued the conservative political agenda of his predecessor in office, making speeches and issuing statements on a number of issues. For example, when the Center for Medical Progress released a series of videos alleging that Planned Parenthood had attempted to sell organs from aborted fetuses, in violation of federal law, Paxton launched an investigation into Planned Parenthood's activities. In addition, Paxton sided with Kountze High School's cheerleaders who were defending their practice of using quotes from the Christian Bible on signs and posters at their high school's football games. Paxton also initiated lawsuits against the national government, primarily the U.S. Department of Labor, for extending provisions of the Family Medical Leave Act to same-sex couples. Paxton also waded into the debate over rights for transgender persons, consistently backing Lieutenant Governor Dan Patrick in his efforts to limit the rights of transgender persons to use the restroom of their gender identity.

Perhaps the centerpiece of Paxton's social agenda, Paxton consistently supported legal action to defend House Bill (HB) 2. This bill, passed by the Texas Legislature and signed into law by the governor from the 2015 legislative session, placed a number of restrictions on abortion providers including the need for providers to have admitting privileges at a local hospital and for clinics where abortions are performed to be accessible to ambulatory emergency beds. Critics of the bill alleged that the bill caused the closing of half of abortion clinics in Texas and placed an undue burden on women

Should you reveal personal contacts and financial arrangements that potentially conflict with other aspects of your life, just as state government officials are expected to do?

⭐ PERSONAL RESPONSIBILITY

TABLE 5.1 Texas's Plural Executive

Governor of Texas

- Acts as chief executive of the state; is elected by the voters every four years; no term limits
- Makes policy recommendations to state lawmakers
- Appoints the secretary of state and members of the state bureaucracy. The governor also appoints individuals to fill vacancies in elected offices between elections.
- Exercises constitutional and statutory duties of the governor, including the following:
  - signing or vetoing bills passed by the legislature
  - serving as commander in chief of the state's military forces
  - convening special sessions of the legislature
  - delivering a state of the state address
  - proposing a biennial budget
  - executing a line-item veto on the budget approved by the legislature
  - granting reprieves and commutations of punishment and pardons upon the recommendation of the Board of Pardons and Paroles
  - declaring special elections to fill vacancies in certain elected offices
  - coordinating policy and resources during a crisis

Lieutenant Governor

- Acts as presiding officer of the Texas Senate; is elected by voters statewide every four years; no term limits
- Acts as governor temporarily when the governor is out of the state or assumes the governorship if the governor is impeached, resigns, or dies in office
- Cochairs the Legislative Budget Board (with the Speaker of the Texas House) and appoints the senatorial members of that board

Attorney General

- Serves as legal representation for the state in court; is elected by voters statewide every four years; no term limits
- Ensures that corporations in Texas comply with state and federal laws
- Collects unpaid child support and delinquent state taxes
- Issues advisory opinions to the governor's office, the legislature, or other state agencies

Comptroller of Public Accounts

- Collects a variety of state taxes and fees; is elected for four-year terms as the state's accountant, auditor, and tax collector
- Manages and invests state funds
- Estimates the amount of revenue the state will generate each year

Agriculture Commissioner

- Heads the Texas Department of Agriculture and implements all agriculture law; is elected by voters statewide every four years; no term limits
- Inspects the accuracy of market scales and gas pumps, regulates the use of pesticides, and regulates the quality of agriculture products
- Promotes agriculture throughout the state

Land Commissioner

- Heads the General Land Office and administers the state's public lands
- Makes low-interest loans available to veterans
- Oversees the Permanent School Fund (PSF), a major source of revenue for the state

Secretary of State

- Serves as state record keeper; is appointed by the governor, with Texas Senate confirmation, to a four-year term
- Maintains a list of lobbyist and campaign contributions, issues corporate charters, certifies notaries public, and keeps the official state seal
- Administers elections, including conducting voter registration drives and certifying election results
- Acts as chief administrator for the Texas Border and Mexican Affairs Division
- Is designated as the chief international protocol officer who receives international delegations

Source: Compiled by the authors using information from the Office of the Texas Governor at https://gov.texas.gov/governor-abbott/duties (accessed July 10, 2018).

seeking an abortion. The bill was challenged in U.S. federal courts, ultimately being argued before the U.S. Supreme Court. The U.S. Supreme Court ruled in the summer of 2016 that the Texas law violated the highest court's earlier ruling in cases like *Roe v. Wade* (1973) and *Planned Parenthood v. Casey* (1992) because the Texas law placed an "undue burden" on women in Texas seeking an abortion.

Which executive branch official has most responsibility? Why?

⭐ CRITICAL THINKING

Consumer protection is a fundamental function of the Texas attorney general, with an entire division devoted to hearing and investigating consumer complaints. At the forefront of Paxton's agenda on consumer protection in his first and second years in office were investigations at the state level of possible violations by German carmaker Volkswagen for deceptive practices associated with overreporting fuel efficiency in certain car models; prosecution of a diploma mill that took money from high school students and issued illegal high school diplomas; and weighing into a dispute between agriculture commissioner Sid Miller and consumers over whether barbeque restaurants and other immediate-consumption food vendors were exempt from state laws requiring the scales they use to measure food amounts be inspected annually.

One of the more fundamental issues that the attorney general had to issue an opinion about during the 2015 regular session of the Texas Legislature involves the governor's veto power, specifically the governor's line-item veto. After the end of the regular session, Governor Greg Abbott exercised veto over approximately $200 million in state spending. The LBB later questioned, in a fourteen-page letter, whether the governor actually vetoed the spending items or instead vetoed "riders," which direct state agencies to act in particular ways but do not actually make appropriations. According to the LBB, the governor violated the constitution, indirectly expanding the power of the governor, to line-item riders.[21] Since the LBB includes the lieutenant governor, this controversy pitted two statewide elected offices against each other: the governor and the lieutenant governor. This controversy drew into the debate the attorney general, who was asked by the Comptroller of Public Accounts Glenn Hegar to rule on the governor's line-item veto. However, Paxton recused himself from this opinion as well, citing possible conflicts of interest. First Assistant Attorney General Chip Roy issued an opinion indicating the governor did have the power to veto these items.[22]

Finally, Paxton supported the state's efforts to challenge the legality of President Obama's use of executive orders to prevent the deportation of millions of undocumented illegal immigrants under the Deferred Action for Parents of Americans and Lawful Permanent Residents (DAPA) and Deferred Action for Childhood Arrivals (DACA). Under Paxton, Texas argued successfully in federal courts, including the U.S. Supreme Court, that the use of executive orders on DACA was an unconstitutional effort to reinterpret the law and legislate without Congressional action. However, the advent of Donald Trump's presidency led Paxton to embrace the White House. The Trump administration's get-tough stance on immigration, especially on DAPA and DACA, found favor in Paxton's office. Paxton began endorsing and supporting the Trump administration's policies.

Despite his personal legal issues, Paxton ran for reelection in 2018, running unopposed in the Republican primaries in March of 2018. In the November general election, Paxton faced Justin Nelson, the Democratic candidate. Nelson, a Yale University and Columbia Law School educated patent lawyer, also founded an advocacy group whose aim is to abolish the Electoral College.

Despite Paxton's past legal issues, and efforts by Justin Nelson to keep these issues at the center of the election campaign, Paxton won re-election with 50.5 percent of the vote to Nelson's 47.3 percent. However, the margin of victory for Paxton was the lowest for any Republican running for statewide office in 2018.

Comptroller of Public Accounts

comptroller of public accounts collects fees and taxes, invests state funds, estimates revenue, and oversees payments by the state for goods and services

Elected to a four-year term, the Texas **comptroller of public accounts** is the state's accountant, auditor, and tax collector. The comptroller is responsible for collecting a variety of taxes, including the state's sales tax (the largest source of state revenue), fuel tax, franchise tax, alcohol tax, cigarette tax, and hotel tax, to name a few. The comptroller also collects certain fees for the state, including higher education fees, vehicle registration fees, and professional fees. In addition, a 1995 constitutional amendment abolished the office of the treasurer and moved responsibility for managing and investing state funds to the comptroller's office. This action places Texas at odds with the practice in most states, in which a separate state treasurer and state comptroller exist. The state treasurer or equivalent is elected in thirty-eight states. Qualifications for the position vary tremendously, especially in terms of the minimum age to hold the position. Some states, such as Vermont, lack a minimum age for their state treasurer, while Florida and New Mexico represent the other end of the spectrum with a requirement that the officeholder be at least thirty years of age. In Texas, the comptroller must be at least eighteen years old. The comptroller must also be a citizen of the United States and a resident of the state, which are qualifications consistent with other states. In states with a separate treasurer, the office is usually required by the state constitution, as is the practice in Texas with the comptroller.[23] The comptroller makes a base salary of $153,750 per year.[24]

The practices of qualification and selection applied to most state comptroller positions are often quite different. Most state comptroller offices are defined by statutory law passed by the state legislature, not mandated by the state constitution. Texas is only one of fourteen states with an elected comptroller. In terms of qualifications for office, sixteen states require the comptroller to have some sort of specialized education or qualification for the position. For example, Alabama requires the comptroller to have a bachelor's degree, while other states, such as Rhode Island, place the additional requirement of being a certified public accountant (CPA). In Mississippi, the comptroller is expected to have at least ten years of professional experience in order to hold the position. Texas does not place any such qualifications on the comptroller.[25] This lack of professional qualification may reflect the fact that Texas's officeholder serves as both the comptroller and the treasurer. Since state treasurers across the United States are typically elected, the qualifications are often less stringent and reflect the historically longer constitutional basis of the position. In addition, university degree requirements and professional certifications are products of twentieth-century ideas about the professionalization of some government offices and agencies related to the rise of managerial science and public administration. These approaches to government management occurred after the writing of the Texas Constitution. While the merger of the two positions is a more recent development, the intent of the amendment to the Texas Constitution was to streamline state government in order to reduce its size and cost, not to focus on the qualification and training of officeholders.

In Texas, the most significant aspect of the comptroller's job involves estimating the amount of revenue the state will generate each year. This estimate is critical for the development of the state budget by the Texas Legislature. Since the legislature meets once every two years and must pass a budget to last until it meets again in regular session, these estimates give the comptroller significant power over the state budget. Moreover, the legislature is prohibited from exceeding the comptroller's estimations unless four-fifths of both houses approve appropriations that exceed the estimates. Thus, the comptroller exercises a great deal of influence on the state's budget.

This influence can put the comptroller in an unpopular position in the state. Legislators and the governor, often motivated to spend as much money as they can get away with, prefer generous estimates. The comptroller holds the job based in part on making accurate estimates and therefore not creating debt for the state. This situation creates tension, as illustrated in the 2003 battle between Comptroller Carole Keeton-Strayhorn and the Texas Legislature. Strayhorn, the state's first female comptroller, rankled the governor and the state legislature when she informed them that they faced a $9 billion budget shortfall. The feud between Strayhorn and the legislature culminated in legislation that transferred the comptroller's authority over two programs to the LBB.[26] Strayhorn's insult-trading public brawl with Governor Perry culminated with her run against him for governor in the 2006 election.

The current comptroller, Glenn Hegar won election in 2014. Prior to becoming comptroller, Hegar was elected from the Katy suburbs of Harris County to the Texas House of Representatives in 2002, and in 2006 voters elected him to the Texas Senate to represent all or parts of twenty counties in central and south central Texas. Hegar has law degrees from St. Mary's University and the University of Arkansas and is a self-styled conservative who defends gun ownership and advocates pro-life positions. He lists his occupation as a farmer and is the sixth generation to live on the family land.

As comptroller, Hegar has favored reform to the state's Rainy Day Fund, a pool of money set aside to operate state government in emergency situations. In the past, the Rainy Day Fund could only be invested in low-yield bond funds and other low-growth investment opportunities. Thanks to Hegar's efforts, as of 2015 the Rainy Day Fund may be invested in higher yield but also riskier opportunities such as international mutual funds or so-called growth mutual funds. This change permits the comptroller to take greater risks with investments of the fund but carries the promise of potentially higher returns, growing the fund even more if successful. At the time, the fund was estimated to be around $8 billion.[27] In 2017, Hegar advocated additional changes that would essentially convert the fund into an endowment-type investment that, if untapped, would exceed at least $12 billion by 2019.[28] Hegar's plan was supported unanimously by the Texas House of Representatives, passed by the Texas Senate, and signed into law by Governor Abbott, who tweeted his support during debates in the legislature.

Lower tax revenue in 2017 due to lower oil and gas prices and the impact of 2015 tax cuts led to bleak estimates for the state budget during the 2017 legislative session. Calls from some state legislators for tapping into the Rainy Day Fund initially fell on largely deaf ears, but eventually the $217 billion, two-year budget passed and ended up tapping $1 billion of the fund. An additional $2 billion plus in shortfalls was addressed through an accounting trick by moving payments to the Texas Department of Transportation from August 2019, the end of the current biennium budget cycle, to September 2019, the beginning of the next biennium budget cycle. Hegar claimed the trick violated the state constitution, which requires state allocations to occur during the fiscal year that the money is to be spent. The transfer in effect pushed over $2.5 billion onto the next budget, not the current budget. Ultimately, Hegar lost this fight, with the final verdict allowing the $2.5 billion to be paid out under the 2020–2021 budget instead of the 2018–2019 cycle.

Hegar was drawn into the 2015 the controversy between the LBB and the governor involving the latter's line-item veto of several lines of the state budget, as discussed previously. After the LBB issued their letter questioning the governor's power to use the line-item veto on these parts of the budget, the comptroller's office was required to decide whether his office would allow the authorization of spending on the items in the budget or would honor the governor's veto. Hegar sided with the governor, denying funding for those items vetoed by the governor but included in the legislature's budget.[29] In addition, the comptroller asked the attorney general to issue an opinion on the matter.

The impact of Hurricane Harvey provided Hegar another opportunity to highlight the state of Texas's budget situation. Although Hegar predicted a robust economy going into the 2019 Texas Legislative session to prepare the 2020 and 2021 budgets, Harvey was expected to reduce state revenue by a minimum of $2 billion by the end of the 2018–2019 budget in August 2019. Hegar suggested that the impact of Harvey, coupled with the deferred spending to the Texas Department of Transportation and underfunding of Medicaid and Medicare in the current budget cycle, may result in a $5 billion deficit at the start of the 2020–2021 budget process, requiring the Texas Legislature to tap into the Rainy Day Fund even more.[30] By mid-2018, Hegar estimated lawmakers will start the next budget with additional issues to address, including a projected $240 million shortfall to the Texas Tomorrow Fund. This program allowed parents prior to 2003 to prepurchase public university tuition for future use by their children. Other challenges include an unsustainable and unconstitutional funding formula for public schools and underfunding of the Texas Teachers Retirement System, which provides pensions for retired employees of Texas public schools but also many of those who work for the state government. Without action on these items, credit agencies will downgrade the state government, making borrowing and financing of state government more difficult.

Like Paxton, Hegar ran unopposed in the Republican primary election in March 2018, while Joi Chevalier won the Democratic primary with 52 percent of the vote. With degrees in Latin and English from University of Texas at Austin, Chevalier entered the world of venture capital and e-commerce, then launched her own culinary incubator in Austin, the Cook's Nook.

In November, Glen Hagar easily defeated his Democratic challenger, Joi Chevalier 53.3 percent to 47.7 percent, suggesting any Blue Wave of Democratic support during the election did not necessarily trickle down to the Comptroller of Public Accounts election.

Agriculture Commissioner

The agriculture commissioner is head of the Texas Department of Agriculture, which implements all agriculture laws in the state. Unlike the office of the governor or lieutenant governor, the agriculture commissioner is not a constitutionally required position. Instead, the position, like the department that the commissioner leads, exists because the Texas Legislature passed a law creating it in its current format. As a result, the position, its method of selection, and term in office may be changed by the Texas Legislature at any time. However, the strength of the tradition of an elected commissioner is a powerful force that is so ingrained in Texas politicians' minds, there is little chance of changing the method of selection. Currently, the commissioner is directly elected by voters in Texas for a four-year term in office. The commissioner of agriculture receives a base salary of $137,500.[31]

For most Texans, the most common encounter with the agricultural department occurs at the gas station. Under Texas law, the department is responsible for weights and measures, including annual inspections of each and every gas pump in the state. These inspections ensure Texans that one gallon of gas pumped at the gas station is in fact one gallon. The department also measures scales used in the food industry and retail price scanners to ensure accuracy in these devices. In recent years, the department has been given the power to certify organically grown meats, fruits, and vegetables.

The department promotes Texas products through the "Go Texan" branded campaign.[32] The department also protects consumers and agricultural products from harmful pests and diseases, and offers financial assistance to farmers and ranchers in times of economic hardship or natural disaster. In addition, it provides low-interest loans to farmers to start new farms.

The Texas Department of Agriculture administers school nutrition programs in conjunction with programs operated by the U.S. government. The department also carries out a number of functions related to rural development and economic growth. For example, it offers grant programs to rural communities to build infrastructure, such as parks and roads. In a related set of activities, the department administers the Texas Certified Retirement Community Program to help local communities attract and keep retirees, a huge population growth opportunity given the aging of the American population. The department also assists rural areas in acquiring broadband communication services and advocates policies at the state and national levels to benefit Texas farming and ranching interests.

The commissioner's office is often an important rung on the Texas political ambition ladder. After serving three terms as a state legislator, Rick Perry was successfully elected commissioner of agriculture. Perry served two terms before running for lieutenant governor, a position he held until Governor George W. Bush resigned to move to the White House. When Perry vacated the office, Susan Combs became the first woman in the state to hold the position of agriculture commissioner. Combs held the position for two terms before successfully running for comptroller in the mid-2000s.

Incumbent commissioner Sid Miller was elected to the position in 2014, after serving in the Texas House of Representatives. Miller, who has a degree from Tarleton State University, has been active on the rodeo circuit and was named "World Champion of Calf Roping" by the U.S. Calf Roping Association. He is rarely seen without his iconic cowboy hat.

Miller brought a very different style and feel to the commissioner's office than his predecessors. As his first act, Miller granted "amnesty" to cupcakes in public schools, allowing parents to bring these and other treats into public schools for student consumption. However, this decision was criticized by former commissioner Susan Combs, who stated a ban on cupcakes and similar treats never existed but they were merely discouraged.[33] Miller did reverse several actual policies from the Susan Combs era, including the removal of a ban on deep fryers and soda machines on public school campuses statewide. This change was announced by Miller as a way to return power to local school districts to decide whether to ban or serve such products as well as allowing up to six times a year fatty foods and sugary drinks on campus during the regular school day for fund-raising efforts by student groups. Critics of these plans claimed that these policies were a move in the wrong direction, given the higher rates of childhood obesity in Texas compared to the national average. Yet, Miller encouraged schools, especially in urban areas, to develop vegetable gardens on campus, and he launched his "Farm Fresh Fridays." This initiative encourages school districts to use Texas-grown foods, local produce and meats.[34]

Miller entered in the 2015 budget discussions by demanding significant increases in the Department of Agriculture's budget, which had been slashed by about one-third since 2011. According to Miller, the cuts left the department unable to fulfill its basic functions of consumer protection including inspections of every gas pump in the state, verify grocery store scanners work property, verify precious metal scales, and inspect every taxicab meter. Miller also decried the 2,000-case backlog he inherited from his predecessor involving consumer complaints and allegations of fraud by businesses the department regulates. He also noted that the department has $1.5 million owed to it in unpaid penalties levied on businesses for violation of department regulations and state law.[35] Legislators fired back with comments that Miller and his government relations team had engaged in a very aggressive campaign, and perhaps unprecedented, for significant increases in his agency's budget. This approach seemed contradictory to his days in the legislature, where Miller had cultivated a reputation of being a fiscal hawk, keeping a tight rein on the state budget.[36] When the legislature failed to give the Department of Agriculture a major funding increase for the 2015–2017 biennium that satisfied Miller's demands, Miller announced a plan to hike license fees for numerous services and registrations that the department services. His proposal, adding an estimated $22 million to the department budget, provoked a response by Lois Kolkhorst (R–Brenham) of the interim Senate Committee on Agriculture: "Some of these increases, Sid, they're choke-a-horse large."[37]

Like several other members of the Texas executive, Miller faced a number of investigations and lawsuits over practices in the Department of Agriculture and in his personal activities. Shelia Latting, the former deputy chief financial officer of the department, filed a lawsuit alleging that she had been fired from her job and replaced with a Caucasian woman because Latting is African American.[38] Allegations of campaign finance law violations including payments direct to Miller's personal accounts from a loan to his campaign fund emerged in 2016.[39] Most serious were criminal investigations by the Texas Rangers that Miller used state funds to pay for his out of state trips to Mississippi to participate in a rodeo and to Oklahoma to receive medical care, tour the Oklahoma National Stockyards, and meet with Oklahoma officials. Miller later claimed he planned to reimburse the state. Potential charges against Miller were dropped in September 2016 when Travis County prosecutors declared it would be difficult to prove criminal intent on the part of Miller.[40]

A "Battle of Barbeque" developed in 2017 and 2018 over the issue of weights and measures. In 2017, the Texas Legislature passed an exemption to the annual inspections for weights scales at restaurants, grocery stores, and other locations where a scale is used almost exclusively to measure food for immediate consumption. Miller opposed the bill, even urging Governor Abbott to veto the bill after it passed the Texas Legislature. Miller's opposition centered on the need to assure consumers that pound of brisket, or other food, bought at their favorite restaurant or store was in fact a pound. After Governor Abbott signed the bill into law, Miller attempted to interpret the bill to mean the exemption occurred only if the food was to be eaten "on the premises"; the bill's authors fired back claiming Miller misinterpreted the intent of the law. Even attorney general Ken Paxton entered the battle when asked by Sid Miller to issue a legal opinion on the matter.[41]

In a three-way race for the Republican primary in 2018, Sid Miller won renomination with over 55 percent of the vote. Kim Olson, a former colonel in the U.S. Air Force, received the Democratic nomination as the only candidate in the primary election. Her past political experience includes service on the Weatherford ISD board of trustees and on the board for Court Appointed Special Advocates of Parker County. Like other Republican incumbents in Texas's plural executive, Miller won re-election 51.4 percent to Olson's 46.6 percent.

Land Commissioner

Perhaps unique among the fifty U.S. states is the Texas **commissioner of the General Land Office**. The office and related agency are among the oldest in Texas, dating back to the Republic of Texas. At the time of independence from Mexico, the Republic of Texas created the office to manage public land, provide maps and land surveys, and to raise money through land grants to finance the Texas Revolution.[42] When Texas joined the United States in 1845, the U.S. Congress would not take over the public debts that the Republic of Texas owed to its creditors. As a result, Texas kept its debt, but it was also allowed to keep its public lands. These public lands included tidelands out to three marine leagues from the shore, unlike other states that border the Gulf of Mexico. This experience sets Texas apart because other than the original thirteen states, any unowned land belonged to the U.S. government. Today, the land commissioner's office manages just over 13 million acres of land.

To be elected land commissioner, a candidate must be eighteen years old, a citizen of the United States, and a resident of Texas. The land commissioner receives a salary of $140,938 per year. Although the head of the general land office contains the title of commissioner, the commissioner does not serve on or answer to a board or commission, unlike the Railroad Commission or the SBOE.

Proceeds from the sale of state lands and revenue from the extraction of minerals and other resources from state lands go to the **Permanent School Fund (PSF)**. The management of this fund was the primary responsibility of the land commissioner for decades. Money in the PSF is used to build and maintain public schools in Texas. As of August 2017, the fund contained over $41.4 billion in assets and had distributed almost $1.06 billion to Texas schools in 2017 alone. In addition, the fund guaranteed over $72.8 billion in bonds issued by over 800 Texas public school districts, and the fund has underwritten over $1.4 billion in bonds for charter schools.[43]

The land commissioner has historically been charged with supervising mineral leases. Yet the scope of the commissioner's duties has expanded over time. For example, the discovery of oil and natural gas in Texas increased the revenue stream into the PSF. In addition, the office defended an attempt by the U.S. government to take over the tidelands of Texas. One duty added to the office is to ensure the quality of life for impoverished and disabled veterans in Texas. As a result, the General Land Office makes low-interest loans available to veterans in the state to purchase land and homes. The office also maintains state cemeteries and skilled-care facilities for Texas veterans. These tasks are assigned to an agency of the office called the Texas Veterans Land Board.

The land office also consists of a number of other offices and agencies that help the land commissioner with the tasks assigned to this executive office. Day-to-day operations

commissioner of the General Land Office
this office administers state-owned lands, controls the Permanent School Fund (PSF), and controls leases for the development of mineral and other resources on public lands; the office is sometimes called the land commissioner

Permanent School Fund (PSF)
a fund set aside to finance education in Texas; the state's largest source of investment income

are managed by the chief clerk, whose office dates back to the creation of the General Land Office and the commissioner's position in 1836. The School Land Board provides governance for the PSF and coordinates disbursements with the Texas Education Agency. The Coastal Coordination Advisory Committee coordinates coastal policies and activities with local and U.S. governments in coastal areas. A series of boards manage leases of state property owned by the Texas Parks and Wildlife Department, Texas Department of Criminal Justice, and various public universities. Conservation programs in rural areas are managed by the Texas Farm and Ranch Lands Conservation Council.

The General Land Office recently began harvesting another natural resource—wind. The vast plains of West Texas produce a lot of wind, and Texas has built large banks of wind turbines in the area. In 2006, Texas surpassed all other states to become the nation's leader in wind production.[44] In 2007, Commissioner Jerry Patterson added offshore wind leases to Texas's already profitable offshore oil industry. Texas has begun leasing wind rights in the Gulf Coast, which will generate millions of dollars for the state over the life of the leases. Reflecting the General Land Office's traditional role as income generator for the state, Patterson boasted that "the future of offshore wind power in the [United States] is right here in Texas, and the Land Office is open for business."[45]

The current commissioner is a familiar name in Texas politics: George Bush. George P. Bush, grandson of former President George H. W. Bush, is the son of Jeb Bush and Columba Garnica Gallo, a naturalized U.S. citizen from Mexico. Elected in 2014, Bush's tenure as land commissioner saw a number of issues come to the forefront of the land office. One of the more interesting issues involved that iconic building associated with Texas independence, transformation, and tradition: the Alamo, as noted at the beginning of this chapter. A major effort by Commissioner Bush was to reorganize the General Land Office that Bush himself called a reboot. Bush's motivation was to streamline the office by eliminating and streamlining duties and jobs, as well as consolidating its internal organization. Part of the reason for the changes was a result of a report critical of the agency issued by the state auditor.[46] Bush's efforts were criticized in part for firing and hiring practices in his office, including the same severance package and emergency leave issues surrounding Attorney General Ken Paxton.

In the wake of Hurricane Harvey, the land office found itself in the middle of the recovery efforts along the Gulf Coast. Governor Greg Abbott negotiated a new approach the federal disaster aid and recovery efforts, placing much of the recovery in the hands of the land office, with the Federal Emergency Management Agency (FEMA). As a result, the role of the commissioner expanded significantly, as Bush attempted to tackle how to manage the state's disaster relief efforts, how to distribute funds to counties and cities, and how to coordinate efforts across federal, state, and local governments. In the latter case, Bush's approach often placed him and the GLO at the center of criticism by cities and counties in the affected area for how funds were allocated. This conflict is explored more thoroughly in Chapter 11.

Former commissioner Jerry Patterson challenged George P. Bush in the Republican primary. In a four-candidate election, Bush prevailed, winning a majority on primary day and avoiding a run-off. In November, Miguel Suazo was the Democratic challenger to Bush. Suazo, a lawyer with degrees from Georgetown University and University of New Mexico School of Law, has no prior experience in elected office.

Jerry Patterson endorsed Suazo rather than fellow Republican George P. Bush in the general election. However, Bush won re-election decisively, performing better over his Democratic opponent than most other Republicans running for statewide executive office. Bush received 53.7 percent of the vote to Suazo's 43.4 percent.

Secretary of State

The Texas Constitution specifically created the office of secretary of state. Unlike the other key offices in the Texas executive branch, which are elected, the Texas secretary of state is appointed by the governor with Senate confirmation to a four-year term. This appointment process places Texas at odds with the normal practice throughout the United States. Most states elect their secretary of state to ensure the position is directly accountable to the voters; in three states, the secretary is chosen by the state legislature, while a few states have the governor appoint the secretary subject to confirmation by one or both houses of the legislature. A few states such as Alaska and Hawaii lack this position.[47] Texas is the only state to have a secretary appointed by the governor without confirmation by the legislature. The Texas secretary of state receives a base salary of $132,924 per year.[48]

Traditionally, the function of the secretary of state is that of state record keeper for the executive branch, chief protocol officer, and foreign affairs chief. This function was given to the office under the Constitution of the Republic of Texas after independence in 1836. At that time, President Sam Houston appointed Stephen F. Austin as the first Texas secretary of state. Unfortunately, Austin died of pneumonia only three months after taking office.[49] After statehood, the roles of protocol officer and foreign affairs chief were removed from the position. In addition to recordkeeping, the position eventually received new duties and responsibilities as the size and scope of state government increased. One of the most important sets of records that the secretary of state's office maintains is related to elections. The office is responsible for administering the Texas Election Code, keeping statewide voter registration lists, certifying voting systems and equipment, and maintaining registration lists of candidates and political parties. The office also oversees Project V.O.T.E. (Voters of Tomorrow through Education), which is designed to teach school-aged children about the process and importance of voting.[50] The requirement that the secretary of state serve as the chief election officer in Texas is consistent with the practice in thirty-nine of the states.

The office is also responsible for keeping records concerning banking and other business activities. All legal corporations, including businesses, must file with the office, and in return each business receives a charter or license to operate in Texas. This duty also extends to nonprofit and charitable organizations operating in the state of Texas. The secretary's office also certifies all notaries public and keeps the official state seal. Any registered trade names that a company uses or any registered trademarks are filed with the secretary of state's office. The *Texas Register*, a weekly update of all rules, regulations, meetings, opinions, and proclamations associated with official state business, is published in the secretary's office. Again, these practices are consistent with the office of secretary of state in most states.

Recent governors have expanded the job of the secretary of state through executive orders, adding three roles to the office. First, the secretary of state is now the chief administrator for the Texas Border and Mexican Affairs Division, which is charged with overseeing border issues and Mexico–Texas relations. Second, the secretary has also been designated the chief international protocol officer; in this capacity, he or she receives international delegations. Note that some of these roles restore earlier

secretary of state
this position is responsible for business licensing and regulation and also administrates and supervises elections; also serves as the chief protocol officer of Texas

Compare the Texas secretary of state's responsibilities to those of the U.S. secretary of state.

★ **CRITICAL THINKING**

Appointed by Governor Greg Abbott in January 2017, Rolando B. Pablos serves as the 111th Texas secretary of state.

functions of the office from the time of the Republic of Texas.

Given the long history of the position, it is not surprising perhaps that many holders of the office have gone on to hold other political positions. Three secretaries later became governor of the state, while another three became lieutenant governor. Six secretaries of state were later elected attorney general. In addition, the office has been somewhat more diverse than other state executive offices. This office was one of the first to feature a woman in a highly visible state position after Ma Ferguson appointed Emma C. Meharg as the first female secretary of state. A leader in the women's suffrage movement in Texas, Jane McCallum holds the distinction as being the longest-serving secretary; she served from January 1927 until 1933. In January 2014, Governor Perry appointed Nandita Berry as the 109th secretary of state; she was the first Indian American to serve in a major statewide office.

BOARDS AND COMMISSIONS

The Texas bureaucracy is a complex system of elected and appointed officials working in conjunction with a wide range of boards and agencies. There are close to 300 boards and commissions in the state; some are specified in the constitution, such as the Board of Pardons and Paroles, but most, such as the Department of Agriculture, have been created by the legislature. Depending on the political mood and particular needs during the period when a board or commission was created, the membership, size, and autonomy of these entities vary greatly. Some boards are elected, providing them a good deal of autonomy from the rest of the executive branch; others are appointed and therefore obligated to the governor or the legislative leadership that appointed them. Six of the most important state agencies are the TxDOT, the DSHS, the Texas Department of Criminal Justice, the Railroad Commission of Texas, the SBOE, and the Public Utility Commission of Texas.

Texas Department of Transportation

One of the best-known agencies of Texas government is TxDOT. This agency is responsible for overseeing the construction and maintenance of state highways and roads, as well as federal interstate highways and roadways within the borders of Texas. Like other state agencies, the TxDOT is governed by a commission, in this case the Texas Transportation Commission. The commission members are appointed by the governor and confirmed by the Texas Senate. The commission plans and makes policies for the location, construction, and maintenance of roads. The commission also develops a statewide transportation plan that integrates road, rail, and water traffic, and it awards state contracts for the building and maintenance of state and federal highways in Texas. Finally, the commission is charged with developing public mass transportation in the state.

The committee relies on strategic priorities developed with input from communities and citizens across the state to assist it in its work. Much of the work on roads across Texas involves local improvements or new routes; these projects must fit into the strategic priorities and must compete with jobs from across the state to receive funding. Such projects include improvements to the I-35 corridor throughout Texas, improvements to interstate highways in downtown Dallas, and completion of the I-69 project. The I-69 project eventually will, when completed, begin as three separate corridors: I-69W in Laredo, I-69C in McAllen, and I-69E in Brownsville. Near Corpus Christi, the three corridors converge into a single roadway, I-69, that will then extend northeast along the existing U.S. 59 highway through Houston and into the Piney Woods of East Texas. Just northeast of Nacogdoches, the interstate will cross into Louisiana. Extensions in Louisiana, Arkansas, and Tennessee will link to the existing I-69 in Kentucky. When completed, I-69 will allow travelers to drive over 2,600 miles from the U.S.–Mexico border in Texas to the U.S.–Canada border north of Detroit, Michigan; approximately one-third of the mileage will be in Texas.

Another priority is the I-14 corridor. In Texas, this route is intended to begin in west Texas at Fort Stockton, generally following the route of U.S. 190 across Texas, attempting to provide some relief to I-10 and bypassing the San Antonio and Houston metropolitan areas. If built and completed, I-14 will traverse from Fort Stockton across Texas through central Louisiana, into southern Mississippi and Alabama, and terminating at Savannah, Georgia. The I-14 designation is both pragmatic because an I-12 and I-16 exist already and symbolic since the interstate will cross through part of the Deep South, with the "14" in the highway number recalling the role of the Fourteenth Amendment's Equal Protection Clause in the civil rights era ensuring equality for African Americans. On January 26, 2017, the first segment of I-14 was completed between Copperas Cove and Belton.

However, TxDOT also develops a strategic plan that goes beyond listing specific road projects and their priorities for the department. For example, the 2017–2021 plan emphasizes the implementation of information technology to improve commute times in urban areas, sets goals for worker safety, addresses methods to improve community and citizen involvement in department decisions, and sets benchmarks to measure the performance of the department.[51] The department also oversees construction and improvement of the state's rail network. This area of policy includes possible high-speed rail connections between San Antonio, Houston, and the Dallas–Fort Worth metroplex and improvements to freight rail, especially from the Rio Grande valley to the Oklahoma border.

All transportation projects funded and directed by the TxDOT go through a similar process. First, the project is proposed, then an open comment time occurs. During this time, the TxDOT may hold open meetings, or hearings, at which citizens, organized interests, and others may offer suggestions to improve the project or voice criticism of it. In the latter case, the goal may be to prevent the project from moving forward. Some of these meetings may occur in the communities that the project is going to affect. For

FIGURE 5.1 Texas Department of Transportation Organizational Chart

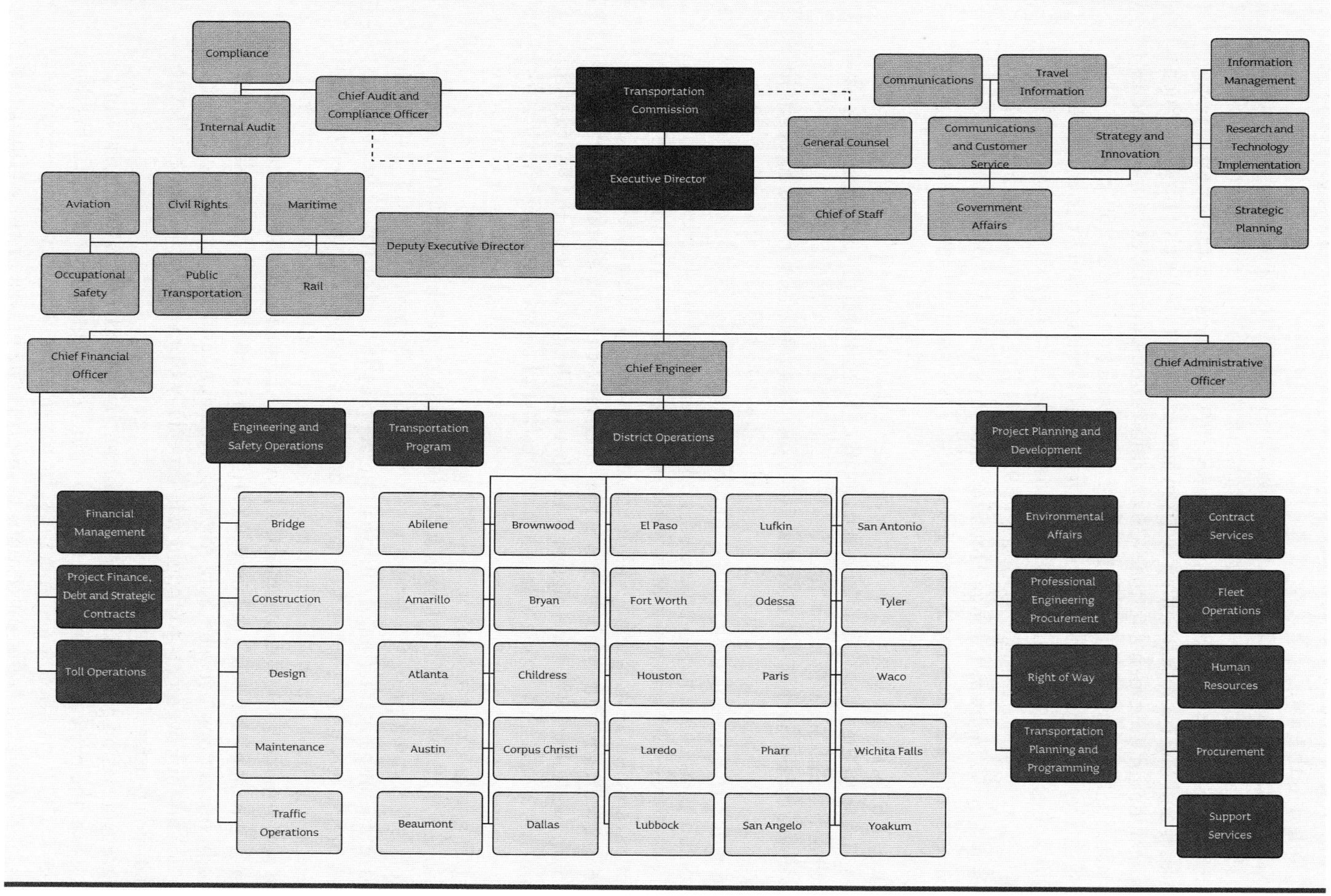

Source: Texas Department of Transportation, "Organization Chart," January 26, 2018, http://ftp.dot.state.tx.us/pub/txdot/admin/txdot-org-chart.pdf.

example, meetings in affected communities have been held with regard to the proposed upgrades to several existing highways to transform them into I-69. A constitutional amendment passed by Texas voters in 2015 requires that the state set aside $2.5 billion annually in sales tax revenue to fund transportation projects.

Which functions and agencies within the Texas Department of Transportation are most surprising to you? Why?

⭐ CRITICAL THINKING

Road and rail construction funding comes from a variety of sources, including the federal government. Depending on the road, up to 80 percent of construction or maintenance costs may come from the U.S. government. Other funding comes from project-specific funding as a rider attached to a bill passed by the Texas Legislature, from the general state budget, from fuel taxes, and from the sale of public bonds.

In order to balance local priorities with state and national needs, the department divides the state into four broad regions. The regions are further divided into districts of around ten to twenty counties. There are twenty-five of these districts across Texas. Each one has an office whose staff is responsible for overseeing all TxDOT projects in that district. The department is headed by an executive director appointed by commission. The executive director oversees the day-to-day operations of the department. In many ways, the director is really in charge of the TxDOT since the Texas Transportation Commission meets only a few times a year, mostly to provide overall guidance for the department. The director is assisted by an executive staff that includes separate agencies for legal affairs, engineering, planning, finance, communications, and administration. Some of the department's road and highway budget is distributed to each district for district-level construction projects.

Figure 5.1 illustrates the structure of the TxDOT, which is typical of the structure of various state departments and agencies. Most departments have a legal affairs office to handle legal issues, such as challenges to decisions and policies of the department, and to handle contracts with outside, private companies that provide services to the department. In the case of the TxDOT, the legal affairs office has additional responsibilities. It handles the acquisition of land for the construction of new roads and highways and manages contracts for the planning, building, and maintaining of those roadways.

The finance division is a division common to many Texas agencies as well. It handles the accounting of the department, including making payments to contractors and vendors and dealing with payments received by the TxDOT for its services and work. The administration division handles day-to-day operations, human resources issues, and logistics for meetings and conferences sponsored by the TxDOT. The communications division handles public relations for the department and communicates information to the public about the safety and conditions of Texas roads. This division also deals with letting the public know about upcoming projects and construction. The TxDOT has some divisions that are unique to it. These include the engineering and planning offices. These divisions deal with how Texas develops new roads and highways, from project proposal through construction, and eventually manage long-term maintenance of the roadways.

A chief of staff assists the director in administration of the office. Reporting to the chief of staff are two other important officials. One of these officials, the state legislative affairs officer, ensures that TxDOT priorities are communicated to the Texas Legislature. The other official is in charge of the TxDOT relationship with the U.S. government. This latter function is somewhat unique to the TxDOT and is necessary because highway and road construction is not conducted in isolation to the rest of the

TEXAS GEORGIA

Recently, a small section of I-85 in Atlanta, Georgia, was expanded to include toll lanes; cars and trucks driving in these lanes pay a premium or toll on the use of those less congested and traveled lanes. These lanes are the only tolled roads in Georgia. At one point, Georgia experimented with roads. Georgia Highway 400 in the Atlanta area had been constructed as a toll road, but Texas has numerous toll roads in major metropolitan areas and increasingly in other areas of the state, and often freeways increasingly have toll lanes similar to those on I-85 in Atlanta.

The Georgia State Transportation Board, the equivalent of the Texas Transportation Commission, is selected by the state legislature and is required by law to consist of one person from each of Georgia's congressional districts. Thus, as the number of representatives from Georgia in the U.S. House of Representatives changes due to reapportionment every ten years, so does the state's transportation board. In 2018, the board had fourteen members. In contrast, the Texas Transportation Commission consists of five members, appointed by the governor for six-year terms. If Texas followed the Georgia model, then Texas's commission would consist of thirty-six members.

In Georgia, the entire state legislature does not choose the entire board. Instead, members of the state legislature divide into small groups based on the fourteen congressional districts. All members of the state legislature from a congressional district select one member of the state transportation board. Each board member serves a five-year term.[i] Once selected, the Georgia

State Transportation Board selects one of its members to be the chair, and another member is selected as the vice chair. The chair and vice chair serve one-year renewable terms. In Texas, the governor appoints one member of the Texas Transportation Commission as the chair of the commission.

The Georgia board serves a similar function to its Texas equivalent. The board in Georgia hires a commissioner to oversee the Georgia Department of Transportation (GDOT). The board also designates which roads are part of the state highway system, approves long-range transportation plans, oversees administration of construction contracts, and authorizes lease agreements.[ii]

Does the system used in Georgia provide a way to fund and build roads that helps all parts of society?

⭐ **SOCIAL RESPONSIBILITY**

How would gerrymandering congressional districts in Georgia shape or change transportation policy?

⭐ **CRITICAL THINKING**

i. Georgia Department of Transportation, "State Transportation Board," accessed June 6, 2018, http://www.dot.ga.gov/AboutGDOT/Board.

ii. Ibid.

country. Much of the TxDOT work is linked to interstate travel and traffic. As a result, coordination of the TxDOT work with neighboring states and with the U.S. government is essential to provide seamless transportation networks nationwide.

Department of State Health Services

The DSHS is one of the largest and most important agencies of state government. The department oversees a budget of around $3.0 billion and employs over 12,000 people. An appointed executive committee, consisting of the heads of various agencies within the department, provides broad guidance and direction for the department. The DSHS is led by a commissioner, an individual appointed by the governor to oversee the day-to-day operations of the department. The current commissioner is John Hellerstedt, a medical doctor. Prior to assuming his duties as the commissioner in 2015, Dr. Hellerstedt spent eighteen years serving as a pediatrician in the Austin area, and then as vice president for Dell Children's Medical Center of Central Texas.[52]

The department is organized into a series of offices and divisions that cover a wide range of health-related issues, including consumer affairs, border health, mental health, and emergency preparedness. Like other state agencies, the department also contains offices that deal with personnel issues and with finances. The department also collects vital statistics on the health of Texans, including birth and death rates, abortion statistics, infant mortality, and child fatalities. In addition, the department maintains databases on epidemiological issues, such as rates of cancer, diabetes, and infectious diseases among Texans. Some of these activities are conducted with the assistance of county health departments and county clerk offices in each of Texas's 254 counties.

Another important area of concern for the DSHS is the licensing and overseeing of hospitals and other medical facilities in the state. In addition to hospitals, the DSHS regulates birthing centers, outpatient surgery centers, medical laboratories, and substance abuse facilities. In each of these areas, the department ensures the quality of care provided meets or exceeds state guidelines.

The DSHS is also charged by the Texas Legislature to ensure public health through the regulation of drugs and various foods, such as dairy products and seafood. As new trends have emerged in the population, the health department's mission has expanded to overseeing businesses engaged in tanning, tattooing, and body piercing. Again, the goal here is to ensure those who access the services provided by these businesses may be certain that the risk to personal health is minimized.

Finally, an important task assigned to the DSHS is the oversight of licensing for some important professions in Texas. This oversight is to ensure that those who practice these professions meet the minimum qualifications for their jobs, engage in ongoing training, and maintain the ethical standards of their professions. Some of the professions that DSHS oversees the licensing for include athletic trainers, social workers, emergency medical technicians (EMTs), midwives, opticians, social workers, and speech pathologists. In many cases, the DSHS works with professional organizations, universities and colleges, and vocation training programs to coordinate the licensing programs.

Railroad Commission of Texas

The Railroad Commission of Texas was created by Governor James Stephen Hogg to regulate the railroads, decrease corruption, and protect the state's large agrarian population from crooked railroad practices. The commission was the first regulatory agency in the state and one of the most important commissions in the state's history. It is composed of three members, each independently elected in a statewide contest. The members serve overlapping six-year terms, with one member reelected every two years. By custom, the chair rotates every two years and is the member who is in the last two years of his or her term. Originally created to regulate railroads, the commission's mandate has expanded over time to include regulation of the oil and gas industry, protection of the environment, and promotion of alternative energy sources. There have long been charges that oil and gas interest groups exert too much influence over the commissioners, and the commission struggles with a reputation for emphasizing protection of the oil and gas industry at the expense of environmental protection. Such concerns became a focal point of debate within the Republican primaries for the railroad commissioner candidates in early 2016. Ultimately, the debate became largely moot, as Republican candidates favoring the oil and gas industry won the primaries.

TEXAS *Legends*

Railroad Commission of Texas

AP Photo

One of the legends of Texas government is the Railroad Commission of Texas. While the commission is the oldest regulatory agency in Texas and one of the few elected regulatory agencies in the nation, today the commission fails to live up to its name. In November 1890, Texas voters approved an amendment to the Texas Constitution that empowered the legislature to create an agency to regulate railroads. While the state had initially encouraged the railroads, by the 1890s many Texans, especially farmers, had grown to resent them. The Texas Traffic Association, an organization made up of the major railroads, set the rates, and due to poor roads and

unnavigable rivers, Texas farmers had no real alternatives for shipping goods. In 1891, the legislature followed up by establishing the Railroad Commission of Texas. Initially, commissioners were appointed by the governor. However, voters in 1894 approved an amendment making the commissioners officials who were elected to six-year terms. Since that time, the Railroad Commission has had the unique designation of being a regulatory agency headed by elected officials.

Attorney General James Stephen Hogg had made the call for the creation of a railroad commission the centerpiece of his campaign for governor. The railroads labeled Hogg "communistic," but his reforms proved popular and his election represented the first stirrings of a populist reform movement in Texas. The creation of the Railroad Commission was proclaimed to be a way of producing fair competition, but in its actual workings, the commission was used more to restrict

out-of-state railroads and protect Texas-based businesses from international competitors.

In the 1920s, the Railroad Commission was given responsibility for regulating motor carriers in addition to railroads. However, the responsibility for motor carriers ended in 1994 when trucking was deregulated and responsibility for trucking safety moved to the Texas Department of Transportation (TxDOT).

Today, about three-quarters of the commission's efforts are focused on regulating oil and natural gas exploration and production. The Railroad Commission also oversees natural gas and hazardous liquids pipeline operations, natural gas utilities, LP gas service, and coal and uranium mining.

In 2005, the commission's responsibility for rail safety was transferred to the TxDOT, the last step in removing the railroads from the responsibility of the Railroad Commission. While the commission retains the distinction of being the state's oldest regulatory agency, nothing remains of its original mission and the Railroad Commission of Texas no longer regulates railroads.

Almost every session of the legislature since 2005 has contained debate over the name, purpose, and conduct of the Railroad Commission. During the 2015 session, the Railroad Commission faced intense scrutiny as the Texas Sunset Advisory Commission released a report suggesting the name be changed to "Texas Energy Resources Commission," improve its monitoring and enforcing of state laws overseeing the oil and gas industry, and transfer natural gas utility rate oversight to the Public Utility Commission of Texas.[53] The 2017 session of the Texas Legislature saw the passage of a reform bill that made minor changes improving enforcement tracking, requiring strategic plans, and improving pipeline safety. However, a proposed name changed to the Texas Energy Resource Commission failed to meet approval again.[54]

The Railroad Commission selects an executive director and other key staff, including a chief financial officer. The commission is organized into several agencies that oversee specific areas of energy policy, such as alternative energy, natural gas services, and oil and gas. In addition, as in other state commissions and departments, there is a legal affairs office, a human resources office, and an information technology office.

JIM WATSON/AFP/Getty Images

Freight transportation is vital to the economic vitality of Texas. Texas's trade with Mexico exceeded $187 billion in 2017, with Texas enjoying a $6 billion trade surplus with its neighbor to the south.

Texas Department of Criminal Justice

The Texas Department of Criminal Justice oversees the state's prisons, jails, and other correctional facilities. It also supervises processes for offenders released from prison, on parole, or on mandatory suspension. A nine-member board is in charge of the department. This board is appointed by the governor for staggered six-year terms. The board hires the executive director of the department, sets rules and policies that guide the agency, and serves as the board of trustees for the Windham School District, the school district created by the state to handle the education of juvenile offenders.

The department consists of five key divisions that report directly to the board. The divisions are the office of the inspector general, the Windham School District, the internal audit division, the office of the state counsel for offenders, and the ombudsman. The executive director also directly reports to the board and heads the other work of the department, including the control of correctional facilities, parole, and victim services. The director also controls offices that carry out routine activities common to all state agencies, such as a human resources office for hiring of staff and information technology. Like other states, Texas attempts to help integrate prisoners into normal life after prison, and the department maintains a prison labor operation that teaches inmates skills associated with manufacturing and industry through its Texas Correctional Industries (TCI). Products made by prisoners through TCI, such as desks and tables, may be used by public universities or other state agencies.

Also associated with the department is the Texas Board of Pardons and Paroles. This board is appointed by the governor to determine which prisoners are due to be released on parole, determine the conditions of parole, determine if parole is to be suspended, and recommend cases of clemency to the governor.

elected board
a directly elected board, such as the Railroad Commission of Texas, that oversees a specific department of Texas government

State Board of Education

The SBOE is another example of an **elected board**, like the Railroad Commission. The SBOE is composed of fifteen members, each elected from single-member districts

(SMDs). The education board's main jobs include approving state curriculum and textbooks, determining passing scores for state educational testing, and managing the PSF. The board is led by a commissioner of education who is appointed by the governor, with Texas Senate approval, from a list of candidates supplied by the board. The board and its commissioner administer the Texas Education Agency, the state's primary and secondary education department. The Texas Education Agency develops curriculum standards, administers state testing requirements, and accredits and rates schools in the state. The Texas Education Agency also distributes state and U.S. government funds to public schools across Texas, which is discussed further in Chapter 14.

Since at least 2010, the SBOE has made news related to curriculum standards. In 2010, the board made national news when it adopted new social studies curriculum standards. These new standards questioned the basis for the separation of church and state, stressed the Christian background of the founding fathers, and emphasized states' rights as a cause of the Civil War. Because Texas is such a large textbook market and publishers accordingly tailor their textbooks to its standards, the board's actions have stirred controversy, as Texas's new standards translate into textbook changes across the nation. One controversy surrounded language in a high school geography textbook that suggested Africans brought to the United States between the 1500s and 1800s were immigrants who came as workers, not as slaves. In 2016, the board voted to keep language in science curricula that critics claim open the door to creation science. Proposals to create a course and related curriculum standards for Mexican American studies were adopted in April 2018, with controversy surrounding the name of the course; this approval occurred after several years of discussion and several votes against the course by the board.

The Texas Education Agency contains a number of offices and units to assist in its work. Key units include standards and programs, educator leadership, assessment and accountability, accreditation and school improvement, and grants and compliance. In addition to the commissioner, the agency is led by a chief deputy of education, a deputy commissioner for policy and programs, and a deputy commissioner for finance and administration. Like other agencies of state government, there is a chief financial officer, a human resources office, and an ombudsman office.

Public Utility Commission of Texas

appointed regulatory commission
an agency of the state government whose members oversee a specific department of state government, are appointed by the governor, and are confirmed by the Texas Senate

The Public Utility Commission of Texas is an example of an appointed regulatory commission in the state. The commission is made up of three members, each appointed by the governor, with Senate approval, for overlapping six-year terms. The commissioners oversee the electric and telecommunications industries in Texas. The commission focuses on protecting customers from unreasonable rates from electric and telecommunication companies and on promoting competition in wholesale and retail markets. The scope of its work expanded in 1996 with the federal Telecommunications Act, which ended local monopolies in telephone service, allowing national long-distance companies to offer local telephone service. Prior to this act, companies such as AT&T that offered long-distance service could not offer local phone service. The act also paved the way for cell phone, local, and long-distance telephone service; cable television; and other forms of communication to be provided by the same company.

Success in the telephone market led the state government, including the Public Utility Commission of Texas, to examine whether the same was possible in electrical markets. The Texas Legislature passed deregulation in 2001, allowing competition in electrical markets. Prior to this bill, the state of Texas, like other states, assumed that electricity production and transmission was too costly to be a functioning market. This assumption led to the creation of monopolies granted to companies to operate in specific areas and communities in Texas. For example, Texas Power and Light, a forerunner of TXU Energy, was given the exclusive right to provide electricity in north central Texas. After 2001, companies were allowed to compete against each other statewide by selling electricity to customers over the same power lines. The power lines are maintained by a separate company with monopoly power, Oncor. In rural areas, exemptions were granted to user owned cooperatives to maintain their local monopoly over the production and sale of electricity. Currently, the Public Utility Commission of Texas regulates the rates that electrical utilities charge customers and ensures that competition occurs in electrical markets throughout Texas.

The Public Utility Commission of Texas hires an executive director to run the agency. The agency is divided into two units: (1) Administration, Operations, and Fund Management and (2) Oversight and Regulation. Each of these units contains several subdivisions. For example, Administration, Operations, and Fund Management contains offices that handle the fiscal operations of the commission, general legal affairs, relations with other state agencies, and human resources. Oversight and Regulation contains offices that oversee competition, regulation enforcement, and consumer protection.

Staffing the State Government

The state of Texas employs over 360,000 Texans to staff the various state boards, agencies, and commissions. This figure includes individuals working directly for the governor, the Texas Legislature, and public universities and colleges throughout the state. Approximately 40 percent of these employees—the largest share—work for Texas's public universities. The next largest category is corrections, or those working in law enforcement agencies and prisons. This area accounts for 14 percent of state employees.

To staff these and other state agencies, Texas uses a mixture of the **patronage system** and the merit system. The patronage system, sometimes called the spoils system, allows individuals to give jobs as political favors, which means that people receive government jobs based on who they know and the connection they have to a powerful political figure. Most patronage positions in Texas government are appointed by the governor himself and total around 3,000 positions. As mentioned in Chapter 4, the governor possesses significant appointment power and is able to use this power to shape key agencies of state government. Other key members of the Texas executive branch possess similar powers for some positions within their department. Within some state agencies, the board or commission that heads the agency may also possess some freedom to choose who works in key jobs within that agency. Thus, securing a government job is dependent upon who you know, not whether you are qualified for the job. The principle also applies to giving promotions and raises and to increases in job duties.

An advantage to the patronage system is the ability of an executive to shape and model the executive branch to his or her liking. In addition, jobs may be given as

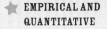

TABLE 5.2 Staff Size for Major State Government Functions

Function	Employees	Percentage
Higher education	135,512	44.5%
Criminal justice, corrections	39,332	12.9%
Public welfare	23,850	7.8%
State hospitals	23,304	7.7%
Transportation	12,806	4.2%
Parks, wildlife, etc.	10,725	3.5%
State finance	7,793	2.6%
State police	6,772	2.2%
State courts and justice	5,686	1.9%
Other education	4,416	1. 5%

Source: Audrey S. Wall, ed., *The Book of the States*, vol. 48 (Lexington, Ky.: Council of State Governments, 2017), 413, Table 8.5. Reprinted with permission of The Council of State Governments.

merit-based civil service system
a system in which people receive government jobs based on a set of qualifications and formal training; job promotion and pay raises are based on job performance

Do merit system employees have a responsibility to promote policies for the benefit of the whole society, or to promote only those policies favored by the governor or head of their department?

⭐ **SOCIAL RESPONSIBILITY**

political rewards to one's loyal supporters during an election campaign. Finally, the patronage system encourages accountability to officials directly elected by the people.

In contrast, a merit-based civil service system gives individuals a government job based on qualifications and merit. The merit system attempts to depoliticize the bureaucracy. First, merit system employees are supposed to be neutral in the services that they provide to the public. This means that government workers are not supposed to treat friends or relatives differently from others. Second, government agencies are hierarchical, with a clear chain of command from entry-level workers up to the head of the agency. Third, there is a division of labor. Certain tasks are assigned to specific individuals to perform, while other tasks are done by other workers. Fourth, the employees follow standard operating procedures. Guidelines and rules govern how employees carry out their jobs, standardizing routine decisions and limiting the power of employees to make decisions on their own. Note that the merit system is often also used in the private sector by business and companies. Walmart and McDonald's both operate using these principles.

The merit system in public service (government agencies) means that government workers are not dependent on who is currently holding office and will not lose their jobs when someone new is elected to office. Supporters of the merit system point out that this system allows the government to be staffed by experts in their jobs who are free to operate government agencies with a focus on efficiency and professionalism. Furthermore, the creation of merit systems at the national and state levels was associated with the rise of public administration and managerial sciences as new approaches to workplace efficiency. Interestingly, the Texas Government Code limits the merit system only to state agencies that are required by U.S. government law or regulation to use such a system.[55] However, the sheer size of U.S. government grants, cost-sharing programs, and other activities means that much of the Texas government is staffed by a merit system.

HOW TEXAS GOVERNMENT WORKS

A State Employment Comparison

Percentage of State Government Employees Working in Key Sectors

Higher Education

State	Percentage
California	39.5%
Colorado	55.3%
Florida	36.4%
Michigan	52.7%
Texas	44.5%

Corrections

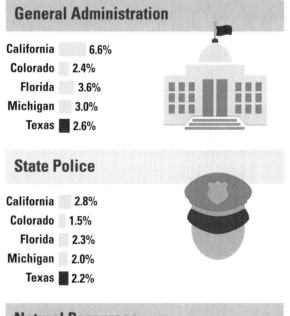

State	Percentage
California	13.6%
Colorado	9.0%
Florida	13.1%
Michigan	8.5%
Texas	12.9%

Highways

State	Percentage
California	4.7%
Colorado	3.8%
Florida	3.6%
Michigan	1.7%
Texas	4.2%

General Administration

State	Percentage
California	6.6%
Colorado	2.4%
Florida	3.6%
Michigan	3.0%
Texas	2.6%

Public Welfare

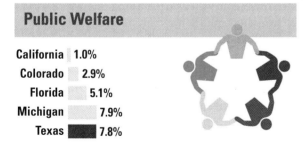

State	Percentage
California	1.0%
Colorado	2.9%
Florida	5.1%
Michigan	7.9%
Texas	7.8%

State Police

State	Percentage
California	2.8%
Colorado	1.5%
Florida	2.3%
Michigan	2.0%
Texas	2.2%

State Health & Hospitals

State	Percentage
California	10.9%
Colorado	7.5%
Florida	2.2%
Michigan	11.6%
Texas	7.7%

Natural Resources

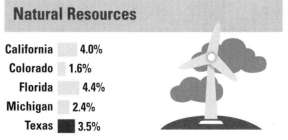

State	Percentage
California	4.0%
Colorado	1.6%
Florida	4.4%
Michigan	2.4%
Texas	3.5%

Source: Audrey S. Wall, ed., *The Book of the States*, vol. 48 (Lexington, KY: Council of State Governments, 2017), 413, Table 8.5: "State Government Employment (Full-Time Equivalent) for Selected Functions. By States. 2017."

BUREAUCRATIC ACCOUNTABILITY

As we have seen, the bureaucracy of Texas is a complex and diverse array of agency heads, board members, and commissioners that may be elected or appointed to their posts. Executive control of the bureaucracy is tenuous at best. As a result, several tools have evolved in Texas that aid the executive in exerting this control.

Texas utilizes so-called sunshine laws, or laws designed to make government transparent and accessible to the people. One such law, the Texas Public Information Act, grants citizens access to government records in the state. Similarly, the Texas Open Meetings Act generally requires governmental bodies to notify the public of the time, date, and nature of scheduled meetings and to open those meetings to the public. City council members from smaller cities have challenged the constitutionality of this requirement in federal court since for a small council it may mean that two people cannot discuss city business in private. When he was attorney general, Greg Abbott adamantly defended the Open Meetings Act. Sunshine laws received a significant boost in November 2007 when Texas voters overwhelmingly passed an amendment that requires both houses of the Texas Legislature to record the final vote on a bill and make that vote available on the Internet.

In addition, the state enacted a sunset review process (see Figure 5.2) to assess all of the statutory boards and commissions in the state. The Texas Sunset Advisory Commission was created by the Texas Legislature in 1977 to review the effectiveness of agencies. The commission is made up of twelve members; five are from the Texas House, appointed by the Speaker of the House, and five are from the Texas Senate, appointed by the lieutenant governor. The other two members are public members, one appointed by the Speaker and one by the lieutenant governor.

The sunset review process requires most governmental commissions or agencies to be reviewed every twelve years. The commission examines a self-evaluation report submitted by the agency under review, as well as developing its own reports and holding a public hearing. The commission can then recommend that an agency be continued, reorganized, or merged with another agency. If the commission takes no action, the sun automatically sets on that agency. According to the Texas Sunset Advisory Commission's estimates, since its inception, thirty-seven agencies have been abolished and forty-six have been consolidated. Estimates from the period 1977–2015 suggest that the commission has saved the state over $980 million in that time span.[56]

WINNERS AND LOSERS

The plural executive offers the citizens of Texas greater direct control over the members of the executive branch through a wider number of elected state government officials. Texans' ability to choose for themselves key offices, such as the attorney general and commissioner of agriculture, should result in greater democratic accountability of the Texas executive compared to the U.S. government. In addition, Texans are not bound to a single slate of executive officers but may pick each officeholder individually, regardless of party affiliation. That key boards and commissions, such as the Railroad Commission and the SBOE, are elected offers Texans more

sunshine laws
laws designed to make government transparent and accessible

What are the advantages of Texas's sunset laws and review process?

 CRITICAL THINKING

sunset review process
a formal assessment of the effectiveness of all statutory boards, commissions, and state agencies

Which states are most comparable to Texas in terms of the distribution of state employees? Are these results surprising?

EMPIRICAL AND QUANTITATIVE

FIGURE 5.2 Sunset Review Process

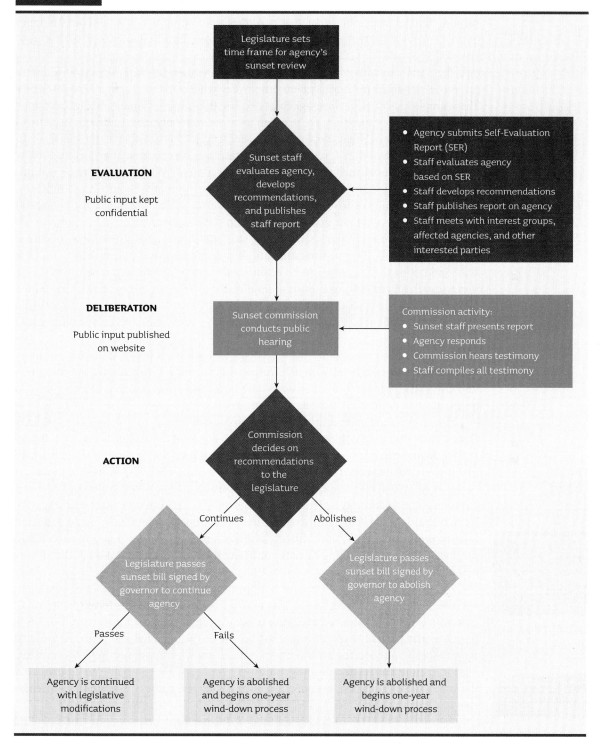

EVALUATION

Public input kept confidential

DELIBERATION

Public input published on website

ACTION

Legislature sets time frame for agency's sunset review

Sunset staff evaluates agency, develops recommendations, and publishes staff report

- Agency submits Self-Evaluation Report (SER)
- Staff evaluates agency based on SER
- Staff develops recommendations
- Staff publishes report on agency
- Staff meets with interest groups, affected agencies, and other interested parties

Sunset commission conducts public hearing

Commission activity:
- Sunset staff presents report
- Agency responds
- Commission hears testimony
- Staff compiles all testimony

Commission decides on recommendations to the legislature

Continues

Abolishes

Legislature passes sunset bill signed by governor to continue agency

Legislature passes sunset bill signed by governor to abolish agency

Passes

Fails

Agency is continued with legislative modifications

Agency is abolished and begins one-year wind-down process

Agency is abolished and begins one-year wind-down process

Source: Texas Sunset Advisory Commission, "How Sunset Works," accessed June 28, 2018, https://www.sunset.texas.gov/how-sunset-works.

direct, democratic control over those agencies as well. In this sense, Texans are clear winners. Politicians with political ambition are often winners as well. Practice gained running for statewide offices, such as comptroller of public accounts or commissioner of the General Land Office, serves as a training ground for higher offices, such as governor, U.S. senator, or U.S. president.

The Texas executive branch produces other winners as well. Texans win due to the professionalism of merit system employees who work for various state agencies. These employees work in these agencies because they are well-qualified, highly trained individuals, not because they are partisan loyalists who only have their jobs because of whom they know or what they have done politically. On the other hand, elected officials are losers when they lose control over state agencies because they lack the ability to appoint personnel throughout the state government. While the highest positions in most state agencies and departments are often accountable to an elected official—usually the governor—through an appointment process, elected officials cannot expect absolute obedience to their political goals from state workers.

If state government has increased in size and scope, such growth has occurred because it is responding to the demands that we Texans place on it. From building state and national road networks to ensuring the safety of tattoo parlors to providing statewide standards for curriculum in public schools, the state government has added new responsibilities over the past century or so. All Texans are winners in the sense that our state government is responding to what we have asked it to do. If we are concerned about the expanding size and scope of state government, the sunset review process allows for regular review of all state agencies and offers an opportunity for Texans—through our elected officials—to determine which agencies are outdated and unnecessary. Thus, the potential for a runaway state government is tempered by our ability to terminate specific agencies through this process.

However, our state executive branch produces losers in some other ways. Rather than creating an institutional structure in which an energetic legislature and executive each possesses enough power to check the other, the Texas system creates an institutional arrangement designed to keep the executive weak. As a result, members of the executive branch are often at odds with each other on key issues and policies. Paradoxically, voters have greater control over the executive yet face an executive branch that lacks an efficient, streamlined operation. The myriad of state agencies, boards, committees, and departments seems daunting at times. Each part seems to have its own agenda, leaving Texans confused and concerned about what the state is actually doing.

In 2014, a phenomenal transformation of Texas politics occurred as every statewide elected office changed hands. This new era of Texas politics features the arrival of individuals with no statewide executive office experience, save the governor. This inexperience may partially explain some, but not all, of the personal and professional legal issues that surrounded the attorney general and land commissioner. Yet, this transformation continued the decade-plus tradition of conservative, Republican control over the state executive branch, keeping and intensifying the conservative political orientation of many state policies.

Although some Democratic candidates did perform better in the 2018 general election in Texas, the Blue Wave that many Democratic voters hoped for did not

What contradictions are apparent in the growth of state government and Texas's traditions of independence and small government?

⭐ CRITICAL THINKING

How much do Texans benefit from the services the state provides?

⭐ CRITICAL THINKING

produce a tidal wave of change for the Texas executive. Instead, the blue wave hit a Red Wall of Republican support in Texas. This wall is evidenced by the ability of all Republicans running for office in the Texas executive to achieve at least 50 percent of the vote automatically, thereby guaranteeing a win, even among tarnished candidates like Ken Paxton. Thus, in 2018 Texas continued its tradition of Republican domination over the executive.

CONCLUSION

The current structure of the Texas executive was created over 100 years ago in a state that was far less complex than the one of today. It derives from a political preference for a weak executive that is a legacy of both colonial Americans' dislike of centralized power and a desire to make the executive branch more accountable to the citizens of the state. The growth of state government since the Texas Constitution of 1876 was adopted has brought new administrative agencies and organizations. Texans now find that their notion of small government is at odds with the practice of state government. Boards and commissions now regulate public utilities, supervise public health and safety, oversee public education, and control a host of additional services. These agencies were the result of public demands for government action in areas that mattered to us Texans. In addition, the advent of a merit system for organizing the state government, where implemented, results in a more professional staff in state government but one that is less eager or less dependent on pleasing the politicians of the day.

Want a better grade?

Get the tools you need to sharpen your study skills. Access practice quizzes, eFlashcards, video, and multimedia at **edge.sagepub.com/collier6e**.

KEY TERMS

appointed regulatory commission (p. 182)

attorney general (p. 161)

bureaucracy (p. 174)

commissioner of the General Land Office (p. 171)

comptroller of public accounts (p. 166)

elected board (p. 181)

lieutenant governor (p. 157)

merit-based civil service system (p. 184)

patronage system (p. 183)

Permanent School Fund (PSF) (p. 171)

plural executive (p. 156)

secretary of state (p. 173)

sunset review process (p. 186)

sunshine laws (p. 186)

ACTIVE LEARNING

- In a small group, develop a list of the advantages of a merit-based system for staffing the state's bureaucracy. **Teamwork**

- Develop a PowerPoint or similar slide show to explain the sunset review process in Texas. **Communication**

CHAPTER REVIEW

1. An executive branch in which the functions have been divided among several, mostly elected, officeholders is called a _____
   a. presidential system
   b. bureaucracy
   c. cabinet
   d. plural executive

2. The Texas _____ is the chief legal adviser for the state in court who also issues advisory opinions on legal matters.
   a. attorney general
   b. lieutenant governor
   c. solicitor general
   d. chief justice

3. Collecting taxes, investing state funds, estimating revenue, and overseeing payments by the state for goods and services are the duties of the _____.
   a. lieutenant governor
   b. commissioner of the general land office
   c. comptroller for public accounts
   d. commissioner of agriculture

4. In the state of Texas, the _____ is an unelected, statewide office.
   a. railroad commission
   b. secretary of state
   c. commissioner of agriculture
   d. lieutenant governor

5. The office of the _____ was created by state law, not the Texas Constitution (1876).
   a. commissioner of agriculture
   b. commissioner of the general land office
   c. comptroller for public accounts
   d. attorney general

6. The oldest office in Texas, dating back to the Republic of Texas, which oversees oil, gas, and mineral leases on state land, is that of the _____.
   a. governor
   b. attorney general
   c. comptroller for public accounts
   d. commissioner of the General Land Office

CHAPTER REVIEW (CONTINUED)

7. Which of the following activities is not regulated by the Railroad Commission?
   a. the environment
   b. oil and gas industries
   c. railroads
   d. alternative energy

8. The largest percentage of Texas state government workers are employed in ______.
   a. higher education
   b. highways
   c. natural resources
   d. state police

9. When individuals receive a state job based on whether they supported a candidate for public office, this system is called a ______.
   a. bureaucracy
   b. patronage system
   c. merit system
   d. regulatory commission

10. The effectiveness of all statutory boards, commissions, and states agencies is assessed by (the) ______.
    a. bureaucracy
    b. patronage system
    c. regulatory commission
    d. sunset review

CHAPTER 6

TEXAS JUDICIAL SYSTEM

Chapter Objectives

★ Identify the different types of local, state, and appellate trial courts.

★ Discuss the issues of representation within the Texas judiciary.

★ Identify problems with the Texas judiciary and give alternative means of judicial selection.

★ Describe the Texas criminal justice system.

Wallace Jefferson, one of the most respected judges in the country, resigned as chief justice of the Supreme Court of Texas in October 2013. Jefferson was not the first member of his family involved in public service. His great-great-grandfather served two terms on the Waco City Council after the Civil War granted him his freedom. Jefferson, who earned his law degree from the University of Texas (UT), was appointed to the Supreme Court of Texas by Governor Perry in 2001. Jefferson was the first African American to serve on the state's highest civil court and within a few years became the first African American chief justice of the Supreme Court of Texas. When he resigned, Jefferson left an impressive record behind. He often spoke of justice for all, advocating increased legal assistance for poor and middle-class families and expanded protection of children. Jefferson worried that "the courthouse door is closed to many who have lost their jobs, veterans and women who struggle with physical abuse."[1] He also promoted increased access to and transparency of the court. Due to Jefferson's leadership, Supreme Court of Texas documents and live webcasts of arguments before the court are now posted online. Jefferson's greatest legacy, however, may well be the reform he never saw.

As chief justice, Jefferson continually advocated for the elimination of partisan races in Texas judicial contests. Many of his speeches focused on the corrosive influence of money in judicial elections. As Jefferson told the 81st legislature in his state of the judiciary address in 2009, "sadly, we have now become accustomed to judicial races in which the primary determinants of victory are not the flaws of the incumbent or qualities of the challenger, but political affiliation and money."[2] Although Jefferson repeatedly had to compete in those partisan elections, he was well aware of the way judicial elections worked in Texas, once stating the following:

Wallace Jefferson resigned from his post on the Supreme Court of Texas in 2013. During his time as chief justice, Jefferson promoted transparency in the court in an effort to advance justice for all.

You don't know who I am. I don't blame you. I have been on the statewide ballot three times, in 2002, 2006 and 2008. I was elected each time by impressive margins. Yet a July 2008 state-wide poll found that 86 percent of the electorate "never heard of" me. I won because Texans voted for Rick Perry, Kay Bailey Hutchison and John McCain.[3]

Jefferson was reelected not because Texans were familiar with his record but because of Texans' reliance on straight-ticket partisan voting in judicial contests. And, according to Jefferson, "a justice system based on Democratic or Republican judging is a system that cannot be trusted."[4]

When Jefferson resigned as chief justice, Governor Rick Perry appointed Nathan Hecht to the position. Like Jefferson, Hecht immediately began calling for the end to partisan elections of the state's judiciary. In his 2017 state of the judiciary address, Hecht pointed out the folly of the highly politicized process Texas uses to select its justices:

In November, many good judges lost solely because voters in their districts preferred a presidential candidate in the other party. These kinds of partisan sweeps are common, with judicial candidates at the mercy of the top of the ticket. I do not disparage our new judges. I welcome them. My point is only that qualifications did not drive their election; partisan politics did. Such partisan sweeps are demoralizing to judges and disruptive to the legal system. But worse than that, when partisan politics is the driving force, and the political climate is as harsh as ours has become, judicial elections make judges more political, and judicial independence is the casualty.[5]

Despite most judges in the state favoring reform, the state's politicians resist change, not wanting to lessen the influence of parties on the process. Texans' deep-seated distrust of government has long translated into an unwillingness to fix the system, even if it is badly broken.

In this chapter, we begin by outlining the structure of the Texas judiciary. This structure is central to a consideration of justice in Texas as the system reflects ad hoc changes rather than a cohesive system of justice. Next, we examine the different levels of courts in the state, explore the costs and benefits of electing judges in Texas, and consider alternative forms of judicial selection. The chapter concludes with a discussion of the criminal justice system in the state.

JUDICIAL FEDERALISM AND TEXAS COURTS

The American court system is based on judicial federalism, in which judicial authority is shared between levels of government. The U.S. Constitution gives the national Congress the authority to create a supreme court and the lower federal courts. The U.S. Supreme Court's jurisdiction is spelled out in the Constitution and includes issues of constitutional law, treaties, and cases involving ambassadors and public ministers, among others. The states created their own state and local court systems. This means that in the United States we have a dual system of jurisprudence in which questions of federal or constitutional law are heard in the national judicial system and questions of state law are heard in the state judicial system. The vast majority of cases are heard at the state level. The Texas judicial system is one of the largest, most complex in the country, and determining which court will hear which case is far from straightforward. The Texas Constitution says this about the state's court system:

> The judicial power of this State shall be vested in one Supreme Court, in one Court of Criminal Appeals, in Courts of Appeals, in District Courts, in County Courts, in Commissioners Courts, in Courts of Justices of the Peace, and in such other courts as may be provided by law.

> The Legislature may establish such other courts as it may deem necessary and prescribe the jurisdiction and organization thereof, and may conform the jurisdiction of the district and other inferior courts thereto.[6]

For early Texans, life on the frontier led to a political culture that was independent of government. Being on the frontier often meant if there was justice to be had, Texans would have to make it for themselves. Where courts and lawmen were scarce, frontier justice would fill in the gaps. Frontier culture produced a preference for local rule and neighbors to decide and mete out justice. Texans wanted to directly choose their judges. Moreover, Texans' view of justice has also long demanded jury trials to ensure ordinary Texans acted as gatekeepers of justice and protection against governmental excess. Texans fought to ensure that the right to a jury trial was protected under Mexico. Its repeal in 1827 was a key grievance that contributed to Texas's fight for independence. Today, Texans can choose a jury trial in both civil and criminal cases. Frontier Texans also preferred local courts. As the state's population grew, the legislature would create new courts, sometimes to fulfill the needs of two neighboring counties, sometimes to fill in the gap in underserved areas, and sometimes to meet a particular need. The resulting court system in Texas, shown in "How Texas Government Works" on pages 200–201, is a highly complex, confusing, and muddled one.

The state constitution establishes two high courts, other appellate courts, district courts, commissioners courts, and justice of the peace (JP) courts. It also empowers the state legislature to establish other courts. Over the years, the legislature created municipal courts, the county courts at law, probate courts, and a variety of specialized courts including drug courts, youth courts, and veterans courts. Courts in Texas are divided by their jurisdiction, their origin, and their geographical coverage. A court's **jurisdiction** refers to its sphere of authority. One issue of authority concerns whether a case is at the original or appellate stage. Courts with **original jurisdiction** hear the initial cases. Typically, courts of original jurisdiction hear evidence and establish the record of the case. Courts with **appellate jurisdiction** hear appeals of cases for which a decision has previously been rendered by a lower court. Rather than hearing new evidence, appellate courts are restricted to reviewing the court record from the original trial and determining whether specific points of law or procedure were applied correctly. In addition, courts are sometimes given **exclusive jurisdiction**, meaning a particular level of court has the sole right to hear a specific type of case.

A second issue of jurisdiction distinguishes whether a case is a criminal case or a civil one. In a **criminal case**, the state charges an individual with violating the law. In a **civil case**, an aggrieved party sues for damages based on claims that he or she has been wronged by another individual. In Texas, the lower-level courts (the municipal courts, JP courts, and county courts) are limited to handling the least serious criminal and civil cases. By contrast, the most serious criminal charges, called felonies, and civil suits over a certain dollar amount are heard in state-level courts called district courts.

A third issue of jurisdiction concerns geographical coverage. Jurisdiction in the Texas lower courts is based on the geographical municipality, precinct, or county where the court is located. There are 469 district- or state-level courts in the state, ninety-eight of which overlap more than one county. The geographic jurisdiction of district courts therefore often overlaps with county courts. Small counties might share a district court, such as Loving, Reeves, and Ward Counties, which all constitute a single district. Conversely, larger counties can have multiple district courts, such as Harris County, which is home to sixty district courts. The state is further divided into fourteen appellate districts. The two highest courts, the Supreme Court of Texas and the Texas Court of Criminal Appeals, serve the entire state. These distinctions often become muddled because, depending on the population of a city or county, courts have evolved to serve different functions and often have overlapping jurisdiction. Since the legislature can create courts with particular jurisdiction to meet the needs of diverse communities in the state, to ascertain the jurisdiction of a particular court in the state of Texas it is often necessary to look at the actual legislation that created that court.

Courts in Texas are further distinguished by their origin. Courts in Texas are either specified in the constitution or created by the state legislature. Courts that are specified in the state's constitution, including JP courts, county courts, district courts, appellate courts, and the two highest courts, are called constitutional courts. Courts that the legislature creates are referred to as statutory courts. The legislature creates all municipal courts, statutory county courts, and probate courts, along with specialized courts, such as veterans courts and juvenile courts.

jurisdiction
the court's sphere of authority

original jurisdiction
the authority to hear the initial case; the evidence and the case record are established in this court

appellate jurisdiction
the authority to hear an appeal from a lower court that has already rendered a decision; an appellate court reviews the court record from the original trial and does not hear new evidence

exclusive jurisdiction
a particular court given the sole right to hear a specific type of case

criminal case
a case in which an individual is charged by the state with violating the law and the state brings the suit

civil case
a case in which an aggrieved party sues for damages claiming that he or she has been wronged by another individual

The end result is a judicial system that is ill defined, confusing, costly, and inefficient. Jurisdiction is often unclear as district courts overlap in many counties in Texas. The state court system is even more confusing since courts often have overlapping original jurisdiction, called concurrent jurisdiction. The distinction between original and appellate jurisdiction is further blurred in Texas, since lower-level courts often do not keep official records, meaning that the appellate court must treat the case as if it were new.

LOCAL TRIAL COURTS

t the local level there are two types of trial courts, each with limited jurisdiction: the municipal courts and JP courts.

Municipal Courts

Municipal courts are courts created by the state legislature for cities in Texas. There are currently 938 municipal courts in the state, with larger cities often having more than one municipal court. Municipal courts have original and exclusive jurisdiction over violations of municipal ordinances—those that typically deal with zoning requirements, fire safety, litter laws, noise violations, traffic, or zoning laws. Municipal courts can impose fines of up to $2,000 for violations of municipal ordinances. In addition, municipal courts have jurisdiction over class C misdemeanors (criminal matters punishable by a fine of $500 or less, with no possible jail time). Municipal courts share jurisdiction over class C misdemeanors with JP courts, which is called concurrent jurisdiction. Typically, if a city police officer issues the citation, then the case is heard in municipal court; citations issued by county officers (such as a sheriff) are heard in the JP court. Municipal courts generally have no civil jurisdiction except in cases involving owners of dangerous dogs. By custom, the municipal courts also perform magistrate functions. As magistrates, municipal courts can issue search and arrest warrants, conduct preliminary hearings, and set bail for more serious crimes. The magistrate functions allow municipal courts to help decrease the workload of higher-level courts. Today, the vast majority of the cases heard in municipal courts, approximately 72 percent, deal with traffic or parking violations.[7]

Appeals from municipal courts are typically heard in county-level courts. If the municipal court is a court of record, then the county-level court exercises appellate jurisdiction. However, most municipal courts, 82 percent, are not courts of record, meaning no official transcript is recorded in cases that are brought before them.[8] Absent an official record, appeals from municipal courts are heard de novo, or with a new trial, in county-level courts.

Municipal judges are typically appointed by city councils to two-year terms. The city council also determines the salary for municipal judges, which varies substantially throughout the state. When the state legislature passes statutes creating municipal courts of record, the statutes require that the judges presiding over those courts be licensed attorneys in the state of Texas. Since most municipal courts are not courts of record, however, most municipalities do not require their judges to be attorneys. In the absence of specific requirements, only 67 percent of all municipal judges graduated college, and only 57 percent are licensed attorneys.[9]

concurrent jurisdiction
a system in which different levels of courts have overlapping jurisdiction or authority to try the same type of case

magistrate functions
the authority to conduct the preliminary procedures in criminal cases, including issuing search and arrest warrants, conducting preliminary hearings, and setting bail for more serious crimes

de novo
to hear an appeal with a new trial in the absence of an official case record

TEXAS KANSAS

While the Texas court system is multilayered and complex as a result of the many different types of courts and courts with concurrent jurisdiction, the court system in Kansas is much less challenging to understand. The Kansas court system contains only four types of courts: municipal, district, a court of appeal, and a supreme court. Compare this to Texas with its municipal courts, JP courts, county courts, district courts, fourteen courts of appeal, and two supreme courts. Unlike in Texas, courts in Kansas typically have exclusive jurisdiction over cases. Thus, jurisdiction in Kansas's court system is much more straightforward than that of Texas.

The lowest level of court in Kansas is the municipal court. As in Texas, municipal courts in Kansas try cases arising from violations of city ordinances, such as traffic violations. Unlike municipal courts in Texas, Kansas municipal courts do not have juries. There are over 370 such courts in Kansas, compared to 938 in Texas. At the next level are district courts, which serve as original jurisdiction courts for violations of state law, both civil and criminal. District courts in Kansas have exclusive jurisdiction over cases involving minors and domestic relations, even when they arise under municipal ordinances; they also hear appeals from municipal courts. Cases at the district level are typically heard by a jury. There are thirty-one district courts, each covering one or more counties in Kansas. Approximately 250 judges serve these courts. District courts in Texas have original jurisdiction over divorces, land title claims, slander, and contested elections, but do not hear appeals from local or county level courts. Compared to Kansas, their jurisdiction is much less clear, since they have concurrent jurisdiction with both JP courts and county courts, and their jurisdiction can vary depending on what other courts are in the area.

The next level of court in Kansas is the court of appeals. Unlike Texas, which has fourteen courts of appeal that hear cases from lower courts in specific geographic areas of Texas, Kansas has a single court that hears appeals from all district courts across the state. The only cases that this court does not hear are cases involving the death penalty and other major felonies. As in Texas, these cases are appealed from the district court directly to the state's highest court. Significant questions of rights of citizens and powers of the state government are appealed directly from the district court to the Kansas Supreme Court as well. A total of fourteen judges sit on the Kansas Court of Appeals, hearing cases in panels that usually comprise three judges.

Kansas also differs from Texas in that it has a single supreme court. The Kansas Supreme Court hears both civil and criminal appeals from the Kansas Court of Appeals as well as death penalty cases appealed from district court. The court contains seven justices who sit en banc, meaning all seven justices sit for all cases that the court hears. The court also hears appeals on decisions made by administrative agencies of the state. For example, a decision by the Kansas Department of Health and Environment to deny a child from a low-income family access to the state's insurance program would be appealed to the Kansas Supreme Court.

Kansas Court System

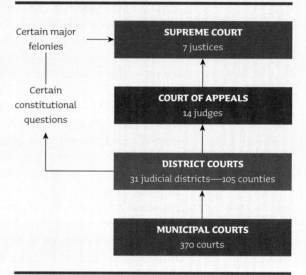

The figure in this box shows the organizational structure of the Kansas court system. Compare this box with "How Texas Government Works" on pages 200–201, which illustrates the complexity of the Texas court system.

What is the benefit to a judicial system where the courts exercise exclusive jurisdiction?

⭐ **CRITICAL THINKING**

Is Texas better served by having two high courts, or is Kansas better served by having a single court?

⭐ **CRITICAL THINKING**

Justice of the Peace Courts

Counties are divided into precincts, and JP courts are precinct-level courts. The number of judicial precincts in a county depends on the size of the county's population. Currently, there are 802 JP courts. The constitution provides that each county have between one and eight JP courts:

> JP courts shall have original jurisdiction in criminal matters of misdemeanor cases punishable by fine only, exclusive jurisdiction in civil matters where the amount in controversy is two hundred dollars or less, and such other jurisdiction as may be provided by law. Justices of the peace shall be ex officio notaries public.[10]

Like municipal courts, JP courts are courts of original jurisdiction only. Civil jurisdiction of JP courts extends to cases that involve $10,000 or less. This jurisdiction is exclusive in civil matters where the amount in controversy is $200 or less and concurrent with county and district courts in cases involving amounts of $200 to $10,000. The criminal jurisdiction extends to class C misdemeanor cases, concurrent with municipal courts. Approximately 81 percent of all JP court cases are criminal cases, and 86 percent of these are traffic cases.[11]

The presiding officials of JP courts perform marriages, act as notaries public, and serve as magistrates for higher courts. JP courts also serve as small claims courts. JP courts are not courts of record, so any appeals are heard de novo in the county courts. One of the more interesting responsibilities of the JP is to act as coroner in counties without medical examiners. The job of the coroner is to determine cause of death, even though justices do not generally have any medical training. Since Texas has only thirteen medical examiner's offices in the state, the JP is often left to determine the cause of death and sign the death certificate. This put Texas in the national news when, in 2016, U.S. Supreme Court Justice Antonin Scalia died while visiting a ranch in a remote part of West Texas. When the local JPs were deemed too far away, a county judge verified the death over the phone. The use of JPs as coroners fills the gap between a handful of medical examiners and the remotest parts of the state.

Justices of the peace, like other Texas judges, are elected in partisan elections to four-year terms. Lack of educational requirements is one of the most consistent criticisms of JP courts. There are no formal qualifications for JP judges. As of 2017, 95 percent of JP judges graduated from high school, 34 percent graduated from college, and a mere 8 percent are licensed attorneys.[12] Salaries vary significantly by county and are set by the county commissioners court.

How does electing judges with limited qualifications affect justice in Texas?

⭐ **CRITICAL THINKING**

COUNTY-LEVEL TRIAL COURTS

Trial courts are courts where evidence is introduced, testimony is presented, and a verdict is rendered. The trial-level court is generally where the original case record is established. At the county level, there are three types of trial courts: constitutional county courts, county courts at law, and statutory probate courts.

Constitutional County Courts

The constitution requires a county-level court in each of the 254 counties in the state; these courts are sometimes referred to as constitutional county courts. The constitution mandates that:

There shall be established in each county in this State a County Court, which shall be a court of record; and there shall be elected in each county, by the qualified voters, a County Judge, who shall be well informed in the law of the State; shall be a conservator of the peace, and shall hold his office for four years, and until his successor shall be elected and qualified.[13]

Constitutional county courts exercise exclusive and original jurisdiction over misdemeanors where fines can exceed $500 and jail time can be imposed (class A and class B misdemeanors). Original civil jurisdiction extends to cases involving amounts from $200 to $10,000 and is concurrent with JP courts and district courts. These courts can also exercise probate jurisdiction, including cases involving guardianship, uncontested wills, and determination of mental competency. Constitutional county courts also possess appellate jurisdiction over cases from either the JP or municipal courts. Appeals from these courts are by and large de novo, which increases the workload of the state court system.

Most of the cases heard in constitutional county courts are criminal cases (51 percent), with another 19 percent of the cases dealing with probate issues. Since the

TEXAS Legends

Judge Roy Bean

Roy Bean, a legend of the Texas judiciary, reflects the lax nature of frontier justice in Texas and the state's fondness for amateur justice. Born in Kentucky in 1825, Bean had no formal education that prepared him for service as a judge. However, Pecos County needed a judge, one that would allow the Texas Rangers to clean up the area without having to make a 400-mile round trip to the nearest courthouse and jail. Thus, for lack of a better choice, Roy Bean became a Texas judge on August 2, 1882.

Prior to serving as a judge, Bean's legal experience had been on the other side of the bench and cell door. After fleeing legal trouble in several states, Bean settled briefly in San Diego, California, where his brother was mayor. In 1852, he was arrested and charged with assault with intent to murder for participating in a duel over a woman. He eventually escaped from jail, allegedly using a knife smuggled inside some tamales to dig himself out. After relocating to San Gabriel, California, Bean became involved

in another duel in 1854, killing a romantic rival. This time, he didn't appear before a court; instead, he narrowly escaped lynching by his victim's friends.

In Texas, Bean supplemented his judicial earnings by running a bar called Jersey Lilly, named for Lillie Langtry, a British actress with whom Bean was obsessed. (Contrary to rumor, Langtry, Texas, was not named after her. The city, originally named Eagle Nest, was renamed in honor of George Langtry, an area railroad engineer.)

While occasionally voted out of office, Bean mostly held on to the position of judge until his retirement in 1902. Despite his lack of training and his possession of only one law book, Bean's justice was creative. Because he lacked a jail, he favored setting fines over requiring jail time when sentencing. Horse thieves were generally released after payment of a fine if the horses were returned. When a man died after falling off a bridge, Bean discovered that the man had been carrying forty dollars and a concealed pistol. He

fined the man forty dollars for carrying a concealed weapon and used the money to pay for his funeral expenses.

Bean's legal and bartending careers complemented each other nicely; Bean required that jurors buy drinks at his saloon during every judicial recess. His most famous venture came in 1896 when he organized a world championship boxing title match. Since boxing matches were illegal in Texas, Judge Bean arranged for Bob Fitzsimmons and Peter Maher to box on an island in the Rio Grande. While the fight lasted fewer than two minutes, word of the match and its promoter spread throughout the United States.

Portraying himself as the "law west of the Pecos," Judge Roy Bean epitomized Texas justice in its infancy. He died in 1903, but his legacy continues to shape the town of Langtry. In 1939, the state of Texas purchased Bean's Jersey Lilly, making it the centerpiece of Langtry's Old West tourism business, and it has had over 1 million visitors to date.

HOW TEXAS GOVERNMENT WORKS

State Court Structure

State's Highest Appellate Courts

Supreme Court
(1 court, 9 justices)

Statewide Jurisdiction

• Final appellate jurisdiction in civil cases and juvenile cases

Court of Criminal Appeals
(1 court, 9 justices)

Statewide Jurisdiction

• Final appellate jurisdiction in criminal cases

Civil Appeals

Criminal Appeals

Death Sentence Appeals

State's Intermediate Appellate Courts

Courts of Appeals
(14 courts, 80 justices)

Regional Jurisdiction

• Intermediate appeals from trial courts in their respective courts of appeals districts

County-Level Appeals

State's Trial Courts of General and Special Jurisdiction

District Courts
(469 courts, 469 judges)

360 districts containing one county
98 districts containing more than one county

Jurisdiction

• Original jurisdiction in civil actions over $200,* divorce, title to land, contested elections

• Original jurisdiction in felony criminal matters

• Juvenile matters

• Thirteen district courts are designated criminal district courts; some others are directed to give preference to certain specialized areas

*The dollar amount is currently unclear.

Source: Office of Court Administration, "Annual Statistical Report for the Texas Judiciary, Fiscal Year 2017," accessed July 2, 2018, http://www.txcourts.gov/media/1441398/ar-fy-17-final.pdf.

Texas Local Court Structure

County-Level Courts
(516 courts, 516 judges)

Constitutional County Courts (254 courts, one court in each county)	Statutory County Courts (244 courts, established in 89 counties, plus one multi-county court)	Statutory Probate Courts (18 courts, established in 10 counties)
Jurisdiction	**Jurisdiction**	**Jurisdiction**
• Original jurisdiction in civil actions between $200 and $10,000	• All civil, criminal, original, and appellate actions prescribed by law for constitutional county courts	• Limited primarily to probate matters
• Probate (contested matters may be transferred to District Court)	• Jurisdiction over civil matters up to $200,000 (some courts may have higher maximum jurisdiction amount)	
• Exclusive original jurisdiction over misdemeanors with fines greater than $500 or jail sentence		
• Juvenile matters		
• Appeals de novo from lower courts or on the record from municipal courts of record		

County Trial Courts of Limited Jurisdiction

Justice Courts[1]
(802 courts, 802 judges)

(Established in precincts within each county)

Jurisdiction

- Civil actions of not more than $10,000
- Small claims
- Criminal misdemeanors punishable by fine only (no confinement)
- Magistrate functions

Municipal Courts[2]
(938 courts, 1,326 judges)

Jurisdiction

- Criminal misdemeanors punishable by fine only (no confinement)
- Exclusive original jurisdiction over municipal ordinance criminal cases[3]
- Limited civil jurisdiction
- Magistrate functions

Local Trial Courts of Limited Jurisdiction

1. All justice courts and most municipal courts are not courts of record. Appeals from these courts are by trial de novo in the county-level courts, and in some instances in the district courts.

2. Some municipal courts are courts of record; appeals from those courts are taken on the record to the county-level courts.

3. An offense that arises under a municipal ordinance is punishable by a fine not to exceed: (1) $2,000 for ordinances that govern fire safety, zoning, and public health or (2) $500 for all others.

workload of JP and municipal courts is, for the most part, traffic related, and county-level courts tend to be overworked, lawyers often use a strategy of appealing traffic offenses in an attempt to get these cases dismissed. Often traffic appeals are not a priority in an overworked county-level court. Constitutional county courts are required to be courts of record.

The constitution requires county judges to be "well informed of the law," which has been interpreted to mean that they do not have to have law degrees. Currently, 65 percent of county judges have graduated from college and 16 percent are licensed attorneys.[14] In addition to judicial responsibilities, the county judge exercises administrative duties over the county government. In larger counties, the county judge often works exclusively on administrative duties and acts as a judge in name only. In those counties, the legislature creates additional county-level courts, called county courts at law, for judicial duties. County judges are elected in partisan elections to four-year terms. Their salaries vary by county and are set by the county commissioners.

What are the costs of having an overly complex judiciary?

⭐ CRITICAL THINKING

County Courts at Law and Statutory Probate Courts

Statutory courts, also called county courts at law, are so called because they are created by legislative statute rather than by the constitution. In larger counties where the constitutional courts are occupied with administration of the county, the legislature establishes statutory courts to handle judicial responsibilities. There are 244 statutory county courts, concentrated in larger counties. Jurisdiction of these courts varies greatly according to the statute but is generally consistent with part or all of the constitutional county courts. However, civil jurisdiction in county courts at law extends to controversies up to $200,000, which is concurrent with district courts. When the legislature creates a statutory court, it can confer civil, criminal, or probate jurisdiction, or all of these on that court. The legislature has created eighteen statutory probate courts in ten of the state's largest metropolitan areas. These courts deal exclusively with **probate** cases, which involve legally validating and administering a will. Like constitutional county courts, all statutory courts are courts of record. Statutory judges are elected in partisan elections to four-year terms. They are required to be trained in the law, and all of these judges have law degrees.[15]

probate
the process by which a deceased person's will is validated by the court, and can be legally executed

DISTRICT COURTS (STATE-LEVEL TRIAL COURTS)

State-level trial courts in Texas are called district courts. Every county in the state is served by at least one district court, while more populated areas often have several. There are 469 total district courts in the state. According to the Texas Constitution, district court jurisdiction is as follows:

> Exclusive, appellate, and original jurisdiction of all actions, proceedings, and remedies, except in cases where exclusive, appellate, or original jurisdiction may be conferred by this Constitution or other law on some other court, tribunal, or administrative body.[16]

The jurisdiction of district courts can vary according to the jurisdiction of other courts in a particular area. In some areas of the state, there are family district courts, criminal district courts, or civil district courts. District courts are granted civil jurisdiction in cases involving $200 or more (concurrent with JP and county courts). District courts exercise original jurisdiction over divorces, land title claims, slander, and contested elections. Their original criminal jurisdiction includes all felony cases. They also have jurisdiction over misdemeanors when the case involves a government official. Forty percent of cases in district courts are matters of family law, and another 31 percent are drug cases. In a district court, those charged with crimes can choose between having a judge decide the case and having a jury trial. In 2017, district cases decided before a judge resulted in a 95 percent conviction rate, whereas district cases decided by a jury resulted in a 79 percent conviction rate. Appeals from district courts are heard at the courts of appeals, with the exception of death penalty cases, which go directly to the Texas Court of Criminal Appeals.

A district court judge must be at least twenty-five years of age, a resident of Texas, and a U.S. citizen. In addition, the judge must be a licensed attorney with at least four years' experience as either an attorney or a judge. District judges are elected in partisan elections to four-year terms.

APPELLATE COURTS

The Texas judiciary has two levels of appellate courts. Initial appeals are heard at the courts of appeals. After the initial appeal, cases can be appealed to one of the state's two highest courts. Texas is one of only two states with two high courts (the other is Oklahoma). The Supreme Court of Texas hears final appeals in civil cases, and the Texas Court of Criminal Appeals hears final appeals in criminal cases. Appellate judges must be at least thirty-five years of age, residents of the state, and U.S. citizens. An appellate judge is also required to have at least ten years' experience as a lawyer or a judge and be a licensed attorney. Judges are elected in partisan elections for six-year terms.

Appellate courts hear cases from lower courts based on the evidence and testimony presented at the original trial. Appellate courts do not hear new evidence or new witnesses. Instead, judges make their decisions based on a review of the written record from the original trial, as well as from written briefs and oral arguments by attorneys arguing legal or procedural points. Upon reviewing the written briefs and oral testimony, appellate courts can **affirm**, or uphold, the lower court's decision or **reverse** part or all of it. In addition, appellate courts can **remand** the case, or send it back to the lower court, typically with instructions from the appellate court.

All appellate courts in Texas decide cases with a majority vote. The appellate court may then issue an opinion or written explanation of the decision. A **majority opinion** represents the official decision and the reasoning behind that decision. A **concurring opinion** can be written by justices who agree with the decision but disagree with the reasoning of the majority. Justices who disagree with the decision in a case can write a **dissenting opinion**. A **per curiam opinion** is an opinion of the court as a whole without individual judges signing the opinion.

Courts of Appeals (Intermediate Appellate Courts)

The state is divided into fourteen districts with a court of appeal in each district. Each court of appeal has between three and thirteen judges, including one chief justice. With the exception of death penalty cases, all civil and criminal appeals from the county and district courts are initially heard in the courts of appeals. Typically an appeal is heard

affirm
appellate court upholds the lower court's decision

reverse
appellate court rejects the lower court's decision

remand
appellate court sends the case back to the lower court to be reexamined

majority opinion
the official decision and reasoning of the appellate court

concurring opinion
an opinion written by a justice who agrees with the decision but not with the reasoning of the court

dissenting opinion
an opinion written by a justice who disagrees with the decision of the court

per curiam opinion
an opinion issued by the court as a whole; these opinions are not signed by individual justices

en banc

an appeal that is heard by the entire court of appeals rather than by a select panel of judges

Is Texas better served by having two high courts?

⭐ **CRITICAL THINKING**

by a panel of three judges, although they can be heard **en banc**, meaning by the entire court. A panel of judges, rather than a single judge, is traditionally used in appeals courts since there are no juries. Including more than one judge limits the power of any single judge. A majority vote by the panel can affirm, reverse, or modify a lower court's decision, or it can remand the case to the trial court for reconsideration. Civil cases heard by a court of appeals can be appealed to the Supreme Court of Texas, while criminal cases can be appealed to the Texas Court of Criminal Appeals.

Texas's Highest Appellate Courts: The Court of Criminal Appeals and the Supreme Court

Texas has two high courts to hear appeals from the courts of appeals: the Supreme Court of Texas, for final civil appeals, and the Texas Court of Criminal Appeals, for final criminal appeals, including automatic appeals in death penalty cases.

Texas Court of Criminal Appeals

The Texas Court of Criminal Appeals is the state's highest court for criminal appeals. Like other appellate courts, the Texas Court of Criminal Appeals hears no new evidence and is limited to reviewing the trial record and briefs filed by the lawyers in the case. The court consists of nine judges, including a presiding judge. The court can hear appeals in panels of three judges, though most cases are heard en banc. Cases are decided by majority vote. While the court has some discretionary authority over the cases it hears, the vast majority of its caseload comprises cases that receive mandatory review. In 2017, 81 percent of all the cases heard by the court were mandatory and nearly all of those cases involved petitions for the court to issue a writ of habeas corpus for felony convictions. In this case, a writ of habeas corpus petitions the court to throw out the conviction, typically on the grounds the defendants' rights were violated. Appeals in death penalty cases are mandatory for the court, and the court typically considers such cases en banc. Although arguably the most important job of the Texas Court of Criminal Appeals, death penalty cases represented less than 1 percent of their caseload in 2017. This court is also the final court of appeals for questions involving

The Texas Court of Criminal Appeals, headed by presiding judge Sharon Keller (front, center), is the court of last resort for criminal cases in the state.

Courtesy of the Texas Court of Criminal Appeals

state law and the state constitution. However, cases involving questions of federal law or the U.S. Constitution can ultimately be appealed to the U.S. Supreme Court.

Supreme Court of Texas

The Supreme Court of Texas is the highest court in the state for civil cases. It consists of eight justices plus one chief justice. If the supreme court chooses to review a case from the lower courts, that case is decided by majority vote. The supreme court also makes procedural rules for lower courts, approves new law schools in the state, and appoints members of the Board of Legal Examiners. It monitors the caseload of the fourteen appellate courts and can move cases between those courts to equalize the caseload. As with the Texas Court of Criminal Appeals, the cases from the Supreme Court of Texas can be appealed to the U.S. Supreme Court if they concern issues of federal law or the U.S. Constitution.

JUDICIAL SELECTION

One of the more controversial aspects of the Texas judicial system is the selection process for judges. With the exception of most municipal judges, judges in Texas are elected in partisan contests. To become a judge, a candidate must raise enough money to win the election. Once on the bench, judges need to continue raising money for reelection. Texas is one of only nine states that select judges for their highest courts with partisan elections, and it is one of only nine states that choose their appellate judges with partisan elections.[17]

The argument for the direct election of judges is rooted in democracy. Texans, who tend to distrust government, prefer to keep choice at the individual level. Unfortunately, there are several impediments to actual popular influence on judicial elections. Foremost, Texans are faced with a long ballot that features almost every major office in the state. In addition to choosing the country's president and the state's national congressional delegation, Texans elect members of the plural executive and other bureaucratic offices, members of the state legislature, and a wide range of judicial offices in the state. So, in 2010, Texas's biggest county, Harris County, had "the largest ballot in the country," which featured eighty-eight races.[18] In that election, every single race was contested, including some involving third-party candidates. One of the main reasons for the length of the ballot was the election of judges, as judicial races made up 81 percent of the Harris County ballot.[19] In the 2016 primary election, one Houston poll worker noted that some voters took thirty minutes to fill out their individual ballots.[20] The democratic charge for the average Texan can be overwhelming, and the issues in judicial selection are often relatively subtle. The result is that most Texans simply do not pay much attention to judicial campaigns. Rather than voting based on judicial competency, voting in judicial elections often amounts to little more than voting on the basis of partisan labels, image, or name recognition.

Historically, Texans have responded to the long ballot with straight-ticket voting. Straight-ticket voting allows a voter to check a single box to vote for all candidates from one party. In 2016, the Texas legislature voted to eliminate the straight-ticket voting option beginning in 2020. Texas judges will still be identified by party, but now Texans will have to check each individual race. Texans tend to be the least familiar with judicial candidates, and are often unable to name any of the judges on the state supreme court.

What are the implications of a long ballot for society?

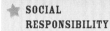
SOCIAL RESPONSIBILITY

If Texas continues to elect judges, do Texans have a responsibility to be informed of the people running for judgeships?

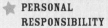
PERSONAL RESPONSIBILITY

straight-ticket voting the practice of selecting all the candidates for office who are running under a party label simply by checking off a single box marked with the party label

Historically, faced with a long ballot and limited knowledge of judicial credentials, Texans often rely on **name recognition** when deciding whom to vote for or vote on names they recognize or even names that simply sound respectable. For example, in the 2016 Republican primary, relative unknown Scott Walker, who shares his name with a well-known Wisconsin governor, won a surprise victory over Sid Harle, "who has been widely praised as one of the greatest legal advocates in the state."[21]

Texas votes are often driven by party rather than candidates' legal expertise or judicial experience. Critics of partisan judicial elections argue that running based on partisan credentials undermines the perception of impartiality that is at the core of the legal system. Moreover, for many Texans, party labels are less meaningful in judicial races than in other political contests. For instance, Republican judges tend to favor businesses and defendants in civil trials, whereas Democratic judges are more likely to side with plaintiffs. According to a study by Court Watch, the Republican Texas Supreme Court overturned jury decisions in favor of corporate interests 74 percent of the time.[22] Thus, one unintended consequence of partisan voting has been a significant contraction of individual rights in the state—rights most conservative Texans still vigorously seek to protect.

Democratic selection of judges has been hampered by a tendency for judicial candidates to run unopposed. This is exacerbated by the long campaign season, which creates disincentives to oppose incumbents, according to retired Supreme Court of Texas chief justice Thomas Phillips:

> Filing deadline is a year before you take office if you win, and so a lot of lawyers feel like they really don't want to be running against the judge—it's not going to be the best way to attract business for a year. So most of our rural judges, literally a majority, have never been opposed.[23]

The long ballot and the tendency for candidates to run unopposed means the perception of popular control on the judiciary remains largely a myth. Moreover, the **incumbency advantage** in Texas is especially robust. Most incumbents run unopposed since they tend to win reelection, which undermines the effectiveness of popular control on the judiciary.

Judicial Appointment

Although judicial selection in Texas technically occurs with partisan elections, a large number of judges initially reach the bench through appointment. The constitution provides that the governor can appoint judges to fill vacancies on district and appellate courts, including Texas's highest courts. These gubernatorial appointments must be confirmed by the Texas Senate. In 2017, 44 percent of judges on the state's highest court and 56 percent judges on Texas's intermediate appellate court originally assumed office by gubernatorial appointment. The fact that the governor ends up making judicial appointments in a system that purports to leave the choice of judges up to the voters

The 2010 Houston ballot was one of the longest in the state. A long ballot creates a high democratic cost, as citizens are overwhelmed with all the offices they have to elect.

name recognition
making a voting choice based on familiarity with or previous recognition of a candidate's name

incumbency advantage
the advantage enjoyed by the incumbent candidate, or current officeholder, in elections; the advantage is based on greater visibility, a proven record of public service, and often better access to resources

is an important aspect of the judicial election system in Texas. A significant number of the judges chosen by the governor may run unopposed in future elections where voters essentially rubberstamp the governor's choice. The vast majority of judges, once in office, continue to win reelection. For example, in the 2014–2015 biennium, 71 percent of judges left office by resigning or choosing not to seek reelection.[24]

Judicial Removal

There are three primary means of removing judges in Texas. The most common means is for the voters not to reelect a judge in the next election. About 20 percent of judges who left office in the 2014–2015 biennium lost their bids for reelection.[25] In addition, the constitution grants the Supreme Court

Judicial campaign signs line the side of the road. Most judges in the state of Texas are elected rather than appointed.

of Texas the power to remove district judges for incompetence, official misconduct, or negligence. Judges can also be impeached by a two-thirds vote in the Texas House and tried in the Texas Senate, with a two-thirds vote necessary for conviction.

To investigate allegations of misconduct, a 1965 amendment to the state's constitution established the Commission on Judicial Conduct. The thirteen-member commission consists of one member from each of the following court levels: municipal, JP, county court at law, constitutional county, district, and appellate; two lawyers appointed by the state bar; and five citizens appointed by the governor who are neither attorneys nor judges. According to the Texas Constitution, judicial misconduct includes the following:

> Willful or persistent violation of rules promulgated by the Supreme Court of Texas, incompetence in performing the duties of the office, willful violation of the Code of Judicial Conduct, or willful or persistent conduct that is clearly inconsistent with the proper performance of his duties or casts public discredit upon the judiciary or administration of justice.[26]

If the commission finds a judge guilty of misconduct, it can issue a public or private censure or warning, issue an official reprimand, order additional information, or make a recommendation that the judge be removed from office.

Of the 1,333 cases disposed of by the Commission on Judicial Conduct in 2017, 53 percent evidenced no judicial misconduct.[27] Some level of discipline, including public sanction, additional education, or suspension, was ordered in fifty-one cases. In eight cases, the judges agreed to voluntarily resign to avoid disciplinary action. The extent of judicial misconduct in the state is largely unknown, since nearly all cases brought before the commission are dismissed without any public record—96 percent between 2008 and 2011.[28] The nature of the commission's work was significantly altered in 2012 when the commission refused to cooperate with a Sunset Advisory Commission audit. The Commission on Judicial Conduct claimed that its proceedings were confidential,

To what extent is there popular influence on the state judiciary?

⭐ **CRITICAL THINKING**

TEXAS *Legends*

Raul A. Gonzalez Jr.

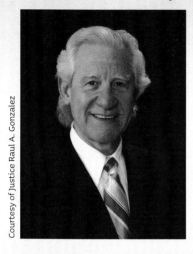

Courtesy of Justice Raul A. Gonzalez

Raul A. Gonzalez Jr. rose from picking crops alongside his parents to serving on the state's highest court. Along the way, he earned a reputation as a hardworking judge who was never afraid to speak his mind. Whether picking crops or serving on the Supreme Court of Texas, Gonzalez was determined to do whatever it took to achieve success, once stating, "I've got big hands and a big drive to succeed."[i]

Born in 1940, Gonzalez grew up in Weslaco, Texas, near the Mexican border. After graduating from the University of Texas (UT) in 1963, he earned a law degree at the University of Houston in 1966. Gonzalez first became a judge in 1978, and over the course of his career won the support of both Republican and Democratic governors. Governor Dolph Briscoe appointed him to fill a vacancy in the 103rd District Court, and he was elected to serve a full term the following November. Gonzalez was soon appointed associate justice on the Thirteenth Court of Appeals by Governor Bill Clements in 1981, becoming the first Hispanic to serve in that role. One year later he won election to a four-year term in the same position, but before it could be completed, Governor Mark White in 1984 appointed him to the Supreme Court of Texas, and Gonzalez made history by becoming the court's first Hispanic member. Gonzalez became the first Hispanic elected for statewide office in Texas in 1986, when he won election to the Texas Supreme Court.

Gonzalez's focus and determination paid off in 1994 when he was challenged in the Democratic primary by Rene Haas, a well-funded challenger backed by powerful trial lawyer groups. While Gonzalez eventually won the nomination and reelection, the race was one of the most expensive judicial races in the state's history, with almost $4.5 million spent by both sides. Like many veterans of the state's highest court, Gonzales is uneasy with the expensive, partisan races that the state uses to elect judges.

Gonzalez's service on the court was more than a symbolic victory for Hispanics. As one historian of the court noted, "not merely a Latino in surname, Gonzalez's life embodied the struggle of Mexican Americans."[ii] The court had a justice who understood the general challenges of being Hispanic in Texas. As a child he had labored in the fields with his family. As the son of parents born in Mexico, Gonzalez understood the plight of immigrants as they found their way in a new country. Gonzalez brought more than a Hispanic surname to the court; he brought a broad understanding of the needs and challenges of a population moving from the fields of South Texas to the highest posts in the state's justice system.

---

i. Robert B. Gilbreath and D. Todd Smith, "An Interview with Former Justice Raul A. Gonzalez," *Appellate Advocate*, 2004, www.hptylaw.com/media/article/24_rob.pdf, 25.

ii. James L. Haley, *The Texas Supreme Court: A Narrative History, 1836–1986* (Austin: University of Texas Press, 2013), Kindle edition, 214.

What are the costs and benefits of keeping investigations of judicial misconduct confidential?

⭐ **SOCIAL RESPONSIBILITY**

even to state auditors. As attorney general, Greg Abbott issued an opinion upholding the idea that the commission can act with complete confidentiality.

TEXAS JUDGES

Historically, the Texas judiciary, like other elected positions, was dominated by Democrats. Since the late 1980s, however, Republicans have dominated, holding all the judicial posts on the state highest courts. In addition, judges in Texas today come largely from upper-middle-class families. Recall that microcosm theory (introduced in Chapter 3) stipulates that true representation occurs only when the makeup of a society's institutions mirrors the makeup of the society as a whole. Although women account for about half of the Texas population, the vast majority of judges in the state are men. In terms of the lower courts, female judges constitute 38 percent of municipal, 39 percent of JP judges, 10 percent of constitutional county court judges, and 31 percent of statutory court judges. Women do not fare much better in state-level courts, composing 35 percent of district judges and 46 percent of judges serving on the intermediate appellate courts. In the state's highest courts, females currently compose 22 percent of the Supreme Court of Texas and 44 percent of the Texas Court of Criminal Appeals.

The racial distribution of the courts is even more troublesome, particularly given the overwhelmingly low representation of both Hispanics and African Americans in the judicial system (see Figure 6.1). Hispanics make up approximately 39.1 percent of the state's population, but their representation in the Texas judiciary remains well below this figure. Hispanic representation on lower-level courts ranges from a mere 9 percent on county courts to 20 percent on JP courts. Hispanics compose 17 percent of the judges at the district level and 15 percent at the appellate level. There is currently one Hispanic on both of the state's high courts. Although the Hispanic population in Texas is almost equal to the state's white population, the only Hispanics to sit on the state's highest courts were first appointed by the governor. Elsa Alcala, who was appointed to serve on the Texas Court of Criminal Appeals by Rick Perry

Justice Darlene Byrne, of the Family Court at Law, handles a child custody case in her courtroom in Austin, Texas.

and unanimously confirmed by the Texas Senate, announced she would not seek reelection, since her "Hispanic unfamiliar surname" would be a liability.[29] In fact, a group of lawyers and voters are currently challenging the statewide election of judges to the state's highest courts in federal court, arguing that it dilutes the voting power of Hispanic voters.

Although African Americans compose about 12.6 percent of the state's population, African American judges remain relatively rare in lower-level courts in the state, never reaching more than 6 percent of any court. There are currently no African Americans on either of the state's high courts. For Asian and Native American groups in the state, representation in the court system is nearly nonexistent.

The issue of minority representation in Texas remains a major concern, and the manner in which judges are selected is a starting point for critics of the system. Some minorities charge that partisan elections and the dominance of the Republican Party in the state make it difficult for minorities to get elected. According to this perspective, merely removing party labels from the ballot would increase the likelihood that a minority candidate would be elected to the judiciary.

The nature of judicial districts may also prove to be an important impediment to minority representation in the state. Large counties in particular often treat the county as one district and then elect quite a few judges from that district as a whole. Minorities

Why does minority representation in the state judiciary matter?

⭐ SOCIAL RESPONSIBILITY

Which level of court is the most representative; which is the least representative? Why?

⭐ EMPIRICAL AND QUANTITATIVE

at-large election
an election in which a city or county is treated as a single district and candidates are elected from the entire district as a whole

contend that using an **at-large election** system to select district and county judges makes it less likely that minorities will win those positions. (See Chapter 11 for more information on at-large elections.)

An alternative to at-large election rules is **cumulative voting**. Cumulative voting allows voters to take the total number of positions in a district and divide their votes for those positions among a few candidates or even give all of those votes to a single

FIGURE 6.1 Diversity in the Texas Judiciary

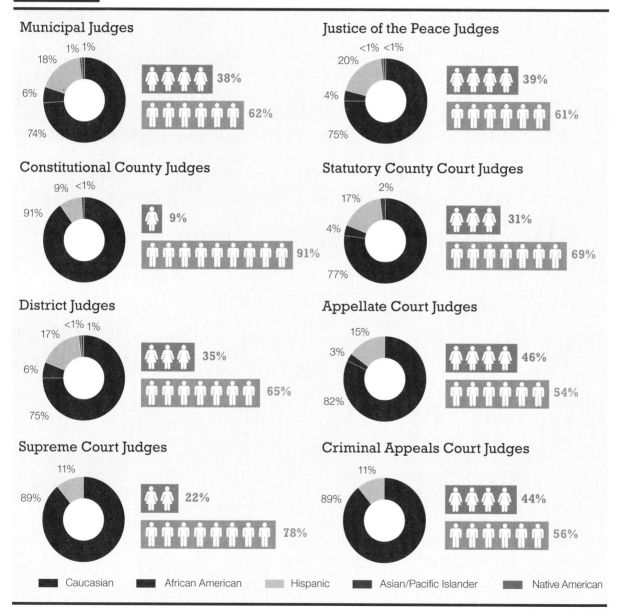

Source: Compiled by the authors from the Annual Statistical Report for the Texas Judiciary, 2017.

candidate. For example, in Harris County, which has sixty-six district judges, a voter could vote for sixty-six candidates, or vote sixty-six times for one candidate. This system would allow voters to concentrate all of their votes in a district on one or two candidates, increasing the likelihood that a minority candidate will be elected. (See Chapter 11 for a discussion of cumulative voting.)

PROBLEMS WITH THE TEXAS JUDICIARY

As we can see, one of the most significant problems of the Texas judiciary is the lack of a coherent court structure. Overlapping and unclear jurisdictions, coupled with ad hoc creation of courts to serve specific functions or particular geographic areas, produce one of the most cumbersome legal systems in the country. In 1991, the nonprofit Texas Research League concluded that the "Texas court system really is not a system at all. Indeed, Texas's courts are fragmented without a central focus and are going along in their own direction and at their own pace."[30] Two years later, a commission established by the Supreme Court of Texas concluded that "the Texas trial court system, complex from its inception, has become ever more confusing as ad hoc responses are devised to meet the needs of an urban, industrialized society. No one person understands or can hope to understand all the nuances and intricacies of Texas's thousands of trial courts."[31] The lack of a clear system is exacerbated by problems in the lower courts, which operate without official records and thereby create the need to hear appellate cases de novo.

In addition, a significant number of judges in the state have no legal training. The lack of trained judges at the city and county levels creates real questions about the quality of justice meted out across the state. Texas judges are infamous in the nation for sleeping during hearings; making inappropriate comments; cleaning their guns during trials; using a stun belt to shock a defendant who won't answer questions; and employing sock puppets to communicate to the court. In rural areas where medical examiners are not available, the use of JP judges, most of whom have no medical training, to determine cause of death undermines the validity of death certificates. When judges perform duties absent professional training or expertise, it serves to further undermine the credibility of the entire judicial system to the people of Texas.

Perhaps even more detrimental is the need for judicial candidates to raise campaign funds to compete for judicial positions. This opens the Texas judiciary up to potential influence by campaign donors. Since the average Texan doesn't pay attention to judicial races, special interests, big business, and attorneys are the primary source of campaign contributions. The appearance of influence is particularly troubling in Supreme Court of Texas races, where campaign costs can exceed $1 million. Between 2000 and 2010, Texas was fifth in the nation for fund-raising by Supreme Court candidates, with the biggest donors being the law firms and businesses that regularly appeared before the court.[32] Justices on the state's supreme court raise a considerable amount of money to pay for those campaigns, and law firms and businesses make sizable contributions, sometimes as large as six figures. The Texas Supreme Court's tendency to overturn jury verdicts that favor those firms generates real questions regarding the court's independence. In a recent example, Leonel Garza's family sued the pharmaceutical company Merck after he died suddenly while taking one of their painkillers, Vioxx. A jury ruled in favor of Garza, and his family was awarded $7.75 million. Merck appealed to the state's supreme court, which overturned the verdict. The justices who sided with Merck

How might cumulative voting change representation in the state's judiciary?

★ CRITICAL THINKING

cumulative voting a system that allows voters to take the total number of positions to be selected in a district and concentrate their votes among one or a few candidates

had all received at least $85,000 in contributions from Merck's law firm in the preceding decade.[33] Notably, races for seats on criminal courts are much less likely to attract large donors. The Texas Court of Criminal Appeals raised around one-hundredth the amount the state's supreme court raised, since, as one critic put it, bottom lines of companies are unlikely to be damaged by criminal proceeding but "are affected by whether a large scale lawsuit is upheld or overturned."[34]

Since the mid-1980s, every chief justice on the Texas Supreme Court has supported abolishing partisan elections in judicial contests. The need to raise substantial sums of money to compete in a judicial race in the state opens judges up to undue influence, or at the very least, the potential for such influence. Justices on the state's highest court are quick to point out that the appearance of influence is sufficient to warrant change. The 85th legislative session saw legislation that would require judges who have received more than $2,500 from a party to recuse themselves. However, this legislation died in committee. The result is the perception, if not the reality, that the judicial system in Texas protects businesses at the expense of the individual.

Texas lawmakers continue to resist eliminating partisan elections completely. However, the 1995 Judicial Campaign Fairness Act represents an attempt to partially limit the influence of money in judicial campaigns. The purpose of the act is to limit contributions of individual donors to no more than $5,000 per election for statewide judicial campaigns. The primary election and general election are treated as separate elections, meaning that an individual can contribute up to $5,000 to a candidate in each election. Contributions from law firms are limited to $30,000 per election for judicial candidates. Additionally, candidates are prevented from receiving more than $300,000 total from a political action committee (see full discussion of political action committees in Chapter 10). A candidate's participation in the limits set by the Judicial Campaign Fairness Act is voluntary. Any candidate who consents to these voluntary limits can advertise their compliance in their campaign materials and media.

ALTERNATIVE SYSTEMS OF JUDICIAL SELECTION: APPOINTMENT AND MERIT

A simple alternative to the current Texas system is to remove partisan labels from judicial candidates. Judges would continue to run in competitive elections but would more likely be assessed based on their merits. Thirteen states currently use nonpartisan elections to select their top judges. Other states use some variation of appointment or merit systems to choose judges.

Appointment

At the national level, undue influence of the federal judiciary is stymied by lifetime appointment of judges. The advantage of appointing judges rather than electing them is that the judiciary can remain independent and free from political pressure. Five states use a gubernatorial appointment model to select their state's appellate and supreme court justices.

Merit System

One alternative to electing judges in partisan elections is use of a merit system to select judges. Sometimes referred to as the Missouri Plan, the merit system is seen

FEDERALISM IN Action

Civil Forfeiture

Civil forfeiture occurs when the government takes cash and property from someone who is suspected of wrongdoing. Unlike criminal forfeiture, in which the government obtains assets after an individual is convicted of a crime, civil forfeiture does not require a guilty verdict. Texas has some of the most permissive civil forfeiture laws in the country, allowing local law enforcement to keep up to 70 percent of any assets seized and requiring only a preponderance of evidence standard in order to seize the property. In many cases, once the property has been seized, formal charges are never actually brought against the accused and the burden is on the accused to prove their innocence in order to reclaim their property. In civil forfeiture cases, individuals do not get a state-appointed attorney, so they must bear the cost of attempting to reclaim their property. Texas brings in an average of $41.5 million in civil forfeitures every year.[i]

Critics of civil forfeiture charge that it deprives individuals of their property without due process, places the burden of proof on the accused rather than the government, and creates perverse incentives for law enforcement agencies that reap the financial rewards of forfeiture. One of the worst examples of abuse comes from the town of Tenaha, Texas. In 2007, James Morrow was pulled over in Tenaha, Texas, for driving too close to the white line. The police officer asked Morrow if he had any cash, and when Morrow indicated he had $3,900 in the car, the cash was seized and Morrow was arrested. Morrow was told that if he didn't agree to forfeit the money, he would be charged with money laundering.[ii] Tenaha, a small town in East Texas, sits on a highway often used to drive to casinos in Louisiana. The town routinely pulled over cars with out-of-town plates, threatened to charge the drivers with money laundering, and even threatened to place their children in foster care in order to coerce them into signing over their assets. The town took an estimated $3 million between 2006 and 2008, while the district attorney gave out "light sentences to those caught with drugs, or laundered money, in exchange for seizing their assets."[iii] For the average law enforcement agency in Texas, civil forfeitures amount to around 14 percent of its budget, and the money has been used for everything from trips to Hawaii, visits to casinos, and a margarita machine.[iv]

Civil forfeiture can also occur in a federal case. If a local official seizes property in pursuant of a federal crime, the federal government allows the local office to keep up to 80 percent of value of assets taken. The forfeiture can allow local officials to circumvent state and local laws to pursue the federal case. This type of civil forfeiture, called equitable sharing, has netted Texas nearly $25 million a year on average from the Department of Justice and another $12 million from the Treasury Department.[v] From a federalist perspective, equitable sharing allows local law enforcement agencies cooperating with federal agencies to do an end run around state laws. For example, in states where marijuana has been legalized, citizens can still be charged by local law enforcement of violating laws if the local police are working with a federal agency. Legislators in Texas have proposed several bills to limit civil forfeiture in recent sessions, but so far have been reluctant to limit the practice. The state does require that the attorney general publish the annual forfeiture totals. Two states, New Mexico and Nebraska, have now banned civil forfeiture. Other states have passed laws requiring a conviction for forfeiture to occur and disallowing local agencies from profiting from such forfeitures.

How do the current civil forfeiture laws limit individual rights?

 CRITICAL THINKING

Should local law enforcement be able to circumvent state laws in pursuit of civil forfeiture?

 CRITICAL THINKING

---

i. Dick Carpenter, Lisa Knepper, Angela Erikson, and Jennifer McDonald, *Policing for Profit: The Abuse of Civil Asset Forfeiture*, 2nd ed., http://ij.org/wp-content/uploads/2015/11/policing-for-profit-2nd-edition.pdf.

ii. James Drew, "East Texas Town Faces Civil Rights Lawsuit without Government Help," *Dallas Morning News*, November 26, 2010, http://www.dallasnews.com/news/crime/headlines/20100122-East-Texas-DA-faces-civil-rights-860.ece.

iii. Forest Wilder, "When it Comes to Civil Forfeiture in Texas, You Have No Property Rights," *Dallas Observer*, May 12, 2014, https://www.texasobserver.org/preying-innocent-civil-forfeiture.

iv. Nick Sibilla, "Cops in Texas Seize Millions by Policing for Profit," Forbes, June 5, 2014, http://www.forbes.com/sites/instituteforjustice/2014/06/05/cops-in-texas-seize-millions-by-policing-for-profit/#141cff123aa8.

v. Carpenter et al., *Policing for Profit*.

as a happy medium between electing and appointing judges. This system relies on a panel of experts in an attempt to balance the need for judicial independence with the accountability associated with electing judges. The panel of experts typically includes judges, lawyers, legal scholars, and sometimes ordinary citizens who are charged with reviewing potential candidates and developing a list of potential judicial nominees. The governor then nominates judicial candidates from the list. In the most common version of the merit system the judges face periodic retention elections and are able to keep their jobs as long as a majority of voters approve. A retention election allows voters to vote to retain or remove a judge without the competition that would make campaigning and, thus, fund-raising necessary. Moreover, recent research shows that using the merit system to select a state's judicial candidates is more likely to result in minority and female judges than other methods of judicial selection.[35] Twenty-one states use some version of a merit system to select judges for their highest courts.

TABLE 6.1 Texas Penal Code: Offenses with Graded Penalties

Offense Level	Examples	Maximum Punishment	Court with Original Jurisdiction
Capital felony	Capital murder; murder of a child	State execution or life in prison without parole	District court; automatic appeal to Texas Court of Criminal Appeals
First-degree felony	Murder (except under the influence of sudden passion); aggravated sexual assault	Life in prison and $10,000 fine	District court
Second-degree felony	Manslaughter; aggravated kidnapping; online solicitation of a minor	Imprisonment for 2 to 20 years and $10,000 fine	District court
Third-degree felony	Kidnapping; child abandonment; terrorist threat; discharging a firearm toward a building; theft of more than $30,000 but less than $150,000	Imprisonment for 2 to 10 years and $10,000 fine	District court
State jail felony (fourth-degree felony)	Criminally negligent homicide; dog fighting; theft of more than $2,500 but less than $30,000	Imprisonment for 180 days to 2 years and $10,000 fine	District court
Class A misdemeanor	Online impersonation; possession of marijuana (more than 2 oz. but less than 4 oz.); attending a dog fight; theft of more than $750 but less than $2,500	Confinement in jail for 1 year and $4,000 fine	Constitutional county court/county court at law
Class B misdemeanor	Driving while intoxicated; indecent exposure; possession of marijuana (2 oz. or less); theft of more than $100 but less than $750	Confinement in jail for 180 days and $2,000 fine	Constitutional county court/county court at law
Class C misdemeanor	Public intoxication; possession of alcohol in automobile; theft of less than $100	$500 fine	Justice of the peace (JP) court/municipal court

Source: Data from Office of the Attorney General, "Penal Code Offenses by Punishment Range: Including Updates from the 85th Legislative Session," March 2018, https://www.texasattorneygeneral.gov/files/cj/penalcode.pdf.

Although the United States has long embraced the necessity of an independent judiciary, and many Texans support changing the current process in the state, the businesses and professions that benefit most from the current system continue to forcefully—and effectively—oppose change. Proposals to abandon partisan elections have "passed the State Senate four times . . . it's never been allowed to have a vote in committee much less on the floor of the House of Representatives, and that's due to the power of political parties."[36] For now, there appears to be sufficient political opposition to thwart the adoption of a merit-based judicial selection system.

CRIMINAL JUSTICE IN TEXAS

Texas political culture tends to favor politicians who are tough on crime and thus a criminal justice system that metes out swift and severe punishment. Criminal cases deal with individuals charged with violating criminal laws or committing crimes that, although there may be a victim, are technically crimes against the state. The lawyer that makes the state's case is called a **prosecutor**. The **criminal defendant** is the person charged with committing a crime. In criminal cases, a twelve-member **grand jury** determines whether there is enough evidence to warrant a trial, unless the defendant waives his or her right to a grand jury. If nine of the twelve jurors on the grand jury agree that there is sufficient evidence to warrant a trial, the grand jury issues an **indictment**. An indictment is issued in the form of a true bill, which details the defendant and the alleged crime, formally charges the individual with the crime, and initiates the case. If the grand jury determines there is not enough evidence to warrant a trial, the grand jury returns no bill, there is no trial, and the accused goes free.

Criminal law ranges from traffic violations to robbery, sexual assault, or murder. The criminal justice system in Texas is based on a graded penal code in which harsher punishments are awarded for more serious crimes and for repeat offenders (see Table 6.1). Lower-level criminal violations, such as public intoxication or resisting arrest, are referred to as misdemeanors. The severity of misdemeanors is distinguished in Texas law by three classes, with class C misdemeanors being the least severe and class A misdemeanors representing the most serious. Misdemeanors are typically nonviolent crimes and involve fines or prison sentences of less than a year. Felonies are more severe criminal offenses, such as sexual assault or murder, and entail harsher punishments. The capital felony is the most serious transgression which could result in a death sentence. First-degree, second-degree, third-degree, and state jail felonies compose the lesser felonies, distinguished by the seriousness of the crime. The Texas penal code also provides for **enhanced penalties**, which allow offenders to be charged with the next higher degree or class in certain cases, including when the accused is a repeat offender. So, for example, a person arrested for driving while intoxicated (DWI) would be charged with a class B misdemeanor, whereas a person arrested for a second DWI could be charged with a class A misdemeanor.

According to Texas law, the defendant has a right to a jury trial, although that right can be waived in all criminal cases except death penalty cases. The trial jury, also called the **petit jury**, determines whether or not an individual is guilty. Petit juries are guaranteed in criminal cases and may also be used in civil cases if requested by either party. In the criminal case, the defendant enters a plea of either guilty, not guilty, or nolo contendere (literally, no contest). The prosecutor will present the state's case by entering

prosecutor
a lawyer who represents the government and brings a case in criminal trials

criminal defendant
a person charged with committing a crime

grand jury
a panel of twelve jurors that reviews evidence, determines whether there is sufficient evidence to bring a trial, and either issues an indictment or returns no bill

indictment
a document (in the form of a true bill) issued by a grand jury that indicates there is enough evidence to warrant a trial

enhanced penalties
a penal code provision that specifies conditions under which the accused can be charged with a higher-degree offense

petit jury
a trial jury; jurors attend a trial, listen to evidence, and determine whether a defendant is innocent or guilty

evidence and witness testimony into the official record. The defendant can challenge the evidence and testimony. The accused is presumed innocent, and the state must prove that the individual is guilty. In order to determine guilt, the burden of proof in a criminal trial is based on whether the state submitted sufficient evidence to prove the guilt of the accused **beyond a reasonable doubt**. Texas requires a unanimous verdict in criminal cases. If an individual is found guilty in a criminal case, the punishment can include fines paid to the government, imprisonment, or, in certain cases, the death penalty. If found guilty, convicted criminals can appeal the conviction to the appellate courts. Death penalty cases are automatically reviewed by the Texas Court of Criminal Appeals.

Civil cases, by contrast, involve disputes between individuals. The **plaintiff** in a civil case claims to have been wronged by another party, the **civil defendant**. Civil law cases often involve breach of contract and other contractual disputes, but they also include family law issues, such as divorce, neglect, custody, or probate questions. Civil cases also include tort cases claiming personal injury or property damage. Civil cases can be tried by a jury or, if both parties agree, can simply be decided by the judge. The burden of proof for civil cases is based on a much lower standard than for criminal cases. To win a civil case, a plaintiff merely has to show through a **preponderance of evidence** that the defendant is likely to be guilty. Whereas criminal cases may result in jail time, plaintiffs in civil cases may ask the court to redress the grievance or award monetary damages. **Compensatory damages** are monetary awards designed to compensate the injured party for loss associated with medical bills or lost income due to missed work. If the court wants to send a message, it may also award **punitive damages**, which are typically larger monetary awards intended to punish the defendant. Decisions in civil cases can be appealed to the appellate courts.

WINNERS AND LOSERS

The Texas judiciary is fraught with impediments to justice for the average Texan. The system is overly complex and unnecessarily confusing, making it difficult for most Texans to understand. In addition, electing many judges creates an excessive cost to the average voter. As a result, it is not surprising that democratic mechanisms to protect individuals in the state provide very little protection in practice. Ironically, Texans resist change in the judiciary largely because they distrust government and want to guard their individual rights, such as the right to choose judges. But more often than not, that right buckles under the weight of the system's complexity and the regular onslaught of judicial campaigning. Texans are simply overwhelmed by the number of public officials they must elect. Texans—fiercely protective of their independence and their influence on government—in the end relinquish their authority over judicial selection to big donors in judicial campaigns. Those big donors are perceived to exert undue influence on government and individual Texans lose. While Texas juries often rule in favor of those who have suffered individual harm or face losing their property at the hands of business interests in the state, judges often do not. The state's Supreme Court consistently overturns jury verdicts in favor of big businesses at the expense of individual rights.

Minorities also lose. Minorities hold few judicial posts in a state that is tough on crime, has one of the largest prison populations in the country, and is rarely sympathetic to appeals. The judicial system in Texas remains dominated by middle- and

beyond a reasonable doubt
the standard burden of proof necessary to find a defendant guilty in a criminal trial; the defendant is presumed innocent

plaintiff
the party who is bringing a civil suit and claiming to have been wronged

civil defendant
the party alleged to have committed the wrong at issue in a civil suit

preponderance of evidence
the burden of proof in a civil case, which is lower than that in a criminal case; the plaintiff must show merely that the defendant is likely to have committed the wrong

compensatory damages
monetary damages designed to compensate the injured party

punitive damages
larger monetary awards designed to punish the defendant and, perhaps, send a message to the larger society

Does a Supreme Court that consistently overturns jury decisions undermine perceptions of justice in Texas?

⭐ **CRITICAL THINKING**

upper-middle-class white males, even as the state's population becomes more diverse. The current system of electing judges, particularly in partisan elections, ensures that minorities will continue to be underrepresented in Texas. The perception that the Texas judicial system is unjust endures for good reason: the prevailing system harms all Texans.

Does the high number of judicial seats that citizens are asked to vote for have a chilling effect on an informed electorate?

⭐ CRITICAL THINKING

CONCLUSION

Justice in Texas is a complicated affair. The judicial system is complex and confusing, and jurisdiction is often unclear. The lack of lower-level courts of record often requires cases that are appealed to be tried as if new. While Texans proclaim a strong desire for justice, in fact the current judicial system rarely satisfies. In order to develop a more responsive judicial system, Texans may need to reevaluate how their preferences are represented in the current system. For instance, the preference of voters to retain control of judicial selection via the long ballot entails a high cost. The overwhelming job of selecting nearly all of the judges in the state comes with very little payoff. More generally, Texans' resistance to change means that the state's judiciary, like other of its institutions, evolves in a piecemeal manner. The result is a system that in many ways no longer makes sense for the state.

SAGE edge™
for CQ Press

Want a better grade?

Get the tools you need to sharpen your study skills. Access practice quizzes, eFlashcards, video, and multimedia at **edge.sagepub.com/collier6e**.

KEY TERMS

affirm (p. 203)
appellate jurisdiction (p. 195)
at-large election (p. 210)
beyond a reasonable doubt (p. 216)
civil case (p. 195)
civil defendant (p. 216)
compensatory damages (p. 216)
concurrent jurisdiction (p. 196)
concurring opinion (p. 203)
criminal case (p. 195)
criminal defendant (p. 215)

cumulative voting (p. 211)
de novo (p. 196)
dissenting opinion (p. 203)
en banc (p. 204)
enhanced penalties (p. 215)
exclusive jurisdiction (p. 195)
grand jury (p. 215)
incumbency advantage (p. 206)
indictment (p. 215)
judicial federalism (p. 194)
jurisdiction (p. 195)

(Continued)

magistrate functions (p. 196)
majority opinion (p. 203)
name recognition (p. 206)
original jurisdiction (p. 195)
per curiam opinion (p. 203)
petit jury (p. 215)
plaintiff (p. 216)

preponderance of evidence (p. 216)
probate (p. 202)
prosecutor (p. 215)
punitive damages (p. 216)
remand (p. 203)
reverse (p. 203)
straight-ticket voting (p. 205)

ACTIVE LEARNING

- Break into groups of five. Given the expense of judicial elections and lack of diversity in judges' backgrounds, should reforms of the state judicial system be considered? What changes would your group propose? **Teamwork**

- Design a meme that depicts an aspect of the Texas judiciary. **Communication**

CHAPTER REVIEW

1. Jurisdiction of courts in Texas is defined by
   _____.
   a. whether the court hears civil or criminal cases
   b. whether the case is original or on appeal
   c. geographical location
   d. all of these

2. Most municipal courts _____.
   a. are courts of record
   b. hear felony cases
   c. are not courts of record
   d. are overburdened with civil cases

3. Which court hears cases related to city ordinances and class C misdemeanors?
   a. Texas Supreme Court
   b. statutory county court
   c. justice of the peace Court
   d. municipal court

4. Most justices of the peace _____.
   a. have not graduated from high school
   b. have not graduated from college
   c. are practicing attorneys
   d. have a medical license

5. District courts hear more _____ than other types of cases.

   a. family law

   b. drug cases

   c. DWIs

   d. traffic citations

6. Which court hears all death penalty appeals?

   a. Texas District Court

   b. Texas Court of Appeals

   c. Texas Court of Criminal Appeals

   d. Texas Supreme Court

7. According to the Constitution, Texas uses which method to select their judges?

   a. appointment by the governor

   b. appointment by the legislature

   c. election in partisan elections

   d. election in nonpartisan elections

8. Most judicial candidates in Texas _____.

   a. run unopposed

   b. have to run in highly competitive elections

   c. run against one other candidate

   d. are chosen by the president

9. Civil forfeiture occurs when local law enforcement seizes an individual's property _____.

   a. while waiting for a criminal trial

   b. without charging them with a crime

   c. after they have been convicted of a crime

   d. after they were imprisoned by the federal government

10. A grand jury hears evidence in a case and _____.

   a. decides guilt or innocence

   b. determines what the punishment should be

   c. decides which court will hear the case

   d. determines whether a trial is warranted

CHAPTER 7

TEXAS-SIZED JUSTICE

H ow old should a person be to be held accountable for their actions? Ancient English common law held that a boy reached adulthood for the purposes of the law at age seven. As a result, it was acceptable under English common law in medieval times to execute a boy of eight or ten for a crime that carried the death penalty as punishment for those guilty of a crime. In the court case *In re Gault* (1967), the U.S. Supreme Court accepted a minimum age of fourteen for individuals to be treated as an adult for trial.[1] In the realm of American civil society, a person is mature enough to operate and drive an automobile with his or her own license at the age of fourteen to eighteen, depending on the state. One can serve in the military and vote at age eighteen, and alcoholic beverages may be purchased and consumed at age twenty-one. In contrast, modern neuroscience finds that the human brain does not reach full development until about the age of twenty-five. The last areas to develop in the brain are those associated with moral reasoning and judgment.

The issue of age and mental capacity is a critical issue in criminal justice policy, both in the United States and in the state of Texas. Debates surround the heinousness of certain crimes, such as premeditated murder; the appropriate forms of punishment (e.g., the death penalty); and the ability of those accused and found guilty of understanding the seriousness of their actions and the consequences of their actions. In 1643, the first youth was executed in the English colonies in Plymouth, Massachusetts. Between 1642 and 1973, almost 350 youth were executed in the United States, with half of those executed being between ten and fifteen years of age.[2] Since 1973, Texas has executed twelve minors, all age seventeen when the crime they committed occurred.

Nikki Kahn/*The Washington Post* via Getty Images

The death penalty enjoys widespread support in Texas, and the state leads the nation in the execution of criminals annually. Texas in the past has executed women, juveniles, and the mentally ill.

None were executed prior to the age of twenty-four years of age. The U.S. Supreme Court has stepped into this issue several times in the last decade or so, forcing states to drop support for the juvenile death penalty and eliminating life without parole sentences for minors. This has forced the state of Texas to change its laws and practices, including what to do with individuals like Scottie Forcey, who was convicted of shooting and killing Karen Burke, a convenience store clerk, in Alvarado in 2009. Forcey at the time was seventeen when he committed the crime and received a life sentence without parole. He will now be eligible for parole after forty years in prison.[3]

A related issue is the willingness of Texas to execute the mentally ill. Consider Scott Panetti, who has been on death row in Texas for over twenty years for killing his mother-in-law and father-in-law in 1992. Panetti has been hospitalized numerous times over a forty-year period for delusions, hallucinations, and schizophrenia. He represented himself at his initial trial in 1995 and demanded testimony from Jesus Christ, John F. Kennedy, and the pope. Panetti believes the gold filling in his mouth is a Bluetooth device, that singer-actress Selena Gomez is his daughter, and that CNN reporter Wolf Blitzer has his prison ID card.[4] Panetti's case eventually went to the U.S. Supreme Court, in which the high court ruled that criminal defendants sentenced to death cannot be executed unless they understand the reason for their imminent death.[5] However, the court left it up to the states to determine when an inmate has a "rational understanding" of their punishment. While Texas courts have attempted to interpret the language broadly, the state continues to hold Panetti in a kind of limbo, detaining Panetti yet denying any funding to provide an up-to-date examination of his mental competency. Panetti's case is headed back to the Fifth Circuit Court of Appeals in New Orleans to determine whether Texas must provide an up-to-date mental health screening before moving forward with the attempt to execute Panetti. As of June 2018, Panetti remains on death row in Texas.[6]

In 2016, Texas executed Adam Kelly Ward, who at the age of twenty-four shot and killed a housing and zoning code officer in Commerce, Texas. The officer, Michael Walker, was taking pictures of Ward's house after numerous violations of city housing codes, including unsheltered storage. Ward had a history of mental illness dating back to age six and court-related mental cases from age fifteen. Whether or not Ward truly possessed a rational understanding of his actions is still a matter of debate.[7] At least two other men on death row in Texas have a history of mental illness, including Robert Robertson, who killed his two-year-old daughter in 2003. Robertson has a well-documented brain injury that his lawyers contend leaves him with lapses in mental capacity. Robertson lacks the usual history of diagnosed mental illness associated with other cases.[8]

These cases, and those involving juveniles, raise the disturbing question of when a person is accountable for a crime and the extent to which one's own awareness of the implications and consequences of one's actions matter. In this chapter, to explore the nature of justice in Texas, we will start by discussing the state's political culture regarding justice and how that culture translates into policies, including Texans' historical support for get-tough-on-crime approaches to justice. We will explore some of those policies through the lens of justice. Specifically, we examine incarceration in Texas, privatization of prisons, and rights of the accused. We will then explore the effect of tort reform on issues of justice and conclude the chapter with a discussion of the death penalty.

JUSTICE IN TEXAS

Texas has a reputation of being tough on crime, and most Texans prefer it that way. Even before Texas was independent, keeping the peace along the frontier was fraught with danger. Comanches, Wichitas, Caddos, and other native tribes faced loss of land and bison as Anglo settlements increased rapidly. The frontier with Mexico was marked by continuous fights with Texas, particularly along the Texas-Mexico border. Life on the frontier was hard, and settlers suffered their share of horse and cattle theft and stagecoach robberies. Settlements in Texas lacked much in the way of formal law enforcement. Instead, early Texans learned to fend for themselves, a way of life referred to as frontier justice. It is not surprising, then, that the political culture that developed in Texas is one that is tough on crime and romanticizes vigilante justice. The belief that people should be able to take care of problems on their own persists in modern-day Texas. Public opinion and juries in the state tend to be sympathetic toward people who take the law into their own hands to protect their families and belongings and shoot trespassers on their property. Texans still by and large distrust government and believe that sometimes for justice to prevail, individuals have to act. As a lobbyist for the Texas District and County Attorneys Association stated, "There's an unwritten rule in Texas courthouses: it ain't against the law to kill a son of a bitch."[9] The resulting political culture has clear implications for the policies of the state, including widespread support for permissive gun laws, the castle doctrine, and the death penalty. Texans also enact tough and unyielding laws, criminalizing more behaviors than other states. A tendency persists to assume the accused are likely guilty, and Texans tend to be weary of complaints about prison conditions or a prisoner's access to health care. The result is that Texas today has one of the largest incarceration rates in the country and the world.

Texans' fascination with the need to punish the guilty reflects a tradition of emphasis on several approaches to criminal justice. This need to punish the guilty often focuses on retribution theory—punishment is justified because it is deserved. This eye-for-an-eye approach sees the rules of society as reflecting a moral order; violating those rules requires one to be punished.[10] Retribution approaches the criminal justice system as one of vengeance; with social factors like income and education or relative deprivation being irrelevant, so, too, is social change.[11] According to this approach, some people are just bad and must be punished. Circumstances are irrelevant. A related approach is "just deserts," in which the purpose of criminal justice systems is to inflict a punishment proportionate to the crime, with a scale or gradation of offenses, the most serious punishments being associated with the most serious crimes.[12] As a corollary, punishment should be consistent across all offenders, with no or little room to take into account the individual circumstances of the crime or the person found guilty. Another theory is that of incapacitation—that is, removing the guilty from society to prevent additional crimes. This theory holds that a certain number of those found guilty will ultimately be "career criminals" and should be removed from society for long periods.[13] These approaches stand in contrast to the theory of rehabilitation: that the purpose of the criminal justice system is to reform the guilty into understanding why his or her conduct was wrong to prevent the offender from returning to a life of crime. Crime is seen as a symptom of a social disease that requires treatment.[14] This theory requires punishments to be tailored to the individual offender and focuses on interactions between the individual and the wider society. A final theory is that of restorative justice, which views crime as a fundamental break in society and in the offender and is based on an overriding need to heal victims, communities, and offenders. All three must be actively involved in the justice process to bring closure to all three while simultaneously placing the offender in society, under social control, with appropriate social support.[15]

INCARCERATION IN TEXAS

Everything is bigger in Texas, including the prison system. Several things contribute to the Texas-sized prison system. First, Texas, and more broadly, U.S. political culture, emphasizes retribution and just deserts approaches to criminal justice. These approaches lead to a higher number of acts that are criminalized compared to other countries and, as a result, high incarceration rates. According to the International Center for Prison Studies, the United States currently holds more prisoners than any other country in the world.[16] America imprisons more of its citizens than any other country, both in absolute terms and after controlling for population. The United States contains around 4 percent of the world's population yet holds 25 percent of the world's prisoners.[17] In 2016, Texas had the seventh-highest per capita incarceration rate in the country, with 157,000 persons in prison. That same year, the Texas prison incarceration rate was 584 inmates per 100,000 residents.[18] If Texas were a country, it would rank third in incarceration rates, below El Salvador and Turkmenistan; Texas would be above Iran, China, Cuba, and Russia.[19] Texas further has over 375,000

MAP 7.1 Incarceration Rates by State

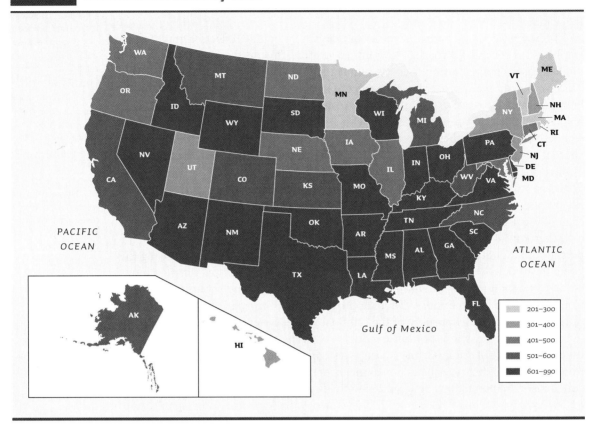

Note: Rates are per 100,000 people.

Source: Bureau of Justice Statistics, Annual Surveys of Probation and Parole, Deaths in Custody Reporting Program, and National Prisoner Statistics program, 2016; and U.S. Census Bureau, unpublished U.S. resident population estimates within jurisdiction on January 1, 2017.

people on probation and another 111,000 on parole.[20] This high rate of incarceration reflects our political culture's demands for politicians and policies to be tough on crime. The result is Texas policies that tend to criminalize more types of behavior and favor tougher sentences than policies of other states. In addition, as the state's population has increased over the last two decades, stiffer immigration and drug laws have combined with this growth to produce a glut of potential prisoners. However, in the past decade all of these rates have fallen, in part because Texas has reformed its criminal justice system and other states have increased their rates of incarceration.

In the 1970s, President Richard Nixon declared a war on drugs, created the national Drug Enforcement Agency, and called for a national policy to address drugs in the United States. In the 1980s, the war on drugs intensified during the administration of President Ronald Reagan. Texas's preference to be tough on crime meant that the state was eager to follow suit. The Texas Legislature responded by adopting stiffer antidrug laws, harsher penalties for possession, and stricter guidelines for probation and parole.[21] The war on drugs directly led to a proliferation of people incarcerated in the state.

Why do southern states have higher rates of incarceration?

★ **CRITICAL THINKING**

In the last few years, many states have legalized marijuana possession, for recreational and medical uses. Currently, possession of even a small amount of marijuana in the state is illegal. While Texans are increasingly in favor of some form of decriminalization, the Texas Legislature resists. In a 2017 *Texas Tribune* poll, 30 percent of Texans favored legalization for medicinal purposes, 32 percent favored legalization for small amounts, and another 21 percent supported legalization of any amount of marijuana.[22] The number of Texans who favor some form of legalization is now 83 percent, with only 17 percent being opposed to legalization under any circumstance. This suggests that Texas, like the rest of the country, may be on the road to legalization.

Why has public opinion shifted on the issue of legalization of marijuana?

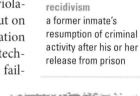 **CRITICAL THINKING**

Shift to Rehabilitation

At the start of the 2007 legislative session, Texas faced the need for over 17,000 new prison beds, projected to cost $1.6 billion by 2012. State representative Jerry Madden (R–Richardson) and state senator John Whitmire (D–Austin) proposed a shift from Texas's traditional approach of punishment and toward rehabilitation, which requires the allocation of resources to alternative types of treatment and correction. In that year, the legislature allocated money for 8,000 treatment beds, allowing judges to place some offenders in much-needed drug, alcohol, and mental health treatment facilities instead.[23]

A majority of those in Texas prisons are nonviolent offenders, and the new approach opened up halfway houses and created specialty courts, such as drug courts and veterans courts, which replaced a long prison stay with mandatory treatment. The new approach also gives the courts leeway in dealing with technical probation violations, which traditionally come with mandatory imprisonment. An individual put on probation, either after serving time or in lieu of serving time, can have that probation revoked if he or she is charged with a new offense or for a technical violation. A technical violation could include missing a meeting with the assigned parole officer, fail-

recidivism
a former inmate's resumption of criminal activity after his or her release from prison

ing to pay a parole fee, or failing a drug test. The underlying idea of the change in approach is that expensive prison stays should be reserved for violent criminals rather than those with substance abuse problems. Rather than focusing on punishment, the shift toward rehabilitation is designed to reduce recidivism, or a return to crime after release from prison. The Texas mantra of being tough on crime was being replaced with the idea of being smart on crime.

The shift from punishment-focused criminal justice to a focus on rehabilitation came at a time when Texas was facing budget shortfalls and an ever-expanding prison population. The traditional approach of building more prisons, while popular, has been costly to the state

LAWRENCE JENKINS/KRT/Newscom

As Texas shifts from its tradition of retribution and incapacitation of offenders, one alternative for drug-related cases is rehabilitation through state-run or private drug counseling and addiction treatment.

over the years. The proposal of Madden and Whitmire cost the state a $241 million investment in alternative treatment courts and facilities rather than $1.6 billion in new prisons.[24] This policy position, untenable a little more than a decade ago, is now seen as fiscally responsible. As Madden put it, "one thing we have in prison: they get free room, free board and free healthcare, at the public's expense. And if we put them out there as a person who has a job and working and living with their family, they may end up paying taxes."[25]

The change in approach has already saved Texans millions of dollars at a time when the legislature is looking for places to cut spending. In 2016, it cost Texas roughly $20,275 a year to imprison someone, not including medical expenses—about $55.55 a day.[26] A study by the Legislative Budget Board in 2018 found that supervised probation costs only $1.06 a day.[27] The shift toward more probation and parole has allowed Texas to contain its spending on criminal justice, allowing balanced budgets to be somewhat easier for the legislature to achieve in recent years.

Prison Conditions

The political culture in Texas tends to be largely unsympathetic to the conditions inside the state's prisons. Texas has long had the reputation of having one of the toughest prison systems in the country. A 1972 case filed on behalf of Texas prisoners represented a second change that enlarged the prison system. In *Ruiz v. Estelle*, Texas prisoner David Ruiz filed a handwritten suit against the director of the Department of Corrections, William Estelle, claiming that conditions in the Texas prison constituted cruel and unusual punishment. Ruiz alleged harsh conditions including lack of adequate medical care, overcrowded conditions, and insufficient security. At that time, Texas prisons were undermanned and prison staff often relied on prisoners to keep other prisoners in line. Judge William Wayne Justice eventually ruled that conditions in Texas prisons were unconstitutional and ordered federal oversight of Texas prisons for the next two decades. The *Ruiz* decision ushered in the most sweeping prison reforms to date. One of the state's responses to this federal intervention was to spend the 1980s building prisons. At the time *Ruiz* was filed, Texas had eighteen prisons. Today there are over 110 prisons in the state, including parole facilities and medical facilities dedicated just to inmates. The prison population ballooned, however, and Texas could not build prisons fast enough.

For decades, prisoners in the state have complained about the lack of timely medical care. As the state faced a budget crisis in recent years, the 82nd Texas Legislature cut spending on prisoner health care by $75 million. At the same time, health care costs have been rising, both in general and for Texas prisons, particularly as the prison population is graying. Elderly prisoners, who make up 8 percent of the prison population, take 30 percent of the health care budget. This has led some in Texas to advocate releasing them. The chair of the Texas Senate Committee on Criminal Justice, John Whitmire, has argued that "in times of fiscal concern, we're spending $1 million or more on inmates who can't get out of bed or are really sick individuals. It's just nuts."[28] Nonetheless, the Texas Board of Pardons and Paroles has so far been reluctant to consider this option for most aging prisoners.

Another long-term complaint has been the lack of air-conditioning in most Texas prisons. Of Texas's state prisons, only twenty-one of them are completely air-conditioned.

TEXAS *Legends*

The Texas Rangers

Bettmann Collection/Getty Images

The iconic Texas Rangers vividly illustrate the power of a state's legends both inside and beyond its own borders. The Texas Rangers have become a defining symbol of law enforcement, originally galloping through serials such as *The Lone Ranger*. They were featured in early radio and television programs and in the movies, where they were played by Western stars such as Roy Rogers, Gene Autry, and Tex Ritter. Long after the early Western stars rode off into the sunset, the Texas Rangers have continued to capture the imagination of viewers across the country on shows such as *Walker, Texas Ranger* and in movies such as *Man of the House*, starring Chuck Norris and Tommy Lee Jones.

The Rangers can trace their origins back to Stephen F. Austin, who first referred to the citizens asked to protect his settlements as "rangers" because they had to range over the countryside. The Rangers became an official extension of the temporary government of Texas in 1835 when they were called upon to protect the frontier during the Texas Revolution.

While they have been generally revered, the Rangers' image has suffered from time to time. When Sam Houston wanted to move the state's capital out of Austin, the two Rangers who went to Austin to retrieve the archives met resistance from the local citizens and returned with their horses' manes and tails shaved. In 1918, Governor William P. Hobby allegedly used the Rangers to suppress voter turnout for James Ferguson in South Texas during that year's Democratic primary. During the 1932 election, the Texas Rangers made the mistake of backing Governor Ross Sterling. When Miriam "Ma" Ferguson won office, she retaliated by firing the entire force of forty-eight Rangers and replacing them with 2,300 "special" Rangers, many of whom were criminals. The legislature responded by authorizing the hiring of just thirty-two Rangers, leaving Texas virtually unprotected as Bonnie Parker and Clyde Barrow (the infamous Bonnie and Clyde) roamed the state robbing banks. The Rangers' image was further tainted when they were accused of being instruments of discrimination and intimidation against Tejanos. Captain Leander McNelly, whose tactics included piling the bodies of dead Mexican rustlers in the Brownsville town square, made the Rangers particularly unpopular among Tejanos in the 1870s.

The Rangers' image today combines independence with law and order—qualities on which all Texans can agree. While the details of the story vary, a common tale depicting the Rangers' uncanny abilities involves citizens of a town who called for a company of Rangers to stop a prizefight. When the local people arrived at the train station to greet the twenty Rangers they had anticipated would be needed to quell the expected riot, they were disappointed to see just one Ranger get off the train: legendary Ranger captain Bill McDonald. When the citizens' disappointment over the arrival of only a single Ranger became evident, McDonald responded by saying, "Hell! Ain't I enough? There's only one prize-fight!"[i] Since that time, "One riot, one Ranger" has been a common slogan associated with the Rangers.

Today, the Texas Rangers are a highly professional and modern law enforcement organization that has been part of the Department of Public Safety since 1935. Perhaps less colorful than many of their predecessors—and their television and cinema image—today's Rangers are trained to meet the demands of a high-tech state. The Rangers include 144 commissioned officers, twenty-four noncommissioned administrative support personnel, a forensic artist, and a fiscal analyst. Rangers assist local law enforcement with criminal investigations, help with the suppression of major disturbances, and conduct special investigations. While twenty-first-century Texas Rangers may look little like their predecessors, they still abide by the creed set down by Captain McDonald: "No man in the wrong can stand up against a fellow that's in the right and keeps on a-comin."[ii]

---

i. Texas Department of Public Safety, "Silver Stars and Six Guns," accessed June 14, 2018, www.txdps.state.tx.us/TexasRangers/silverstars.htm.

ii. Ibid.

Most prisons in Texas do not have air-conditioning in the cells. This means that prisoners are held in their cells even when the temperature reaches triple digits, without windows and without any means of escaping the heat. Prison officials' records indicate that the heat index in prisons can top 150 degrees in the summer, which is dangerous for both the prisoners and the prison staff. After four inmates died of heat-related illnesses in 2011, a 2012 lawsuit was filed in federal courts arguing that the conditions are inhumane. In 2014, the state installed coolers in seven of its prisons, though state officials continued to assert that heat in the prisons poses no threat to inmates. Some prisons received fans. By 2016, reports indicated that 70 percent of Texas's prisons still lacked air-conditioning. The U.S. Fifth Circuit Court of Appeals in New Orleans signaled that the lack of air-conditioning was a form of cruel and unusual punishment in a case related to Louisiana's infamous Angola Prison.[29] At the impetus of federal district court judge Keith Ellison, the state government and a group of prisoners who sued the state under the "cruel and unusual punishment" clause of the Eighth Amendment came to an agreement that will commit the state to air-conditioning state prisons.[30]

Texas prisons have also received national attention for having some of the highest instances of prison rape in the country. Although compiling good data on prison rape is notoriously difficult, as inmates are often threatened if they report rape, in 2014, Texas ranked in the top five in the U.S. in terms of substantiated rates of staff-on-inmate and allegations of inmate-on-inmate rape.[31] The Texas Department of Criminal Justice points out that official rape complaints for the same year were actually much lower than the Bureau of Justice estimated.

While issues such as food, medical care, air-conditioning, and rape all raise concerns about cruel and inhumane treatment within Texas prisons, Texans and Texas lawmakers generally remain unsympathetic. For Texans, justice is black and white, and people who break the law get what they deserve. Most Texans also know hardship and believe that prisoners should have an uncomfortable life. The prevailing attitude in the state is that a prisoner's three square meals and access to television and a college education does not amount to punishment.

Privatization of Prisons

One way Texas tried to deal with its increasing prison population was by embracing the **private prison** option. In the 1990s, Texas firmly got on board the privatization movement, and it currently leads the country in utilizing privately-run prisons. By the end of 2016, over 13,000 prisoners in Texas were housed in private prisons. This number exceeds the private prison population of any U.S. state. Florida came closest at the time to Texas, with over 12,000 private prison inmates. Although only 3,000 prisoners in neighboring New Mexico were in private prisons, this figure accounts for over 43 percent of prisoners in that state.[32] That means New Mexico relied on private prisons for a larger share of where its prisoners were housed, compared to only 8.4 percent in Texas and 12.2 percent in Florida.

In addition, private prisons based in Texas have often had contracts with other states, meaning violent criminals from those states are transferred to Texas. Defenders of privately owned prisons argue that the costs for the state are significantly lower than for locally or state-run facilities. They often point to jobs created by private prisons, which are built in rural areas of the state. Opponents point to the poor conditions,

private prison
a private, for-profit prison corporation that staffs and runs prison facilities in a state

FEDERALISM IN *Action*

Marijuana Policy

Texans favor a justice system that's tough on crime, and social conservatives have long warned against the potential dangers of marijuana use. Yet one of the current significant trends across the country is a move away from the criminalization of marijuana. About one-third of states have decriminalized marijuana, meaning possession is now treated as a minor offense involving a small fine. Ten states, along with the District of Columbia, have legalized marijuana. When these states first chose to legalize marijuana, it created an interesting paradox, since possession of the substance was still against federal law. Since then, however, the federal government has said it will prosecute possession in those states only if it is tied to other criminal activity or involves minors in possession. Toward the end of his administration, President Obama

referred to marijuana policy as a states' rights issue. Also, over twenty states have enacted legislation allowing some form of marijuana to be used for medicinal purposes.

However, the U.S. government's approach changed under President Trump when Attorney General Jeff Sessions took control of the U.S. Justice Department in January 2017. Sessions launched a crackdown against marijuana, and even threatened states where marijuana had been legalized under state law. Pushback from several states, including Colorado, ultimately led President Trump to unilaterally reverse the crackdown without informing his own attorney general.[i]

The choice to incarcerate people for possession and use of marijuana entails significant costs. In 2014, it cost Texans an estimated $378,820 a day to incarcerate people for simple drug possession.[ii] While Texas law no longer deems it a felony to possess even a small amount of marijuana, state law can still seem draconian. Jacob Lavoro made national headlines in 2014 when he was arrested for making a batch of pot brownies. Although Lavoro used 2.5 grams of THC in his brownies, the Texas teen was originally charged for the entire weight of the brownies—one and a half pounds—which carried with it a maximum punishment of life in prison.

Although more Texans are embracing the notion of decriminalization, social conservatives still vehemently oppose any move toward legalization. Governor Abbott has clearly stated that he favors existing drug laws and prefers focusing on compliance. While Texas has made a few small steps away from harsh punishment and absolute criminalization, in 2016 the Texas Legislature legalized marijuana for a limited number of medicinal uses like the treatment of epilepsy. However, the state has been slow to license and approve places to dispense marijuana, specifically marijuana oil, with only three dispensaries having been opened by mid-2018.

> How likely do you think it is that marijuana will be decriminalized or legalized in Texas in the next decade?
>
> ⭐ **CRITICAL THINKING**

> How does the federal government's authority over security clash with state governments' power over marijuana laws?
>
> ⭐ **CRITICAL THINKING**

i. Evan Halper, "Trump Administration Abandons Crackdown on Legal Marijuana," *Los Angeles Times*, April 13, 2018, http://www.latimes.com/politics/la-na-pol-marijuana-trump-20180413-story.html.

ii. "High Time for Texas to Decriminalize Marijuana," *Daily Texan*, January 30, 2014, www.dailytexanonline.com/opinion/2014/01/30/high-time-for-texas-to-decriminalize-marijuana.

underpaid and poorly trained guards, and high-profile scandals involving the largest private prison corporations. Because these prisons are motivated by profit, providing adequate facilities and services to the prisoners often takes a back seat to the bottom line. Moreover, research suggests that the few jobs created by a private prison facility are outweighed by negative job growth, as private prisons have actually impeded economic growth overall.[33] In addition, critics contend that inmates moved to private facilities from other states and faced with poor conditions at the private prisons are often more likely to be clinically depressed and are less likely to have access to family or other visitors, making rehabilitation more difficult and recidivism more likely. Recent years have seen a slight decline in the use of private prisons in Texas, including the closure of at least one facility.

> What are the advantages and disadvantages of using private prisons for the incarceration of inmates?
>
> ⭐ **CRITICAL THINKING**

Several high-profile scandals have drawn attention to these private facilities. For example, the GEO Group, Inc., prison company was fired in 2007 by the Texas Youth Commission (TYC) for squalid conditions after one prisoner (transferred from Idaho) committed suicide.[34] Shortly after the suicide, Idaho corrections officials visited the facility and concluded it was the worst correctional facility and that it was incapable of being repaired or corrected. In spite of chronic questions regarding the conditions in these private jails, a *Dallas Morning News* study found "only a few instances of TYC not renewing contracts because of poor performance" and no cases where the TYC had fined for-profit contractors for problems, though it has the authority to assess such fines.[35]

The business model of private prisons is based on continued increases in the prison population. Not surprisingly, these prisons have actively lobbied for longer sentences and tougher laws. Critics of the "prison industrial complex" argue that this trend is not really about privatizing. Private prisons are still paid for by taxpayer money and are thus not actually shrinking government. Instead, they are "giving a monopoly rent to a private contractor who then goes about the same business the state would have provided."[36] One analyst has called this "faux privatization." As Texas's prison population has begun to decline in recent years, the change means that a lot of companies that built new private prisons speculating on an ever-increasing prison population are now stuck with half-empty prisons. Some prisons received contracts with the U.S. Department of Justice to keep themselves in business; however, by 2015, reviews of the prison conditions prompted the U.S. government to end those contracts.[37] Some of those prisons held immigrants detained by the U.S. government.

The closure of private prisons has brought with it a new set of problems. Take the West Texas town of Littlefield. In 2000, the small town issued $10 million in bonds to build the Bill Clayton Detention Center to be run by the GEO Group. For several years, the detention center housed prisoners from Idaho. However, after the suicide scandal, Idaho began to transfer its prisoners out of Texas. Not surprisingly, lacking customers, the GEO Group pulled out of its contract. The town of Littlefield still owed about $9 million on the now-empty facility. To pay its loan, Littlefield has had to raise fees on water and sewer usage and increase property taxes, all while its credit rating has been falling.[38] The town thought it had sold the prison in July 2012 for $6 million, but that sale fell through. Several other attempts to sell or to find contracts for the prison failed until late July 2015, when a contract was reached with Correct Care Solutions of California to house approximately 200 sex offenders from California at the prison.[39]

RIGHTS OF THE ACCUSED

In the United States, our criminal justice system is rooted in the strongly held belief that people are innocent until proven guilty. This means that individuals accused of crimes have certain rights. In the Texas Constitution, many of these rights are contained in Article 1, Section 10, which states, in part:

In all criminal prosecutions the accused shall have a speedy public trial by an impartial jury. He shall have the right to demand the nature and cause of the accusation against him, and to have a copy thereof. He shall not be compelled to give evidence against himself, and shall have the right of being heard by himself or counsel, or both, shall be confronted by the witnesses against . . . and no person shall be held to answer for a criminal offense, unless on an indictment of a grand jury.

Other rights found in Article 1 of the Texas Constitution (1876) either mirror or parallel rights of the accused in the U.S. Constitution. Historically, these rights in the Texas Constitution ensured that Texans received a set of rights in state courts similar to those guaranteed in U.S. courts. These include the writ of habeas corpus, protection from double jeopardy, and the due process of law. Texans are also assured of the right to bail in criminal cases, with noted exceptions depending on the seriousness of the alleged crime.

The right of the accused to have legal counsel has long been the tradition in Texas. Long before the U.S. Supreme Court ruled in *Gideon v. Wainwright* that the Sixth Amendment to the U.S. Constitution entailed a right to counsel in criminal cases, that right was protected by the constitutions in Texas. Every Texas constitution since 1836 has guaranteed the right to counsel to those who cannot afford it, a requirement called **indigent defense**.[40]

indigent defense
the requirement that governments provide legal counsel to those charged with serious crimes who cannot afford representation

In practice, Texas political culture has not been overly supportive of the rights of the accused, and the ability to get a decent defense has varied greatly across the state. In 2001, Texas passed the Fair Defense Act, which requires minimum standards for defense lawyers, the prompt appointment of lawyers, and financial resources to hire experts and investigators in indigent cases. Only fourteen counties in Texas have created a county public defender's office within the structure of county government. A public defender's office is an agency of the county government that provides legal counsel to those accused of a crime who cannot afford a lawyer. Some counties provide a wide range of services, while others focus narrowly on juvenile defense or mental health issues. Another approach to public defender's offices is for multiple counties to join together to provide such services. There are four such regional public defender's offices that cover as few as three counties and as many as 177 counties.[41] All other Texas counties rely on contracts with private practice lawyers who receive some support from the county for their expenses associated with indigent defense or who contract with private lawyers to provide the defense of the poor for free.

However, the victims of crime are also guaranteed certain rights in the Texas Constitution in Article 1, Section 30. This section was added and amended to the state constitution in 1989. These rights include the right to dignity and privacy during the trial; protection from the accused; the right to present in court; the right of restitution; and the right to information about the conviction, sentence, imprisonment, and release of the accused. In the last set of rights of victims, these provisions allow the family and friends of murder victims to be present at the killer's execution. For example, the father and daughter of Michael Walker attended Adam Kelly Ward's execution in early 2016.

In the past few years, the issue of excessive bail, especially for lower-income citizens, has become an area of criticism of Texas criminal justice policy. An example is linked to the shootout between rival biker groups at the Twin Peaks establishment in Waco, Texas, on May 17, 2015. When a dispute arose between the Bandidos and Cossacks, two rival biker groups, over Texas-themed distinctive patches or "cuts" worn on jackets by members, the dispute quickly escalated into a shootout between the groups, and later encompassed a Waco police SWAT team. While disputes between the groups had occurred in recent years, none had remotely reached this level of violence. In the end, nine bikers, mostly Cossacks, died. Over 192 arrests were made on the spot or soon after the shootout, mostly white males. All suspects had bail set at $1 million, with some as high as $2 million.[42] Since Texas requires bail bonds be met at a minimum of 10%, this meant that suspects had to come up with $100,000 cash. Several of those arrested eventually sued the Waco police department and the city of Waco claiming a violation of fundamental rights guaranteed by the U.S. and Texas constitutions, including prohibitions on excessive bail. The bikers claimed that their arrest and bail were due to the fact that they were bikers and had been at Twin Peaks when the shootout occurred.[43] While prosecutors have begun to drop cases against many of the bikers, a number of individuals identified by police as key figures in the fight are still facing trial.

To highlight the issues surrounding excessive bail and its impact on the Texas criminal justice system, chief justice of the Texas Supreme Court Nathan Hecht specifically mentioned this issue in his 2017 address to the Texas Legislature. Hecht noted that those who cannot afford a bail bond remain in jail awaiting a hearing, and are more likely to lose their job and reoffend compared to those who make bail. In addition, individuals held in prison on excessive bail cost Texas taxpayers $1 billion per year. He also noted that defendants who cannot pay fines and court costs, often for traffic violations, end up serving prison time in Texas, a practice called debtors' prison, which is illegal under the U.S. Constitution. Excessive court fees in Texas include fees for using a payment plan to pay court fees rather than a single payment, a fee for missing a payment, and a fee to make a payment.[44] Later in the 2017 legislative session, a bill was passed by both houses and signed by the governor to end jail time associated with the inability to pay court fees.

Another issue is the emphasis on victims' rights. This issue is in some ways an extension of retribution. By being allowed to attend court and even the execution of the accused, victims and victims' families participate in the state's retribution and punishment of the accused. However, these rights are also consistent with a move, if ever so small, toward restorative justice, allowing victims and their families to achieve a sense of closure on a traumatic part of their lives.

Texas political culture remains tough on crime, and Texans by and large believe in swift justice. The emphasis in the state on individual responsibility means that if you find yourself on the wrong side of the law, Texans are unlikely to be sympathetic. Texans distrust government in most policy areas but exhibit a high degree of trust in the state when it comes to meting out justice. This culture has resulted in more criminalized behavior and thus higher incarceration rates than other states. The fiscal cost has also been high. Recent moves away from punishment and toward rehabilitation appeal to the fiscally conservative Texan but run counter to our sense of retribution and "just deserts." Recent moves by the legislature allow drug abuse and mental health cases to be treated as public health concerns rather than as criminal acts, but the extent to which these moves will be embraced by judges, juries, and the average Texan remains to be seen.

LAW AND PUNISHMENT

What happens when Texas's idea of rugged individualism and its "pull yourself up by your bootstraps" attitude meet its keen sense of right and wrong? Individual responsibility has always been central to Texans' strong sense of justice. Yet, as a state, we struggle with how to balance protecting individual rights against preventing the behavior of individuals who might take advantage of the system. As we will see, when Texans' sense of right and wrong collides with the rights of individuals, the rights of individuals often lose. Justice remains highly valued and sometimes requires harsh punishment. Texans feel justified in using lethal force to protect their homes, which is the ultimate manifestation of frontier justice. They also prefer the use of capital punishment as the most efficient means of retribution for the most serious crimes. The movement toward tort reform represents a desire to avoid frivolous lawsuits that upset Texas's sense of justice. Texas justice seems harsh to observers outside the state, but to most Texans, the punishment fits the crime.

Tort Reform

One of the biggest changes in justice in Texas occurred as a result of changes in tort law. Tort law allows individuals who have been wronged due to negligence or malpractice to sue for damages. The idea of tort law is to protect individuals against companies, government, or other individuals' wrongful action that results in injury. The difficulty in tort law is to balance the needs of individuals who are wrongfully injured against frivolous lawsuits that cost businesses, and in turn consumers, a lot of money. In the 1980s, Texas saw a surge of malpractice suits with large settlements, including a dramatic rise in medical malpractice, which drove up malpractice insurance rates for doctors in the state. This led to a decrease in the number of doctors in the state, and, by 2003, Texas ranked forty-fourth out of the fifty states in the ratio of doctors to citizens. However, tort reform had rebounded the state to only forty-first out of the fifty states by 2016.[45]

tort
a wrongful act by a person that results in injury to another person or property in civil law

Tort reform in Texas began with legislation in 1987 and again in 1995 that imposed limits on the amount of damages litigants could collect. In 2003, the Texas Legislature passed the most sweeping tort reform legislation, limiting the amount of noneconomic damages (i.e., pain and suffering) in civil suits to $250,000 for a physician or hospital. The goal was to stop frivolous lawsuits. Supporters of the law said the limit would lead to fewer lawsuits and lower insurance costs for doctors. Those lower costs would be passed on to the average Texan. Opponents of tort reform argued that the $250,000 cap would also discourage genuine claims and deny Texans their constitutional right to a jury trial. Since the Supreme Court of Texas had previously ruled that such limits were unconstitutional, the same legislative session approved a constitutional amendment allowing the legislature to set such limits.

In 2011, the Texas Legislature passed additional tort reform, the so-called loser pay law, which requires certain litigants who lose their lawsuit to pay the legal costs of the person who was sued. The law requires litigants to pay if they turn down a settlement offer and the final jury award is less than the settlement amount offered. Under the law, the Supreme Court of Texas establishes guidelines for judges to dismiss what appear to be frivolous lawsuits (under $100,000) earlier in the process, and allows a judge to dismiss a lawsuit at the beginning of the process. A reform in 2017 reduced the fines that insurance companies pay for failure to compensate policyholders for hail and wind damage.[46]

loser pay law
Texas law that requires litigants to pay those they sued if they lose their lawsuits in certain cases

For Texans, juries awarding millions of dollars and people suing over everything just rankles us. Texans also have a keen sense of fairness and believe they should be able to get a fair trial if they are the victims of an egregious act. The balance between these two values is difficult. In 2008, when twenty-five-year-old Vanessa Samudio was struck by a police car traveling eighty miles per hour with no lights or sirens, she

HOSPITAL MEDICAL ERRORS KILL 98,000 AMERICANS EACH YEAR. -- HEARST NEWS INVESTIGATION

suffered permanent brain damage.[47] Samudio's medical bills were significantly more than the $250,000 cap. Unfortunately, since the 2003 reform, even Texans with legitimate claims have had a difficult time getting an attorney to agree to take their case. This is particularly true of those on limited incomes, such as the elderly, who have little means to pay for legal services absent an award. To make the case that someone got cancer because of a company's negligence or that malpractice in the nursing home led to a senior's death, costly expert witnesses and assessments are needed in addition to legal fees.

Since the passage of these reforms, results have been mixed. Proponents of tort reform argue that it has largely ended frivolous lawsuits, helped create a business-friendly environment, stemmed the tide of lost physicians, and decreased the cost of medical malpractice insurance. From this perspective, the average Texan benefits from easier access to physicians and lower costs for medical services (since physicians pay less for malpractice insurance). Critics of tort reform, on the other hand, say these benefits have never been realized. In particular, claims that Texas has seen an increase in the number of doctors do not take into account population growth. According to Texas Department of State Health Services statistics, the number of physicians per capita actually grew at a faster rate between 1996 and 2002 than in the years immediately after the 2003 reforms.[48] In addition, a University of Texas study found no evidence that health care costs had declined after 2003, even after accounting for the average increase in those costs compared to all other states. Moreover, Texans who are the victims of negligence or malpractice face much higher costs when seeking compensation, and even if awarded, that compensation will be limited while the costs associated with their injuries may not be. The threat of paying the other side's legal fees will further be a deterrent to poorer Texans in seeking compensation. In contrast, Texas is now viewed as a state favorable to physicians. According to one industry publication, Texas is among the best states in which to practice medicine.[49] Clearly, Texas will continue to struggle with the balance between individual rights and decreasing frivolous lawsuits for the foreseeable future.

Castle Doctrine

castle doctrine
Texas law that allows the use of deadly force to defend your home, or "castle"

Consistent with Texas's culture of frontier justice, since 2007 the state has had a fairly permissive castle doctrine (Texas's version of the stand-your-ground doctrine). The castle doctrine derives from English common law and is based on the idea that deadly force is sometimes necessary to defend your home, your "castle." In 1973, the Texas Legislature passed a law that deadly force could be used so long as a reasonable person would not have retreated. However, in 1995, and more recently in 2007, the legislature broadened the castle doctrine and removed the duty to retreat. According to the Texas Penal Code (Section 9.01), use of deadly force is permitted in one's home, vehicle,

TEXAS (VS) MINNESOTA

The Texas criminal justice system historically focused on the need to punish the criminal, seeking retribution and revenge on the accused for the crime as well as deterring crime in the first place through harsh sentences for crimes. This get-tough-on-crime approach reflects the traditionalist-individualist political culture of Texas that emphasizes the role and responsibility of the individual. Government is to enforce the laws and extract punishment, taking on the role of the individual protecting his or her property with a gun on the frontier.

Minnesota's history, including its settlement patterns, is quite different. Mostly settled by German and Scandinavian immigrants, Minnesota lacks the hard-core frontier experience idealized in Texas history. Instead, Scandinavians in Minnesota brought a more communitarian philosophy that focuses on promotion of the good society and public well-being consistent with moralistic political cultures. As a result, Minnesota's criminal justice system has long focused on rehabilitation—and in more recent decades, restorative justice. Minnesota attempts to work with the victims and criminals to minimize a return to a life of crime, or recidivism.

Do these orientations in Texas compared to Minnesota produce different outcomes? Evidence can be found to support both sides of the equation. However, many measures demonstrate that Minnesota's system is producing a very different set of results. Minnesota in most categories ranks below Texas, indicating a lower rate of crime. In several categories, Minnesota has among the lowest crime rates in the U.S., for example in violent crime, murder, and aggravated assault.

> How do the statistics in the table provide evidence in favor of Minnesota's approach to criminal justice, including rehabilitation and restorative justice?

 CRITICAL THINKING

> To what extent do the differences between Minnesota and Texas reflect the broader political cultures of these two states?

 SOCIAL RESPONSIBILITY

Rates of Crime and Crime-Related Statistics, 2016

	Minnesota Rate (Rank in U.S.)	Texas Rate (Rank in U.S.)
Violent Crime	231.40 (42)	421.90 (18)
Violent Crime with Firearm	52.30 (33)	148.50 (14)
Robbery Rate	67.50 (34)	119.60 (8)
Rape Rate	31.40 (20)	35.40 (14)
Property Crime Rate	2,133.30 (33)	2,759.80 (19)
Murder Rate	1.80 (49)	5.30 (25)
Motor Vehicle Theft Rate	158.10 (32)	247.80 (18)
Larceny Theft Rate	1,638.10 (29)	1,978.10 (19)
Aggravated Assault Rate	134.70 (44)	261.60 (23)

Source: *SAGE Stats* using reported data from the Federal Bureau of Investigation, http://data.sagepub.com/sagestats/index.php.

Does the castle doctrine address the balance between the right of individuals to protect their property and the rights of individuals to a fair judicial process when accused of a crime? Why or why not?

⭐ **PERSONAL RESPONSIBILITY**

place of work, and anywhere "a person has a right to be present." The law presumes the *reasonableness* of the use of deadly force. Previously, the law in Texas required a person faced with imminent danger to retreat, if possible. The new law no longer requires an individual to retreat so long as he or she does not provoke the person and is not engaged in criminal activity above a class C misdemeanor, which is the least severe criminal category. Now you can use deadly force in Texas to protect yourself or your property.

The castle doctrine remains largely popular in Texas, yet questions remain. For instance, shortly after Texas passed the 2007 law, Texan Joe Horn called 911 because someone was breaking into his neighbor's house. Although he was told by the dispatcher to stay inside, Horn was familiar with the new law and told the dispatcher, "The laws have been changed . . . since September the first, and I have a right to protect myself." Horn said, "I ain't gonna let them get away with this shit. I'm sorry, this ain't right, buddy. . . . They got a bag of loot. . . . Here it goes buddy, you hear the shotgun clicking and I'm going."[50] Horn shot the two men seconds before the police arrived. Under the new castle doctrine, Horn was not arrested nor was he indicted by a grand jury, even though he had to leave his house to defend his neighbor's castle. Proponents of the castle doctrine argue that homeowners have the right to defend themselves and that the castle doctrine is fundamental to that right. Critics of the law charge that individuals now have the right to shoot to kill someone in instances where even the police do not and that it threatens the presumption of innocence. When James Green was shot and killed after accidently entering the wrong house (he thought it was his friend's house), the homeowner who killed him was not charged under the castle law. When a twenty-four-year-old stole the tip jar (containing around $20) from a taco truck, the owner ran after him and killed him while he tried to flee. Under the castle doctrine, the killing was ruled a justifiable homicide. Indeed, the castle doctrine raises significant questions about presumption of innocence and when use of force is necessary. Texans will continue to grapple with the appropriate balance between protection and the taking of a life.

Capital Punishment

In 1923, Texas adopted the electric chair (referred to as "Old Sparky") as the state's official method for carrying out **capital punishment**. Prior to the 1920s, hanging was the preferred method of state execution. In 1972, the U.S. Supreme Court ruled that the imposition of capital punishment amounted to "cruel and unusual punishment" since its selective application violated due process.[51] Up to that point, Texas had electrocuted 361 people. Following the court's ruling, some states, including Texas, began to change their procedures to make them less arbitrary. The most significant change was the adoption of a two-stage process: first, guilt or innocence is decided, then, where a guilty verdict has been pronounced, appropriate punishment is decided separately. By the time Texas implemented its new procedures for imposing the death penalty, lethal injection had become its official means of execution.

The state may implement the death penalty if a person is found guilty of the murder of a public safety officer, firefighter, correctional employee, or child under the age of six, or if the person is found guilty of multiple murders. Other actions that may invoke capital punishment include committing murder during a kidnapping, burglary, robbery, sexual assault, arson, or prison escape; committing murder for payment; or murdering a prison inmate serving a life sentence for murder, kidnapping, aggravated sexual assault, or robbery. The decision to implement the death penalty occurs at the local level. The district attorney must seek the death penalty, and the jury determines whether or not the death penalty is warranted in the punishment phase of the trial. In Texas, application of the death penalty is not consistent across the state. Instead, the largest urban centers account for the lion's share of death penalty cases. Of the inmates on death row in 2018, seventy-eight inmates, or 34.7 percent, came from Harris County alone. The next highest was Dallas County with twenty-five inmates, or 11.1 percent, followed by Tarrant County with sixteen inmates, or 7.1 percent.[52]

The U.S. Supreme Court has recognized some significant limits on the death penalty. In 2002, the court ruled in *Atkins v. Virginia* that it is unconstitutional for the state to execute defendants who are "mentally retarded."[53] However, the U.S. Supreme Court left it to the states to develop standards to define "mental retardation." In response, the Texas Court of Criminal Appeals developed criteria in *Ex Parte Jose Garcia Briseño* (2004).[54] Among the criteria the court developed was consideration of several questions, including: "Did the commission of that offense require forethought, planning, and complex execution of purpose?" and "Has the person formulated plans and carried them through, or is his conduct impulsive?" However, the court also drew an analogy to the character of Lennie Small from John Steinbeck's *Of Mice and Men*. According to the Texas Court of Criminal Appeals, only a narrow, limited number of people are exempted from the death penalty based on intellectual

FIGURE 7.1 Executions in Texas since 1983

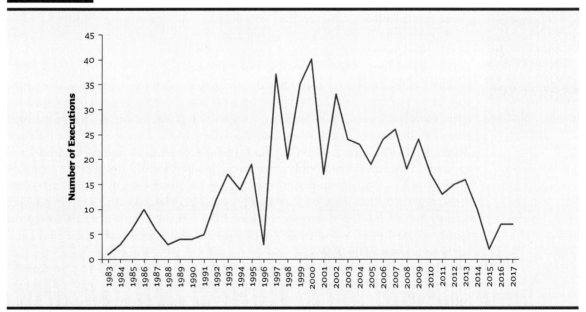

Source: Death Penalty Information Center, "Death Sentences in the United States from 1977 by State and by Year," accessed October 30, 2018. http://www.deathpenaltyinfo.org/death-sentences-united-states-1977-2008.

disability. Exemptions occur when the accused is considered similar to Lennie Small; for example, did other people think the accused was intellectually disabled, or can the person lie effectively? In spite of these court decisions and despite a national outcry, in 2012 Texas executed Marvin Wilson, who had an IQ of sixty-one, well below the cutoff point of seventy for "mental retardation."[55]

Since that time, the U.S. Supreme Court has continued to narrow who can be executed. A few years after *Atkins*, in *Roper v. Simmons*,[56] the U.S. Supreme Court further ruled that juveniles could no longer be subject to the death penalty. The case of Scott Panetti, discussed briefly in the opening of this chapter, led to the follow-up case that requires the individual to be executed to have a "rational understanding" of why he or she is to be executed. This is a requirement that applies to juveniles and adults.[57] Furthermore, in *Hall v. Florida* (2014), the U.S. Supreme Court limited states' abilities to execute the intellectually disabled. Individuals who before age eighteen have low IQ scores and lack fundamental social and practice skills may not be executed.[58] Moreover, Texas must now reconsider the criteria found in *Ex Parte Jose Garcia Briseño* because the U.S. Supreme Court found the criteria too subjective in *Moore v. Texas* (2017).[59]

Describe the pattern of execution in Texas over time.

⭐ **EMPIRICAL AND QUANTITATIVE**

Should Americans, and Texans, be concerned that our embracing the death penalty places us in a category of countries whose political systems and values have historically been vastly different from our own?

⭐ **CRITICAL THINKING**

Texas stands at a crossroads with regard to death penalty convictions. On the one hand, Texas continues to favor and utilize the death penalty more than other states and most other countries in the world. Between 1982 and July 2018, Texas executed 551 individuals, far more than any other state in the United States. Texas has carried out almost 37 percent of all executions in the country since 1976. The next two states are Virginia with 113 executions and Oklahoma with 112. Most executions in the United States occur in the South. These executions account for approximately 82 percent of all executions in the country since 1976. Texas not only leads the nation in executions but also consistently ranks among the top ten countries worldwide (see "How Texas Government Works: Justice and the Death Penalty" on the next page).

On the other hand, Texas's use of the death penalty has decreased in recent years and the death penalty is becoming less popular across the country. Nineteen states have abolished the death penalty, with one-third of those instances occurring since 2007. Internationally, the death penalty has also become increasingly unpopular. Currently, over 140 countries ban the death penalty, including all Western industrialized countries except the United States. In Europe, opposition to the death penalty has become so potent that European countries now refuse to sell to U.S. correctional facilities the drugs used in lethal injection. While Texas is still a leader in the use of the death penalty and no state politician would campaign on the abolition of it, the rate of executions in the state has decreased in recent years. Figure 7.1 shows a steady decline in the use of the death penalty. Of course, Texas still has 243 people on death row, yet even that number has declined in recent years. Since 2010, Texas has sentenced an average of twelve people a year to death row, compared to twenty-one a year in the 2000s and thirty-four a year in the 1990s.

Although the number of executions in Texas has decreased in recent years, consistent with the rest of the United States, Texas continues to lead the country in state executions. Why does Texas execute significantly more people than other states? Texans have a strong sense of right and wrong and are deeply attached to the idea of the death penalty as a deserved punishment. Whereas other states that use the death penalty may see it as a necessary evil, Texas culture embraces the state's right to execute its citizens

HOW TEXAS GOVERNMENT WORKS

Justice and the Death Penalty

Texas Compared: Countries with the Highest Number of Confirmed Executions, 2017

United States
23

Texas
4

Pakistan
60

China
1,000+

Iran
507

Iraq
125

Egypt
35

Saudi Arabia
146

Somalia
24

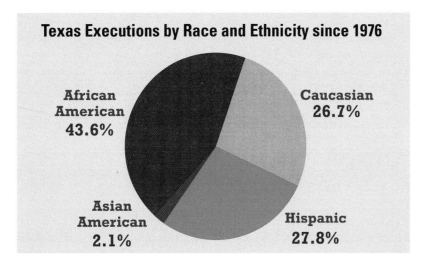

Texas Executions by Race and Ethnicity since 1976

African American
43.6%

Caucasian
26.7%

Asian American
2.1%

Hispanic
27.8%

Sources: Death Penalty Information Center, "Current Death Row Populations by Race," accessed August 6, 2018, https://deathpenaltyinfo.org/race-death-row-inmates-executed-1976?scid=5&did=184; Death Penalty Information Center, "Executions and Death Sentences around the World," accessed August 6, 2018, https://deathpenaltyinfo.org/death-penalty-international-perspective#interexec.

for the violation of certain laws. Texans' attachment to the death penalty remains as strong as their attachment to guns. Frontier Texans were often left to secure their own towns—indeed they preferred it that way, suspicious as they were of governmental interference. Imposition of the death penalty is viewed as a right, one in keeping with Texans' sense that there are no gray areas: Right is right, and wrong is wrong. This attitude still prevails throughout most of the state. It can be found among Texans sitting on juries, among Texans sitting on the Texas Court of Criminal Appeals, and among Texans serving on the Texas Board of Pardons and Paroles. A former Smith County district attorney put it this way:

> The death penalty in Texas is primarily a function of the fact that it is in our law. We have conservative jurors and district attorneys run for election and so it's very important that DAs . . . [who come up for reelections] make decisions on cases that are consistent with the feelings of their constituents.[60]

How does Texas's view of the death penalty reflect frontier culture?

⭐ CRITICAL THINKING

Support for the death penalty in the state remains strong. While national polls indicate that 60 percent of Americans support the death penalty, a 2014 *Texas Tribune* poll indicates that 71 percent of Texans continue to do so.[61] This faith in the death penalty stands at odds with national trends. As DNA evidence has increasingly revealed that innocent people in the United States have been put to death, national support for the death penalty has waned. More recently, budget crises have motivated some states to abolish the death penalty due to the expense associated with it. Texans' preference for the death penalty remains so strong that often the actions of Texas courts seem downright odd to the rest of the country. In one infamous case, a panel of three judges from the Fifth Circuit Court of Appeals upheld a death penalty sentence even though the defendant's attorney had slept through portions of the trial. The panel ruled that since they could not determine whether the attorney had slept through critical parts of the trial, there was no basis to overturn the conviction. Although the full Fifth Circuit Court later overturned this ruling, the initial ruling is indicative of prevalent attitudes toward justice in Texas. Texas again made national news when, in 2007, the U.S. Supreme Court announced it would consider for the first time since 1972 whether the death penalty constituted cruel and unusual punishment. Michael Richard was scheduled to be executed in Texas that same day, and his lawyers scrambled to put together a request to stop his execution until the court made its ruling on the constitutionality of lethal injection. Richard's attorneys were working on their appeal late in the day when their printer malfunctioned. The attorneys called the Texas Court of Criminal Appeals, the highest criminal court in the state, and requested that the court stay open an extra twenty minutes so they could file the appeal. Texas courts have stayed open in the past to hear last-minute appeals, and three judges were at the appeals court in anticipation of a last-minute filing. In spite of that, presiding judge Sharon Keller reportedly told the attorneys that the Texas Court of Criminal Appeals "close[d] at 5:00."[62] Michael Richard was executed that day.

Although Texas's criminal justice system has shifted somewhat away from retribution in practice, Texans in general tend to favor retribution, and the death penalty is viewed as the fitting punishment for the crime of murder. Proponents of the death penalty in the state and elsewhere argue that it acts as a deterrent on crime.

This argument manifests itself at the ballot box in the election of politicians, including state court judges in Texas, who are tough on crime. In addition, this approach to criminal justice reflects our frontier experience of self-reliance and self-administered justice.

Critics of the death penalty continue to emphasize that minorities disproportionately receive the death penalty. In July 2018, the Texas Department of Criminal Justice reported that since 1983, 44 percent of executed prisoners had been African American, 27 percent white, and 28 percent Hispanic.[63] (See "How Texas Government Works: Justice and the Death Penalty.") Texas has also executed six of the sixteen women executed in the United States since 1976. Moreover, opponents point out the added expense of death penalty cases, which involve automatic appeals to the state's high court, among other things. The average time spent on death row is slightly over ten years, although the longest time spent there was twenty-four years. In 1992, a *Dallas Morning News* study estimated that taxpayers pay $2.3 million for the average death penalty case in Texas, compared to $750,000 to imprison someone in a single cell at the highest level of security for forty years.[64] This higher cost comes in every case, even those in which the death penalty only *might* be imposed. The cost of the death penalty, coupled with the comparatively large number of executions in the state each year, places a significant burden on Texas's taxpayers.

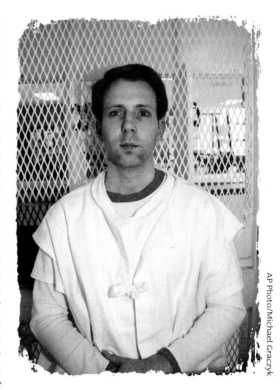

AP Photo/Michael Graczyk

Adam Kelly Ward, whose case is mentioned earlier in this chapter, was executed in March 2016. Ward's history of mental illness raised important questions about who is executed in Texas.

WINNERS AND LOSERS

In many ways, Texans' preference for a tough approach to crime, demands for justice, and ardent support of the death penalty sets them apart from much of the rest of the country. Texans believe the punishment must fit the crime and that the death penalty represents the ultimate symbol of justice. However, these political preferences come at a high cost to the average Texan. Money spent on imprisonment rather than rehabilitation means that Texas's high imprisonment rates translate to significantly higher state taxes. Private prisons are often cited for poor conditions, and Texans have been willingly taking on other states' criminal populations. Movement away from private prisons, a function of the inadequate conditions and security problems in and overall growing distrust of private prisons, has left Texas where is started over a decade ago. However, the move by the Texas Legislature toward rehabilitation rather than punishment may help Texans become winners. As incarceration rates have leveled and over $1 billion has been saved, the increased focus on rehabilitation for nonviolent criminals clearly makes taxpayers winners.

Texans win and lose with the death penalty. Although it is increasingly unpopular nationwide, in Texas the death penalty is revered. On the one hand, Texans, in

Are traditional Texan views on justice worth the burden to taxpayers? Is the shift to rehabilitation a good one for the state?

⭐ **CRITICAL THINKING**

Do concerns that Texas has executed innocent people make you reconsider your views on the death penalty? Why or why not?

⭐ **SOCIAL RESPONSIBILITY**

persisting with their policy preference for justice and retribution, "win" in terms of leading the country in number of executions carried out. On the other hand, Texans pay the high costs associated with ensuring that potential death penalty cases follow due process. In appropriating to themselves this cost—one that is significantly higher than the cost of life imprisonment—Texans lose.

CONCLUSION

Justice in Texas is a complicated affair. The political culture in the state favors policies that are tough on crime, and Texans trust other Texans even more than the judicial system to mete out punishment rather than working to rehabilitate the criminal into a productive life outside prison. The state's prevailing culture often puts it at odds with the rest of the country, and Texans pay a significant price for their preferences. In the coming years, the state's prison population will once again start to climb, and Texans will have to ask themselves if it is worth it to continue to criminalize so many behaviors. Many countries, and other states, have begun to view drug use as a public health issue rather than a criminal one. The move toward rehabilitation represents a sea change for justice in the state. As future budget and population pressures increase, Texas will have to decide if that sea change is more or less important than its long-standing views of justice on the frontier.

for CQ Press

Want a better grade?

Get the tools you need to sharpen your study skills. Access practice quizzes, eFlashcards, video, and multimedia at **edge.sagepub.com/collier6e**.

KEY TERMS

capital punishment (p. 236)

castle doctrine (p. 234)

incapacitation (p. 223)

incarceration rate (p. 223)

indigent defense (p. 231)

just deserts (p. 223)

loser pay law (p. 233)

private prison (p. 228)

recidivism (p. 225)

rehabilitation (p. 223)

restorative justice (p. 223)

retribution (p. 223)

tort (p. 233)

- In small groups, discuss what, if any, limits there should be on an individual's ability to defend his or her home, or "castle." Were you able to reach a consensus? **Teamwork**

- Write a paragraph explaining the various costs and benefits associated with the death penalty. **Communication**

CHAPTER REVIEW

1. _____ is an approach to criminal justice that emphasizes punishment because the guilty violated societal rules.

   a. Incapacitation

   b. Just deserts

   c. Retribution

   d. Restorative justice

2. _____ is an approach to criminal justice that emphasizes removing the guilty from society to prevent new or additional crime.

   a. Incapacitation

   b. Just deserts

   c. Retribution

   d. Restorative justice

3. _____ is an approach to criminal justice that sees crime as a break in society between the community, the perpetrator, and the victim, and focuses on healing this break.

   a. Incapacitation

   b. Just deserts

   c. Retribution

   d. Restorative justice

4. In contrast to Texas, which state mentioned in the chapter focuses on restorative justice as a key part of its criminal justice policy?

   a. Alabama

   b. Minnesota

   c. Missouri

   d. Utah

5. Key problems facing Texas's prisons include _____.

   a. overcrowding

   b. role of private prisons in Texas

   c. lack of air-conditioning during summers

   d. all of these

6. The right to a lawyer in Texas for those who cannot afford one is most often handled in criminal cases by _____.

   a. the Texas Department of Justice

   b. a county public defender's office in each of Texas's counties

   c. the U.S. district attorney's office in each county

   d. free legal counsel from lawyers in the community or reimbursement of local lawyers

(Continued)

7. A law that requires litigants to pay those they sued if they lose their lawsuit is called _____.

   a. the loser pay law

   b. excessive bail

   c. tort reform

   d. the castle doctrine

8. In other states, the castle doctrine is referred to as _____.

   a. just deserts

   b. restorative justice

   c. stand your ground

   d. tort

9. In which court case did the Texas Court of Criminal Appeals attempt to define when those with intellectual disability may be exempted from the death penalty?

   a. *Atkins v. Virginia* (2002)

   b. *Ex Parte Jose Garcia Briseño* (2004)

   c. *Roper v. Simmons* (2005)

   d. *Moore v. Texas* (2017)

10. In which case did the U.S. Supreme Court rule that juveniles cannot be executed?

   a. *Atkins v. Virginia* ((2002)

   b. *Ex Parte Jose Garcia Briseño* (2004)

   c. *Roper v. Simmons* (2005)

   d. *Moore v. Texas* (2017)

CAMPAIGNS AND ELECTIONS, TEXAS STYLE

Chapter Objectives

★ Discuss the barriers to minorities' voting rights in Texas.

★ Describe the different types of elections held in Texas.

★ Explain the trends of voter turnout in Texas elections.

★ Explain the impact campaign finance has on Texas elections.

★ Assess who wins and who loses when voting barriers exist.

★ Assess who wins and who loses as a result of low voter turnout in Texas.

The face of Texas is changing rapidly. Over the past two decades, the percentage of Texas's population that is Hispanic has been growing, as have been the Asian American, Arab American, and other ethnic group populations. While Anglos have continued to grow in numbers—for example, from 2000 to 2010 the Anglo population has grown by over 400,000—the rate of growth among other groups has been much greater. According to data from the Office of the State Demographer, the Hispanic population expanded by over 40 percent while the Asian American population grew by over 60 percent.[1] By 2020, Texas is expected to add 2.5 million Hispanics, an additional 30 percent over 2010. In the same time frame, the Anglo population will add another 325,000 Anglos, or about 3 percent more. Increases in the number of African Americans in Texas and Asians in Texas, while expected to be higher than that of Anglos, is projected to be much less than that of Hispanics.[2] Moreover, the trend of population concentration in urban areas and suburbs within the state is expected to continue.

How do these trends in the makeup of Texas's population influence politics in the state of Texas? For example, the Hispanic population in Texas is now the second largest in the United States and accounts for over one in every four persons eligible to vote in Texas. Hispanic voters also tend to be younger than the average Texas voter and tend to be less educated but are only slightly less likely to own their own home.[3] In general, Hispanics in Texas and across the United States tend to identify with the Democratic Party, an estimated 46 percent in Texas. Compare that figure with the 26 percent of Anglos who identify with the Democratic Party. In addition, Texas Hispanics are more

A voter registration booth in Austin, Texas, includes an electronic voting machine for newly registered voters to try. Registration efforts aimed at Hispanics attempt to boost the number of Hispanic voters in Texas.

likely to declare themselves as an independent voter than their Anglo counterparts. However, Hispanics are much less likely to vote on Election Day than their Anglo counterparts.[4] Expectations are for the Hispanic population to continue to grow, while the African American population is expected to remain stable and the Anglo population to begin to decline within twenty years. Moreover, the Hispanic population is growing throughout the state. Growth is not limited to the Rio Grande Valley and areas near the border with Mexico. In southeast Texas, both Hardin and Orange Counties have among the ten fastest-growing Hispanic populations in the state. Also on this list are Ector and Midland Counties in West Texas and Randall Counties in the panhandle.[5]

Media reports often focus on the impact that the Hispanic population will have in shifting the state of Texas from a "red" state that is heavily Republican to a "blue" state that is Democratic.[6] These projections are based on assumptions that Hispanics over time will consistently vote Democratic, in part assuming their party identification and/or affiliation remains consistent over time. This assumption is reinforced by the fact that more Hispanics are being elected to the Texas Legislature and the fact that most of these Hispanics are Democrats. In 2014, the first Hispanic woman to run for statewide elected office, Leticia Van de Putte, performed as well as or better than other Democrats for statewide office that year. By 2018, the Texas Democratic party was willing to nominate an openly lesbian Hispanic, the former sheriff of Dallas County, Lupe Valdez.

The only Hispanics who currently vote Republican on a regular business are Cuban Americans, and in Texas, Cuban Americans are only a small minority in the overall Hispanic population. While U.S. senator Ted Cruz is a prominent Cuban American, very few Hispanic elected officials are Republican. So, the Republican Party in Texas would appear to need to change its positions on several issues or prepare to lose elections in Texas soon. Yet, half a century ago, Roman Catholics in Texas and the United States were heavily Democratic voters. By the 1980s, Roman Catholics in the United

States had experienced significant gains in income and economic prosperity; Roman Catholics began to shift toward the Republican Party as their economic status began to mirror the wider Protestant Christian population. As Hispanics gain economically and see significant increases in their standard of living, will they follow their pocketbooks into the Republican Party?

In addition, conservative positions on social issues like abortion and traditional marriage shifted many Roman Catholics toward the Republican Party. Hispanics tend to be more likely to support laws that restrict abortion and more likely to prefer marriage to be defined as one man, one woman, although there has been some shift toward support for same-sex marriage since 2015.[7] Hispanics tend to be more religiously observant than Anglos and tend to adopt issues on social policy similar to their religious beliefs. In the case of Hispanics, many remain committed to the Roman Catholic Church. Growth in Protestant Christianity among Hispanics has mainly been in the more socially conservative Evangelical and Pentecostal branches of Christianity. Emphasis on social conservativism on political issues may help Republicans reach out to more Hispanic voters. Only time will tell.

In this chapter, we will review the history of voter registration and voter qualifications. Discussion will focus on the expansion of voting rights to African Americans, Hispanics, women, members of the armed forces, and younger voters. In the case of African Americans and Hispanics, attention is paid to the challenges of securing voting rights in the face of legal and social barriers and to the need for U.S. government action to rectify this situation in light of white majority popular opinion during the 1950s and 1960s. We will also place Texas in context with the wider American South. We then turn our attention to the various types of elections—primaries, general elections, and direct democracy elections—before discussing the ways people in Texas can vote, including early voting and electronic voting. The rates of voter registration are examined, and we include a discussion of the demographics of who votes in Texas elections. The chapter concludes with a discussion of campaigns in Texas, from how candidates and political parties get on the ballot to styles of campaigning, trends in campaigning, and the campaign finance system. Throughout the chapter, we will study the attempts to maintain tradition in Texas while a fundamental transformation of the electoral landscape is occurring.

DEMOCRACY, REPRESENTATION, AND ELECTIONS IN TEXAS

Democracy and representative government imply mechanisms for citizens to make decisions about how to govern themselves directly or through agents chosen to represent them in the various branches and levels of government. At the heart of American and Texas government is the electoral system, which includes various types of elections, processes to determine who may vote, processes to determine who may run as a candidate for office, activities associated with campaigning to win an election contest, and the system of paying for electoral contests.

The health of a democracy hinges on electoral competition. Electoral competition is the interaction between candidates, voters, electoral systems, political parties, and organized interests. A system of fair competition, access to the ballot box, and free elections are essential to democratic, representative government. Campaigns must be meaningful, offering candidates, political parties, and organized interests an opportunity to provide information on their ideologies, issue positions, and prescriptions for action to the electorate. Participation in the electoral process must be free of coercion and intimidation while simultaneously allowing free expression of voter preferences. It must also ensure that the number participating in the electoral process is maximized to ensure no systematic bias in who is participating and who is not. When some voices are heard but others stifled, when some voices are allowed to participate while others are not, the result is a distorted image of what is wanted and needed. The outcomes of the election, the decisions made by the government branches so elected, and the legitimacy of the political system are distorted.

Voter Qualifications and Registration

Access to the voting booth is a vital issue in a democracy. The rules of who may vote, how they vote, and under what conditions they vote significantly impact the legitimacy of the government and its responsiveness to the people. Thus, voting rights and qualifications are essential to determining who gets what, when, and how. For example, if voting rights are denied to a group of people based on their race, candidates running for office might ignore the issues and concerns of people of that race.

At the Constitutional Convention of 1787, the framers of the U.S. Constitution largely left to state governments the conduct of elections. Article 1, Section 4 left the "Times, Places and Manner of holding Elections for Senators and Representatives" to the states. As a result, states determine who is qualified to vote in an election, how potential voters register to vote, how candidates and parties get onto a ballot, and what types of voting equipment are used to collect and count votes. This tradition remains at the basis of the constitutional order in the United States. However, since the Civil War (1861–1865), states have faced some degree of national oversight, first through a series of amendments to the U.S. Constitution and later through U.S. Supreme Court decisions. National supervision of elections became even more prominent during the civil rights era of the 1950s and 1960s when the U.S. government attempted to rectify past discrimination in the area of voting rights. This supervision gave several national government agencies, such as the U.S. Department of Justice, greater power over state election processes and began a transformation to include new voices in the electoral process.

After the Reconstruction Era (1865–1877), the state of Texas attempted to deny African Americans the right to vote through a variety of laws and practices. Candidates often ignored issues of concern to African Americans, such as the condition of African Americans' schools and crime in their neighborhoods. As a result, government policy made upgrading schools in white communities or addressing crime in white areas the priority. This attempt to deny minorities a voice is a tradition of white dominance in Texas.

Because state governments in the United States are responsible for voter registration, there are fifty different sets of voter registration processes, procedures, and qualifications. For example, North Dakota lacks any formal voter registration process. On Election Day, a voter simply shows a driver's license or state identification card indicating that he or she lives in the state and community in order to vote. However, each county shares its list of voters with the state to ensure voters do not vote in multiple locations on Election Day. Fifteen states, including Minnesota, Montana, and Wisconsin, allow same-day voter registration, meaning if a person is qualified to vote, then that person may register to vote and vote in an election on the same day. A few states, such as Iowa, allow same-day registration but limit the election contests in which the voter may participate. For example, in some cases the voter may vote only in the U.S. national election for president.

Voter registration in Texas is a bit more complicated. To register to vote, a person must be a citizen of the United States, be at least eighteen years of age, and have resided in Texas for at least thirty days. To vote in a county or other local government election, the thirty-day residency requirement applies, even if a voter is already a resident of Texas. So, a voter who moves from San Antonio to Amarillo must live in Amarillo for at least thirty days before voting in an Amarillo city election. If a voter owns property in several locations within Texas, the voter chooses which address serves as his or her primary residence for the purpose of voting.[8] To register to vote, a voter registration form must be completed. The form is available from county voter registration offices or online from the Texas secretary of state. The completed form must be submitted in person or by regular mail to the voter registration office in the county in which the voter resides. Electronic submissions are not allowed. Thirty-seven states, including several southern states, allow online voter registration, but not Texas. Since 1993, residents of Texas may register to vote when applying for a driver's license or when renewing a license. This development occurred when the U.S. Congress passed the National Voter Registration Act, more popularly known as the Motor Voter Act. As an election nears, some local civic organizations, such as the League of Women Voters or a university's student government association, often hold voter registration drives to get more people registered to vote. Those interested in registering to vote fill out the form and return it by mail, or the civic organization returns all of the cards to the county elections office. Some public libraries and schools make voter registration forms available. Regardless of how a person registers to vote, the form must be submitted to the county voter registration office no later than thirty days before an election. In 2016, Oregon extended the Motor Voter Act at the state level to automatically include anyone who gets a state driver's license, renews a license, or applies for any other state identification card.[9]

In addition to age and residency requirements, Texas maintains other qualifications to vote. Individuals determined by a court to be partially or totally mentally incapacitated may be denied the right to vote. Likewise, convicted felons over the age of eighteen are stripped of the right to vote until they have completed their sentence, including any required parole or probation.[10] This limitation reflects the traditionalistic political culture of Texas, which emphasizes the need to punish criminals and the idea that the rights of citizenship are not automatic.

Texas is one of eleven states to require registration at least thirty days before an election. Under the Voting Rights Act of 1965 passed by the U.S. Congress, this time limit of thirty days is the maximum a state may impose between the end of the registration period and the actual election. As discussed previously, states vary on when a voter may register before an election. The U.S. government, while limiting how far out a state may require a resident register to vote, still allows states significant control over the exact time frame for registering to vote. In addition, Texas's deadline is not unusual and is the most common deadline in the United States.

Motor Voter Act
the National Voter Registration Act, which allows citizens to register to vote when applying for or renewing their driver's license

Voting Rights Act of 1965
a federal statute that eliminated literacy tests as a qualification to vote, greatly increasing African Americans' access to the ballot box

TEXAS *Legends*

Landslide Lyndon

Today, visitors to the Lyndon B. Johnson Presidential Library and Museum in Austin can watch a mechanical figure of the former president lean on a split-rail fence and spin yarns about Texas. Johnson occupies a unique position in that he has both starred in and recounted many Texas legends.

The career of Lyndon Baines Johnson saw his rise from a teacher in a poor school in Pearsall, Texas, to president of the United States. When "Pappy" O'Daniel, in what one newspaper called the "most constructive act" of his career, retired from the U.S. Senate, the battle to succeed him pitted Johnson against former governor Coke Robert Stevenson. Stevenson was considered unbeatable by some, but Johnson won the endorsement of many of the state's newspapers and "Ma" Ferguson, who remembered that Johnson had attended the funeral of her husband while Stevenson skipped the service. Johnson concentrated on the large urban areas and zipped around the state campaigning via helicopter while Stevenson was content to drive around in an old Plymouth sedan.

Stevenson finished first in the primary, easily besting Johnson by a vote of 477,077 to 405,617 in a multicandidate race. However, lacking the majority needed to win the nomination, the top two candidates faced off in a runoff election. Official returns from the runoff took three days to compile before the Texas Election Board announced that Stevenson had won by 362 votes. However, "late returns" were still coming in, including what would become the legendary Box 13 from Alice, Texas, which belatedly revealed 203 uncounted ballots, 202 of them for Johnson. Upon further examination, the poll lists showed that Box 13's voters had signed in and voted in alphabetical order and in identical handwriting. Amended returns gave Johnson a margin of eighty-seven votes statewide and the nickname "Landslide Lyndon."

The State Democratic Executive Committee had the final word on the primary returns and voted 29–28 to certify the Johnson victory. While some of Johnson's critics have pointed to evidence of voter fraud in Alice, others point out that there was evidence of similar voter fraud on behalf of Stevenson in East Texas. As T. R. Fehrenbach concluded in his classic history of Texas, "Johnson's men had not defrauded Stevenson, but successfully outfrauded him."[i]

While Johnson's leadership of the nation as it tackled landmark civil rights legislation, including the Civil Rights Act of 1964 and the Voting Rights Act of 1965, has given him a well-deserved place in history, it's worth remembering that Johnson, like many other leaders of his time, came to power under the wing of powerful party bosses and sometimes won high office by taking the low road.

i. T. R. Fehrenbach, *Lone Star: A History of Texas and the Texans*, updated ed. (Cambridge, MA: Da Capo Press, 2000), 659.

Since 1972, Texas has maintained a permanent list of voters. The maintenance of the voter registration list is the responsibility of county governments. In most of Texas's counties, the responsibility is retained by the county tax assessor, a relic of the pre–civil rights era when the tax assessor was responsible for collecting poll taxes as a prerequisite to voting. Having the same office collect the poll tax and maintain voting records made sense. Other counties have shifted this responsibility to the county clerk's office. Because the county clerk is responsible for keeping other records, such as birth records and marriage licenses, placing voter registration in that office makes sense also. Finally, some counties have created a separate county elections office that in addition to maintaining the voter registration list also trains poll workers, sets up polling places, counts votes on election night, and performs other election-related duties.

VOTING RIGHTS IN TEXAS

Under the Republic of Texas Constitution, the right to vote in Texas elections extended only to white males. In fact, no free person of African descent was permitted to reside permanently in the Republic of Texas without the consent of the Texas Congress. The status of Hispanics varied across Texas and over time. In some localities, Hispanics were considered to be white, which allowed them to register to vote and cast ballots in an election. In other localities, Hispanics were considered nonwhite and therefore not entitled to vote. Women, Native Americans, and African Americans were denied suffrage, or the legal right to vote. The Texas Constitution of 1845, adopted when Texas joined the United States, continued to deny access to voting to these groups. The Civil War and its aftermath spurred an increased role for the national government in state election processes, primarily in securing to African American males the right to vote through the Fifteenth Amendment. The expansion of the role of the national government in the area of voting rights continued into the twentieth century with the addition of women's suffrage and the passage of voting rights legislation during the civil rights era.

Legal Barriers to Voting in Post-Reconstruction Texas

After the U.S. Civil War, the U.S. Constitution was amended to include the Thirteenth, Fourteenth, and Fifteenth Amendments. The Fifteenth Amendment specifically requires that state governments ensure the right to vote regardless of race or prior status as a slave. Here we see the first steps by the national government to regulate voting rights of all Americans and to transform the electoral landscape by ensuring equal rights for all to vote. With the end of military occupation of the southern states and the end of Reconstruction in 1876, states such as Texas officially maintained the right of African Americans to vote even as they imposed a series of barriers to effectively bar former slaves from actually exercising that right. The exact barriers used varied by state, but collectively states in the South used five types of barriers to prohibit African Americans from voting. A grandfather clause prohibited them from voting by restricting the right to vote to those whose grandfathers had the right to vote. Given that most African Americans in the American South were former slaves, as were their fathers and grandfathers, they were barred from voting. While the grandfather clause was important in several states, including Louisiana, Texas never used it. Another technique was the literacy test, a test of the prospective voter's ability to read and understand aspects of American government. The poor state of public education in African American communities throughout the South from the end of Reconstruction into the 1950s ensured that many African Americans were denied the right to vote. In some communities, African Americans were given different, harder tests than whites. Unlike other southern states, such as Alabama, Texas never used the literacy test.

A third legal barrier instituted to prevent African Americans from voting was the poll tax, an annual tax that had to be paid before one was allowed to vote. In Texas, the poll tax proved to be an important barrier. The Constitution of 1869 permitted

suffrage
the legal right to vote

grandfather clause
the granting of voting rights only to those citizens whose grandfathers had the right to vote; used to bar African Americans from voting in the South after the end of Reconstruction; used in other southern states but not used in Texas

literacy test
a test of a prospective voter's ability to read and understand aspects of American government; used to bar African Americans from voting in many parts of the post-Reconstruction South but not used in Texas

poll tax
an annual tax that had to be paid before one was allowed to vote; used in Texas

the use of poll taxes as a method of funding public education in Texas. Our current state constitution, adopted in 1876, also permitted the Texas Legislature to impose poll taxes on Texans.[11] The state imposed a rate of $1.50 per voter annually, while counties could impose a tax of up to $0.25 on each voter. Since most African Americans in Texas earned lower incomes than whites, African Americans faced the choice between purchasing basic necessities and participating in politics. Further, these taxes had to be paid well in advance so that anyone who wanted to vote had to save up to pay the tax, and these taxes were often levied in the spring, long before most people thought about the **general election** in November.

The poll tax prevented many poor whites from voting as well. Disenfranchising poor, rural white voters served a useful purpose: diluting the strength of the Populist Party. The Democratic Party feared the growing challenge of the Populist Party in the late 1800s, which was based in farmer and labor movements throughout the United States and directly challenged wealthy interests in Texas politics. Populists focused on the economic plight of poor, small- and medium-sized family farms and sought to shift the race-based politics of the Civil War, Reconstruction, and post-Reconstruction eras to a class-based politics in which the lower and middle classes could effectively vie with the upper classes for political power. As such, the poll tax served the Democratic Party well: African Americans and potential populist voters were eliminated from voting, and consistent with Texas's traditional political culture, it was the "better" elements of society that were given the right to rule. The poll tax was instrumental in allowing the Democratic Party in Texas to stave off any serious challenge to its supremacy and maintain its status as the majority party for decades. Racial appeals by traditional Democrats continued into the late 1940s and beyond. For example, Governor Allan Shivers in 1948 complained of "creeping socialism" by the national Democratic Party leadership and the need for "moral regeneration" or a "spiritual awakening" to prevent integration of the races.[12] He relied upon similar themes to confront integration of public schools in the 1950s as well.

Another important technique for disenfranchising African American voters in the southern states was the **white primary**. Essentially, participation in primary elections to nominate candidates for office was restricted to members of the party only, and membership in the party was limited to white voters. Because the **primary election** determined the Democratic Party nominee for the general election and because the primary was restricted to white voters, the white primary guaranteed that parties and candidates responded only to issues of concern in the white population.

Among the states that used the white primary, Texas was unusual in that its use of such a primary occurred because of state law. All other states implementing the white primary did so as a matter of party rules or custom rather than law.[13] This legal use of the white primary in Texas became a key barrier preventing African Americans from voting in our state.

Finally, violence and intimidation were also used in Texas to discourage African Americans, although the extent of violence against African Americans seems to have been less than in other southern states like Mississippi. Yet, the use of these techniques against Hispanics also set Texas apart from other southern states simply because, until recently, other southern states lacked any substantial Hispanic population to be targeted by the white majority. However, the extent to which violence and intimidation were used to suppress voting varied by county and over time.

general election
an interparty election in which candidates from two or more political parties and independent candidates compete for actual political office

white primary
the attempt by the Democratic Party in Texas and other southern states to limit the voting in party primaries only to party members; in Texas, this practice was codified in state law

primary election
intraparty election in which candidates compete to determine who will win the party's nomination in the general election

Eliminating Barriers to Voting for African Americans

Ultimately, the removal of barriers to voting gave the national government significant control over state voter registration processes and in so doing took power away from the states. This nationalization of voter registration occurred because elected officials in southern states refused to ensure African Americans' equal rights, including the right to vote. The assumption of control by the national government was a necessary step on the road to equality. Restoration of voting rights for African Americans occurred through court cases and legislation passed by the U.S. Congress.

The grandfather clause was eliminated when the U.S. Supreme Court issued its ruling in *Guinn v. United States* (1915). To eliminate this barrier, the court relied on the equal protection clause of the Fourteenth Amendment to the U.S. Constitution. This clause of the Constitution requires that state laws and state constitutions treat all citizens the same. Because the grandfather clause treated African Americans, whose grandfathers clearly did not have the right to vote, differently from whites, it violated the idea that the law must treat all citizens the same. The literacy test used in other states as an important barrier to voting was removed by the passage of the Voting Rights Act of 1965. This act is also important for other reasons that are discussed later in this section.

Eliminating the poll tax proved to be more complicated. The poll tax in national elections was eliminated by the Twenty-Fourth Amendment to the U.S. Constitution in 1964. However, states assumed that state and local elections, which clearly did not involve the national government, remained solely the domain of state law. Payment of the poll tax continued to be required for state and local elections for another year. Then, in *Harper v. Virginia State Board of Elections* (1966), the U.S. Supreme Court struck down the poll tax in Virginia state and local elections as a violation of the equal protection clause of the Fourteenth Amendment to the U.S. Constitution.[14] Challenging the white primary also initially proved difficult, especially in Texas. In the Texas-based case *Nixon v. Herndon* (1924),[15] the U.S. Supreme Court invalidated the white primary where required or sanctioned by state law. In response, the Texas Democratic Party declared itself a "private organization" and therefore exempt from the standards of equity applied to elections run by the state. Twenty years later, the court threw out the white primary in *Smith v. Allwright* (1944).[16] The court declared that the vital function of nominating candidates for office meant that political parties were public organizations. Not accepting this decision, the Democratic Party in Fort Bend County attempted a "Jaybird" preprimary in which only whites cast informal votes to consolidate support behind a single candidate, whom all whites would then back in the official primary. Seeing through this attempt at coordination and control, the U.S. Supreme Court outlawed the practice in *Terry v. Adams* (1953).[17] One estimate suggests that removing the poll tax and white primary had the immediate impact of allowing as many as 200,000 African Americans in Texas to vote.[18]

After decades of wrangling with a host of discriminatory practices, the U.S. Congress passed the Voting Rights Act of 1965. The act barred any "qualification or prerequisite to voting, or standard, practice, or procedure" that served to deny or abridge the right of a citizen to vote based on race or color. The law's broad language was a response to states whose practices discriminated against black citizens. Many of these practices remained in effect until the courts struck them down. Under the act, a

---

equal protection clause clause of the Fourteenth Amendment to the U.S. Constitution requiring that state laws and state constitutions treat all citizens the same

---

Why did Texas rely on the poll tax and white primary to limit voting rights of African Americans? Why did Texas not rely on either the grandfather clause or literacy test?

⭐ **CRITICAL THINKING**

state that was found to have a pattern of discrimination against a group was required to get preclearance before instituting new procedures or practices that could also have the effect of discriminating against minorities. This provision included changes in polling locations, dates for elections, qualifications for voting, and district lines drawn for state legislatures and local governments, such as city councils, county commissions, and school boards. Another provision of the act addressed the issue of violence and

The poll tax was used to deny the right to vote to many African Americans in Texas. This poll tax receipt from Wood County in 1955 shows that the poll tax had been paid in full by a white couple, thereby allowing them to vote in upcoming elections.

intimidation when African Americans attempted to register to vote or to cast their votes on Election Day. The act required the U.S. government to send election monitors into areas with a history of discrimination. The monitors, who were employees of the U.S. Department of Justice, would report any harassment or activities used to intimidate African Americans to local government officials and to state government authorities. If these local and state officials refused to stop the violence and/or intimidation, they could be charged with a federal crime for failing to enforce the act and could be prosecuted in federal court.

While most of the provisions of the act remain in force, critics have raised concerns about the preclearance provision, particularly the question of how long a state or local government is subject to such preclearance. A section of the act does allow local governments, but not states, to apply for an exemption to the preclearance provision based on the percentage of the minority population registered to vote and percentage that votes in elections. In *Northwest Austin Municipal Utility District No. 1 v. Holder* (2009), the U.S. Supreme Court affirmed the right of local governments to apply for an exemption.[19] A few years later, the court declared the entire preclearance process to be unconstitutional in *Shelby County v. Holder* (2013),[20] in part because enforcement of the preclearance provisions relied upon data and practices from the 1960s, not current information.

Hispanics and Voting Rights

The history of voting rights for Hispanics in Texas is a complex story. In the days of the Republic of Texas and early statehood, some discrimination against Hispanics existed, but not to the extent faced by African Americans.[21] Texans of Mexican descent had an uncertain political status in a state that reserved voting for white citizens but did not define *white*. In 1897, a federal district court affirmed the civil rights of Texas Mexicans to vote after Richard Rodríguez challenged the claim that he did not qualify for citizenship since he was not "a white person, nor an African, nor of African descent, and [was] therefore not capable of becoming an American citizen."[22]

The extent of discrimination against Hispanics is somewhat uncertain, as illustrated in the contrast between the impact of the poll tax compared to the white primary. The poll tax did disenfranchise many Hispanics, just as it did poor whites and African Americans, because so many Tejanos were involved in the kind of subsistence farming and ranching that might feed their family but did not produce much cash. Therefore, the removal of the poll tax in national and state elections provided an opportunity for more Hispanics to register to vote. However, scholars debate the impact of the white primary on Hispanic voting. In some counties, Hispanics were apparently allowed to vote in the white primary when they formed an important base of support for the Democratic Party, as they did in southern parts of Texas. As evidence of this, some scholars note that along the Mexican border many local elected officials were Hispanic. Yet some scholars assert that the white primary did prohibit Hispanic voters.[23]

Although the Voting Rights Act of 1965 originally applied only to attempts to disenfranchise African American voters, the renewal of the act in 1975 extended its protection to Hispanic voters in states or counties with a history of low levels of Hispanics voting, where elections were conducted only in English, or where more than 5 percent of the voting-age population was part of a language minority.[24] Half of all states, including Texas, are required to provide bilingual ballots that encourage Hispanic voters who are citizens to participate in elections. A provision for a bilingual ballot has also been applied to benefit Native Americans in twelve states, with specific languages varying by state according to the tribal languages spoken. In Texas, this provision applies only to El Paso county, which must provide Pueblo language ballots. Asian Americans also are covered by this provision in ten states across the United States. Harris County, Texas, is required to provide ballots in Chinese and Vietnamese, and Tarrant County is required to provide Chinese ballots.[25]

One source of the disenfranchisement of Hispanics appears to have been economic harassment. Whites boycotted Hispanic businesses, linked bank loans to support for white candidates in elections, and fired Hispanics who engaged in political campaigns. In addressing discrimination against Hispanic voting in Bexar County, the U.S. Supreme Court identified the sources of discrimination to be primarily economic, educational, and linguistic in nature, rather than the result of law.[26] However, the use of economic and other tools to disenfranchise Hispanics varied by county.[27] Thus, rather than the formal and legal barriers that African Americans faced, the primary barriers to voting for Hispanics were intimidation tactics.

The expansion of voting rights to African Americans and Hispanics ushered in a transformation of the Texas electorate to be more inclusive of all residents of Texas. However, the recent issue of voter fraud, or concerns about possible voter fraud, has led to a wave of states passing voter identification (ID) laws. These laws require that a voter present some form of voter ID or other document on Election Day as he or she goes to the polls. Proponents of these laws state that they are necessary to ensure that only the registered voter actually casts the vote, rather than someone attempting to impersonate the voter. They claim such fraud could shift election outcomes, causing the winner—a person supported by actual registered voters—to lose to a candidate who wins as a result of support from unregistered voters. Often, unauthorized immigrants are identified as a potential source of fraudulent voters. Opponents of the identification requirement point to the lack of evidence that unauthorized immigrants vote or that the number of fraudulent ballots is sufficiently large enough to change election outcomes. They also point out that the law exempts mail-in ballots, which can be another source of voter fraud. In addition, voter ID opponents raise the issue of the intimidation of minority voters.[28] Another concern is the impact on minorities, especially those with low incomes, since such a law requires a state identification card or a state driver's license in order to vote. Racial and ethnic minorities are often less likely to possess either of these forms of identification because they cost money.[29] Thus, the requirement that a voter present a state-issued photo ID becomes a tax akin to a poll tax, which was one of the techniques used in Texas and other states to prevent African Americans from voting in the past.

In 2011, the Texas Legislature passed a voter ID law that requires a voter to show one of several forms of ID, including a state-issued driver's license, state identification card, or state voter ID card, when he or she votes in an election. The last option can only be used for the purpose of voter ID and can be issued upon the request of a registered voter free of charge.[30] This law paralleled similar laws passed

Explain why providing ballots in multiple languages is essential in a representative system of government. What potential drawbacks exist?

 SOCIAL RESPONSIBILITY

FEDERALISM IN Action

Voter Identification

Texas spent the decades following the Civil War passing a variety of laws attempting to disenfranchise minority voters and undermine the Fifteenth Amendment. To counter this discrimination, the federal Voting Rights Act of 1965 included a provision in which any change in election laws had to be precleared—or approved in advance—by the U.S. Department of Justice to ensure that it had neither the intent nor the effect of disenfranchising minorities. This clearance requirement ended in 2013 after a ruling by the U.S. Supreme Court. On the same day the Supreme Court handed down its decision, Texas declared that its recently passed voter identification (ID) law, which had been denied preclearance by the federal government, would take immediate effect.[i] The Texas voter ID law, which is considered one of the strictest in the country, requires voters to produce one of a few approved forms of identification at the polls in order to vote. Driver's licenses, state ID cards, passports, and concealed handgun licenses are approved, but student ID cards, even those issued from a state university, are not. The approximately 600,000 Texans who lack approved identification can obtain a free identification, but they still have to pay for the documents necessary to acquire the card.[ii]

For many in Texas, having to get proposed changes in election laws precleared by the national government rankled; and it was a question of federalism. Texas authorities applauded the abolition of the preclearance requirement, which then-governor Rick Perry described as "a clear victory for federalism and the states. Texas may now implement the will of the people without being subject to outdated and unnecessary oversight and the overreach of federal power."[iii] Moreover, Republicans in the state argued that the voter ID law was necessary to address voter fraud.

Opponents of the voter ID law argued that it disproportionately affected minority voters, who are less likely to have one of the approved forms of identification. For those Texans, critics have charged that the law acts as a poll tax. Moreover, opponents suggest that voter fraud is extremely rare, with fewer than three cases for every 1 million votes cast.[iv] Opponents worry that voter ID laws will keep people from the polls. A recent study by the University of Houston and Rice University found that in a 2014 congressional election, the Texas voter ID law, through misunderstanding and misinformation, suppressed the vote even among Texans who possessed approved identification.[v] In 2016, the U.S. Fifth Circuit Court of Appeals ruled that Texas's voter ID law violated the Voting Rights Act. The court found that the small number of acceptable IDs and the "lackluster educational efforts" by the state regarding the new requirement created excessive burdens on Texas voters.[vi] The court did not strike down the entire law but instead ordered Texas to fix it. The Texas Legislature made changes to the law during the 2017 session to comply with the federal appeals court, but these changes did not completely satisfy civil rights groups. Challenges to the updated law were eventually appealed back

to the U.S. Fifth Circuit Court of Appeals, which ultimately ruled that the Texas law was now constitutional.

How can Texas weigh the possibility of voter fraud against potential disenfranchisement of voters?

⭐ **CRITICAL THINKING**

When should the federal government get involved in a state's election laws?

⭐ **CRITICAL THINKING**

i. Greg Abbott, "Statement by Texas Attorney General Greg Abbott," June 25, 2013, https://texasattorneygeneral.gov/oagnews/release.php?id=4435.
ii. Jim Malewitz, "Texas Voter ID Law Violates Voting Rights Act, Court Rules," *Texas Tribune*, July 20, 2016, https://www.texastribune.org/2016/07/20/appeals-court-rules-texas-voter-id.
iii. Todd Gillman, "Supreme Court Strikes Down Formula That Puts Heightened Scrutiny on Texas under Voting Rights Act; Voter ID Law Could Go into Effect Soon," *Dallas Morning News*, June 25, 2013, https://www.dallasnews.com/news/politics/2013/06/25/breaking-supreme-court-strikes-down-formula-that-puts-heightened-scrutiny-on-texas-under-voting-rights-act.
iv. Ross Ramsey, "Analysis: Scant Evidence for Abbott's 'Rampant' Voter Fraud," *Texas Tribune*, March 15, 2016, https://www.texastribune.org/2016/03/15/analysis-scant-evidence-abbott-rampant-voter-fraud.
v. Bill Hobby, Mark P. Jones, Jim Granato, and Renée Cross, "The Texas Voter ID Law and the 2014 Election: A Study of Texas's 23rd Congressional District" (white paper from University of Houston Hobby Center for Public Policy and Rice University's Baker Institute for Public Policy, August 2015).
vi. Malewitz, "Texas Voter ID Law Violates Voting Rights Act, Court Rules."

by other state legislatures in states like Indiana and Georgia. In *Crawford v. Marion County Board of Election* (2008), the U.S. Supreme Court affirmed the requirement that voters show a photo ID in order to vote. Because the Texas law passed prior to the U.S. Supreme Court decision in *Shelby County v. Holder* (2013), it was subject to preclearance as discussed previously. After denying preclearance because Texas could not show the law did not deny or limit the right to vote on the basis of race,[31] U.S. Attorney General Eric Holder called the law essentially a poll tax.[32] In August 2012, a federal district court in Washington, DC, struck down the Texas voter ID law, calling it racially discriminatory. However, the U.S. Supreme Court's decision in *Shelby County v. Holder* (2013) had the immediate effect of allowing Texas to implement the new voter ID law. Civil rights groups then sued Texas to block the law. Eventually, the U.S. Fifth Circuit Court of Appeals in New Orleans struck down part of the law, but then required the U.S. Department of Justice and Texas government to resolve the issue. An agreement allowed a wider number of documents to prove residence and allowed those without a photo ID to swear an affidavit attesting to their citizenship. In 2017, Governor Abbott signed a law that updated the 2011 law to meet the appeals court decision. However, several civil rights groups believed the state had not fully met the requirements and again sued the state. Ultimately, the U.S. Court of Appeals in New Orleans found Texas in compliance with their earlier rulings.

Voting Rights for Women, Members of the Armed Forces, and Younger Voters

Texas proved slightly more progressive in its extension of voting rights to women. The Wyoming Territory in 1869 was the first area of the United States to grant women the right to vote. Women's suffrage in Wyoming continued after statehood in 1890, making Wyoming the first state in which women could vote. In 1893, Colorado became the first state in which a state legislature granted women the right to vote. The Texas Legislature first considered the issue of women's suffrage in 1915, and by 1918 it had authorized women to vote in primary elections. The 1918 election saw the first woman to win statewide office: Annie Webb Blanton was elected Texas superintendent of public instruction. Also, Nellie Gray Robertson defeat her male opponent 446–2 to become Hood County Attorney. In all of these states and territories, women possessed the right to vote in some or all state and local government elections only. Two years later, in 1920, the Nineteenth Amendment to the U.S. Constitution gave women the right to vote in U.S. national elections. Texas also proved somewhat forward-thinking by being the first state in the Old South—and the ninth in the nation—to ratify the Nineteenth Amendment.

Historically, members of the U.S. military and their families were denied the right to vote in some states if they were not residents of that state prior to joining the military. In Texas, a provision of the original 1876 state constitution prohibited voting by all "soldiers, marines and seamen, employed in the service of the army or navy of the United States." Because residency is a requirement to vote, members of the military were effectively denied the right during a tour of duty because they were large populations considered to be transient that could overwhelm local voters. In 1965, the U.S. Supreme Court ruled in *Carrington v. Rash* (1965) that while states can impose reasonable residency requirements for voting, it cannot deny someone the right to vote because he or she is a member of the armed services. It said that members of the military who have established residency and intend to make the state their permanent home must be allowed to vote.[33] Members of the military and their families were then allowed to establish residency like any other person moving to Texas and exercise the right to vote in state and local elections.

A further extension of voting rights concerned young adults. The right to vote was associated with being an adult—historically defined as having attained the age of twenty-one. However, in 1971, the Twenty-Sixth Amendment to the U.S. Constitution lowered the minimum voting age to eighteen in federal elections. States quickly followed suit, lowering the minimum voting age to eighteen for state and local elections. This extension of voting rights stemmed in part from U.S. involvement in Vietnam. Young men of this era were fighting—and losing their lives—for their country in the Vietnam War but were unable to vote in national or state elections. The discrepancy between being able to die for one's country and not being able to participate in the selection of one's political leaders struck many as wrong, spurring ratification of the Twenty-Sixth Amendment.

The voting rights of college students represents an issue related to both the youth of these students and their transient nature. Today, Texas state law guarantees college students the right to choose where they will vote if the student spends weeks or months in different locations each year, including the community in which he or she attends college.[34] In the past, state and local governments attempted to prevent college students from registering to vote where they attended school if that location was different from their parents' residence. Since most votes in Texas occur on a weekday during the school year, students often find that voting in the community where they attend college is easier than returning home to vote. The argument against the participation of college students in local elections was similar to that against the participation of members of the military: they were viewed as large numbers of transients rather than permanent members of the community. However, because college students use local government services, such as roads, and pay local taxes, such as sales taxes, they often do have an interest in the politics of the community in which they attend school. In addition, once a student votes in an election, he or she is more likely to vote in future elections. Thus, by allowing students to vote in the community where they attend college, a lifelong pattern of voting is encouraged.

The objection to college students' voting may evidence a deeper distrust. Some area residents view them as outsiders who might displace local political elites and change local ordinances in the community. In any case, when students go off to college, they have the right to choose whether to vote at their permanent home address or at their college address, but they must choose one or the other.

An interesting quirk regarding the rights of voters in Texas centers on the conduct of the voter on Election Day. With the exceptions of treason, felony, or disturbing the peace, voters in Texas are exempt from arrest while going to or returning from voting.[35]

The history of voting rights in Texas appears to be periodic attempts to restrict the right to vote to only the "right" kinds of voters: white and, at times, Hispanic males with better education and more money. The Democratic Party of the post-Reconstruction era sought to maintain its power base by writing the "rules of the game" to exclude African Americans and to prevent the state government from responding to the demands of all citizens. As a result, state politics and policy reflected primarily the wishes of those able to vote, rather than those of all the citizens of Texas. Only after the civil rights era of the 1950s and 1960s took root did significant numbers of poorer whites and African

Americans gain access to the ballot box, transforming Texas politics as the electorate became more inclusive. Efforts to include women, members of the military, and young voters in the election process proved less controversial. More recently, legal attempts to include Hispanics in Texas politics more completely—as voters, candidates, and elected officials—have proved increasingly effective.

TYPES OF ELECTIONS IN TEXAS

Voters can participate in several types of elections. A primary election is essentially an intraparty election. In these elections, candidates compete to represent a particular political party in a general election. Thus, the winner of a primary "wins" the party's nomination and a place on the ballot in the general election. A primary election may be a **direct primary** in which the winning candidate automatically receives the party nomination, or it may be a **preference primary**. In a preference primary, voters indicate their choice of candidate to hold office, but the actual selection is left to the political party elites, usually at a state or national party convention.

direct primary
a primary election in which the winning candidate directly receives the party nomination

preference primary
a primary election in which voters indicate their choice to hold office but the actual selection is left to the political party elites

Primary Elections versus General Elections

The winner of a political party's primary next moves on to compete in the general election as that party's candidate. General elections see candidates from two or more political parties vie for elected office. These elections are interparty elections in which voters choose among several candidates representing different political parties and independent candidates. The winner of the general election wins office, for example, as governor, member of the state legislature, or judge.

In Texas, primary elections, in most instances, are direct primaries. Political parties use direct primaries to nominate candidates for all state offices, plus the U.S. House of Representatives and the U.S. Senate. In the presidential primaries, Texas and many other states use an indirect primary to nominate candidates. An alternative to the indirect primary is the caucus. In some states, parties are allowed to pick how their delegates are selected. In Texas, the two major parties must use a primary election, according to state law.

Three types of primaries exist: closed primaries, open primaries, and blanket or wide-open primaries. A **closed primary** restricts the voters who participate in the primary to party loyalists. Typically, prior to the primary, often when registering to vote, each individual voter must declare or list a party affiliation. At the primary, when a voter shows up to cast a ballot, the voter's name is checked against a list of registered party supporters. Obviously, this approach limits the number of voters in the primary to those willing to specify a party affiliation, thereby excluding independent voters and those affiliated with another political party. An advantage of the closed primary is the fact that candidates who win the party nomination more closely reflect the beliefs and ideas of the party faithful. On the flip side, candidates may not reflect the beliefs of the entire electorate because independent voters and supporters of other political parties are excluded from voting. A closed, enforced primary ensures that only the registered party supporters vote in the primary. However, some states and localities use a closed, unenforced primary. In this case, although voters register with a specific party affiliation, at the actual primary election a voter's name is not checked against a list of

closed primary
an electoral contest restricted to party loyalists that excludes supporters of other political parties and independent voters

registered party supporters. A voter may therefore be registered with the Democratic Party but vote in the Republican Party primary or vice versa. In states with closed primaries, political parties may hold their primaries on different days.

In an **open primary**, a voter is not required to declare a party affiliation. At the primary, the voter requests a specific party's ballot. The ballot contains only those candidates from the party that the voter requested. Once a voter participates in a specific party's primary, he or she is prohibited, usually by law, from participating in another party's primary. As with closed primaries, in some states the parties may hold their open primaries on different days. Independent voters often prefer the open primary because they may be allowed to participate in at least one party's primary. Moreover, cross-party voting often occurs because Republicans may vote in the Democratic Party primary and vice versa. Of course, if a Republican chooses to vote in the Democratic primary, that voter is then barred from participating in the Republican primary. Also, open primaries are more subject to manipulation. For example, if a Democratic Party candidate is running unopposed in the Democratic primary, party officials may encourage Democratic voters to show up for the Republican primary and help the most extreme or easiest-to-defeat candidate win the Republican nomination. Republicans may likewise engage in the same behavior in a Democratic primary.

A few states use the **blanket or wide-open primary**. In popular media, this primary is often called the jungle primary. In this system, voters do not register a party affiliation. At the primary, voters receive ballot papers containing the names of all candidates from all political parties running for office. Voters still may choose only one candidate per office, not one candidate per political party. There are two subtypes of blanket or wide-open primaries. The first type is the partisan blanket primary. In this system, the Democratic Party candidate with the most votes moves on to the general election as the Democratic nominee, and the Republican candidate with the most votes competes in the general election as the Republican nominee. The same results hold true for any and all other parties holding primary elections. Currently, no states use the partisan blanket primary. Louisiana pioneered the second type of blanket or wide-open primary, called the nonpartisan blanket primary. In this type, the top two candidates, regardless of party affiliation, move on to the general election. In the 1970s and 1980s, a common outcome of the primary saw two Democrats competing in the general election, with no Republicans on the ballot. Another unusual aspect of Louisiana's system is the fact that if a candidate wins a majority of the vote in the primary election, the candidate wins the office and no general election ensues. In effect, the primary becomes a general election. Note that Louisiana uses this primary system only for state and local elections. In 2004, voters in Washington adopted an amendment to the state constitution to change their partisan system to a nonpartisan blanket primary like Louisiana's. The U.S. Supreme Court upheld the use of this type of primary in 2008. More recently, California voters approved Proposition 14 in June 2010. This ballot measure amended the California constitution to require the use of the nonpartisan blanket primary in state and many local elections. A legal challenge to the new system failed in federal district court in late 2010, and the system was first used in California's June 2012 primaries.

Currently, Texas's primary system is technically a closed one, as required by state law. In practice, however, Texas's system is considered semi-open.[36] The designation semi-open is appropriate because, as in an open primary, voters in Texas do not have

TEXAS OREGON

While Texas serves as a pioneer in early voting, Oregon followed a different path in encouraging voter turnout by allowing vote by mail. In the vote-by-mail system, the state of Oregon mails a ballot to every registered voter about two weeks before the election. At their leisure, voters mark the ballot and mail the ballot back in a special envelope. A voter may also deliver the ballot by hand to designated locations throughout the state.

Historically, states allowed voters to receive a ballot early and mail it back only for absentee voting. Absentee voting required that the voter provide a legitimate reason for not being in the community on Election Day in order to cast an early ballot. In 1981, Oregon allowed limited experiments with mail-in ballots for all voters in local elections. In December 1995, the state extended the process to party primaries. By 1998, all elections in Oregon utilized the vote-by-mail system. One review of the research on the impact of voting by mail suggests that voter turnout increases between 5 to 10 percent over traditional in-person voting.[i] Oregon's success with vote by mail led Colorado and Washington State to adopt it as well.

The table presents some statistics comparing turnout in Texas to turnout in Oregon since voting by mail became a statewide process in 1998.

Election	Oregon Turnout	Texas Turnout
2000 Presidential election	61%	44%
2002 November general election	56%	29%
2004 Presidential election	74%	46%
2006 November general election	57%	26%
2008 Presidential election	63%	46%
2010 November general election	53%	27%
2012 Presidential election	63%	43%
2014 November general election	52%	25%
2016 Presidential election	61%	46%

Sources: Texas Secretary of State, "Turnout and Voter Registration Figures (1970–Current)," 2018, http://www.sos.state.tx.us/elections/historical/70-92.shtml; U.S. Census Bureau, "Voting and Registration Tables," 2016, http://www.census.gov/topics/public-sector/voting/data/tables.html. Some calculations were made by the authors.

i.   Paul Gronke and Peter Miller, "Voting by Mail and Turnout: A Replication and Extension" (paper presented at the Annual Meeting of the American Political Science Association, Chicago, IL, August 20, 2007).

How is the vote-by-mail system similar to early voting in Texas?

 **CRITICAL THINKING**

How does vote-by-mail place more responsibility on you, the voter, to be honest?

 PERSONAL RESPONSIBILITY

to declare a party affiliation when registering to vote. However, the system becomes functionally closed on the day of the primary election because when a voter requests a specific party's ballot at the primary, this information is recorded and, in some counties, even stamped on voter registration cards at the time. For the next year, the voters cannot change party affiliation and vote in the regular primary or runoff primary of another party. If the next primary occurs within one year, a voter is forced to vote in the same party's primary as before. If the voter requests another party's primary ballot, he or she is still given the ballot for the party from the earlier primary. Electronic record-keeping has enhanced the ability of local election officials and party election monitors to enforce this provision, because the party affiliation becomes part of your electronic voting registration for a year after the primary.

Another interesting requirement in Texas primary elections is that the election be a **majority election**. In a majority election, the winner of the election must receive a majority of the vote—50 percent plus one additional vote—in the primary election. If the leading candidate does not receive a majority in the initial election, a **runoff election** is held a month later between the first- and second-place candidates in that party's initial primary election. In this way, the Texas primary system becomes essentially a single-member district majority (SMDM) election system, as discussed in Chapter 11. This designation of SMDM reflects the fact that a single winner must be chosen by the party faithful in the election district, in this case a specific political party's nominee for a single office like U.S. senator or Texas House of Representatives District 148. In the case of primaries, the use of SMDM means that the winner receives the right to run as the political party's candidate in the general election. Simply put, candidates must receive a majority of the political party's primary votes, not just the most votes. The advantage to SMDM is that the winner selected is the preferred candidate among the voters who show up. Therefore, the winner can safely claim to represent the majority of the party faithful on Election Day.

Note that in Texas, general elections are plurality elections. In a **plurality election**, the candidate with the most votes wins, regardless of the percentage of the vote received. As a result, Texas general elections use the single-member district plurality (SMDP) election system. For example, in a race for Texas House of Representatives District 148, the general election could feature a three-candidate race between a Republican, a Democrat, and a Libertarian. It is theoretically possible for the Republican to receive 33.4 percent of the vote, the Democrat 33.3 percent of the vote, and the Libertarian 33.3 percent of the vote. The Republican wins, despite the fact that a majority of the voters voted for other candidates and the winner did not receive an outright majority. The SMDP system is the most common election system for legislative elections across all levels of government in the United States, with only a handful of states like Georgia and Louisiana using SMDM for general elections. A variation of SMDM is called **instant runoff**. In this election, voters indicate a first choice, a second choice, etc. If no candidate receives a majority of the first-place votes, rather than declaring the plurality winner elected or holding a runoff election for SMDM, a winner is determined based on the rank ordering of the first- and second-place votes. This system is used to elect the lower house of the Australian national parliament. Instant runoff is sometimes called ranked-choice voting, and voters in Maine adopted the system in a statewide referendum in 2016. In November 2018, Maine used the system statewide for the first time.

The history of primaries in Texas is riddled with political manipulation to produce certain outcomes. In an effort to stave off defection to the Republican Party as national Democratic Party leaders began to emphasize civil rights legislation in the 1950s, election reforms in 1951–1952 allowed **cross-filing**. In cross-filing, a candidate may run simultaneously as a Democratic candidate and as a Republican, essentially competing

majority election
a type of election in which a candidate must receive 50 percent of the vote plus one additional vote to be declared the winner; simply winning the most votes is not sufficient

runoff election
a type of election in a SMDM that is held when an election fails to yield a clear majority winner in the initial balloting; the runoff is limited to the top two vote-getters from the initial election, ensuring a majority win

plurality election
a type of election in which the candidate with the most votes wins the election

instant runoff
a type of election in which second-place votes are considered in instances where no candidate has received a majority of the vote; a winner is determined by adding together the first- and second-place votes

cross-filing
a system that allows a candidate to run simultaneously as a Democratic and a Republican candidate, essentially competing in both parties' primaries

in both parties' primaries.[37] This tactic allowed Democrats to maintain control of the Republican Party as it held its first presidential primary election in Texas. Democratic voters were able to cross over to support Republican candidate Dwight Eisenhower for U.S. president, all the while ensuring that state and local candidates who won the Republican primary were also loyal Democrats. Republicans labeled these Democratic voters "One-Day Republicans."[38] This practice seems unusual, but as recently as 1948, Texas Republicans approached prominent Democrats, including candidates for governor, and requested that they run as Republicans.[39] Note that some states today allow a related practice called electoral fusion, in which more than one party nominates the same candidate in the general election and the candidate carries both party labels on the election ballot.

Direct Democracy Elections

A final type of election is the direct democracy election, which emerged during the era of the progressive reforms. At the state level, three of the Progressive Party's ideas associated with direct democracy and voter input into the decision-making process have been adopted: the referendum, the initiative, and the recall. Opening the political system through direct democracy elections was promoted by progressives in the early twentieth century as a method to break the power of organized interests, labor unions, and big business and return the power to the average citizen-voter.

Normally, a law is passed by having the state legislature approve a bill; the bill is then signed by the governor to become a law. In a referendum, the state legislature proposes a new law and places it on an election ballot. At the next election, citizens vote statewide to determine whether the new law is adopted or rejected. As of 2017, twenty-six states used the referendum for approving new laws.[40] Texas lacks this referendum process to enact laws. Another use of the referendum, as discussed in Chapter 2, is to approve formal amendments to a state constitution. In this instance, a state legislature submits the amendment to the voters of the state for approval. Forty-nine states, including Texas, require that amendments to the state's constitution be approved by voters through this second use of referenda.

Another way to get citizens directly involved in lawmaking is the initiative. An initiative takes shape when citizens propose a new law by writing it out and then collecting the signatures of registered voters who support the law on an initiative petition form. When a set number of registered voters, which varies by state, has signed the form, the form is submitted to the state's chief elections officer for certification. Once certified, the proposed new law is placed on an election ballot for voters statewide to accept or reject. Sometimes the initiative petition is called simply a proposition. States use the initiative petition, like the referendum, to propose new laws or to amend the state constitution. As of 2017, twenty-four states allowed the initiative petition,[41] but Texas was not one of them.

The recall petition serves as a method for removing a sitting elected official before his or her term of office has finished. The recall operates in a manner similar to a petition: A specified number of signatures is collected on a petition calling for immediate removal of an elected official from office. Once enough signatures have been gathered, the petition is submitted to the state's chief elections officer for certification. Following the certification, voters at the next election determine whether the official remains in office. Eighteen states allow the recall petition for elected officials. Texas does not. However, local officials in Texas may be recalled in some cities and other local governments depending on the locality's plan of government and the Texas Local Government Code. The limited use of direct democracy elections reflects two realities of Texas politics. First, the Texas Constitution of 1876 predated the rise of the progressive movement and its championing of direct democracy. Yet the lack of citizen and voter inclusion maintains the Texas tradition of limiting political input by those deemed less important by political elites.

Too Much Democracy?

In Texas's general elections, voters are confronted with the long ballot, one Progressive Era reform adopted by Texas that made as many state and local offices as possible subject to direct election by the voters. The long ballot is so called because it is just that—long. A long ballot may contain choices for all of the following: the governor, the lieutenant governor, the comptroller of public accounts, the commissioner of the General Land Office, the commissioner of agriculture, the attorney general, a state senator, a state representative, a member of the U.S. House of Representatives, a U.S. senator, members of the Railroad Commission of Texas, members of the Texas Board of Education, a justice of the peace (JP), county commissioners, county tax assessors, a mayor, members of the city council, city judges, county judges, and state court judges (including district court, appeals court, and the two high courts). All of this is quite an undertaking.

The sheer number of elected offices and candidates running for office means that voters are often overwhelmed at the polling place. One result is that voters tend to vote for the offices that appear higher on the ballot while ignoring and leaving blank offices that are farther down. When doing so, voters typically vote for the most "important" offices, such as the U.S. president, state governor, or U.S. senator, and leave "lesser" offices at the county and local levels blank. This phenomenon is called **roll off**.[42] For example, in Texas, almost 209,000 fewer votes were cast for Texas Railroad Commissioner in 2016 compared to the number of votes cast for U.S. president—a difference of approximately 2.3 percent. Yet both of these offices are a statewide vote.

Another effect of the long ballot is **party-line voting**, also known as straight-ticket voting. Party-line voting occurs when a voter selects candidates on the basis of his or her party affiliation—that is, the voter records a vote for all Democratic candidates or all Republican candidates. In this way, the voter avoids having to make tough decisions on an office-by-office or candidate-by-candidate basis. In some states, party-line voting still requires a voter to go through the entire ballot, marking each candidate of their preferred political party. More common is for a state to have a place at the top of the ballot for the voter to mark the ballot once, indicating a vote for all Democratic candidates only, all Republican candidates only, etc. Once the top of the ballot is marked, a vote is recorded for every candidate from that voter's preferred political party. This approach is used in Texas.

The advantage of the long ballot is, of course, greater accountability of elected officials to the voters in the state, county, city, or other agency of state government.

roll off
process in which voters mark off only the "more important" offices on a lengthy ballot—usually national or statewide offices—and leave the county or local office choices blank

party-line voting
process in which voters select candidates by their party affiliation

However, the long ballot, if used as intended by the progressives, requires that voters ignore partisanship as a guide to selecting a candidate in the election. Instead, voters are expected to be well informed about all candidates and issues in the election, selecting wisely the most qualified candidate or the candidate with views closest to the voter's. Such expectations may be unrealistic given the sheer number of races to be decided on a lengthy ballot. Thus, the expectation of civic education and progressive thought, which focus on virtuous voters who willingly and eagerly seek information on their own to make well-reasoned and informed decisions at an election, confronts the reality of the busy lives of most voters, who lack time to become informed about a multitude of candidates running for the large number of offices. Instead, voters may rely on heuristics, or "shortcuts," to aid them in making their choices.[43] Shortcuts include use of party labels,[44] name recognition, and ideology. Overall, the increase in the number of elected offices contributes to voter fatigue and raises the costs of voting. The unintended consequence is fewer voters turning out on Election Day.

Concerns over party-line voting were raised after the 2016 election. An article in the *Texas Tribune* highlighted the fact that in the state's ten biggest counties by population, 64 percent of voters cast party-line votes for a political party.[45] Republican lawmakers seized upon this information and other analyses that suggested rates of party-line voting were increasing to pass legislation in 2017 abolishing the option of a party-line vote at the beginning of the ballot. Signed into law by Governor Abbott, the law takes effect in 2020. Republican leaders assumed that party-line voting benefits Democratic voters, and that such voting is more likely among racial and ethnic minorities as well as lower-income voters. Yet, in four of Texas's most populous counties, Republican voters are routinely more likely to cast party-line votes.[46]

VOTING, VOTER REGISTRATION, AND TURNOUT

National elections are required by federal law to be held on the first Tuesday following the first Monday in November. State and local elections in Texas are also typically held on a Tuesday, and polls are open from 7:00 AM to 7:00 PM. While these hours might seem extensive, in fact, for many people who work from 8:00 AM until 5:00 PM, with time needed for commuting to and from work, these hours may not be enough. To help Texans turn out to vote, Texas began in 1988 to experiment with advanced or early voting, which allows a voter to cast a ballot before an election without giving a specific reason. Historically, to cast a ballot before Election Day, a voter had to qualify for an absentee ballot by documenting a specific reason for being absent on Election Day: for example, being on vacation, being on a business trip, or being away at college. In early voting, the local elections administrator opens polling to voters during specified times and days in the weeks leading up to the election. In Texas, early voting days include weekends. Voting is made easier and occurs at the leisure of the voter, who can now avoid a hectic workday scramble to get to the voting booth before it closes on Election Day. Texas was an early adopter of such voting; its experiences and those of a handful of other states led to the expansion of early voting nationwide, and many states now have some form of it. As shown in Figure 8.1, early voting has become quite popular in Texas, especially in presidential election years.

advanced or early voting a voting system that allows a voter to cast a ballot before an election without giving a specific reason, thus making voting more convenient for the voter

The nonpartisan blanket primary system used in Louisiana often seems attractive to voters from outside the state. The system differs from the closed primary by allowing independent and third-party voters to participate in the primary election because voters do not need to register a political party affiliation. In addition, the nonpartisan blanket primary differs from the traditional open primary in that voters do not have to choose a specific political party's primary in which to participate. Instead, a registered voter simply arrives at the polling place on Election Day and receives a ballot with all the candidates from all the political parties with all offices to be chosen listed. Here, voters can maximize cross-party voting by, for example, choosing a Republican for president, a Democrat for U.S. senator, a Libertarian for U.S. House of Representatives, and so forth. This ability to cross-party vote by office, which is impossible in other types of primaries because the ballot contains only candidates from a specific political party, is attractive to many voters. Since all registered voters may participate in the primary, proponents maintain that the system should produce more centrist or moderate candidates. This ability to produce such candidates was important in the California campaign to adopt the nonpartisan blanket primary.[i] After all, by restricting the ballot to registered party supporters, the closed primary essentially limits participation to conservative or right-of-center voters in the Republican primary and liberal or left-of-center voters in the Democratic primary. Independent voters are forced to choose a side or stay at home.

Does the nonpartisan blanket primary in Louisiana produce centrist or moderate candidates that reflect the views of the entire electorate rather than those of a smaller number of partisan voters? Unfortunately, evidence from Louisiana's elections for governor suggest that Louisiana's primary system does not necessarily produce centrist or moderate officeholders. For example, in 1991, the centrist incumbent governor Buddy Roemer, a one-time Democrat who became a Republican, received 27 percent of the vote to finish third in a twelve-candidate field. Roemer's third-place finish meant he was eliminated. In second place, with 32 percent of the vote, was David Duke. Duke, a former member of the state legislature and once grand wizard of the Knights of the Ku Klux Klan, was clearly more extremist than Roemer. Edwin Edwards, a former state governor who had been indicted and tried several times for a variety of violations of federal racketeering laws, finished in first place with 34 percent of the vote. Edwards and Duke moved on to the general election in November. Edwards defeated Duke with 61 percent of the vote.

The 2015 election of Louisiana's current governor, John Bel Edwards, offers another example. Edwards, who is unrelated to Edwin Edwards mentioned previously, won 40 percent of the primary vote as a centrist Democratic with a proven bipartisan record. Second place went to Republican David Vitter, a U.S. senator whose voting record in state and national office placed him on the far right. Vitter received 23 percent of the vote. Vitter also faced a scandal involving his past association with a Washington, DC, prostitution madam. Two Republicans who were more moderate than Vitter finished third and fourth with 19 and 15 percent of the vote, respectively. In the runoff election, Edwards won with 56 percent of the vote to Vitter's 44 percent. The fourth-place primary finisher, Jay Dardenne, who had a reputation for being a moderate, ultimately endorsed Edwards, not fellow Republican Vitter.

INSTRUCTIONS TO VOTER
Read the following before marking your ballot:
1. Use ONLY a pencil containing black lead to mark your ballot.
2. Completely fill in oval to the right of each of your selections. Any other type of marking may void your ballot.

CORRECTLY MARKED BALLOT:
John Doe

INCORRECTLY MARKED BALLOT:

3. DO NOT vote for more than the number to be elected for each office.
4. If you incorrectly mark this ballot, erase the incorrect mark completely and make a new mark.

ABSENTEE BALLOT

October 24, 2015

East Baton Rouge Parish

17-001A

Ballot Page 1 of 3

Official Ballot
Prepared and Certified by

Tom Schedler
Secretary of State
STATE OF LOUISIANA

Governor (Vote for ONE)	
Scott A. Angelle — Republican	1
Beryl Billiot — No Party	2
"Jay" Dardenne — Republican	3
Cary Deaton — Democrat	4
John Bel Edwards — Democrat	5
Jeremy "JW" Odom — No Party	6
Eric Paul Orgeron — Other	7
S L Simpson — Democrat	8
David Vitter — Republican	9

Lieutenant Governor (Vote for ONE)	
Elbert Lee Guillory — Republican	10
Melvin L. "Kip" Holden — Democrat	11
"Billy" Nungesser — Republican	12
John Young — Republican	13

Secretary of State (Vote for ONE)	
"Tom" Schedler — Republican	14
"Chris" Tyson — Democrat	15

Attorney General (Vote for ONE)	
Geraldine "Geri" Broussard Baloney — Democrat	16
James D. "Buddy" Caldwell — Republican	17
Isaac "Ike" Jackson — Democrat	18
"Jeff" Landry — Republican	19
"Marty" Maley — Republican	20

Treasurer (Vote for ONE)	
John Kennedy — Republican	21
Jennifer Treadway — Republican	22

Commissioner of Agriculture and Forestry (Vote for ONE)	
"Charlie" Greer	23
Adrian "Ace" Juttner — Green	24
Jamie LaBranche — Republican	25
Michael G. "Mike" Strain — Republican	26

Commissioner of Insurance (Vote for ONE)	
"Jim" Donelon	27
Donald Hodge, Jr. — Democrat	28
Charlotte C. McDaniel McGehee — Democrat	29
Matt Parker — Republican	30

TURN BALLOT OVER

VOTE BOTH SIDES OF BALLOT ➡

Courtesy of Louisiana Secretary of State Tom Schedler

The evidence suggests that centrist candidates are often crowded out in Louisiana's primary system by more extreme candidates. Simply put, centrist and moderate candidates, if sufficient in number, can split the middle vote, which has the effect of allowing more extreme candidates to get just enough votes to move on to the general election.

Hypothetically, a six-candidate race in which the candidates evenly split the votes could produce a result in which the top two candidates move on to the general election having received no more than 16 or 17 percent of the vote. What matters in Louisiana is finishing in the top two regardless of party in the primary. Compare this with Texas's semi-open system in which the Republican and Democratic candidates moving on to the general election must have received a majority of the votes in their respective political party's primary.

What are the advantages to Louisiana's nonpartisan blanket primary?

 CRITICAL THINKING

What are the advantages to Texas's current semi-open system? (See text for details on Texas's system.)

CRITICAL THINKING

---

i.   John Howard, "Voters Approve Prop. 14, 'Open Primary,'" *Sacramento Capitol Weekly*, June 8, 2010, http://capitolweekly.net/voters-approve-prop-14-open-primary.

Electronic Voting in Texas

Also of concern for state and local governments is ensuring that the votes cast are accurately counted. In the wake of the 2000 presidential election, which saw a large number of irregularities in the state of Florida, Congress acted to create a single national standard for election procedures for presidential and congressional elections by passing the Help America Vote Act (HAVA) in 2002. Ultimately, many states and local governments began adapting procedures for nonfederal elections to comply with the HAVA simply because those elections are often held simultaneously with federal elections. Therefore, the act has had the effect of standardizing procedures for all elections—federal, state, and local—and in so doing has given the national government a degree of control in states' election affairs.

Help America Vote Act (HAVA)
a federal statute enacted after the 2000 presidential election to effectively standardize election procedures

The HAVA mandates that all polling stations utilize electronic voting equipment and have at least one voting booth that is accessible for those with a disability. It also requires that state and local voting officials conduct educational activities and equipment demonstrations to allow voters to become familiar with the electronic voting equipment. While the act does not specify the exact equipment to be used, standards have nevertheless been set for the equipment. Congress, recognizing the expense of purchasing new equipment, provided limited funds to states and local governments to implement the act. In Texas, the secretary of state's Elections Division certified several types of equipment, including optical scanners, touch-screen voting machines, and dial-controlled computer voting (eSlates). County governments may select from one of four companies to supply the equipment.

The shift to electronic voting is meant to overcome the perceived problems of other forms of balloting. Traditional paper ballots are subject to ballot-box stuffing, in which additional paper ballots are placed in the box to ensure a particular candidate wins. When questions arise about the final vote totals, paper ballots are recounted by hand—a process that is not particularly reliable. Lever-operated voting machines, if not maintained properly, can cause errors in tabulating vote results,

Do the rates of early voting in Texas suggest a trend or pattern in the data over time?

EMPIRICAL AND QUANTITATIVE

FIGURE 8.1 Early Voting in Texas, 1996–2018

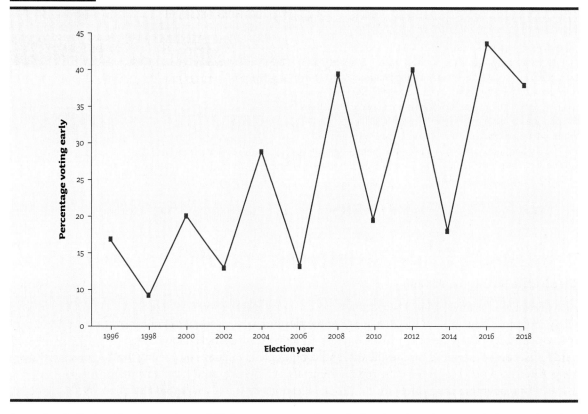

Source: Compiled by the authors based on data available from Texas Secretary of State, "Early Voting Information," accessed July 13, 2018, http://www.sos.state.tx.us/elections/historical/earlyvotinginfo.shtml.

and these machines do not have a paper record of the vote for comparison later if results are questioned. Punch-card ballots, which were a primary cause of the difficulties in the 2000 presidential election in Florida, are among the least reliable, with high error rates both in counting the ballots and determining which candidate on the ballot was actually selected by the voter.[47] However, electronic voting methods, such as touch screens and eSlates, are also not without problems, including the possibility of software tampering, the lack of a paper ballot to verify results,[48] errors in saving votes to a database, and voter distrust of computer-based voting.[49]

When Congress passed the HAVA in 2002, about one-third of Texas's counties still used the paper ballot. Fourteen counties employed punch-card systems, and three counties used lever machines. All of these counties were required to replace their voting equipment with electronic systems. In 2000, the majority of counties employed optical scanners. With optical scanners, a voter marks a ballot, the ballot is scanned, and the results are added by the scanner's software to the database. Although optical scanners were allowed to continue under the HAVA, counties

270 LONE STAR POLITICS

using them were still mandated to have at least one eSlate or touch-screen system available at each polling place for those with disabilities. The passage of the HAVA, then, meant that almost all of Texas's 254 counties needed to upgrade their equipment, with a substantial proportion of them needing to replace their equipment entirely.[50]

The cost of these upgrades has been high. Estimates from the Texas secretary of state's office suggest that more than $170 million was needed to comply with the HAVA.[51] Funds were made available to counties from the state based on a formula that included the number of voting precincts and the voting-age-eligible population. Loving County, the smallest in population, with only fifty-four age-eligible voters at the time, received $27,000 in 2003 and $40,000 in 2004. Implementation of the HAVA in Harris County, with its almost 2.5 million voters, cost over $6 million in 2003 and $12 million in 2004. In the trade-off between ensuring the accuracy of the vote and the need to fund elections, Congress chose ensuring accuracy but passed most of the cost on to states and local governments. The limited funds provided by Congress were nowhere near the total cost to states and local governments to purchase the new voting equipment. Again, the role of the national government in promoting change in Texas elections becomes evident. The transition to electronic voting resulted from laws passed by the U.S. Congress.

Contemporary Voter Registration and Turnout

The measures just discussed are all directed at making voting easier. The health of democracy is often measured, correctly or incorrectly, by using participation in elections as a benchmark. To some extent, this approach makes sense because efforts at civic education often stress voting as the "best" or "most important" form of having one's voice heard. The denial of the right to vote to African Americans has placed additional focus on exercising one's right to vote. Finally, elections are essential to concepts of modern representative democracy, and thus turnout is important to ensuring representation.

Figure 8.2 tracks the rate of voter registration from 1970 to 2018 among the age-eligible population in the state of Texas. Beginning in 1974 and continuing into the 1990s, the rate of registration remained relatively stable, hovering in the low to mid 60 percent range for most of the period. Registration peaked during presidential elections. From a high of 71.2 percent in the wake of the Watergate scandal in 1976, participation trended downward, reaching 70 percent in 1984. In 1994, the trend was toward higher rates of voter registration, leveling off in the low 80 percent range by the mid-2000s. Why did voter registration spike in the mid to late 1990s? One important explanation is the impact of the 1993 Motor Voter Act. In addition, the implementation of online voter registration forms made access to registration easier for many potential new voters, leading to potentially higher registration rates. The advent of some new technologies, such as computerized databases, and better training of local election officials influenced the rates of voter registration as well. In the last decade, voter registration has declined, falling by 2010 to about 70 percent. This trend may reflect only the improved ability to update and purge voter registration records. The 2016 and 2018 elections saw a slight increase in registration to the mid to upper 70 percent range.

Why do states often report voter turnout based on the total number of registered voters rather than the age-eligible population?

★ CRITICAL THINKING

FIGURE 8.2 Rate of Voter Registration, 1970–2018

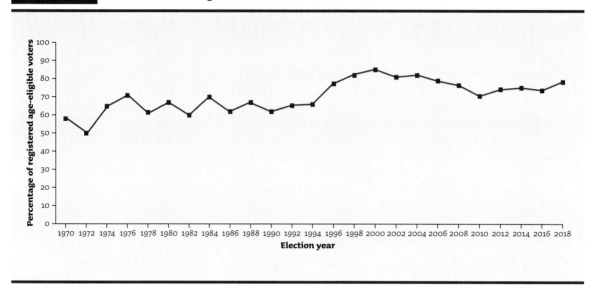

Source: Compiled by the authors based on data from Texas Secretary of State, "Turnout and Voter Registration Figures (1970–Current)," accessed July 13, 2018, http://www.sos.state.tx.us/elections/historical/70-92.shtml.

voter turnout
the number of people casting ballots in a given election

Another important consideration during elections is **voter turnout**. In Texas, voter turnout, or the number of people actually casting ballots in an election, resembles trends from across the United States. Voter turnout tends to be higher in presidential election years than in off-year, midterm elections. Moreover, special elections and local elections tend to have very low levels of voter turnout.

Voter turnout is calculated one of two ways: as the percentage of ballots cast in the election based on (1) the total number of registered voters or (2) the total population aged eighteen and over (the voting-age-eligible population). Often, government officials like to report turnout based on the first method, in part because rates of turnout are inflated when using it. Obviously, the total number of registered voters is normally lower than the total number of people who are of eligible voting age.

This issue of using registered voters or the age-eligible population to determine turnout is important when comparing voter turnout rates over time or across states. States sometimes change the eligibility requirements; for example, southern states, such as Texas, have clearly manipulated registration requirements to exclude African Americans, as discussed earlier. Also, registration processes and voter eligibility vary from state to state. North Dakota, as noted earlier, lacks any form of registration, so that anyone showing up on Election Day with a valid state driver's license or other proof of residency is allowed to vote. In neighboring Minnesota, voters are allowed to register to vote up to and on Election Day. These differences produce variations in the percentage of the age-eligible population that is registered to vote.

Thus, the more accurate figure, especially for comparison purposes, is to use the total population eighteen and over (the voting-age-eligible population). In general, voter turnout among the age-eligible population hovers in the 40 to 50 percent range for presidential elections but declines to the high 20 or low 30 percent range for midterm, off-year elections. Recent elections have adhered to these trends. However, the 2018 midterm elections in Texas, similar to the rest of the United States, experienced unusually high rates of voter participation. In 2018, 52.8 percent of registered voters cast a vote in the election, or 41.9 percent of age-eligible voters.[52]

AP Photo/Eric Gay

Students at the University of Texas in Austin wait with other community residents to vote in the March 2018 primary. UT hosts one of the polling places in Travis County, allowing students a convenient location to vote.

Interestingly, the gap between turnout among the age-eligible population and actual registered voters narrowed between 1992 and 2004. This narrowing of the gap between turnout and age-eligible population reflects the trend toward increased voter registration, whether as a result of the Motor Voter Act, ease of online registration, improvements in database management, or some other cause. Since 2004, the gap has grown wider again.

What about voter turnout in special elections? Figure 8.3 shows the trends in voter turnout in special elections in Texas since 1977. With the exceptions of the May and June elections of 1993, all other special statewide elections since 1977 concerned amendments to the Texas Constitution. In general, voter turnout in special elections is quite low, never reaching higher than 35 percent of registered voters or 20 percent of age-eligible voters. In the special elections in 2007 and 2009, the rate of voter turnout fell to around 5 percent. In 2017, 4.5 percent of age-eligible voters cast ballots in the special election to amend the state constitution. Why is voter turnout typically very low in these special elections? Usually, amendments to the state constitution are largely technical matters that do not generate a significant amount of interest by the media or in the public. When controversial, like the 2005 vote to amend the state constitution to define marriage as limited to only couples consisting of one man and one woman, turnout still remains low. Since the U.S. Supreme Court decision in *Obergefell v Hodges* (2015) legalized same-sex marriage, this amendment to the Texas constitution is now invalid.

So why is voter turnout typically higher for presidential elections than for midterm elections for governor, members of the U.S. House of Representatives, and the state legislature, and why do midterm elections in turn have higher voter turnouts than special elections? One answer lies in what scholars who compare elections across

FIGURE 8.3 Turnout in Texas Special Elections, 1977–2017

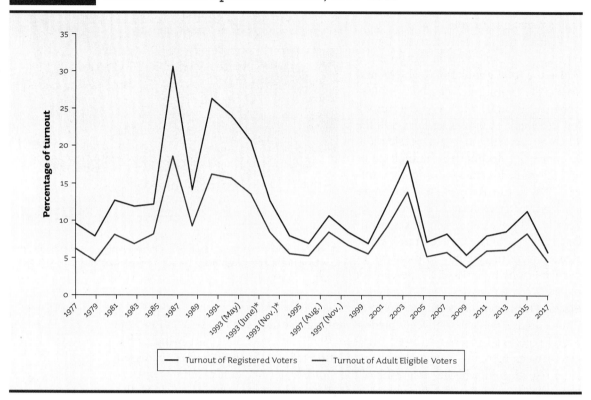

*The June 1993 election was a runoff for the U.S. Senate; a constitutional election occurred in November 1993.

Source: Compiled by the authors from data available from Texas Secretary of State, "Election Results," accessed July 13, 2018, http://www.sos.state
.tx.us/elections/historical/index.shtml.

What do you think is
the biggest reason voter
turnout is so low in
special elections?

⭐ **CRITICAL THINKING**

second-order elections
elections for offices below
the national executive
level in countries with
presidential systems like
the United States' or the
national legislature level in
parliamentary countries like
Great Britain; generally viewed
as less important in scope
and impact on a country

different countries refer to as **second-order elections**.[53] Second-order elections are
elections for offices other than the national executive in presidential systems like the
United States' or the national legislature in parliamentary systems like Great Britain's.
The term *second order* refers to the fact that these elections are simply less important
in scope and impact on the country, with less ability to shift the direction of the entire
political system. Because the stakes are lower, voters see fewer benefits from voting
and view the act of voting in these elections as less important. Another explanation
is the issue of mobilization. Presidential elections in the United States are more likely
to be discussed in the media and often more intensely advertised. What is more, the
political parties and the candidates themselves, through their campaign organizations,
are more aggressive in contacting potential voters to go out and to cast votes.

Voting behavior in Texas is in a state of transition. More and more Texans are now
on the voter registration list, but this upward trend in registration is not reversing the
general trend in low voter turnout. Voter turnout remains alarmingly low in special
elections. Congressional and statewide elections not held in conjunction with presidential elections tend to have low voter turnout as well.

Who Votes?

In general, Texas typically ranks near the bottom in voter turnout compared to other states. Low voter turnout is a result of several factors. Certainly the long ballot, with its many races and candidates, is a deterrent for some voters. The focus on charismatic candidates and "personality" approaches to campaigns offers entertainment but little serious focus for some voters. While the process is relatively easier than in the past, actually taking time to register to vote may be a deterrent, especially when a potential voter realizes that the list of registered voters is used by state and local courts to call people for jury duty. Lower turnout is also a result of Texas's traditionalistic political culture, which tends to cast a negative view on politics and political life in general; the state's strain of extreme individualism can make voting seem more of a chore than a right to be exercised. Finally, the relatively weak organizational nature of Texas's political parties limits their ability to mobilize voters.

The rate of turnout in Texas is not consistent across demographic groupings such as race or ethnicity, gender, and age. To illustrate these differences, the 2016 presidential election provides an example of the patterns of turnout in an election in Texas. Table 8.1 provides comparisons between Texas, the U.S. average, Minnesota, and Hawaii. Minnesota had the highest turnout in 2016, and Texas had the lowest.

Note the differences in the rates of voter turnout between various demographic groups. For example, men are less likely to vote than women at the national level. That trend holds in each of the three states in the comparison. Non-Hispanic whites typically voted more than other ethnic groups. These trends are consistent with national trends on turnout by gender and ethnic group. However, the presence of Barack Obama on the presidential ballot energized the African American community, and many communities and states saw significant gains in African American voter turnout in 2008 and 2012.

Throughout the United States and in Texas, voter turnout varies considerably by age group. The youngest voters, ages eighteen to twenty-four, consistently vote at levels much below the national or state average. While some improvement occurs in the twenty-five to thirty-four age bracket, the highest rates of voting occur among those over the age of forty-five, especially among those in the sixty-five and older age bracket. The trends in the 2016 election were consistent with prior presidential elections. These differences in turnout by age level are important. Older Americans' propensity to vote leads candidates and parties to address disproportionately the concerns of older voters relative to those of younger voters.

Low voter turnout has consequences for Texas politics. Assuming there are differences in the policy preferences, party identifications, and other characteristics of voting behavior between the various ethnic groups, low voter turnout among African American and Hispanic voters in Texas means that fewer government decisions reflect these groups' beliefs. Similarly, government decision makers are less responsive to the concerns of younger voters because, as a group, younger voters tend to vote less. In addition, lower turnout among various ethnic groups reduces the likelihood that minority candidates are elected to office. As a result, the system is less representative of the population as a whole.

TABLE 8.1 Voter Turnout Rates across Demographic Groups in the 2016 Presidential Election

Characteristic	Texas	United States	Minnesota	Hawaii
Sex				
Men	45.7%	53.8%	63.2%	41.5%
Women	49.6%	58.1%	67.1%	45.0%
Race/Ethnicity				
White, non-Hispanic	47.8%	64.1%	70.6%	60.2%
African American	54.9%	55.9%	58.0%	N/A
Asian	28.0%	33.9%	37.4%	37.0%
Hispanic (any race)	30.4%	32.5%	19.4%	N/A
Age				
18–24	27.3%	39.4%	49.6%	20.4%
25–34	37.5%	46.4%	61.4%	30.8%
35–44	42.9%	51.8%	64.1%	42.8%
45–64	55.5%	61.7%	69.7%	49.7%
65+	65.0%	68.4%	72.3%	55.8%

Note: N/A = Not available.

Sources: U.S. Census Bureau, "Reported Voting and Registration by Sex, Race, and Hispanic Origin, for States, November 2016," *Current Population Survey*, accessed July 13, 2018, https://www.census.gov/data/tables/time-series/demo/voting-and-registration/p20-580.html, table 4b; U.S. Census Bureau, "Reported Voting and Registration of the Total Voting-Age Population, by Age, for States: November 2016," *Current Population Survey*, accessed July 15, 2018, https://www.census.gov/data/tables/time-series/demo/voting-and-registration/p20-580.html, table 4c.

Do the differences in voter turnout across Texas's demographic groups, such as age and ethnicity, matter in state politics?

★ CRITICAL THINKING

independent candidate
a candidate running for office without a political party affiliation

party primary
an electoral contest to win a political party's nomination for the right to appear as its candidate on the ballot in the general election

GETTING ON THE BALLOT IN TEXAS ELECTIONS

Who gets on the ballot is an important aspect of elections. Elections imply choice and, ideally, ideological diversity as well as demographic variety among the candidates. Everyone running for office in the state of Texas must be a resident of Texas and of the relevant election district. A candidate must also be registered to vote. Beyond these requirements, getting on the ballot as a candidate results from one of two processes: nomination by a political party or qualifying as an **independent candidate**.

For candidates running with a party nomination, the candidate gets on the ballot either by competing in and winning a primary election or by being selected from a party convention. Political parties that won 20 percent or more of the vote in the last governor's election must hold primary elections. To qualify for the primary election, a candidate must pay a filing fee. The filing fee varies from $5,000 for a candidate for U.S. senator to $300 for candidates for the State Board of Education (SBOE). In lieu of paying the filing fee, candidates may qualify for a **party primary** by filing a petition with a set number of signatures from registered voters. This number varies from 5,000 signatures to the number of signatures equivalent to 2 percent of the vote in the governor's election in the state, county, or election district. If a political party receives 5 percent or more of the vote but less than 20 percent, the party may use a primary election or nominating convention to place candidates on the general election ballot. However, the filing fee requirements remain in place. Parties with less than 5 percent of the vote in the most recent governor's election must first register with the secretary of state's office by collecting the signatures of registered voters who support the party. A party must secure enough signatures to equal 1 percent of the total votes for all candidates for governor at the last election.

An independent candidate, a candidate running for office without a political party affiliation or nomination, must submit an application for a place on the general election ballot. In addition, the candidate must gather signatures of registered voters willing to sign a petition that the candidate's name should appear on the ballot. The number of signatures needed varies from 1 to 5 percent of the total votes for all candidates for governor at the last election. If the independent candidate is running for a countywide office, the candidate needs to collect 1 to 5 percent of the total votes for governor in that county. Because they lack a party affiliation, independent candidates do not compete in primary elections in Texas. In fact, independent candidates cannot declare their intention to run for office until after primary elections are over and cannot have voters who participated in the primary elections sign the petition form that puts them on the ballot. Write-in candidates qualify by either paying a filing fee or, like independent candidates, completing a nomination petition. Once a candidate decides to run for a party nomination either by party primary or party convention, he or she cannot run as an independent candidate in the general election. This provision is called a sore loser law.

Even as Texas maintains its tradition of ballot access for major-party candidates, independent candidates, and write-in candidates, another tradition endures in the state, one whereby rules and procedures are used to make access to the ballot for minor-party candidates more challenging. The rule requiring minor parties to constantly reapply to have their party name and label on the ballot based on statewide totals in the governor's election clearly favors the established Democratic and Republican Parties. The hurdles put in place by Texas's ballot-access rules and procedures reflect the traditional political culture that dominates much of the state: a desire to keep the "wrong" kinds of candidates and political parties off the ballot. Denying access to the ballot to these candidates and political parties minimizes challenges to existing political elites and ensures the tradition of Democratic and Republican domination of state politics. Of course, periodically, a political party such as the Libertarians or Greens does qualify automatically for access to the ballot.

Of course, getting on the ballot is only an early step in the electoral process, and merely holding an election to fill an office does not equate to democratic, representative government. Many authoritarian and totalitarian political systems often hold elections to create the illusion of democratic legitimacy. Truly democratic elections require some degree of real choice. A ballot with only one candidate hardly offers a choice. More importantly, the choice must be between viable alternatives. In other words, elections imply not just a choice between A and B but that both A and B have

HOW TEXAS GOVERNMENT WORKS

Characteristics of Eligible Voters in Texas

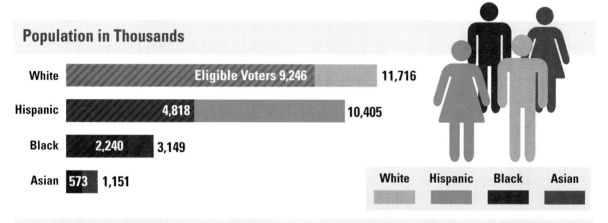

Population in Thousands

White	Eligible Voters 9,246	11,716
Hispanic	4,818	10,405
Black	2,240	3,149
Asian	573	1,151

White Hispanic Black Asian

Language Use (Percentage of Eligible Voting Population)

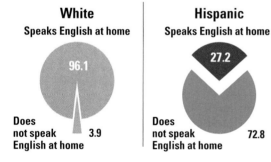

White
Speaks English at home
96.1
Does not speak English at home 3.9

Hispanic
Speaks English at home
27.2
Does not speak English at home 72.8

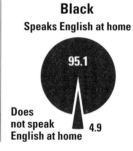

Black
Speaks English at home
95.1
Does not speak English at home 4.9

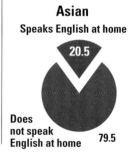

Asian
Speaks English at home
20.5
Does not speak English at home 79.5

Education (Percentage of Eligible Voting Population)

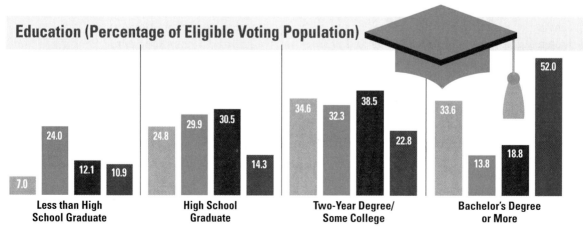

Less than High School Graduate
7.0 · 24.0 · 12.1 · 10.9

High School Graduate
24.8 · 29.9 · 30.5 · 14.3

Two-Year Degree/ Some College
34.6 · 32.3 · 38.5 · 22.8

Bachelor's Degree or More
33.6 · 13.8 · 18.8 · 52.0

Source: Gustavo Lopez and Renee Stepler, "Latinos in the 2016 Election: Texas," Pew Research Center, January 10, 2016, http://www.pewhispanic.org/fact-sheet/latinos-in-the-2016-election-texas/.

some possibility of actually winning the race.[54] This concept of two or more choices, each with some possibility of winning—or what is called electoral competition—is important for another reason. Electoral competition has been linked to higher rates of voter turnout.[55] Does Texas meet this standard of democratic elections? If not, what can be done to create a truly competitive Texas democracy?

In 1998, Republicans won control of the Texas Senate, and in 2002 they won control of both houses of the Texas Legislature for the first time since 1876. By 2006, Republicans controlled all six statewide elected offices and both houses of the Texas Legislature, and they dominated other statewide elected offices, such as both of the state's high courts, the Railroad Commission of Texas, and the Texas Board of Education. This domination continued through the 2018 election, during which the Democrats were unable to beat the Republicans in any statewide race. Despite his broad appeal and significant campaign funds, even U.S. Senate candidate Beto O'Rourke was unable to win election. Statewide, Democrats remained locked out of key executive offices. In most elections in which an **incumbent**, or current office-holder, is running, the incumbent possesses a significant advantage over his or her challengers. The incumbent, by virtue of already holding office, is well known to voters. The advantage of having voters be familiar with the identity of a candidate is called *name recognition*. Name recognition is also enhanced by media coverage of the incumbent's activities, speeches, and public appearances before and during the election campaign. Of course, challengers with previous experience in other elected positions will also have a degree of name recognition.

Incumbents are also advantaged by having an existing record of positions on issues, both from previous elections and in the context of decisions made while in office. This advantage is known as **position taking**. For executive branch offices, position taking taps into an incumbent's record of accomplishments, including programs created or abolished, new initiatives created, and so forth. In the legislature, incumbents are advantaged by having a record of votes on specific bills and resolutions. The legislator's position is therefore known based on his or her voting record in the legislature. Presumably the incumbent has attractive positions to some of the voters—otherwise he or she would not likely have been elected in the first place.

Another positive aspect of incumbency is the ability to engage in **credit claiming**. Credit claiming occurs when an incumbent points out positive outcomes for which he or she is responsible. Credit claiming could include obtaining state funding for new buildings at a local community college or state university, sponsoring a bill that changes the penalties for underage consumption of alcoholic beverages, or taking a stand against perceived runaway spending by the legislature.

In elections to a legislature such as the Texas Legislature or U.S. Congress, incumbents are also favored by **casework**, or solving problems for the people back home. However, the most important advantage of incumbency may be the advantage an incumbent possesses in raising money for an election campaign. Incumbents typically raise much more money than nonincumbents during an election cycle. Organized interests, knowing the advantages that the incumbent has, contribute willingly to his or her reelection campaign to remain in good standing or court new relationships with the incumbent.

Calculate the percentage of each racial and ethnic group registered to vote from the infographic "How Texas Government Works: Characteristic of Eligible Voters in Texas." Which groups have similar rates of registration and which ones are different? Why do you think such differences continue to exist in Texas?

★ CRITICAL THINKING

incumbent
the current officeholder

position taking
an incumbent's advantage in having an existing record of positions on issues, both from previous elections and in the context of decisions made while in office

credit claiming
the advantage derived from incumbents' ability to point to positive outcomes for which they are responsible

casework
the process of solving problems for constituents

Finally, incumbents often find it much easier to raise money, since lobbyists and the organized interests they represent will use fund-raising as an opportunity to gain access to elected officials. Special interest groups are especially fond of legislators who hold important positions in leadership or on committees, and these incumbents can use the money to enhance the other advantages of incumbency that they possess.

Campaigns in Texas History

Election campaigns in Texas have regularly been the stuff of legends, starting in the era of the Republic of Texas. While running for his second term as president of Texas, Sam Houston was attacked by Vice President David Burnet, who described Houston as a drunken coward who failed to fight the Mexican Army before San Jacinto and possessed "beastly intemperance and other vices degrading to humanity."[56] Houston responded by calling Burnet a hog thief. When Burnet became enraged and challenged Houston to a duel, Houston laughed off the challenge, in part because he "never fought down hill."[57]

After statehood, this trend continued. In his 1857 run for the governorship, Houston gave speeches, sometimes with an antislavery message, that ranged from two to four hours. When prosecession candidates attacked him, Houston responded by telling his audience that one candidate had left a political career in Arkansas because of a banking fraud scandal and that the other had killed two men in South Carolina before coming to Texas.

Race has been an issue in many Texas campaigns. However, the races under attack have not always been the same ones. Playing off the distrust of Germans that resulted from World War I, opponents of James "Pa" Ferguson claimed that the improper loans that had led to Ferguson's impeachment were from the kaiser of Germany. Ferguson retorted that William P. Hobby, his opponent, had put "full-blooded Germans" in key government positions. When another of Ferguson's opponents claimed to be a solid prohibitionist but belonged to the Houston Club for its literary pursuits, Ferguson publicized the club's recent spending, which included $10,483 for liquor but only $112 for books.[58] The U.S. Civil War as a political issue still lingered as late as 1912. Governor Oscar B. Colquitt struggled in his reelection bid because he had criticized the state textbook board after it rejected a history book because it contained a photograph of Abraham Lincoln. Many Texans also flocked to see Colquitt's opponent, William Ramsay, who played upon southern sentiments in his speeches and had bands play "Dixie" during campaign events.

Radio and television have played a role in Texas, as they have in other states. Wilbert Lee "Pappy" O'Daniel used his radio show to launch his campaign for governor. The years since have seen the broadcast media of radio and television become the central tool of candidates' campaigns. While candidates still travel the state and personally interact with voters, the battles of advertising and of efforts to get covered by news organizations have become the primary concern of campaigns. While O'Daniel made the most of the new technology of radio, his campaign platform (the Ten Commandments) and his motto (the Golden Rule) were decidedly ancient. He cashed in on these sentiments by sending his children through the audience to gather contributions.[59]

Campaigns in Texas Today

Today's campaigns are modern, featuring high-tech use of the Internet and other media. In the 2006 gubernatorial election, independent candidate Kinky Friedman used the Internet to show Texans his "Kinkytoons" commercials that portrayed what the defenders of the Alamo would have done if led by today's parties. While not as colorful as Friedman, the other independent candidate, Carole Strayhorn, took to the television airwaves to paint herself as "one tough grandma." Trying to live up to the larger-than-life legacy of earlier Texas politicians, Democrat Chris Bell appeared in an ad as a giant figure looming over Texas landmarks such as the capitol building and the Alamo. The larger-than-life Texas campaign is alive and well.

In general, campaigns in Texas are very much like those in the rest of the nation. The state's large size does require that candidates come up with more cash and produce more style. To run a campaign in Texas means to advertise in not a handful of media markets but around twenty separate television markets. Major metropolitan areas such as Austin, Dallas–Fort Worth, Houston, and San Antonio have a local newspaper that dominates the market, but these papers lack significant circulation outside their cities. Compare this to neighboring Arkansas, where the Little Rock television market covers almost all the state. To campaign in Arkansas, one needs to run ads in only five or six television markets. In addition, the *Arkansas Democrat-Gazette*, based in Little Rock, circulates widely across the entire state. Texas voters also remain connected to the legends of Texas history, meaning that candidates will continue to use icons such as the Alamo and the cowboy heritage. Ironically, campaigns embrace the larger changes in the state by adopting new technologies, such as the Internet, to transmit these time-tested messages of traditional Texas mythology.

The Costs of Campaigns in Texas

What do the millions spent on campaigns buy candidates in Texas? For decades, most campaigns have spent most of their budget on advertising. Getting candidates' names and messages in front of the voters has taken a variety of forms, with campaigns using mail, newspapers, radio, and television to reach voters. However, the ways of reaching Texas voters are as diverse as Texans themselves.

Because campaign finance reports are not finalized until at least six months to a year after the election, the 2014 gubernatorial election is the last statewide election with complete information as of this writing. In the 2014 gubernatorial election, Republican Greg Abbott reported contributions totaling over $44 million, while Democrat Wendy Davis raised almost $9 million. Combined, however, these two candidates received enough money to make the 2014 campaign one of the most expensive in Texas history. The lieutenant governor's race included $43 million in contributions. Eventual winner Dan Patrick received over $18 million, while his key rival in the Republican primary and incumbent lieutenant governor David Dewhurst raised almost $11 million alone. These candidates raised significantly more money than Democratic nominee Leticia Van de Putte, who raised just over $8 million.

Other statewide offices varied widely in terms of campaign funds raised by candidates. The race for agriculture commissioner included $3.6 million raised by ten candidates competing in the primary elections and general election collectively. These campaign dollars pale in comparison to the $20 million raised by candidates for attorney general, the $7 million raised by candidates for comptroller of public accounts, and the $5.5 million raised by candidates for commissioner of the General Land Office. In the last case, at least $5.2 million was contributed to the election campaign of one candidate, Republican George P. Bush, the winner.[60] Patterns of contributions also tell us a significant amount of information about the status of the political parties in Texas. Individual and group contributions to candidate campaigns totaled $317 million, with $256 million being given to Republican candidates alone. In fact, Republicans running for state offices including executive, legislative, and judicial offices outdid their Democratic rivals; Republicans raised over $4 for every $1 that Democrats raised.[61] Moreover, incumbents for office raised significantly more money than their challengers, with incumbents raising $140 million to just $21 million for challengers. Clearly the money in state legislative, U.S. House of Representatives, and state judicial elections favored those already in office.

Campaigns and the Media

The future of campaigning could look very different. The rise of digital media, coupled with massive databases and social media, has already shifted the priorities of campaigns, and campaign consultants are closely watching these trends to see how much they transform the process. Traditionally, campaigns spent a lot of their money getting their message to voters. This generally meant buying as much advertising space in newspapers or time on radio or television as possible in hopes that their message would reach the public. Today, citizens can use social media sites, such as Facebook, Twitter, or Snapchat, to spread messages they like. This means that campaigns can now spend more time and effort on producing different messages and leave the task of spreading that message to supporters. The traditional media strategy was to take what the campaign thought would be its most popular ad and put it on the air over and over again in hopes that it would eventually reach the right audience members and catch them when they were paying attention. Today, campaigns produce a variety of commercials, share them through YouTube or Facebook, and then hope that you pass along to your friends the ad that you most like. This technique fits Texans, with their big personalities and often unique messages, very well.

Yet, social media campaigning is fraught with the potential for abuse, just like any other medium. Revelations about activities by groups like Cambridge Analytics using back-door and hidden methods to collect data to profile individual voters and sell that information during the 2016 presidential election season raised concerns about online campaigning. These concerns were only heightened by additional ones about Facebook data collection and sharing methods in the 2015 Canadian national election campaign that may have favored the Liberal party. Additionally, allegations over similar activities in the 2016 referendum campaign over continued British membership in the European Union (EU) may have swayed the results in favor of leaving the EU; British election authorities fined Facebook over $650,000. The ability of Russian-based Internet trolls to spread disinformation during the 2016 U.S. presidential election campaign raised additional concerns about the security and validity of elections in the United States and abroad. Only time will allow sufficient investigation, action by social media outlets, and legislative action to address these concerns.

While television remains an important source of entertainment and information for Texans, it operated in a very different fashion just a few decades ago. First, television is no longer dominated by the big three networks. There was a time when Americans had only three choices for the evening news and prime-time entertainment: ABC, CBS, and NBC. Today, there are many more choices, which creates both challenges and opportunities for campaigns. On the one hand, candidates can no longer find one place where they can reach a large audience, since the viewing audience is scattered over the wide range of broadcast and cable options. On the other hand, the shows we pick may help smart campaigns target specific audiences. Most obviously, conservatives watch Fox News, while liberals favor MSNBC. Beyond that, cable channels target specific audiences, such as Lifetime's appeal to women or Velocity's appeal to men. BET specializes in television for African Americans, while Univision, geared toward the Hispanic community, contains elements of a traditional broadcast network and a cable presence. This targeting allows a campaign interested in talking specifically to a certain group of people to find the right audience.

Additionally, television has changed thanks to the rise of cable television and addressable cable boxes. Cable companies can now target ads to specific neighborhoods and to specific homes. This means that in a few years, you and the people next door could be watching the same television show at the same time but see different commercials during the breaks. These ads are targeted based on databases that political campaigns and commercial marketing companies build based on information they gather on the magazines you buy, the church you attend, the car you drive, and a host of other information that firms have been gathering on you. These data-mining operations operate in a very similar way to the advertising on Facebook. The advent of on-demand television delivered through web-based streaming services like Amazon Prime, Netflix, and Sling has opened additional opportunities for political campaigns to target individuals and households. Your IP address on your tablet, computer, gaming system, or smart TV allows this targeting to occur. Even traditional broadcast networks like CBS, NBC, and ABC have responded by

Governor Greg Abbott addresses supporters as he announces the launch of his reelection campaign. Abbott won the Republican primary in March 2018 and the general election in November.

starting apps with ads tailored to your interests. Candidates and political parties have moved away from traditional yard signs and newspaper ads into digital ads on social media and on-demand streaming services.

We have seen Texas political ads move from television to computers to handheld devices within the span of a single generation. While most campaigns will probably continue to make some use of traditional campaign items, such as bumper stickers, yard signs, lapel buttons, and balloons, it may be possible to win office using only digital advertising through Facebook, YouTube, Snapchat, and whatever comes next. Thus, new media seem to be transforming the method of campaigning, but whether the style and substance are changing is yet to be seen.

CAMPAIGN FINANCE IN TEXAS

Inevitably, the discussion of elections turns to the issue of money. Campaign finance is important because, without money, candidates and political parties have trouble getting out their message, and voters have a difficult time gathering information and making decisions about which candidate they will vote for. Money also provides essentials for election campaigns, such as television and radio advertising and travel throughout the state or election district. It also pays for office space, telephones, websites, public opinion polls, and campaign staff.

The issue of campaign finance is important to a discussion of the health of American democracy, voter participation, and outcomes of elections. In a large, diverse state such as Texas, a well-funded campaign is often viewed as crucial. However, the sources of campaign money raise important concerns, such as who is giving money to candidates and what those candidates may be doing in return. When an organization gives a candidate a contribution, it is typically doing so with the expectation that the candidate will at least listen to the group's concerns. The issue of campaign finance also raises the question of whether organized interests "buy" favorable legislation, court rulings, and executive decisions.

Regulating Campaign Finance

Because money matters, the issue of free speech comes to the forefront of the debate. On the one hand, campaign contributions are a form of political speech, because, by contributing to a candidate's campaign, individual citizens or interest groups are expressing their political position. On the other hand, the cost of modern campaigns virtually guarantees that those with more money to contribute are "heard" more often, regardless of the opinions of the entire electorate or even a majority of voters. The issue of money in elections also raises serious concerns about potential quid pro quo—that is, organized interests receiving favorable laws as a result of campaign contributions.

On January 30, 1976, the U.S. Supreme Court in *Buckley v. Valeo* struck down limitations on expenditures on the grounds that "it is clear that a primary effect of these expenditure limitations is to restrict the quantity of campaign speech by individuals, groups and candidates. The restrictions . . . limit political expression at the core of our electoral process and of First Amendment freedoms."[62] While the court struck down limits on how much campaigns could spend, it upheld limitations on contributions because they safeguard the integrity of the electoral process, and according to the court, "expenditure ceilings impose significantly more severe restrictions on protected freedom of political expression and association that do its limitations on financial contributions."[63] The court extended the protection of free speech to unions and corporations in *Citizens United v. Federal Election Commission* (2010),[64] and as we will see in Chapter 10, this opened up many interesting new channels of money.

While the court's protection of the right to spend money on behalf of a person's views was a victory for free speech, it contributed to inequalities that concern some reformers. For example, the court has ruled that limiting what an individual contributes to his or her own campaign violates the First Amendment of the U.S. Constitution. This means that while the government might limit how much an individual gives to another person's campaign, wealthy candidates can spend unlimited amounts of money from their own accounts. For example, David Dewhurst put about $19 million of his own money into his failed candidacy for the U.S. Senate in 2012. Likewise, what an individual or organized interest spends on their own, independent of a candidate's campaign, cannot be limited. Thus, if money is equal to speech, then those with more money have more freedom of speech, thus limiting the rights of those without money.

Some countries, such as Germany, have addressed this issue by providing **public financing** of elections. Essentially, the government covers the costs of campaigning by providing subsidies to parties and candidates or by providing a reimbursement for campaign costs. Thus, parties and candidates do not have to raise money for the campaign from private citizens or organized interests, such as labor unions, special interest groups, or corporations. A public finance system contrasts with the reliance on **private financing**. Private financing occurs when individual citizens, interest groups, labor unions, or corporations make donations to candidates and political parties to cover the cost of an election.

The United States possesses a mixture of systems, with most elections being privately financed. An exception is the U.S. presidential election, which features some public financing. Presidential candidates can qualify for federal matching funds during the presidential primary season as long as they accept federal spending limits. Similarly, the presidential nominees of the two major parties can receive large lump-sum grants ($96 million in 2016) to pay for their campaigns provided they do not accept other funds. While these grants are attractive, candidates have recently declined them so they can spend as much as they can raise, because federal campaign finance law uses these funds as incentives to get presidential candidates to voluntarily accept the campaign spending limit the court ruled would be unconstitutional if required by law. In 2016, only one major party candidate, Martin O'Malley, sought public financing of his primary election campaign. He withdrew from the Democratic primaries after he failed to win a single delegate in the Iowa caucuses, the first test of the nomination process for president. All other candidates, Democratic or Republican, refused public financing. Thus, most of the $96 million remained unspent.

Campaign finance laws in the United States tend to emphasize reporting the sources of campaign finance, the size of donations, and the patterns of candidate spending rather than limiting campaign spending. The idea is that voters can hold candidates accountable for excessive spending or accepting money from unsavory donors if those candidates have to publicly disclose this information. The responsibility for

public financing
a system of campaign financing in which the government covers the cost of elections for political parties or candidates

private financing
a system of campaign financing in which citizens, interest groups, labor unions, and corporations donate funds to cover the cost of elections for political parties or candidates

collecting this information and providing it to the public rests for state elections with the Texas Ethics Commission (TEC). Candidates are required to file reports with the commission every month once they begin to campaign. After an election, a final report must be filed within three months of the election. The TEC maintains a searchable database for citizens on its website: www.ethics.state.tx.us.

To provide context, Canadian campaign finance laws were largely modeled on U.S. laws and experiences. While Canada also focuses on disclosure, it chooses to emphasize spending limits rather than donation limits. In Canada, political parties, organized interests, and individual candidates may collect as many as and as large of donations as they can. However, all campaign spending is limited. Maximum limits in national election campaigns are set based on a formula that considers the size of the electorate in each single-member district (SMD) for the lower house of the Canadian parliament, the rate of inflation since the last election, and the performance of officially registered parties and independent candidates in the last election. These limits apply to national political parties, individual candidates, and organized interests. Several of Canada's provinces, such as Ontario, have replicated the national campaign finance laws for provincial elections.

Contribution Disclosure

All state and local elections in Texas are privately financed, and Texas state law places few restrictions on how much can be given. In Texas, there is an emphasis on disclosure. Disclosure is the idea that each candidate reports who has contributed money to the campaign and how much has been contributed by an individual or group. Texas does not place limits on how much an individual, interest group, labor union, or corporation may contribute. However, candidates must disclose the source of any contribution over $50. Texas election law does prohibit members of the legislature and most statewide officers from accepting political contributions during a period beginning thirty days before a regular legislative session convenes and ending twenty days after final adjournment. These officials are allowed to accept contributions during a special session but must file a special report within thirty days of the end of the session. Candidates cannot accept contributions from labor organizations or corporations. However, as we'll see in the next chapter, labor unions and corporations can spend their own funds advocating for candidates and issues as long as they act independently of the candidate's official campaign.

Political action committees (PACs) from within the state are allowed to give as much as they want. However, the law mandates that a PAC have at least ten contributors before it makes a political contribution. Political organizations outside the state are limited to a $500 contribution unless they provide documentation listing every donor who gave $100 or more to the organization in the previous twelve months. While some Texans wonder about the wisdom of allowing out-of-state PACs to give any money to Texas political campaigns, having a mailing address from outside Texas does not mean that the committee does not represent citizens of the state, as many Texans support national organizations, such as the National Rifle Association (NRA). Similarly, the designation of "in state" means only that the group has filed for organization under Texas law, and such a group could receive large amounts of funds that originated outside Texas.

---

disclosure
the reporting of who contributes money to a campaign and how much is contributed by an individual or corporation

Judicial Campaign Contributions

Because state and local judges are elected in Texas, judicial elections are also covered by campaign finance laws. Texans hope their judges will be as impartial as possible, and to alleviate fears that justice in Texas can be "bought" through campaign contributions, additional regulations limit the size of all contributions made to a candidate's campaign to get elected as a judge. The limits on individual donors depend on the size of the judicial district and range from $1,000 for judicial districts with a population of 250,000 or less to $5,000 for judicial districts with a population of 1 million or more; individual donors to candidates for statewide judicial offices are limited to $5,000 as well. Law firms may contribute up to six times the individual limits, but individual members of the law firm are limited to $50 contributions. Similarly, statewide candidates may accept only $300,000 from PACs.

Judicial candidates may also opt to accept voluntary spending limits. Like contribution limits, the voluntary limit for a judicial office is based on the size of the judicial district. For example, the limit begins at $100,000 for districts that have less than 250,000 people and eventually rises to $500,000 for districts with more than 1 million people. The contribution limit for statewide office is $2 million. Candidates accepting these limits enjoy an unusual reward—if their opponent exceeds the expenditure limits, the candidate is no longer subject to limits on contributions and expenditures. While the law has been considered a success by some, a 2012 race for a state district court in Marshall saw challenger Brad Morin reject the voluntary limits when he entered the race. This rejection left some reformers concerned because they had hoped pressure from voters and rival candidates would be enough to nudge judicial candidates into accepting the voluntary limits.[65]

WINNERS AND LOSERS

Campaigns and elections in Texas are clear examples of transition in Texas as the right to vote, diversity of the electorate, and nature of political campaigns continue to evolve in the first half of the twenty-first century. Because politics involves decisions about who gets what, it is not surprising that those groups that participate in politics are more likely to be the winners in a state's distribution of resources. In theory, the strength of a democracy lies in the ability of all citizens to exert pressure on the political system. When representative democracies are working, public policy reflects compromises that take into account the needs of a wide range of groups in society. Historically, differences in participation were created by institutional barriers to voting, ranging from the outright denial of suffrage to some groups to obstacles such as white primaries and poll taxes designed to stifle a particular group's participation. These actions produced winners among the white elites in Texas, while causing Hispanics and especially African Americans to be the losers, lacking representation and public policies that reflected their attitudes, beliefs, and values. Removing these barriers to voting has occurred slowly and often as a result of federal imposition of election standards. Thus, the state of Texas and other state government became losers as their unwillingness to allow peacefully the inclusion of minority voters forced the national government to act where state governments failed. This nationalization of election laws, voter registration oversight, and election administration made the national government winners by gaining power over the states.

Unfortunately, in spite of the enfranchisement of minority groups in the state, minority participation in the electoral process remains significantly lower than white participation. Asian and Hispanic groups in particular exhibit extremely low levels of voting participation. Minorities will continue to struggle to make their voices heard as long as they keep their distance from the voting booth. Texas is one of the most diverse states in America, but this is not reflected in its voting patterns. Until participation rates become more uniform, minorities continue to lose influence over the state government.

Voter turnout is also significantly lower among certain age groups. College-age voters are the least likely to show up at the polls and, therefore, the least likely to be represented by state policies. Because policies in Texas often ignore the needs of college-age voters, in times of budget crisis, college students are often the first group that legislators target. The deregulation of tuition at state universities and the state legislature's failure to restore funding to state universities to pre–financial crisis, 2008 levels despite the recovery of the Texas economy and the state government's finances are two recent examples. Groups in the state who remain apathetic about voting will continue to be the first sacrificed in times of budget cuts. Thus, older voters, especially those over sixty-five, are clear winners in voter turnout and influence over state government politics.

Ballot access in Texas also produces winners and loser. The two dominant parties, Republican and Democrat, are winners by engineering electoral rules to their favor, ensuring that they only need worry about competition from each other. Minor political parties, such as Libertarians and Greens, as well as independent candidates, are the primary losers, with more difficult times getting on the ballot for an election.

Finally, the long ballot in Texas exerts a palpable cost by increasing voter apathy throughout the state. Ironically, Texans resist changes to the election system, preferring to keep many of the most important public offices elected because of their distrust of government. Elected officials are theoretically more accountable to the people. Yet, in any given election, most Texans are not exercising the option to have a say in who wins that election. In some instances, voters face noncompetitive elections at the level of the state legislature. The result is that average Texans are becoming increasingly disconnected from the political process.

CONCLUSION

Texas elections, like all election systems, are designed to produce certain types of outcomes. Historically, election rules and voting rights were designed to disenfranchise African American voters and, to a lesser extent, poor, rural white voters. The rules historically were also designed to allow the Democratic Party to maintain control over the election system. Now, Republicans seem to design rules to keep their party in power. The transition of Texas politics toward inclusion of minorities and women occurred in large part through the actions of the national government in securing voting rights for disenfranchised groups, especially African Americans and Hispanics. By increasing the national government's role, a second transition was spurred: Congress and the U.S. Supreme Court moved into the area of elections by establishing over time a set of standards that all states must follow in the conduct of

Who wins and who loses with voter ID legislation in Texas? Why might such a requirement be a good idea? What are the disadvantages?

★ CRITICAL THINKING

Is the U.S. Supreme Court correct in declaring campaign contributions to be free speech? Why or why not?

★ CRITICAL THINKING

national, state, and local elections. The mandated use of electronic voting equipment is the latest example of this transition. However, this transition developed from a fundamental constitutional design. The framers of the U.S. Constitution designed a political system to prevent a passionate majority from tyrannizing the minority, thereby stripping away their rights through electoral success. Historically, the state's passionate majority of white voters kept minorities at bay, forcing the national government to act using the tools of federalism to open up the state's electoral rules and practices. This balancing of state and national government power is part of the constitutional architecture of our system of federalism. In some cases, the states do hold the national government in check.

The emergence of the Republican Party in the 1960s altered Texas politics, bringing greater electoral competition in the state for the first time since the end of the Reconstruction era. Periods of alteration between Republican and Democratic dominance of statewide elected offices in the executive branch and various commissions have been replaced since 2002 by Republican dominance. Yet, these transformations are being influenced by two additional transformations in Texas. Rapid demographic transformation of the state is reshaping the electorate. A more ethnically and racially diverse Texas may end the area of Republican dominance unless significant change occurs in the Republican coalition, its political agenda, or how it engages Hispanic voters especially. In addition, the rapid transformation of political campaigns to include new media outlets like social media and on-demand entertainment have shifted how candidates and political parties reach voters. The long-term impact on voter registration, voter turnout, and election outcomes remains to be seen.

for CQ Press

Want a better grade?

Get the tools you need to sharpen your study skills. Access practice quizzes, eFlashcards, video, and multimedia at **edge.sagepub.com/collier6e**.

KEY TERMS

advanced or early voting (p. 267)

blanket or wide-open primary (p. 262)

casework (p. 279)

closed primary (p. 261)

credit claiming (p. 279)

cross-filing (p. 264)

direct primary (p. 261)

disclosure (p. 286)

equal protection clause (p. 254)

general election (p. 253)

grandfather clause (p. 252)

Help America Vote Act (HAVA) (p. 269)

(Continued)

incumbent (p. 279)
independent candidate (p. 276)
instant runoff (p. 264)
literacy test (p. 252)
majority election (p. 264)
Motor Voter Act (p. 250)
open primary (p. 262)
party-line voting (p. 266)
party primary (p. 276)
plurality election (p. 264)
poll tax (p. 252)
position taking (p. 279)

preference primary (p. 261)
primary election (p. 253)
private financing (p. 285)
public financing (p. 285)
roll off (p. 266)
runoff election (p. 264)
second-order elections (p. 274)
suffrage (p. 252)
voter turnout (p. 272)
Voting Rights Act of 1965 (p. 250)
white primary (p. 253)

ACTIVE LEARNING

- Develop a meme explaining the approach to campaign finance in Texas. **Communication**

- In a small group, come to a consensus on your preferred type of primary election. Then, develop a short PowerPoint or similar presentation explaining why you prefer that type of primary. **Teamwork**

CHAPTER REVIEW

1. To register to vote in Texas, you must register _____.
   a. on election day
   b. one day before the election
   c. two weeks before the election
   d. thirty days before the election

2. Which barriers were used in Texas to deny African Americans access to voting?
   a. grandfather clause and literacy test
   b. grandfather clause and poll tax
   c. poll tax and white primary
   d. white primary and literacy test

3. Unique to their experience, Hispanics in Texas were often subjected to which of the following forms of discrimination?

    a. grandfather clause

    b. poll tax

    c. economic harassment

    d. literacy test

4. A(n) _____ is a type of primary restricted to party loyalists that excludes supporters of other political parties and independent voters.

    a. closed primary

    b. open primary

    c. nonpartisan blanket primary

    d. partisan blanket primary

5. A(n) _____ is a primary in which voters do not register a political party affiliation and receive ballot papers with the names of candidates from all political parties.

    a. closed primary

    b. open primary

    c. nonpartisan blanket primary

    d. partisan blanket primary

6. Which of the following direct democracy elections is used in Texas?

    a. referendum for lawmaking

    b. referendum to amend the state constitution

    c. initiative petition for lawmaking

    d. initiative petition for amending the state constitution

7. A voting system that allows a voter to cast a ballot before an election without giving a specific reason is called _____.

    a. a roll off

    b. advanced or early voting

    c. party-line voting

    d. primary voting

8. Incumbents in an election are often favored due to _____.

    a. name recognition

    b. position taking

    c. credit claiming

    d. all of these

9. Regulating campaign finance in Texas is the responsibility of the _____.

    a. Texas Ethics Commission

    b. Texas attorney general

    c. lieutenant governor

    d. Texas Supreme Court

10. In Texas, campaign finance focuses on _____.

    a. limiting which individuals and groups may give to a candidate or political party

    b. limiting what a candidate or political party may spend during an election

    c. disclosing who gave to a candidate and how much was given

    d. public financing of a campaign from the state budget

POLITICAL PARTIES

I n June 2018, Republicans from around the state gathered in the Henry B. González Convention Center in San Antonio for the party's biennial state party convention. Chosen through a process that began in local precinct conventions, delegates to the party's convention from all walks of life came together from across Texas to conduct the business of the party. While most Texans (and many Republicans) paid little or no attention to the proceedings, the convention was important because it would define what the Republican Party officially stood for and how it would conduct party business.

All the hyperbole of political conflict was on display as delegates began their debates. Outgoing Republican Speaker of the Texas House Joe Straus apparently was compared to Darth Vader, as one delegate declared the end of the old order by saying, "We blew up the Death Star and Joe Straus is gone." Some Trump supporters compared state party chair James Dickey to Benedict Arnold, the American general who defected to the British during the Revolutionary War, by labeling him "Benedict Dickey."[1] The convention quickly became entangled in a battle over whether the convention should reelect Dickey as state chair or replace him with Cindy Asche. Asche argued that a change in leadership was essential to the long-term health of the party, and her challenge stemmed in large part from Dickey's initial resistance to Donald Trump's candidacy. The battle at the convention went through a variety of procedural maneuvers, despite Dickey's win in an early vote of chairs. One delegate complained, "We're doing the most divisive thing possible. We're going to burn the party down so she can be queen of the ashes."[2] While Dickey would prevail in the end by a margin of almost two to one, the Republicans spent a frustrating afternoon carefully working through the party's system of "weighted voting," which required delegations to report their vote out to places beyond the decimal.

The disagreements went beyond who should chair the convention. Some delegates booed land commissioner George P. Bush's mention of his plans for the Alamo, and the party platform they approved explicitly rejected Bush's plans to move some monuments and asserted that "the Alamo should be remembered and not 'reimagined.'"

While the conventions of the state's parties sometimes look like enthusiastic pep rallies for unified teams, the conventions inevitably bring together delegates with very different hopes for their party. The work of the Texas Republican Party in 2018 might appear especially easy, since the party already held all the statewide elected offices and the party's domination of the state elections seemed likely to carry the party through to victory in the 2018 election. However, Texas Republicans have learned that power brings with it the challenges of implementing the vision of a party—the party must move forward even when there is disagreement within it. The Republican Party had a lot on its mind and addressed difficult issues ranging from immigration to transgender rights before adopting a socially conservative platform that included 330 policies, up from 266 on the 2016 platform.[3]

Political scientist Julia Azari has argued that "the defining characteristic of our moment is that parties are weak while partisanship is strong."[4] Thus, citizens have loyalties to a party organization that has little or no control over the candidates it asks party members to support. Azari's point is that while many citizens feel passionate about their parties and their goals, American parties lack the power to get members of the party to work together once in office. Without the cooperation needed to accomplish party goals, voters become disaffected with parties when they don't see the progress they expected.

The strong partisanship of voters is largely built on their views and distrust of members of the other party. Polls have shown that Republicans and Democrats are increasingly distrustful of each other, with some even considering the other party a threat to the nation's well-being. One poll found that 58 percent of Republicans and 55 percent of Democrats had a very unfavorable view of the other party, and 45 percent of Republicans and 41 percent of Democrats described the other party as a threat to the nation's well-being.[5] While these animosities may help mobilize partisans on Election Day, it does little to make sure the people they elect agree on exactly what to do once in office. In the meantime, bipartisanship becomes almost impossible, and nearly everything government does is shaded by the assumption of partisan motives.

The battles at the party conventions are easy to criticize. However, a convention of thousands of delegates representing a large, diverse state confronting the most complicated and divisive issues of the day will inevitably prove to be difficult to manage. Political parties are charged with the task of taking the passions and energies of citizens, pulling them together, and converting them into a single, unified movement. State party leaders often must lead the party through the most compelling state issues while also synchronizing with a national party. Additionally, citizens are reluctant to give parties much formal power to keep candidates and voters in line. Parties are certainly imperfect institutions, but many of the alleged flaws erupt from the pressures of bringing the passions of so many different groups into one team.

In this chapter, we will look at political parties and their contribution to the practice of democracy in Texas. Texans may complain about partisanship, but political parties remain important conduits for citizen participation in state politics. While political parties can help citizens enter into the political process, we will see that the parties are

Texas governor Greg Abbott (center) with wife, Cecilia (right), and daughter, Audrey, at the Texas GOP Convention, Friday, June 15, 2018, in San Antonio.

finding it increasingly difficult to engage citizens, and they face the daunting task of getting people to work together in government.

THE DEVELOPMENT OF POLITICAL PARTIES IN TEXAS

While the battle between political parties has often defined competition in U.S. politics, Texans have rarely enjoyed the benefits of a truly competitive party system. Early Texans were not strangers to political parties, but they initially shunned them. Sam Houston had been a close political ally of Andrew Jackson, whose **patronage** system did much to build the early Democratic Party in the United States. Despite his Democratic roots, however, Houston generally avoided party labels in his Texas campaigns, and the state's earliest elections were dominated by personalities rather than parties.

Just as political parties were taking root in Texas, the national Whig Party collapsed in the mid-1850s. Its replacement, the Republican Party, held antislavery positions that ensured it would find little support in the state. The anti-immigration American, or Know-Nothing, Party, aggressively cultivated Texans, forcing the Democratic Party to become fully organized in Texas for the first time in 1854.[6] Even as the Democratic Party was beginning to take hold in the state, the divisions that would culminate in the Civil War separated Texans into pro-union and pro-secessionist factions and blotted out any chance of Republicans winning statewide office. The bitterness that followed Reconstruction was directed toward the Republican Party, allowing the Democratic Party to dominate the state for decades. Challenges to the Democrats would come from the Greenback Party in the 1870s and 1880s and the Populist or People's Party in the

patronage
when an elected official rewards supporters with public jobs, appointments, and government contracts

1880s and 1890s, but both parties would eventually see many of their most popular ideas co-opted by the Democratic Party.

The Populist Party, also known as the People's Party, backed largely by small farmers looking to democratize the economic system, favored programs such as a graduated income tax, an eight-hour workday, and government control of railroads. While some consider the populists as originating in the politics of the American Midwest, the party had its roots in the Farmers' Alliance (itself an outgrowth of the Grange movement) that had organized in Lampasas, Texas, in the mid-1870s.[7] Texas's Populist Party was built on the foundation of the fundamentalist churches, an especially important social network in early Texas because churches were one of the few networks that brought farm families together. Farmers thus often linked religious themes with their desire for relief from economic pressures.[8] The populists won 44 percent of the vote for J. C. Kearby, their candidate in the 1896 election. Kearby ran with the support of the Republicans, who had not fielded their own candidate that year. Populists' call for government ownership of the railroads and limits on land ownership by corporations was decidedly at odds with the pro-business Republican Party, and the alliance with the Republicans undermined the consistency of the Populist Party's ideological foundations. Meanwhile, some of their more popular ideas were appropriated by Democratic politicians, such as Governor Jim Hogg, who won the favor of many Texas farmers by taking on the railroads.

The next challenge to the Texas Democratic Party emerged from the Progressive Party, a formidable force for reform in much of the country. Because Texas's progressives lacked the targets for reform that energized the party nationally, such as corrupt, big-city **party machines** and unfavorable economic policies, they turned instead to cultural issues, such as alcohol prohibition.[9] The Progressive Party found itself caught up in the prohibition movement, because promoting political reform and banishing alcohol were seen as tools for building a better society, especially in the eyes of Evangelical Christians and women's groups that had been drawn to the progressive cause.[10]

Texas had a few local party machines in which local party officials dispensed patronage, such as government jobs, contracts, and other favors, to party loyalists in return for support at reelection time. Big-city political machines like William M. "Boss" Tweed's "Tammany Hall" in New York in the mid-nineteenth century and Richard J. Daley's Democratic machine in Chicago in the 1960s are the most famous examples. However, the Parr political machine (see page 296) is just one example of how domination by one party led to a lot of creative corruption in Texas.

The Parr machine was not the only corruption coming from political parties in Texas. In 1869, citizens in Navarro County were unable to cast their votes after the county's registrar absconded with the registration lists before the election. In the same year, Milam County ballots were never counted, and in Hill County, an official took the ballots to another jurisdiction to count, with results that surprised many Hill County voters.[11] While Texas needed the reforms championed by the progressive movement, changes were slow to come.

The Republican Party in Texas slowly became viable in the early twentieth century. Republican presidential candidate Herbert Hoover won the state in 1928. However, many Texans eventually blamed the Great Depression on Hoover and the Republican Party and, like much of the nation, switched their loyalty to Franklin Roosevelt and

party machines
state or local party organizations that sustain their control over government by providing jobs, government contracts, and other favors to citizens in return for votes

Do citizens and media today watch local government closely enough to make sure that no corruption exists?

★ PERSONAL RESPONSIBILITY

To what degree should parties be able to give government jobs or contracts to supporters?

★ CRITICAL THINKING

TEXAS *Legends*

George Parr and "Landslide Lyndon"

Associated Press

Texas government was well suited for some forms of corruption at the local level, because the Texas Constitution combined locally elected officials (with control over local budgets) with entrusting the investigation of criminal activity to locally elected judges. This means that corrupt local officials might be part of the same political machine that elected the prosecutors and judges charged with rooting out corruption. Outside law enforcement agents like the Texas Rangers could investigate but had to be invited in by locally elected district attorneys. So, anyone who managed to control local voters could exploit control over local government with minimal risk of prosecution.

The most famous political machine in Texas was the Duval County machine controlled by Archie Parr from 1908 until his death in 1942, then by his son George Parr, who took over and held on to power until 1975. Corralling local voters required some creative governing. To ensure that his supporters were eligible to vote, Archie Parr either had supervisors deduct poll tax payments from the wages of some county

workers or paid the poll taxes of supporters himself. On Election Day, the Parr political machine distributed to supporters ballots that were premarked and kept armed guards around voting locations to intimidate voters not interested in Parr's ballots. Tax collectors were instructed not to accept poll taxes from voters likely to vote against Parr. He slammed the door on competition within the Democratic Party by eliminating local precinct conventions where opponents might wrest control of the party from him. Parr built loyalty with voters by helping them with food, clothes, medical expenses, or funeral expenses in their moments of need, and much of Parr's support came from Tejanos who appreciated his acts of kindness. Further, Parr often stood with Mexican Americans when other politicians turned a blind eye to injustices they faced.

After he inherited control from his father, local Mexican Americans gave George Parr the nickname El Tacuacha ("The Possum") because, "He may pretend he's asleep or dead, but don't be fooled. He's planning his next move."[i] While George Parr may have been quiet, his methods were no less subtle than his father's. During one election, a local deputy went around town taking the keys from the ignitions of cars with anti-Parr stickers. Parr also kept careful track of who had died, giving him a ready source of fraudulent votes in a close election. Businesses owned by political opponents faced harassment. Parr funded his political machine and his personal wealth with money that disappeared from school and county government budgets. A popular saying in Duval County was, "Parr controls everything except the way the wind blows."

George Parr's ability to deliver votes to friendly candidates made him a kingmaker in Texas. In his most famous move, Parr was responsible for pushing local election officials to find the questionable votes

that secured Lyndon Johnson's Democratic primary victory in the 1948 U.S. Senate campaign. Coke Stevenson finished first in the Democratic primary, easily besting Johnson by a vote of 477,077 to 405,617. However, Stevenson lacked the majority required by law to win the nomination, forcing the two candidates to face off in a runoff election. Official returns from the runoff took three days to compile before the Texas Election Board announced that Stevenson had won by 362 votes. However, "late returns" were still coming in, including what would become the legendary Box 13 from Alice, Texas, in Duval County, which belatedly revealed 203 uncounted ballots, 202 of them for Johnson. Upon further examination, the poll lists showed that Box 13's voters had signed in and voted in alphabetical order and in identical handwriting. The amended returns gave Johnson a margin of 87 votes statewide and the nickname of "Landslide Lyndon." While some of Johnson's critics have pointed to evidence of voter fraud in Alice, others point out that there was evidence of similar vote fraud on behalf of Stevenson in East Texas. As T. R. Fehrenbach concluded in his classic history of Texas, "Johnson's men had not defrauded Stevenson, but successfully outfrauded him."[ii]

The corruption of the Parr family would eventually unravel after Lyndon Johnson left the White House and the Parr machine lost its most important ally. In 1974, George Parr would be convicted of tax evasion, and he died of an apparent suicide in April 1975.

i. Anthony R. Carrozza, *Dukes of Duval County: The Parr Family and Texas Politics* (Norman, OK: University of Oklahoma Press, 2017), Kindle, 30–31.

ii. T. R. Fehrenbach, *Lone Star: A History of Texas and the Texans*, updated ed. (Cambridge, MA: Da Capo Press, 2000), 659.

TEXAS VS NEW YORK

In November 2016, New York voters elected one of their U.S. senators, something Texas voters did in 2018. In both states, voters considered candidates from four political parties: Democrat, Republican, Green, and Libertarian. However, New Yorkers also had the option of voting for candidates from additional parties like the Working Families, Women's Equality, Conservative, and Reform parties.

A key difference between the two states is that four political parties selected and listed the same candidate for U.S. senator, Charles Schumer: the Democratic Party, Working Families Party, Independence Party, and Women's Equality Party. Given that Schumer is a high-ranking member of the U.S. Senate's Democratic Party, it may seem self-evident that minor parties might back a known winner and also nominate Schumer. Yet, three parties nominated Wendy Long: the Republican Party, the Conservative Party, and the Reform Party. In New York, the ballot is laid out so every party and candidate appears separately. Thus, Schumer's name was listed on the ballot four times and Long's appeared three times. In addition, the votes for each candidate are calculated by political party, not candidate. So, in some respects, Charles Schumer was running not only against Wendy Long, but also against himself. Schumer won overwhelmingly with 61.3 percent of the vote as the Democratic candidate, but he also received 3.1 percent as the Working Families candidate and another 1.9 percent as the Independence Party candidate.

The practice of two or more political parties legally nominating the same candidate for office is called electoral fusion. Electoral fusion is allowed in a handful of states, including New York. While electoral fusion was once practiced in Texas as a means of protecting Democratic Party dominance, it is now illegal.

U.S. Senate Election in New York, 2016

Candidate	Percentage of Votes	Party
Charles Schumer	61.3%	Democrat
Wendy Long	22.1%	Republican
Alex Merced	5.1%	Libertarian
Wendy Long	3.4%	Conservative
Charles Schumer	3.1%	Working Families
Charles Schumer	1.9%	Independence
Robin Wilson	1.5%	Green
Wendy Long	0.6%	Reform
Charles Schumer	0.2%	Women's Equality

Source: New York State Board of Elections, "NYS Board of Elections U.S. Senator Election Returns November 6, 2012," accessed July 29, 2016, http://www.elections.ny.gov/NYSBOE/elections/2012/General/ USSenator.07292013.pdf; some calculations by authors.

Does electoral fusion give voters a more meaningful way of participating in an election?

 PERSONAL RESPONSIBILITY

How does electoral fusion legitimize voting for third parties and allow more views to be expressed?

 SOCIAL RESPONSIBILITY

Why would the major parties in Texas favor or oppose fusion laws?

 CRITICAL THINKING

the Democratic Party. While the Depression and World War II hurt Republicans seeking statewide office, Texans slowly warmed to Republican presidential candidates. In 1952, the Texas Democratic Party officially supported Republican candidate Dwight D. Eisenhower, and, for the second time in Texas's history, a Republican presidential candidate carried the state. Texas Democrats avoided the Republican tide that swept across the state in 1952, however, when every Democratic nominee for statewide office except one cross-filed for positions on the ballot as both a Democrat and a Republican under the provisions of a 1951 law.

President Donald Trump speaks with secretary of energy Rick Perry during the 140th annual Easter Egg Roll at the White House on April 2, 2018, in Washington, DC.

Texans' loyalty to the Democrats created a strange and uneasy alliance within the party. While the Democratic Party would eventually embrace the civil rights movement, from Reconstruction until the 1960s it often supported segregation. Democratic governor James "Pa" Ferguson proclaimed, "A negro has no business whatever taking part in the political affairs of the Democratic Party, the white man's party."[12] African Americans were barred from participating in Democratic primaries, and since the Democratic Party enjoyed a virtual monopoly in winning statewide general elections, African Americans were effectively shut out of any meaningful role in elections. Eventually, the civil rights issue helped split the Democratic Party in Texas and throughout the South.

The Republicans won statewide office for the first time since Reconstruction when Republican John Tower won the U.S. Senate seat vacated by the election of Democrat Lyndon Johnson to the vice presidency. While Republicans were thrilled by this victory, they would not win the Texas governorship until 1978 when William Clements won a surprise victory. By 2000, Democrats were unable to effectively challenge Republicans for any statewide office. Thus, in less than forty years, Texas went from being a state dominated by the Democratic Party to one dominated by the Republican Party. Exit polls from the 2018 election revealed that 39 percent of Texas voters identified themselves as Republicans, 34 percent as Democrats, and 27 percent as independents.[13] Texas is often considered the least "southern" of the southern states[14] and as such is something of a trend leader in southern development. The "Texafication" of American politics includes an emphasis on low taxes; high-tech, industry-embracing policies; and limited spending on social welfare.[15]

Domination of a state by one party is not always the case in American politics. After the 2017 elections, sixteen states had divided governments, with a governor faced with at least one house of the state legislature in the hands of the opposition party. Among the other states, seven had both the legislature and governor's mansion in the hands of Democrats, while in the other twenty-three they were in the hands of Republicans.

Parties, Competition, and Voter Participation

A general election ballot offers voters a choice, preferably one between viable alternatives. Electoral competition has been linked to higher rates of voter turnout,[16] and in Texas, the choice between viable alternatives is not always on the ballot. Of course, the general election is not the only place where there can be competition and a common joke has been that Texas only has one party but has enough conflict for six. For much of the state's history, its political battles were fought during the process of nominating Democratic candidates. With Republicans unable to mount a serious challenge, Texas politicians understood that the winner of the Democratic nominating primary was effectively the election winner. Today, the dominant parties are the opposite, but the dilemma is the same and the battles to win the primary are often the most hotly contested.

Few voters take part in the primaries of either major party. For example, the 2018 primaries that selected candidates for governor, lieutenant governor, and other state-wide elected officials saw only 5.4 percent of Texans voting in the Democratic primary and 7.8 percent voting in the Republican primary. Spurred in part by the presidential primaries, turnout was slightly higher in 2016, when 7.4 percent of Texans voted in the Democratic primary and 14.7 percent voted in the Republican primary. In contrast, turnout for the Democratic primaries during the 1970s—when that party dominated—was generally between 15 percent and 19 percent. As Figure 9.1 shows, in the 1970s, less than 5 percent of Texans took part in the Republican primaries, a matter of little consequence, since Republican gubernatorial candidates were seen as having little chance of winning office. However, since that time, the stature of the Republican Party has grown tremendously, even though participation rates in the party's primaries have not increased dramatically. It appears that the GOP hasn't grown into its new boots as far as voter electoral participation is concerned, and alongside the Democrats, it is left to contend with the troubling trend of reduced voter participation.

One of the ways of judging how much electoral competition exists is to look at how often voters even have a choice between the two major party candidates. Even if a party has little success in a district, having a candidate on the ballot at least offers voters a choice in November. Candidates from minor parties have never done well in Texas and currently do not seem likely to threaten major party candidates.

As Figure 9.2 indicates, in 2000, voters had a choice between candidates of the major parties in only forty of the 150 Texas House races. That year, fifty-seven Texas House races had only a Democratic candidate, and fifty-three had only a Republican candidate. This means that most Texas voters did not have a choice between the two major parties when they entered the voting booth in 2000.

Things had changed by 2018. After years of being criticized for failing to even get candidates on the ballot, Democrats left only eighteen Texas House races without a Democratic candidate. Meanwhile, Republicans left only thirty-five races without a Republican candidate. The Republican absence from so many races is telling because it reveals that even in a state dominated by Republicans, there are areas of the state clearly dominated by Democrats. Overall, almost two-thirds (ninety-seven) of races had candidates from both parties, meaning that the number of races with major-party candidates had more than doubled since 2000. While having a candidate in more races does not guarantee that a party will win more races, winning is, of course, impossible unless you are in the game.

Third parties, such as the Libertarians or Greens, often field candidates and bring more competition to some elections. Getting on the ballot, however, is a huge hurdle, and candidates of these parties do not often present a real challenge to those of the major parties. For a political party to be included on the ballot, one of its statewide candidates must have won more than 5 percent of the vote in the previous election. The Libertarian Party qualified in 2018 because Mark Miller, their candidate for Texas

Why don't more Texans take part in party primaries?

★ SOCIAL RESPONSIBILITY

What should parties do to encourage young Texans to become involved in political parties?

★ PERSONAL RESPONSIBILITY

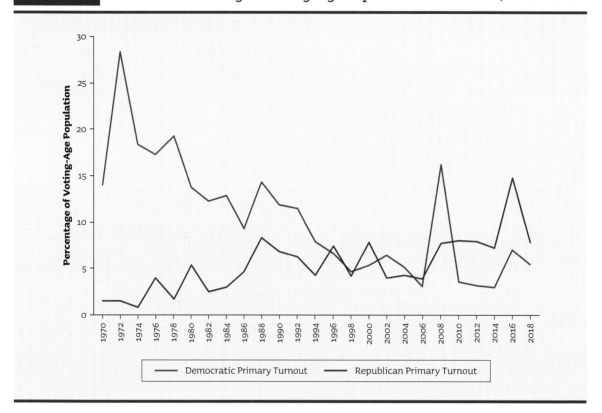

Source: Texas Secretary of State, "Turnout and Voter Registration Figures (1970–Current)," accessed June 1, 2018, www.sos.state.tx.us/elections/historical/70-92.shtml.

What do these trends say about the health of the parties?

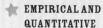 **EMPIRICAL AND QUANTITATIVE**

How can Texas give voters more meaningful choices in the general election?

SOCIAL RESPONSIBILITY

Railroad Commissioner, won 5.3 percent of the vote in 2016. Unfortunately for the Green Party, their candidate with the strongest showing, Martina Salinas, won only 3.2 percent of the statewide vote in the race for Railroad Commissioner that year. The alternative to winning 5 percent of the vote is gathering petitions statewide. This left the Green Party with the task of getting nearly 50,000 valid signatures on petitions. Complicating this task is the requirement that signatures be from registered voters who did not take part in either the Republican or Democratic primary or participate in another party's nominating convention. In addition, the signatures must be gathered over a seventy-five-day period following the March 6 primary.

Ultimately, Texas may see Republican domination decline as the state's demographics continue to change. The Democratic Party had struggled finding candidates to run for some offices, and Texans relied on competition within the nominating process of the Republican Party to produce quality candidates for statewide office. The 2018 campaign showed the stirrings of a revitalized Democratic Party, with the party fielding candidates in more races and Beto O'Rourke putting together a well-funded challenge to U.S. Senator Ted Cruz. While the 2018 election did not produce a wave of Democratic victories in statewide races, Democrats in

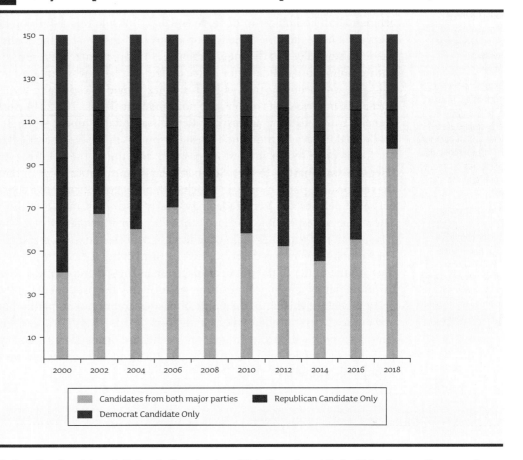

Source: Compiled by the authors from data available from the Texas Secretary of State, "1992–Current Election History," accessed June 12, 2018, http://elections.sos.state.tx.us/elchist.exe.

those races were more competitive and the party gained twelve seats in the Texas House and two in the Texas Senate.

POLITICAL PARTIES IN TEXAS

Texas history has often strained traditional definitions of political parties. One classic definition of a political party comes from eighteenth-century British political philosopher Edmund Burke, who described a party as people "united for promoting by their joint endeavors the national interest, upon some particular principle in which they are all agreed."[17] As we've seen, Texas at times experiences almost as much fighting within its parties as between them, straining the application of the traditional definition of parties to Texas politics. For example, while there is no doubt that today's Republican Party can be labeled a conservative party, Republicans frequently clash on the meaning of conservatism, as conflicts over issues such as trade and education divide Texans who claim the conservative label.

political party
any group, however loosely organized, seeking to elect governmental officeholders under a given label

responsible party model
the view that each party should hold firmly to a clear and consistent set of policies with a coherent ideology distinct from that of other parties in order to present voters with clear choices

electoral competition model
the view that parties make a pragmatic move to the center of the political spectrum as they attempt to win votes, sacrificing the more purely ideological positions

The realities of the **political party** in Texas are best captured by Leon Epstein's definition of a party as "any group, however loosely organized, seeking to elect governmental office-holders under a given label."[18] While this definition does not meet everyone's hopes for the function of a party, it does match the realities of Texas's parties historically and distinguishes parties from organized interests by noting that parties nominate candidates for office under their label while interest groups do not. It is also worth noting that while Texas has provided especially vivid examples of intraparty battles, such troubles are not limited to Texas. The 2016 election featured Donald Trump battling against the Republican establishment while Bernie Sanders challenged Hillary Clinton and the establishment in the Democratic Party.

Texas provides an interesting case for examining the role that many political scientists want parties to play. Some scholars want politics to meet the standards of the **responsible party model**, in which each party holds firmly to a consistent, coherent set of policies and has an ideology clearly distinct from that of the other parties. The virtue of responsible parties is that they provide voters with clear choices and firm positions the parties are pledged to honor if elected. In contrast, political scientist Anthony Downs has described an **electoral competition model** in which parties move to the center of the political spectrum as they attempt to win votes, sacrificing the more purely ideological positions preferred by the proponents of the responsible party model. In this view, the political parties are more pragmatic than ideological and are ready to shift their issue stands from year to year in order to win office. Like American political parties in general, parties in Texas do not match either model perfectly and reflect the tensions between the goals of winning elections and taking strong policy stands.

FIGURE 9.3 Party Competition in U.S. States, 2012–2017

State	Ranney party control index	Ranney competition index	State	Ranney party control index	Ranney competition index
Modified one-party Democratic					
Hawaii	0.833	0.667	Connecticut	0.691	0.809
Rhode Island	0.757	0.743	Oregon	0.682	0.818
California	0.751	0.749	Maryland	0.679	0.821
Massachusetts	0.735	0.765	New York	0.670	0.830
Delaware	0.734	0.766	Illinois	0.646	0.854
Vermont	0.700	0.800			

State	Ranney party control index	Ranney competition index	State	Ranney party control index	Ranney competition index
Two-party competition					
Colorado	0.622	0.878	Montana	0.437	0.937
Washington	0.609	0.891	Pennsylvania	0.424	0.924
Minnesota	0.588	0.912	Iowa	0.413	0.913
New Jersey	0.587	0.913	Louisiana	0.399	0.899
New Mexico	0.537	0.963	Nebraska	0.393	0.893
West Virginia	0.537	0.963	Missouri	0.368	0.868
Maine	0.491	0.991	Wisconsin	0.363	0.863
New Hampshire	0.481	0.981	Arkansas	0.351	0.851
Kentucky	0.468	0.968	Alaska	0.348	0.848
Nevada	0.461	0.961			
Virginia	0.458	0.958			
Modified one-party Republican					
North Carolina	0.340	0.840	Alabama	0.277	0.777
Arizona	0.339	0.839	Kansas	0.271	0.771
Michigan	0.336	0.836	Oklahoma	0.264	0.764
Texas	0.327	0.827	Idaho	0.231	0.731
Florida	0.325	0.825	North Dakota	0.228	0.728
South Carolina	0.324	0.824	Tennessee	0.227	0.727
Mississippi	0.317	0.817	Utah	0.215	0.715
Georgia	0.309	0.809	South Dakota	0.202	0.702
Indiana	0.285	0.785	Wyoming	0.179	0.679
Ohio	0.282	0.782			
Fifty-state mean	0.450	0.836			

Note: The Ranney Index runs from 0 to 1, with 0 indicating complete domination of the state governorship and legislature by Republicans and 1 indicating complete control by Democrats.

Source: Thomas M. Holbrook and Raymond J. La Raja, "Parties and Elections," in *Politics in the American States*, 11th ed., ed. Virginia Gray, Russell L. Hanson, and Thad Kousser (Washington, DC: CQ Press, 2017), table 3–2.

How competitive is politics in Texas?

⭐ **CRITICAL THINKING**

How will Texas politics change as the youngest generation of Texans begins to have more influence?

⭐ **PERSONAL RESPONSIBILITY**

straight-ticket voting
the practice of selecting all the candidates for office who are running under a party label simply by checking off a single box marked with the party label

How many Texans identify themselves as "independent" but vote consistently for one party or the other?

⭐ **SOCIAL RESPONSIBILITY**

What do the terms *liberal* and *conservative* mean to you? Do you think about those terms the same way your parents and grandparents do?

⭐ **CRITICAL THINKING**

Party Loyalty and Identification

If you had to summarize the relationship between Texans and their political parties, you'd have to conclude, "It's complicated." While Texans may be independent in some ways, many remain fiercely loyal to their parties in practice. Texans, after all, elected nothing but Democrats to statewide office for almost a hundred years after Reconstruction, and a century of loyalty has to count for something.

In 2017, the Texas Legislature removed straight-ticket voting effective beginning with the 2020 election. Straight-ticket voting allowed Texans to cast a vote for all candidates from their party by checking one box on the ballot. Advocates of eliminating straight-ticket voting argued that forcing voters to select individual candidates for each race forces them to make more thoughtful choices. In 2016, 62 percent of Texans in the state's largest 20 counties voted straight-party tickets. In those counties, which accounted for almost three-fourths of all votes that year, 29.2 percent voted straight-ticket Republican and 32 percent voted straight-ticket Democrat. Some opponents charged that Republicans backed the removal of the straight-ticket vote because more Democrats made use of the straight-ticket option. In addition, some opponents argued that straight-ticket voting makes more sense than ever in today's highly polarized political environment because the two parties are more differentiated than ever.[19]

A February 2018 poll found that 46 percent of Texans said they identify or lean Republican while 44 percent identify or lean Democrat. While these results led some observers to declare that Democrats had made Texas competitive again, low turnout among Democrats combined with the tendency of many people to vote for incumbents has made it hard for Democrats to win back control of statewide offices. When asked where they place themselves on the ideological spectrum, from extremely liberal to extremely conservative, most Texans placed themselves on the conservative end of the spectrum, with 47 percent describing themselves as either extremely conservative, somewhat conservative, or leaning conservative (see Figure 9.4) and only 28 percent describing themselves as extremely liberal, somewhat liberal, or leaning liberal.

The relationship between a voter and his or her party is almost always complicated. While party identification is the best predictor of how someone will vote, party identification is as much a way of seeing the world as it is a choice that citizens make. Some of the earliest voting studies argued that a voter's choice of candidates is shaped by his or her perception of campaigns and other events, but these perceptions are shaped by the voter's party identification.[20] More recent research has suggested that how we see the world is shaped early in life and may reflect predispositions that we are born with.[21] Both views remind us that members of a political party are resistant to change because they see the world through Republican or Democratic lenses that lead them to discount or completely ignore information coming from the other party. The growth of cable news and social media like Facebook have further enabled this tendency, and citizens today can spend much of their lives never encountering information that might challenge their political views. These theories help us understand why Texans seem locked into political parties, despite the fact that so many harbor concerns about their divisive role in American politics and their inability to produce effective leadership in government.

FIGURE 9.4 Political Ideology and Party Identification in Texas, 2018

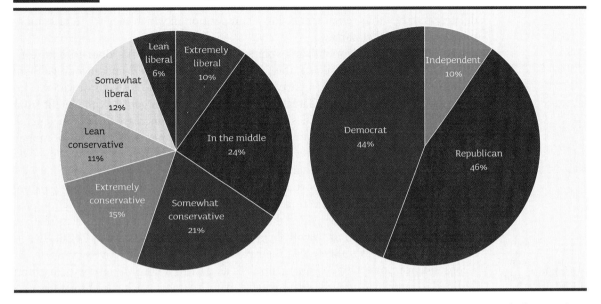

Source: University of Texas/*Texas Tribune* poll, "Texas Statewide Survey," February 1–12, 2018, https://static.texastribune.org/media/documents/ut-tt-2018-02-summary-full.pdf.

Functions of Parties

State and local parties have a variety of important roles in a representative democracy. The most obvious is the nomination of party candidates. Since the distinguishing characteristic of a party is electing candidates under its label, selecting nominees is a central function of the state and local parties.

One of the most important functions of state and local parties is recruitment. As each party attempts to build a winning team, party leaders at the state and local level seek out the most politically talented individuals and encourage them to seek office to help build the next generation of politics. Before he was president, George W. Bush was a Texas governor urged by state Republicans (and some Democrats) to run for president. Before that, he was a businessman urged into state politics by local Republican leaders.

Both state parties provide support for party candidates. Some of the support is financial, with parties providing cash contributions as well as advertising and voter mobilization. The parties also provide training for candidates and their campaign staffs, including training on polling, broadcast media, website development, and social media. One party leader said, "I see the party organization as a sort of quartermaster corps, delivering services that achieve economies of scale."[22] One function that is rapidly expanding may define modern parties: fund-raising. Headlines about presidential involvement in fund-raising in the 1990s clouded the fact that much of the fund-raising being done was actually sending money into state party accounts. Fund-raising and spending in campaigns shifted to the states because federal campaign finance laws restrict how much individuals can give to the national parties. State parties in general faced few such restrictions and thus found themselves the recipients of the big checks their national parties could not legally accept. While fund-raising remains an area of controversy, the parties must raise funds to promote their agendas as well as their candidates, and they thus remain locked in a competition in which they try to raise more money than the other parties.

Another function is mobilizing voters. Through phone banks, door-to-door canvasing, mailings, and advertising, the parties reach out to voters and encourage them to go to the polls. Of course, a party is most likely to reach out to those voters who will support that party's candidates. However, democracy in general can benefit from healthy competition if both parties reach out to voters and increase turnout in general. Today, state leaders like Governor Greg Abbott invest tremendous amounts of money and energy in building volunteer networks and databases that will help them—and other members of their party—win elections.

Parties can also be an important tool for representation. Texas's one-party nature has often meant its general elections were not competitive, and the redistricting process described in Chapter 3 divided the state even further by creating districts that are often heavily Republican or heavily Democratic. This means that many Texans live in districts in which it is unlikely that their party will be able to effectively compete. As a consequence, some citizens see themselves as part of a chronic minority, a group destined to rarely win an election or achieve majority status. Such citizens see few reasons to become actively engaged in politics and have little hope that their views will be reflected by their representatives in Austin. Parties can offer some hope that such views will be heard, even if these views are channeled through an elected official from another area of the state. For example, Democrats in areas that find themselves represented by Republicans in the Texas House and Senate may hope that Democrats from other parts of the state will give voice to their concerns and advance their causes.

The ultimate function of political parties is control of government, since the point of winning elections is getting party candidates into office. In some ways, this function goes against the constitutional order, because our system of checks and balances and separation of powers is intended to keep any one faction from having too much influence. However, parties are elected so they will have influence and get things done, and their ability to coordinate the efforts of officials across the branches of government can be an important tool in creating the kind of leadership a state in transition needs.

The Consequences of Weak Parties

The scholar V. O. Key observed that Texas's geographic size makes it hard for well-formed political networks to function. Without close-knit political networks, it has been harder for parties to maintain enduring political organizations across the broad geographic expanse of the state. Those parties that were able to build organizations often did so through dramatic appeals to the public that were generally short-lived and created a political coalition based more on personality than policy goals. For example, it was his skills as a flour salesman rather than dependence on a well-ordered political machine that brought Wilbert Lee "Pappy" O'Daniel into the governorship. In contrast, other southern states saw the rise of personal political machines, such as the Longs in Louisiana, which spanned several generations.

With no well-organized party organization to provide party insiders a reliable path to statewide victory, political outsiders have often found their way into the Texas

---

chronic minority
a group that rarely wins elections or achieves majority status and thus sees few reasons to become actively engaged in politics

HOW TEXAS GOVERNMENT WORKS

Party Organization

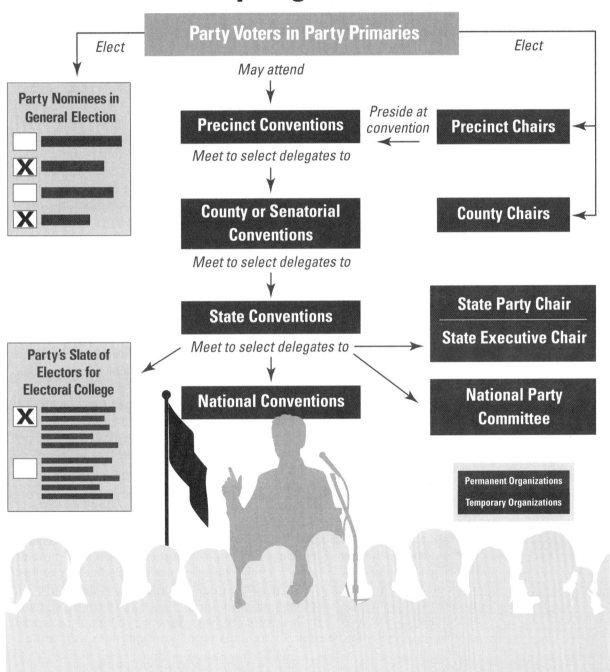

Party Voters in Party Primaries

Elect → **Party Nominees in General Election**

Elect

May attend → **Precinct Conventions**

Preside at convention ← **Precinct Chairs**

Meet to select delegates to → **County or Senatorial Conventions**

County Chairs

Meet to select delegates to → **State Conventions**

Meet to select delegates to →

State Party Chair / State Executive Chair

National Party Committee

National Conventions

Party's Slate of Electors for Electoral College

Permanent Organizations
Temporary Organizations

governor's mansion. While the early twentieth century saw the success of some dynamic outsiders, such as James E. "Pa" Ferguson and Pappy O'Daniel, more recent elections have seen the rise of political newcomers, such as William Clements and George W. Bush, leading the Republican revival in the state.

Changes in national politics have weakened Texas parties further. Early in U.S. history, the lack of communication and the decentralized nature of American government meant that the national parties looked something like a collection of state and local party bosses. They gathered at each party's national conventions to bargain their way to the selection of a presidential candidate for the party, a process that often took several days and repeated ballots.

Several changes combined to alter the nature of the parties and the role of state and local party leaders. First, the creation of party primaries shifted control of the nomination of candidates from party leaders to voters. Also, the rising power of the national government naturally shifted attention from state parties to the national parties and organized interest groups that grappled with these issues in Washington. Later, the rise of mass media campaigns made candidates more reliant on the money needed to air ads than on the local party volunteers who campaigned door to door. Most recently, political power has followed the shifting tracks of political money that came with changes to campaign finance rules. The 2010 U.S. Supreme Court decision in *Citizens United v. Federal Election Commission* and other changes mean that union, corporate, and other funds can more easily be used to purchase political advertising directly without working with political parties.

Rather than giving money to the broad party organization, states are seeing more and more money going into legislative campaign committees, which are fund-raising committees that raise money from individuals and interest groups and then distribute it to candidates at the national political party level. While these committees can help members of a party win election, they may weaken the influence of the state party because these groups need not support the party's agenda and may represent one particular faction of the party at the expense of others. For example, Texans for Lawsuit Reform (TLR) gives millions of dollars directly to candidates. While the group claims to be bipartisan, over a twenty-one-year period from 1994 to 2015, the group gave over 80 percent of its $35.2 million in contributions to Republican candidates.[23] Moreover, its ability to contribute or spend money independently rather than through the party means that it does not have to work with party leaders. Party organizations can still exert influence under these new campaign laws, but the challenges they face continue to grow as the role of money continues to rise and organized interests have fewer reasons to work with them.

PARTY ORGANIZATIONS

Because of the role they play in the practice of democracy, the organization and functioning of political parties is subject to some regulation by the state. The U.S. Supreme Court has ruled that state law can regulate the internal affairs of political parties only if it is "necessary to ensure that elections are orderly, fair, and honest."[24] Texas state law places restrictions on the selection, composition, rules, and meeting dates of the state and local political party committees. In fact, Texas is rated a "heavy regulator," with some of the most extensive laws governing the state's parties.[25]

Political parties in the United States contain both temporary and permanent organizations. The temporary party organizations are occasional gatherings of ordinary party members through primaries and in meetings known as caucuses and conventions. The permanent party organizations are the party officials selected by the temporary organizations to conduct the business of the party in between primaries, caucuses, and conventions.

While the temporary nature of party conventions may make them seem less important, like any democratic organization, America's political parties draw their legitimacy from the participation of citizens. As such, a political party is a grassroots organization, or a group in which power and decision making reside with average citizens. This relationship makes these gatherings of party members the foundation upon which a party claims legitimacy.

Citizens' participation in Texas's two major parties begins at the local level through primaries, which are elections in which ordinary citizens vote to choose the candidates that will represent a party on the ballot in the general election (see "How Texas Government Works: Party Organization" infographic on page 307). Primaries have been part of Texas elections since the Terrell Election Law in 1905 mandated that major political parties use primaries to select their nominees. Prior to that, parties were free to make their nominations however they pleased, with nominees usually being chosen by nominating conventions composed of party leaders without input from average citizens. Progressives promoted primaries as a means to take the choice of candidates away from political bosses meeting behind the scenes and expand participation to ordinary citizens.

Texas law requires that the major parties (those that received 20 percent or more of the vote for governor in the last election) use primaries to choose their candidates for office. Parties whose candidate for governor received between 2 and 20 percent of the vote in the last election have a choice between nominating candidates by convention or by primary. Parties whose gubernatorial candidates received less than 2 percent of the vote must use conventions because of the costs involved in holding primaries. Primaries require separate voting booths for each party in every precinct in the state. To control costs, minor political parties, such as the Libertarian Party, typically choose conventions when given the option of primaries.

For decades, the major political parties operated their primaries as they pleased, claiming along the way that their private status allowed them to set their own restrictions—including barring black voters. Until 1972, political parties paid for primaries, relying on hefty candidate filing fees to fund these elections.

As noted in Chapter 8, Texas party primaries are technically closed primaries, with only party members being allowed to vote. In practice, Texas primaries are much more accessible and function as semi-open primaries in which any voter may participate without having previously registered a party affiliation. When Texans vote in a party's primary, their party affiliation is recorded in the statewide database kept by the Texas secretary of state's Elections Division and is accessible by county election officials. Under state law, this "affiliates" citizens with a specific party for an entire year and thus makes them ineligible to participate in the nominating process of another party or independent candidate that year. However, this affiliation does not obligate a voter to contribute to, vote for, or support in any way that party's candidates. By law, a party

temporary party organizations
gatherings of ordinary party members, such as primaries, caucuses, and conventions

permanent party organizations
the party officials selected by the temporary organizations to conduct party business between the primaries, caucuses, and conventions

grassroots organization
a group in which power and decision making reside with average citizens; the participation of average citizens is the foundation upon which these groups' legitimacy rests

affiliation expires at the end of each voting year; before the primaries in the next set of elections two years later, all voter affiliations are removed from their record. In addition, Texas's "sore loser law" prohibits someone from voting or running in the primary of one party and later running for office under the label of another party in the same year. In 2012, two Democratic candidates in Angelina County were disqualified from the November ballot because they had cast votes in the Republican primary that year.

The flexibility of Texas's primary voting system can create its own set of problems. For generations, many conservative Texans continued to vote in the Democratic primary since they could often nominate like-minded conservatives as Democrats and see them elected in November. Meanwhile, other conservatives sought to make the Republican Party more viable. Today, Democrats face a similar dilemma. Many vote in the Republican primary hoping to make that party's nominee as moderate as possible. Others will seek out the nominee who will most embarrass the Republican Party.

runoff primary
a primary that occurs if no nominee receives the required majority of the votes in the primary; the top two finishers face off in a second primary to determine the nominee for the general election

Under state law, a political party's nominee must receive a majority of the total number of votes in the primary. Races that generate competition from three or more candidates raise the possibility that no nominee will get the required majority, necessitating a **runoff primary** in which the top two finishers from the first primary face off. This was the case in the May 27, 2012, primary for the U.S. Senate, when David Dewhurst won 44.6 percent of the vote, Ted Cruz won 34.2 percent, and seven other candidates divided up the rest of the vote. With neither candidate having a majority, Dewhurst and Cruz then faced off in a runoff primary on July 31 when Ted Cruz won with 56.8 percent of the vote.

The parties may also include nonbinding referendum items on their primary ballot. For example, in 2016, the Republican Party included referendum items on eliminating property taxes; requiring cities, counties, and other local governments to comply with federal immigration laws; prohibiting government entities from taking funds from public employees' paychecks to pay union dues; and having Texas reassert Tenth Amendment rights. These items generally serve little purpose other than as symbolic statements designed to rally voters around shared goals. Meanwhile, Texas Democrats were approving their party's support for allowing public universities to opt out of campus carry, demands for a new voting rights act, calls for comprehensive immigration reform, legislating renewable energy sources, free community college, minimum wage increases, and reform to the criminal justice system.

Local Parties

precinct chair; county chair
a precinct chair is selected by party members in each voting precinct by majority vote; a county chair is selected by countywide vote; these party officials are responsible for managing the local affairs of their party for the next two years

Party primaries also elect local party officers. In Texas, party members in each voting precinct elect by a majority vote a **precinct chair** and in a countywide vote select a **county chair**. These officers are responsible for managing the local affairs of their party for the next two years. To be eligible to be a county or precinct chair of a political party, a person must only be a qualified voter and not hold or be a candidate for any elective federal, state, or county office. To make participation as easy as possible, state law provides that a candidate for county chair or precinct chair not be required to pay a fee to get on the primary ballot.

At the county level, each party has a county executive committee led by a county chair and each precinct in the county has a precinct chair. This committee is the permanent committee that oversees the party's organization, fund-raising, and campaigning within the county. There is often little competition for these positions, and they sometimes go vacant because most Texans are content to leave the business of the parties to others.

The parties hold precinct-level meetings, or conventions (caucuses). In much of the nation, such meetings are called caucuses when held at the local level. Primary conventions are temporary organizations in the party structure that usually convene on the day of the primary election between 7:00 PM and 9:00 PM, usually in the same location as the primary election. Sometimes, Republicans and Democrats hold their precinct conventions in different rooms in the same building, often the same school, church, fire station, or other building that hosted voting earlier that day. State law requires that a written notice at the polling place provide to primary voters the date, hour, and place for convening the precinct convention.

conventions (caucuses)
meetings at which party members participate in a range of party business

While these meetings are open only to party members, recall that party affiliation in Texas requires only showing up for the primary and requesting the party ballot. Thus, citizens in Texas can choose their party the day of the primary election and return in the evening to attend their party's caucuses. Minor parties that do not use primaries to nominate candidates obviously cannot require that citizens vote in their primary to participate in their party's convention. In these cases, a citizen wishing to participate in the convention of a party that has not held a primary may affiliate with that party simply by taking an oath prescribed by law: "I swear that I have not voted in a primary election or participated in a convention of another party during this voting year. I hereby affiliate myself with the _____ Party."

Precinct conventions are used to elect delegates (and alternates) who will attend the party's conventions held later at the county level or Texas senatorial district level. The number of delegates a precinct is allotted is based on how many members of the party voted in that precinct in that election. While selecting those party members to represent the precinct at future conventions is the primary function of the precinct conventions, attendees may also vote on resolutions related to political issues, especially those on which citizens want their party to take an official stand.

On the third Saturday after the primary election, each of the major parties holds its county or senatorial district convention. A county convention is held in a county if the county is not situated in more than one state senatorial district. If a county is in more than one state senatorial district, a senatorial district convention is held in each part of the county that is in a different senatorial district. These conventions select delegates to the statewide convention and deal with other party business.

county or senatorial district convention

a convention in which delegates to the statewide convention are selected; held on the third Saturday after the primary election

State Parties

Texas's political parties hold their state conventions biennially in May or June. The convention includes delegates selected by the county or senatorial district conventions. Nominees for or holders of state or national government offices are entitled by law to attend the state convention of their party, but they may not vote in the convention unless they have been selected to serve as delegates by their county or senatorial district through the usual process.

While the state conventions are temporary party organizations, meeting over a few days every two years, they are important events because state parties really only take form when the parties' members gather in state conventions at this time. For example, state law requires that party rules be approved by the party's state convention. While gathered, each state convention writes and approves their party platform, the document that officially spells out the issue stands of the party. Each issue position of the party platform is referred to as a plank. (See Table 9.1 for excerpts from the 2018 platforms for the Texas Republican and Democratic parties.)

The Republican Party of Texas (RPT) has made a concerted effort in recent years to make its platform more binding. It has done this by creating a system that makes Republicans take clear positions on policies discussed in the party platform and subjecting them to censure for three or more actions in opposition to the "core principles of the Republican Party of Texas." Rule 44 of the Republican Party of Texas (RPT) allows the party to withhold financial or other support from any Republican candidate censured by a two-thirds vote of the State Republican Executive Committee (SREC).[26] In January 2018, the SREC voted to censure Texas House Speaker Joe Straus for failing to adequately support the Republican platform.

Each party's officials are selected by the state conventions. Delegates elect a state party chair and executive committee to carry on the activities of the party between state conventions. By law, each party's state executive committee consists of one man and one woman from each state senatorial district. In addition, each state committee's chair and vice chair positions must include some combination of a man and a woman—either the chair must be a man and the vice chair a woman, or vice versa. Texas's state party executive committee is typical of state party committees, if there is such a thing as a typical state party committee. As one text points out, "so great are the differences between these committees from state to state—in membership selection, size, and function—that it is difficult to generalize about them."[27]

While not officially the head of the Republican Party in Texas, there is no doubt that elected Republican officials like Governor Abbott and Lieutenant Governor Dan Patrick attempt to reshape the party. While the state party chairs officially head each party, the visibility enjoyed by officials like Abbott and their ability to raise and spend money create opportunities to lead the party. During the 2018 Republican primaries, Abbott spent more than a quarter of a million dollars trying to replace three Republican incumbents. Two of the three candidates he campaigned against won their primaries. Abbott's efforts reflect the reality that, while various party leaders may want to direct the party, voters ultimately control the direction of the party when they vote in primaries.

Nominating Presidential Candidates

In addition to conducting the business of the state parties, the state party conventions in presidential election years must also select the parties' delegates to the national party convention and the representatives to the parties' national committee, as well as the slate of electors who will be available to serve in the Electoral College.

Today, state law requires that major parties in Texas hold presidential "preference primaries" in presidential election years, in conjunction with their regular primaries. Texans may use this primary to express their preference for one of the candidates on the ballot, or they may vote "uncommitted." While holding these primaries at the same time as the nominating primaries for other offices makes some sense by consolidating voting dates, it presents a dilemma in national politics as many states attempt to move their primaries earlier in the year to garner as much attention as possible from

TABLE 9.1 Comparison of 2018 Texas Party Platforms

Issue	2018 Texas Republican Party Platform	2018 Texas Democratic Party Platform
Abortion	"The sanctity of innocent human life, created in the image of God. . . should be protected from fertilization to natural death."	"[T]he Texas Democratic Party will. . . preserve confidential, unrestricted access to affordable, high quality, culturally sensitive health care services, including the full range of reproductive services, contraception and abortion, without requiring guardian, judicial, parental, or spousal consent."
Environmental policy	"'Climate change' is a political agenda promoted to control every aspect of our lives. We support the defunding of 'climate justice' initiatives and the abolition of the Environmental Protection Agency and repeal of the Endangered Species Act."	"Texas Democrats recognize that climate change is a real and serious threat that is causing drought, crop failure, heat waves, more extreme hurricanes, torrential storms, and extreme climate events. Recent events have shown how these extreme climate disruptions are ravaging our economy and environment, and it is time for Texas to become a leader in combating climate change."
Local control	"We encourage the Legislature to preempt local government efforts to interfere with the State's sovereignty over business, employees, and property rights. This includes but is not limited to burdensome regulations on short-term rentals, bags, sick leave, trees, and employee criminal screening. We support preemption of city ordinances that dictate sick leave policies to private businesses."	"We oppose any attempts by the Texas Legislature to stifle efforts of municipalities to regulate litter and pollution through city ordinances and regulations that ban bottles, bags, Styrofoam, or other wasteful packaging. "Texas Democrats support. . . the rights of local governments and voters to regulate oil and gas operations within their communities, including the right to establish setbacks and bans on hydraulic fracturing near residences, businesses, schools and hospitals."
Same-sex marriage	"We oppose homosexual marriage, regardless of state of origin. We urge the Texas Legislature to pass religious liberty protections for individuals, businesses, and government officials who believe marriage is between one man and one woman."	"[W]e oppose. . . efforts to defy the U.S. Supreme Court decisions which guaranteed marriage equality and the full benefits of marriage to all couples."
School choice	"Texas families should be empowered to choose from public, private, charter, or homeschool options for their children's education, using tax credits or exemptions without government constraints or intrusion."	"Texas Democrats. . . believe 'school choice' is a deceptive marketing frame that purports to advocate something that already exists—school choice—but whose true purpose is to divert public school funds to vouchers on tax credit systems supporting private and sectarian schools."
Women in combat	"We oppose the use of women in military combat units."	"We believe in America. . . made stronger by the men and women who put their lives on the line when it is necessary to engage our military to secure our nation."

Sources: Excerpted from the 2018 Republican Party of Texas Platform, accessed July 6, 2018, https://www.texasgop.org/platform, and from the 2018–2020 Texas Democratic Party Platform, accessed July 6, 2018, https://www.txdemocrats.org/our-party/texas-democratic-party-platform.

presidential candidates. Texas, which held its primaries in June for many years, moved its primary date up to early March in 1988 and joined the ranks of "Super Tuesday" primaries, so named because many of the large states held their party primaries on that Tuesday. In 2007, in response to moves by other states to hold their primaries even earlier, the Texas Legislature considered moving its primary to February to avoid being left to vote on presidential nominations after a candidate had already won enough state and local votes to lock up the nomination. Since 2008, the Texas Republican and Democratic parties have held their primaries on the first Tuesday in March. However, many citizens prefer to nominate their candidates a little closer to Election Day in November, and moving the nominating process earlier in the year only extends a campaign season that is already too long for many Texans. Some states hold separate presidential primaries at different times from the primaries used to select other offices. Other states, such as Kansas and Iowa, have opted not to hold a presidential primary in their state and rely on a caucus instead.

Texas's presidential primary has not always been binding. When voters filed through the voting booths during the day to vote in the primary, the number of delegates that their favorite candidate was allocated was decided by party members who attended the precinct conventions that evening and other conventions later in the spring. Today, while the party conventions select which individuals will be sent to the party's national convention as delegates, the allocation of these delegates between the competing candidates for president is determined by party rules, which use results from the presidential preference primary to allocate candidates on a districtwide or statewide basis. Currently, state law requires that at least 75 percent of delegates representing the state at the party's national convention be allocated based on the votes in the presidential primaries. However, the law does not dictate exactly how the parties use the results of primary voting in allocating those delegates. For example, the Republicans have an elaborate system of allocating delegates using the vote counts at the congressional district and statewide levels. A candidate who receives more than 50 percent of the votes within a congressional district is entitled to all of the delegates to the Republican convention from that district. When no candidate gets 50 percent, the delegates are divided between those candidates who received more than 20 percent of the vote.

In 2008, Texas came under scrutiny for its system of delegate allocation because candidate Hillary Clinton won the popular vote in the state's Democratic presidential primary but did not win the majority of the 228 delegates Texas sent to the Democratic National Convention. The controversy resulted from Texas's complicated allocation process. **Allocation** refers to how delegates at the national convention pledged to vote for a specific candidate or attend as undecided. Because the Texas Democratic Party wanted to encourage participation in all stages of the party's process, delegates are actually allocated in three ways: (1) allocation based on primary day votes, (2) allocation based on convention attendance, and (3) unpledged superdelegates. Dividing delegate allocation between the primary and caucus makes some sense because it encourages people to take part in both voting in the primary elections and the face-to-face meetings that make up the caucus.

In 2016, the Texas Democratic Party had been allocated 222 delegates for the Democratic National Convention and another twenty-nine superdelegates. Of the 222 regular delegates, 145 were distributed among the thirty-one election districts for the

allocation
the process by which party rules designate how many of the state's delegates to the national party convention will be pledged to vote for a specific candidate or will attend as undecided

Texas State Senate. Each district receives between two and ten delegates, depending on the Democratic Party turnout in recent statewide elections. Any candidate receiving 15 percent of the vote in the Democratic primary in that district receives a share of the delegates proportional to their vote total. The remaining seventy-seven delegates are distributed proportionally based on the statewide vote, but a candidate must receive 15 percent of the statewide vote to receive delegates.[28] On primary election night, Clinton won 147 delegates to Sanders's seventy-five. Of course, this process sounds complicated and may seem to a new candidate to presidential elections like Sanders or his supporters as being "rigged." However, the system was enacted and modified over time to produce certain outcomes in the wake of presidential election failures like Walter Mondale's disastrous defeat in 1984, the failure of various Super Tuesday primaries to produce a clear Democratic winner, and the poor showing of John Kerry in the 2004 election.

Democrats were not the only party to tinker with their rules. In 2016, Donald Trump complained at times of rigged rules. The 2016 Texas Republican Party selected 155 delegates to the Republican National Convention that met in Cleveland, Ohio. Each of Texas's thirty-six U.S. House of Representatives election districts is allocated three delegates. A candidate winning a majority of the vote in the district wins all three delegates, but if one candidate receives at least 20 percent of the vote and no candidate wins over 50 percent, the delegates are split between the top two candidates. If no candidate receives over 20 percent of the voting in the district, the top three candidates each receive one delegate. An additional forty-seven delegates are allocated based on the statewide vote, with all forty-seven going to a candidate winning a majority of the statewide vote. If no majority occurs, then delegates are allocated in a manner similar to the formula for each U.S. House of Representatives district.[29] On primary election night 2016, Ted Cruz won 44 percent of the vote, Donald Trump 27 percent of the vote, and Marco Rubio 18 percent of the vote. Once the district conventions met and at-large delegates were selected, Cruz won 104 delegates (67 percent of Texas delegates), Donald Trump won 49 delegates (31 percent), and Marco Rubio won 3 delegates (2 percent).

The State Parties and the National Parties

Although citizens generally consider parties to be consistent across all levels of government, there are actually significant differences between the expressed opinions of the parties. Because American parties are grassroots organizations in which power flows from the bottom up, the national parties are not able to impose their views on the state parties. Texas political parties vividly illustrate the inability of the national parties to control party members. For example, for years the national Democratic Party championed civil rights while some of the conservative Democrats who controlled the Texas Democratic Party vigorously opposed civil rights legislation. More recently, the Texas Republican Party platform has consistently "demanded" the elimination of presidential authority to issue executive orders and the repeal of all previous executive orders, despite the fact that the executive order was used frequently by George W. Bush and other Republican presidents.

Many of the differences between the national party and state parties have been overlooked because the national party conventions have come to be dominated by the campaign organizations of the presidential candidates rather than by the state parties. Because delegates to the national convention are selected based more on attachment to national presidential candidates than on service in the state or local party, the local party's role has received little attention. This undermines some of the representational role of parties as state and local concerns disappear in the shadow of national politics.

While local party leaders remain important actors in recruiting party candidates and building the parties at the local level, the rise of mass media and candidate-centered campaigns has taken away some of the local parties' most important functions as vehicles for raising money and getting candidates' messages out. Some have called state and local parties "Mom-and-Pop Shops in the Information Age,"[30] and as citizens make more use of television and the Internet to learn about candidates, local parties may find less to do. This represents one way in which changes in the state may permanently transform the way the parties operate and who in the parties holds significant power.

WINNERS AND LOSERS

Although the primaries and conventions may technically be open to any eligible voters willing to declare themselves members of a party, Texans generally seem increasingly uninterested in participating in the business of parties. With just over 10 percent of eligible Texans voting in the primaries at any time, how representative are the nominees of the two major parties? V. O. Key argued that "over the long run, the have-nots lose in a disorganized politics."[31] According to Key, when there are no strong parties, no one has the incentive and ability to mobilize disorganized interests. Without well-organized parties, some citizens will remain disorganized and their interests diffuse. Organization is especially important to anyone wishing to promote serious reform, since reform efforts require battling an entrenched status quo.

TEXAS (VS) IOWA

While most states require parties to hold primaries to nominate candidates for the general election, Iowa uses a system of caucuses. The word *caucus* allegedly comes from a Native American word for a meeting between tribal leaders.[i] The Iowa caucus system developed in the late 1800s within political parties as a method of selecting delegates to political party conventions. The Iowa caucuses operate similarly to a closed primary in that the participants must be registered with a political party. This process effectively limits the Republican caucuses to Republicans and the Democratic caucuses to Democrats.

On the night of the Iowa caucuses, participants gather in over 2,000 local, precinct-level meetings. Historically, these meetings occurred in the homes of local party activists, creating a feeling of neighborliness among participants. In recent years, the meetings have occurred at a local school, library, church,

or similar place. To some extent, the caucuses still take on the flavor of a giant precinct party.

The two major parties have slightly different rules concerning how the caucus proceeds. For the Republican Party, the caucus consists of participants dropping the name of a candidate in a hat. Results are then tabulated. At a separate meeting, participants choose delegates to attend a state convention where the official nomination of party candidates for the general election takes place. At the Democratic caucus, participants break into groups based on which candidate they support. Note that "undecided" is an acceptable grouping. If any group consists of less than 15 percent of the total number of participants, then those group members must realign with another group. Participants then lobby and persuade members of the other groups or the groups with less than 15 percent to change their preference. When all remaining groups supporting

Results of the Iowa Caucuses since 1972

Year	Democratic Party Iowa Caucus Winner	National Party Nominee	Republican Party Iowa Caucus Winner	National Party Nominee
2016	Hillary Clinton	Hillary Clinton	Ted Cruz	Donald Trump
2012	Barack Obama	Barack Obama	Rick Santorum	Mitt Romney
2008	Barack Obama	Barack Obama	Mike Huckabee	John McCain
2004	John Kerry	John Kerry	George W. Bush	George W. Bush
2000	Al Gore	Al Gore	George W. Bush	George W. Bush
1996	Bill Clinton	Bill Clinton	Bob Dole	Bob Dole
1992	Tom Harkin	Bill Clinton	George H. W. Bush	George H. W. Bush
1988	Richard Gephardt	Michael Dukakis	Bob Dole	George H. W. Bush
1984	Walter Mondale	Walter Mondale	Ronald Reagan	Ronald Reagan
1980	Jimmy Carter	Jimmy Carter	George H. W. Bush	Ronald Reagan
1976	Uncommitted	Jimmy Carter	Gerald Ford	Gerald Ford
1972	Edmund Muskie	George McGovern	Richard Nixon	Richard Nixon

Source: Compiled from "Caucus History: Past Years' Results," *Des Moines Register*, accessed August 3, 2016, http://caucuses.desmoinesregister.com/caucus-history-past-years-results.

(Continued)

(Continued)

a candidate are above 15 percent of the total participants at that location, delegates to the party county convention are allocated based on the size of the groups. The table on the previous page contains a comparison of the results of the party caucuses since 1972, when the Iowa caucuses gained their reputation as a presidential bellwether and grabbed the attention of candidates and the nation alike.

By tradition, the Iowa caucuses are the first caucuses held in the United States. Because winning, or at least doing well or "better than expected" in, an Iowa caucus creates momentum for a candidate's campaign and encourages financial support from donors, the Iowa caucuses are very important to candidates running for U.S. president. For example, Rick Santorum's narrow win in the 2012 Republican Iowa caucus gave his campaign a boost that helped him be seen as one of the primary challengers to Mitt Romney. Because so much attention is paid to Iowa's caucus results, critics suggest that Iowa carries too much weight in presidential elections, especially considering the state's relatively small and homogenous population.

While turnout for Texas primaries has been low in recent decades, the turnout rates for the Iowa caucuses appear to be increasing. However, turnout for the Iowa caucuses is harder to determine simply because, in contrast to closed primaries, lists of registered Democratic or Republican voters do not exist. Estimates indicate that the percentage of the population that participates in the caucuses is increasing over time.[ii]

Do caucuses or primaries produce the most meaningful participation for party members?

⭐ **SOCIAL RESPONSIBILITY**

What do you think the advantages or disadvantages of a system such as the Iowa caucuses would be if Texas changed to that system?

⭐ **CRITICAL THINKING**

i. "Frequently Asked Caucus Questions," *Des Moines Register*, www .desmoinesregister.com (accessed November 5, 2007).

ii. Ibid.

What elements in the Texas political process inhibit voters from participating more widely in state politics?

SOCIAL RESPONSIBILITY

How have changes in national politics impacted Texas's state politics? Are they for the better?

CRITICAL THINKING

Domination by one party complicates matters. Without groups to mobilize the masses, there is no policy debate, leaving voters less informed and the meaning of election victories less clear. This means that new Texans looking to take their place in politics and any Texans interested in reforming the system will both need to be especially well organized if they want to see change.

Ironically, while Texans value their independent nature, independent Texans suffer the most in this setting. While these voters could legally show up and vote in either the Republican or Democratic primary, the strong partisans that currently dominate voting in Texas primaries often create choices too extreme for the tastes of moderate Texans. Thus, such voters may stay home during the primary and then find themselves equally uncomfortable with the choices they have in the general election.

CONCLUSION

The importance of political parties in Texas is not in dispute. However, their contribution to competitive elections and effective governing is less certain. V. O. Key, who defined much of our understanding of Texas and southern politics, noted, "As institutions, parties enjoy a general disrepute, but most of the democratic world finds them indispensable as instruments of self-government, as means for the organization and expression of competing viewpoints on public policy."[32] While Texans continue to grumble about parties, their reliance on parties persists, and, like most Americans, Texans are growing more partisan and more polarized.

They may express frustration and proclaim their political independence, but the citizens of Texas have proved unswervingly loyal to first the Democratic Party and now the Republican Party. Despite their disdain and doubts, Texans continually turn to these political institutions, ensuring them a place in the future of Texas politics.

for CQ Press

Want a better grade?

Get the tools you need to sharpen your study skills. Access practice quizzes, eFlashcards, video, and multimedia at **edge.sagepub.com/collier6e**.

KEY TERMS

allocation (p. 314)

chronic minority (p. 306)

conventions (caucuses) (p. 311)

county chair (p. 310)

county or senatorial district convention (p. 311)

electoral competition model (p. 302)

executive committee (p. 312)

grassroots organization (p. 309)

party machine (p. 295)

party platform (p. 312)

patronage (p. 294)

permanent party organizations (p. 309)

plank (p. 312)

political party (p. 302)

precinct chair (p. 310)

responsible party model (p. 302)

runoff primary (p. 310)

state party chair (p. 312)

straight-ticket voting (p. 304)

temporary party organizations (p. 309)

ACTIVE LEARNING

- Draft a plank of the platform for either the Republican or Democratic party that reflects an issue you feel deserves more attention. **Communication**

- As a class, identify five important issues in Texas politics, then break into two

or more groups representing different hypothetical political parties. Each group should draft a stand on the five issues. The goal for each party is to become cohesive enough that each member of the party is willing to sign onto the party's platform. **Teamwork**

1. _____ is the process by which parties reward supporters with jobs or government contracts as a way of perpetuating their power.

   a. Patronage
   b. Hierarchy
   c. Allocation
   d. Delegates

2. Political parties in Texas are defined as _____.

   a. organized interests focused on a few narrow issues
   b. any group, however loosely organized, seeking to elect governmental officeholders under a given label
   c. organizations of political elites and elected officials who choose candidates and policy stands for members

3. While the responsible party model values parties that present clear and consistent sets of policies, the electoral competitions model emphasizes a party's need to _____.

   a. win elections by moving toward more moderate positions
   b. define itself in a way that is very different from that of other parties
   c. move away from moderate positions in order to win elections
   d. avoid taking stands on issues

4. The precinct caucuses in Texas are an example of _____ party organizations.

   a. permanent
   b. temporary
   c. elite

5. Parties in Texas are grassroots organizations because _____.

   a. average citizens have little or no role in choosing the candidate or policy positions of the party
   b. they are permanent organizations with set membership
   c. power and decision making reside with average citizens

6. To win a primary in Texas, a candidate must win _____.

   a. a plurality of votes cast in the primary
   b. a majority of votes cast in the primary
   c. two-thirds or more of the votes cast in the primary
   d. unanimous support of party caucuses

7. Party members selected to attend their party's conventions at the county level or the Texas senatorial district level are known as _____.

   a. representatives
   b. tributes
   c. primaries
   d. delegates

8. The individual positions in the party platform are known as _____.

   a. stalks
   b. line items
   c. delegates
   d. planks

9. _____ is the process by which the parties designate how many delegates to the national party convention will be pledged to vote for a specific candidate or attend as undecided.

   a. Allocation

   b. Gerrymandering

   c. Realignment

   d. Patronage

10. Texas state parties _____.

    a. must adopt the platform of their national party

    b. may adapt the party platform of the national party to address state issues

    c. must get their party platform approved by the national party

    d. can write whatever they want in their platform

ORGANIZED INTERESTS

CHAPTER **10**

Chapter Objectives

★ Describe the role of organized interests in Texas.

★ Identify the ways in which organized interests seek to influence policy.

★ Assess who wins and who loses when organized interests are involved in Texas politics.

or many Texans, $114 sounds like a lot to spend on someone else in a day. However, that's how much a lobbyist can spend on a state official before he or she must report it to the Texas Ethics Commission (TEC). This includes food and beverages (but not taxes or tips), transportation, and lodging provided for a state official. Lobbyists have found loopholes that allow them to get around even these generous limits and sometimes avoid even reporting their favors by having several lobbyists work together and divide their spending on a legislator between them. While one lobbyist spending $200 to buy a legislator a very expensive meal would be subject to reporting requirements, two lobbyists spending $100 each does not have to be reported. Lobbyists are allowed to pay for transportation and lodging on "fact-finding trips" for legislators when the trips "explore matters related" to official duties. While Texans might generally applaud their legislators' finding facts, citizens would hope that elected officials will pursue the facts even when lobbyists are not paying for the trip.

The impact of "The Lobby" has been an important part of the lore of Texas politics for generations. At times, lobbyists have been so influential that they have been referred to as the "Third House" of the Texas Legislature. While the excesses of expensive meals and trips today may seem troublesome, it may be comforting to know that these treats pale in comparison to the appetites of earlier legislators. Some observers joked about the three Bs of lobbying—beef, blondes, and booze—but the excesses of the lobby often matched the jokes. Legend has it that lobbyists followed legislators to Hattie's and Peggy's, two of the best brothels in Austin, ready to pick up the tab for legislators who were feeling lonely during the session. Other politicians were offered more practical considerations. Oilman Sid Richardson once allegedly told Governor John Connally, "I'm going to put you in a way to make a little money, John."[1]

lobbying
direct contact with members of the legislative or executive branch to influence legislation or administrative action

Lobbyist Robert Culley (center) takes notes while waiting with other lobbyists for legislators outside the Texas House of Representatives.

While some of the most colorful stories about lobbying might be in our past, Texans are right to keep worrying about the impact of organized interests in Texas. Texans see millions of dollars spent on lobbying every session and millions of dollars in campaign contributions going to candidates in the elections between sessions. While Governor Greg Abbott once again declared ethics reforms one of his primary goals during the 2017 session, very little changed. As it turns out, legislators do not like to mess with rules about the gifts and campaign contributions they may want.

If we judge the intensity or importance of political battles in Texas by the volume of rhetoric, Texans might conclude that issues like abortion, transgender bathrooms, and gay marriage dominate the legislature. However, if we measure these battles by the amount of money invested by special interests, we come away with a very different picture. As we will see, ideological groups like Empower Texans pour huge amounts of money and effort into lobbying the state legislature on a wide variety of issues. We see those battles echoed in headlines and political speeches. What we are much less likely to notice is the effort by individual industries to see laws that favor their bottom line, and Texans might wonder why issues that seem so small to them generate such expensive lobbying efforts. If AT&T is spending millions on lobbying, they must see something pretty important at stake.

In this chapter, we will look at the impact that organized interests and the money they provide has on the practice of democracy in Texas. Lurking in the shadows of the three branches of Texas government, organized interests remain indistinct but important players in state politics. While organized interests can help bring citizens into the political process and provide important issue information to voters or legislators, we will see that they often fail to fully represent the citizens of the state and can become a hindrance to state government's ability to keep pace with change.

ORGANIZED INTERESTS IN TEXAS POLITICS

With Republicans winning every statewide election since 1994, as Democrats did a few decades earlier, some of the state's political battles have moved from between the parties to between organized interests. These battles are played out publicly in the primary election battles of candidates and privately in the struggle for control of the legislative process. Some organized interests have done well working with members of both parties, while others have worked consistently with just one party.

In this text, we use the term *organized interests* for what many textbooks, journalists, and citizens would refer to as special interests or interest groups. Many of the forces tugging at the political system today are not the large membership organizations that we generally think of as interest *groups*.[2] Many important players in politics are individual citizens or businesses rather than groups. Nowhere is this more evident than in Texas, where many individual businesses, such as AT&T and TXU Energy, spend millions of dollars lobbying the Texas Legislature without benefit of joining a group, and where some individual citizens, such as the Koch brothers, pour millions of dollars into political causes.

An **organized interest** is any organization that attempts to influence public policy decisions. *Organization* in this sense does not mean a collection of individuals.[3] Instead, organization reflects the direction of systematic efforts aimed at influencing the political process. Thus, *organized interest* sometimes refers to the systematic efforts of an individual. In addition, it should be clear that many of the organizations in politics represent corporations, not individuals. For example, the Chamber of Commerce, a very important group at the state and federal level, is a collection of businesses, not individual citizens.

Our definition is well suited for some of the key issues in this chapter. As we will see, many interests in the state may be special, but they are not organized and will not have a meaningful impact on the state's politics. In fact, one of our key arguments is that the failure of some interests to organize is fundamental to understanding who wins and who loses in Texas politics.

Those interests that are well organized in Texas benefit from the part-time nature of Texas government. Legislators meeting during the busy 140-day legislative session often find themselves moving through legislation quickly and needing help to understand the issues. With little professional staff available, lawmakers become more reliant on the kind of information and assistance lobbyists dish out. The part-time commissioners who head bureaucratic agencies provide another entry point for interests' influence in the state. As governors look for citizens to occupy the boards that oversee so much of the Texas bureaucracy, they are likely to turn to wealthy donors—especially those with a connection to the policy area being regulated.

Interest Group Formation

A variety of factors play into Texans' decisions to join interest groups. Some of Texas's early organized interests were held together by the provision of solidarity benefits, which are social interactions that individuals enjoy from joining a group and from working together for a common cause. Texas's size shaped its politics from its earliest days, as the Patrons of Husbandry, more commonly known as the Grange, formed in

organized interest
an individual, group of people, or group of businesses that organizes its efforts to influence public policy

solidarity benefits
the social interactions that individuals enjoy from joining a group and from working together for a common cause

1867, largely to escape rural isolation and address the educational and social needs of the farmers who found themselves widely dispersed across rural areas. Over time, the Grange became more engaged in economic matters and farmer protests. By 1875, the Grange had more than 1,000 lodges in Texas, claiming over 40,000 members in a state with about 250,000 voters.[4] When the Grange faded, it was replaced by the Farmers' Alliance, which got its start in 1877 as an attempt by farmers to sell their goods without intermediaries. While modern Texans may not be as isolated as their ancestors, they may still join a group to make new friends, find a little romance, or simply enjoy the sense of connection that comes from working alongside others with similar interests.

The advantage of organizing political interests on preexisting social networks is evident today. In modern Texas, churches, already homes to groups of people connected through religious communion, are particularly effective at mobilizing their members for political action. The large impact of conservative Christians on the state stems from groups such as the Texas Christian Coalition, the Texas Restoration Project, the Texas Eagle Forum, and the American Family Association of Texas tapping into the networks already fostered by churches.

Another motivation for group membership is the **expressive benefits** individuals enjoy by taking action to express their views. Many individuals and groups protest even in the face of widespread antipathy or hostility. While this behavior may seem unproductive or irrational at some level, so is yelling at the television during sporting events—a behavior that is not limited to Texans. Thus, Texans may want National Rifle Association (NRA) stickers on their vehicles or American Civil Liberties Union (ACLU) cards in their wallets as a way of expressing themselves in a political system that seems too large to notice them very often.

According to **disturbance theory**, organized interests have become more numerous as society has changed. As society and the economy develop, becoming more complex and diverse, new interests emerge. These new interests begin to voice their concerns, which leads to the mobilization of established interests that seek to protect themselves from the challenges posed by the emerging interests.[5] This theory helps to explain the large number of organized interests active in politics in conjunction with the ongoing transformation of the state.

One of the challenges to getting people to join political groups is the **free-rider problem**. The free-rider problem occurs in the case of citizens who do not contribute to the efforts of a group even though they enjoy the results of those efforts. The problem arises because groups labor for **collective goods**, which are benefits that, once provided, go to everyone and cannot be effectively denied to others—even those who did not contribute to the effort. Those who do not organize or work to advance their interest still enjoy as many benefits as those who do. The dilemma of the free-rider problem is that citizens will see little point in making an individual contribution to political efforts since their individual contribution is small and the work will go on without them. For example, all students may enjoy lower tuition, better facilities, and similar benefits even if they do not belong to any student-oriented group or contribute to student organizations in any way.

The free-rider problem is common in politics as well as in the rest of life. Government itself is a partial solution to the free-rider problem. It creates rules and compels citizens to share the burden of the advancement of a common good. Government partially

expressive benefits benefits that arise from taking action to express one's views; motivates group membership

disturbance theory a theory of group formation that states that as societies become more complex and more diverse, new interests emerge to voice their concerns, prompting established interests to mobilize to protect the status quo

free-rider problem occurs when citizens who do not contribute to the efforts of a group nevertheless enjoy the results of those efforts

collective goods benefits that, once provided, go to everyone and cannot be effectively denied to others, even those who did not contribute to the effort

solves the free-rider problem by jailing citizens who refuse to pay taxes or abide by common rules. College students are familiar with their own free-rider problem: roommates who eat groceries that another roommate paid for or who don't do their share of cleaning chores.

Two things can happen when Texans leave politics to others and fail to get involved. First, nothing gets done. When only a few people who take an interest in an issue become active, their impact will be minimal. Second, when only a narrow slice of interested citizens becomes involved, the few who do take action may poorly represent the views of others. In a process known as unraveling, a relatively small number of people take over an organization and define its goals in a way that drives away more moderate members. As moderate members leave, the group becomes increasingly radical, driving away still more moderates until the organization no longer reflects the views of the majority of those interested in the issue.

Given these problems, what keeps like-minded Texans working together? One solution to the free-rider problem is the provision of **selective incentives**, or benefits that can be given to members but effectively excluded from nonmembers. For example, the Texas State Teachers Association proudly proclaims it is "Fighting for Public Schools." However, new members are drawn into the organization with the promise of savings on services ranging from shopping to snowboarding. Current members are encouraged to log in for updates by monthly drawings for "free stuff." Similarly, while many Texans join the NRA to protect their gun rights, the NRA also offers its members an official NRA membership ID card; a choice of three magazines; $5,000 of accidental death and dismemberment coverage; and $2,500 in insurance for their firearms against theft, accidental loss, and damage. Because these kinds of benefits go only to members, they can help organizations build membership, and they are common to many of the nation's most successful interest groups. However, many observers may worry about the moral authority of groups built on free tote bags and discounted travel. For example, the American Association of Retired Persons (AARP) is known for using its political muscle to protect Social Security benefits and other programs that profit senior citizens. However, it attracted some of its estimated 38 million members with discounted travel and insurance, even though some of these members oppose the AARP position on health care reform and other important issues.

The fundamental dynamics of interest group organizations often leave the citizens with the greatest needs facing the greatest barriers to getting organized. Because they lack the resources to organize members or the money needed to finance large campaign contributions or professional lobbyists, some Texans will remain at a disadvantage. For example, college students are impacted tremendously by decisions made by the Texas Legislature, Texas Higher Education Coordinating Board (THECB), and other officials who control the costs and content of higher education in Texas. Students who wish to organize and be heard, however, are faced with apathy and a lack of resources on the part of their peers. In contrast, administrators and regents of the schools are well represented because these schools often have their own lobbyists, and university presidents can often be found in Austin testifying before committees or meeting with members of the legislature. As a result, it is easy for legislators to overlook students' views.

selective incentives benefits exclusively available to members of an organization

Types of Interests in Texas

Probably the most visible organized interests in Texas are economic interests. These organizations attempt to produce economic benefits for group members. They might be corporations working individually or collectively to lower taxes, reduce regulation, or alter some other business policy to help their bottom line. As Table 10.1 indicates, many of Texas's businesses hire lobbyists to represent them in Austin. The large dollar amounts reflected in the table often conceal the full effort of these businesses, since some business leaders will lobby on behalf of their businesses without additional compensation.

Economic interests also include labor unions, which seek better pay or working conditions for their membership. For example, in 2017, the Houston Professional Fire Fighters Local battled a pension reform plan in the Texas Legislature that would have dramatically reduced retirement benefits for Houston city employees, including police and firefighters. The Texas AFL-CIO works on issues such as raising the minimum wage and improving the quality of schools on behalf of about 500,000 labor union members in Texas. In a similar fashion, professional associations, such as the Texas State Teachers Association and the Texas Medical Association, represent the needs of professionals who are not represented by unions. Some businesses work collectively through trade associations, which are organizations of similar businesses working together to advance shared goals. For example, the Texas Hospitality Association (THA) is a coalition of restaurants and bars that lobbies on state laws related to how the food and beverage service sector does business. The THA mission statement calls for the repeal of the state law that requires distilled spirits to be purchased only from a retail store.

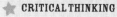

Why do some companies lobby much more aggressively than others?

CRITICAL THINKING

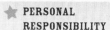

What can citizens do to make sure that a broader range of interests are lobbying in Austin?

PERSONAL RESPONSIBILITY

labor unions organizations that represent the interests of working people seeking better pay and better working conditions

professional associations organizations that represent the needs of professionals not represented by unions

trade associations organizations of similar businesses that work together to advance shared goals

TABLE 10.1 Top 10 Companies or Groups Spending on Lobbying, 2017 Session

1.	AT&T	$4,195,020
2.	Texas Central Rail Holdings	$1,395,005
3.	American Electric Power	$1,200,000
4.	Texas Association of Realtors	$1,118,565
5.	Blue Cross Blue Shield of Texas	$1,100,005
6.	Houston Professional Fire Fighters Local	$1,050,005
7.	Texas Trial Lawyers Association	$1,050,003
8	NextEra Energy	$990,009
9.	CenterPoint Energy	$960,004
10.	Oncor	$910,007

Source: FollowTheMoney.org, accessed September 6, 2018, https://www.followthemoney.org/show-me?dt=3&lby-f-fc=2&lby-s=TX&lby-y=2017#[{1|gro=lby-y,lby-f-eid.

In contrast, public interest groups pursue noneconomic policies on behalf of the general public (even if not all members of the general public agree on the issues, policies, or solutions). For example, Texans for Public Justice attempts to promote better government by scrutinizing campaign finance and lobbying, while Texans for Lawsuit Reform (TLR) seeks to reduce the abuse of the legal system. Some single-issue interest groups might also be considered public interest groups since the issue their members are grouped around is one that impacts the public in general. For example, the Texas Right to Life Committee and the Texas Abortion and Reproductive Rights Action League focus their efforts primarily on the issue of abortion, while the Texas State Rifle Association (TSRA) and Texans for Gun Safety square off over gun rights.

Another type of interest is other governments, often referred to as the intergovernmental lobby, in which different levels of government lobby each other. As a state, Texas sits in the middle of the intergovernmental lobby, lobbying the national government and being lobbied by cities, counties, and school districts. Some of the biggest spenders in 2017 include the cities of Austin ($625,000) and Houston ($340,000), while the Houston Port Authority spent about $320,000 on its own lobbying effort. In addition, the state is lobbied on behalf of state institutions, such as universities. While some of this lobbying is done on a contract basis with professional lobbyists, many institutions, such as the universities, rely on their upper administration to represent them in Austin. Meanwhile, about 40 private schools combined their efforts under the umbrella organization of Independent Colleges and Universities of Texas and spent about $500,000 lobbying the legislature in 2017.

Texas state government works closely with members of the U.S. Congress to maximize federal grants coming into the state. Questions were raised about $1.2 million that Texas had paid for lobbying contracts spanning the period between 2003 and 2007. While the idea of governments lobbying each other may sound odd, and the prospect of Texas paying millions of dollars for representation in Washington may seem wasteful, keep in mind that Texas receives about one-third of its budget—almost $34 billion in the 2018 fiscal year budget—from the national government. This means that if the state paid lobbyists $1 million a year, and those lobbyists' efforts contributed to increasing the state's federal grants by only 1 percent, the state would receive a roughly thirty-fold return on the money it spent on the lobbyists.

What Organized Interests Contribute to the Political Process

Organized interests in Texas play the same kinds of roles they do in other states and countries. However, given the condition of Texas's parties, some of these functions are especially important in the state.

One of the primary functions of organized interests is to provide *representation* for groups to complement the geographic representation provided by elected officials. In an essentially one-party state such as Texas, group representation may be especially important to many Texans who live in areas in which no one from their party holds office. Beyond that, Texans have interests that may be best served based on something other than the geographic representation provided by legislative districts. For example, Texas's teachers come together through groups such as the Texas State Teachers Association to work on educational issues. Public school teachers, while a small part of any one community, constitute a huge bloc of voters across the state. Likewise, farmers may constitute a small percentage of the population in any one legislative district, and they have interests that are often very different from those of the rest of their communities. To make their voices heard, they join collectively in farmers associations that help promote their interests.

The *education* function is also very important, since many of the issues that impact Texans' lives lie beyond their everyday experiences and knowledge. Organized interests in Texas help bring attention to issues and educate citizens about what their government is doing and how it impacts their lives. For example, environmental groups draw citizens' attention to environmental issues and help them understand the scientific and technical aspects of these issues and the potential impact of the issues on their physical or economic health.

Terry Holcomb, executive director of Texas Carry, displays his customized holster at a rally supporting "Open Carry" on the south steps of the Texas State Capitol, January 1, 2016.

Similarly, Texans may benefit from *program monitoring*, which occurs when organized interest groups invest their efforts in keeping an eye on the many large bureaucratic agencies and small boards that do much of the work of governing in the state. The average citizen has little time to do this and may lack the expertise to track levels of pollution or deal with budget issues. Organized interests serving as watchdogs can help uncover bureaucratic misbehavior in some cases and deter it in others.

Organized interests can also play an important role by providing program alternatives. In education, for example, teacher groups and other organized interests have put forward alternative reforms to public schools in Texas and helped give citizens options that might never emerge from the education bureaucracy. Organized interests may not seem like the best source of reform, but in some cases they may prove more supportive of reform and innovation than bureaucrats and elected officials.

INFLUENCING POLICY IN TEXAS THROUGH ORGANIZED INTERESTS

Organized interests utilize several strategies for influencing policy: electioneering, litigation, and lobbying. With electioneering, interests try to shape public policy by influencing who is elected to office. Seeking a statewide office such as governor or the Texas Supreme Court necessitates getting your message to every corner of the state, which requires lots of advertising dollars. New candidates often find they cannot raise enough money for such a campaign from individual donors contributing small amounts; therefore, donors able to supply large amounts, such as organized interest groups, can become especially important in deciding which campaigns get off the ground.

electioneering
method used by organized interests to try to shape public policy by influencing who is elected to office, especially by serving as sources of campaign funding

FEDERALISM IN *Action*

Campus Carry

On August 1, 1966, Charles Whitman climbed to the top of the clock tower at the University of Texas at Austin (UT Austin) and started shooting people in what is widely considered to be the first mass shooting in the United States. Exactly fifty years later, in 2016, a new law went into effect that required all public universities in Texas to allow individuals with concealed carry licenses to bring guns onto college campuses. The law, commonly referred to as campus carry, was passed in 2015 by the Texas Legislature.

Among the issues in the campus carry debate is which level of government should pass laws relating to guns. The federal government has enacted several laws restricting guns, such as the National Firearms Act of 1934, mandating the registration and restricting the sale of certain types of firearms, and the Gun Control Act of 1968, regulating interstate commerce of firearms. Individual states have passed additional legislation, such as Texas's campus carry law. The matter of gun legislation in Texas isn't just one between the federal and state governments, however. Campus carry also involves a fight over elements of local control.

The original campus carry legislation included a provision that allowed public universities to opt out, and several campuses across Texas indicated they would likely do that. But when the legislation was reintroduced in the 84th legislative session, that option was notably absent. In the Texas debate over campus carry, much of the pushback concerns the opt-out option. During public hearings, universities appealed to the need for their campuses to reflect their diverse preferences and realities.[i] Campuses across Texas have diverse student bodies and political cultures, and they face widely disparate issues depending on their geography and demography. After the public hearing, the campus carry bill was changed to allow universities to declare some spaces as gun-free zones, but public schools could not opt out completely. Twelve student body presidents from Texas universities signed a letter to Governor Abbott, urging the inclusion of an opt-out clause in the legislation. Private schools in Texas can opt out, and so far all private universities in Texas but one have chosen to do so. Yet public universities do not have that choice.

A number of organized interests mobilized in support of or opposition to the proposed campus carry legislation. At the outset, two powerful interest groups—the Texas State Rifle Association (TSRA) and the National Rifle Association (NRA)—declared campus carry a priority. In fact, the 84th legislature saw a large number of TSRA- and NRA-supported legislation, including legislation permitting campus carry, legalizing open carry, decreasing the training requirements for a concealed handgun license, and requiring hotels who do not allow guns to notify individuals during the reservation process.[ii] The state legislature seemed poised to pass a lot of gun legislation, including the bill on campus carry. The TSRA and NRA worked diligently to see the campus carry legislation become law, including contributing campaign dollars to many Texas legislators and state leaders, calling on their organizations' members to directly contact their representatives, and testifying at the legislature's public hearing on the proposed legislation. When Governor Abbott signed the campus carry bill into law, he thanked the NRA and the TSRA for keeping pressure on the legislature to get the bill passed.

Although campus carry was popular among conservatives in Austin, it was often unpopular on college campuses. University groups across the state organized against campus carry, including the Texas Association of College and University Police Administrators. A new grassroots group called Gun Free UT was created on the UT Austin campus to oppose the legislation with organized protests, a petition to the legislature, and even a teach-in in an attempt to pressure the legislature to vote down the policy.

> **Should the power to decide campus carry in Texas reside with federal, state, or local officials?**
>
> ⭐ **SOCIAL RESPONSIBILITY**

> **What is the federal government's role and responsibility when it comes to gun rights and restrictions in the states?**
>
> ⭐ **CRITICAL THINKING**

i. The Texas Senate Committee on State of Affairs, Streaming Video Player, accessed August 3, 2016, http://tlcsenate.granicus .com/MediaPlayer.php?clip_id=9093.
ii. Texas State Rifle Association PAC, "TSRA Legislative Goals," accessed August 2, 2015, http://www.tsrapac.com/legislation.

Organized Interests' Spending on Elections

Organized interests influence elections in a variety of ways. The most visible and perhaps the most important is through spending. Some individuals have the resources to make large donations and through them can have a major impact. When individuals do not have the amounts of money it takes to make large financial contributions, they can contribute to campaigns as part of a group in order to bring together enough money to have an impact on the candidates. These contributions pass through interest groups— usually a **political action committee (PAC)**. PACs are essentially the fund-raising arms of organized interests set up to meet the requirements of state and federal campaign finance laws. During the 2013–2014 election cycle, the 1,991 PACs registered with the Texas Ethics Commission reported expenditures of just over $207 million.[6]

The biggest-spending PAC (independent of political parties) in 2016 was the Texas Association of Realtors, which spent $5.6 million; the Texas Association of Realtors Issues Mobilization spent an additional $1.3 million promoting the interests of real estate agents and brokers. That same year, TLR spent 3.7 million to elect legislators and judges who supported its desire to reduce the cost of nonmeritorious lawsuits. That amount is much smaller than the $7 million spent in 2014.

Organized interests often spend money on their own advertising or on providing materials that others can distribute. Such **independent political expenditures** have been protected by the courts because they reflect the free speech of political interests. Thus, individuals and groups can spend as much money as they want—as long as they do not coordinate with the candidates' campaigns. The courts have allowed limitations on contributions to candidates (even though Texas law places no such limits) because they might help safeguard the fairness and integrity of the electoral process, but they have rejected limits on independent expenditure because they impose more severe restrictions on freedom of political expression than do limitations on financial contributions. These independent expenditures are not inconsequential. In 2010, the NRA spent $534,034 independently in the Texas governor's race.[7] Spending by an independent group can be an asset or a liability. For example, during the 2010 election for governor, a full-page newspaper ad paid for by Back to Basics PAC attacked Governor Rick Perry by calling him a coward for refusing to debate Bill White. The ad was criticized as "grade-school name calling" and may have helped Perry by shifting news coverage away from his unwillingness to debate to the nature of the attacks against him.[8]

Organized interests find other ways of winning voters. The Christian Coalition produces voter guides, brochures that list the candidates' positions on issues important to the group that members can print and distribute at their own expense. Texans for Fiscal Responsibility and Empower Texans have often succeeded in defining the debate on budget issues with their Fiscal Responsibility Index that grades legislators on their stands on spending and business issues identified by these groups.

Many people believe that politics was transformed by the U.S. Supreme Court's 2010 ruling in *Citizens United v. Federal Election Commission*.[9] In that decision, the court ruled that the First Amendment's guarantee of free speech prohibits the government from restricting independent political expenditures by corporations and unions. At the same time, the court upheld the ban on campaign contributions by unions and corporations. Union members and corporate officers have always been allowed to make contributions as individuals, but such campaign spending directly from union and corporation accounts had been prohibited since Congress passed the Taft-Hartley Act in 1947. This act made permanent a wartime ban on labor union contributions in federal elections and extended the ban on contributions by national banks, corporations, and unions to include a prohibition on any expenditures in connection with

political action committee (PAC)
the fund-raising arm of an interest group that has been organized to raise and spend money under state and federal campaign finance rules

independent political expenditures
spending on behalf of a candidate that is done without coordination with the candidate or his or her campaign

TEXAS *Legends*

The League of United Latin American Citizens

The League of United Latin American Citizens (LULAC) began in 1929 in Corpus Christi, Texas, when delegates from Alice, Austin, Brownsville, Corpus Christi, Encino, Harlingen, La Grulla, McAllen, Robstown, and San Antonio came together to lay the foundation for an organization that would bring together the various groups that had been working on the rights of Mexican Americans. While LULAC initially brought together three of the best-known Hispanic groups in Texas—the Knights of America, the Order of Sons of America, and the League of Latin American Citizens—other groups were reluctant to join. LULAC seeks to promote Hispanic pride in a society that is bilingual and bicultural. Some groups have advocated civil disobedience or even rebellion against Anglo authorities, but LULAC emphasizes assimilation into American culture and loyalty to the United States and its government. LULAC has gone so far as to make "America" its official song, English its official language, and "George Washington's Prayer" its official prayer. Further, membership is limited to native-born or naturalized citizens of

Mexican American extraction, and members are required to take an oath of loyalty to the government of the United States as well as to its Constitution and laws.

The LULAC moderate approach to politics has left them disdained by some activists who deride them as "middle-class assimilationists." LULAC, which is largely composed of older, middle-class Hispanic citizens, has met resistance from much of the Anglo community throughout the organization's history. Sometimes its complaints about inequality were simply ignored. At other times, attempts to organize were met with threats at gunpoint.

The organization was especially active in the years after World War II when members returned from military service and sought to more fully participate in American life. In 1948, LULAC filed suit in the case of *Delgado v. Bastrop ISD*, which helped end segregation in the public schools. The organization also helped end the exclusion of Mexican Americans from juries and party primaries in Texas. Most recently, LULAC has been involved in lawsuits challenging redistricting in Texas that it argued reduced

Hispanic representation in Congress and the Texas Legislature.

While part of the organization's work involves filing lawsuits seeking the protection of voting rights through the courts, LULAC has also created a number of its own programs. The LULAC Little Schools of the 400 project began in 1957 to teach forty-four basic English words to Hispanic preschoolers. The program became the model for Texas's Preschool Instructional Classes for Non-English Speaking Children and the federal government's Head Start program. LULAC has also helped build affordable housing for low-income families and has provided job training through forty-three employment centers in the United States. It has also worked with Fortune 500 companies to create partnerships between these companies and the Hispanic community.

While LULAC has grown to national prominence and maintains an office in Washington, DC, its Texas roots remain strong. It has an executive office in San Antonio and a large office in El Paso that manages the organization's finances, membership materials, and group archives. Today, LULAC has more than 900 local chapters or councils that serve their communities through scholarship and other programs. It maintains an active agenda that includes a broad range of issues from foreign policy and marriage equality to energy independence. However, the group remains close to its original promise to "eradicate from our body politic all intents and tendencies to establish discrimination among our fellow-citizens on account of race, religion or social position as being contrary to the true spirit of Democracy, our Constitution and Laws."[i]

---

i. Cynthia E. Orozco, *No Mexicans, Women, or Dogs Allowed: The Rise of the Mexican American Civil Rights Movement* (Austin: University of Texas Press, 2009), Kindle, 66–67.

federal campaigns. Texas laws contained a similar prohibition. However, immediately after the *Citizens United* decision, the TEC issued an advisory opinion stating that the state's ban on independent spending by corporations and unions was unenforceable in light of the decision, and, in 2011, the Texas Legislature passed a bill (HB 2359) formally removing the corporate and union ban on political expenditures from the state's election code. In 2014, the state's labor-related PAC, Texas Organizing Project (TOP) PAC, spent $2.5 million on communicating directly with voters.

The *Citizens United* decision added the deep pockets of unions and businesses to independent political expenditures, giving rise to new super PACs. A **super PAC**, a technically independent expenditure-only committee, may raise unlimited sums of money from corporations, unions, associations, and individuals and then spend those sums to overtly advocate for or against political candidates. A poll performed in the summer of 2012 found that only 40 percent of Americans could correctly identify the term *super PAC* and that nearly half (46 percent) did not know what the term referred to. Another 14 percent gave incorrect definitions of the term.[10]

One of the newest issues in campaign finance is **dark money**. Dark money is money spent on political activities by organizations that do not have to report their sources of funding because they declare themselves nonprofit (rather than political) under Internal Revenue Service (IRS) rules associated with charities. In fact, these groups are often referred to as 501(c)(4) and 501(c)(6) organizations, in reference to the specific areas of IRS code. While many of these groups are purely charitable, they also include clearly political groups like the Democratic Socialists of America, Planned Parenthood, and the NRA. In 2013, Governor Perry vetoed legislation that would have required these groups to report their donors, and a provision requiring the disclosure of contributors to dark money groups led to the demise of an ethics reform bill in 2015. While dark money has generated a lot of discussion in Texas, its impact is unclear. In 2014, the ten largest dark money groups combined spent $1.7 million on independent expenditures in Texas elections.[11]

Reformers say that voters have the right to know who is behind campaign spending in state elections and that transparency is essential in order for voters to hold organized interests and candidates accountable. Those defending dark money say that donors want their privacy protected because they fear reprisals for their political activities.

Citizens worried about elections being bought by large donors may be comforted by the reality that that spending buys only as much democracy as voters allow it to, and citizens can (and do) ignore political advertising.

Perhaps a greater concern is that super PACs and dark money will have an impact on elected officials pursuing the support of well-financed interests. Just because these donors are not buying voters doesn't mean they're not buying politicians. While the impact of the *Citizens United* decision may be less dramatic than some critics contend, there is no doubt that the case will provide additional avenues into elections for corporate and union money. Large donors that spend millions of dollars on campaigns will likely remind any candidate they helped win about those efforts.

There is also the concern that spending by these outside groups will drown out the candidates themselves. Citizens often fail to notice the difference between advertising sponsored by candidates and that sponsored by outside groups. Further, these outside groups often favor negative ads. The Center for Responsive Politics estimated that the

super PAC
an organized group that can raise and spend unlimited amounts of money as long as it does not coordinate with candidate campaigns

dark money
money spent on political activities by a nonprofit organization that does not have to report its sources of funding

top fifteen independent expenditure groups spent more than $600 million nationally in the 2012 election cycle, with $520 million (86 percent) of that being spent on negative ads.[12] These groups are largely unaccountable because they can move on or change their names before the next election, while candidates and elected officials are left to attempt to work with the animosities and misrepresentations left behind by such advertising.

From Activism and Litigation to Lobbying

Organized interests may also provide other kinds of assistance to candidates, such as volunteering time to help candidates, challenging legislation in court, or seeking to influence policy through lobbying. Labor unions and other groups with large memberships may provide volunteers to help staff phone banks, campaign door to door, stuff envelopes, or provide other kinds of help with campaigns. This is one area in which student groups hold an advantage. While they seldom have enough money to make large cash contributions, student groups can provide much-needed volunteers to campaigns. Students can help work phone banks, distribute campaign brochures, put up yard signs, and perform other essential campaign work.

Sometimes organized interests turn to the courts for assistance and use litigation to advance their causes. While an individual who believes his or her rights have been violated may lack the resources to take the case to court, groups of people can band together to file lawsuits. For example, the League of United Latin American Citizens (LULAC) filed a lawsuit challenging the Texas Legislature's redistricting plan on the grounds that it violated the voting rights of the Latino community in Texas according to the Voting Rights Act of 1965. The case resulted in a 2006 U.S. Supreme Court decision, *LULAC v. Perry*, that struck down the redistricting plan; the justices cited diluted representation in violation of the Voting Rights Act.[13]

An ad by Back to Basics PAC created a backlash by calling then-Texas-governor Rick Perry a coward.

AP Photo/Eric Gay

In Texas law, lobbying is defined as contact by telephone, telegraph, or letter with members of the legislative or executive branch to influence legislation or administrative action. This form of direct lobbying is what people generally think of when they think about how groups try to influence government. Disagreement over the exact meaning of lobbying persists. In 2014, Michael Quinn Sullivan was fined $10,000 for failing to register as a lobbyist in 2010 and 2011. The TEC found that Sullivan had communicated directly with members of the legislature about bills being considered and thus met the legal definition of lobbying.[14] Sullivan's lawyer argued that requiring lobbyists to register is unconstitutional. In addition, he argued that Sullivan merited an exemption because his contribution to newsletters from his organization, Empower Texans, made him a journalist and not a lobbyist.

Lobbying embraces a wide range of efforts. Writing about lobbying in *Texas Monthly* in 1974, Richard West noted that "to lobby successfully requires a great deal of energy from a man who must wear many different hats. Lawyer. Educator. Entertainer. Friend and companion. And if the occasion arises, procurer."[15] For example, during the legislative session, TLR offers massages, manicures, and pedicures on top of the usual food and drink to the "ladies of the legislature" at their "Girls Night Out" event at the Four Seasons Hotel in Austin. While the legislators and staffers in attendance are not offered money, sixteen of the roughly eighteen legislators who attended in 2007 won $1,000 scholarships to be donated to the school of their choice.[16]

Legislators benefit from a cozy relationship with organized interests in a variety of subtle ways. During the legislative sessions, carts of food zip around the Texas capitol building, and legislative offices find that they can feast upon meals and snacks provided by lobbyists. In the evening, legislators and their staffers can always find receptions and dinners funded by organized interests. Table 10.1 on page 327 illustrates the substantial investment companies put into lobbying, with many big names in Texas industry spending well over $1 million. Unfortunately, precise reports on spending on lobbying are unknown because the state only requires that Texas lobbyists report values in ranges (e.g., $100,000 to $149,999). However, it is clear that the state's top spenders invest a great deal in trying to influence the legislative session.

Lobbying is often a bipartisan affair, since many of the big issues that separate the two parties have little to do with the narrow interests of a particular industry or other special interest group. For example, according to Richard West, the Wholesale Beer Distributors of Texas worried little about the broader political leanings of candidates and instead thought only about their views on alcohol: "Does he drink an occasional beer or is he high tenor in the Baptist Church choir who denounces demon rum every Sunday? It doesn't matter if he is a Commie-Red-Pinko-Symp or worships the spirit of Joseph Goebbels. Will he vote wet or dry?"[17]

One technique is not entirely new but has expanded with advances in mass communication. Via **grassroots lobbying**, groups will attempt to influence legislators by shaping public opinion. One version of grassroots lobbying is when a large group mobilizes its members to contact officials. For example, the Texas State Teachers Association has members in every legislative district (plus family and friends) who can be counted on to write letters, call legislators, or attend legislative committee hearings. While social media has made this much easier, groups have been using grassroots lobbying to keep their members looking over legislators' shoulder for decades.

grassroots lobbying attempts by organized interests to influence legislators through public opinion; extension of democratic principles in which groups of citizens spontaneously mobilize to build support for a cause

HOW TEXAS GOVERNMENT WORKS

Lobbying

Who Lobbies

- Labor unions
- Professional associations
- Trade associations
- Public interest groups
- Single-issue interest groups
- Different levels of government
  (intergovernmental lobby) from local to federal

Types of Lobbying

Grassroots lobbying
Groups' attempt to influence legislation through public opinion, such as by mobilizing group members to contact officials

Astroturf lobbying
Elite spending of large sums of money to generate an appearance of public support for their agenda

Grasstop lobbying
Attempts to influence legislators through key constituents or friends of the legislators

Planting sod
Tactic that transfers grassroots grown in one place to other issues

Top 5 in Texas

Political Contributors*

Texas Association of Realtors (Austin)
$9,132,640

National Association of Realtors (Chicago)
$4,145,366

Texans for Lawsuit Reform (Austin)
$3,936,560

Farris C & Jo Ann Wilks (Frac Tech Services) (Cisco)
$3,259,734

Associated General Contractors of TX (Austin)
$2,116,675

* Amount Spent

Source: Texans for Public Justice, "Texas' Top Contributors: Texas' Top Contributors in 2016," accessed September 6, 2018, http://info.tpj.org/reports/Top%20 Donors%202016.pdf.

One narrower version of grassroots lobbying is grasstop lobbying, which is an attempt to influence legislators through key constituents or friends of legislators. Rather than calling upon thousands of citizens to contact their elected officials, grasstop lobbying efforts rely on the influence of a few key citizens to sway elected officials. One example of grasstop lobbying in Texas is the use of oil and gas industry executives, who are often prominent members of their communities or large contributors to campaigns.

Grassroots lobbying is a legitimate extension of democratic principles in which groups of citizens spontaneously mobilize to build support for a cause. However, the misuse of public opinion has stirred concerns, as some groups have used negative or misleading information to advance their cause. One variation of grassroots lobbying is often described as Astroturf lobbying. As the name implies, Astroturf lobbying simulates grassroots support in an attempt to influence legislators. Often manufactured by specialized lobbying firms, Astroturf lobbying involves spending large amounts of money to create the illusion of public support behind a group's agenda. Sometimes this involves large donors using phone banks to urge citizens to contact legislators based on misleading or incomplete information. In *Grassroots for Hire*, Edward Walker describes how Students for Academic Choice (SAC) mobilized students to fight rule changes to student grants and loans that they claimed would harm "single mothers, veterans, and adult students who work full time while attending school."[18] As it turned out, the SAC was sponsored and funded by the Career College Association, the leading trade association working on behalf of for-profit colleges and universities. Thus, a group whose face is ordinary students may actually be directed by large businesses. Walker goes on to argue that there has been a rise in a "subsidized" public in which "select citizens are targeted and trained for participation," and he argues that this is more like "planting sod" than Astroturf because these professional advocacy consultants are not creating false grassroots but transferring grassroots grown other places to their issues.[19] As was the case with the SAC, the interest behind the student needs was legitimate. However, those students would have found it much more difficult to organize and could not have traveled to Washington to meet with federal officials without the sponsorship of the group funded by the schools they attended. Lawmakers heard from only those student interests that aligned with those of the universities. This reflects the concern that the people with the most resources get the most effective representation. We often think of grassroots activism as a tool that ordinary citizens use to challenge the power of government, corporations, and other powerful players. However, the interests of ordinary citizens are most often heard when they align with the interests of those who already enjoy the most influence.

Lobby Regulation

For most of its history, Texas has had little meaningful regulation of lobbying activity, which is reflected in legends such as those about poultry magnate Lonnie "Bo" Pilgrim passing out $10,000 checks on the floor of the Texas Senate in 1989. In 1957, the Representation Before the Legislature Act required that lobbyists disclose certain activities and began the process of reform. Today, Texas law prohibits legislators, statewide officers other than judges, and certain political committees from accepting campaign contributions thirty days before and twenty days after the legislative session. For example, the moratorium on accepting contributions surrounding the 2019 regular

grasstop lobbying
the attempt to influence legislators through key constituents or friends

Astroturf lobbying
a simulation of grassroots support, usually conducted by specialized lobbying firms

session of the legislature began December 8, 2018, and continued through the legislative session until June 17, 2019.

Texas law requires that a person seeking to influence policy register as a lobbyist if he or she expends more than $500 or receives more than $1,000 in compensation in a three-month period. Because lobbyists in Texas must file reports that disclose their salaries only in category ranges (such as "$50,000 to $99,999") rather than in precise dollar amounts, we cannot determine exactly how much they spend or receive. However, with millions of taxpayer dollars at stake, it should come as no surprise that lobbying is a well-developed industry in Austin. Texans for Public Justice estimates that 2,932 clients paid 1,704 Texas lobbyists up to $349 million during the legislative sessions in 2013.

Monitoring lobbying in Texas is the TEC, created by a constitutional amendment approved by Texas voters in 1991. The TEC is composed of eight members, with no more than four members from the same party. Four of the commissioners are appointed by the governor, two by the lieutenant governor, and two by the Speaker of the Texas House. The legislature has given the commission legal responsibility for administering laws related to political contributions to candidates and the election of the Speaker of the House. The TEC also regulates lobbyists, oversees the personal financial disclosure reports required of state officials, and handles other matters related to integrity in state government. The commission meets roughly every two months and has an executive director selected by the commissioners to manage the commission's staff and daily work. The Texas Constitution also gives the TEC the authority to recommend—subject to approval by the voters—the salary and per diem payments of members of the legislature, the lieutenant governor, and the Speaker of the Texas House.

TEC rules prohibit officeholders from accepting certain gifts, and the commission tracks what government officials receive. Elected officials and other state employees are barred from soliciting or accepting any gift, employment, business opportunity, or other favor that might influence their official duties. Officials may accept noncash items of less than $50 in value from a lobbyist. However, if a lobbyist provides officials with food, beverages, entertainment, lodging, transportation, etc., the lobbyist must be present at the event. Officeholders are not allowed to accept honoraria or other compensation for speaking if the invitation is related to their status as an officeholder. While travel expenses to a speech can be accepted, the officeholder may not accept any pleasure travel from a group.

Lobbyists' Relationship with Texas Legislators

While there is some debate about how much influence these large lobbying contracts actually have, there is no doubt that the millions of dollars invested in lobbying has some impact. These companies did not become large enough to spend millions of dollars on lobbying by making investments that did not produce returns. Clearly, they have reaped some reward in keeping their views before the legislature.

While there is a debate about the impact of lobbyists in Austin, there is no doubt about their visibility during the legislative session. Legislators and staff find themselves wined and dined by lobbyists, and free meals are not hard to come by during the session. The rule that lobbyists be present explains why you will often see the staff of a lobbying firm tending a table of breakfast burritos or lingering in an Austin restaurant. Of course, winning a legislator's vote is not as easy as buying him or her a meal, and state officials consistently deny that their support can be bought with gifts, travel, or campaign donations. However, giving elected officials campaign contributions or sharing a meal with them is a means of getting access and creating a friendly connection between official and lobbyist. With so many constituents and professional lobbyists competing for a legislator's time, simply having access to the legislator or his or her staff is a fundamental part of winning influence.

Access can be promoted in several ways beyond traditional lobbying or campaign contributions. Former House Speaker Tom Craddick was criticized for raising over $1 million for renovation and upkeep on the Speaker's apartment in the Texas capitol building after both AT&T and Dallas oilman T. Boone Pickens led the list of donors, each chipping in $250,000 for the apartment. While the money was controlled by the State Preservation Board, many people were concerned that gambling interests and other special interests were the source behind the money used for the Speaker's living quarters.

Legislators are especially likely to rely on lobbyists, given the short sessions and limited staff assistance in Texas. With only 140 days in the session and a staff of only a few full-time people, legislators find themselves needing information on a wide variety of issues on very short notice. The familiar face of a lobbyist may be the easiest source of information for a hurried legislator or staff person trying to sort out complicated issues such as health care or education funding. This is one of the reasons that former officials or staffers are the more prominent and successful lobbyists. These veterans of the process are familiar with the problems of the legislators, if not the legislators themselves.

There are also lobbyists who are experts in their field. Anyone who has read through state law knows that much of the language is highly technical and involves

Sandra Haverlah (center), lobbyist for the Environmental Defense Fund, talks with Colin Meehan (left), director of regulatory and public affairs for First Solar, and Cyrus Reed (right), conservation director of the Lone Star Chapter of the Sierra Club, after their testimony before a committee of the Texas House of Representatives.

the details of business and other practices that legislators will find difficult to master in a short period of time. Some legislative issues are extremely complex, such as the environmental impact of different types of oil and gas production or the intricacies of health care insurance. For this reason, some lobbyists are recruited from the ranks of regulatory agencies or the businesses they oversee as organized interests seek out someone who can put together a strong factual case for their cause.

Lobbying has long been a concern in Texas, and there has often been disagreement about the proper relationship between lobbyists and legislators. For example, at one time it was considered acceptable for large companies to keep legislators who were also lawyers "on retainer." In this arrangement, members of the Texas Legislature would accept payments from companies even as they deliberated over legislation impacting that company. One textbook published in 1964 matter-of-factly described this as an "especially common and possibly effective method of exerting influence" for businesses, because "when a bill comes up involving the industry or business concerned, their representative is already sitting in the legislature, ready to care for the interests of his clients."[20]

The fluid movement of people between public service and private lobbying concerns many Texans. This movement, known as the revolving door, sees legislators and members of the executive branch shift quickly from government office to lobbying firms, where they are able to use the access they have developed through years in public service for private gain. According to the Center for Public Integrity, between the close of the 2005 legislative session and the start of the 2007 session, eight former legislators became lobbyists, helping Texas lead the nation in lawmakers-turned-lobbyists, with seventy having made the transition.[21] Many of the state's best-paid lobbyists had previously served as a state official or staff person. Texas is one of eleven states with no "cooling off" period between serving in the legislature and working as a lobbyist.[22] Every session, legislation is introduced that would require that members of the Texas Legislature be prohibited from becoming paid lobbyists for at least two years after they leave office. Stopping the revolving door, or even slowing it down, has proved difficult because it asks state legislators to support laws limiting their future careers. Also, limits on what officials do after their years of public service are limits on their First Amendment rights that could face court challenges.

Some relatives of legislative leaders have found jobs as well-paid lobbyists, suggesting that interest groups are buying influence through family members. One study found that at least six well-paid lobbyists had members of their families serving in high-level positions in Texas government.[23] One member of the legislature, Jim Pitts, had a twin brother, John, who worked as a lobbyist. While the two claimed to have avoided discussing issues during the legislative session, the close connection illustrates the concern that many observers had about the relationship between legislators and relatives.

The Relationship between Organized Interests and Parties

As discussed in the previous chapter, the relationship between organized interests and parties can be troublesome. While some organized interests consistently support one party over the other, they can also highlight differences within the party and challenge the party establishment. This was vividly illustrated in the 2012 U.S. Senate nominating contest between Lieutenant Governor David Dewhurst and Ted Cruz. Cruz's candidacy received massive amounts of support from the Club for Growth, most of it in the form of independent expenditure ads attacking Dewhurst as "big spending and tax raising." The criticism of Dewhurst's record did not go over well with the Republican legislators and governor who had signed off on those budgets. More recently, Empower Texans endorsed thirty-four candidates in the 2018 Republican primary, often endorsing challengers to Republican incumbents. Such efforts present challenges for the party organization, which would rather maintain control of as much of the money and campaign message as possible. The challenge is compounded when the special interest group is national and allows people from outside Texas to shape the campaign. The job of the party is to elect as many people as possible under the party's label, but the mission of an organized interest may be much narrower. In contrast, the organized interest is more likely to promote its agenda regardless of how narrow that agenda or its appeal might be.

WINNERS AND LOSERS

One important debate in the area of organized interests is always who wins and who loses. One perspective on this issue is the **pluralist perspective**. This perspective looks at politics as a collection of interests and argues that democracy is best practiced when citizens participate through groups. When many interests are represented, pluralists see wide participation and a healthy democracy. The leading voice of pluralism was political scientist Robert Dahl, who, in his classic *Who Governs?*, concluded that no single interest dominated and that politics was open to broad participation with organized interests representing the needs of real people.[24]

pluralist perspective
a view of politics that argues that democracy is best practiced when citizens participate through groups; a greater number of organized interests means wider participation and a healthier democracy

Critics of pluralism disagree with the idea that the presence of a large number of interest groups means that citizens are well served; some people, they argue, will be better represented by organized interests than others. C. Wright Mills maintained that the "power elite," the wealthy and powerful interests, were better represented than ordinary citizens.[25] As one scholar colorfully suggested, "the flaw in the pluralist heaven is that the heavenly chorus sings with a strong upper-class accent."[26] Most Texans don't have enough money to contribute to an interest group or hire the lobbyists and other staff needed to build support for their agenda. There are some groups that represent poor Texans, but ironically, these groups are generally funded and led by people who are not themselves poor. That is, poor Texans remain reliant on wealthy patrons to advocate for them.

One of the challenges to the pluralist view is that we have gone beyond simple pluralism and evolved into a system of **hyperpluralism** in which many narrow groups are represented, often at the expense of the broader public interest. For

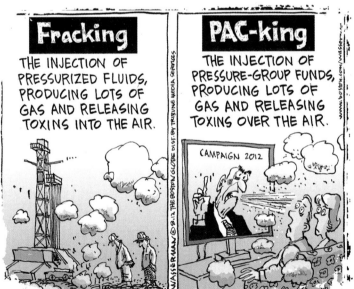

TEXAS (VS) ALASKA

The state of Alaska tackles the issue of lobbying very differently than Texas. In 2015, one rating of regulation of lobbyists and their activities awarded Alaska the highest grade of A as best in the nation, while Texas got an F.[i] While Texas has refined its lobbying rules, the rules and the structure of the Texas Ethics Commission (TEC) have greatly limited the ability of the commission to monitor and punish lobbyists. Court rulings have made it difficult for the TEC to impose fines, while officials in Alaska have been able to issue large fines.

When it comes to defining and registering lobbyists and their activities, the two states differ in a number of areas. As the table comparing Texas with Alaska shows, Alaska's regulatory environment provides a more detailed and transparent accounting of the activities of lobbyists who attempt to influence the state government than does that of Texas. Most importantly, the follow-up is more extensive in Alaska. In Texas, lobbyists' reports are not audited, and the TEC has not been able to consistently investigate abuses and punish those who break the rules. While the TEC did fine Michael Quinn Sullivan $10,000 in 2014 for failing to register as a lobbyist, it is telling that this was the first time a complaint alleging that a lobbyist had failed to register had gone through the entire process since the commission had been created almost a quarter of a century ago.

> **How should states balance concerns about lobbyists' freedom of speech with concerns about honest government?**

 SOCIAL RESPONSIBILITY

> **How do you think such provisions would change the dynamics of money in Texas politics?**

 CRITICAL THINKING

---

i.   Center for Public Integrity, "In Your State—Washington" and "In Your State—Texas," accessed August 11, 2010, www.publicintegrity. org/hiredguns/iys.aspx.

Lobbying in Texas and Alaska

Activity Regulated	Texas	Alaska
Register if lobbying executive branch	Yes	Yes
Register if paid to lobby	Yes	Yes
Minimum spent to qualify as a lobbyist	$5,000	Any amount
Lobbyists file detailed registration forms within a few days of initiating lobbying activity	Yes	Yes
Employers/principals list on spending reports the compensation/salary of all lobbyists they hire	Yes	No
Employers or principals of lobbyists required to fill out spending reports	Yes	No
Citizens can access lobbying disclosure documents at no cost	Yes	Yes
Lobbying disclosure information is made available in an open-data format	Yes	No
Lobbying disclosure records are independently audited	Yes	No
Penalties are imposed as necessary when lobbying-reporting requirements are violated	Yes	Inconsistent

Sources: Compiled by the authors from data available at Center for Public Integrity, "State Integrity 2015," accessed August 6, 2018, https://www.publicintegrity.org/accountability/state-integrity-investigation/state-integrity-2015, and Texas Ethic Commission, Texas, "Lobbying in Texas: A Guide to the Law," January 1, 2017, https://www.ethics.state.tx.us/guides/lobby_guide.pdf.

example, the NRA may effectively represent many Texans on the issue of gun ownership, but that does not mean its members are heard on issues unrelated to the narrow focus of the NRA. Hyperpluralism was given a boost with the *Citizens United* decision, because now corporations and labor unions can put money directly into political advertising without working with the political parties or candidates. The rise of dark money may allow even more narrow interests to have a larger voice. As is evident from looking over the groups functioning in Texas, many businesses and groups labor in Austin on behalf of narrow interests, while very few work on behalf of citizens in general. While the two-party system may be divisive, at least it encourages the interests within each party to work together.

Some of the arguments implicating organized interests have little to do with class or party. One view is that special interests have made it impossible to get rid of a government program that is no longer needed, whether it's a social program benefiting the poor or a subsidy benefiting businesses.[27] In this argument, organized interests have been successful at protecting their own spending, even if it is at the expense of everyone else's pocketbooks. While all organized interests win in this state of affairs, they also all lose, as taxpayers remain burdened with programs that are ineffective.

The ability of some groups to effectively organize while others cannot produces clear winners and losers in the state. In Texas, businesses, and often individuals, have effectively organized. Once organized, the relatively loose laws governing lobbying make it easy for them to exert considerable influence in Austin. Other groups, perhaps due to apathy or a lack of money or both, fail to effectively organize and pay a high price. For instance, the vast majority of college and university students in Texas consistently show little interest in politics. In recent years, the state of Texas has deregulated tuition, capped the number of courses students can withdraw from, and limited the number of hours Texans can enroll in before they pay out-of-state tuition. Students might well ask what kind of voice they had when these issues that are impacting them directly were being debated in the legislature.

CONCLUSION

Parties and organized interests can be both allies and enemies in the political process. While organized interests often support political parties, there are times when narrow interests will abandon the broader goals of the political parties and feed divisions within the parties. However, while the two political actors may at times clash, their impact on Texas politics is undeniable.

The factions that James Madison sought to muzzle with our system of checks and balances are alive and well in Texas. Like citizens of other states, Texans generally express disdain for "special interests" while enthusiastically joining their favorite groups. Whether for or against gun control, education reform, or other issues, Texans are never shy about taking sides.

Although Texans scorn "special-interest" groups, few states have systems in which their lobbyists play a stronger role. The citizen government that Texans want representing them in Austin finds itself surrounded by professional lobbyists and other members of the influence industry, and the part-time nature of the legislature makes its members willing to rely to some extent on former colleagues and other lobbyists for information when facing policymaking decisions.

hyperpluralism
a view that the system today has evolved beyond simple pluralism and is now one in which many narrow interests are represented, often at the expense of the broader public interest

Do organized interests create hyperpluralism and polarization?

 SOCIAL RESPONSIBILITY

How well do organized interests in Texas represent the needs of average Texans?

 SOCIAL RESPONSIBILITY

for CQ Press

Want a better grade?

Get the tools you need to sharpen your study skills. Access practice quizzes, eFlashcards, video, and multimedia at **edge.sagepub.com/collier6e**.

KEY TERMS

Astroturf lobbying (p. 337)

collective goods (p. 325)

dark money (p. 333)

disturbance theory (p. 325)

electioneering (p. 329)

expressive benefits (p. 325)

free-rider problem (p. 325)

grassroots lobbying (p. 335)

grasstop lobbying (p. 337)

hyperpluralism (p. 341)

independent political expenditures (p. 331)

intergovernmental lobby (p. 328)

labor unions (p. 327)

lobbying (p. 322)

organized interest (p. 324)

pluralist perspective (p. 341)

political action committee (PAC) (p. 331)

professional associations (p. 327)

public interest groups (p. 328)

revolving door (p. 340)

selective incentives (p. 326)

single-issue interest groups (p. 328)

solidarity benefits (p. 324)

super PAC (p. 333)

trade associations (p. 327)

ACTIVE LEARNING

- Write a memo or message that a lobbyist could use to advocate for a student-related issue. **Communication**

- Work in groups to create a hypothetical organization related to an issue important

to the members of your group. Draft rules that prevent the free-rider problem. **Teamwork**

CHAPTER REVIEW

1. An *organized interest* is defined as _____.
   a. a large group of people with a shared political perspective
   c. any organization that attempts to influence public policy decisions
   d. an organization that nominates candidates and tries to get them elected under a shared label

2. The solidarity benefits of group membership include _____.
   a. winning specific political victories that produce economic benefits
   b. meeting and working with other people who have similar interests
   c. membership cards and other benefits organized interests give to individual members
   d. the natural advantage that large organized interests enjoy

3. An example of a free-rider problem is _____.
   a. students who do not help with a group project but still get a good grade on the assignment
   b. people who go to a party and do not chip in on food or drink
   c. people who do not pay their taxes but enjoy the benefit of programs like national defense
   d. all of these

4. Selective benefits are _____.
   a. public policies that help specific groups
   b. public policies that help all citizens
   c. benefits that only go to members of an organized interest
   d. tax cuts that only benefit certain businesses

5. A public interest group _____.
   a. pursues noneconomic policies on behalf of the general public
   b. promotes the interest of business and trade organizations
   c. works only on issues related to narrow groups of citizens
   d. involves one level of government lobbying another level of government

6. The intergovernmental lobby _____.
   a. involves citizen groups working with only one branch of government
   b. involves different levels of government lobby each other
   c. is money given to political parties supporting candidates for different offices
   d. includes lobbyists who are not registered with the Texas Ethics Commission

(Continued)

7. Political action committees are _____.

    a. the part of political parties involved in raising and spending money on behalf of candidates

    b. the part of organized interests involved in raising and spending money to influence elections

    c. groups of candidates working together to raise money

    d. groups of legislators who share common goals

8. Independent expenditures involve _____.

    a. money given directly by citizens to political candidates

    b. money raised and spent by candidates not affiliated with one of the two major parties

    c. money spent by the government to subsidize political campaigns

    d. spending by organized interests without coordinating with the campaigns of candidates

9. In *Citizens United v. Federal Election Commission*, the Supreme Court ruled that the right to free speech extended to allowing _____ to make direct contributions to campaigns.

    a. corporations and unions

    b. individual citizens

    c. foreign nationals

    d. residents of other states

10. Dark money involves campaign spending by a group that _____.

    a. goes toward write-in candidates who do not appear on official ballots

    b. goes toward parties and not to individual candidates

    c. goes toward social media advertising

    d. does not have to be reported to the group's donors

LOCAL GOVERNMENT IN TEXAS

The unprecedented flooding along the Texas Gulf Coast and Houston metropolitan area from Hurricane Harvey in August 2017 exposed Texans to important problems affecting local governments throughout Texas and the country. One issue is the coordination, or lack thereof, between the U.S., state, and local governments in regions affected by a natural or manmade disaster. While the impact of Harvey on areas like Corpus Christi, Victoria, Beaumont, Rockport, and other coastal communities cannot be understated, the size and scope of its impact on the greater Houston area illustrates the problem of coordinating relief efforts.

At the national level, the Federal Emergency Management Agency (FEMA) provides the first, immediate response by the national government. Other U.S. government agencies are also involved, like the Department of Agriculture for food support, the Department of Housing and Urban Development for rebuilding homes, and the Small Business Administration for loans to support businesses. Initially, Texas governor Greg Abbott praised FEMA's quick response and coordination with state officials in the immediate aftermath of Harvey.[1] This contrasts with the intense criticism in 2005 of FEMA's response to Hurricane Katrina in Louisiana and Mississippi.

Governor Abbott empowered the General Land Office (GLO) and its commissioner, George P. Bush, to coordinate state disaster coordination. Traditionally, FEMA takes a leading role in disaster relief, with state agencies taking a secondary role. However, true to the spirit of Texas independence, Governor Abbott insisted that the

Hurricane Harvey left unprecedented flooding and destruction in its wake. Efforts to cope with the disaster strained local and state government budgets and created conflicts between levels of government over control of the rebuilding process.

GLO be in charge. This change rewrote the federal disaster aid playbook in terms of how relief is carried out. The GLO, notified just days before the announcement of the decision, faced a significant learning curve, as GLO officials had to become familiar with federal procedures, regulations, and funding processes. Problems arose over how the GLO would implement immediate and long-term recovery efforts. Coordination with local governments suffered as the GLO first had to learn how to provide disaster relief, and then how to provide relief within FEMA's guidelines. Local governments across the affected area complained about delays, lack of access to data, and high turnover of individuals working on relief efforts.[2] Coordination between the state and local governments quickly began to deteriorate.

Demands by Governor Abbott for sufficient funding also ran into problems. In the immediate aftermath of Harvey, the national media attacked Texas—and Houston in particular—for its libertarian approach to urban planning and development, including limited zoning, allegations of overdevelopment, and poor consideration of flood plains. Criticism also extended to the political culture of Texas. The emphasis on small government, resistance to federal government overreach in state and local affairs, and low taxes were all singled out as ironic, given Texas's requests for U.S. government assistance in rebuilding. However, Texas's congressional delegation has typically provided strong support to similar natural disaster relief efforts in other states.[3]

Because the Texas Legislature meets only biennially, the legislature itself was unable to take direct action. Moreover, Governor Abbott refused to call a special session of the Texas Legislature to address the issue, even though spending on disaster relief was estimated to exceed $4 billion.[4] Without the legislature to approve spending, the governor relied on his emergency powers to manage the crisis. Ultimately, local governments faced a stressful fall and winter wondering when, and if, rebuilding efforts might be completed.

Complicating matters further was the decision by Governor Abbott to place John Sharp, chancellor of the Texas A&M system, in charge of the "Rebuild Texas" initiative. This decision set up a conflict between the General Land Office and the "Rebuild Texas" program, with both claiming a mandate to lead the recovery efforts.

Additional struggles developed between the state government and local governments over the relief and rebuilding process. As early as September 2017, Governor Abbott released $50 million to Houston mayor Sylvester Turner in disaster assistance, which allowed the city to avoid increasing property taxes to pay for hurricane relief. However, local government officials from Harvey-affected areas complained that much of the current budget money was being spent and that the lack of timely funds from the state or U.S. government slowed recovery efforts.[5] It remained unclear to cash-strapped cities and counties from where the necessary financial resources for recovery would come.

In November 2017, Governor Abbott approved funding from the state's general revenue rather than the Rainy Day Fund, a state account reserved for emergency spending. These emergency funds helped cities and counties pay for debris cleanup. Local governments used this money toward the 10 percent of the total cleanup costs they are expected to pay under FEMA guidelines (the U.S. government picks up the other 90 percent). However, those funds were distributed months after they needed to be spent, forcing cities and counties to engage in creative bookkeeping to maintain day-to-day operations such as police, fire protection, and public works. The 90 percent federal/10 percent local cost sharing is unusual; normally, local governments must contribute 25 percent of the total costs. Governor Abbott struck an agreement with the Trump administration to shift Texas local governments to these more favorable terms.[6] Yet, the governor left local governments out of the negotiations, even though local governments are expected to pay part of the costs.

Planned spending priorities on housing recovery also led to conflicts between the General Land Office and the governments of the City of Houston and Harris County. The GLO wanted to use some U.S. Department of Housing and Urban Development (HUD) funds to match federal funding for other housing recovery programs. While such diversion of funds is allowed under federal law, the local governments in Houston and Harris County pushed back, demanding that all HUD funds be used as originally intended. Ultimately, the GLO relented to the wishes of Houston and Harris County. This episode points to the need for coordination between levels of government in relief efforts.[7]

Conflicts continued well into the spring of 2018. Houston Mayor Turner continued to register complaints that the GLO was not consulting with local officials to coordinate the distribution of federal funds from HUD. In a letter to the GLO, the mayor stated that the GLO had not asked Houston to contribute to rebuilding plans, had not specified what data were being used to allocated funds, and had not distributed funds directly to the city.[8]

The need to provide large-scale disaster relief surpasses the capacity of any local government and strains the resources of state governments. Because the U.S. government has deeper pockets, it inevitably gets involved in disaster relief of this magnitude. However, conflicts over the priories of different levels of government, over process control, and over how funds are sourced and spent become inevitable. As we will discover later in this chapter, some local governments, like county governments, exist solely to carry out tasks the state needs to accomplish. These governments are merely convenient tools for the state. While cities are designed to provide key services for its citizens, the state still dominates the form of government and the specific powers of cities in Texas. Thus, local governments often get caught between what the residents of the city or county want versus what the state needs done.

In this chapter, we will review the fundamentals of the myriad local governments in Texas, discussing the creation, powers, and organization of county government. Then we will review city government, focusing on the differences between general law and home rule cities. We will also examine the functions of city governments and survey their elections processes. We will conclude with a review of other forms of local government, including public education and special districts such as **municipal utility districts (MUDs)**.

municipal utility district (MUD)
a special district that provides water, sewer, or similar services to individuals and businesses outside city limits

LOCAL GOVERNMENT: THE BASICS

Local government involves a wide range of entities. Most often, we think of local government as referring to cities and counties. In Texas, local government also includes school districts, community college districts, MUDs, water conservation districts, and airport districts, among others. Numerous local governments exist to provide for public schools, hospitals, parks and recreation, economic development, ports, libraries, and fire protection. For example, residents of the Cypress-Fairbanks area of northwest Harris County have at least eight local governments governing their lives, providing necessary services and levying taxes to fund those services. These separate and distinct local governments include the Cypress-Fairbanks Independent School District (ISD), Harris County Flood Control District, Port of Houston Authority, Harris County Hospital District, Lone Star College System, Harris County Department of Education, Harris County Emergency Services District 9, and a MUD. One reason for the large number of local governments is that Texas's counties often do not provide the same services that counties in other states provide. In the absence of strong county governments, Texans have found other ways to obtain the services they desire, in part by creating many other types of local governments.

In 2012, Texas had the second-highest number of local governments of any state in the United States (see Table 11.1), ranking behind another large-population state, Illinois, and ahead of Pennsylvania and California.[9] In contrast, Hawaii has the fewest local governments. Hawaii's low number of only twenty-one local governments reflects the fact that Hawaii has no incorporated cities and lacks school districts in the way that other states organize their school systems. On one hand, large-population states may be expected to generate more local governments. However, comparing the total number of local governments to the size of the population shows that Texas has 20.5 local governments for every 100,000 residents. This ratio is lower than in many other states in the region, such as Oklahoma, which has a significantly smaller population. Therefore, for a state the size of Texas, we may have fewer local governments than other states. As a result, Texans may have a lower level of public services, such as water, sewer, and trash collection, or Texas may rely on fewer governments to provide the same services that residents of other states receive.

The common characteristic of all of these local governments is that each exists as an arm of the state government. Regardless of the type of local government, all local governments are creatures of the state government, a concept known as Dillon's Rule. In an 1868 case before the Iowa Supreme Court, Justice John Forrest Dillon affirmed the principle that local governments have only those powers specifically granted to them by the states.[10] The U.S. Supreme Court later echoed this view. The court ruled that states may change the powers of their cities, even if the residents living in the city do not approve.[11] By extension, this concept applies to all forms of local government within a state, including county governments and special districts. In other words, the powers, duties, and very existence of every local government are determined by the state government. This legal status between local governments and their respective state governments is the same in every state in the country.

In Texas, the constitution provides a basic framework to define the types, powers, and responsibilities of local governments in the state. Statutory laws, such as the Texas Local Government Code, Texas Education Code, Texas Utilities Code, and even the Texas Water Code, supplement the framework found in the Texas Constitution. For example, the Texas Constitution specifically grants to the Texas Legislature "the power to create counties for the convenience of the people."[12] These constitutional provisions and statutory laws go so far as to specify how local governments elect officials, which administrative offices must exist, and what types of taxes local governments may use to fund their activities.

Because there are fifty states in the United States, essentially fifty different systems of local government have developed. States diverge tremendously in the structure and functions of their local governments. As examples, Connecticut and Rhode Island lack county government in the sense that Texas and other states use it. In both of those states, counties serve primarily as a method of reporting population for the U.S. Census. Most functions that Texans associate with county government are performed in Connecticut by township governments and in Rhode Island by cities and towns. Ohio and several other states maintain township governments to provide specific services, such as snow removal and cemetery maintenance. Other states, such as Georgia, maintain countywide school districts. Arkansas allows school district boundaries to cross county lines. A number of states, such as Tennessee and Louisiana, allow cities and counties to merge into a single local government, and in Virginia some cities are independent of or outside counties; these cities in Virginia existed prior to the creation of counties after the American Revolution.

Because local governments of all types are extensions of a state government, a second relationship necessarily exists: the relationship between local governments and the national government in Washington, DC. This relationship is more complex. The U.S. Constitution mentions explicitly only state governments and the national government. On a legal and technical level, then, local governments do not exist in the eyes of the U.S. Constitution. In practice, however, the national government recognizes that state governments and state constitutions create local governments and that such governments exist within states. The norm is to hold state governments responsible for the policies and procedures of their local governments. For example, if local school districts are unable or unwilling to comply with a federal law or federal court decision, the U.S. government ultimately requires the state government to solve the problem. A dramatic

TABLE 11.1 Units of Local Government Compared to State Population, 2012

Number of Local Governments		
State	Number	Governments per 100,000 People
Top Five		
Illinois	6,963	54.4
Texas	5,147	20.5
Pennsylvania	4,897	38.6
California	4,425	11.9
Ohio	3,842	33.4
Bottom Five		
Delaware	339	37.7
Nevada	191	7.1
Alaska	177	1.5
Rhode Island	133	25.3
Hawaii	21	1.5
States Bordering Texas		
Oklahoma	1,852	52.9
Arkansas	1,556	53.7
Louisiana	529	11.8
New Mexico	863	41.1

Source: U.S. Census Bureau, Census of Governments, "Local Governments by Type and State: 2012," accessed March 12, 2018, https://www.census.gov/data/tables/2012/econ/gus/2012-governments.html; population per 100,000; calculated by authors.

example involved the failure in the 1970s and 1980s of the Kansas City, Missouri, public school system to integrate its schools following the U.S. Supreme Court's ruling in favor of desegregation. The federal courts went so far as to hold the Missouri state government responsible for the problem and to require the use of statewide taxes to pay for integration of Kansas City schools.[13]

A federal system of government, as described in Chapter 2, exists where the powers of government are divided between a national government and state governments, with each level of government having an independent base of power. This arrangement contrasts with a unitary system of government in which all power is centralized and other levels of government are allotted power at the discretion of the central government. The exact division of powers in a federal system may be dual federalism, in which each level has distinct and separate powers, or cooperative federalism, in which the state governments and the national government jointly carry out some tasks.

In addition to Dillon's Rule, the relationships between the U.S. government, state governments and local governments are shaped by fiscal federalism and administrative federalism. Under fiscal federalism, the U.S. government sets goals and objectives or develops new programs, then the national government provides financial incentives

fiscal federalism
use of national financial incentives to encourage policies at the state or local level

administrative federalism
the process whereby the national government sets policy guidelines then expects state governments to pay for the programs they engender without the aid of federal monies

for the state governments to participate in the programs. In response, states begin to develop their own programs or change their own policies to match the goals of what the national government wants. States typically receive money from the national government to cover some of the costs of these programs. For example, if the U.S. Congress and the president believe that providing computers and Internet access to students in elementary, middle, and high schools is essential to learning, then they will fund a federal program that provides money to those states that decide to buy new computers and equip new and existing schools with Internet access. The money provided by the national government is matched with contributions from the state and local governments and then given to schools for implementation. There are numerous examples of this type of program, spanning a variety of policy areas that include health care for the disabled, immunization programs for poor children, road construction, and draining and sewer system improvements, among others.

Administrative federalism works in a similar manner—minus financial input, however. The national government sets up guidelines for policy and then expects the state governments to pay for the programs on their own without matching funds from the national government. Under administrative federalism, for example, the national government may wish to improve K–12 public education. To do so, the U.S. Department of Education may set minimum standards for student achievement for each grade level, then states are expected to bear the costs to change school curricula, including courses and subjects taught at each grade level, to meet the national standards. States may also exceed these minimal standards set by the U.S. government.

How do fiscal and administrative federalism connect to local government? In fiscal federalism, the national government provides money in the form of grants, or sums of money given to state or local governments to fund a program or policy. Usually, states allow local governments to apply to the state for a share of the money, often through a competitive process. Thus, local governments must develop the skills and staffs to write the applications, provide evidence of the need for the funds, and develop budgets. In addition, once a local government receives a grant, it must report back in detail to the state government how the money was used. In terms of administrative federalism, local governments again serve as agents of implementation. However, state governments establish how best to achieve the national government's objectives, outlining an approach that is then handed to local governments to carry out. Yet, cash-starved state governments may pass the costs of implementation onto local governments like school districts or cities.

Some Texans and Texas politicians stir the political waters of "Texas independence" by questioning the U.S. government's relationship to the state and sometimes go so far to raise the specter of a "Texit" or secession. An important issue in this scenario is the money local governments like cities, counties, and especially school districts receive from the U.S. government in grant money. While reducing or eliminating much oversight, and administrative rules and regulations, from the U.S. government might seem appealing to many Texans, would the average Texan be willing to increase the size and scope of Texas state government and state taxes to offset the money lost from the U.S. government? While talk of secession occurred during the presidency of Barack Obama, the advent of the Donald Trump administration has lessened such discussion.

TEXAS OHIO

When the U.S. Congress began to address the issue of lands beyond the original thirteen states, it passed the Northwest Ordinance. In 1785, as part of that law, the territory that would become the state of Ohio was surveyed. The survey was used to set aside plots of land six miles by six miles, for a total of thirty-six square miles per plot, and each plot of land became a township.[i] Variations on this standard size were allowed when the survey encountered a natural land feature, such as Lake Erie, or a political boundary, such as the border with Pennsylvania. Each township was subdivided into sections, with one section per township set aside for public schools and four set aside as payment to veterans of the American Revolution. These townships sat as a level of governmental administration between the county government and municipal governments, such as cities and towns. The remnants of these townships are the school districts in rural parts of Ohio.[ii]

The concept of the township later became used in Ohio for another type of local government entity: the civil township. Civil townships provide a number of services to residents in Ohio, including cemetery maintenance, trash collection, road and bridge maintenance, and snow removal.[iii] These townships in Ohio are created by county governments, and all areas of the county not in a city or town are part of a township. A county's board of commissioners may divide or consolidate any township within the county. However, voters may also, through a home rule provision, consolidate or divide a township.[iv] Any new township created by voters can only include land that is not in an existing city or town. When an area of a township is incorporated, or annexed, into a city or town, the township may be dissolved. If only part of the township is incorporated, the area of the township not incorporated may consolidate with another township, or the township may continue to function within the city.

A civil township is governed by an elected board of trustees comprising three members who serve four-year terms in office.[v] The trustees may hire an administrator to oversee day-to-day operations of the township. Trustees have the power to levy taxes to pay for township government and services,[vi] and the township may provide services above and beyond those listed previously. Some additional services include demolition of derelict property, solid waste disposal, the hiring of a resident physician, the operation of airports, the development of harbors and port facilities, the provision of public libraries, and the creation of township parks. Interestingly, in Ohio, when services provided by a county government conflict with or duplicate those of a township government, by law the township continues to provide the services, while the county must stop the activities.[vii] Townships may consolidate or transfer their powers to a county government after a vote of the residents of the township.[viii]

Currently, a total of 1,308 township governments exist in Ohio. These townships account for 35 percent of all local governments in the state. In contrast, Texas lacks township governments. Services typically provided by Ohio townships are often provided in Texas by cities. If a person does not live in a city in Texas, the county government may provide such services. However, municipal utility districts (MUDs) in Texas can be created to provide these services, or individuals may contract with private companies to provide them.

> **What is the advantage of creating township governments in Ohio?**
>
> **CRITICAL THINKING**

> **How are MUDs in Texas similar to and different from townships in Ohio?**
>
> **CRITICAL THINKING**

i. Ohio History Central, "Township," accessed March 14, 2018, www.ohiohistorycentral.org/w/township.

ii. Ohio Revised Statutes (2012), chap. 501.

iii. Ohio Revised Code (2012), chap. 503, sec. 02.

iv. Ohio History Central, "Township."

v. Ohio Revised Statutes (2012), chap. 505, sec. 03.

vi. Ohio Constitution (1851), art. 10, sec. 2.

vii. Ohio Constitution (1851), art. 10, sec. 3.

viii. Ohio Constitution (1851), art. 10, sec. 1.

COUNTY GOVERNMENT, TEXAS STYLE

Texas counties vary tremendously in population, natural resources, and land areas. However, all Texas counties are structured the same way, and this structure is grounded in historical development and constitutional provisions. As a result, Texas county government exhibits a one-size-fits-all approach. The lack of variation in government structure makes Texas unusual compared to some states.

History and Function of Counties in Texas

Local government in Texas is rooted in the old municipality system of the Mexican Republic. Under Mexican rule, Texas contained four municipalities, large areas containing a town and surrounding rural areas. Initially, the four municipalities were San Antonio, Bahia (Goliad), Nacogdoches, and Rio Grande Valley. The number of municipality governments increased as the population and settlements grew. When the Republic of Texas was established, twenty-three counties were created based on the existing Mexican municipalities, including Nacogdoches, Bexar, and Brazos. At statehood in 1845, the county system was retained. The Confederate Constitution of 1861 created 122 counties, and the number of counties continued to increase under subsequent state constitutions. In 1931, Loving County became the last county to be established. Interestingly, the organization of Loving County marked its second era of existence. The first Loving County had originally been carved in 1893 from Reeves County as part of a get-rich-quick scheme to defraud landowners and the state of Texas by the organizers of the county. The scandal surrounding Loving County, which involved falsified county records, illegitimate elections, and low population, prompted the Texas Legislature to abolish the county in 1897. The arrival of the oil industry to western Texas later spurred its reestablishment.[14]

Texas today has 254 counties, more than any other state. Georgia is the next closest with 159 counties. Hawaii and Delaware have the fewest, with three counties each. In Texas, counties are created by laws passed by the state legislature, subject to a few limitations from the Texas Constitution. For example, new counties may not be smaller than 700 square miles, and existing counties from which a new county is created cannot be reduced to less than 700 square miles.[15] Historically, county boundaries were drawn so that a county's citizens could travel to the county courthouse and return home in a single day.[16] By population, Harris County is the largest county in Texas, with over 4.1 million people. Only two counties in the United States are larger in population: Cook County, Illinois, and Los Angeles County, California. The smallest county in Texas by population is Loving County, with just eighty-two people. In addition, Loving County holds the distinction of being the smallest county in terms of population in the country as a whole. In terms of geographic area, Brewster County is the largest in Texas at 6,204 square miles, an area larger than the states of Connecticut and Rhode Island combined. Rockwall County, near Dallas, is the smallest at 127 square miles.[17] County names in Texas reflect a variety of historical and cultural influences. In addition to the county names derived from Mexican municipalities, twelve counties are named for defenders of the Alamo, including Bowie, Fannin, and Taylor Counties. Several reflect geographic features like rivers, streams, and landforms, such as Pecos and Sabine Counties. Some are named for governors and other figures in Texas politics, such as Coke County and Lamar County. Panola County is named for the Native American word for cotton, while Lampasas County comes from the Spanish word for lilies. Freestone County is named for a variety of peach.

County government is essential in Texas because counties carry out many duties for the state government. In this respect, counties are essentially extensions of the

Local Governments in Perspective

Number of Local Governments by State as of 2012

Highest

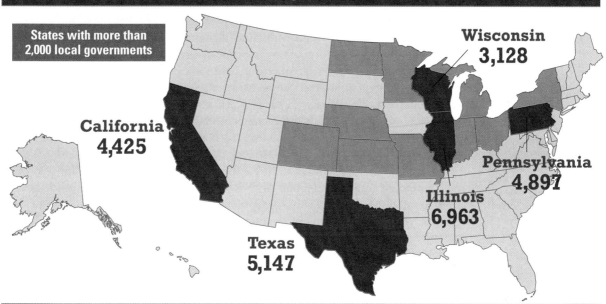

States with more than 2,000 local governments

Wisconsin 3,128

California 4,425

Pennsylvania 4,897

Illinois 6,963

Texas 5,147

Lowest

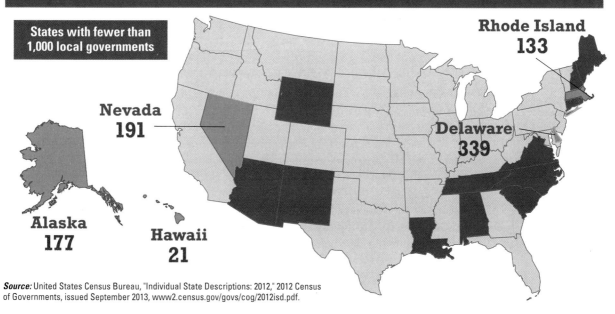

States with fewer than 1,000 local governments

Rhode Island 133

Nevada 191

Delaware 339

Alaska 177

Hawaii 21

Source: United States Census Bureau, "Individual State Descriptions: 2012," 2012 Census of Governments, issued September 2013, www2.census.gov/govs/cog/2012isd.pdf.

state government. The role and function of counties are especially important in rural areas of the state where cities and towns are few and far between. In the days before well-maintained roads and highways, the state government in Austin was largely inaccessible to many Texans. So county government was designed to bring state government closer to the people. County government is also essential to the function of both administrative and fiscal federalism because counties are often the front line for the delivery of a variety of policies.

Texas's counties perform at least six key functions for the state government. Counties operate courts for the state, including justice of the peace (JP), county, and district courts. Counties make available public health clinics, conduct immunization programs, enforce state health regulations, and inspect restaurants. They also maintain vital records for the state, including marriage licenses, death certificates, birth certificates, and property deeds. Another function of counties is to collect funds for the state government, for example, in the form of property taxes, license plate fees, and motor vehicle title fees. Counties are also responsible for conducting elections; they maintain election equipment, oversee the registration of voters, and operate polling places. Finally, counties work jointly with state government to carry out other functions. For example, counties help with law enforcement by maintaining sheriff or constable offices and operating county jails. They also build roads and bridges that connect to the state's network of roads and highways.

In a strange twist on Texas politics, the Texas Constitution contains a strong provision against imprisonment for debt. However, the constitution also allows each county to provide a "Manual Labor Poor House and Farm, for taking care of, managing, employing, and supplying the wants of its indigent and poor inhabitants."[18] This is perhaps a legacy of the frontier experience where rugged individuals were expected to provide for themselves. This provision of the state constitution is an arcane one that counties have replaced with a variety of national, state, and local programs to provide assistance to the poor. The state permits counties to carry out certain activities that may also be provided by other forms of local government, including cities and special districts. Counties sometimes operate parks, run libraries, own airports, and manage hospitals, but these functions are optional for counties.

Governing Texas Counties

All Texas counties are governed the same way. This means that counties are controlled directly by state laws, the most important being the Texas Local Government Code. Adherence to state law means that all 254 counties in Texas have the same form of government (see Figure 11.1). Every county government is led by a **commissioners court**. This court consists of four elected commissioners and the county judge from the county constitutional court. The selection of the commissioners and the county judge is conducted by **partisan election**—that is, an election in which each candidate's name and party affiliation are listed on the ballot. The elections for the four commissioners in every county are by the single-member district plurality (SMDP) system. (See Chapter 3 regarding the state legislature and later in this chapter in reference to city council elections.) The county judge is elected by voters across the county. The members of the court, including the county judge, are elected for four-year terms. Commissioners are elected to staggered terms of office.

Is there a relationship between the size of a state's population and the number of local governments in a state?

EMPIRICAL AND QUANTITATIVE

commissioners court
the governing body for Texas counties, consisting of four elected commissioners and the judge from the county constitutional court

partisan election
a type of election in which candidates' names and party affiliations appear on the ballot

FIGURE 11.1 The Structure of County Government in Texas

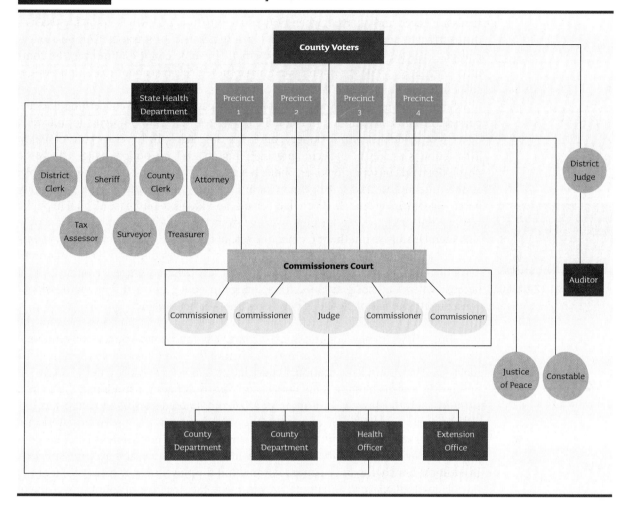

Source: John A. Gilmartin and Joe M. Rothe, *County Government in Texas*, issue 2 (Texas A&M University, Texas Agricultural Extension Service, V. G. Young Institute of County Government, 2000).

Students of Texas politics are often confused by the term *commissioners court*, which implies a judicial function. This confusion is increased by the presence of the county constitutional court judge on the commissioners court. In fact, the commissioners court serves as a legislative body for the county not as a judicial body. The commissioners court passes ordinances that govern the county, determines types and rates of taxes to fund the county government, and passes the annual county budget. It administers state and federal funds for local government use, oversees the various county departments and agencies, and holds final responsibility for the conduct of elections in the county. The county constitutional court judge serves as the presiding officer of the commissioners court, certifies elections, and appoints temporary replacements when a commissioner resigns.

Beyond their duties as a legislator, each commissioner is responsible for the maintenance of roads and bridges in their district. Each commissioner determines which roads are paved and repaved, when bridges are repaired, and which company receives the contract to perform road projects in his or her district or precinct. Commissioners may act solely in the interest of their precincts. In some counties, however, the commissioners agree to pool resources and make these decisions about roads and bridges collectively in the interest of the whole county.

County commissioners may also collectively pass ordinances concerning the sale, possession, and consumption of alcoholic beverages. State law, however, permits residents to override the commissioners court regarding alcoholic beverage control policy. This action is usually in a specific precinct, though, and any policy change affects the possession and consumption of alcoholic beverages only in that precinct. For example, at one time in East Texas's Angelina County, alcohol policy varied across the county because voters in one precinct voted to permit individuals to purchase alcohol in public places if the purchaser was an adult over age twenty-one and had also bought a private club membership. In another precinct, the sale of beverages was permitted only in restaurants and bars to those over age twenty-one who showed a valid ID. In still other parts of the county, the sale and possession of alcoholic beverages remained illegal because voters had not petitioned for a change in policy, nor had that commissioner consented to the sale of alcoholic beverages in his or her precinct.

The county constitutional court judge also serves several functions beyond the presiding officer of the commissioners court. Obviously, the county constitutional court judge sits as the judge hearing cases before the county court, a typical judicial function. The county constitutional court judge also serves as the chief executive of the county, overseeing the county budget and day-to-day administration of the county.

Although the Texas Constitution of 1876 and its predecessors mirrored the U.S. Constitution's separation of powers at the state level, similar provisions were not included for county government. The structure of county government in Texas does just the opposite by giving the county judge judicial, legislative, and executive powers. In addition, few checks and balances exist to limit the power of county judges. In a state that prides itself on small and limited government, the structure of county government seems at odds with the prevailing political culture.

To assist the commissioners court, the voters elect a variety of other county officers. Typically, these officers are elected for four-year terms. Voters elect a county sheriff to oversee law enforcement in the county. The sheriff appoints deputy sheriffs and operates the county jail. The county clerk is responsible for maintaining county records, including birth and death reports and marriage licenses. In some counties, the county clerk also serves as the county elections officer and registrar of voters. The county attorney serves as the chief prosecuting attorney for misdemeanors in local courts, represents the county in legal activities, and offers legal advice to the county government. The county tax assessor collects property taxes and license plate fees; issues title certificates for cars and trucks; and, in some counties, acts as the registrar of voters and chief elections administrator. Since 1978, many counties have created a unified tax assessor district that provides property tax assessment and collection for the county and the cities and school districts in it. The county tax assessor's involvement with voter registration is a holdover from the days of the poll tax (see Chapter 9).

What are the advantages and disadvantages of Texas's "one size fits all" approach to the structure of county government?

★ CRITICAL THINKING

sheriff
the elected county official who oversees county law enforcement

county clerk
the elected county official who maintains county records and in some counties oversees elections

county attorney
the county official who represents the county in legal activities and offers legal advice to the county government

tax assessor
the elected county officer who collects county taxes and user fees

The justice of the peace (JP) serves as an elected judicial officer for minor criminal and civil cases. Normally, each of the four precincts or districts of the county has a JP. The JP is assisted by a constable, also elected at the precinct level; the constable serves a law enforcement capacity that includes investigating crimes and serving warrants. Large-population counties may also have deputy constables in each precinct.

Several other officers may be elected or appointed. A district clerk maintains court records for county and district courts. For larger counties, an auditor is appointed by the district judge to oversee county finances, a county public health officer directs local public health clinics, and a county agricultural agent assists with the needs of the farming community in rural counties. Some counties have a county elections administrator.

These officials are assisted by a host of employees that work for the various departments of the county government. From receptionists and administrative assistants to county land surveyors, counties employ thousands of Texans to perform the day-to-day operations of county government. In all but a handful of Texas counties, these jobs are essentially patronage. In a patronage system, elected officials give out government jobs to whomever the elected official wishes to have them—often loyal supporters. A person hired for a government job then serves at the wishes of the elected official and may be fired at will for any reason. Historically, under patronage, government jobs were handed out as political favors by the person who won an election. In some cases, the person who got a job in government service lacked any qualifications for the position. Of course, many of the men and women who work for county governments throughout Texas are competent, qualified people. They hold jobs without the protections of a merit-based civil service system. In a merit system, people receive government jobs based on a formalized system of qualifications and usually have formal training for the position, including college degrees or vocational certification. Often, merit systems require an applicant to take a test or examination to determine if he or she is qualified. Individuals receive promotions and salary increases based on a standard scale or series of performance goals. A patronage system may mimic the merit system by mandating qualifications for offices or setting minimal standards for getting a job, but the fact remains that these standards are not mandated by anything other than the decisions of county commissioners.

The Texas Local Government Code allows counties with 190,000 or more people to create a merit-based civil service system. Counties with less than 190,000 retain a patronage system. The creation of a merit system may be initiated by a vote of the county's commissioners court or by the county's voters.[19] In counties with over 500,000 people, a civil service system may be limited to the county's sheriff's department. A civil service system for a county is administered by a county civil service commission. The commission is appointed by the commissioners court for a term of two years. The civil service commission develops job definitions, qualification processes, classification of employees, and requirements for promotion. Additional responsibilities of the commission include developing disciplinary procedures for employees who violate policies and procedures and constructing a grievance process to handle employee complaints.

County Finances and Operations

To provide for day-to-day operations, counties in Texas rely on property taxes as their primary source of income. Other sources of revenue are motor vehicle license fees,

justice of the peace (JP)
an elected county officer who acts as a judicial officer for minor criminal and civil cases

constable
an elected county officer who acts as a judicial officer for minor criminal and civil cases; assists the justice of the peace (JP) with his or her duties

auditor
a county officer appointed by the district judge to oversee county finances

merit-based civil service system
a system in which people receive government jobs based on a set of qualifications and formal training; job promotion and pay raises are based on job performance

county civil service commission
the agency administering the county's civil service system; develops job definitions, qualification processes, employee classifications, and other aspects of the system

How should members of your county's commissioners court balance the need for providing public goods (e.g., sheriffs, county jails) with keeping residents' property tax rates reasonable?

★ SOCIAL
RESPONSIBILITY

privatization
a process whereby a government entity sells off assets or services to a private company that is then responsible for providing a service; for example, a school district sells its buses to a private company and then allows the company to provide transportation to schools

contract outsourcing
a process whereby a government entity contracts with a private company to perform a service that governments traditionally provide, such as a contract to collect trash and garbage

service fees, and federal aid. Service fees include the costs of obtaining official documents, such as marriage licenses and birth certificates, as well as court fees required to file a case with the county court.[20] In counties without incorporated cities or transportation districts, the county may also use sales taxes to finance the county government. While county governments face an upper limit on the rate that may be assessed for property taxes, voters may agree to additional property tax rates to fund roads and bridges in the county or for additional special services that the county may provide, such as flood control. Additional services that citizens desire beyond those financed by the county budget may be funded by creating special districts to fund hospitals, libraries, ports, airports, and so forth. In some counties, residents have created special districts called MUDs to provide basic utilities such as water, sewers, and electrical delivery. However, such districts may be created to provide services in only parts of a county. Special districts are discussed later in this chapter.

In some counties, the county government contracts with private businesses to provide the basic services counties normally offer through their budgets and related property taxes. This process involves either privatization or contract outsourcing of government services. Often services such as trash collection and recycling are targeted for privatization and contract outsourcing. Another outsourcing trend is the building of toll roads. In some counties, a private company is contracted to build and maintain a highway for the county or state. Individuals who use the highway pay a fee to drive on the road. This fee helps to repay the private company for the cost of building the highway and for routine repairs to it. Harris, Dallas, Tarrant, Bexar, Travis, and Smith Counties all now have toll roads.

Property taxes provide the primary source of funding for county governments in Texas. However, rates of property taxes vary tremendously in the state. In addition, property taxes include two categories of taxes. Counties impose general revenue taxes to fund basic county functions, activities, and services. In addition, counties may levy additional property taxes for a specific task or function. These property taxes do not go into the county's general revenue fund but instead go to a specific fund to pay for those activities. For example, a county might create a special property tax to fund road and bridge construction rather than rely on the funds from the general county revenue fund. Thus, property tax money from the special tax goes to a separate account to fund only road and bridge construction. Designated funds like these may be in addition to normal funds.

In 2016, Midland County represented the low end of property tax rates in Texas, with rates at $0.16 per $100 of the assessed value of the property, while Jim Hogg County maintained the highest rate at $1.20 per $100. In Jim Hogg County, $0.85 per $100 of assessed value went to the county's general fund for the county budget, and $0.35 went to other designated activities, such as flood control and farm-to-market road maintenance (see Table 11.2).

In Texas, real estate is the only property that is routinely taxed for the purposes of funding local governments. Other states assess personal property taxes as well. Personal property may include recreational vehicles, furniture, electronic appliances, and animals. Some states include the cars and trucks that a family or business owns in their personal property tax assessments. In states such as Missouri and Kansas, the tax on cars and trucks can be quite substantial. Note that in Missouri and Kansas, these taxes are levied by many forms of local government including counties, cities, fire protection districts, and school districts. In Texas, while other local governments, such as school districts and cities, may levy property taxes, just like with counties in Texas, property taxes are levied only on real estate, not personal property. The use of property taxes as the primary source of funding for county government is not without controversy. For counties with high property values, the use of property taxes provides ample revenue to fund county services. The reliance on property taxes stems in part from the inability of many counties to levy sales taxes to fund local government. In addition, property taxes permit the state of Texas to avoid the imposition of income taxes, common in many states. However, property values vary tremendously across the state's coun-

An Austin police officer staffs a recruiting booth at a local church fair. Community engagement and community relations are increasingly important for police across Texas.

ties, and in many rural areas without significant natural resources or economic development, lower property values might mean an inability to raise adequate revenue. In some instances, property tax rates are substantially higher in these counties to compensate for the relatively lower value of property in the county. Critics of property taxes

TABLE 11.2 Property Tax Rates in Texas, 2016

County	Total Tax Rate Per $100	General Fund	Other Provisions
Five Highest Rates			
Jim Hogg	$1.20	$0.85	$0.35
Cochran	$1.10	$0.80	$0.30
Throckmorton	$1.03	$0.75	$0.28
King	$1.03	$0.75	$0.28
Concho	$1.02	$0.84	$0.18
Five Lowest Rates			
Tarrant	$0.25	$0.25	$0.20
Denton	$0.25	$0.25	$0.00
Dallas	$0.24	$0.24	$0.00
Collin	$0.21	$0.21	$0.00
Midland	$0.16	$0.16	$0.00

Source: Texas Comptroller of Public Accounts, "County Rates and Levies," accessed March 12, 2018, controller.texas.gov/taxes/property-tax/rates/index.php.

also point out that the taxes are paid only by individuals who actually own property. If an individual does not own property, he or she does not pay taxes but still has use of public services. In some communities, 30 percent to 35 percent of residents do not own property and therefore enjoy services provided by counties, cities, and local governments without contributing directly to the provision of those services, though costs may be passed on to them indirectly through higher rents.

The structure of county government in Texas reflects the continuity and tradition of the state. Although the number of counties has increased, as have their populations, the Texas Constitution and statutory law prevent variation in the structure of the commissioners court and its powers. This lack of variation is true for most other county officials and their duties as well. As a result, Harris County and Loving County essentially share the same system of government, despite their tremendous difference in population and demand for government action. While Harris County's government is larger in terms of total staffing and size of budget, it basically does what Loving County's government does, and in about the same way. County governments cannot adapt to the realities of their situation or the changes that occur over time. For counties to significantly adapt and update the uniform, single approach to county government required in Texas, the state legislature would have to either alter the Texas Local Government Code or propose amendments to the state constitution.

CITIES

Although counties serve Texans as an extension of the state government, cities develop more directly from citizen input. In addition, the Texas Constitution and statutory laws give cities more discretion than counties to adapt to change in such areas as city organization, election system, local laws, and form of government. Given the wide divergence in population size, geographic location, and resource base among cities, the flexibility given to them better equips them to carry out local government functions in a rapidly changing state.

A city is created in Texas when the population of an area that is not already incorporated as a city reaches at least 200 people. To form a city, the residents must also define its exact boundaries and negotiate with the county regarding the services the new city government will provide versus those the county already provides to the residents. At this point, residents in the area of the proposed city may gather signatures of others living there who support the creation of a city. After gathering the required number of signatures—up to 10 percent of the registered voters of the proposed city—the petition is presented to the county constitutional court judge, who places the issue on the ballot at the next county election. A city may also be created when residents living within an existing city receive permission to leave it and form a new one. Once a city is created, it continues to exist even if the population drops below 200 people. Only a majority vote by the registered voters living in the city can dissolve it.

The Texas Constitution provides for two categories of status for cities: general law and home rule. A city is normally a **general law city**. In other words, the default status of cities when created is general law. The Texas Local Government Code specifies the exact forms of government, **ordinance** powers, and other aspects of

general law city
the default organization for Texas cities, with the exact forms of government, ordinance powers, and other aspects of city government specified in the Texas Local Government Code

ordinance
a law enacted by a city government

city government. However, general law cities often find that this arrangement is too rigid to adapt to the demands of population growth, demographic change, and economic development.

Three types of general law cities exist in Texas. These are Type A general law, Type B general law, and Type C general law cities. Type A general law cities are typically larger cities that contain at least 600 residents. They must have the strong mayor form of city government discussed next; the Texas Local Government Code calls this system the aldermanic form.[21] Type A cities may choose between SMDP and at-large election systems (discussed later in the chapter) and are required to have a wider range of city officials, either appointed or elected, than the other types. For example, Type A cities must have a tax assessor, a treasurer, a city secretary, and a city attorney. Type A cities may change their form of government to a council-manager system by vote of the residents. In contrast, Type B general law cities contain between 201 and 9,999 residents. These cities are governed by the weak mayor system described below. The city council, confusingly called the city commission in the Texas Local Government Code, must be elected using an at-large election system.[22] Type C general law cities have between 201 and 4,999 residents. These cities are required to have a commissioner form of government/ weak mayor form of government, unless in an election the residents vote to adopt the council-manager system described next.[23] The mayor and commission normally serve two-year terms in office. In addition, a Type C city must have a city clerk and a city tax assessor.

In 1912, an amendment to the Texas Constitution began to give cities more flexibility by allowing some to become home rule cities. A home rule city is a city that has been granted greater freedom in the organization and function of its city government. A general law city with 5,000 or more people may choose to become a home rule city through a proposal by the city government and a vote of the residents of the city. The advantages of home rule include the ability to adopt any of the three forms of city government, change the administrative structure by creating or abolishing departments, and alter systems of electing city officials without seeking the permission of the state. Home rule cities are governed by a city charter, subject to voter approval.[24] A city charter is a plan of government that details the structure and function of the city government. The city charter also discusses land usage within the city limits, specifies the election system for elected city officials, and details the types of ordinances, or laws passed by a city government, the city may enact. General law cities of all types lack a city charter and are governed directly by state law and city ordinances. Home rule cities have more freedom to pass ordinances and have some influence over land usage just outside the city boundaries. This land-usage power varies from half a mile for cities over 1,500 people to five miles for cities over 25,000. Home rule cities have greater powers of annexation, or the addition of areas adjacent to it into the city limits. Once a city becomes a home rule city, it retains this status even if the population falls below 5,000. Two cities in Texas—Josephine in Collin County and Latexo in Houston County—are neither home rule nor general law. This exemption seems to be related to the fact that both cities were originally created as railroad company towns.

home rule city
a city that has been granted greater freedom in the organization and functioning of city government; it can make structural and administrative changes without seeking permission from the state

city charter
a plan of government that details the structure and function of the city government; similar to a constitution

annexation
a process whereby areas adjacent to a city are added to the city, thereby extending the city limits

The Galveston Hurricane

While Hurricane Harvey has had a recent, major impact on local governments in Texas, we often overlook an earlier natural disaster that occurred over a century ago. In 1900, about 37,000 people lived in Galveston, and the city was often referred to as the "Queen City of the Gulf." The prosperous city enjoyed such luxuries as gas streetlights and theaters, funded by the commerce gained from being one of the nation's leading ports and from the investments flowing through its twenty-three stock companies. Until a few years earlier, it had the largest population in the state, briefly edging out San Antonio. Galveston reflected the optimism of the time. It had been hit by hurricanes in 1867 and 1875 but continued to rebuild and thrive, despite dire warnings about future storms.

The storm that hit on September 8, 1900, proved to be more powerful than any before, producing winds of 120 miles per hour and a fifteen-foot storm surge on an island whose highest point was only nine feet above sea level. The storm killed about 6,000 people and destroyed 3,600 buildings—more than half the buildings in the city.

After the devastation created by the hurricane, residents feared that Galveston would suffer the same fate as Indianola, which went from being the second-largest port in the state to obscurity after being hit by storms in 1875 and 1886. In response to the crisis, the citizens of Galveston created a new system of government designed to facilitate the rebuilding. Under the so-called Galveston Plan, the city was initially governed by five commissioners that were partly elected and partly appointed by the governor, although later the legislature modified the system to require citywide election of all commissioners. Commissioners were chosen citywide to promote cooperation across parts of the city and minimize the corruption brought by localized "bosses," who might dispense jobs in return for political support. Collectively, the commission wrote the basic policies of the city as did other city councils. However, in addition to these general duties, each commissioner administered a specific portion of the city's functions, such as safety or public works.

The city's recovery under the Galveston Plan was considered remarkable. The city constructed a seawall seven miles long and seventeen feet high. Thirty million cubic yards of sand were pumped from the Gulf of Mexico to raise the ground level of the city by seventeen feet, and the houses that survived the storm were raised and placed on new higher foundations. These preparations would help the city survive subsequent hurricanes in 1909 and 1915.

The Galveston Plan became one of the most widely adopted reforms of the Progressive Era. Houston adopted the system in 1905, and by 1917, about seventy-five Texas cities and 500 cities nationwide were using the commission form, which was embraced by reformers, including presidents Theodore Roosevelt and Woodrow Wilson.

Ironically, the Galveston Plan can no longer be found in Galveston or anywhere in Texas. The city, like many others, has adopted the council-manager form of government. Economically, Galveston lost much of its luster after Houston succeeded in dredging a ship channel that allowed it to create a port that brought railroads and ships together in a safer inland location. While Galveston's charming historic residences and buildings have kept it a popular tourist destination, the city is no longer a major commercial center. In addition, Galveston is once again facing a challenge as recent surveys have indicated that the island is gradually sinking, meaning that the city will once again have to band together to hold off the sea.

Forms of City Government

There are three basic forms of city government in Texas: the weak mayor-council system, the strong mayor-council system, and the council-manager system (see Figures 11.2–11.4). The strong mayor-council system occurs when the voters of the city elect a mayor as the chief executive and a city council to serve as the city's legislature. The mayor serves as the head of the city's executive branch, develops the city budget, appoints the heads of the departments of city government, sets the agenda for the council, and serves as chief administrator of the city's departments. The mayor also serves as a symbol of the city at important functions such as opening new businesses, speaking on behalf of a city's residents, attending conferences with other mayors, and negotiating on behalf of the city. In many cities, the mayor may veto ordinances passed by the city council. The city council serves as the representative of the city residents. As the legislative branch of city government, the city council is responsible for passing ordinances; in some cities, the council may override a veto by the mayor. In addition, the council approves the city budget. In small cities, the mayor and council members may be part-time positions. In large cities, both positions may be well compensated because serving as mayor or sitting on the council is a full-time job. In Texas, the strong mayor system is sometimes called the mayor-council, mayor-commission, or mayor-aldermanic form of government.

The advantage of the strong mayor system is the concentration of power in the hands of the mayor. The mayor provides leadership on issues of the day and sets the priorities of the city. The mayor's control over the city budget and over the city's departments allows for greater harmony and efficiency in policy implementation. In addition, the strong mayor system mirrors the separation of powers between the executive and legislative branches of government found in the national government. However, the concentration of power in the hands of the mayor may lead to personality-driven politics, to the detriment of the city. The power of the mayor also reduces the influence of the city council, which is designed to be the representative branch of city government.

In contrast, the weak mayor-council system features a directly elected mayor whose powers are much more diluted relative to those of the city council. Although the mayor still oversees the day-to-day operations of the city, the mayor and city council share power over the creation and adoption of the city budget. Collectively, the mayor and city council choose the heads of the various city departments and jointly oversee the city bureaucracy. In some cities, voters directly elect the heads of the various city

FIGURE 11.2 Mayor-Council Form of City Government with a Weak Mayor

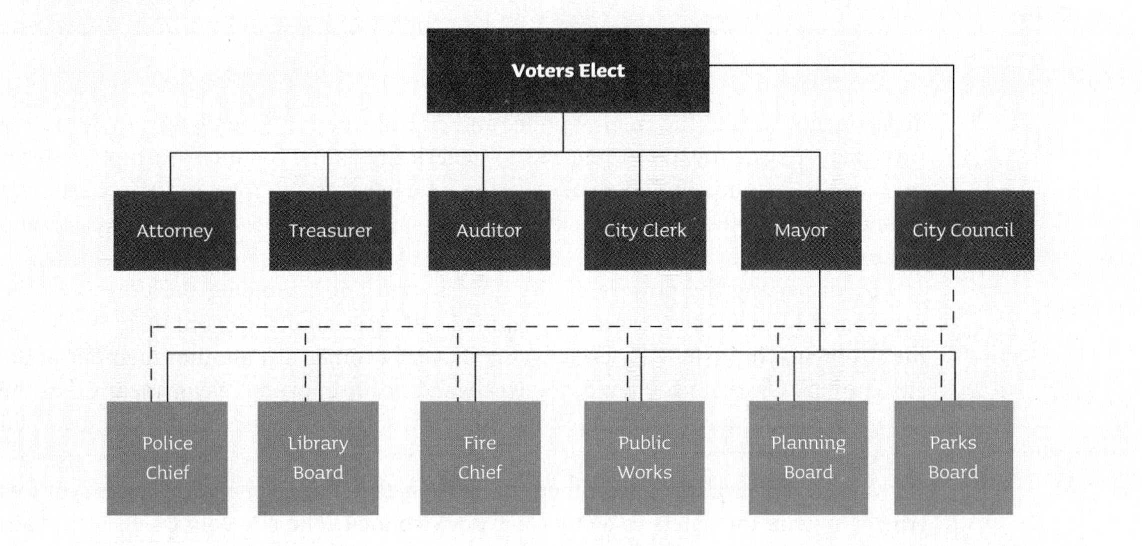

FIGURE 11.3 Mayor-Council Form of City Government with a Strong Mayor

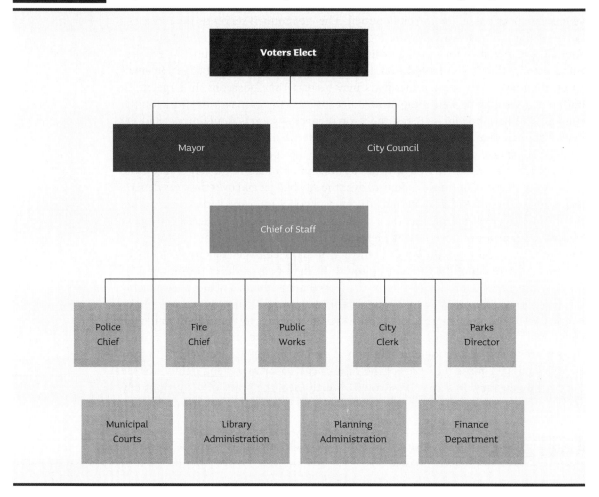

departments, such as the chief of police and city attorney, independently. In Texas, the weak mayor system is often referred to generically as the "council" form of government or the "commission" form of government. However, this form of city government should not be confused with the city commissioner system once used by Galveston and some other cities in Texas.

By dispersing the powers of city government and balancing the powers of the mayor and council, the weak mayor-council system attempts to avoid the problems of the strong mayor system. Essentially, the mayor becomes just another member of the city council. On the other hand, the weakened position of the mayor means that the city government may be less able to act quickly, since in essence the city is governed by a committee.

A third form of city government in Texas is the council-manager system. In this type of system, the voters in a city elect a city council. The city council, in turn, then hires a manager to run the day-to-day administrative functions of the city. The manager

FIGURE 11.4 Council-Manager Form of City Government

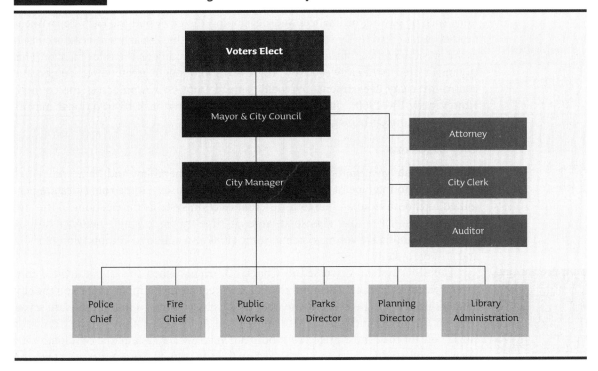

proposes new ordinances for the city council to consider and develops the city budget. The city manager also hires the heads of the city departments and oversees those departments. The city manager is essentially chief executive officer (CEO) of the city, similar to a business. Usually, the city manager is hired based on professional qualifications, including prior experience in city government and an academic background in public administration or political science. Confusion sometimes arises when a council-manager system includes an elected "mayor." In this situation, the mayor is actually elected to the city council just like every other member. The "mayor" serves merely as a figurehead and holds no significant power beyond that of a member of the city council. In some cities, the "mayor" serves as the presiding officer of the city council. Council-manager systems, sometimes called commission-manager systems, are most common among Texas's home rule cities.

The advantage of the council-manager system is the removal of day-to-day administration of the city from the turmoil of politics. Routine decisions can be made outside partisan politics or personality politics common to the elected offices of the mayor-council system. The resulting management of city government in a council-manager system is assumed to be both more professional and more efficient than in alternative systems. However, because city managers are involved in formulating policies for the city and are charged with initiating the city budget, in practice they almost inevitably become involved in politics as well.

A final form of city government, pioneered by Galveston after the 1900 hurricane that devastated the city, contains a city council comprising the heads of the various city

Research the form of city government used where you live or attend college. Is the city governed by home rule or general law? Is the city government mayor-council or council-manager? Is your city best served by this form of government?

⭐ CRITICAL THINKING

departments. Thus, the chief of police, chief of the fire department, commissioner of streets and bridges, head of the library, etc., sit as the city's legislature to perform functions such as passing ordinances and developing the city's budget. Each department head is elected directly by voters throughout the city. One department head is chosen as the presiding officer of the city council, sometimes taking on the title of mayor. This system, favored in the early 1900s by progressives who sought greater direct democratic control over city departments by voters, spread from Galveston across the country. However, by the 1960s, cities in Texas began reverting back to traditional mayor-council and council-manager systems.

City Elections

The Texas state government distinguishes between general law and home rule cities with respect to the type of election system that a city uses. Home rule cities are permitted to choose from among four different election systems for elections to the city council. These cities may choose at-large, at-large by place, single-member district (SMD), or cumulative voting systems. Some cities also employ a combination of SMD and at-large systems.

The SMD system, discussed in Chapter 3, occurs when the city is divided into several election districts. The number of districts equals the number of seats on the city council. Each district elects one member of the city council so that if there are seven seats on the city council then, there are seven districts. Voters in each district cast a single vote for their most preferred candidate. In an SMDP system, the candidate with the most votes in the district wins the seat on the city council. Some cities adhere to the single-member district majority (SMDM) system, which requires the winning candidate to win a majority of the votes, or 50 percent of the votes plus one additional vote.

In an at-large system, candidates compete for seats on the city council without reference to specific districts or seats on the council. Instead, voters are allowed to vote for as many candidates as there are seats on the council. For example, if there are seven seats on the city council and eighteen candidates running for office, each voter will vote for up to seven of the eighteen candidates. The candidates with the most votes, up to the total number of seats on the city council, win election to the council. If there are seven seats on the council, the seven candidates with the most votes of the eighteen are elected to the council.

A variation of the at-large system is the at-large by place system. In this system, candidates declare that they are running for particular positions or seats or "places" on the city council. The candidate for each seat that receives the most votes wins that seat. Thus, if there are seven seats on the city council, a candidate decides for which seat he or she is running. At the election, a voter has seven votes and chooses one candidate running for each of the seven seats. The key difference between the at-large and the at-large by place system is the fact that in the at-large by place system, candidates are grouped into different seats or "places" on the ballot. In contrast to the SMD system, the seats or places for which candidates compete lack any connection to specific geographic areas or neighborhoods in the city. Instead, candidates select which of the positions or places on the council for which to run.

The final system is the cumulative voting system. Like an at-large election, all candidates compete for seats on the city council without reference to specific seats, places, or districts. Voters possess a number of votes equal to the number of seats on the council. However, voters may choose to give all of their votes for the same candidate or may spread their votes among several candidates. Thus, if the city council contains seven seats, a voter may give all seven votes to the same candidate or may give three votes to one candidate and four votes to another candidate. The voter may spread the votes among as many or few candidates as the voter desires, so long as the voter casts no more votes than there are seats on the council. The candidates with the most votes, up to the number of seats on the council, win election to the city council. Again, if there are seven seats, the top seven candidates win.

Advocates of the SMD system suggest that the direct connection between a member of the city council and the voters is an advantage. Each voter knows that a specific member of the council represents the voter's area of the city. If a problem occurs, the voter knows exactly whom to approach. Thus, government should be more responsive to citizens. Another advantage is that SMD city elections appear to increase racial and ethnic diversity among the candidates that are elected to the city council. This prospect for minority representation is an outgrowth of the Voting Rights Act of 1965 (discussed in Chapter 3). Since the 1970s, many cities in Texas have moved from at-large systems to SMD systems, including El Paso, Fort Worth, and San Antonio. However, district systems suffer from the same issues of partisan gerrymandering that occur with the state legislature and U.S. House of Representatives. In the late 1800s and early 1900s, the SMD system became associated with city-based machine politics, in which political organizations headed by a local party boss controlled specific seats on the city council by using city jobs, government contracts, and other giveaways. The party boss ran the city for personal power and gain.

machine politics
a system of patronage whereby political organizations, led by a local party boss, disperse city jobs, government contracts, and other benefits to maintain control of city governance; power, once acquired, is typically used for personal gain

The advantage of the at-large system is the ability of the city council to act on behalf of the entire city and to consider ordinances and policies from the perspective of the whole city, not the particularistic views of an area or neighborhood in the city. Citywide campaigns may also produce better-qualified candidates with broad-based, citywide appeal. At-large systems served in the past as a method of solving the machine politics problem associated with SMD systems. However, at-large systems have been used in Texas to suppress minority votes, especially those of African American and Hispanic voters. Very simply, the Caucasian majority historically voted exclusively for white candidates, effectively overwhelming minority voters and candidates. In some cities, members of the council have consistently come from wealthy areas in town, and less well-off and minority voters have found themselves governed by officials who see or understand little about where minority voters live. In contrast, the SMD systems allow creation of majority-minority districts to boost minority representation, as discussed in Chapter 3.

Cumulative voting advocates point to the ability of voters to express intensity of preference among the candidates running for the city council. By giving three or four votes to the same candidate, a voter indicates a greater preference for that candidate than if the voter gives only one or two votes for a candidate. Another advantage is the ability to enhance minority voting by concentrating votes. If minorities concentrate their votes among one or two candidates, while whites disperse votes among several candidates, the likelihood of minority candidates winning is increased. Evidence from school board elections in Texas suggests that minority representation is enhanced under cumulative voting.[25] However, because few local governments use this system, the question remains whether or not minority representation is actually increased. Also, the concentration or dispersal of votes creates a greater possibility of spoiled ballots, especially in comparison to SMD systems. A spoiled ballot occurs when a voter mismarks a ballot in such a way as to invalidate the ballot, causing it not to be counted. In an SMD system, a voter simply chooses the most preferred candidate and casts only the single vote. In cumulative voting, the voter must be careful not to cast more votes than positions to be elected. If there are six seats on the city council, accidentally casting seven votes would spoil the ballot. The ballot and the votes on the ballot would not be counted. Because a voter may give multiple votes to candidates and may spread the votes across several candidates, the likelihood of spoiled ballots increases relative to the SMD system.

Some cities attempt to have the best of both worlds by creating a hybrid of the SMD system and at-large system. Houston is an example of a city that pursues a hybrid approach. The fourteen-member city council in Houston consists of nine members elected from SMDs and five members elected at large. A candidate chooses to either run in the district in which he or she lives or conduct a citywide campaign for an at-large seat. Proponents of this system point to the ability to balance the geographic link between a particular neighborhood or part of the city and a specific member of the city council found in the SMD system and the broader, citywide orientation of the at-large members that a hybrid system allows. In addition, ethnic and racial minorities continue to benefit from the preservation of the district system in electing minority candidates to the city council.

Election systems in city politics remain an area of change and transition in Texas. City governments, especially those that utilize home rule, are more successful than county- or state-level governments in securing more representative outcomes—for example, the election of minorities to the city council. The shift away from at-large and at-large by place systems to SMDs is indicative of this change. In some cities, experiments with hybrid systems containing both at-large and SMD seats also demonstrate the adaptability of Texas cities. Whether cities will make additional changes to election systems based on the recent success of cumulative voting in producing more diverse city councils and school boards remains uncertain.

Issues in City Government

Because city government is typically the level of government closest to the people, cities address a large number of issues that will most directly and immediately affect Texas residents. Most of the streets within a city's boundaries are maintained by the city government. Cities often provide a variety of services to residents, including libraries, museums, and parks. Cities offer public health and safety services, such as police protection, fire protection, restaurant inspections, and child care facility inspections. Many also engage in policies to attract new businesses to the community for the purposes of economic development.

Zoning and Planning Policies

Zoning and planning policies are among the most controversial issues that cities confront. Given the average Texan's attitudes toward land, including a commitment to the idea that individuals retain maximum rights to use their property as they see fit, conflicts between individual property owners and the broader needs of the city are inevitable. This desire to allow individual owners to maintain absolute control over their property is a key reason why Houston, despite being among the largest cities in the United States, has largely avoided the issue of zoning. In zoning policy, the city restricts what property owners may do with their property. Most often, zoning involves designating parts of a city for residential use, commercial use, and industrial use. Residential-use restrictions may include designating an area single-family housing only, limiting the number of houses that can be built per acre, or permitting apartments and condominiums only in certain areas. Commercial zoning restrictions may include specifying where large-scale shopping centers and shopping malls may be built, limiting the number of entrances or exits to businesses' parking lots, or restricting the location of establishments that serve alcoholic beverages. Industrial zoning restrictions involve identifying where large factories, industrial plants, and high-tech firms may build their facilities. Other issues addressed by zoning policies range from the size of signage that a business may erect to regulations on how residential homes are built.

Zoning and planning often pit those seeking to develop property, build new shopping centers, or construct more houses against established neighborhoods. These battles are usually played out in local politics. Often, individuals do not want certain types of zoning in their neighborhood like a shopping center, public school, or airport. While these services are needed, city officials get caught in the middle of such disputes. The term NIMBY, or "not in my backyard," refers to the tendency of individuals to want certain services and businesses in their community but not in their neighborhood. Zoning and planning plays a role in historic preservation. Historic districts require that changes to buildings in the area be approved by a review board so that they conform to the historic look of the area.[26] In some instances, local zoning laws in historic areas have prevented developers from buying older homes, tearing down the homes, and building McMansions, large homes over 3,000 square feet in size.

Zoning and planning also became important during the impact of and recovery from Hurricane Harvey. True to Texas's rugged individualism, Houston remains a largely deregulated metropolitan area in terms of land use policy. This approach empowers large scale developers of industrial, commercial, and residential property to build with a maximum amount of freedom, without significant city or county oversight.

After Harvey, the Houston city council began to rethink some policies, including imposing new regulations to reduce the impact of future floods. For example, new homes in some flood-prone areas

How does the NIMBY ("not in my backyard") problem in local government relate to, or contradict, the role of personal responsibility of citizens to their neighbors?

★ **PERSONAL RESPONSIBILITY**

Photo Courtesy City of Texarkana, Texas

The Texarkana City Council poses for a photo. Texarkana is one of many Texas cities that are experiencing gains in minority and women's representation, reflecting the state's increasing diversity.

must be raised up to eight feet higher, and the impact of new developments is being considered against the 500-year floodplain, not the current 100-year one.[27] Moreover, substantially damaged homes with repairs costing 50 percent of the home's value are to be flagged, and requests for building permits are to be reviewed for compliance with the 500-year floodplain height requirements.[28] Other communities in the greater Houston area, including Waller County, Montgomery County, and the City of Humble, have adopted similar regulations. Also under consideration are measures to change the density of development, flood control management, and reliance on roadways as a channel for runoff water.[29]

Annexation and Economic Development

Another issue related to zoning and planning is annexation. When a city wishes to expand its borders, the expansion may occur for several reasons. The residents of the area that the city plans to expand to may want to be annexed. The residents may see benefits to being within the city limits, including access to services the city provides—perhaps the city has a good police department or excellent fire protection, or maybe the city's water system is superior to that of the county.

Economic development may be spurred by annexation, making annexation an attractive prospect. The city adds new territory in order to entice new businesses to locate in the area. Similarly, cities seek to expand to prevent themselves from becoming hemmed in, surrounded by other cities. Once a city is surrounded on all sides by other cities, it is developmentally, and hence perhaps economically, limited. Population growth and economic development can then occur only within the existing city's land capacity. Cities may also annex areas to increase revenue. Newly annexed areas provide new sources of property and sales taxes. Cities especially desire to annex areas that are economically and financially well-off. In addition, the annexation of new areas allows cities to receive more money from the state and national governments. Often, funding formulas for grants are tied to a city's size. Politically, larger cities receive more seats in the state legislature as well. State law permits cities to annex up to 10 percent of their land area each year. If a city annexes less than 10 percent, then the difference may be carried over to another year. However, a city may not annex more than 30 percent of its land area in any given year.[30]

Economic development in cities may occur through means other than annexation. Attracting the right businesses into a community produces the rewards of population growth and economic growth. These results, in turn, may allow a city to attract even more businesses. New businesses generate new jobs and pay taxes, giving city governments more reason to welcome newcomers. To attract businesses, cities often provide incentives, such as rebates on city sales tax and reductions on property tax rates. Cities often build infrastructure for businesses as well: access roads to the business, water lines to the property, and other essentials that the business may require. On the downside, more development means more traffic to channel, more children to educate, more garbage to collect, and more services of every kind to provide.

City Government versus State Laws

An ongoing controversy in city government in Texas is the efforts by Texas cities to supersede or go beyond state laws. These efforts have included a diverse range of topics including hydraulic fracking, sanctuary cities, and civil rights for lesbian, gay, bisexual, and transgender (LGBT) people. From the cities' perspectives, state law creates a minimum, or floor, for various policies areas, but cities are free to act above and beyond state law, adding additional policies, acting where the state has not acted, or extending civil rights beyond that of the state of Texas. From the state's perspective, state law creates a ceiling or maximum for these policy areas, and cities should not act beyond what the state allows.

The city of Denton illustrates the issue of city-state conflict in the area of hydraulic fracking. Hydraulic fracking is a method of using pressurized liquids to create small fractures in deep rock to allow natural gas or petroleum to migrate to a well to be pumped to the surface. While the liquid, often a brine solution of water and chemical additives, is kept at a pressure level to replace the rock formation that is fractured, the practice of fracking has become controversial for its potential contamination of ground water and other water supplies, noise pollution, spills and backflows, and possibility of causing earthquakes.

In the spring of 2014, opponents of fracking began to campaign for a petition to allow residents of Denton, located north of the metroplex, to vote in November of that year to ban fracking outright. This drive by an organized interest, the Denton Drilling Awareness Group, came after the city of Denton expanded its required zone to 1,200 feet between a residence and a proposed well. While not as restrictive as Dallas's 1,500 feet, the Denton ordinance resulted in allegations that Eagle Rock Energy had violated the law by drilling wells within city limits without permits.[31] When the petition was submitted to the city government, the city placed a temporary ban on the drilling of new wells. Voters approved a permanent ban on fracking in the November 2014 election. However, within days of the election, lawsuits challenging the ban had been filed in state courts. By the 2015 session of the Texas Legislature, the issue of Denton's ban, combined with actions and possible actions by other city councils, prompted the Texas Legislature to pass House Bill (HB) 40, which Governor Greg Abbott signed into law. That bill prohibits cities from passing ordinances that ban fracking. Shortly thereafter, the Texas Oil and Gas Association and the general land office filed suit in state courts to overturn the Denton ordinance banning hydraulic fracking because the ban now violates state law and cities may not pass ordinances that conflict with state laws and constitution. After a state judge placed a moratorium on the city of Denton from enforcing the fracking ban ordinance, the city council repealed the ban on a 6–1 vote.[32] The state of Texas then withdrew the lawsuit against Denton.

Local governments attempt to use their ordinance-making powers to protect local homeowners and reflect the public policy beliefs of the local citizens who elect them. Local voters often oppose fracking in their communities for the drawbacks that were just listed. However, these innovative uses of zoning and planning policies place city ordinances in conflict with state lawmakers in Austin. State lawmakers tend to reflect broader public interests, including general majority public opinion in the state. Some lawmakers support fracking because it allows local property owners to sell or lease the mineral rights to their property to a company that will drill on their property and neighboring properties. Thus, bans on fracking conflict with property ownership.[33] (Chapter 13 addresses the economic and environmental impacts of fracking in greater detail.)

Immigration Policy

This attempt to use city ordinance-making power to supersede or move beyond state law has occurred in other policy areas as well. In immigration policy, some cities in Texas have declared themselves sanctuary cities. These cities have enacted ordinances that prohibit city police and other law enforcement agencies from complying with national immigration laws related to illegals—for example, working with the U.S. government to identify illegal immigrants and to aid in the deportation of illegal immigrants. Such sanctuary cities include Austin, Dallas, Denton, Katy, and McAllen. After an attempt to pass a bill limiting or prohibiting Texas cities from passing sanctuary cities ordinances in the 2015 session of the Texas Legislature failed, the debate has reemerged. In November 2015, when Dallas County sheriff Lupe Valdez announced she was going to honor requests from the U.S. Immigration and Customs Enforcement (ICE) agency to hold ICE detainers on a case-by-case basis, the reaction from the state government was quick. Governor Abbott denounced Valdez's case-by-case approach and indicated calling for total and complete compliance with the U.S. government in rounding up illegals. Abbott called for legislation in the 2017 session to ban sanctuary city ordinances and make it a violation of state law to fail to turn over an illegal immigrant to ICE when requested.[34] The Texas Legislature complied, passing Senate Bill 4, which makes it a Class A misdemeanor subject to fines of up to $25,500 for failure to comply with U.S. government authorities or for not honoring requests to hold noncitizens subject to deportation. However, the bill went further to allow law enforcement officials in Texas to question a person's immigration status during questioning, not just after arrest. This "show-me-your-papers" provision was heavily opposed by Democrats and the Hispanic community in Texas as implicating all persons of color.[35] The law also requires public colleges and universities to comply with federal authorities.

Dallas County sheriff Lupe Valdez challenged state lawmakers when she refused to work with federal officials attempting to deport illegal immigrants. Valdez later agreed to work on a case-by-case basis to turn certain immigrants over to federal authorities. Her efforts led to prominence in state politics, allowing Valdez to run for and to receive the Democratic party nomination for Governor in 2018.

A battle ensued as cities including Houston, Dallas, San Antonio, Austin, and El Paso filed lawsuits against the new law. El Paso County and Maverick County filed lawsuits as well. Texas attorney general Ken Paxton filed a preemptive lawsuit against the City of Austin and Travis County, but that lawsuit was dismissed by judge Sam Sparks of the U.S. District Court for the Western District of Texas.[36] Shortly thereafter, a case filed by several cities and counties challenging the constitutionality of the law was heard by judge Orlando Garcia; the judge suspended many parts of the law, awaiting actual oral arguments before his bench. However, Texas appealed Garcia's opinion to the Fifth Circuit Court of Appeals in New Orleans, where the court overturned most of Garcia's ruling and allowed most of the law to become enforceable.[37]

FEDERALISM IN *Action*

LGBT in the Workplace

Although the Supreme Court has ruled that all states must recognize same-sex marriage, other rights for same-sex couples are still denied by many states and local communities. Texas has an estimated 429,000 lesbian, gay, bisexual, and transgender (LGBT) individuals active in the workplace, and those individuals face a wide range of discrimination.[i] Complaints and lawsuits indicate the LGBT community faces open hostility and harassment, such as the Austin police detective who accused male colleagues of showing her pornographic pictures of women, making inappropriate comments, and asking if she wanted to have sex with female detainees.[ii] Discrimination in hiring practices and pay and promotion are also alleged, with same-sex couples earning a median income that is 9 percent less than that of different-sex couples.[iii]

There is no statewide law prohibiting discrimination based on sexual orientation or gender identity, but a handful of cities in Texas have passed local ordinances protecting the employees in that city. In 2000, Fort Worth became the first city in the state to pass an ordinance outlawing discrimination based on sexual orientation; that law was later expanded to include gender identity.[iv] While a growing number of cities, counties, and school districts have passed ordinances and adopted policies to protect LGBT persons, these decisions often vary in terms of who is covered and what is protected. In addition, some private companies, including most of the large companies headquartered in the state, have prohibited discrimination as well as the University of Texas (UT) and Texas A&M systems. Still, nearly 86 percent of Texas's workforce is not protected from such discrimination.[v]

At the state level, there seems little momentum to protect LGBT individuals against workplace discrimination. In fact, several anti-LGBT bills were introduced in the 85th state legislature, ranging from prohibiting individuals to use the bathroom that corresponds to their gender identity to nullifying and banning local laws designed to prevent LGBT discrimination. Although none of these bills passed, the special session in the summer of 2017 attempted to pass anti-LGBT legislation. This issue is certain to reemerge in the 2019 session of the Texas Legislature. As the 2015 battle in Houston over the Houston Equal Rights Ordinance (HERO) amendment illustrates, state legislators appear unwilling to let local communities pass LGBT antidiscrimination laws. The Equality Act has been introduced in the national Congress to expand the Civil Rights Act of 1964, which prohibits discrimination in hiring based on race and sex, to include sexual orientation and gender identity. So far, though, the national government has not been able to pass such legislation.

> Should the national, state, or local government be the primary level of government addressing LGBT rights? Why?

 CRITICAL THINKING

i. Christy Mallory and Brad Sears, "Employment Discrimination Based on Sexual Orientation and Gender Identity in Texas," Williams Institute, April 2015, http://williamsinstitute.law.ucla .edu/wp-content/uploads/Texas-ND-May-2015.pdf.

ii. Ciara O'Rourke, "Austin Detective Sues City over Sexual Harassment, Retaliation Claims," *Austin American-Statesman*, December 29, 2014, http:// www.mystatesman.com/news/ news/crime-law/austin-detective-sues-city-over-sexual-harassment-/ mHsdyWrn1xaOZSvHRvp8zK/.

iii. Mallory and Sears, "Employment Discrimination Based on Sexual Orientation and Gender Identity in Texas."

iv. Alexa Ura, Edgar Walters, and Jolie McCullough, "Comparing Nondiscrimination Protections in Texas Cities," *Texas Tribune*, June 9, 2016, https://www.texastribune.org/2016/06/09/ comparing-nondiscrimination-ordinances-texas.

v. Mallory and Sears, "Employment Discrimination Based on Sexual Orientation and Gender Identity in Texas."

The sanctuary cities debate is mirrored in California; however, the relationship is reversed. California state lawmakers passed a bill declaring the entire state to be a "sanctuary," opposing the deportation of perceived illegal immigrants by the U.S. government under President Donald Trump. California's law limited the ability of local government to work with U.S. federal authorities and to comply with requests to detain or check the status of suspected illegal residents.[38] In response, the city of Los Alamitos revolted, officially passing an ordinance in opposition to the state law. Over a dozen cities and two counties passed similar ordinances.[39] Lawsuits have been filed against the state government by California's cities and counties as well.

LGBT Rights

A final, major issue that involves conflicts between Texas cities and state government surrounds the rights of LGBT people. At least twelve cities with populations over 100,000 have passed ordinances that protect LGBT people. Bexar, Dallas, and Walker counties have passed county-wide ordinances, and at least seven school districts have non-discrimination policies as well. These ordinances ban discrimination in employment, housing, and public accommodation. The purpose of these ordinances is to ensure that LGBT persons have the same civil rights and protections from discrimination as other classifications of persons—for example, racial and ethnic groups like African Americans or Hispanics. Cities enacting such ordinances see their actions as moving beyond the existing civil rights protections endorsed by the state into new areas of emerging civil rights. In some way, one may see the state law and constitution as establishing a floor of civil rights, while these cities are attempting to move beyond the floor to maximize rights for others as well. These cities are acting in addition to and in absence of state law, constitution, and policy. Moreover, these cities are acting as representatives of their residents who elected them into positions of city government like city councils and city mayors. If power is localized, then city governments are acting in the interest of local preferences.

However, state leaders including Governor Greg Abbott and Lieutenant Governor Dan Patrick have denounced these efforts. Their actions certainly represent a defense of traditional concepts of sexuality and gender identity. Moreover, attempts by the city of Houston to pressure religious conservatives during the debate over the HERO ordinance only encouraged more resistance by state government officials. During the HERO debate, the city of Houston issued subpoenas to pastors of religiously conservative, mostly Protestant Christian churches for their sermons and office correspondence. Since these churches and their leaders reflect traditional views of marriage and human sexuality, the city of Houston sought evidence that the opposition to HERO coming from religious conservatives violated regulations prohibiting churches and other non-profit organizations from engaging in direct political campaigning. Religious leaders from these churches denounced the actions as government intimidation. In 2017, the Texas Legislature passed a law, signed by Governor Abbott, protecting sermons from government subpoenas.

Finally, the state successfully argued before the Texas Supreme Court in 2017 that the landmark *Obergefell v. Hodges* (2015) case legalizing same-sex marriage nationwide does not require Texas, or its local governments, to extend marital like health care to spouses of same-sex couples. In this case, brought by the city of Houston, the city tried to force the state into extending benefits to same-sex couples. After losing in the Texas Supreme Court, the city of Houston appealed to the U.S. Supreme Court, which refused to hear the case.

Since cities are ultimately creations of the state government, arguably, state officials are also indicating that issues like civil rights are best defined statewide, creating a single statewide policy or law. Such a statewide, single-policy approach moves power from the level of government closest to the voters like cities to a more removed level of government: the state. To date, the state however has not taken actions to limit cities' abilities to pass such ordinances.

City Budgets

City budgets are often a source of conflict. Budgets are generated by a variety of sources. Cities levy property taxes just like counties do. They may collect franchise fees, for example, which are fees paid by cable television, electrical power, and natural gas providers operating within the city limits. Cities also raise revenue from hotel and motel occupancy taxes and from fines from traffic tickets issued by police. They may also raise money by levying sales taxes on purchases made within the city limits. To fund special projects, such as acquiring land for parks, building city courthouses, or establishing a city museum, cities may issue **municipal bonds**, which are certificates of indebtedness. When a city issues municipal bonds, it is essentially pledging to pay back a loan over time with interest. Regardless of the sources of revenue, the city must prioritize how to spend what it raises. Because revenues are limited, emphasizing the expansion of the city park system or the building of new sidewalks inevitably means less money for other projects, such as public health initiatives or erecting new streetlights.

A variety of contrasts between cities and counties exist in Texas. At a basic level, counties are the creation of the state government and exist solely to carry out specific functions the state legislature and constitution designate. Cities, in contrast, are created by citizens and residents who seek additional services from local government that counties are not able to provide. While the Texas Legislature and Texas Constitution ultimately determine what cities may or may not do, cities are established by citizens.

Another key difference is that cities, unlike counties, are allowed some flexibility in the form of government and election system they employ, which allows them a degree of transition and change to adapt to new circumstances. As Texas continues to experience high population growth rates in the early twenty-first century, the needs of citizens for more, better, and faster services require flexibility. The concentration of the state's population in metropolitan areas, including the development of massive suburbs and bedroom communities on the sites of former pine forests, farms, and ranches, has created—and continues to create—profound challenges to city and county governments. Although flexibility is most evident in home rule cities, Type B general law cities possess a degree of flexibility as well. Because cities can collect revenue from a wider variety of sources, they can adapt to change more readily than counties. They can also exert influence on the zoning and use of land just outside their boundaries. Counties lack this ability. In fact, a city's influence may infringe on the rights of property owners outside the city limits and on the ability of counties to regulate land use within unincorporated areas of the county near the city's boundaries. Larger cities with home rule status are also freer of state control over their plan of government, the content of city ordinances, and the process of changing these arrangements.

municipal bond
a certificate of indebtedness issued by a city that serves as a pledge by the city to pay back the loan over time with interest; used to raise money for services and infrastructure; may also be issued by other forms of local government, such as counties, school districts, and special districts

Homeowner Associations: Not Quite a Government, but Close

While not technically a form of government, homeowner associations (HOAs) exercise powers similar to cities and counties in Texas. HOAs are legally chartered institutions under Texas law. Typically, an HOA is created by a developer or builder of homes to ensure that an aesthetic look and feel to a neighborhood is maintained. HOAs also provide services to residents, such as golf courses, swimming pools, walking trails, clubhouses, and other amenities that enhance the quality of life. Some HOAs even employ their own security services to handle minor issues that arise in the neighborhood. HOAs may also be created by those who own houses or property in the neighborhood.

An HOA is usually governed by a board elected by those who own houses or vacant lots in the neighborhood. Votes are determined by the amount of land owned. If all lots are the same size throughout the neighborhood, then once the neighborhood is complete, each person will have the same vote. However, if some lots are bigger than others, votes may be allocated proportionally to the amount of land owned. To illustrate, if a neighborhood is going to cover twenty acres of land, and ten acres will be divided into one-acre lots, then each of the owners of those lots will receive one vote. If the remaining ten acres will consist of five two-acre lots, then an owner of a five-acre lot will receive two votes (one for each acre) in the HOA. Often, a developer or builder retains significant control over the HOA during the actual building and development process, since he or she retains ownership of the land until houses are built and sold. To follow the previously given example, in our twenty-acre neighborhood, if all ten of the one-acre lots are sold and none of the two-acre lots are sold, then there will be ten people with one vote and the developer with ten votes (two votes for each of the five lots of two acres).

The HOA governing board is responsible for the upkeep of any amenities provided by the HOA, ensuring that bills are paid and seeing that dues are large enough to cover expenses. The board also checks to make sure the rules and covenants of the HOA are followed by homeowners. Some of these rules are often very specific, such as the color of paint you may use on your house, the architectural style of any additions to your home, or even the types of plants in your flower beds. If individuals fail to pay their dues or violate the rules, the HOA is legally able to rectify the situation. These remedies may include sending letters and notices; levying fines; and, in extreme cases in Texas, filing liens on homeowners, garnishing wages, or seeking foreclosures. Some HOAs have architectural committees that approve new homes, monitoring the style of the home, size of the home, number of stories, and how the home fits on the lot. Other HOAs may have the entire board act to approve new construction. These approval processes may also apply to outbuildings such as detached garages or storage units on the property, types of fencing materials used, and even plantings in flower beds.

Following the Texas Legislature's investigation of potential abuses by HOAs in 2010 and 2011, new laws were passed to reform HOA activities. Open records requirements are now in place to ensure homeowners are

Tim Weir

Nancy Hentschel ran afoul of her HOA when she placed these dinosaur statues on her lawn. Her neighborhood in Sugar Land tightly regulates homes and lawns, almost like a government.

TEXAS Legends

Tommy Joe Vandergriff

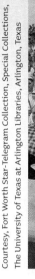

When Tom Vandergriff became mayor of Arlington, Texas, in 1951, the city of 7,000 residents spread over four square miles and was described by some as "the 'dash' between Dallas and Fort Worth." Only twenty-five years old when he was elected, Vandergriff might have seemed an unlikely candidate to transform his community. In his almost twenty-six years of service, however, he played a central role in the transformation of Arlington into a business, sports, entertainment, and education hub in North Texas.

One of Vandergriff's first endeavors was to help bring a $33 million General Motors auto assembly plant to Arlington. This required negotiating a deal for a 250-acre plot of land big enough to host the plant and forging an agreement for the state to build a highway to the site in order to ensure materials could be shipped in and new cars could be shipped out efficiently. The plant opened in 1953 and by 2014 employed 4,500 workers who built about 1,140 Escalade, Tahoe, Suburban, and Yukon sport utility vehicles daily.

To put the city on the map with regard to higher education, Vandergriff played a role in turning Arlington State College into a four-year school in 1959 and brought the school into the University of Texas (UT) system in 1965. UT Arlington is currently designated an emerging research university, offering numerous degrees to more than 33,000 students.

Vandergriff's plans did not end there. After visiting Disneyland in the 1950s, Vandergriff decided to bring a theme park to Arlington. With his encouragement, developer Angus Wynne Jr. led the building of Six Flags Over Texas. The historically themed park opened in 1961, and in the half century since its inception it has become the anchor of one of the world's largest theme park chains, with eighteen parks spread across the United States, Mexico, and Canada. The park attracts more than 3 million visitors every year.

Vandergriff believed that making Arlington a major city also required Major League Baseball. In 1959, he won voter approval of a $9.5 million bond issue to construct a baseball stadium, and he set about looking for a Major League Baseball team. His first choice was the Houston Astros, but he was met with opposition from Astros owner Judge Roy Hofheinz, who received support from his friend, President Lyndon Johnson. The president spent more than an hour on the phone with Vandergriff, trying to convince him that Texas had room for only one major league team. The young mayor simply remarked, "I just listened."[i] And bided his time. In 1971, Vandergriff went after the Washington Senators, but again he faced presidential opposition, this time from Richard Nixon. According to legend, Vandergriff happened to be in the office of Senators owner Bob Short when Nixon's son-in-law David Eisenhower arrived. Vandergriff hid in a closet until the man finished explaining Nixon's concerns. In the end, Vandergriff prevailed, and the team moved to Arlington in 1972, becoming the Texas Rangers.

Not everything Vandergriff touched turned to gold. After a failed venture at a marine park, which left the city in debt from millions of dollars provided in bond money, Vandergriff resigned from the Arlington City Council. He went on to serve in Congress as a Democrat from 1983 to 1985 but lost his House seat to Republican Dick Armey amid the Republican landslide behind Ronald Reagan's 1984 reelection. He returned to politics as a Republican in 1990 and was elected Tarrant County judge.

By the time of his death, Vandergriff had seen Arlington grow to a population of over 365,000, covering almost ninety-six square miles. The city sees an estimated 6.8 million visitors every year and has played host to World Series baseball games, Super Bowl football games, NCAA Final Four basketball games, and other major sporting events. It also entertains millions annually at Six Flags, Hurricane Harbor, and other vacation destinations.

---

i. Gerry Fraley, "Presidents Were No Match for Tom Vandergriff," *Dallas Morning News*, January 2, 2011, www. sportstoday.dallasnews.com/texas-rangers/rangersheadlines/2011/01/02/farley-presidents-were-no-match-for-tom-vandergriff.

aware of actions and decisions by HOAs. Open meeting laws now require HOAs to hold open, public meetings that all homeowners can attend; such meetings must be publicly announced at least seventy-two hours in advance.[40] Additional requirements include the need to obtain a court order before foreclosing on a home and a prohibition of HOAs banning solar panels.[41] However, some ambiguity exists in the law still, mostly surrounding the activities of HOAs in which the developer or builder still owns at least half of the land and therefore half of the votes.[42]

OTHER FORMS OF LOCAL GOVERNMENT

In addition to counties and cities, Texas contains a variety of other forms of local government. These include districts to handle the conduct of K–12 public education across the state. Special districts such as community college districts and MUDs also complete the variety of local governments in Texas.

Public Education as Local Government

An important function of state government is the education of its citizens. Like other state constitutions, the Texas Constitution of 1876 makes specific references to education, including public schools, universities, and community colleges.[43] Texas, like other states, uses several forms of government to provide for the education of its citizens through universities, community colleges, state technical schools, elementary schools, middle schools, and high schools.

One of the local governments most familiar to Texans is the local school district. In most instances, these are referred to as ISDs. Basic elementary and secondary education is the responsibility of the local board of education. These boards exist at the discretion of the Texas Legislature and operate under the authority of the Texas Constitution. The Texas Education Code, a statutory law passed by the legislature and signed by the governor, provides additional guidelines for K–12 education. Most students enrolled in K–12 education in Texas attend a school that falls under the jurisdiction of one of the more than 1,000 separate ISDs. However, a handful of public schools continue to operate under the pre-ISD system. Under the Texas Education Code, preexisting school systems such as common schools, county schools, and municipal schools may still operate.[44] County and city governments, and the voters in these counties and cities, determine whether or not a preexisting school should continue to stand or be converted into an ISD. Municipal schools are owned and operated by a city government directly and educate only those students living within a city's boundaries. Similarly, a county school system occurs when a county government directly owns and operates all public schools within the county. County and municipal school districts may have an elected board of education or may have a board chosen by the county or city government.

ISDs in Texas refers to local public school districts that are governed separately from, or independent of, any other form of local government or state government control. An ISD is governed by a board of trustees that is elected by the voters living within the boundaries of the school district. Boards are elected by at-large, at-large by place, or cumulative voting systems.[45] Members of the board serve four-year terms in office, with staggered elections so that half the board is elected every two years. The board of trustees of an ISD consists of three to seven members. To be a trustee, a candidate must reside within the school district and must be registered to vote. The boundaries of an ISD may be contained within a county, may include parts of two or more counties, and may include a city or parts of a city.

The ISD system is not unique in the United States, although the term to describe the system is. Under federalism, states are allowed to create school systems however they choose, and education policy is largely considered the domain of state governments. Two neighboring states illustrate differing approaches to education. Arkansas's school districts are similar to those of Texas. School districts are independent of local governments. In Arkansas, school district lines may cross county lines or may be contained within a single county. District lines may also be limited to a single city or include several cities. Some school districts in Arkansas are drawn based on the proximity of a road or highway to a school. In the Ozark and Ouachita Mountains, sometimes the closest school via highway or road may be in another county. Louisiana, by contrast, has parishwide (countywide) school districts. All public schools in a parish are part of the same public school system. Most school systems are parishwide, with just a handful of exceptions, such as the cities of Monroe, Bogalusa, Baker, Central City, and Zachary. Even in Louisiana where, with a handful of exceptions, parishwide school systems exist, local school boards are elected separately from parish and city governments. The parish school boards make decisions independent of the parish government. To give another example, the nation's largest school system is the public school system for New York City. Rather than a separate school district, the public schools in New York City are owned and operated as a department of the city government. Finally, Hawaii lacks school districts. All public schools are operated directly by the state government through its Department of Education.

In Texas, the board of trustees of an ISD oversees the schools of the district by authorizing construction of schools, selling bonds to finance projects, collecting property taxes to fund operations, and providing guidelines for schools. Guidelines may include directions on the hiring of teachers and administrators, curriculum decisions, discipline policies, and budget decisions.[46] In effect, the board of trustees runs the schools in the district.

Although the ISD system is designed to give citizens local control over their schools, the state of Texas exerts control in specific areas. In particular, the state uses its power over the creation, existence, and support of school districts to enforce statewide policies. These policies include the classes that students must take, the textbooks that students use, and the structure of district budgets.[47] To this end, the Texas Constitution provides for the State Board of Education (SBOE).[48] The SBOE consists of fifteen members elected from SMDs across the state. A commissioner, appointed by the governor and confirmed by the Texas Senate, heads the board. The structure, function, and policy implications of the SBOE are discussed in Chapter 14.

An example of the power of the state to control local school districts occurred in Galveston County. La Marque ISD sat on the southeast end of the county, along the I-45 corridor just before crossing Galveston Bay and onto Galveston Island. Beginning in 2011, La Marque schools were among the lowest rated schools on the Texas Assessment of Knowledge and Skills (TAKS) and later the State of Texas Assessments of Academic Readiness (STAAR). After comprehensive plans to improve the school districts performance on standardized tests, and plans to improve the financial transparency and health of the school district failed, Texas Education Commissioner Michael Williams unilaterally announced the closure of La Marque ISD in November 2015. This action was undertaken without the consent of the La Marque ISD Board of Trustees, students and parents, or residents of the school district. The school district's elected board was replaced with an unelected board of commissioners in December 2015. Texas City ISD, an adjacent school district, agreed to annex La Marque ISD territory. In August 2017, Hurricane Harvey disrupted the area, with devastating rains and flooding forcing the temporary relocation of schools and shifts in attendance zones as Texas City ISD coped with damaged and destroyed schools in both Texas City and La Marque.

Special Districts

Special districts are created when the residents within the proposed boundary of the district petition to create one. Examples of special districts are airport authorities, library districts, MUDs, and community college districts. The process is similar to the process of creating a city. In contrast to a city or county, however, a special district provides a single service or a limited number of services to the residents of the district. The creation of a special district can be complicated, depending on the type of district. Hospital districts are created by first passing an amendment to the Texas Constitution, then by the approval of voters in the proposed district. Community college districts are first authorized by the Texas Legislature. The Texas Commission on Environmental Quality (TCEQ) approves the creation of MUDs. Special districts have even been created to build and manage sports stadiums for professional sports teams in Texas, even though the primary beneficiary is a private business.

Normally, special districts are created when a county or city government is unable or unwilling to provide a service itself, or when the existing local government prefers to allow a special district to provide the service. Because counties face limits on the amount of property tax they levy, special districts allow counties to overcome this limit by essentially "farming out" new services to a special district. In some instances, residents of a county may choose to join a special district that exists in another county. In this case, the residents take a vote to join the special district, or a local government may request that the special district start providing services in the area. Special districts are funded primarily by property taxes that residents agree to pay to provide the services. If the district crosses county lines, then arrangements are made for the tax assessors in each county to collect the taxes and transfer the funds to the district. Thus, special districts often can overcome the problems of coordinating services across multiple cities and counties. This approach is very useful in major metropolitan areas like the Dallas–Fort Worth metroplex, for example. Some special districts are authorized by voters to issue municipal bonds, while others charge user fees for their services.

Special districts are governed by a board of usually five members. The board is often elected by voters in the district. In some instances, it is appointed, usually by the mayors, city councils, and commissioners courts operating within the district. The board oversees the regular operation of the special district, hires necessary staff and professionals, and makes policies regarding the provision of services. For example, the Port of Houston Authority is governed by an appointed board of seven members. Some members are appointed by the Harris County Commissioners Court, while others are appointed by cities within Harris County. The authority oversees the collection of public and private dock facilities along the Houston Ship Channel and monitors ship traffic on the channel and in Galveston Bay. For community colleges, its board of trustees hires the chancellor or president of the college. The board decides, within state guidelines, the degrees that will be offered and the coursework that is required. The board also enters into agreements with four-year universities to determine the transferability of courses, harmonization of degree programs, and ease of transfer to four-year institutions. It establishes pay scales for faculty and staff, qualifications to be on faculty, and rates of tuition and fees for students. In some cases, community colleges have service areas defined by a law passed by the Texas Legislature. Angelina College in East Texas has the exclusive right to operate in all or parts of thirteen East Texas counties. In contrast, Harris County contains several community college districts, including Houston Community College, Lone Star College, and San Jacinto Community College. Currently, fifty separate college districts exist in Texas. Community colleges educate over 550,000 Texans each year.

The advantage of a special district is the ability to provide services that ordinarily might not be provided. In addition, the services may be provided to promote economic development. In the case of MUDs, which provide water, sewer, and similar services to individuals and businesses outside city limits, these services may entice new businesses to relocate to the area or developers to construct new homes. Again, in some instances, the special district aids in bridging disputes between cities or counties over the provision of services. However, like other local government elections, special election district elections are low-turnout events, and thus the decisions made by voters may reflect the wishes of only a few. Also, the proliferation of special districts in an area creates confusion among residents, who may not know who is responsible for what. Special districts also encourage conflict among local governments as multiple districts compete for property tax resources and pursue contradictory goals.

WINNERS AND LOSERS

As we have seen in previous chapters, choices about the structure of government, the distribution of powers within government and between levels of government, and how government is selected directly impact citizens. In Texas, various levels of local government provide different services and create additional tax burdens on citizens. To the extent that local government in Texas creates flexibility, citizens win. To the extent that each level of local government creates additional, obscure taxes, citizens lose.

Cities are clear winners in the state because they are relatively powerful entities that provide a significant number of government services to citizens. Home rule cities are even bigger winners. They have tremendous freedom to choose their form of government, election system, and organization of city government. However, counties are often losers. Counties, especially large-population ones, are strapped with the same form of government that all other counties in Texas possess. Little freedom exists for them to tailor their plans of government and structures to their needs. However, cities can also be losers when cities assume state laws create a floor, not a ceiling to enact policies. While such approaches may be successful, perhaps with sanctuary cities, as residents of Denton have learned in the fracking debate, the state legislature is more than willing to strip power away from cities.

The winners in education are often the residents of the districts. In ISDs, residents benefit by having local school boards that govern smaller areas than might otherwise occur under a countywide system. This arrangement reinforces the small-town and rural bias common in Texas political history. School boards should be more responsive to voters and parents, especially in smaller-enrollment school districts. This arrangement allows policies and programs to be tweaked to the wishes of local concerns. For example, Hudson ISD, located just outside of Lufkin in East Texas, operates the largest high school in Texas without a football team. Hudson High School is classified as a 4A school for University Interscholastic League (UIL) athletic and academic competitions. However, residents are wary of the football culture of many other towns and communities of Texas, including nearby 5A football powerhouse Lufkin High. Again, if the state government decides, however, that local school boards are not providing academic, or other, services up to the level of state expectations, residents may find their school district abolished without their consent, as exemplified by La Marque ISD's recent forced annexation into Texas City ISD.

Both of these situations also suggest an interesting dichotomy for Texas. While our state government consistently bemoans what is perceived as power grabs by the U.S. national government in Washington, DC, and demands power to be concentrated at the level of the state government, which is closer to the residents of Texas, it simultaneously seems increasingly willing to curb power of cities, school districts, and other local governments that are closer to the residents and voters.

Residents are also often winners with regard to special districts if they are willing to create a district and to see their property taxes raised to cover the additional services that the special district provides. In addition, residents within a city or in part of a county may elect to create the district to provide selected services to a particular area, even if the majority of residents in the entire city or county do not want those services. Thus, the creation of special districts gives Texans the freedom to choose whether to accept certain services and the corresponding taxes and to reject those services (and taxes). However, this buffet-style approach produces significant variation in the services that residents receive and results in divergent rates of property taxes across the state and even within cities and counties. Residents also find themselves subject to several local governments, a confusing array that offers little coordination of services throughout a county or metropolitan area.

Moreover, the heavy use of property taxes to fund all of these services may depress property values in some parts of the state, causing significant variation in taxation levels between rural and wealthy areas of the state; it also places the burden of paying for services largely in the hands of property owners.

Reliance on property taxes to fund local governments, discussed here and in Chapter 12, overburdens citizens who live in larger metropolitan areas or rural areas where property tax rates are significantly higher to compensate for lower property values than in wealthier suburban areas. The property tax is a distinct burden on retirees, whose spending and income often decrease while property taxes remain at the same level. By amendment to the Texas Constitution, retirees are protected from increases in property tax rates. Texans may also be losers because each ISD, MUD, community college district, etc., must bear the administrative costs of operating the district, including such expenses as office space, office equipment, and staffing. Local governments in

Texas ultimately raise their costs of operation to pay for these administrative expenses, passing these costs on to citizens of Texas, who pay higher taxes in the process. For example, a countywide school district in Georgia or Louisiana requires one central office administration, not the five, six, or even nine that each school district in a county in Texas may have. Government in Texas is clearly proving unnervingly complex and, arguably, costly. In the end, the citizens of Texas lose.

CONCLUSION

Local government in Texas is a diverse set of governments. Ultimately, all local governments are dominated by the state government, which determines the powers of local governments and the organizational structure of them. Local government, in the form of cities, counties, and special districts, exists to aid the state of Texas in delivering public policies and public services in areas such as transportation, education, and public health. Citizens also create, with the permission of the state, some forms of local government, such as cities and special districts, to provide specific services that the citizens want. Texas provides little flexibility to its local governments, although cities are afforded more freedom under home rule provisions than other forms of local government. However, residents of cities of sufficient size must choose to adopt home rule status before they can take advantage of it. In the end, Texans are confronted with a set of overlapping jurisdictions providing a variety of public services and overseeing a plethora of public policies with various degrees of effectiveness.

SAGE edge™
for CQ Press

Want a better grade?

Get the tools you need to sharpen your study skills. Access practice quizzes, eFlashcards, video, and multimedia at **edge.sagepub.com/collier6e**.

KEY TERMS

administrative federalism (p. 353)

annexation (p. 365)

auditor (p. 361)

city charter (p. 365)

commissioners court (p. 358)

constable (p. 361)

contract outsourcing (p. 362)

county attorney (p. 360)

county civil service commission (p. 361)

county clerk (p. 360)

Dillon's Rule (p. 352)

fiscal federalism (p. 353)

(Continued)

general law city (p. 364)
home rule city (p. 365)
justice of the peace (JP) (p. 361)
machine politics (p. 371)
merit-based civil service system (p. 361)
municipal bond (p. 379)
municipal utility district (MUD) (p. 351)

ordinance (p. 364)
partisan election (p. 358)
privatization (p. 362)
sheriff (p. 360)
tax assessor (p. 360)
zoning policy (p. 373)

ACTIVE LEARNING

- Write an essay or develop an oral presentation explaining the role and function of each type of local government in Texas. **Communication**

- Divide into groups. Select a state other than Texas. Research the similarities and differences in county governments between your selected state and Texas. **Teamwork**

CHAPTER REVIEW

1. Which of the following is not a type of local government in Texas?

    a. county

    b. city

    c. school district

    d. township

2. The form of county government in Texas is called the ____.

    a. commissioners court

    b. common court

    c. county council

    d. quorum court

3. Which principle of U.S. and Texas state government is violated by the structure of Texas's county government?

    a. limited government

    b. representative government

    c. separation of powers

    d. individual rights

4. A city in Texas that has a city charter, more freedom in ordinance making, and more freedom in how to structure the city government is called a ____.

    a. village

    b. home rule city

    c. general law city

    d. constitutional city

5. Which is a form of city government with an elected city council and a hired professional who oversees day-to-day operations?
   a. city commissioner system
   b. strong mayor-council system
   c. weak mayor-council system
   d. council-manager system

6. An election system for local government in which voters have multiple votes and may give all to one candidate or spread votes among many candidates is called ____.
   a. at large
   b. at large by place
   c. cumulative voting
   d. single member district plurality

7. ____ is the policy by which the city restricts what individuals and entities may do with their property, usually by designating certain areas for specific use.
   a. NIMBY
   b. Annexation
   c. Privatization
   d. Zoning

8. Most Texas school districts are ____.
   a. independent
   b. county districts
   c. consolidated
   d. city districts

9. What type of special district provides services like trash collection in areas outside a city or where another government does not provide the service?
   a. commissioners court
   b. municipal utility district
   c. special services district
   d. township

10. Which of the following is a responsibility of county government in Texas?
    a. recording keeping, such as birth certificates, death certificates, and marriage licenses
    b. registering voters and conducting elections
    c. maintaining law and order through county courts, county jails, and sheriff departments
    d. all of these

FISCAL POLICY

Chapter Objectives

★ Describe the basic steps in the policymaking process.

★ Identify the different types of taxes that Texans pay.

★ Assess who wins and who loses under the Texas tax system.

★ Describe other state revenue resources, including the role of the federal government.

★ Explain how tax expenditures and subsidies work as fiscal policy tools.

★ Assess who wins and who loses under Texas's fiscal policy.

During the Great Recession, which was marked by a contraction in the U.S. gross domestic product, a stock market crash, and unemployment reaching 10 percent, Texas led the country in job creation and the idea of the Texas miracle was born. The Texas miracle tells the story of a state with low taxes, few regulations, and business-friendly policymakers who continued to create jobs as the rest of the country struggled. Texas did create more jobs between December 2007 and 2016 than the next six states combined.[1] However, by mid-2014 the price of oil and natural gas has collapsed, and critics question how much of the Texas miracle was merely driven by the increased price of oil that accompanied the Great Recession. The oil and gas bust cost Texas over 80,000 jobs and 2016 saw three quarters of negative job growth. By 2017, the price of oil and gas began to bounce back as did the state's economy. In that year, the Texas economy was the fastest growing and the second biggest in the country. As Texans reflect on the Texas miracle in the coming years, the state government's intervention in the economy and the role of oil and gas will no doubt receive greater scrutiny.

What is striking is how much the Texas miracle reflects a fundamental change in Texas's attitude toward business. The Texans who wrote the early constitutions, including the current one, held a deep distrust of big business. They worried about businesses taking advantage of individuals. The current Texas Constitution originally held a number of specific clauses designed to limit big businesses in the state. For example, the 1876 constitution did not allow branch banking; that was true until the constitution was amended in 1986. Even as you drive through Texas today, you still see a

Governor Greg Abbott announces the relocation of Mitsubishi Heavy Industries' headquarters from New York to Texas. This relocation of one of the world's leading industrial firms was one example of the Texas miracle, which brought jobs to Texas while other states struggle to recover from the Great Recession.

hometown bank in every small town. If you are looking for a Bank of America, Wells Fargo, or Chase Bank, you will likely have to drive to a bigger city. The current Texas Constitution also severely limited the rail companies, regulating everything from how much they could charge to forbidding grants of money to railroads. It further contained a provision that prevented Texas rail companies from consolidating with rail companies outside the state. Similarly, Texas laws encouraged small oil companies and did not allow integrated oil companies to operate in the state until 1917. The constitution also reflected a preference for local control, constraining the state government's ability to tax and spend and specifically creating limited institutions at the state level.

It is worth reflecting that today's Texas is dramatically different from what the framers of the constitution intended. The Texas miracle did not merely require the state government to give big businesses a free hand but often to give them a hand up. The lack of regulations and limits on tort (discussed in Chapter 7) mean, in practice, businesses gain at the expense of individuals. Elected officials proselytizing about the Texas miracle often forget to confess to the state's dalliance with subsidies and tax breaks, discussed at the end of this chapter. As you read the chapter, the difficult choices of who to tax and where to spend will become evident. The fundamental change in the character of Texas, represented by the Texas miracle, will also become apparent.

In this chapter, we will describe the policymaking process and examine types of taxes that Texas utilizes and how they compare to other states. Next, we explore where the state spends its money. We will also look at how fiscal policy is used to encourage and discourage certain behaviors and promote certain industries. As we will see in the discussion of the budget, policy solutions are difficult because Texans often do not even agree on whether there is a problem. Texas's government under different flags and constitutions has been struggling for generations to find solutions to the problems Texans face. However, a rapidly changing population continually redefines our old problems and generates new problems as immigration from other countries and other states continues to bring new people and new politics to Texas.

THE POLICYMAKING PROCESS

There is little more difficult than deciding who to tax and where to spend. Nothing more clearly represents the state's priorities and nothing more decisively picks winners and losers. Policy is determined through a variety of actors in the state government. Some policies result directly from the actions of the Texas Legislature as it gathers every two years to write new laws. Many policies result from executive orders and other actions of the governor or other elected executives. Others emerge from the bureaucracy as it interprets the laws enacted by the legislature. Finally, local policies result from the actions of city or county governments. Government is seldom tasked with problems that have easy solutions.

Policy, or the actions and activities of government, is the bread and butter of governance. Scholars have identified five stages in the policymaking process: agenda setting, policy formation, policy adoption, policy implementation, and policy evaluation. The first step, the agenda setting stage, refers to policymakers prioritizing the various problems facing the state. The policy agenda takes shape as policymakers identify their priorities based on their own everyday experiences, or issues are brought to their attention by citizens, interest groups, media reports, or formal hearings. Agenda setting represents a choice of what issues policymakers are going to focus on at any given time, and the order in which the issues will be considered. In the policy formation stage, possible solutions are developed and debated. Next, in the policy adoption stage, formal government action takes place with approval of the legislature or through administrative action by a member of the executive branch. The policy implementation stage occurs when which state agencies follow up on the actions of elected officials. In this stage, bureaucratic agencies develop rules and regulations that detail the guidelines for how the policy will be carried out. Finally, in the policy evaluation stage, government agencies, the legislature, and interest groups assess the implementation of the policy to determine if their goals are being met.

Political scientists have categorized policies into three types: redistributive, distributive, and regulatory. Redistributive policy moves benefits (usually in the form of money) from one group to another in an attempt to make society more equal generally by taxing people with higher incomes to provide benefits to people with fewer resources. Distributive policy is similar except that it attempts to meet the needs of citizens without targeting any one group as the source of money. As a result, distributive policies are easier to implement because their costs are widely dispersed, and such policies face less opposition since no group is identified as the source of funds. Regulatory policy attempts to limit or control the actions of individuals or corporations. Regulation is typically used either to ensure a fair market, as in antitrust laws, or protect the public from negative consequences of business activity, such as the health consequences of lead in paint. For example, businesses may face fines or other penalties as a disincentive for polluting or causing other socially undesirable outcomes. Thus, policy is at the heart of politics as policymakers resolve the question of who gets what from government.

policy
the actions and activities of government

agenda setting
the stage in which various actors attempt to prioritize the problems facing the state

policy formation
the stage in which possible solutions are developed and debated

policy adoption
the stage in which formal government action takes place

policy implementation
the stage in which the policy is carried out in state agencies

policy evaluation
the stage in which the implementation of a policy is examined to see if policy goals are being met

redistributive policy
moves benefits, usually in the form of money, from one group to another in an attempt to make society more equal

distributive policy
moves benefits to meet the needs of citizens but does so without targeting any one group as the source of money

regulatory policy
attempts to limit or control the actions of individuals or corporations

SOURCES OF STATE REVENUE: TAXES

Perhaps the most obvious way of looking at who gets what from government is examining the money that Texas takes from its citizens (taxes) and puts into various programs (spending). While the intentions and effectiveness of specific policies the state spends money on will be discussed in Chapters 13 and 14, we need to first look at fiscal policy, which is how government seeks to influence the economy through taxing and spending, including subsidies. Fiscal policy includes policies intended to shape the health of the economy overall as well as policies the state uses to encourage specific businesses and activity and discourage others.

fiscal policy
how government seeks to influence the economy through taxing and spending

subsidies
incentives designed to encourage the production or purchase of certain goods to stimulate or support some businesses

Taxes in Texas History

Texans, not surprisingly, have never liked taxes. Settlers in Stephen F. Austin's colony complained about the per-acre tax of 12.5 cents Austin charged to pay for survey fees and the militia needed for the settlers' defense.[2]

Early in the state's history, Texas financed much of its activity through a property tax. The Constitution of 1845 specified a property tax, but it allowed the legislature to exempt from taxation $250 worth of the household furniture or other property belonging to each family. Around the time of World War I, the state got about three-fourths of its revenue from the property tax. Texas had also begun taxing corporations in 1893, oil production in 1905, inheritances in 1907, motor vehicles in 1917, and gasoline in 1923. Over time, Texas shifted away from the property tax as a source of revenue for state government, passing it down to local governments, who now rely on it.

State Taxes Today

Though Texan distaste for taxes continues, the state still has to pay for roads, education, hospitals, and other basic services. Texas tax policy represents a choice between different types of taxes, each of which involves a different set of trade-offs. Today, Texas employs a complicated mixture of over sixty separate taxes. Texas is one of nine states with no general income tax, a tax calculated as a percentage of income earned in a year. While the idea of avoiding income tax is appealing, Texas has demonstrated that there are many other ways of raising revenue for the state. As Bob Bullock quipped while he was serving as the state's comptroller, "there are only certain taxes known to civilized man, and Texas has nearly all of them, except the income tax."[3]

income tax
a tax calculated as a percentage of income earned in a year

General Sales Tax

By far, the largest source of tax revenue in the state comes from the general sales tax, which is based on what individuals buy rather than what they earn. In 1961, Texas implemented its first general sales tax, a tax imposed on goods and services, when it imposed a tax of 2 percent on many goods sold. Over time, that tax rate increased to 6.25 percent and expanded to include more goods and services. Today, the state sales and use tax is added to certain services, retail sales, and the leases and rentals of most goods. Food products for human consumption are exempt from the sales tax unless they are candy, soft drinks, or prepared meals. In 1967, the Local Sales and Use Tax Act authorized cities to add a local tax of 1 percent on all retail sales. Today, Texas cities, counties, transit authorities, and other special-purpose districts have the option of imposing an additional local sales tax for a combined possible maximum for all state

general sales tax
an across-the-board tax imposed on goods and services sold within a jurisdiction

What are the trade-offs of
taxing income compared
to consumption?

⭐ CRITICAL THINKING

and local sales taxes of 8.25 percent. Cities are allowed a maximum of 2 percent, counties a maximum of 1.5 percent, transit authorities 1 percent, and special purpose districts 2 percent. By 1967, the sales tax had become the largest source of tax revenue for Texas. In 2017, the state sales taxes brought in $28.9 billion, accounting for 58 percent of Texas's taxes, by far the biggest source of tax revenue for the state.

Comparing the sales taxes of the forty-five states that use a statewide sales tax is difficult because each state uses a different mixture of state and local sales taxes. In fact, thirty-eight states allow local governments to collect sales taxes. For example, the state of Louisiana imposes a sales tax rate of only 4 percent, but local governments in Louisiana can collect up to 7 percent in additional sales tax. Alaska has no statewide sales tax but allows as much as 5 or 7 percent in Juneau and Kodiak, respectively. Other states, such as Connecticut, have a state-level sales tax of 6.35 percent with no local sales tax added on. Texas's sales tax of 6.25 percent is tied for the thirteenth-highest state sales tax rate in the nation, more than a point behind California's sales tax of 7.25 percent. However, California does not allow as much to be added by local governments. Once all the local sales taxes are added in, the average sales tax rate in Texas (8.17 percent) is only slightly lower than in California (8.54 percent). The highest combined rate for state and local sales taxes is Louisiana (10.02 percent).[4] Four states have no sales tax at the state or local level.

While the Texas sales tax covers a wide range of products and services, there are many exemptions that encourage some activities over others. Professor Lori Taylor noted in her analysis of the Texas sales taxes that Texas families are encouraged to eat at home because the prepared food served at restaurants is taxed while food to be prepared at home is not. Taylor notes that numerous exemptions are buried so deep in the tax code that we seldom notice them. For example, Texans must pay taxes on getting their dishwashers repaired but not their cars. Similarly, Texans pay a sales tax on getting their clothes washed but not on getting their car washed. Taylor goes on to conclude that "we could lower the sales tax rate by nearly a third and return revenues to current levels—simply by following the basic principles of good governance and refusing to play favorites with the tax code."[5] Taylor's analysis demonstrates how exempting some goods and services from our "general" sales tax comes at a price and that taxing more goods and services could allow Texas to reduce the tax rate we pay on each item without reducing what the state brings in. In addition to the general sales tax, Texas has a separate tax of 6.25 percent on the sale, rental, or lease of motor vehicles. There is also a tax of 3.25 percent on the sale of manufactured housing. These taxes bring in another $4.5 billion per year, or 9 percent of the state's taxes.

Gasoline and Severance Taxes

Texas has a separate tax on the sale of gasoline. Unlike the general sales tax that is a percentage of the cost of the product, the gasoline and diesel fuel tax charges consumers in Texas a fixed rate of twenty cents on every gallon of gasoline purchased (on top of 18.4 cents a gallon in federal taxes). Texas's gas tax rate is one of the lowest in the nation (forty-third out of the fifty states and the District of Columbia), coming in at nearly a third of Pennsylvania's 58.2 cents a gallon but considerably more than Alaska's 12.25 cents a gallon. This tax generates over $3.6 billion each year, or 7 percent of the state's tax revenue. As automobiles have become more fuel efficient and as electric vehicles become more common, the ratio of miles driven to gas taxes collected continues to rise. To make matters worse, the Texas Legislature has not raised the gasoline tax since 1992, and these

TEXAS CONNECTICUT

Every year, the Tax Foundation, a nonpartisan tax research group based in Washington, DC, calculates Tax Freedom Day to illustrate what portion of the year citizens must work to pay their federal, state, and local taxes. In 2018, it estimated that the average American works about 109 days out of the year to pay his or her taxes, making Tax Freedom Day fall on April 19.

By the Tax Foundation's estimate, Tax Freedom Day comes a few days earlier (April 14) for Texans, placing Texas twenty fourth among the fifty states in terms of total state taxes paid per capita. The most heavily taxed states, according to the Tax Foundation, are New York, Connecticut, and New Jersey.[i] One of the reasons for Connecticut's high taxes is that its citizens are relatively prosperous, with a median household income of $71,755, compared to Texas's median household income of $54,727 and the national average median of $55,322.[ii] Because families in Texas have lower incomes, they naturally pay lower federal income taxes than families in higher-income states. In addition to the federal income tax, Connecticut has a separate state income tax with six brackets and a top rate of 6.99 percent. Other states, such as California (13.3 percent) and New York (8.82 percent), have even higher state income taxes. Texas has no state income tax, but its average combined state and local sales tax is 8.05 percent sales tax along with an average $1,731 per capita property tax. Connecticut's state and local sales tax is 6.35 percent, and their citizens pay $2,847 on average in property taxes.[iii]

Overall, the states with the highest total state and local tax rates per capita are generally found in the Northeast, with New York (#1), Connecticut (#2), and New Jersey (#3) having the three highest rates in the nation (see Map 12.2). In contrast, taxes are generally lower in the far North with Alaska (#50), South Dakota (#49), and Wyoming (#48) among the least-taxed citizens. Southern states with Mississippi (#41), Louisiana (#45), and Tennessee (#47), also tend to have comparatively lower taxes.

> **What are some advantages of living in a state with a high income tax, such as Connecticut?**
>
> ⭐ **CRITICAL THINKING**

> **Identify issues in Texas that might be better addressed if the state had more revenue?**
>
> ⭐ **SOCIAL RESPONSIBILITY**

i. Scott Greenberg, "Tax Freedom Day 2016 Is April 24th," Tax Foundation, April 2016, http://taxfoundation.org/sites/taxfoundation.org/files/docs/TaxFreedomDay_2016..pdf.

ii. U.S. Census Bureau, www.census.gov.

iii. Ibid.

funds are not keeping up with the increasing costs of building and maintaining Texas roads. Currently, 75 percent of the state's motor fuel tax is set aside for construction, maintenance, and policing of the state's roads, while the remaining 25 percent is deposited in the Available School Fund. Some legislators have suggested that devoting a higher percentage of the gas tax to transportation spending is preferable to raising the tax rate.

After oil erupted from the Spindletop well on January 10, 1901, ushering in an era of petroleum, taxes on Texas's oil production became a huge source of revenue that kept many Texans from having to pay much in the way of taxes. By 1905, the state was raking in $101,403 a year from oil production alone. Texas still taxes the production of oil and gas with a **severance tax**, which is a tax on natural resources charged when they are produced or "severed" from the earth. These severance taxes, similar to the value added tax (VAT) common in Europe, take the form of Texas's oil production tax that takes 4.6 percent of the market value of oil produced. In the 1950s, this severance tax and related taxes generated about one-third of the state's tax revenue. After that, increased competition from overseas and other factors lowered oil production and forced the state to

severance tax
a tax on natural resources charged when the resources are produced or "severed" from the earth

MAP 12.1 Combined State and Average Local Sales Tax Rates, 2018

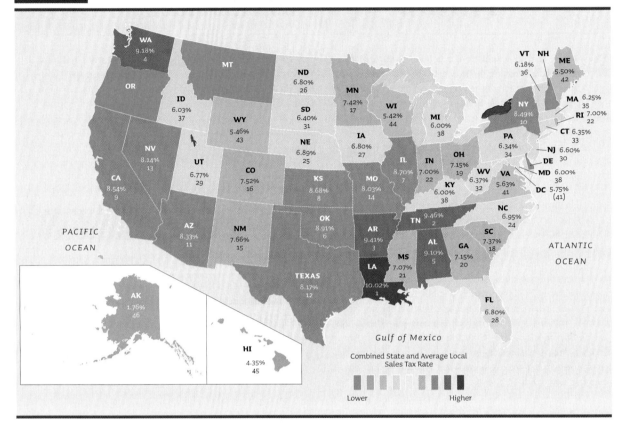

Source: Tax Foundation, "How High Are Sales Taxes in Your State," accessed August 6, 2018, https://files.taxfoundation.org/20180313143458/Tax-Foundation-FF572.pdf. Tax Freedom Day® 2016.

shift to other sources of tax revenue. Today, oil production taxes accounts for less than 4 percent of the state's tax revenue.

The state also taxes the production of natural gas at 7.5 percent of market value. In addition, liquefied gas is taxed at a rate of fifteen cents a gallon. While once a much larger portion of the state budget, the state's tax on natural gas production today accounts for only about 2 percent of all state taxes. Since the oil and gas tax is based on market value rather than the volume produced, a rise in the price of oil or gas can bring a windfall in state revenues; when prices fall, budget cuts often follow. In 2014, at the height of the market, Texas oil produced just under $4 billion in revenue and natural gas produced another $2 billion. The sharp decline in the price of oil and gas that followed meant that, even as the state produced more, revenues fell sharply. By 2017 revenue from oil was down to $2 billion and natural gas revenue fell to under a billion.

Franchise Tax

Texas's **franchise tax** is its primary tax on business. This tax was significantly revised in the 2006 special session to help fund Texas public schools by expanding the types of

franchise tax
the primary tax on businesses in Texas, which is based on the taxable margin of each company

businesses taxed. At the same time, the method of calculation of the tax was changed. Today, the franchise tax is based on the taxable margin (a variety of measures designed to approximate profit) of the company and has been labeled the margins tax by some. In fact, the franchise tax is complicated and can be based on either the net taxable capital or net taxable earned surplus of a business. While Texas generally enjoys a reputation as a business-friendly state, the franchise tax has been described by one critic as "one of the most destructive taxes on corporate and small businesses in the country" because it imposes a higher burden on some industries than others.[6] One problem is that the franchise tax can be imposed on businesses even when they're not profitable. The 84th Texas legislature voted to reduce the franchise tax by 25 percent, which decreased state revenue by just over $2.2 billion in the following budget cycle.

Sin Taxes

Like other states, Texas brings in revenue through so-called **sin taxes**, which are taxes on products or activities that some legislators want to discourage. The objects of sin taxes make inviting targets, as elected officials look for places to impose taxes on the least sympathetic products possible. Sin taxes are generally attached to activities that the government wants to discourage, often because they are unhealthy. Governor Milo Roberts instituted the state's first sin tax in 1879, creating a two-cent tax on each drink and a half-cent tax per beer drawn. To ensure that the taxes were being paid, every saloon had to have a hand-cranked counter that rang a bell to register the tax being paid.[7] While the federal government has its own **excise tax** on alcoholic beverages, which is a tax paid at the time of purchase with the cost of the tax usually included in the price of the product, Texas has separate tax rates on liquor, beer, wine, malt liquor, and mixed drinks. Wine and beer are taxed by volume; mixed drinks are taxed at nearly 15 percent of sales. In 2017, Texas's taxes on alcohol totaled about $1.2 billion. This is a small portion (2 percent) of the total state taxes, but Texans might be surprised to realize that they drink enough to average over $6 in alcohol tax annually for every Texan of drinking age and generate $1 billion in tax revenue.

The rise in the state's tax on cigarettes, passed in May 2005 to help pay for schools, illustrates the complexities of the sin tax. On January 1, 2007, the state's tax on a pack of cigarettes leaped a full dollar for a total tax of $1.41 a pack, driving the cost of most packs of cigarettes to over $6 and making the state's tax much higher than in Missouri ($0.17) or Mississippi ($0.68). Some Texans contemplated quitting smoking, an effect intended by groups such as the American Cancer Society that lobbied for the increase. Some saw the tax increase as a way of offsetting the health care costs to a state that sees over 20,000 people a year die from smoking-related illnesses. Since about half of the revenue from the tobacco tax is designated for the funding of public schools, imposition of the tax may seem an easy way to raise revenue at the expense of unpopular products. While Texas's tobacco tax may seem high compared to other southern states, it has not gone as far as states such as New York where cigarettes are taxed at a rate of $4.35 a pack.

The state's newest sin tax is a $5 fee for each person entering a business that provides live nude entertainment and allows consumption of alcoholic beverages. Referred to under tax policy as the fee on sexually oriented businesses, the fee has become better known as the "pole tax" (named for the tendency of strippers to utilize poles in their dancing routines). Sin taxes employed in other states, such as taxes on soda or vaping, are notably absent in Texas.

sin tax
a tax on products or activities such as cigarettes or gambling that some legislators would like to discourage

excise tax
a tax paid at the time of purchase, with the cost of the tax included in the price of the product

property tax
a tax on the value of real estate that is paid by the property owner; used by county and local governments to fund such programs as public schools

The state's mixture of taxes in 2017 is spelled out in Table 12.1. As the table demonstrates, while Texas's tax rates may be low, the system is far from simple as the state looks to a wide variety of sources for its tax dollars.

Property Taxes

While Texas's state taxes are lower than most other states, local governments impose a significant local property tax, which is a tax on the value of real estate that is paid by the property owner. The Texas Constitution forbids a statewide property tax and limits property taxes charged by local governments. Texas cities, counties, and local school districts, and special districts such as water districts, hospital districts, and community college districts, charge property taxes that they rely heavily on for their revenue. In 2006, the Texas Legislature reduced school property taxes by one-third. The plan traded lower school property taxes for higher taxes on businesses, smokers, and used-car purchasers. While the legislature's reform promised significantly lower property tax rates, about two-thirds of local school boards in the state opted to increase the rates after the legislature had reduced them.[8] Those increases were relatively modest, and within the limits created by the law, and they served to reduce the size of tax cuts the legislature sought. Further, with state funding for public schools reduced by budget cuts in recent years, local school districts are even more dependent on property taxes.

These complications reflect the challenges of a mixed-funding system that leaves local school boards dependent on the state for much of their money while remaining subject to state rules on how they raise remaining revenues. Many local school boards are faced with growing student populations, rising utility bills, and increasing staff costs, even as the legislature has cut state education funding. Locally elected school boards are left with few alternative sources of revenue and have little choice but to raise property taxes or cut budgets.

A similar problem plagues county government in areas that experienced a boom in oil and gas production. The severance tax on oil and gas goes to the state coffers while counties must rely on property taxes that change slowly. During the boom, county roads in Texas experienced a considerable increase in traffic volume, including drilling haulers and other heavy machinery that played havoc on the roads. According to the Texas Department of Transportation (TxDOT), a single oil or gas well requires 1,184 loaded trucks to start production, 353 loaded trucks a year to maintain production, and another 997 loaded trucks every few years to refrack the well.[9] The agency estimates the total cost to the state from drilling damage is an additional $4 billion a year just to maintain the roads. The increase in traffic and damage to local roads also increases the number of fatalities around fracking sites. For example, TXDOT estimates that the Eagle Ford Shale experienced a 40 percent increase in fatalities in 2012.[10] While the fracking boom has left its mark on county roads across Texas, the funding formulas that the state uses to distribute road maintenance funds give the counties little revenue to work with to deal with the damaged roads.

In 2015, the approximately 4,000 taxing entities in Texas levied around $52.2 billion in property taxes, an increase of about 6.3 percent from the year before. A little over half of that ($28.2 billion) was levied by school districts, while counties collected about $8.7 billion and cities brought in another $8.4 billion. The remaining $7.0 billion in taxes were levied by a wide range of special districts.[11] By and large Texas pays for local services such as roads and education with property taxes, and Texas relies more

FEDERALISM IN Action

Minimum Wage

As the Great Recession has seen wages stay relatively flat while inflation continued, people around the country increasingly talked about raising the minimum wage. The national government sets a minimum wage, which was increased to $7.25 in 2009. Many state and local governments around the country see this as too low, and thirty states have adopted higher minimum wages. The states with the highest minimum wage are Washington ($11.50), Massachusetts ($11.00), and California ($11.00). In addition, California, Massachusetts, and New York have passed laws that will continue to gradually increase their minimum wage to $15 in the next few years. Some cities have surpassed their state's rates, such as Seattle and San Francisco, which are both incrementally increasing their wages to $15. Minimum wage in the state of Texas is based on the federal minimum of $7.25 an hour.

In 2003, the Texas Legislature passed a law that prohibited local governments from adopting their own minimum wage. Localities cannot adopt minimum wages for everyone in their district, although some local governments have recently adopted minimum wage laws for their employees. For instance, Bexar County adopted a $13 minimum wage for all county employees. The city of Austin also has a $13 minimum wage for its city employees. San Marcos went further, passing a law that requires any business that receives local grant money or local tax breaks to pay a minimum wage of $15 an hour. San Marcos city manager Jared Miller stated that the goal was to pay people enough so that the city sees a reduction in the number of schoolchildren who receive free or reduced cost lunches, which is currently almost three-fourths of the total school children.[i] San Marcos councilman John Thomaides pointed out that, although San Marcos wants new jobs, if businesses are paying "poverty-level wages, we're not going to give [them] subsidies."[ii] As Texas cities increasingly debate the merits of raising the minimum wage, there will undoubtedly be more related city ordinances.

Should the national government be able to force states to raise their minimum wage? Should state governments be able to preempt local governments from setting a minimum wage?

 CRITICAL THINKING

What are some arguments in favor of raising the minimum wage? What are arguments against minimum wage?

 CRITICAL THINKING

---

i. John Austin, "Small Texas City Adopts $15 Minimum Wage," CNHI News Service, February 16, 2016, www.cnhi.com/featured_stories/small-texas-city-adopts-minimum-wage/article_10d9e1a2-d5b1-11e5-926a-13f7cd67e41f.html.
ii. Ibid.

---

on local property taxes to pay for local services than any other state.[12] Not surprisingly, then, while Texans enjoy having no income tax, they make up much of the difference with a higher sales tax from the state and higher property taxes levied at the local level, as indicated in Figure 12.1.

Setting property tax rates may seem like a simple process. However, the property tax is an **ad valorem tax**, a tax based on the value of property. Even if the property tax rates remain the same, governments may raise the tax paid by citizens by increasing the amount of the **appraisal**, the official estimate of a property's value. This problem is especially serious in rapidly growing areas where property values rise quickly as new residents increase the demand for housing. This creates what critics call a "stealth tax increase" as citizens see the value of their homes increase even though they are not offering their houses for sale. Texas population continues to grow, leading to increased demand for housing and city services; property values rise with it.

ad valorem tax
a tax based on property value, which is subject to periodic appraisals

appraisal
the official estimate of a property's value

Is the Texas tax system overly complicated? Why or why not?

CRITICAL THINKING

From "In the Heart of The Eagle Ford Shale, The Roads To Perdition," Eileen Pace, Texas Public Radio, January 15, 2015. Reprinted with permission from Eileen Pace, freelance writer based in Texas.

A rural road in Texas after the fracking boom. Fracking dollars generate economic growth across the state, but damage to rural roads is one of the unanticipated costs.

Disagreements over appraisal values often create tension between residential property owners and the owners of commercial properties. Fairness has become an important issue in appraisals because many people feel that the process in Texas undervalues commercial and industrial properties, leaving homeowners to pick up more than their share. Reformers argue that the owners of large commercial properties are more likely to hire lawyers to challenge property valuations. Assessment of residential property values is relatively easy to establish based on the prices paid for the large number of homes sold each year with the price of each home publicly available.

What are the costs to Texas's heavy reliance on property taxes?

⭐ CRITICAL THINKING

TABLE 12.1 Texas State Taxes by Source, Fiscal Year 2017

	2017 Revenue	Percentage of Total Tax Revenue	Percentage of All Sources of Revenue
Tax Collections			
Sales tax	$28,900,035,304	58.2%	26.0%
Motor vehicle sales/rental taxes	$4,532,348,585	9.1%	4.1%
Motor fuels taxes	$3,583,733,917	7.2%	3.2%
Franchise tax	$3,242,218,796	6.5%	2.9%
Insurance taxes	$2,376,091,985	4.8%	2.1%
Natural gas production tax	$982,762,914	1.9%	0.9%
Cigarette and tobacco taxes	$1,522,827,788	3.0%	1.4%
Alcoholic beverages taxes	$1,217,710,832	2.5%	1.1%
Oil production tax	$2,107,335,182	4.2%	1.9%
Utility taxes	$439,065,387	0.9%	0.40%
Hotel tax	$530,715,704	1.0%	0.5%
Other taxes	$208,575,065	0.4%	0.2%
Total taxes	$49,643,421,639	100.00%	44.6%

Note: Totals may not sum due to rounding.

Source: Texas Comptroller, "Revenue Sources for Fiscal Year 2017," accessed July 28, 2018, https://comptroller.texas.gov/transparency/reports/revenue-by-source/.

A receipt for $16.25 in state and county taxes that Thomas W. Grayson owed in 1852 for taxable property. This property included 660 acres on Salado Creek in Bexar County, two "negros," thirty-five head of cattle, one wagon, and one carriage. Ironically, freed slaves would go from being taxable property to being discriminated against with a poll tax.

Currently, the state caps the annual increase in a home's taxable value at 10 percent. This benefits senior citizens and others living on fixed incomes who may have trouble keeping up with the taxes on their homes as property values rise. As one resident of Austin complained, "I am now paying as much in property taxes as I used to pay for my entire mortgage payment when I first bought the house in 1988."[13] Texas offers a cap on school taxes, and the Texas Constitution was amended in 2003 to allow (but not require) cities and counties to cap seniors' taxes. While this may give retired Texans some protection against rising rates, it shifts the burden for taxes to others and may present a serious problem for areas with high numbers of retirees. In 2015, the legislature passed, and voters approved, a constitutional amendment that increased the homestead exemption from $15,000 to $25,000. The impact is relatively modest, since the average Texan will save only about $125 a year.[14]

Commercial properties are often valued on the revenue that they generate from rents or other revenue that may be confidential information not available to tax assessors. The Texas Constitution was amended in 1997 to require property taxes be equal and uniform. That allows business to argue that their tax bills are unfair based on comparable rates. Since the state does not require the sales price for the property and it can be difficult to compare dissimilar businesses, it is unclear what is "comparable." The result is that companies routinely sue tax collection entities, arguing their taxes are not equitable, sometimes based on the value of businesses hundreds of miles away.[15] Many big businesses in the state have used that language to drastically lower their tax bills. For example, Valero, which owns refineries across Texas, routinely sues local tax authorities over what it calls unfair tax bills. The difficulty arises in comparing one refinery to another, as the actual business and volume varies dramatically from

FIGURE 12.1 Sources of Tax Revenue: Texas and the National Average

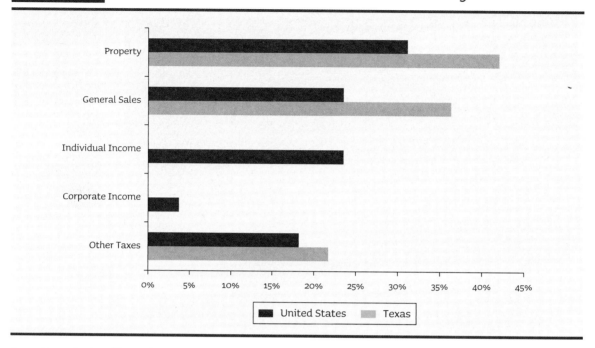

Source: Morgan Scarboro, "Facts & Figures 2018: How Does Your State Compare?," Tax Foundation, table 8, accessed July 29, 2018, https://files. taxfoundation.org/20180411102900/Facts-Figures-2018-How-Does-Your-State-Compare.pdf.

refinery to refinery. Valero has sued and won tax refunds in the amount of $7.5 million from Dumas School District and Moore County, $5 million from Texas City, and $32 million from Port Arthur's school.[16] Those funds had to be payed from the local tax base. Moreover, as more and more businesses in the state regularly sue to lower their taxes, the median value for all business lowers, and as former state senator Rodney Ellis explains, "The result is a constant and growing erosion of the tax base."[17] Because comparables are typically difficult to assess and large businesses enjoy the resources to keep local governments in court over the long term, critics worry that this loophole allows businesses to shift much of their share of taxes onto local homeowners.

WINNERS AND LOSERS

progressive tax
a graduated tax, such as an income tax, which taxes people with higher incomes at higher rates

regressive tax
a tax that takes a higher proportion of income from people with lower incomes than from people with higher incomes

The type of taxes Texas uses creates obvious winners and losers. A **progressive tax**, such as the federal income tax, places higher rates on people with higher incomes. A **regressive tax**, in contrast, takes a higher proportion of income from people with lower incomes than from people with higher incomes. Texas main sources of income are based on what Texans spend rather than what they earn. These types of taxes are more likely to be regressive taxes. Although everyone pays the same tax rate on purchases, people with lower incomes tend to spend a larger share of their income on the kind of items taxed at sale. A 2015 study by the Institute on Taxation and Economic Policy described Texas as the third most regressive tax system in the country where the poorest Texans paid 12.5 percent of their income to state and local taxes compared to only 2.9 percent by the state's top 1 percent.[18]

Some Texans have advocated an income tax like those used by other states to shift more of the state's tax burden to people with higher incomes, creating a more equitable tax system. While critics complain about the complexity of an income tax system with exemptions and schedules of deductions, the vast array of current state taxes is evidence that Texas has already created a complicated system without an income tax. Even some conservative legislators privately concede that replacing some of Texas's long list of taxes with a single income tax based on calculations already done for federal income taxes would simplify taxation in the state. However, these legislators worry that if the state does away with small taxes in favor of an income tax, nothing would prevent the state from gradually reinstating these small taxes whenever the government needed more money.

Choosing how much to tax and who to tax is a clear example of who wins and who loses. With so many taxes, it should not be surprising that almost every Texan finds something to dislike about them. And, with voters already unhappy, it is easy to see why the legislature has not been anxious to look at new taxes. When the political price of new taxes is so high, our elected officials tend to avoid updating the system altogether because changes will inevitably shift the tax burden and be seen as new taxes, even when they are designed to replace old taxes.

> To what degree should individual citizens advocate taxes that promote their personal wealth, and to what degree should they advocate tax policies that are the most equitable?
>
> ★ CRITICAL THINKING

> Which states have the greatest and the least state and local tax burden, per capita? How does Texas compare?
>
> ★ EMPIRICAL AND QUANTITATIVE

MAP 12.2 State and Local Tax Collections Per Capita

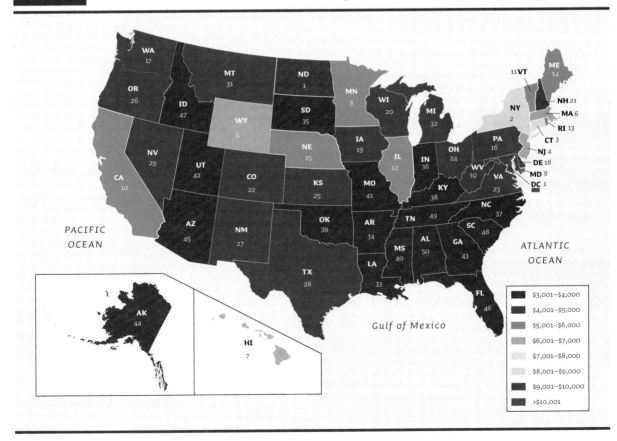

Legend:
- $3,001–$4,000
- $4,001–$5,000
- $5,001–$6,000
- $6,001–$7,000
- $7,001–$8,000
- $8,001–$9,000
- $9,001–$10,000
- >$10,001

Source: Tax Foundation, "Facts and Figures: How Does Your State Compare? 2018," 2018, https://files.taxfoundation.org/20180411102900/Facts-Figures-2018-How-Does-Your-State-Compare.pdf.

TABLE 12.2 Texas State Revenue by Source

Revenue by Source	2017 Revenue	Percentage of All Sources of Revenue
Tax collections	$49,643,421,639	44.6%
Federal income	$38,365,630,033	34.5%
Licenses, fees, fines, and penalties	$10,378,557,433	9.3%
Interest and investment income	$1,691,191,616	1.5%
Net lottery proceeds	$2,053,243,707	1.8%
Sales of goods and services	$308,230,150	0.3%
Settlements of claims	$527,518,330	0.5%
Land income	$1,694,312,814	1.5%
Contributions to employee benefits	$57,253	0.0%
Other revenue	$6,533,309,363	5.9%
Total revenue	**$111,195,472,338**	**100.0%**

Note: Totals may not sum due to rounding.

Source: Texas Comptroller, "Revenue Sources for Fiscal Year 2017," accessed July 29, 2018, https://comptroller.texas.gov/transparency/reports/revenue-by-source/.

SOURCES OF STATE REVENUE: OTHER RESOURCES

While the taxes outlined so far generated almost $49 billion in 2017, they accounted for just under 45 percent of state revenue. This raises the question of where the state gets the rest of its money. As Table 12.2 indicates, tax revenues are only part of the funding picture.

Federal Grants

The large share of the state budget that comes from the federal treasury might surprise many Texans. In 2017, Texas received over $38 billion from the federal government, which accounted for over one-third of the state's finances. As Figure 12.2 illustrates, the share of the Texas budget coming from federal funds has increased dramatically over the last two decades. In the 1980s, federal funds accounted for less than one in four dollars in state spending, but by 2003 that rate had increased to one in three. The drop-in sales tax revenue associated with the economic downturn, combined with the surge in federal spending in the stimulus program, brought the federal contribution to the state budget to over 42 percent in 2010. However, while some of the increasing federal role in the state's budget reflects the Obama administration's programs, the long-term shift reflects a growing federal role under both Republican and Democratic administrations.

As the discussion of fiscal federalism in Chapter 2 illustrates, these federal monies often come with strings attached. In some cases, they pay for programs in which the

Does the state's tax system place more of an undue burden on specific groups of citizens or types of businesses?

 SOCIAL RESPONSIBILITY

Should Texas have an income tax? Why or why not?

 CRITICAL THINKING

state and federal government partner. The large dollar amounts account for much of state leaders' willingness to accept federal rules.

Interest, Licensing, and Lottery Funds

Rounding out the revenue picture for Texas are various funding sources that together account for about 10 percent of all state revenue. Some of this money comes from the licensing of various professions and businesses. While these fees resemble taxes on certain professions, the argument that they simply offset some of the specific expenses associated with licensing justifies counting them as something different from taxes. In addition, the state receives money from fines paid by those found guilty of traffic and other violations.

In 2017, the state received just under $1.4 billion in income from returns on its bank balances and other investments. The largest source of investment income came from the state's Permanent School Fund (PSF), a fund set aside to finance education in Texas. The state received another $1.5 billion from income derived from land.

Texas also makes money from a state lottery. Some of the proceeds of lottery ticket sales go into the prizes, with the state and retailers dividing the rest. In 2017, about $5.1 billion in lottery tickets were sold, and about $3.3 billion in cash prizes were awarded by the state. After about $276 million in commissions and other payments to retailers and $220 million in administrative expenses, the lottery brought in almost $1.3 billion for state use. Most of that revenue ($1.2 billion) went to a fund to support Texas public schools, while another $17.8 million went to support the Texas Veterans Commission, and another $75.8 million went into the state's general revenue fund.[19] While unpopular with a wide variety of groups, the lottery remains a part of Texas state finances for the same reason as the other taxes and fees: no one has found a more popular way to replace the money it generates. For example, many social conservatives in the Texas

> **Permanent School Fund (PSF)**
> a fund set aside to finance education in Texas; the state's largest source of investment income

> What are the main sources of revenue for the state?
>
> ★ EMPIRICAL AND QUANTITATIVE

FIGURE 12.2 Federal Funds as a Share of Total Texas State Revenue, 1980–2017

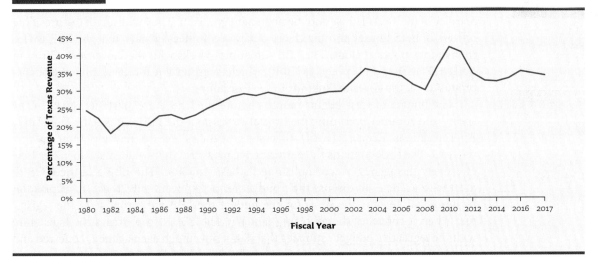

Source: Texas Comptroller, "Texas Net Revenue by Source: Fiscal Years 1980–2017," accessed July 29, 2018, https://comptroller.texas.gov/transparency/reports/revenue-by-source.

Legislature find the state's profits from gambling distasteful or immoral. However, eliminating the Texas Lottery would require increasing taxes or cutting popular programs to offset the revenue lost. Thus, taking this revenue source off the books would be politically difficult.

SPENDING AND BUDGETING

Texas government has not always been frugal. During the three years of Mirabeau Lamar's presidency, the government of Texas spent about $4.85 million while taking in only about $1.08 million.[20] Lamar had reversed Sam Houston's policy of cooperating with the Native American tribes, and the hostilities spawned by Lamar's desire to remove Native Americans cost Texas dearly. By contrast, Houston's administration spent only about a half million dollars in the three years after Lamar's presidency.

The Texas budget determines how much money Texas will spend and where it will spend it. While budgeting in Texas has always been political, it is also a clear representation of priorities in the state. Texans hate taxes and have long preferred little government. In recent years, lawmakers have been hesitant to raise taxes and often reluctant to spend money on even the most basic of services. Since the state legislature only meets every two years, Texas is one of twenty states that have a two-year budget cycle. That means, for example, that in a year where oil revenues suddenly rise, Texas may have cut spending on things like education and healthcare only to have unexpectedly higher revenues than anticipated. Likewise, in a year where the economy contracts without warning, Texas may be spending money it will have to make up the following year when the legislature meets.

The Legislative Budget Board

The Legislative Budget Board (LBB) was created in 1949 to help coordinate the budgeting process in Texas, a process that had previously been a haphazard collection of individual appropriations bills. As outlined in Chapter 3, the LBB is cochaired by the Speaker of the Texas House and the lieutenant governor. The inclusion of the presiding officers of both houses and the chairs of key committees ensures that the LBB wields tremendous political clout. The LBB sometimes works with the Governor's Office of Budget, Planning, and Policy (GOBPP), which is responsible for developing the budget proposal that the governor submits to the legislature.

The budget process begins months before the legislature starts its work. In the spring and summer preceding the legislative session, the LBB sends out a Legislative Appropriations Request (LAR) that state agencies use to develop their budget requests. The LAR contains the performance measures that will be used to gauge how effectively the agency is accomplishing its basic mission. The LBB and the GOBPP meet with agencies to discuss their budget requests. Eventually, these appropriation requests will become the basis for the budget the LBB will propose to the legislature when it convenes the following January. The LBB also provides the legislature with the legislative budget estimates that detail how much each agency requested and how much funding it received in previous budgets. The legislature is not completely dependent on the LBB analysis. During the legislative session, the Senate Committee

A man buys lottery tickets at a Texas convenience store. The sale of lottery tickets has become an important but controversial source of revenue for the state.

on Finance and the House Committee on Appropriations independently hold hearings and hear testimony from the state agencies. These committees often amend the proposed budget, and these amendments continue through consideration by the full House and Senate.

The state budget faces scrutiny even after it has been approved by the House and Senate. After the appropriations bill is passed, the comptroller must certify that sufficient revenue will be available to pay for the budget. The budget then goes to the governor for his or her signature. The Texas governor has line-item veto authority that allows him or her to remove or veto individual items in the appropriations bill. If the legislature is still in session when the governor vetoes a line in the appropriations bill, it may override the veto by a two-thirds majority vote in each house. As discussed in Chapter 4, Governor Abbott greatly expanded the governor's item veto power, vetoing riders attached to budget lines. This power suggests that the governor will play a much more active role in the budget process.

Once passed, the appropriations bill becomes the budget for the state for the next fiscal year. The fiscal year in Texas begins September 1, meaning that the state's budget year runs from September 1 through August 31 and does not coincide with the calendar year.

Traditionally the LBB has enjoyed tremendous influence because it prepares the initial budget estimate that will be considered during the legislative session, and its work continues beyond the initial proposal. During the legislative session, the LBB staff provides analysis for the legislative committees involved in spending. Texas law requires each bill in the legislature to have a fiscal note prepared by the LBB staff that estimates the cost of the bill. Because elected officials tend to want to spend more than they have, many critics feel that the fiscal notes have become politicized and that they often ignore the true costs of bills favored by the leadership. At the end of the 2007 legislative session, Governor Perry complained that fiscal notes were no longer providing accurate pictures of the costs of legislation and warned that he would no longer sign bills with inaccurate fiscal notes (see Figure 12.3).[21]

Between sessions, the LBB or the governor may recommend prohibiting a state agency from spending money appropriated to it by the legislature. The LBB or the governor may also transfer money from one state agency to another or change the purpose for which an appropriation was made. Such recommendations by the LBB must be approved by the governor in order to go into effect, while recommendations by the governor require approval by the LBB. This was the process used by state leaders in 2010 when they instructed state agencies to reduce their spending and to "give back" money that had previously been appropriated by the legislature in 2009. They did this so that the budget could remain balanced when tax revenues failed to live up to expectations.

State Budgeting

Texas political culture tends toward fiscal conservativism and distrust of government. When Texans drafted the current constitution in 1876, they specified that no debt could be created by the state, except to "repel invasion, suppress insurrection, or defend the State in war," and then not to exceed $200,000. Since then, the state constitution has been amended to further constrain state budgeting, including requiring limits on increased appropriations, caps on welfare assistance, "pay-as-you-go" budgeting, and limits on debt. Since Texans prefer little government with little spending, Article 8 of the Texas Constitution stipulates that biennium increases in state appropriations cannot exceed the expected rate of growth in the state's economy. This is a clear statement that Texans don't want more government; government spending cannot grow faster than the state's economy. Article 3 of the Constitution further mandates that the state can spend no more than one percent of the budget on "needy dependent children."

In addition to attempting to limit spending, the state's constitution also endeavors to limit debt. Texas has a **"pay-as-you-go" system** that requires a balanced budget, meaning appropriations cannot exceed available revenue. The constitution stipulates that the pay-as-you-go requirement can be suspended with a four-fifths vote of both the Texas House and Senate.[22] Texas further limits authorization of any debt if the state's debt exceeds general revenues by five percent.

While many Texans might assume that balancing the state budget is relatively simple, the system created to ensure that the budget stays balanced has spawned some unique features in Texas government, especially in the role of the comptroller of public accounts. At the beginning of each legislative session, the Texas Constitution requires that the comptroller certify how much money will be in the state's accounts in the two years that the legislature is budgeting for. This means the comptroller needs relatively good forecasting models to keep the legislators within their limits. Since the Texas Legislature meets only every two years, it also means that the comptroller's crystal ball needs to be able to anticipate changes in the economy two years out. These provisions put the Texas comptroller in a unique—and powerful—position. Former comptroller Carole Strayhorn pointed out the following:

"pay-as-you-go" system a fiscal discipline, adopted by Texas and many other states, that requires a balanced budget and permits borrowing only under very few circumstances

FIGURE 12.3 Texas Biennial Budget Cycle

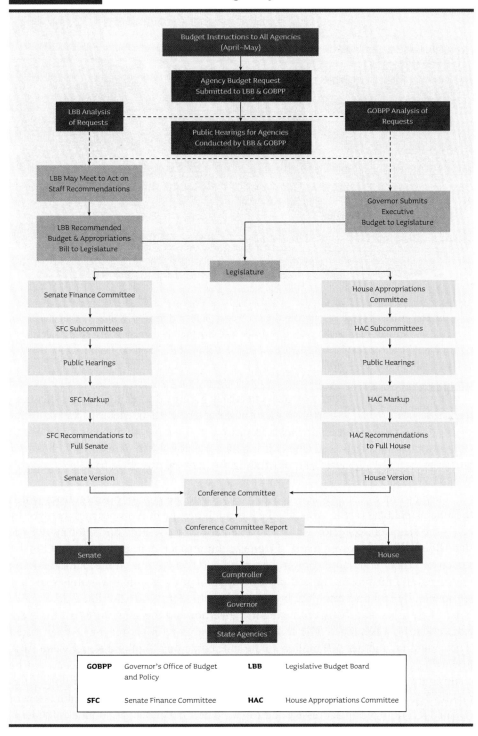

Source: Senate Research Center, "Budget 101: A Guide to the Budget Process in Texas," January 2017, https://senate .texas.gov/_assets/srcpub/85th_Budget_101.pdf.

Governor Greg Abbott (center) signs House Bill 32, a franchise tax cut, during a bill signing ceremony in Austin, Texas.

Rodolfo Gonzalez/Austin American-Statesman via AP

> The comptroller's office is a constitutional office; there's nothing like it in any other state. I tell the legislature what they can spend, and I certify that the budget is balanced. Unless and until I certify that budget, there is no appropriations bill, and there is nothing for the governor to line-item veto.[23]

The estimate from the comptroller effectively became the ceiling for state spending that the legislature had to operate under. The comptroller, then, wields particular influence but also faces unique minefields in office. For example, then-comptroller Susan Combs was roundly criticized when during the recession she underestimated the state's budget by over $8 billion in 2011, illustrating the political minefield that the comptroller has to navigate.

The position of comptroller does not seem to be the kind of position from which to launch a political career. After all, the job combines the dubious warmth enjoyed by being the state's tax collector with the excitement of accounting and auditing for the state. Bob Bullock, however, made his time as comptroller an important part of his rise to power. When he became comptroller in 1975, the office ran on mechanical adding machines, and the most advanced piece of equipment in the office was an electric letter opener. Bullock increased the budget for his office from $16.5 million to $46 million in four years, largely by promising the governor and the legislature that for every extra dollar he was budgeted he could bring in ten more in tax revenue. When asked if he could find another $10 million so the state could buy Big Bend Ranch State Park, Bullock is said to have replied that he couldn't find $10 million for the park, but he could find $11 million for the park so long as it also included $1 million for pay raises for the Texas Rangers. Bullock increased tax collections through a combination of updated technology and aggressive auditors who became known as "Bullock's Raiders." Bullock and his auditors made some of his raids on television, a tactic that motivated other businesses owing back taxes to pay up. The process was not always smooth or

TABLE 12.3 State Spending by Function, Fiscal Year 2017

Government Function	Amount	Percentage of Total
General government: executive departments	$2,783,421,232	2.5
General government: legislative	$150,078,901	0.1
General government: judicial	$345,837,980	0.3
Total general government	**$3,279,338,116**	**2.9**
Education	$35,504,880,963	31.5
Employee benefits	$4,755,179,125	4.2
Health and human services	$49,075,263,713	43.6
Public safety and corrections	$4,927,729,972	4.4
Transportation	$10,260,658,371	9.1
Natural resources/recreational services	$2,045,995,022	1.8
Regulatory services	$349,818,908	0.3
Lottery winnings paid	$557,026,044	0.5
Debt service: interest	$1,255,690,046	1.1
Capital outlay	$613,540,131	0.5
Total net expenditures	$112,625,120,411	

Source: Texas Comptroller, "Texas Net Expenditures by Function—Fiscal 2017," accessed July 31, 2018, https://comptroller.texas.gov/transparency/reports/expenditures/function/.

genteel, and Bullock was sued by the Texas Council of Campfire Girls after he forced them to pay $13,284 in sales taxes.

One of the ways the state's legislators can get around the requirement to balance the budget is take on debt by selling bonds. The constitution allows the state to sell revenue bonds to finance activities specified in Article 3. As stated above, bonds that are paid back from the state's general revenue must not exceed five percent of the state's general revenue. Bonds that are sold to investors and then paid back with the revenue from the services they provide are not subject to the constitutional debt limit. For example, Texas often issues tuition revenue bonds that may pay for new buildings on college campuses with student fees set aside to pay back the debt. As of 2015, Texas had about $41 billion in outstanding state bonds.[24]

While the public debt in Texas is relatively low compared to other states, the debt of Texas local governments has been increasing in recent years. As state budgets have slashed money for education and roads, local governments have had to pick up the slack. Local governments in Texas issue bonds for everything from road construction, new school development, sewage system expansion, to new sports arena development. Total debt for Texas local governments was just over $212 billion at the end of the 2015 fiscal year.[25] An analysis from the comptroller's office revealed that local government

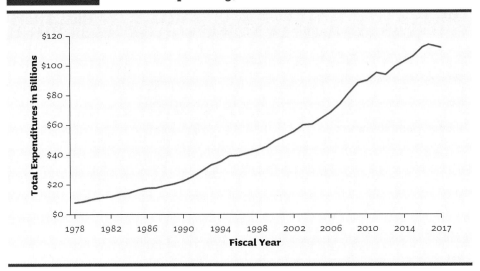

FIGURE 12.4 Trends in Spending, 1978–2017

Source: Texas Comptroller, "Texas Net Expenditures by Function–Fiscal 2017," accessed July 29, 2018, https://comptroller.texas.gov/transparency/reports/expenditures/function.

debt had more than doubled in the decade from 2001 to 2011, rising from $87.6 billion to $192 billion.[26] While the comptroller's report was somewhat critical of localities for this borrowing, it's only fair to point out that some of this borrowing resulted from efforts to keep up with explosive growth. Communities with rapid growth have trouble keeping up with this growth because their tax rates are constitutionally limited and new schools, roads, and water systems are expensive.

State Spending

As the Texas economy changes and Texans' expectations for government change, spending in Texas shifts. One of the fundamental causes of a growing state budget is a growing state population. As Table 12.3 details, Texas spends its money on a wide array of functions. Health and human services account for the largest outlays in the state, amounting to nearly 44 percent of the total budget. This includes Medicaid, mental health spending, Children's Health Insurance Program (CHIP), Temporary Assistance for Needy Families (TANF), unemployment, and worker's compensation. Funding for most of these programs is shared with the federal government. Education makes up the second largest expenditure in the state and accounts for nearly 32 percent of the budget. This includes primary and secondary education in the state, which supplements local taxes. It also includes funding the state's community colleges and universities. State spending on transportation makes up 9 percent of the overall budget to maintain around 80,000 miles of road. State spending on public safety, employee benefits, natural resources, and general government each amount to less than 5 percent of the state's total spending.

While the state's constitution establishes numerous barriers to state debt, these provisions have not stopped increased state spending. Even though Texas is a conservative state, spending continues to rise. As Figure 12.4 demonstrates, spending in the state has been increasing steadily for the past thirty years. Much of this increase can be

FIGURE 12.5 The Rainy Day Fund

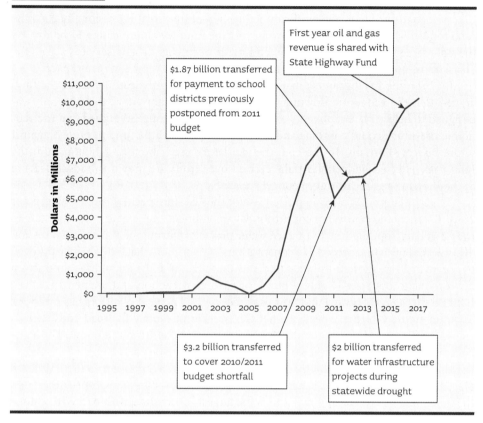

First year oil and gas revenue is shared with State Highway Fund

$1.87 billion transferred for payment to school districts previously postponed from 2011 budget

$3.2 billion transferred to cover 2010/2011 budget shortfall

$2 billion transferred for water infrastructure projects during statewide drought

Source: Texas Comptroller of Public Accounts.

explained by inflation and the fact that the state's population has roughly doubled in the same time frame. However, Texas's government has grown dramatically under both Republicans and Democrats, and this enlargement reflects the increased demands of a growing and changing state.

The Rainy Day Fund

The Economic Stabilization Fund (ESF), often referred to as the Rainy Day Fund (see Figure 12.5), was set up by a constitutional amendment approved by the voters in 1988 to help offset the effect of a sometimes erratic oil and gas market on the state's budget. The ESF receives an amount equal to 75 percent of the amount of oil production tax collections in excess of 1987 levels and 75 percent of the amount of natural gas tax collections in excess of 1987 levels. The fund also receives one-half of any unused general revenue funds at the end of each biennial budget. In addition, the Texas Legislature may also add revenue to the fund whenever it wants.

Using the funds is much more difficult. Under certain circumstances, such as when the comptroller certifies a budget deficit, the legislature may appropriate money from the ESF with a three-fifths vote of each house. Otherwise, the legislature can use funds from the ESF for any purpose with a two-thirds vote of the members present in each

How has the state's Rainy Day Fund been affected by large transfers of money during the Great Recession?

★ EMPIRICAL AND QUANTITATIVE

Under what conditions should lawmakers tap into the Rainy Day Fund?

★ CRITICAL THINKING

house. The ESF became a political football in recent years as the oil and gas boom led to unprecedented growth in the fund. In 2007 the ESF exceeded $1 billion for the first time and continued to grow significantly throughout the Great Recession. By 2008 the fund topped $4 billion, and the following year the fund was approaching $7 billion. As the state struggled with the recession and made deep cuts to state services across the board, most notably education, the state's Rainy Day Fund grew at a record pace.

By 2011, the ESF became a major source of conflict. Advocates of using the fund argued that the economic downturn was the kind of "rainy day" that the ESF was designed to help with. Proponents of leaving the fund untouched argued that the economic downturn could continue and that the state needed the fund to protect against future budget shortfalls. In the end, the legislature used about $3.2 billion from the fund that reflected budget shortfalls carried over from the previous budget, leaving $6.3 billion in the ESF for future budget shortfalls.

The legislature has also supported use of the ESF for specific uses. In November 2013, Texas voters approved a constitutional amendment that would allow the state to use $2 billion from the ESF to finance water projects. During the third special session of 2013, the legislature agreed to a constitutional amendment that, after being approved by voters in 2014, allowed the state to divert up to half of ESF's oil and gas production tax revenue to the State Highway Fund for road construction and maintenance. The ESF and the State Highway Fund now each receive 37.5 percent of oil and gas revenues. That amendment further specified that the transfer of money for road construction would continue until 2024, provided the ESF maintain a "sufficient" amount. The legislature determines what a sufficient amount is prior to the start of the legislative session. For the 2018–2019 biennium, the legislature established $7.5 billion as the ESF floor. Since the fund's creation, the state has authorized $11.6 billion in appropriations from the fund. Still, Texas's Rainy Day Fund is the largest of any state, with over $10 billion.

FISCAL POLICY TOOLS

 hile the basic issues of taxing and spending occupy the minds of most Texans, there are some fiscal policy tools that require special attention.

Tax Expenditures

tax expenditures
any reductions in tax liabilities that result from tax benefits to particular taxpayers rather than taxpayers in general

One form of subsidy that is especially difficult to measure is tax expenditures. Tax expenditures include any reductions in tax liabilities that result from tax benefits or exclusions applied to particular taxpayers rather than taxpayers in general. These kinds of selective incentives can be used to encourage certain types of businesses yet are different from other kinds of government support because they do not show up on a budget since they reflect taxes never collected.

For the 2017 fiscal year, Comptroller Glenn Hegar estimates that the total value of tax exemptions from sales, franchise, motor vehicle sales, and oil production taxes is $43.7 billion.[27] The largest share of this is sales tax exemptions, which are granted to a wide variety of industries. In addition, another $11.8 billion in tax exemptions or special appraisals is granted to local school district property taxes. For example, the oil and gas industry can qualify for tax expenditures for low producing wells, utilizing

Should the state exempt some businesses from paying part or all of its sales taxes?

★ SOCIAL RESPONSIBILITY

previously inactive wells, and using enhanced oil recovery methods. The largest tax incentive for natural gas is a high cost tax reduction on natural gas wells, which can be applied retroactively. A contraction in the oil industry in 2014 and 2015 and the appeal of the high cost tax reduction led to a spike in the number of applications to reclassify oil wells as natural gas wells.

The tax-free holiday celebrated annually in Texas since 1999 is another kind of tax expenditure because it exempts certain items from the sales tax each year as Texans are getting ready for the start of school. In 2007, the Texas Legislature added another tax-free weekend for the purchase of energy-efficient items such as appliances and lightbulbs, and in 2015 the legislature added a third sales tax holiday for emergency preparation supplies. The comptroller estimates that the three tax holidays will save Texans nearly $100 million in 2017. While these millions will never show up as dollars spent by a program, they resulted in lower government revenues and financial advantage for citizens willing to face the crowds that weekend. Research from the Tax Foundation suggests that the holidays only serve to shift shopping from one day to another and that some businesses actually increase their prices during the holiday. The Tax Foundation also argues that the tax holidays generate additional administrative costs for government and small businesses, which have to reprogram their registers to comply, and that they tend to be championed by a few large businesses that view them as a form of free advertising.[28]

Tax breaks for certain professions may seem the stuff of modern politics, but they are not new to Texas. In fact, the constitutions of 1845, 1861, 1866, 1869, and 1876 all authorized an income or occupational tax, but with the provision that agricultural or mechanical pursuits were exempt. Thus, we can see a preference for farm income extending back to the origins of the state.

Local governments sometimes provide tax abatements that exempt certain businesses from some of their property taxes. For example, in 2011, Fort Worth put together a package that reportedly included $13.5 million in tax breaks for Bell Helicopter as incentive for the helicopter maker to remain in the area.[29] According to another story, California chain In-N-Out Burger got its own tax break, meaning that Whataburger (a Texas institution) could be paying higher taxes to fund incentives to bring in competition.[30] Many cities offer grants and tax breaks to businesses thinking about relocating. While bringing jobs to an area might seem popular at first glance, these incentives shift the tax burden to existing businesses that may not enjoy paying the tax bill for their new neighbors. In addition, tax dollars might be used to bring in businesses that are controversial (e.g., nuclear power plants).

Local governments in Texas have not always found managing growth an easy task. Communities often scramble to keep up with the growing need for more schools, roads, and water. As Frisco school superintendent Jeremy Lyon noted, "state leaders have done an excellent job creating an environment that interests companies in moving here. What gets lost is that you need a vibrant school system to attract the families that also will move."[31]

Subsidies

While we often think of the federal government as being much more activist than the Texas state government, the state of Texas and many of its cities are not shy about subsidizing activities they want. Texas utilizes a wide range of subsidies to attract certain businesses and events to the state. In 2004, then-governor Perry championed the creation of a Texas Enterprise Fund (TEF) to attract businesses to the state. Since its inception the fund has awarded more than $500 million to various businesses. When Perry announced that Toyota would relocate its North American headquarters to Plano, he cited a "combination of low taxes, fair courts, smart regulations and [a] world-class workforce [that] can help businesses of any size succeed and thrive."[32] However, Perry was offering Toyota something beyond the traditional Texas fare of low taxes and minimal business regulation: $40 million in funds from the TEF. To sweeten the deal further, the city of Plano agreed to a grant of $6,750,000 and offered Toyota a 50 percent tax abatement for ten years and a 50 percent rebate on taxes for the ten years after that. Since taking office, Governor Abbott has also regularly tapped the TEF, giving $9.75 million to a pharmaceutical company, McKesson, to build a campus in Irving. While Abbott calls the TEF a deal closing fund, it has not been without controversy. A 2014 state audit found that more than $222 million had been awarded to companies that had not actually applied for the funds.[33]

Since its inception, the fund has awarded more than $600 million to various businesses. However, TEF awards typically require local governments to include economic incentives. Local government incentives are frequently in the form of Chapter 380 (city), Chapter 381 (county), and Chapter 313 (local school board) economic development agreements that provide additional tax exemptions or grants to businesses. The TEF awards are often dwarfed by the accompanying local subsidies and the cumulative total for a business that gets a TEF grant is significant. It is difficult to assess the total cost of any incentive package, the details of which are often shrouded in secrecy. According to a recent study, once you add the local subsidies with the TEF awards, Texas spends *at least* $1.76 billion a year subsidizing private businesses.[34] The TEF has clearly brought jobs to the state. However, the total cost of the economic incentives can be excessive. For example, a 2006 $118 million grant to Samsung Electronics was accompanied by a Chapter 313 grant of another $204 million, a property tax rebate, and an ad valorem tax rebate, among other incentives. Overall, the benefit to Samsung Electronics was $321 million for a promised 900 new jobs, which worked out to $356,000 per job.[35]

The state also has three funds used to attract events to the state: the Events Trust Fund, the Major Events Reimbursement Program, and the Motor Sports Racing Trust Fund. In both 2012 and 2013, the state paid out just over $25 million to support the United States Grand Prix, with local governments chipping in another $4 million each per year. The comptroller's office considered these subsidies important to encouraging development of a $242 million racetrack that was estimated to pump $400 million into the Texas economy.[36] The subsidies came from the state's event trust funds, which have paid out amounts ranging from the $26,856,950 provided to support the 2011 Super Bowl to the $2,727 the state paid to help bring the 2011 Little Dribblers' Basketball National Tournament to Texas. Along the way, the state of Texas paid $2,175,247 to host the 2018 NFL draft in Arlington (with another $348,040 provided by local governments) and $1,800,595 to host MegaFest 2013 (a two-day, family-oriented fellowship event), with host city Dallas chipping in another $288,096. Generally, contributions from local government must match the state's contribution by providing one dollar of local funds for every $6.25 in state funds. Funds are available only for an event that is competitively bid and involves a community competing with cities outside Texas for the right to host it.

In 2005, the Texas Legislature created the Texas Emerging Technology Fund (TETF) to support start-up companies in cutting-edge fields. In 2015, Governor Abbott pushed to have the TETF abolished and replaced by a University Research Initiative. The 84th Texas Legislature funded the new initiative with $40 million with the goal of attracting major researchers including Nobel laureates to Texas state universities.

It is telling that when the Future Business Leaders of America met in San Antonio in June 2012 to prepare young people for careers in business, the organization did so with the help of $322,157 in state and local subsidies. While Texas is a conservative state, even a conservative state engages in a variety of partnerships between the public sector (government) and the private sector (businesses). This may not seem consistent with the conservative legends of Texas, but in reality the state has always had a hand in encouraging economic development. For example, after World War II, the state began construction of a farm-to-market road system designed specifically to help Texas farmers and ranchers move their products to market. The state also offers tax breaks for certain types of high-cost natural gas production to help encourage energy production.

WINNERS AND LOSERS

Texans are generally big fans of the system of free enterprise, and many think the free market and not the government should be picking economic winners and losers. In June 2007, the Texas Legislature created the Texas Moving Image Industry Incentive Program that provides grants and tax breaks to films, television programs, commercials, and video games produced in the state in the name of creating jobs. In signing the bill, Governor Rick Perry noted neighboring Louisiana's success with a similar program and told Texans that the entertainment industry "creates jobs, builds the economy and serves as an incubator for the development of the creative arts industry."[37] In 2009, when Perry signed a revision of the law, he held the bill-signing ceremony at Robert Rodriguez's Troublemaker Studios and boasted that the law was "strengthening our state's investment in a vital industry."[38] The law, to some degree, has had its desired effect and, according to Robert Rodriguez, brought production of his movie *Machete* to Texas.

Help for companies extends beyond the entertainment industry. In 2012, the state of Texas finalized a plan to give Apple $21 million over ten years from its TEF, while the city of Austin offered $8.6 million in grants and Travis County promised an additional grant of at least $5.4 million over 15 years.[39] This plan was expected to help bring a $304 million investment from Apple that could create more than 3,600 jobs. Anyone familiar with Apple knows that the company did not need much help in 2012.

While we often think about "winners versus losers" as pitting big companies against consumers or small businesses, there are times when the state makes winners of some companies at the expense of others. The problem is that when state and local governments give grants or tax breaks to bring a company into the area, the company's arrival does not diminish the need for government revenue. In fact, it likely increases the demand for services because the company and its employees will need additional infrastructure, such as roads, housing, and education. This means that existing companies, and citizens, must pay more taxes to make up the difference.

Having the state picking economic winners and losers runs contrary to Texans' support for free enterprise. However, other states are providing incentives and failing

State Spending in Perspective

Total State Expenditures Per Capita

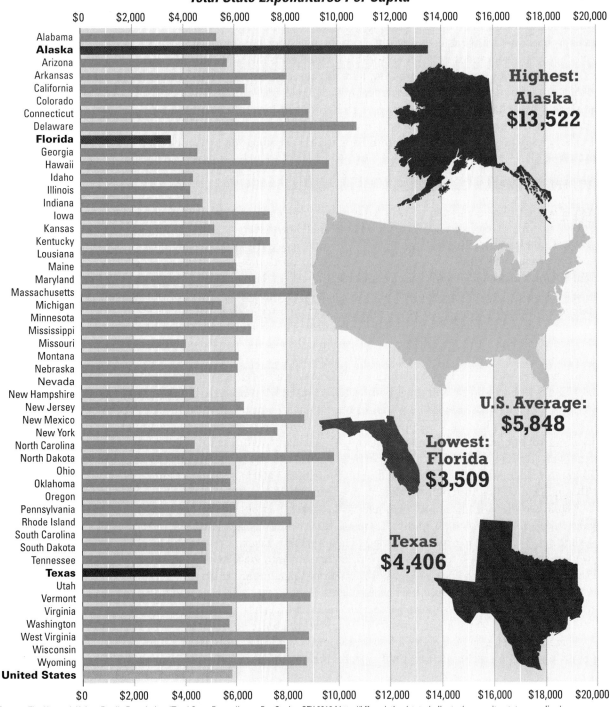

Highest: Alaska $13,522

U.S. Average: $5,848

Lowest: Florida $3,509

Texas $4,406

Source: The Henry J. Kaiser Family Foundation, "Total State Expenditures Per Capita, SFY 2016," http://kff.org/other/state-indicator/per-capita-state-spending/.

to do the same could put Texas at a huge disadvantage in its competition with other states. So, in Texas politics, how free your enterprise is depends on your enterprise and how well represented it is in Austin. As we have seen, even a conservative government like Texas's is actively engaged in trying to shape the economy. Inevitably, this will lead to the state picking economic winners and losers.

CONCLUSION

Politics is how we decide who gets what, and nothing is a clearer statement than a state's budget. Texas continues to struggle with how to allocate state resources and Texans prefer a government that stays out of their lives and keeps taxes limited. Still, most Texans agree that some programs, like education funding in the state and road construction, continue to be underfunded. In a 2017 poll that asked what the legislature's top budget priority should be, 17 percent identified redesigning K–12 education funding, 13 percent said increasing CHIP funding, and 12 percent wanted increased funding for border security.[40] In that same poll, 20 percent of Texans said lowering property taxes should be the top priority and another 16 percent said approving no new taxing or spending. Texans will continue to face tough budget choices. While the state's leaders enjoy bragging about how many people and businesses come to Texas, they know that these newcomers will create the demand for more water, new roads, more schools, and other government services. Attracting new businesses sometimes involves tax breaks or other incentives, the costs of which fall on existing taxpayers. Thus, the tension between old and new Texas finds its place in the state's tax code and budget.

> Should the state's tax system or spending be revised? How?
>
> ★ CRITICAL THINKING

> Are tax breaks useful in bringing business to Texas, or are the costs of luring business to the state too high?
>
> ★ SOCIAL RESPONSIBILITY

for CQ Press

Want a better grade?

Get the tools you need to sharpen your study skills. Access practice quizzes, eFlashcards, video, and multimedia at **edge.sagepub.com/collier6e**.

KEY TERMS

ad valorem tax (p. 399)

agenda setting (p. 392)

appraisal (p. 399)

distributive policy (p. 392)

excise tax (p. 397)

fiscal policy (p. 393)

franchise tax (p. 396)

general sales tax (p. 393)

income tax (p. 393)

"pay-as-you-go" system (p. 408)

Permanent School Fund (PSF) (p. 405)

policy (p. 392)

(Continued)

KEY TERMS (CONTINUED)

policy adoption (p. 392)
policy evaluation (p. 392)
policy formation (p. 392)
policy implementation (p. 392)
progressive tax (p. 402)
property tax (p. 398)
redistributive policy (p. 392)

regressive tax (p. 402)
regulatory policy (p. 392)
severance tax (p. 395)
sin tax (p. 397)
subsidies (p. 393)
tax expenditures (p. 414)

ACTIVE LEARNING

- Break up into small groups and discuss the various "hidden" taxes in Texas. Can you identify some of them? **Teamwork**

- In what areas, if any, should Texas spend more money? Prepare a two- to three-slide presentation to make your case. **Communication**

CHAPTER REVIEW

1. Most of Texas's tax revenue comes from _____.

   a. sales tax

   b. property tax

   c. income tax

   d. sin tax

2. A policy that attempts to make society more equal is called _____ policy.

   a. tax

   b. distributive

   c. redistributive

   d. regulatory

3. Texas utilizes all of the following taxes *except* _____.

   a. sales tax

   b. property tax

   c. income tax

   d. sin tax

4. Texas's oil and gas tax is calculated based on the _____.

   a. amount of profit an oil company makes in a year

   b. market price of oil and gas produced

   c. amount of oil and gas that is produced

   d. average fuel efficiency of automobiles

5. Texas taxes which of the following?

   a. cigarettes

   b. alcohol

   c. nude entertainment

   d. all of these

6. How much does Texas utilize local property taxes?

   a. less than most other states

   b. about the same as most other states

   c. more than most other states

   d. not at all

7. A tax that takes a higher portion of income from people with lower incomes is called a _____ tax.

   a. progressive

   b. regressive

   c. poor

   d. severance

8. On the whole, Texas's tax system is generally _____.

   a. more regressive than most states

   b. more progressive than most states

   c. about as regressive as most states

   d. equally paid across different groups

9. The Texas Constitution limits the state budget in which of the following ways?

   a. Appropriations cannot exceed the state's expected rate of growth.

   b. The state can spend no more than 1 percent of the budget on "needy dependent children."

   c. Appropriations cannot exceed available revenue.

   d. All of the above

10. Texas's Rainy Day Fund _____.

    a. was set up to offset the erratic prices of oil and gas

    b. was completely emptied during the Great Recession and Hurricane Harvey

    c. gets 100 percent of the state's oil and gas tax

    d. is smaller than most states

ENERGY, ENVIRONMENT, TRANSPORTATION, AND TRADE POLICIES

Transforming Texas

Chapter Objectives

★ Discuss how oil and natural gas shape Texas politics and identity.

★ Explore the costs and benefits of a boom-and-bust economy.

★ Assess who wins and who loses in the way Texas manages its natural resources.

★ Identify ways in which Texas's transportation infrastructure is stressed by the state's population and economic growth.

★ Assess who wins and who loses in the state's approach to managing its infrastructure to meet the demands of a growing populace.

★ Assess who wins and who loses from Texas's trade policy.

Texas has long been associated with oil or "Texas Tea." Most people don't think of Texas as a leader in green energy. For more than a decade, Texas has led the country in wind energy. The rapid growth of the wind market, which involved building new transmission lines, allowed Texas cities to use renewable energy. In 2016, Georgetown became the first city in Texas and the largest city in the country to be powered completely by renewable energy. According to the town's mayor, the decision was economic. When it came time for the city to renew its power contract, wind and solar prices had become competitive with traditional fossil fuels.

View of downtown Georgetown, Texas. Georgetown is the first city in Texas to be powered completely by renewable energy.

Moreover, those prices are not subject to the same dramatic market volatility as oil and gas, so "the city can sign a contract today and know what the bill is going to be for the next 25 years."[1] The move to green energy has been so popular in this conservative town, where electricity rates have decreased, that Georgetown is doubling down on green energy—in residential solar panels with the goal of creating a virtual power plant. As the price of renewable energy continues to plummet, other Texas cities will follow. Denton has already announced its intention to become 100 percent renewable by 2020. This is significant, since Denton is twice as large as Georgetown. As wind and solar are reshaping the Texas landscape, they are also proving an economic boon. According to the Bureau of Labor Statistics, the two fastest-growing jobs in the country are solar installer and wind turbine technician.[2] Texas has long been a state of tradition, but Texas has also consistently had to reinvent itself with ever-changing economic realities. The wind rush may represent the face of Texas's future.

In this chapter, we explore Texas policies that celebrate traditions and change. We examine Texas's rich history of oil and natural gas discoveries and how this helped shape the state's economy and identity. We further explore the current natural gas boom, including the costs and benefits of fracking, to understand how it has shaped energy politics in the state. Next, we look at the state's environmental policy, specifically regarding air and water, and the growing field of alternative energy, as well as the state's new foray into hazardous waste disposal. The evolution of transportation policy, from railroads to roads to mass transit, will then be reviewed. We end with an examination of Texas's trade economic policy and how that continues to shape the state.

OIL AND GAS IN TEXAS

Nothing has done more to transform Texas than the discovery of oil. Agrarian Texas, defined by vast plains of land and scarce resources, gave way to Texas as oil country, dominated by its booms and busts. Early settlers spotted oil seeping from the ground, but they could find little use for it beyond the occasional boat repair. All of that changed with the American oil boom in the 1800s, which started in Pennsylvania and flourished in the eastern part of the country. Texas's earliest discoveries of oil, in Nacogdoches County in 1866 and in Corsicana in 1894, were relatively modest, and few people expected the state to figure in the oil boom. That changed in 1901 when a well drilled at the Spindletop oilfield in Beaumont struck oil. The world took notice when Lucas No. 1 erupted, shooting oil 100 feet into the air and producing 100,000 barrels a day for the next nine days before finally being capped. As oil collected around the area, it caught a train on fire, creating a cloud of smoke that hovered over the city and returned to earth via a rain that ruined the paint on the houses in town.[3] Word of the discovery made its way across America, and Texas's towns were soon overrun by those wanting to strike it rich. The Texas oil rush had begun.

Oil's Influence on Texas

As a result of the discovery of oil, Texas's population got a boost in the early 1900s as people flooded the state in search of oil. As we recall from Chapter 2, the 1866 Texas constitution allowed individuals to retain the mineral rights to their lands. Some Texans suddenly found ranch land that had barely sustained their herds highly prized by oil companies. Predicting the location of oil was (and still is) an uncertain business, and many investors bought up land or mineral rights in the hope of finding oil. Initially, Texas law favored individual prospectors, called wildcatters, and discouraged large oil companies. Texas antitrust laws did not allow integrated oil companies until 1917. That meant that companies that refined, stored, and transported oil were not allowed to produce it.[4] Under these rules, many small oil companies flourished in Texas, although many more produced only dry wells and quickly went out of business. In 1901, there were 491 new oil companies that were granted charters by the state.[5] Moreover, oil discoveries soon reached across Texas and supported a wide range of oil-related businesses, including oil refineries and manufacturers of drill bits and other related machinery.

How did early Texas oil laws reflect Texas political culture?

⭐ CRITICAL THINKING

As many Texas oilmen went from rags to riches, so did the state treasury. In 1905, the Texas Legislature passed its first tax on oil production, at 1 percent of the value. The discovery of oil led to a significant stream of income for the state. In 2017, the tax on oil production was 4.6 percent, and natural gas was taxed at 7.5 percent, amounting to $3.09 billion of the state's revenue.[6] Not all gas production pays the 7.5 percent rate. To encourage natural gas production, Texas tax code allows wells designated by the Texas Railroad Commission as high-cost wells to get a tax credit for up to ten years. While Texas has benefited from oil and gas, the tax code also significantly subsidizes the industry. In 2006, the state comptroller estimated that 96 percent of the state's $1.4 billion in subsidies went to the oil and gas industry.[7]

The oil boom also directly benefited the University of Texas (UT) and Texas A&M. As early as 1839, the Republic of Texas Congress set aside fifty leagues of land to establish two universities. When the national government passed the Morrill Land-Grant College Act in 1862, Texas added even more land, and in 1876, the Texas Legislature created the Permanent University Fund (PUF). Much of the land used to endow the fund was in West Texas and generally thought to be of little value until the discovery of oil in the Permian Basin. In 1931, the legislature passed a law that allocated three-fourths of the fund's money

TEXAS Legends

Hot Oil

While Texans often think of oil producers as solid citizens who may enjoy a cozy relationship with elected officials, this hasn't always been the case. In fact, the state's early relationship with oil producers was rocky. Writing about the Texas oil industry in the 1930s, Wayne Gard declared, "Oil is the toughest baby the New Deal has tried to civilize. It is still one of the most obstreperous American industries, though it has become the third largest. It is shot through with lawlessness and with flagrant disregard for the public interest."[i]

The trouble erupted in the 1930s when a glut of oil came onto the market. During this decade, when the East Texas oil fields began producing, the surplus of oil drove down prices to a few pennies per barrel. The East Texas oil fields, which were not discovered until October 1930, were populated with 15,271 wells by 1935.[ii] To stabilize the situation, the governor asked the Railroad Commission of Texas to put together a proration plan

that would force producers to cut back how much oil came from their wells. In August 1931, when producers ignored an order from the Railroad Commission to stop production, Governor Ross Sterling, himself a former chair of Humble Oil, announced East Texas oil producers were in "rebellion," declared martial law, and sent in the National Guard to shut down oil fields in Rusk and Gregg Counties.[iii]

Despite the governor's decree, many small drillers continued to operate in defiance of limits imposed by law and smuggled "hot oil" in what became known as the "hot oil wars," which continued for almost four years. Oilmen created phony wells next to real wells to win the right to produce more oil. Gasoline was smuggled out of eastern Texas in oil trucks disguised as moving vans or through hidden pipelines. Some producers hired their own "rangers" to approach federal officials with both guns and cash.[iv] Illegal "moonshine" refineries sprouted to serve the hot oil market.

The federal government was eventually drawn into the battle after members of the Railroad Commission of Texas appealed to the newly elected U.S. president. Franklin Roosevelt signed an executive order in July 1933 that sent hundreds of federal agents into the field to enforce it.

Some of the lawlessness was driven by simple greed, but some oilmen were pushed to the limits because they had purchased oil rights and equipment on credit. Unlike independent oilmen, the large oil companies could afford to leave the oil in the ground and resume drilling when the price rebounded.

---

i.   Wayne Gard, "Hot Oil from Texas," *American Mercury*, May 1935, 71.

ii. Ibid., 73.

iii. Bryan Burrough, *The Big Rich: The Rise and Fall of the Greatest Texas Oil Fortunes* (New York: Penguin Press, 2009), 77.

iv. Gard, "Hot Oil from Texas."

---

to UT Austin and the remaining one-fourth to Texas A&M University. The state's recent oil and gas boom significantly increased the value of the fund. Annual oil and gas contributions to the PUF increased from $83 million in 2000 to around $512 million in 2016. The 2014 yearly contributions marked a high point, generating $1.1 billion for the fund.[8] The PUF has more than doubled since 2000 and is worth more than $20 billion today.

The Texas economy continued to be driven by the oil industry throughout the twentieth century. Oil helped move Texas from an agrarian state to an urban one. Perhaps more importantly, oil gave Texas a boom-and-bust economy. A familiar pattern emerged where oil discoveries would bring a booming economy marked by a surge in oil wells and jobs. The rapid production of oil would bring riches, but inevitably the resulting glut in oil would cause the price of oil to plummet. Oil jobs disappeared and wells were abandoned. For a small town, the discovery of oil brought with it immediate jobs and the people to fill them. Roads, housing, and schools strained under the rapid influx of people. The rush to build new infrastructure to keep up with the rapid growth rarely anticipated the inevitable busts, where buildings were left vacant and people were left jobless. Overall, the Texas economy rose as the price of oil surged, and the state faltered as the price fell. Oil cushioned Texas from the worst of the Great Depression. Along the way it made (and broke) many small towns. In 1981, oil and gas made up 26.5 percent of gross state product (GSP). By the mid-1980s, the price of oil plunged to $11 a barrel, and the Texas economy fell with it. The result was significant migration out of the state and a smaller oil and gas industry.[9] Following the 1980s recession, Texas diversified its economy, and oil and gas dropped to a mere 7.4 percent of GSP by 1999. The technologies that facilitated the most recent natural gas boom in the state (discussed next) are also being used to drill for oil in addition to natural gas, giving new life to old oil fields. As the United States dealt with the Great Recession that started in 2008, record prices of oil per barrel helped soften the blow to Texas's economy. In 2008, rising prices and technological advances helped oil and gas account for 16.5 percent of Texas's GSP.[10] Today, oil and gas remains a significant portion of the state's economy, although it has contracted as the price of oil has dropped. In 2013, oil was 13.5 percent of the state's GSP, and that percentage is expected to decrease further still.[11] In the most recent bust, the price of oil plummeted from over $100 a barrel in 2014 to $27 a barrel by 2016, upending the oil and gas industry. Independent oil operators in the state shuttered their doors; wells were abandoned and jobs lost. By the end of 2016, Houston had lost more than 81,000 oil and gas jobs, 100 oil and gas companies had gone bankrupt, and the number of rigs in the state had dropped by 80 percent. By 2018, the price of oil had rebounded, as had the industry.[12] In that year, Texas's Permian Basin was producing more oil than its pipelines could handle, costing oil companies in the area billions.[13] New pipelines will take years to build and could be further slowed by looming steel tariffs.[14] Unlike the 1980s, the recent bust was less devastating to the overall economy. Today's economy continues to lead the country in oil production and oil-refining capacity. Yet Texas has diversified significantly, now as likely to operate in computer chips, telecommunications, and finance as in oil and gas. Still, oil remains a powerful industry as well as a powerful source of identity for the state.

The politics of oil continues to be a part of Texas politics. The United States has been trying to move away from dependence on oil from the Middle East, and in 2008, a Canadian company called TransCanada proposed a pipeline that would make importing Canadian oil easier by extending the Keystone pipeline into Texas. In 2015, President Obama rejected completion of the northern portion of the Keystone XL, but the pipeline from Oklahoma to the Gulf Coast of Texas was operational as of early 2014. Supporters argue it will help stabilize the oil supply and generate construction jobs necessary to build the pipeline. Opponents contend the pipeline will create only a few, temporary jobs, the benefits of which are outweighed by environmental and property rights concerns. Along with concerns about the amount of water the pipeline will use, the pipeline has generated controversy because of the use of tar sands, which are more corrosive than conventional oil. Environmentalists worry that the tar sands make leaks in the pipeline more likely, increasing the possibility of contaminating groundwater along the pipeline. These concerns have been borne out by the numerous Keystone pipeline leaks, the latest of which spilled around 400,000 gallons in South Dakota. Several East Texas landowners along the route refused to grant TransCanada the right to put the pipeline through their properties, which raised interesting questions about the power of a foreign company to assert eminent domain. Although Texas property

What happens to Texas during a boom? What are the effects of a bust?

⭐ CRITICAL THINKING

eminent domain
the power of the government to take private property for public use, generally for public functions, such as roads

owners were able to get a temporary restraining order against TransCanada, in August 2012, a Lamar County court at law judge ruled that TransCanada did in fact have eminent domain rights to the land. The Supreme Court of Texas refused to hear the case, allowing the Canadian company to seize land from Texas farmers to complete the pipeline. The issue of eminent domain is likely to increase in importance in the near future as discoveries of natural gas lead to more pipelines being built across the state.

The Natural Gas Boom and Fracking

Today, Texas is experiencing a second boom—the natural gas rush. The oil crisis of the 1970s created a national push to explore ways to decrease America's dependence on oil. The resulting decades of research by the U.S. Department of Energy yielded improvements in technology that have made it economically viable to extract natural gas trapped in shale formations (a type of sedimentary rock). Hydraulic fracturing, or fracking, involves extracting natural gas from shale formations underground. The shale rock is fractured and injected with millions of gallons of water and chemicals that cause the natural gas to rise to the surface of the well. Although fracking has been used by the oil and gas industry for a long time, modern fracking is significantly different from traditional fracking. Advances in technology allow what is called horizontal fracking, which extends oil drilling horizontally underground. Horizontal fracking uses significantly more water and chemicals to get the natural gas deposits out of the shale. The Barnett Shale in north central Texas led not only the state but the country in a natural gas boom. With China's growing energy demands, Texas's fracking boom stands to continue for the foreseeable future.

Fracking remains controversial in Texas, since it promises economic prosperity to its proponents and environmental doom to its detractors. For proponents, fracking allows companies to access natural gas that was previously too expensive to obtain. Fracking has brought new life to the oil and gas industry, driving Texas's economic miracle. Certainly, the oil and gas industry has a vested economic interest in the practice of fracking. But so do Texas landowners—many of whom have signed over the rights for a company to frack on their property in exchange for monthly royalty checks. At the height of the price of natural gas, those checks were substantial, and initially Texans didn't ask too many questions.

The economic impact on the state has been considerable. Texas accounts for almost one-fourth of the country's natural gas production and holds almost a quarter of the country's natural gas reserves. Texas is home to some of the largest natural gas reserves, including the Permian Basin, the Barnett Shale, the Eagle Ford Shale, the Haynesville Shale, and the Granite Wash. Proponents of fracking advocate natural gas as a means of decreasing America's dependence on oil and coal, stating that the natural gas boom creates jobs and generates economic growth across the state.

Texans' excitement about fracking soon changed to concern as people began to question its safety. Opponents of fracking are concerned about the damage it can do to the state's air and water quality. People are increasingly worried that fracking releases methane and volatile organic compounds, including cancer-causing benzene, into the air and water. Critics of fracking argue that the air quality around shale sites has significantly worsened, and cities have noticed a marked increase in smog. Opponents of fracking also charge that the chemicals used to extract the natural gas are contaminating the state's drinking water. These chemicals are unregulated by the government and are generally treated as a trade secret. Many believe that fracking releases methane

What limits, if any, should there be on eminent domain?

⭐ CRITICAL THINKING

fracking
fracturing underground rock formations and using high-pressure injections of chemicals and water to cause natural gas to rise to the surface

Rosenberg Police Department via AP

A massive sinkhole in Rosenberg, Texas, in 2017. Research suggests that fracking is causing new sinkholes in oil production areas.

into the water supply. A 2015 study of 550 water samples from the Barnett Shale revealed elevated levels of metals and chemicals associated with fracking, including benzene, toluene, ethyl benzene, and xylenes.[15]

Fracking also uses a large amount of water, estimated to be between 1 million and 5 million gallons in a five-day period. Texans began paying attention to the amount of water that oil and natural gas companies were using when the state experienced a severe drought in 2011. The city of Grand Prairie became the first to adopt water restrictions that included fracking industries. In response, Chesapeake Energy simply started bringing in water from neighboring Arlington, which angered residents there. In response to water use concerns, oil and gas companies have vowed to recycle the water they use to frack. However, a 2014 study revealed that about 92 percent of the water used in fracking is consumed rather than returned to the reservoir.[16] Not only does fracking consume large quantities of water, but oil and gas companies pay the same tax-subsidized price for water as a town's residents.

In addition, Texans are becoming increasingly worried about earthquakes in areas where they are not typical. In areas such as Cleburne in North Texas and Timpson in East Texas, minor earthquakes have occurred in places that historically have not had earthquakes. Between 1970 and 2008, Texas averaged one to two earthquakes a year; since 2008, that number has jumped to twelve to fifteen earthquakes per year.[17] A study from UT and Southern Methodist University found that wastewater disposal from fracking had triggered most of the earthquakes since 2008.[18] Critics argue that these minor earthquakes are particularly problematic since gas pipelines in these areas are not required to be built to withstand earthquakes. The Texas Railroad Commission, which is responsible for regulating the oil and gas industry, ruled that the study amounts to insufficient evidence to alter oil company policies at present. More recent research points to a rise in sinkholes in the state resulting from injection wells.[19]

For Texas, a lot is on the line. The recent economic boom abetted by the oil and gas industry reflects the essence of the Texas cultural identity. Fracking is also politically attractive to oil companies that have long been political powerhouses in Texas politics. Environmental stewardship in the state has often taken a back seat to economic interests. So far, state politicians have been hesitant to do anything to curb fracking. One exception came with the 82nd legislature, which passed a law requiring oil and gas companies to disclose many of the chemicals, as well as the amount of water, used to frack a well. In practice, the law has made little difference, as it does not require prior notice and many of the chemicals remain undisclosed because the industry claims they are trade secrets.

Should the state require fracking companies to report chemicals used in fracking?

★ SOCIAL RESPONSIBILITY

FEDERALISM IN Action

Fracking

Since horizontal hydraulic fracking ushered in a new economic boom for the state, the question of regulation has loomed large. Which level of government should regulate fracking? The federal government has a wide range of laws that could limit fracking-related pollution, including the Clean Air Act and the Clean Water Act. Elected officials in Texas, whose state economy was poised to win big from fracking, have consistently held that the federal government should not regulate fracking, and they have spent millions suing the U.S. Environmental Protection Agency (EPA). Other states landed on the opposite side of the coin and sued the EPA for failing to regulate methane emissions from fracking, which they charged was a violation of the Clean Air Act. Texas attorney general Ken Paxton called the emissions standards "a gross demonstration of federal overreach."[i] State officials worried about the effect of regulations on the oil and gas industry, since the recent success of the Texas economy had been largely driven by the boom.

While the federal and state governments engaged in a near-decade-long battle over who should regulate the oil and gas industry, Texas city governments joined the fray. Should local governments be able to adopt laws that limit fracking? In 2014, almost 60 percent of citizens in Denton voted to ban fracking within the city limits. Citizens in Denton worried about air quality, water quality, and noise pollution. In the 84th legislative session, state politicians responded by adopting a bill that preempts any local regulations and asserts the state's exclusive jurisdiction to regulate the oil and gas industry. According to the Texas Municipal League, more than 300 Texas cities adopted some local ordinances regulating oil and gas, mostly limiting how close rigs could be put to homes and schools but also including twenty-nine cities that barred fracking within city limits.[ii] Citizens in Denton were surprised to find they could not adopt local ordinances to limit or ban fracking. After Tom Phillips, a lawyer for the oil and gas industry (and former chief justice of the Texas Supreme Court), informed the city council that they would likely be sued, council members voted to repeal the ban.

The question of local control over fracking is both a legal one and a question of tradition. Texas has long championed local control over centralized policy. The 1876 Texas constitution showed a clear preference for local over state control. When Texans amended the state's constitution to allow for home rule, the goal was to protect local control and give cities more freedom to adopt ordinances that reflect the values of their residents.

In the past, Governor Greg Abbott, who signed the fracking bill into law, has said the state needs to "get out of the way" in other policy areas and allow "genuine local control" rather than "one-size-fits-all solutions [that] are pushed down from the top."[iii] More recently, Abbott seemed to reverse himself, expressing the need for a ban on local regulations and a move to centralize control with the state.

Is the federal government's approach regarding fracking-related pollution an "overreach" of its powers?

 CRITICAL THINKING

Should local governments be allowed to adopt laws designed to protect air and water quality?

 CRITICAL THINKING

i. James Osborne, "Texas Sues EPA over Methane Emissions Crackdown," *Houston Chronicle*, August 1, 2016, http://www.houstonchronicle.com/business/article/Texas-suing-EPA-over-methane-crackdown-9008109.php.

ii. Jim Malewitz and Ryan Marphy, "See How Local Drilling Rules Vary Across Texas," *Texas Tribune*, March 27, 2015, https://www.texastribune.org/2015/03/27/see-how-local-drilling-rules-vary-across-texas.

iii. Greg Abbott, guest columnist, "Strengthening Local Control of Our Schools," *Waco Tribune-Herald*, May 1, 2014, http://www.wacotrib.com/opinion/columns/guest_columns/greg-abbott-guest-columnist-strengthening-local-control-of-our-schools/article_6681ccf0-e415-5347-beea-cd8ca9b28517.html.

TEXAS ENERGY

Everything is bigger in Texas, and Texas energy production is no exception. Texas leads the country in the production of oil, natural gas, and wind. Texas is the only state that has its own energy grid, a symbol of Texas's love of independence and distrust of federal government. A separate grid keeps Texas's energy largely outside the jurisdiction of the Federal Energy Regulatory Commission, which regulates interstate energy transmission. The Texas energy grid, called the Electric Reliability Council of Texas (ERCOT), provides energy to nearly the entire state except for the western-most point, around El Paso, the northernmost point in the panhandle, and the eastern border region. In 2017, the main sources of that energy continued to be natural gas and coal, which provided nearly 39 percent and 32 percent of the state's energy usage, respectively.[20] However, those numbers are likely to change significantly as the boom in natural gas makes it much cheaper than coal. In early 2018, four of Texas's coal plants closed their doors.

Coal is also being squeezed out by wind, which according to ERCOT surpassed coal in generation capacity in 2017. Texas has led the country in wind energy since 2006. According to the American Wind Energy Association, Texas has 22,799 mega-watts of total wind capacity, more than three times that of any other state in the country.[21] Wind power has become increasingly popular in Texas, since it allows the state to capitalize on its vast endowment of land. Windmills have emerged on dried-up oil fields and struggling farms across the plains of West Texas. The increased viability of wind energy has become an engine of development in rural areas such as in Nolan County, where property values have surged in recent years thanks to wind farms.[22] In 2017, wind energy accounted for more than 17 percent of the total electricity gener-ated in Texas.[23] Wind production in Texas grew so rapidly that as early as 2006, West Texas wind farms were producing far more wind than they had the ability to deliver. In 2008, the Texas Legislature authorized a $7 billion, 3,600-mile transmission line to transmit wind power from West Texas to metropolitan areas that use the most energy, such as Dallas, Austin, and Houston. The recently completed lines can transmit 18,500 megawatts of power. This helped Texas set a record in 2016, when wind energy pro-vided 45 percent of the state's energy demands for seven-teen straight hours.[24] Advances in turbine technology and improvements in batteries have resulted in a substantial decrease in the price of wind energy. Today, the levelized (removing subsidies and tax breaks) cost per kilowatt hour of wind energy is competitive with the levelized cost of natural gas.[25] The result is a "wind rush" contributing to a booming industry and an exploding job market.

As investment in wind technology has taken off across the state, Texas is now seeing the kinds of boomtowns pre-viously associated with oil discoveries. For example, in Sweetwater, Texas, the population is increasing and unem-ployment is down. Sweetwater is in Nolan County, which is now home to four of the country's ten largest wind farms; it hosts 1,371 wind turbines, creating 2,060 megawatts of wind energy.[26] The tax base grew so fast in Nolan County that in 2012 the county cut its taxes.[27] In addition to the sharp increase in sales tax and hotel occupancy taxes it collected, Sweetwater reported $23 million in school prop-erty taxes and another $4.8 million in property taxes paid by wind companies between 2002 and 2007.[28] A bit farther north in Hale County, they are also feeling the impact of the wind energy rush. Hale County's executive director of economic development described the construction of

FIGURE 13.1 Energy Use in Texas by Source, 2017

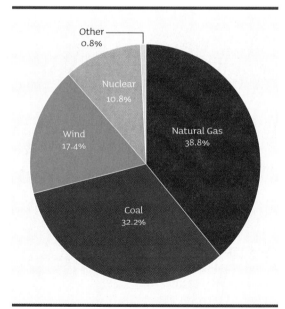

Source: ERCOT, "2017 State of the Grid Report," accessed July 9, 2018, http://www.ercot.com/content/wcm/lists/144926/ERCOT_2017_State_of_the_Grid_Report.pdf.

the wind farms as creating "a tremendous impact on our local sales tax because these [workers] are staying at our hotels, they are eating at our restaurants, they're buying fuel and they're doing routine things that you do consumption-wise when you live in a community that has had a sizeable impact . . . Our sales tax numbers are up to double digits for both the city and the county over the last fiscal year."[29]

While Texas has made significant progress with wind energy, its progress in using other types of alternative energy has been more limited. As the Texas power grid strains under record heat, finding alternative energy sources is extremely important. Thanks to its vast plains, Texas has considerable solar resource potential. However, although Texas leads the country in oil, natural gas, and wind production, solar development remains limited in the state. Texas recently dropped from fourth to seventh among states' total solar capacity, producing only 11 percent of what California—which leads the country—produces.[30] Policies that have generated support for solar energy in other states are notably absent in Texas. There are no state tax incentives for solar development, and Texas is one of only a handful of states without a net-metering policy, which allows residents to sell their excess electricity back to the grid. Solar advocates argue that solar has a considerable advantage over wind in Texas since it produces the most power on hot summer days when the energy grid experiences peak usage. Still, Texas solar capacity has swelled in the last decade, reaching 2,000 megawatts in 2018.[31] According to the Solar Energy Industry Association, the price of solar in Texas has fallen by 53 percent in the last five years, and the state now has nearly a quarter of a million homes with solar installations.

Texas also has two nuclear power plants that supply about one-tenth of the state's power. The state held its collective breath as Harvey narrowly missed the state's South Texas Project plant. That plant, which continued to supply power throughout Hurricane Harvey, was recently granted a twenty-year license extension as its original forty-year license was set to expire. Texas continues to be oil country, but Texas is also seeking diverse ways to power its energy grid in the future.

> To what extent should Texas policy support alternative energy production?
>
> ★ SOCIAL RESPONSIBILITY

ENVIRONMENTAL POLICY

Given its wide, open spaces and the individualistic nature of its citizens, it is perhaps not surprising that concern about the environment has been slow to develop in Texas. Even in such a conservative state, however, there is some need for regulation. Regulation can occur when governments make and enforce rules intended to protect citizens from harm by private firms. While federal regulations generally attract the most attention, much of the regulatory task is left to the states.

In the language of economics, government regulation protects citizens from negative externalities. An externality occurs when costs are imposed on someone who is not participating in a transaction. For example, a citizen who does not make, own, drive, or ride in an automobile still must live with the pollution created by cars. This is a problem in a free-enterprise system, which assumes that costs and benefits involve just those people buying and selling a product. Those people involved in a transaction express their desire for cleaner or safer products by favoring products with those qualities and avoiding those without them. An individual not taking part in a transaction has no influence on shaping the characteristics of a product through market participation, thus creating the need for government involvement. Many Texans own houses

regulation
government rulemaking and enforcement intended to protect citizens from being harmed by private firms

negative externality
an unintended cost imposed on someone who did not participate in the economic transaction

Texas Commission on Environmental Quality (TCEQ)
the agency that oversees state environmental policy, including air and water quality

on land that others own the mineral rights to. When individuals not living on the land possess and sell the rights to drill for natural gas, for instance, the Texas homeowners have no say in the transaction. In short, if you're not buying or selling a product, you have no way of dealing with its impact on your own life without regulation.

Texas has long tended to emphasize business interests over environmental protection. Twentieth-century Texas was a state defined by the oil boom, and today's state politics continue to be dominated by oil interests. When it comes to environmental regulations, the interests of big oil coincide with the frontier preference for small and unobtrusive government. Texans prefer little regulation of business and have long been skeptical of policies designed to protect the environment. Texas politicians have tended to stress making the state friendly to big business, which translates into little regulation. When Rick Perry was governor and Greg Abbott was attorney general, the state was openly hostile to attempts by the federal government to protect the environment. In fact, by the time he left office, Abbott had sued the EPA over thirty times, costing Texas taxpayers millions of dollars. In his first three years as attorney general, Ken Paxton has kept with that tradition, filing twenty-seven suits against the federal government.

The agency in Texas responsible for protecting the state's environment is the **Texas Commission on Environmental Quality (TCEQ)**. The agency consists of three commissioners who are appointed by the governor, with Senate approval, and an executive director hired by the commissioners. The commissioners serve staggered, six-year terms. Environmental policy in Texas is also a product of federal regulations. The federal Clean Air Act and Clean Water Act, for example, set minimum pollution standards that the EPA, along with the TCEQ, must enforce.

TEXAS AIR QUALITY

So what does the air quality in Texas look like? On the one hand, Texas has dramatically improved its air quality in recent decades. On the other hand, the state continues to be one of the largest polluters in the country. Improvements, while remarkable, have occurred in part because Texas has been polluting at a considerably higher rate than other states. As one environmental lawyer put it, "for the most part, Texas has lowered its toxic emissions, but so has essentially every other state in the country."[32] In spite of these improvements, Texas leads the country in carbon dioxide emissions; in fact, according to the EPA, Texas emissions are nearly twice those of California, the second-largest emitter.[33]

While environmental policy has most often been the concern of the federal government, many states have taken their own paths, even regarding problems such as climate change that reach beyond state lines. As governor and attorney general, respectively, Perry and Abbott took on the EPA and EPA standards in the state on an unprecedented scale. One of the most visible examples of this has to do with air quality. The federal Clean Air Act limits the amount of certain pollutants industries can produce from each source. In 1994, the TCEQ began allowing industries in Texas to meet that limit using flexible permits. Flexible permits measure a facility's overall pollution levels rather than measuring individual units within the facility. In 2010, the EPA ruled that flexible permits allow companies to emit pollution levels in violation of the Clean Air Act, since pollutants concentrated in one area can be harmful to nearby neighborhoods. Texas responded by suing the EPA. In 2014, the EPA reached a new deal with the TCEQ that allows the agency to issue conditional flexible permits. Texas also sued the EPA over regulations meant to address pollution that drifts into neighboring states. In 2014, the U.S. Supreme Court upheld EPA rules that require states to address pollution that crosses borders into other states.

In response to federal regulations designed to decrease carbon emissions, Texas unsuccessfully sued the EPA to try to prevent the national government from regulating greenhouse gases.[34] Although air quality in most metropolitan areas in the state has improved over the previous decade, many Texas cities have struggled to meet federal ozone standards. A 2018 American Lung Association study that examined air quality in thirty-four Texas counties gave fifteen of those Texas counties an F for ozone pollution and ranked Houston–The Woodlands and Dallas–Fort Worth eleventh and sixteenth, respectively, for worst ozone pollution in the country.[35]

How should the state balance economic gains associated with oil and natural gas against environmental dangers?

⭐ CRITICAL THINKING

DROUGHTS AND FLOODS

After several years of drought, water sources in Texas came under a new threat with recurring flooding in 2015 and 2016. While the initial storms were welcome relief for waterways across the state, the increased frequency and severity of the storms, resulting in many cases in extreme flooding, brought a new set of problems. In 2011, Texas experienced a severe drought that dried up lakes and rivers, causing strains in everything from cattle ranching to cotton growing. The drought meant that farmers didn't have sufficient water to keep horses or cattle, and the lack of rain sent the price of hay through the roof. Many Texas farmers sold off their cattle, and around the state, stories of horses being given away at auction or abandoned on the side of the road became common. Texas, for the first time in history, cut off water to rice farmers in the state due to low water levels. The Ogallala Aquifer, which provides water from West Texas to South Dakota, experienced the largest decline in twenty-five years because of the drought.[36] Towns across the state were dangerously low on water, and in 2012, Spicewood Beach became the first town in Texas to officially run out of water. By 2014, an estimated twenty towns were within ninety days of running out of water. In what some dubbed "toilet to tap," Wichita Falls became the first city in the country where half of the city's drinking water came from recycled waste water.

The drought left most of the state parched. During the drought, desperate water districts across the state pumped water out of the ground. The result of pumping groundwater is subsidence, where the ground loses elevation. For example, the U.S. Geological Survey estimates that parts of Harris County have dropped ten to twelve feet since 1920.[37] One of the dangers of subsidence is flooding becomes more severe. After several years of drought, the water situation in Texas changed rapidly in the spring of 2015. After four weeks of rain, so much of the state was flooded that Governor Abbott declared thirty-seven counties disaster areas. Extreme storms and flooding quickly replaced the drought as the new norm in the state, and in 2016 the governor again found himself declaring more than thirty counties disaster areas after one week of rain and flooding. In that year, the Brazos River crested at an all-time high of fifty-five feet, and the crested Sabine River closed most of the border between Texas and Louisiana. In 2017, Texas again saw extreme flooding followed by severe drought. When Hurricane Harvey hammered the Texas coast in August 2017, it caused unprecedented flooding across the state. But by January, nearly 40 percent of the state was experiencing a moderate drought that persisted throughout the summer.

subsidence
loss of elevation over time that results when water districts pump groundwater and the affected area sinks

What, if anything, should Texas do to ensure the state does not run out of water?

★ **SOCIAL RESPONSIBILITY**

rule of capture
Texas law that says property owners own the water below their property

As water rights have become an increasingly salient issue, the state has had to prioritize water access. In Texas, water that is aboveground is owned by the state. However, underground water rights in Texas are based on the **rule of capture**, which comes from English common law. Rule of capture says if you own property in the state, you own the water underneath that property. Thus, unlike in most other states, in Texas landowners can deplete water under their property, including shared underground water, without any legal liability to adjacent landowners. Years of drought followed by years of extreme weather and massive flooding have increased calls by environmental groups for the legislature to address the state's water needs. The 84th legislature funded research for desalination and required the Texas Water Development Board to conduct a statewide study of groundwater. On the heels of Harvey, the 85th legislature passed legislation that would provide funds to create an underground water storage reservoir to take advantage of the next deluge. That legislation was ultimately vetoed.

HAZARDOUS WASTE

In the spring of 2012, Texas became the first state in thirty years to open a low-level radioactive waste site. The site, located in West Texas's Andrews County, is only the fourth radioactive waste site in the country, and the first in Texas. Previously, hazardous waste from Texas's companies was shipped to Utah. The site accepts class A low-level radioactive waste and is the only site in the country authorized to accept B and C classifications of low-level radioactive waste, which are more hazardous than other sites will take. The Texas site is particularly controversial since it sits atop the Ogallala Aquifer, and scientists worry about its potential for contaminating the groundwater.

During the TCEQ review process, scientists and engineers unanimously concluded that the dump was too close to the Ogallala Aquifer and that radioactive contamination of the aquifer was a risk. Despite that, TCEQ executive director Glenn Shankle issued the permit for waste control specialists to develop the site. Within a week, Shankle was hired as a lobbyist for the company. While the original deal was to accept waste only from Texas and Vermont, in 2011, the state legislature authorized the site to accept waste from thirty-six additional states. In 2015, waste control specialists successfully lobbied the TCEQ to allow them to increase by threefold the capacity the site could hold. Under the expansion, the site can now take up to 9 million cubic feet of radioactive waste. At the same time, the TCEQ voted to reduce the financial accountability waste control specialists would have in the event of an accident.[38] In 2015, waste control specialists again sought to expand the site. This time they sought

Radioactive waste site in West Texas. The location of the site atop an aquifer and the level of waste it holds have caused controversy.

AP Photo/Betsy Blaney

permission from the federal Nuclear Regulatory Commission to take the country's high-level radioactive waste. As governor, Rick Perry advocated bringing the country's high-level radioactive waste to West Texas. Now energy secretary Perry will have considerably more say in where that waste goes. Proponents argue that rural Andrews County stands to gain considerable economic advantage from the site. Opponents worry about the potential for groundwater contamination, the danger of handling the spent nuclear material, and having numerous trucks loaded with hazardous materials driving across the state.

WINNERS AND LOSERS

Texas is a state endowed with abundant natural resources. Since the first discovery at Spindletop, oil has been a significant engine of economic growth for the state. The discoveries of natural gas shales across Texas promise to help spur economic growth for the foreseeable future. Texans are committed to oil and natural gas because the state's natural resources make its citizens winners.

However, the state's strong devotion to the use of its natural resources for economic development has often meant policy that ignores larger environmental concerns. As water stress continues and periods of drought increase subsidence and worsen the effects of flooding, real questions about how we manage our water need to be explored. Technologies such as fracking need to consider the potential public health impact. If Texans allow their groundwater to be irreversibly contaminated, Texans clearly lose. The cost to the health care system and to individuals in the form of increased asthma and cancers related to increased pollutants will be shared by all Texans. On the other hand, Texans emerge as the winners as new energy sources help relieve the stressed energy grids in the state. As the price of solar continues to fall, more solar farms will further decrease the cost of energy to Texans. The Texas economy stands to win big as well, as depressed land in West Texas finds renewed value with windmills. The wind industry employs more than 24,000 Texans, while the solar industry employs nearly 12,000. Texas's growing wind industry is on track to help residents access cheap energy without the ups and downs of oil or gas prices. Texas consumers and the Texas economy are the winners in a strong and diverse energy market.

TRANSPORTATION POLICY

Getting around Texas during the state's early years was notoriously difficult. From the early days of the frontier, travel was unreliable, since Texans depended on waterways or undeveloped trails, both of which were highly susceptible to the state's notoriously unpredictable weather. Too much rain meant muddy, impassable roads, and too little rain left waterways too shallow to be usable.[39] Road development in Texas, the second-largest state, faced serious obstacles, with large swaths of land that were sparsely populated and numerous counties that remained fairly isolated. Texas was also a relatively poor state, and Texans leaned toward fiscal conservatism. Despite these challenges, a rapidly growing state needed a means of moving its people and goods around. This was especially important to the state's farmers, who found

How should Texans balance the potential for economic gain against the possibility for environmental devastation?

★ SOCIAL RESPONSIBILITY

To what extent do you have a responsibility to protect the environment?

★ PERSONAL RESPONSIBILITY

How should Texas weigh potentially higher health care costs across the state against potential economic gain?

★ SOCIAL RESPONSIBILITY

To what extent should Texas pursue alternative energy sources?

★ CRITICAL THINKING

themselves spread across the large state. Texas's transportation priorities have evolved as the state first relied mostly on railroads, then turned to roads, and is increasingly looking to mass transit to meet the residents' transportation needs.

Railroads

Texans initially had a complicated relationship with the railroads. The state's farmers were dependent on the railroads' ability to move produce, but the monopolies that the railroad enjoyed in most areas left the farmers at the mercy of whatever shipping rates the railroad set. In 1836, the first Congress of the Republic of Texas authorized creation of a company to build a railroad system in the state. However, the financing and engineering of this railroad proved too daunting, and the state would not see its first tracks laid until 1852, when a route was established that ran from Buffalo Bayou to the Brazos River at Richmond.[40] While rail lines connecting the state's cities developed naturally, reaching the farmers in the more remote areas of the state was not worth the financial risk, and the railroads had already grown accustomed to getting help from government as they moved west across America.

Early Texas was cash poor and land rich, so in 1854 the state authorized giving railroads 10,240 acres of land for each mile of railroad completed. In addition, numerous Texas cities began offering deals to the railroads in hopes of bringing them in, along with the prosperity and jobs they brought. Cities competed against each other, and money was often passed under the table. Some towns, such as Abilene, thrived when the railroad arrived, while cities such as Buffalo Gap withered without the arrival of the railroad. Eventually, the state accepted the need to subsidize railroads if they were going to reach across Texas, and the state gave the railroad companies over 32 million acres (an area the size of Alabama).[41] Though initially slowed by the Civil War, rail development eventually took off. Texas had a mere 486 miles of track operating in 1870, but over the next two decades, the railroad added another 8,000 miles of rail connecting every city in Texas that had a population of 4,000 residents (except Brownsville).[42] Once rail lines were laid, both the railroads and the state had incentives to bring in more settlers—even if it took a little creative promotion. New citizens were lured to the "less humid" regions of West Texas, where rainfalls averaged only about fifteen inches a year and farming and ranching were difficult for Anglos schooled in the agricultural techniques of the less arid eastern United States.

In 1890, Attorney General James Stephen Hogg decided that his office was not able to keep up with the enforcement of regulations on the state's railroads. Hogg advocated the creation of a railroad commission, making the call for the commission a centerpiece of his campaign for governor. Although the railroads labeled Hogg "communistic," his reforms were appealing to voters, and Hogg became Texas's first native-born governor in 1891. Today, Texas's Railroad Commission focuses on regulating the oil and gas industry rather than railroads.

Modern-day Texas continues to pay the price of uneven investment in railroads, as large parts of the state remain isolated. Railroads have fundamentally changed from a transportation method primarily used for moving goods to one increasingly moving people around the state. The availability of federal funds for building high-speed rails has encouraged several European firms to propose building these systems to connect major areas of the state. These proposals range from connecting Austin to Houston to a high-speed rail between East Texas and Dallas. Perhaps the plan that has generated the most enthusiasm is connecting Houston to Dallas–Fort Worth. A company named Texas Central Partners has a proposal to build a high-speed rail that would take Texans from Houston to Dallas in about ninety minutes. The company hopes to begin construction by 2020. Although enthusiasm for building traditional railroads in Texas has never been particularly strong, there seems to be growing support for some strategic high-speed rail lines across the state. As the state's population grows and traditional roads struggle to keep up, high-speed rail development has seen support grow in urban areas. However, that support is tempered by folks in largely rural counties whose houses and farms are in the path of proposed routes. Amid pressure from their state representatives, the 85th legislature passed a law that prohibits the use of any state funds for the development of the entire Houston-Dallas line.

Roads

While Texas saw some railroads built in the late 1800s, the building of roads didn't really take off for another half century. For most of its history, Texas left road building and maintenance to fiscally strapped county governments. County governments were authorized to procure ten days of labor each year for building roads and bridges from every male citizen between the ages of eighteen and forty-five and every slave between the ages of sixteen and fifty.[43] However, as they often lacked the financial means to do so, most counties simply did not build roads. There were only a few miles of graded roadway in 1860.[44] Some roadways were little more than a mass of wagon ruts; others were mostly cow trails. The first significant movement in Texas to improve the poor roads occurred when the U.S. Congress passed the Federal Aid Road Act of 1916. Under this act, the national government matched state money with federal money to be used for building roads and bridges. To qualify for the federal money, states had to have a state-managed highway program. Texas, which still left road development to counties, responded in 1917 by creating the Texas Highway Department to coordinate state highway development. Though Texas was relatively slow to prioritize building roads up to this point, the new department wasted no time applying for the newly available funds. Within six months, the Texas Highway Department had submitted its first request for federal money and had spent over $9 million in road construction.[45] At about the same time, Texas set its first speed limits of eighteen miles per hour in rural areas and fifteen miles per hour in the city.[46] Texas quickly became one of the leaders in road building among states.

Early in the twentieth century, Texas built roads on an unprecedented scale. The state paved its first road in 1918 and within ten years had 18,000 miles of roadway.[47] Texas quickly surpassed other states in the miles of roads it built, and, as one historian notes, "[it] went from a horse culture to something resembling an automobile culture in one swoop."[48] In the 1940s and 1950s, Texas tripled its total miles of highways. Like the expansion of railroads, the development of roads across the state often determined the future of small towns, as cities where highways were built flourished and those bypassed by the state highway system stagnated.[49] By the 1970s, however, Texas highway development was no longer keeping up with the needs of the state. The oil crisis of the 1970s led to both inflation and more fuel-efficient vehicles, which hampered the Texas Highway Department's ability to build new roads, since road development relied on a gasoline tax for a significant portion of its revenue. At the same time, the Texas population was seeing significant and unending growth. Compounding the problem, the cost of building roads has substantially increased in recent years. The Legislative Budget Board (LBB) estimates that between 2002 and 2007, the cost of building roads soared, rising 62 percent in a mere five-year span.[50] Or, as one researcher put, in the past forty years, Texas has seen its population increase "by 125 percent, the number of vehicles increase by 172 percent and the number of miles we drive increase by 238 percent. At the same time, the lane-miles of state-maintained roadways (our highways, farm-to-market roads primarily) have increased by only 19 percent over that same period of time."[51] Texas, which once led the country in highway development, has not kept up with the state's population growth, and the highway program has languished.

Funding Roads

One of the most significant obstacles to an efficient road system is the ability to pay for it. Funding roads in Texas has always been a highly politicized affair. The Texas Highway Department originally relied on a vehicle registration tax for money, though it quickly shifted the funding mechanism from this registration to a gasoline tax. In 1923, the state legislature introduced the first tax on gasoline, which was one cent per gallon. Initially, Texas raised the gas tax over the years to keep up with inflation, although the last increase occurred nearly three decades ago. The current state gas tax, which was adopted by the Texas Legislature in 1991, is twenty cents per gallon. With inflation, the twenty-cent tax was worth only about seven cents per gallon in 2014. The national government levies an additional 18.4 cents a gallon tax on gas. That makes the total gas tax for Texans 38.4 cents, well below the national average of 52.49 cents per gallon, and forty-fifth in the country, in spite of the fact that Texas maintains more miles of roads than other states.[52]

In addition to the gas tax, Texas utilizes a variety of other taxes and fees to pay for its roads and bridges. These include vehicle registration fees, title certificate fees, over-size weight permits, motor vehicle sales and use taxes, motor lubricant sales taxes, and, increasingly, tolls.[53] Different types of taxes are discussed at greater length in Chapter 12. Historically, the two greatest sources of money for building roads in Texas were the federal matching dollars and the gasoline tax. Including all taxes and fees related to transportation, the average Texan pays approximately $232 a year toward the state's transportation needs.[54]

In 1946, Texas passed the so-called Good Roads Amendment, which requires the lion's share of these fees be used for road construction. Specifically, Article 8, section 7a of the Texas Constitution requires that three-fourths of all road-user fees, including the gas tax, be used for building and maintaining roads and the remaining one-fourth be used to pay for state education. The Good Roads Amendment was designed to protect money for highway funding from being spent by the Texas Legislature on other services.

Texas legislators have consistently resisted raising the gasoline tax, exacerbating the state's difficulty in creating a transportation network that keeps pace with its urbanization and population growth. In the 1920s, Texas formally adopted a pay-as-you-go funding system for road construction, representing Texans' traditionally fiscally conservative approach to government. This meant that, unlike other states, Texas could not borrow money for road construction but had to fund roads as it built them. The

Should Texas increase the gas tax?

★ **SOCIAL RESPONSIBILITY**

Good Roads Amendment state constitutional requirement that 75 percent of road-user fees be spent on building and maintaining roads and the remaining 25 percent be used for education

pay-as-you-go funding for Texas transportation continued until 2001, when the financial strains of the state's highway department had reached a crisis point. In that year, the Texas Legislature and Texas voters amended the state's constitution to allow the state to issue bonds (borrow money) to keep up with the transportation needs of the state. By the end of 2012, the state had issued approximately $17 billion in bonds to build roads and bridges.[55]

Within a decade, the state's transportation-related debt skyrocketed. Since eliminating the pay-as-you-go system, Texas now pays a significant portion of money each year to finance its debt burden. The Texas Department of Transportation (TxDOT)

TEXAS Legends

Private Property and Takings

One of the most pervasive legends in Texas is that of private property. Most Texans view their property as being exclusively under their own control. However, this is increasingly false.

The idea of "takings" emerges from the Fifth Amendment to the U.S. Constitution, which prohibits the taking of private property "for public use, without just compensation." Traditionally, this clause has been examined in the light of eminent domain, the power of government to take property for public use. Generally, eminent domain has been used to take private property for government use for public services, such as roads. Recently, the limits of eminent domain have been tested as the government has taken private property for public uses such as the Dallas Cowboys' stadium in Arlington, toll roads operated by private firms, and projects such as the Keystone pipeline, operated by foreign-owned firms. In this more expansive use of power, the taking of private property is justified for general economic development that will create jobs and other advantages for the entire community. Thus, "public use" doesn't exclude private profit.

Another use of takings deals with the impact of regulation on the value of private property. One example of regulatory takings would be environmental regulations that place restrictions on the uses of private property designated as wetlands. These rules restricting how individuals use their property may diminish the value of the property. In this case, the government is restricting use of property to promote the general welfare, which is certainly a public concern. For many years the courts did not support compensating citizens for regulatory takings. Restrictions on land use are not unique to environmental regulation. Property owners in cities also face restrictions on how they use their land. For example, zoning rules prohibit building businesses in residential areas. However, environmental regulations reach outside cities to the rural areas where many people have retreated in their attempt to avoid rules imposed by government and their neighbors.

The problem of takings reflects a cost of government that frequently does not show up on the balance sheet of costs and benefits. Sometimes government regulation requires costly action, such as altering coal plants to produce less pollution, with the cost being passed along as higher utility bills. At other times, government policies restrict citizens' uses and enjoyment of their own property.

However, without some ability to extend its authority onto private property, the government would lack the ability to create and enforce meaningful rules related to the environment or public safety, since pollution and other problems don't recognize property lines. Without such rules, individuals could block the flow of creeks and cut off water supplies to, or cause flooding for, other citizens. Neighborhoods could find adult businesses placed next to family homes or schools. Thus, the matter of who wins and who loses involves a balancing act in which the government must weigh the public safety against the rights of individual property owners.

> **Under what conditions should eminent domain be used to acquire land for development?**

 SOCIAL RESPONSIBILITY

estimates that for every billion it borrows, it will have to pay $65 million in annual interest rates.[56]

In less than a decade, Texas's fiscally conservative approach to building roads was history. In 2011, the Texas Legislature for the first time appropriated more money for servicing its transportation debt than it allocated for actually building roads.[57] Since then, the legislature has made three significant changes to funding the state's roads. The 83rd legislature, in its third special session, passed a constitutional amendment designed to improve the state of transportation funding in the state. The legislation required up to half of the money that currently goes to the Rainy Day Fund from the state's oil and gas production tax to be diverted into a fund for transportation. The comptroller estimates that in the 2018–2019 budget cycle, that will amount to $1.37 billion, well short of the $4 billion a year necessary to maintain current Texas roads. The 84th legislature passed, and voters approved, a second constitutional amendment that diverts up to $2.5 billion from the states' sales and use tax revenue to the state highway fund whenever revenue exceeds $28 billion. In the event that sales revenue drops below $28 billion in a year, the transportation department will not get the additional $2.5 billion allocation. The comptroller could further allocate 35 percent of the tax revenue from the state motor vehicle tax that exceeds $5 billion for the state highway fund. After years of inadequate transportation funding, this amounted to the largest increase in transportation funding in Texas's history. Texas now struggles to make up for years of poorly kept roads and lack of new roads. The increased revenue can be used to pay for new road construction or used to pay down the debt on current transportation bonds.

The Texas Department of Transportation

In 1991, the Texas Legislature created TxDOT, which combined the Texas Department of Highways with the Texas Motor Vehicle Commission and the Texas Department of Aviation. The five-member Texas Highway Commission oversees TxDOT. The commissioners are appointed by the governor, subject to Texas Senate approval. The commissioners serve staggered, six-year terms. As of 1991, Texas law requires that at least one commissioner come from a rural part of the state. The commission's job is to plan and oversee construction and maintenance of Texas highways and to develop mass transportation systems. In addition to the commission, TxDOT employs an executive director, who until 2009 was required by law to be a professional engineer. Today, TxDOT comprises around 12,000 employees and enjoys an annual budget of nearly $30 billion.

Public-Private Partnerships

public-private partnerships (PPPs) government infrastructure built by private companies for profit

Faced with increasing populations and decreasing funds to build roads, in 2002 Governor Perry began to advocate for **public-private partnerships (PPPs)**. PPPs allow government infrastructure to be built by private investment entities seeking to profit and create alternative funding in the cash-strapped state. Texas attempted to encourage such projects when the legislature passed the 2011 Texas Public and Private Facilities and Infrastructure Act to help facilitate PPPs. In the case of Texas roads, PPPs would allow private corporations to build roads and charge tolls for use of those roads. The money generated from the tolls goes to the private firm rather than state coffers.

Throughout his tenure, Governor Perry was one of the most vocal advocates for privatizing toll roads. The most ambitious example of a PPP was Perry's proposal for the 4,000-mile Trans-Texas Corridor, which the legislature quickly squashed.

The use of PPP toll roads as a means to build roads in the state has flourished. Toll roads such as Texas State Highway 121 connecting Collin County to Denton County and Texas State Highway 130 in Austin are PPPs. The North Texas Tollway Authority (NTTA), a private company, paid $3 billion for the right to turn Texas State Highway 121 into a tollway. The NTTA updated and extended the highway, which it renamed the Sam Rayburn Tollway. After raising rates several times, the NTTA board voted in 2009 to automatically raise rates every two years. In 2018, a driver who traveled the current length of Texas State Highway 121 from Coppell to McKinney paid $4.24 with a TollTag or $6.37 in cash one way. So for Texans with a TollTag who drove a small car on the tollway to and from work five days a week, the cost was around $42 per week.

Proponents of using PPPs to build toll roads argue that it provides Texas with a means to build desperately needed roads that the state would not otherwise be able to afford. They also claim that private firms will be driven by competition and desire for profit to use new technologies and other efficiencies to provide these routes as cheaply as possible. Opponents contend that tolls amount to a backdoor tax and point out that private firms are free to set their own rates and raise them at will. Texans still pay for the roads, but now they pay to a private firm rather than the state. Critics also point out that the fifty-year contracts are too long and create monopolies rather than fostering private competition. Toll roads remain politically attractive in the legislature, however, as they allow Texas politicians to claim they did not raise taxes. Paying to use a road rankles most Texans. As more and more toll roads replaced public roads, and some parts of the state became difficult to navigate without paying tolls, the backlash against toll roads has been swift.

As stated previously, private companies can raise the prices of tolls annually. For example, builders of toll roads in Central Texas announced that their rates would increase by 25 to 50 percent in January 2013, although the original proposal kept tolls at their initial levels until 2015.[58] By comparison, in the past, Texas toll roads were treated as a public good rather than a for-profit industry. For example, the Texas Turnpike Authority completed Interstate 30 as a toll road in 1957. The highway took seventeen years to pay off, at which point the state took over the road and removed the tollbooths. The potential for a wholly private toll road raises significant questions about the role of government in providing public goods, not the least of which is to what extent a private company can use eminent domain. The 84th legislature passed legislation that removed Texas Turnpike Corporation's eminent domain powers, which appears to have doomed the private toll road. More importantly, there has been a growing backlash in the state to the dramatic increase in toll roads, which now account for over 500 miles of state roads. As quickly as state legislators embraced toll roads as a solution to the state's traffic congestion, legislators have now largely disavowed the use of toll roads for the state. The 84th legislature debated buying back the state's toll roads, but TxDOT estimated it would cost at least $30 billion.[59] The 85th legislature passed several bills that reflect the growing public hostility toward toll roads, including a law blocking free roads from being converted to toll roads and preventing TxDOT from subsidizing future privately owned toll roads. By 2018, Governor Abbott pledged that the state would not approve any new toll roads.

Should Texas use PPPs to build roads in the future?

⭐ **CRITICAL THINKING**

Texas transportation expansion faces increasing financial difficulties, and the state must start preparing for the future. As the recession continued and gas prices soared, many Texans began driving less, thus generating less state revenue for building roads. During the 1990s, Texans preferred big trucks and SUVs, which tend to be fuel inefficient, but Texans have responded to increased gas prices by buying more fuel-efficient cars, which further decreased state revenue generated by the gas tax. An increase in the number of electric and hybrid vehicles will generate little or no fuel tax revenue. Politicians avoided increasing the gas tax by utilizing toll roads and private funding. State senator John Carona advocated indexing the gas tax to inflation, which would allow the gas tax to keep up with increased prices without politicians having to actually vote to raise taxes. However, this proposal has, predictably, been unpopular among state lawmakers. Moreover, ending the pay-as-you-go system in the state has resulted in desperately needed dollars from the existing gas tax being used to pay interest on loans rather than being applied toward building new roads. At the same time, surges in Texas's population and deteriorating infrastructure have contributed to an unprecedented transportation crisis, and addressing transportation needs is becoming politically difficult.

How does the elimination of pay-as-you-go funding requirements affect the state's ability to meet its transportation needs?

⭐ CRITICAL THINKING

Mass Transit

While Texas is facing serious problems with regard to its highway system, the mass transit situation in the state has been slow to get off the ground. Texas recognized its need for mass transportation in the 1850s when a system of stagecoaches moved people around the state. Even then, the stagecoach lines made much of their profit from government contracts to carry mail.[60] Until recently, Texas has paid little attention to developing mass transit infrastructure. Only bigger urban centers have some form of light rail, and even those are relatively recent projects and remain limited. Texas didn't open its first light rail until 1996, when Dallas Area Rapid Transit (DART) opened its first line. Houston's MetroRail opened a 7.5-mile stretch in 2004, and Austin opened Capital MetroRail in 2010. Other major urban areas, including San Antonio and Corpus Christi, still do not have any light rail service. DART has expanded to operate the most miles of light rail in the United States. Former senator Kay Bailey Hutchison points to DART as a model for transportation success in the country today. Houston's light rail system, by contrast, was beset by funding issues and delays and was slower to get off the ground. Fort Worth and El Paso are poised to develop light rail in the next few years, and citizens in Galveston voted to rebuild their trolley system, which was devastated by a hurricane in 2008.[61] Arlington was the biggest city in the country without any form of mass transit until recently. In what is dubbed "microtransit," Arlington contracted a rideshare company to create an app with which customers can schedule a minibus pickup and drop-off for a flat $3 fee.

Texas's neglect of light rail systems significantly costs the state. When the federal government offered grants for high-speed rail as part of a 2010 stimulus package, Texas was caught unprepared. In fact, Texas received only $11 million, or 1.3 percent, of the available grant money.[62] By comparison, California received $2.5 billion of the same federal funds. To attract federal funds, Texas needs a statewide plan for mass transit.

Although the state was unprepared to obtain federal money, some Texas cities have fared much better. DART received a $700 million federal grant in 2006 to help expand its light rail system, and in 2011, Houston received $900 million in federal grants to be

Should the government provide mass transportation systems?

⭐ SOCIAL RESPONSIBILITY

paid over five years. Texas, though late to the mass transit party, is starting to catch up. In 2009, the legislature passed a bill that requires TxDOT to develop a statewide passenger rail transportation plan and creates a rail division within the agency. Nonetheless, it will take time for Texas's mass transit infrastructure to match that of other states.

WINNERS AND LOSERS

Texas's thriving economy, increasing urbanization, and constant population growth create serious stress on the state's roads and highways, with no end in sight. As the state's economy continues to thrive, the state is constantly in need of more roads and road maintenance. More than half the state's roads are in mediocre to poor conditions.[63] The cost of driving on poorly maintained roads, while hidden, is significant. Driving on poor roads isn't just dangerous; it is also expensive. Driving on poorly maintained roads costs every Texas driver an average of $761 a year and is a factor in one-third of the state's traffic fatalities.[64] The recent legislatures' move to increase transportation funding in the state will benefit all Texans and help facilitate future economic development. Yet, Texas continues to have one of the lowest gas taxes in the country. The gasoline tax is a plus, since Texans can see exactly what it is and where it is going. As long as politicians see increasing the gasoline tax as politically unviable, funding roads will be an opaque process involving poor infrastructure and private, sometimes foreign, ownership of infrastructure. Politicians, who like to claim they have not raised taxes, are the winners in this story. The reality, though, is that toll roads amount to a hidden tax. As the state's population booms and transportation infrastructure fails to keep pace, more citizens will be paying that tax. The private companies that operate the toll roads have an incentive to continue to raise tolls, and they don't face the political backlash that politicians do. Those increased tolls do not go to pay the state's bills. Arguably, raising the gasoline tax would be better for Texans, since it is not a hidden tax and would be put toward paying for collective goods. Even a significant increase of the gas tax is unlikely to be as expensive as the costs associated with regular toll road use. Texans, particularly those in large cities who increasingly face the choice of paying the tolls or spending hours in traffic, lose.

More critical for Texans is the move from a pay-as-you-go system of funding transportation to borrowing money to fund the building of roads. This move was designed to allow Texans to keep up with increased demands on roads. In reality, the state now spends much of its meager transportation budget financing its debt. As Texas spends more on servicing the debt rather than on building roads, it is Texans who lose. As urbanization and population pressures continue, Texas will have to look toward expanding its transportation network, which means it will need to pay more attention to mass transit and even high-speed rail. Mass transit and high-speed rail both facilitate economic development, which helps all Texans win.

TEXAS TRADE

The Texas economy is big—really big. The state's $1.7-trillion economy is larger than the economy of South Korea, the Netherlands, and Russia. The Texas economy, which produces the most oil and houses the most refineries in the country, is also home to the second-largest deep-water port. The Houston

What are the costs to Texans if politicians do not raise the state's gasoline tax?

 CRITICAL THINKING

When weighing the pros and cons of highways, mass transit, and high-speed trains, what should Texas's transportation priorities be?

 SOCIAL RESPONSIBILITY

TEXAS (VS) CALIFORNIA

As large states by both population and land area, Texas and California offer natural comparisons in terms of the economic impact each state has on the global economy. In some ways, California and Texas are quite similar. Both states rank in the top two in gross state product, a measure of each state's economic output. In 2017, California ranked first with $2.3 trillion, followed by Texas at $1.7 trillion. If each state were an independent country, California would be the eighth-largest economy in the world, ranking just ahead of Brazil and just behind France. Texas would rank as the tenth-largest economy, ahead of Canada and just behind

Italy. In addition, both countries attracted similar levels of foreign direct investment (FDI) from outside the United States, with California receiving $41.6 billion in 2017 compared to $39.7 billion for Texas. The two states rank first and second in the country in terms of FDI, well ahead of third-place Illinois at $25.9 billion.

There are some significant differences between the two states in terms of international trade, however. California engages in more international trade, with $613 billion in total exports and imports in 2017. Texas's trade accounted for around $527 billion that same year. However, Texas's trade was more

balanced, with $263 billion in imports and $264 billion in exports, leaving Texas with a small trade surplus with foreign countries. California, in contrast, ran a $269 billion trade deficit. California exported only $172 billion in goods and services to the outside world while it imported $441 billion. Another difference exists with the key trading partners of each state. While NAFTA partners Canada and Mexico rank in the top five for both states, other important trading partners for California include Japan, Malaysia, and Hong Kong. For Texas, other important partners are South Korea, Saudi Arabia, and Brazil.

What each state trades is also an important distinction. For California, key imports include passenger cars and digital equipment, while exports include aircraft, integrated circuits, and semiconductors. Key imports into Texas include various types of oil, cellular telephones, and digital processing equipment, while exports include various types of oil, propane gas, and parts and accessories for mechanical equipment.

Category (as of 2017)	California	Texas
Gross State Product	$2.3 trillion	$1.7 trillion
Gross State Product (2007)	$2.0 trillion	$1.2 trillion
Change (2007–2017)	15.0%	41.2%
World Rank	8th	10th
Exports to Rest of World	$172 billion	$264 billion
Exports as % of U.S. Total	11.1%	17.1%
Imports from Rest of World	$441 billion	$263 billion
Imports as % of U.S. Total	18.8%	11.2%
FDI into State	$41.6 billion	$39.7 billion
FDI Rank	1st	2nd

Sources: Federal Reserve Bank of St. Louis, "Gross Domestic Product by State," accessed July 23, 2018, https://fred.stlouisfed.org/release?rid=140; U.S. Department of Commerce, Bureau of Economic Analysis, "News Release: New Foreign Direct Investment in the United States: 2017," July 11, 2018, https://www.bea.gov/newsreleases/international/fdi/2018/pdf/fdi0718.pdf.

Which state is more productive economically? Why?

⭐ EMPIRICAL AND QUANTITATIVE

What do the patterns of trade in Texas and California suggest about each state's geographic location within the United States?

⭐ EMPIRICAL AND QUANTITATIVE

shipping channel, which possesses the largest petrochemical complex in the United States, is a center for international trade. Today's Texas also manufactures computer products, aerospace equipment, and medical supplies. The economic powerhouse that is Texas developed due to a variety of factors. While internal, U.S.-based production and consumption is a chief source of economic activity, the Texas economy is also highly interconnected with the rest of the world. Nothing has shaped Texas's role in the international economy more than the North American Free Trade Area (NAFTA). **NAFTA** is a trade relationship between the United States, Canada, and Mexico that removed tariffs—taxes on imports and exports—among the member countries. NAFTA is based on bilateral agreements that had already been negotiated between the United States and Canada in 1988, with precursory treaties in some areas of the economy like the automobile industry from the early 1960s. Governor Abbott estimates that NAFTA has created one million jobs in the Lone Star State.[65]

Texas is the largest exporting state in the country, exporting more than one and a half times the country's second-largest exporter, California. The state exported $264 billion in goods, in 2017. Texas's top trading partners include its fellow NAFTA partners, Mexico and Canada. Since the trade agreement took effect, Texas exports to Mexico have increased by 13 percent a year, according to Governor Abbott.[66] In 2017, Texas's exports to Mexico accounted for over $97 billion, or 37 percent of Texas's foreign trade. Canada accounted for an additional $23 billion, or almost 9 percent. China ranked third in terms of exports from Texas, at $16 billion. Of the twenty-eight-member European Union (EU), the Netherlands and the United Kingdom rank in the top ten for Texas's exports; Germany, Belgium, and France are in the top fifteen; and Texas exports to the EU collectively exceed that of Texas exports to China.[67] In terms of imports into Texas from the rest of the word, in 2017, Texas's imports from Mexico were valued at almost $90 billion and imports from Canada at $18 billion. In both cases, Texas maintains a trade surplus, exporting more to Mexico and Canada than it imports. Among EU countries, Germany, the United Kingdom, and Italy are among Texas top-fifteen importers. The state maintains a balanced trade relationship with the EU. China's imports into the state are significant, at over $42 billion in 2017, but again, these numbers are smaller than imports from both NAFTA partners and from the EU collectively. The China-Texas trade relationship is a net deficit for Texas, with imports from China exceeding exports to China by $26 billion.[68] It is also interesting to note that U.S. trade with Canada and Mexico under NAFTA is almost entirely without import taxes, or tariffs, imposed by any of the three countries, consistent with a free trade area. Most products traded between the United States (and indeed the entire NAFTA region) and the European Union are already covered by free trade agreements. As governor, Abbott has sought to further Texas trade, traveling to countries such as India, Ireland, and Cuba to try to negotiate new agreements and investment for the state.

Often, our view of foreign trade is that of finished goods crossing national boundaries. However, trade is much more nuanced than that. Trade often involves component parts of a finished product crossing national borders to be integrated into products that cross national borders again to be installed into a finished product. Thus, trade is not just finished goods or raw commodities crossing borders. A more accurate picture of Texas's economic relationship with the outside world includes a focus on **foreign direct investment (FDI).** FDI provides a more complete measure of economic relationships because it involves a commitment by a business to invest in another country, indicating a higher degree of trust in the economic and political relationships between the countries and a higher degree of stability. After all, why invest

Texas Imports, Exports, and Foreign Direct Investment (FDI)

Texas Imports

Top 5 countries, 2017
(Billions of dollars)

Mexico	$89.8
China	$42.7
Canada	$18.3
South Korea	$9.1
Saudi Arabia	$7.3

Texas Exports

Top 5 countries, 2017
(Billions of dollars)

Mexico	$97.7
Canada	$22.9
China	$16.4
Brazil	$10.0
South Korea	$9.7

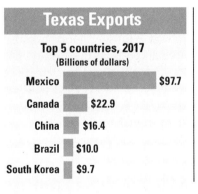

FDI into Texas

Top 5 countries, 2011-2016
(Billions of dollars)

France	$4.5
Japan	$3.1
Germany	$3.0
Canada	$2.7
UK	$2.3

Sources: United States Census Bureau, "State Exports from Texas," https://www.census.gov/foreign-trade/statistics/state/data/tx.html (accessed July 26, 2018); United States Census Bureau, "State Imports for Texas," https://www.census.gov/foreign-trade/statistics/state/data/imports/tx.html (accessed July 26, 2018); Office of the Governor, "Texas Trade and Foreign Direct Investment 2016," https://gov.texas.gov/uploads/files/business/fdi_report.pdf (accessed July 26, 2018)

millions or billions of dollars to build a manufacturing facility in another country if you do not expect to stay?

Between 2011 and 2016 (the latest data available), FDI into the state of Texas was more than $40 billion and generated 84,000 new jobs, with the largest share of FDI coming from EU countries including the United Kingdom, Germany, and France. Canadian investment in Texas added over 9,000 new jobs as well. Other notable countries in new investment include EU members Spain, the Netherlands, and Sweden, non-EU European countries like Norway and Switzerland, Japan (which added over 12,000 new jobs), India, and Australia.[69] While the Texas–China trade relationship is large, Chinese investment in Texas is almost nonexistent compared to European Union and NAFTA investment in Texas. In addition, between 2011 and 2016, Texas-based companies invested over $59 billion abroad, with the biggest investments in the United Kingdom, Germany, and France. While China was a significant location for investment by Texans, investment in Canada was almost five times as large, and investment in Mexico was twice as large. Texas prefers to invest in the EU and NAFTA countries over China.[70]

WINNERS AND LOSERS

Texas, while proud of its independence, is increasingly one of the most integrated states in the global economy. Trade with our NAFTA partners, which brings in billions of dollars and tens of thousands of jobs, makes Texans clear winners. Imports allow Texans to buy cheaper goods, while our exports reflect Texas products sold around the world. Texas exports cheap natural gas and crude oil, but also products like computer chips and airplane parts globally. The state imports crude oil, cell phones, and tractors, among other things. Texans also wins when we create a state that attracts investment from NAFTA partners, EU countries, and others. Texas loses if we adopt trade policy that contracts our existing economic relationships with our largest trading partners. The future of the state depends on continuing to attract investment and encourage trade. As Texas moves into the future, our trade policy, particularly with our biggest partners, is on the whole balanced.

How does Texas fare in the globalized economy?

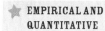 **EMPIRICAL AND QUANTITATIVE**

CONCLUSION

Nothing is more legendary in Texas than the state's relationship with oil. As Texas moves toward the future, its reliance on oil, coal, and natural gas is increasingly augmented by alternative energy sources. Texas has always been blessed by its large endowment of land. The state's vast plains make it ideal for harnessing wind and solar energy, and the state is in the position to lead in green energy, along with oil and gas. Texas also must increasingly look to its strained resources, such as water, as it struggles with how to be a good steward of its greatest endowment. The state's ability to deal with fundamental changes in everything from environmental policy and adequate natural resources to sufficient transportation will define its future. Texas's ability to adapt has helped it become the economic powerhouse it is today. With an economy larger than most countries in the world, Texas is not only the largest U.S. exporter but continues to attract new investment. The state has never stayed the same, yet it remains in the enviable position of being a place where people can find numerous opportunities to better their lives.

Is Texas trade an overall benefit or drain on the state?

★ **CRITICAL THINKING**

for CQ Press

Want a better grade?

Get the tools you need to sharpen your study skills. Access practice quizzes, eFlashcards, video, and multimedia at **edge.sagepub.com/collier6e**.

KEY TERMS

eminent domain (p. 426)
foreign direct investment (FDI) (p. 445)
fracking (p. 427)
Good Roads Amendment (p. 438)
NAFTA (p. 445)
negative externality (p. 431)

public-private partnerships (PPPs) (p. 440)
regulation (p. 431)
rule of capture (p. 434)
subsidence (p. 433)
Texas Commission on Environmental
   Quality (TCEQ) (p. 432)

ACTIVE LEARNING

- Break into groups of five. In each group, discuss what changes the Texas Legislature should make to reform transportation policy. **Teamwork**

- What should policymakers prioritize for Texas future energy needs? Design a meme that represents the future of Texas energy. **Communication**

CHAPTER REVIEW

1. The first Texas oil boom occurred _____.

   a. in the 1700s, when the Spanish began drilling for oil

   b. in 1901, when Spindletop struck oil

   c. in the 1990s, when fracking technology improved

   d. Texas has always had an oil boom.

2. Texas oil and natural gas boom towns have been characterized by _____.

   a. a rapid influx of people in the town

   b. a large increase in jobs

   c. strain on the local infrastructure (schools, roads, housing)

   d. all of these

3. The power of the government to take property for public use is called _____.

   a. eminent domain

   b. oil and gas tax

   c. regulation

   d. rule of capture

4. If a local factory puts dangerous chemicals in the air and there is an increase in asthma and lung cancer, this unintended consequence is called a _____.

   a. market transaction

   b. negative externality

   c. regulation

   d. rule of capture

5. The Texas agency responsible for protecting the environment is called the _____.

   a. Environmental Protection Agency

   b. Texas Commission on Environmental Quality (TCEQ)

   c. Texas Railroad Commission

   d. Electric Reliability Council of Texas (ERCOT)

6. Texas wind energy production is _____.

   a. near zero; this is oil country

   b. number seven in the country

   c. number one in the country

   d. not likely to be around in a few years

7. Texas's hazardous waste facility _____.

   a. was the first to open in the United States in three decades

   b. accepts more hazardous classifications of radioactive waste than other states

   c. has applied to host the country's high-level radioactive waste

   d. all of these

8. Originally, roads in Texas were paid for by _____.

   a. county governments, which were authorized to hire male citizens to complete the work

   b. wealthy landowners

   c. city governments, which could tax citizens for the number of horses they owned

   d. state governments, which could tax railroad companies to pay for the roads

9. Which country imports more goods from Texas than any other country?

   a. Brazil

   b. Germany

   c. Mexico

   d. China

10. Which country invests more money in Texas than any other country?

    a. the United Kingdom

    b. Mexico

    c. Israel

    d. China

SOCIAL POLICY

Education, Health, and Immigration

Chapter Objectives

★ Explain the challenges facing the K–12 and higher education systems in Texas.

★ Assess who wins and who loses when it comes to K–12 and higher education funding.

★ Describe the relationship between the state and federal governments in social policies and programs.

★ Assess who wins and who loses in the politics of state health and human services.

★ Assess the role and impact of immigration in Texas.

★ Assess who wins and who loses in the context of immigration in Texas.

ccess to higher education has become one of the hottest topics in state politics, and as some parents and students become more concerned about a school's prestige, the question of exactly who gets admitted to the state's top schools has become much more important. In 1997, the Texas Legislature approved a law that guaranteed students in the top 10 percent of their high school graduating class admission to any state university in Texas. The idea was to increase diversity at the University of Texas (UT) and other schools by ensuring that the best students from every community could be assured admission to the state school of their choice. The top 10 percent rule appealed to urban schools with large African American populations, South Texas with large Hispanic communities, and rural schools—some of which had never had a student admitted to UT.[1]

One problem was that guaranteeing every top 10 percent student in Texas a place in the incoming class increased the demands on a university already bursting at the seams. In fall 2006, 71 percent of students entered UT through the top 10 percent rule, limiting the school's ability to fill the rest of its freshman class with out-of-state students or those who distinguished themselves through special abilities, such as art or music, that are not always reflected in the student's overall academic performance. In 2009, UT and its supporters won passage of a law that capped the number of students that the

Students await their diplomas during the graduation ceremony at Mission Community College in El Paso, Texas. Texas has about 1.3 million students in its colleges and universities.

university had to accept under this rule at 75 percent of its entering class. This allowed UT to select the other 25 percent through a "holistic review" that might take race into consideration, along with other factors. The cap meant that fewer students were admitted under the top 10 percent rule, and UT admitted only the top 7 percent of Texas high school graduates for the fall of 2016.

While the top 10 percent rule allows every Texas community a chance to place its students in the most exclusive universities, critics complain that it passes over students from highly competitive school districts and private schools. In 2008, Abigail Fisher, a white student from Sugar Land who had been denied admission to UT, filed a lawsuit against the university, arguing that she was penalized because of her race in violation of the Fourteenth Amendment's promise of equal protection. After years of legal battles, the U.S. Supreme Court surprised many observers in the summer of 2016 when it ruled against Fisher in *Fisher v. University of Texas*. The court affirmed that UT could continue to utilize affirmative action as part of its holistic review. The court supported the university's attempt to recruit a more diverse student body as long as it could demonstrate that considerations of race serve the university's educational goals.

The battle over admission reflects a long-fought and complicated battle over higher education in Texas, with both sides pursuing their view of equality. The *Fisher* case represents only a small part of the debate since UT and Midwestern State University were the only two schools in Texas asking to use race as a consideration in admission decisions. And the battle is far from over. As soon as the *Fisher* decision was handed down, members of the Texas Legislature began to discuss ways in which they could alter admission criteria through changes to the law. An analysis by the *Texas Tribune* demonstrates how complicated the issue is by revealing that white and Asian applicants were far more likely to be admitted under the holistic review that allowed consideration of race.[2]

The lack of educational diversity Texas offers is especially problematic in a state with a diverse economy that is seeking to prepare its youth to become the next generation of farmers, ranchers, software engineers, etc. Thus, the drive for control by the state can create costs and inefficiencies of its own, and citizens have to decide how much control elected officials and bureaucracy can or should have.

This chapter will assess the impact of a growing and changing population on state education policy and social policies such as welfare and health care. We first look at how the state attempts to get millions of young Texans from kindergarten to high school graduation. We then turn to a system of higher education designed to take Texans beyond a high school diploma to college degrees. Next, we will look at how the state tries to meet the basic needs of Texans in the areas of food, shelter, and health care. Finally, we will review some of the issues surrounding immigration and Texas politics.

EDUCATION POLICY

Education is important to Texans for several reasons. Outside of family, schools are often the primary influence on children's intellectual, social, and physical development. Education is seen as critical for long-term economic well-being, and the state's educational system energizes the state economy by providing its businesses with the qualified workforce needed to be competitive. Also, the research conducted at the state's universities leads to innovations needed for the future. Further, the state's schools help create a society with citizens ready to engage in civic life and prepared to indulge in the rich cultural pursuits of arts, music, and literature. Often the local public school system is the largest employer in a community, and a community college or public university produces a tremendous economic impact on the surrounding community. For many small towns across Texas, the local public high school is a source of community pride and unity. Even in urban and suburban areas, Texans identify with the "Friday Night Lights" of football, marching bands, high stepping drill teams, and competitive cheer squads.

With education's influences being so wide, it is no surprise that the importance of schools to the state's businesses has increased through the years. This fact was highlighted in 2007 when a new group calling itself Raise Your Hand Texas formed with the purpose of seeking educational reforms, which it felt were needed to keep Texas economically competitive. Although the organization was chaired by a former lieutenant governor, Bill Ratliff, most of the board members are current or former heads of major corporations, such as Texas Instruments, Continental Airlines, and AT&T, reflecting the ongoing interest of business in public education.

Texas's schools have become a major battleground in Texas politics because they represent an essential investment in the state's future, and citizens' desire to see such a large investment handled wisely has subjected Texas schools to scrutiny. The size and scope of public education is daunting, with billions of dollars spent each year by states and local governments, employing several million Texans. Some groups, such as Raise Your Hand Texas, worry that the standardized tests used to hold public schools accountable have discouraged students who face too many tests and teachers who feel that innovative teaching will not be rewarded. At the same time, reformers look at the rising price of education and insist that the state try to ensure that money be spent wisely.

Public Education in Grades K–12

Political battles over public education are nothing new, predating the state and even the Republic of Texas. In fact, the authors of the Texas Declaration of Independence included in their list of grievances that Mexico had "failed to establish any public system of education, although possessed of almost boundless resources (the public domain) and, although, it is an axiom, in political science, that unless a people are educated and enlightened it is idle to expect the continuance of civil liberty, or the capacity for self-government." During his presidency, Mirabeau Lamar earned the nickname of "Father of Texas Education"[3] by championing education in the new republic and setting aside three leagues of land for each county to support elementary schools. Despite Lamar's vision, the limited value of this land, combined with Texans' reluctance to finance schools with tax dollars and the preference of many for private schools, delayed realization of a public school system until the Constitution of 1868 centralized the public schools.

The foundation of the modern public school system in Texas was laid in 1949 when the legislature passed the Gilmer-Aikin laws, named for Representative Claud Gilmer and Senator A. M. Aikin. This act guaranteed Texas children twelve years of school with a minimum of 175 days of instruction per year. The legislation also redesigned the state's governance of public education by replacing the nine-person appointed State Board of Education (SBOE) with commissioners elected by voters in districts. While we take this structure for granted today, it was regarded as revolutionary at the time, and Dolph Briscoe, a member of the Texas House who worked on the legislation and went on to serve as governor, recounted how the bill was attacked as "communistic."[4]

By 2017, Texas had 8,771 public schools in 1,023 school districts and 180 charter operations. These schools educated about 5.3 million students and employed about 342,352,756 teachers, 98,497 administrators, and 253,754 support staff.[5] The state's school system is overseen by the Texas Education Agency, which is run by a commissioner of education appointed by the governor and the State Board of Education (SBOE). The SBOE has grown to fifteen members elected from districts and has a chair appointed by the governor. Members of the SBOE are unpaid but reimbursed for travel

> **What do the trends in enrollment in K–12 schools in Texas suggest about how Texas needs to prepare for the future of higher education in Texas?**
>
> ⭐ **CRITICAL THINKING**

TABLE 14.1 Texas School Enrollment, 2007–2017

Level	Enrollment (2007–2008)	Enrollment (2016–2017)	Percent Change
Early education and kindergarten	574,415	620,069	+7.9%
Elementary (1–5)	1,790,360	2,028,641	+13.3%
Middle (6–8)	1,009,558	1,186,638	+17.5%
High (9–12)	1,297,130	1,523,779	+17.5%
Total K–12	4,671,463	5,359,127	+14.7%

Source: Texas Education Agency, "Enrollment in Texas Public Schools, 2007–2008," January 2009, https://tea.texas.gov/acctres/Enroll_2007-08.pdf; Texas Educational Agency, "Enrollment in Texas Public Schools, 2016-2017," June 2017, https://tea.texas.gov/acctres/enroll_2016-17.pdf.

and other work-related expenses. The board meets every few months and decides broad education issues, such as curriculum and standards for passing state-mandated exams.

While the idea of having an elected board of education suits Texans' desire to have popular control over their government, recent battles in the board have led some to question whether the process has become too politicized. The most visible battle involved the creation of curriculum guidelines for teachers in areas such as science and history. The SBOE has become embroiled in debates over teaching topics ranging from evolution to Mexican American heritage. In 2010, the board drew national attention over changes to the history curriculum guidelines, which, according to comedian Stephen Colbert, "decides which historical figures all of our children will be drawing mustaches and eye-patches on."[6] This debate brought Texas into the national spotlight when the SBOE voted to remove founding father Thomas Jefferson from draft guidelines of the list of political philosophies to be discussed. While some popular media went so far as to suggest Texas was removing Jefferson's presidency from history textbooks, in actuality the SBOE only removed references to Jefferson's political philosophy that mirrored discussions of English philosopher John Locke. Jefferson's presidency was always included in SBOE guidelines.

The ardency of the debate makes clear that the SBOE has become intensely involved in partisan politics and the so-called culture war. Unfortunately, this means that a few narrow issues, such as evolution, will dominate campaigns for the SBOE, while broader issues, such as the value of highly detailed guidelines, are forgotten as candidates try to score partisan points. The disdain and ridicule generated by the debate over curriculum guidelines is compounded by the fact that this debate results in dictating from Washington or Austin what teachers do in the classroom. In the end, both students and teachers may see their efforts devalued as politicians wrangle over which political philosophy gains control over the curriculum.

One of the overlooked issues involving the SBOE is its management of the Permanent School Fund (PSF). The origins of the PSF go back to 1854, at which time the new state of Texas set aside $2 million from the $10 million payment it received from the United States for giving up claims to some of the land it had claimed as the Republic of Texas. The Constitution of 1876 revived the fund and granted the proceeds of the sale of certain public lands to the PSF. Since that time, money from the sales and leasing of these public lands has gone into the PSF, with the returns on the investment of the funds being made available for use in Texas public schools. In 1960, the U.S. Supreme Court recognized Texas's claim to a 10.35-mile seaward boundary of lands off its coast, and proceeds from the sale and the mineral lease rights to these lands have also helped fill the fund. The PSF was valued at about $41.4 billion at the end of 2017, and the SBOE distributed over $1 billion from the interest earned on the fund to support public school education. The PSF has distributed about $27 billion to Texas public schools since 1960.[7]

The SBOE work with consultants and the staff of the Texas Education Agency that oversee the management of these funds led to ethics charges after board members were accused of receiving gifts from firms involved in the fund. Even aside from ethics rules, the challenges the part-time SBOE faces in effectively handling the very different tasks of setting statewide education policy, constructing a public school curriculum, and managing billions of dollars make it unlikely that board members are expert in everything they must do. With a wide range of tasks before them, the SBOE members must master the world of education and high finance to make sure the state gets the most out of its schools and its investments.

Equality in Education

Texas education was further transformed by the civil rights era, although change proved slow. Texas schools had embraced the idea of separate-but-equal schools since the Constitution of 1876, which specified that "separate schools shall be provided for the white and colored children, and impartial provision shall be made for both." This reflected the principle of "separate but equal" upheld by the U.S. Supreme Court in the 1896 decision of *Plessy v. Ferguson.*[8] While the races remained separated, the provisions for their schools remained far from "impartial" in Texas, with many schools for non-white students underfunded.

The reality of equal schools remained elusive even after 1954 when the U.S. Supreme Court issued the landmark *Brown v. Board of Education*[9] decision that declared segregated public schools to be a violation of the equal protection clause

Neither Separate nor Equal: Hispanics in the Education System

While the battle for equal rights has often been played out before the U.S. Supreme Court, the nature of discrimination and the ambiguous legal status of Hispanics in Texas has posed a unique set of challenges for Tejanos.

For decades, the official position of the state of Texas was that Hispanics were not a distinct race from whites and therefore did not need the equal protection for races promised in the Fourteenth Amendment. In the 1930s, about 90 percent of South Texas school districts maintained separate schools for Hispanic students and made no attempt to disguise this segregation. Many of these schools carried the official designation of "Mexican School." Although schools for African American children had some obligation to be separate but equal after

the 1896 decision in *Plessy v. Ferguson,*[i] Mexican schools were generally neglected.

In *Delgado v. Bastrop Independent School District* (1948), federal district judge Ben C. Rice declared that it was unlawful and unconstitutional to segregate Hispanic American children in Texas public schools. The decision did, however, permit the segregation of students based on English proficiency. Thus, because they were judged not fluent in English, Hispanic students could still be placed in inferior schools. Of course, putting these students into crowded, inferior schools helped ensure that they did not improve their English and therefore never moved into the mainstream Anglo schools. Some Hispanic students received bad grades regardless of their actual language skills. And in some cases, students with Hispanic

surnames were placed in Mexican schools even though they spoke only English.

Eventually, in *Herminca Hernandez et al. v. Driscoll Consolidated ISD* (1957), a federal court declared the segregation of Mexican American students unconstitutional. As the case had been with racial segregation following the *Brown v. Board of Education*[ii] decisions, however, local school districts resisted change and equality has remained elusive. Supported by the League of United Latin American Citizens (LULAC) and other groups, parents continue to battle local school districts to guarantee a quality education for Hispanic students.

---

i. 163 U.S. 537.

ii. 347 U.S. 483 (1954); 349 U.S. 294 (1955).

of the U.S. Constitution. The court put aside the possibility of separate facilities being equal and declared that laws separating the races were interpreted as denoting an inferiority of black children that would undermine their motivation to learn. Despite the court's unanimous agreement in the original decision and in a follow-up decision known as *Brown II*,[10] which was handed down in 1955 and called for desegregation "with all deliberate speed," little progress was seen in Texas in the decade after the *Brown* decisions. Texas governor Allan Shivers told local school districts that he saw no need for them to change, and students in many areas remained separated by race.

More pressure came through the federal government via the Civil Rights Act of 1964 and the Elementary and Secondary Education Act of 1965. Eventually, the U.S. Department of Justice filed a lawsuit against the state of Texas that resulted in a 1970 decision by Judge William Wayne Justice, the chief judge of the U.S. District Court for the Eastern District in Tyler, to desegregate the state's public schools. The decision also gave the court authority to oversee the state's implementation of the desegregation.[11]

One of the challenges of education in a changing state is addressing the needs of students who primarily speak other languages. In 2017, almost 19 percent of the state's public school students were classified as having limited English proficiency, with an additional almost 19 percent being classified as bilingual. Note that both classifications include those of all language groups, not simply Spanish speakers. Only about 2 percent, or around 100,000 students, are classified by the Texas Education Agency (TEA) as immigrant, and a much smaller number, around 22,000, are associated with migrant labor. These data suggest that those students with bilingual or limited English language proficiency are overwhelmingly here legally as citizens. In 2014, the League of United Latin American Citizens (LULAC) filed a lawsuit renewing its claim that the state has failed to support programs that help students learn English. According to the LULAC brief, the problem goes beyond recent immigrants: "Contrary to popular belief, a majority of ELL students in secondary schools are not classified as recent immigrants and have been in U.S. schools for at least three years."[12] The LULAC court case alleges that the state has failed to maintain high enough standards for certification to teach languages and that, as a result, a majority of English language learner (ELL) students are not making adequate progress in English and that this is also inhibiting their success in other classes.[13] In addition, the ongoing challenges by LULAC have attempted to force the state, the Texas Education Agency, and local school districts to comply with prior court decisions requiring equality in education for Hispanics that date as far back as 1972.

Funding for K–12

The state's struggles with equality have extended beyond race to include differences created by funding. Education policy in the state's public schools is especially complicated because it brings together the efforts, money, and rules of federal, state, and local governments. In the 2015–2016 school year (the last year complete financial data was available before this book went to press), Texas public schools received 40.8 percent of their budgets from the state, 10.2 percent from the federal government, and 49.0 percent from local sources. As this indicates, while federal laws such as the No Child Left Behind Act (NCLB) and its replacement, the Every Student Succeeds Act (ESSA),

Every Student Succeeds Act (ESSA)
the federal education act that replaced No Child Left Behind and reduced federal government emphasis on mandatory testing to track student progress and evaluate schools based on that progress; states have more freedom under ESSA to develop assessment plans unique to their state

have continued to increase federal involvement in Texas public schools, the financial responsibility for schools remains mostly with state and local officials.

Combined, federal, state, and local governments spent over $64.7 billion on Texas public schools in the 2015–2016 school year, averaging $12,264 per pupil. This amount is actually up from the 2013–2014 school year when spending averaged $10,971 per pupil. Given the large investment of tax dollars, and with the future of the state's children at stake, the education issue is primed for conflict. At the same time, various political groups seeking to bring their concerns into the schools up the ante, triggering debates about emotional issues such as prayer in public schools, access to contraceptives, transgender bathrooms, as well as other societal concerns.

The financial inequality between school districts remains one of the most vexing problems in Texas politics. While the Texas Legislature mandated a statewide curriculum in 1981 and continues to dictate most of what local schools must teach, much of the financial responsibility for these mandates remains with the local school district. In 1949, the state of Texas provided about 80 percent of funding for public schools. However, today that figure has been cut to less than half. This shift to local funding has left the public schools largely dependent on local property taxes, meaning that school districts located in areas with high property values have been able to provide more resources for their students, while school districts with low property values have had to get by with much less.

In 1989, the Supreme Court of Texas's unanimous decision in *Edgewood Independent School District et al. v. Kirby*[14] forced the funding issue into the legislature when the court ruled that Texas's system violated the Texas Constitution's requirement of free and efficient schools. The court noted that two schools in Bexar County illustrated the inequity, as the Edgewood Independent School District (ISD) had $38,854 in property taxes per student, and Alamo Heights had $570,109 in property taxes per student. After three failed special sessions of the legislature, the fourth session produced a bill to raise sales taxes one-quarter of a cent and increase taxes on cigarettes to bolster education funding. While this financing scheme did not fully satisfy the court, it did hold off further reform (thanks to court appeals by the state) until the early 1990s. In 1993, the Texas Legislature again addressed the issue by passing a law that established an equalized wealth level for schools and created a process for redistributing money between districts. This law became known as the "Robin Hood" plan because it took money from "rich" school districts and gave it to "poor" districts.[15] Unfortunately, this has failed to fully equalize funding and has left many school districts frustrated by seeing their tax dollars go elsewhere.

To resolve this issue, the Texas Legislature has attempted to tackle the problem on several other occasions. In 2006, a special session of the legislature expanded the business tax to fund schools, but those increases were offset by bigger cuts to property taxes. In 2012, about 600 school districts that include about three-fourths of the state's students sued the state for its failure to provide an adequate education because the lack of state funding forced local school boards to raise the property tax rate to the maximum allowed by the legislature. This action created the kind of statewide property tax the Texas Constitution forbids. In February 2013, Texas district court judge John Dietz agreed, in a ruling on a related case about school funding. A 2016 Texas Supreme Court ruling upheld the constitutionality of the state's funding system. However, the

What responsibility does each homeowner have to ensure that all Texans have access to a quality education?

★ SOCIAL RESPONSIBILITY

court's decision went on to say that "our Byzantine school funding 'system' is undeniably imperfect, with immense room for improvement. But it satisfies minimum constitutional requirements."[16]

The 2017 regular session of the legislature saw little direct action on school finance, with a looming possibility of some districts losing up to 50 percent of their state funding. At the heart of the debate was a deadlock between the Texas House and Texas Senate over a supplemental fund for public school districts that targeted low enrollment, low property tax districts. The fund, which was set to expire in September 2017 unless renewed, received support in the Senate with the provision that the legislature also fund a private school choice plan, allowing parents sending their children to private schools to receive compensation or reduced taxes to help pay tuition. The Texas House of Representatives rejected the school choice plan.[17]

School financing was a key issue during the legislature's special session in July and August 2017. Again, the House and Senate deadlocked over the level of spending by the state government for public education and the reform of the funding formula. At the end of the session, the Senate, led by Lieutenant Governor Dan Patrick, got much of what they wanted, including less funding than the House had proposed and no changes to the funding formula. During the interim before the 2019 session, the legislature created a commission, the Texas Commission on Public School Finance (TCPSF), to improve the state's funding formula for public education.[18]

As the commission began its work, the commission focused on broader questions such as student outcomes and programmatic considerations, not the fundamental question of how to finance the schools. Proponents of the commission's agenda asserted that before dealing with how schools should be financed, the state needs a better measure of how much needs to be spent. Opponents countered that the agenda of the commission had been derailed by one-sided presentations based on data that assumed the current funding is adequate.[19]

The state's problems with unequal funding are rooted in the local property taxes that schools rely on for much of their funding. Given the wide disparity in the value of property, inequity has proven hard to remove, and the state is certain to grapple with this issue well into the future. As education costs rise, citizens want more information about how well their tax dollars are being spent. Parents worried about their children's futures, employers concerned about quality in the workforce, and taxpayers worried about costs have all contributed to a demand for constant reevaluation of public education. A call for reform was inevitable.

Accountability and Reform in K–12

Education Reform Act
a 1984 statute that requires teachers and school administrators to take a test to assure basic competency before being recertified; students are also tested periodically to monitor progress and are required to pass an exam before being allowed to graduate

Texas has labored to improve the quality of its public schools through various reform movements while still addressing the need for equality. In the 1980s, a committee led by wealthy businessman H. Ross Perot pushed for reforms and saw the Texas Legislature adopt many of its recommendations in a special session in the summer of 1984. The Education Reform Act required that teachers and administrators take the Texas Examination of Current Administrators and Teachers (TECAT) to ensure basic competency before being recertified. Students were also tested periodically, beginning Texas's long experimentation with standardized testing, which ultimately spread across the nation during the presidency of George W. Bush. The act also included the controversial "no-pass, no-play" rule that kept students with an average below 70 in any subject from taking part in extracurricular activities. The new law also called for more funding for poor school districts that lacked resources because of the reliance on local property taxes to fund schools. Some of these reforms proved unpopular, as "no pass" sometimes meant "no play" for high school football players.

While these reforms eventually helped cost Mark White, the governor at the time, his reelection bid, some of the reforms White signed into law endured and became part of a movement toward accountability that has now become nationwide. Part of the Education Reform Act required students in odd-numbered grades to take tests in language arts and math. It also required students to pass an exam before they could receive their diploma. While these tests have occasionally changed names and subject matter, they have become a central part of the state's education policy.

Members of the Texas House of Representatives discuss HB 21, which attempted to address problems with the current public school funding formula, during the 2017 regular session of the legislature.

Ironically, while the reform bill he signed helped end the political career of Governor White, George W. Bush continued to press for more standardized testing, and his rise to the presidency was based partly on his promise to do for the nation's schools what he had done for schools in Texas.

States, and increasingly the national government, have been demanding more accountability from local school districts, making Texas a focal point in this debate because of the state's early embrace of standardized testing. In 1990, the Texas Assessment of Academic Skills (TAAS) was implemented and used to create higher standards for state assessment before being replaced in 2003 by the Texas Assessment of Knowledge and Skills (TAKS). In the spring of 2012, the State of Texas Assessments of Academic Readiness (STAAR) replaced the TAKS, and Texas high school students are now required to take separate end-of-course exams at the end of each school year in the four core subject areas: English, math, science, and social studies. Students have to score an average of 70 on the tests in each subject in order to graduate; the tests must count for 15 percent of a student's final grade in the class. For grades three through eight, the STAAR program assesses the same subjects as the TAKS did. Texas has created (and re-created) these tests to create a standard by which student progress can be tracked and schools evaluated based on that progress. The idea is that these standards create guides that citizens can use to evaluate their schools and hold them responsible.

In 2013, the legislature responded to the concerns of parents and many educators and reduced the number of state-mandated tests required to graduate from high school from fifteen to five. This covered the core course areas of Biology, U.S. History,

Algebra I, and English I and II. Many parents felt that the number of high-stakes exams required to graduate was placing too much pressure on students. However, for many critics of testing, the reforms passed in 2013 did little to deal with the heavy emphasis on test preparation over instruction. In 2015, the U.S. Congress passed the Every Student Succeeds Act (ESSA). This new law replaced No Child Left Behind and permitted states more freedom to develop and tailor public school accountability. In reaction, Texas developed a new plan that ultimately gives every public school and every school district a grade of A through F based on student achievement on STAAR, student progress toward key measures of performance, and efforts to close the gap between Anglo performance and that of minority groups.[20] However, in 2016, the state's testing regime was shaken when a computer glitch caused the loss of some or all of student answers on more than 14,000 STAAR exams. Similar issues plagued the system in 2018; students had problems with logging onto the testing software, and with slow connectivity, and revelations that hundreds of students in several high-performing school districts erroneously received zeros on their English essays.[21]

A new problem with the STAAR exam emerged in areas affected by Hurricane Harvey in August 2017. School districts in those areas were closed for days if not weeks, and some were faced with destroyed facilities, massive cleanup operations, and significant disruption of the academic year. Schools scrambled to petition the state for exemptions to STAAR testing. Eventually, the TEA allowed affected schools to apply for a waiver on the 2018 scores.[22]

Unintended Consequences

These high-stakes exams may have spawned some unintended consequences. For example, in 2012, Texans discovered that state law mandated that students who had failed one of the STAAR tests could not be admitted to the state's four-year universities. The only way students who had failed these exams could enter a four-university as a freshman was to get a high score on the ACT or the SAT. While this appears not to have been the intention of any of the legislators who pushed the bill, it found its way into law and impacted thousands of students.[23] Another unintended consequence of this high-stakes testing is that it may be bringing out the worst in our teachers and administrators. For example, studies funded by the *Dallas Morning News* found evidence of massive amounts of cheating on the 2005 and 2006 exams. According to the newspaper's analysis, more than 50,000 students' exams showed evidence of cheating. Because schools see their ratings tied to test scores, and teachers' raises are also dependent on the scores, concerns go beyond student cheating and extend to "educator-led" cheating, in which teachers or school administrators aid students or change answers after the exam to produce higher passing rates. Evidence of cheating was three times as frequent in schools that had been underperforming—schools where the pressure to cheat would have been greatest. For example, in one previously underperforming school district, science scores went from 23 percent below the state average to 14 percent above; evidence of cheating was found in half of the district's eleventh-grade science exams.[24] Such results were eight times more common in the eleventh-grade exams, which determine graduation, than at other grade levels. Confronted with these figures, Texas officials generally were content to call these results "anomalies" rather than proof of cheating.[25]

How does the high stakes assessment system in Texas impact your responsibility for your own educational achievements?

⭐ **PERSONAL RESPONSIBILITY**

While the state's system of testing was intended to help citizens evaluate local schools, credibility concerns leave Texans doubting the validity and value of high-stakes tests in public schools and worrying that these tests seriously undermine the entire educational process. State officials have little incentive to follow up on the evidence of cheating, since it would undermine the validity of their measures and their claims to progress. With their federal funds and the state's reputation on the line, local and state officials have incentive to ignore evidence of cheating.

Texas's Performance

Overall, Texas's record on public schools has been mixed. Texas has made progress on high school graduation rates. One recent report from the U.S. Department of Education found Texas tied for third in high school graduation rates for the 2014–2015 school year with 89 percent, compared to a national average of 83 percent.[26] The state's performance on other measures lags behind the nation. The average SAT score for Texas students (1020) fell below the national average of 1060.[27] Texas students averaged 20.7 on the ACT exam, just below the national average of 21.[28]

In some ways, it should not be surprising that Texas has struggled in educational attainment. For generations, the state's economy was largely agricultural in an era when farming and ranching usually involved little formal education. For many Texas families, the time young people spent in the classroom was a luxury they could not afford, as they needed their children to help in the fields or pastures. Further, these professions required less formal education in early Texas. Today, fewer Texans live on the farm, and the new economy demands more education than ever. Government is under greater pressure to provide graduates who are ready to tackle college or technical fields that are increasingly demanding. However, the fact that there is a need for a change does not ensure that change will occur rapidly.

The Goals of a Public School Education

The educational reforms passed in 2013 went beyond reducing the number of standardized tests and altered the basic curriculum required of students beginning in the 2014–2015 school year. This law, frequently referred to simply as House Bill (HB) 5, addressed the fundamental issue of the goals of a public school education. Previously, all Texas high school students had to complete four years each of science, English, social studies, and math. Beginning in the fall of 2014, high school students began to take a foundation curriculum that includes four English credits; three credits each in science, social studies, and math; two foreign language credits; one fine arts credit; and one PE credit. Students add a fourth science and math credit when they select one of five diploma "endorsements" in areas including STEM (science, technology, engineering, and math); business and industry; public services; arts and the humanities; and multidisciplinary studies. For example, the public services endorsement includes courses directly related to health occupations, law enforcement, culinary arts, and hospitality. The business and industry endorsement includes courses that support construction, welding, automotive technology, and information technology. Advocates of the change say it will keep more students interested and in school and ready to enter the workforce with useful skills. Critics worry that students who fail to pursue endorsements that do not prepare them for college will find themselves locked out of a college education.

Students in a Texas classroom take the STAAR test. The state embraced tough curriculum standards and standardized testing ahead of the national government, although not without concern from educators and parents. By 2017, Texas had retreated from its model of overemphasis on standardized tests to assess schools and student performance.

The debate over HB 5 often turned on what Texans wanted for their children. While some wanted to ensure that every student was encouraged to prepare for college, others wanted to facilitate moves into careers that might not require a college degree.

In many ways, the struggles of Texas public schools dramatically reflect the basic dilemmas of public policy. Citizens want as much efficiency as possible, and in response legislators create systems of accountability. However, accountability testing is costly and generates unintended consequences, such as cheating, which then leads to more oversight, more bureaucracy, and more expense. Despite the challenges of public education, the demands for a better-educated workforce keep the state focused on continued improvement of public schools.

Even if Texans agree on the structure of the state's schools, finding the money for better teacher pay is and will continue to be a struggle. Texas currently ranks twenty-eighth in teacher pay with an average salary of $50,713, compared to a national average of $57,420.[29] Bill Hobby once wrote that "school finance reform in Texas is like a Russian novel. The story line runs across generations, the plot is complex, the prose is tedious, and everybody dies in the end."[30]

School Choice

Some of the state's leaders, including Lieutenant Governor Dan Patrick, have promoted the idea of school vouchers. A voucher is a check issued to the parents of a school student to allow the parent to pay for a transfer to another school within their district, to

FEDERALISM IN Action

Education Policy

Education policy has traditionally been left to state and local governments. That all changed when President George W. Bush signed the No Child Left Behind Act (NCLB). NCLB was based on the high-stakes testing system developed in Texas for state-wide assessment of K–12 education. Under NCLB, states developed and administered tests to all students at select grade levels in order to receive federal funding. While NCLB did not create a single national test or set of standards, it mandated that each state test its students and demonstrate steady improvement in test scores from year to year. The essential argument behind NCLB was that schools should be held accountable for meeting basic education standards. However, critics of the law argued that NCLB resulted in education that was geared toward teaching to the test. Frustrations with the law led most states, including ironically Texas, to apply for waivers from the federal program.

As NCLB became increasingly unpopular, President Obama advocated the Common Core State Standards (championed by Bill Gates). Common Core attempted to establish consistent education standards across the country. States did not have to participate in Common Core, and so far Texas has opted out. The state legislature passed legislation in 2013 that prohibits Texas from adopting Common Core or using Common Core standards in its classrooms.

Proponents of federal education policy point to uneven education levels across states and argue that states should be held accountable for how they spend federal education dollars. Opponents argue that education and curriculum decisions should be made at a local level. From their perspective, federal management of local education results in an overly complicated policy that rarely fits the needs of the local community. When it comes to education, Americans have their doubts about both the federal and their state governments. In response to state demands (including, ironically, those of the state of Texas), the U.S. Congress passed the Every Student Succeeds Act (ESSA) in 2015. This act, signed by President Obama, gave states greater freedom to develop and tailor assessment plans to their own needs. The law makes Common Core an option, not a requirement. In addition, states are given freedom to define what is success and whether a poor performing school should be subject to state takeover.[i]

While we most often hear about the struggle between the federal and state governments, tensions also exist between Texas government and local school districts beyond battles over school finance and standardized tests. Many teachers and school district officials resist the large number of mandates from the state about what is taught and how it is taught. Greg Abbott campaigned for governor partly on a plan that offered "genuine local control by giving school districts operational flexibility over their schools and by empowering families to make meaningful educational choices."[ii]

> To what extent should local governments be in control of education policy?

 **CRITICAL THINKING**

> If national standards can be sidestepped by states through waivers and other exemptions, how much influence does the federal government really have over policy at the state level?

 **CRITICAL THINKING**

i. Greg Korte, "The Every Student Succeeds Act v. No Child Left Behind: What's Changed," *USA Today*, December 10, 2015, https://www.usatoday.com/story/news/politics/2015/12/10/every-student-succeeds-act-vs-no-child-left-behind-whats-changed/77088780/.

ii. Abbott for Governor, "Greg Abbott's Educating Texans Plan: Governance," https://www.gregabbott.com/wp-content/uploads/2014/04/Greg-Abbotts-Educating-Texans-Plan-Governance.pdf.

another school district with better performing schools, or to a private school to help pay tuition and fees. Advocates of vouchers believe that allowing families to choose schools will create healthy competition that will encourage schools to improve their education in order to attract students. Opponents of vouchers worry that such a program would harm public schools by destabilizing their funding and leaving them with only the neediest students. Overall, vouchers are not popular among all Texans, with only 42 percent supporting state money to be used to support private schools in 2017. However, support is much higher among Republicans, at 55 percent, than Democrats at 26 percent.[31]

Some school choice already exists in Texas. A 1995 revision of the Texas Education Code authorized the creation of charter schools. These schools receive public funds but are set up independently of traditional public schools and have been established by entities ranging from private, for-profit firms to state universities. While charter schools are subject to fewer state rules than traditional public schools, they are subject to the same testing and accountability standards. The idea behind providing flexibility to charter schools is to encourage innovation and efficiencies in teaching that might not emerge through the existing school structure. The charter, or documentation, that allows the school to exist is reviewed by the state on a periodic basis to ensure the school offers a better alternative to public schools. Currently, about forty-two states allow charter schools as an alternative to traditional public schools. In 2014, New Orleans created the nation's first all-charter system.[32] While charter schools are supposed to be about allowing students in underperforming public schools access to more options, they are not without controversy. First, they are often operated by groups with little or no experience running a school. Second, some charter schools are located in suburban areas or in school districts that are not classified as needing improvement. Third, some charter schools are disproportionately middle and upper middle class and more white/Anglo than the wider population, leading some to charge that charter schools are another, modern form of school segregation.

What are advantages and disadvantages to school choice programs like charter schools and vouchers?

★ CRITICAL THINKING

School Safety

The tragic shootings in May 2018 at Santa Fe High School south of Houston, in Galveston County, brought to public attention another issue in public education, the safety of our schools. When Lieutenant Governor Dan Patrick weighed in, he advocated rethinking school architecture, not gun control or mental health. Patrick suggested that schools restrict access to facilities through a single entrance monitored by law enforcement or school personnel. Patrick laid blame on school buildings having too many entrances and exits.[33] This statement, echoed by Governor Greg Abbott, ignores the fact that many Texas public schools already follow this practice and that buildings for several decades have been designed for controlled access. Patrick later donated metal detectors for the entrances to Santa Fe High School.

Governor Abbott quickly assembled a plan to address school safety, but he ruled out a special session of the Texas Legislature. Any legislative action had to wait until the 2019 regular session of the legislatures. Abbott's plan called for increased mental health screenings, red flag measures allowing judges to seize temporarily an individual's firearms, and safe firearm storage practices.[34] Lieutenant Governor Dan Patrick impaneled a Senate select committee to investigate school safety and school violence; the committee is to report findings and recommendations to the Senate at the 2019 session of the Texas Legislature. Meanwhile, public opinion initially supported arming teachers and school officials, with 54 percent of Texans supporting such measures. True to Texas' frontier mentality, support was lower for stricter gun laws at 45 percent. Support for background checks was at 93 percent, and 64 percent of Texans favored requirements to keep guns locked up when not in use.[35]

WINNERS AND LOSERS

Every Texan has a stake in the state's public school system. Parents, teachers, students, employers, and the rest of the community count on the public schools to produce quality graduates ready for the workforce and for civic life. However, Texans bring a wide range of expectations to the system, and the state has struggled to meet the demands of its growing and diverse society. Texas has been committed to attracting high-tech firms. However, these firms require the kind of highly trained workforce that can only be produced by a first-rate educational system. Texas schools struggle to meet those expectations as well as the demands that come with receiving federal and state funds. An important question is how effectively the learning encouraged by the state's standardized testing system meets up with the needs of students preparing to enter the workplace or higher education. While Texas created standardized testing to provide the impetus for improvement in public schools, some parents, students, and employers are questioning the validity of the state's testing regime and the federal government's reliance on it for funding decisions.

The winners in Texas public education are clearly the wealthier, high property value areas of the state, which raise significant funds for education while keeping property taxes low. Until the state fund formula issue is resolved, they will remain the primary beneficiaries to the current system, leaving students in inner city, rural, and other low property value areas of the state on the sidelines. In addition, high-stakes testing as a method of school accountability produces winners at least for school districts willing to teach to the test and invest in priming students on strategies of test taking. Schools and districts who invest in teacher retention, professional development, and innovative teaching may also be winners when such investments produce better test scores. While the state government and Texas residents receive some measure of accountability and adequacy of schools, students may be the real losers as innovative learning strategies are stifled and students are encultured with the idea that learning is simply done to justify the existing structure of their schools. The focus on Every Student Succeeds placed greater emphasis on minority achievement, and Texas has enjoyed some success in closing the gap between minority and low-income college readiness. Here, we have winners as well.

Issues of school choice and charter schools produce winners when underperforming schools are converted into charter schools or are required to compete against other public schools and when such efforts work. Texans also receive these options as appeals to our individualistic political culture and disdain for heavy-handed institutionalism. Yet, communities lose their sense of cohesiveness as their "Friday Night Lights" experience may be diminished with the presences of charter schools or loss of enrollment to nearby public schools in other neighborhoods and communities. Local school districts whose funding is tied to performance on standardized tests and other measures of accountability may be losers as well, with intense pressure to perform better. Ultimately, loss of local control occurs as the state mandates plans for improvement or as the TEA forces the closing of schools, dissolving of school districts, or creating charter schools as a remedy. While the Texas Declaration of Independence called for improved schools, how to make that a reality has puzzled Texas politicians since.

How much should local school districts be directed by the state and federal government?

★ CRITICAL THINKING

What changes do you think should be made to the state's education policy and why?

★ CRITICAL THINKING

Higher Education

The challenges facing higher education are as daunting as those facing the state's public schools. Not only is the state seeing its population increase, but a growing share of that population will seek some kind of education beyond a high school diploma. Today, higher education in Texas brings together a wide variety of institutions seeking to serve students beyond K–12. As Table 14.2 shows, in the fall of 2017, the state of Texas enrolled 1.42 million students in its thirty-eight public universities, fifty public community college districts, three state colleges, two independent junior colleges, four state technical colleges, nine public health-related institutions, and one independent health-related institution. In addition, Texas is home to about forty private colleges and universities with another 128,000 students, approximately. While large institutions such as UT and Texas A&M are the most visible parts of higher education in the state, the system includes a variety of other institutions with widely different goals. As the Texas economy continues to diversify, higher education must meet the demands of the global market by providing the state's citizens with the increasingly wide range of skills required to maintain competitiveness.

Texans apparently love their state-supported universities. In 2017 over 91 percent of Texas's higher education students were in state schools, and about 9 percent attended private schools. Nationally, about 73 percent of college students attend a public university.

The relationship between the state's politicians and UT has become a stormy one as the government subjects its universities to more and more scrutiny. Jay Mathews once commented that "K–12 education is watched as carefully as a third grader crossing the street, but higher education's claims go largely unexamined."[36] As we will see, this may have been true at some point, but the state is becoming increasingly engaged in the inner workings of its institutions of higher education. Located in Austin, right under the nose of the Texas government, UT has proved an appealing target for politicians who have sought to reach across town and squash pesky academics. Governor James Ferguson battled with the UT faculty—a battle that helped lead to his impeachment. Later, in the 1940s, the regents of the university fired four economics professors who had supported federal labor laws, eliminated funding for social science research, and banned John Dos Passos's *U.S.A.* trilogy shortly before it won a Pulitzer Prize. The recent effort of some regents to oust University of Texas at Austin (UT Austin) president Bill Powers and the attempt to impeach UT regent Wallace Hall demonstrate that higher education continues to be a political battleground.

If anything, the state's interest in higher education has become more serious as the state's business and political leaders have seen more need for a highly trained workforce and the cost of a college education has increased.

Funding

Permanent University Fund (PUF)
an endowment funded by mineral rights and other revenue generated by 2.1 million acres of land set aside by the state; investment returns support schools in the University of Texas (UT) and Texas A&M systems

Higher education in Texas has been aided by the Permanent University Fund (PUF). The PUF was created by the Constitution of 1876, which added 1 million acres to the 1 million acres previously granted to UT. Initially, the land, spread over nineteen counties in West Texas, generated little money. Most of the value of that land was in grazing leases that netted about $40,000 in 1900. In 1923, the PUF changed dramatically when the Santa Rita well struck oil on university lands, and by 1925 the PUF was growing at

TABLE 14.2 Higher Education Enrollment in Texas, Fall 2017

Type of Institution	Enrollment
Public universities	651,137
Public community and two-year colleges	726,699
Texas state technical colleges	12,717
Public health–related institution	25,031
Total state higher education	**1,415,584**
Private four-year colleges and universities	124,748
Private junior colleges	581
Private health–related institutions	3,047
Total higher education	**1,543,960**

Source: Texas Higher Education Coordinating Board, "Enrollment—Statewide by Institution Type, Fall 2017," accessed July 25, 2018, http://www.thecb.state.tx.us/reports/PDF/10619.PDF?CFID=82284185&CFTOKEN=33743124.

about $2,000 every day. Today, the PUF totals about $19.9 billion and provides support for schools in the UT and Texas A&M systems. The PUF is an endowment, meaning that the principal from this account cannot be spent and that only investment returns can be used. In 2017, these payments increased to about $838 million a year, which is made available to the eighteen universities and colleges in those systems.[37] PUF funds may be used only for construction and renovation projects or for certain academic excellence programs.

Amendments to the Texas Constitution in 1984 and 1993 allowed the legislature to provide appropriations to universities, health-related institutions, and the Texas State Technical College institutions not funded by PUF. This Higher Education Fund (HEF) is similar to the PUF and can be used only to construct and repair campus buildings or to purchase capital equipment or library materials. The HEF was designed to provide the kind of support previously enjoyed only by schools in the UT and Texas A&M systems.

Calculate the percentage of overall higher education enrollment for each type of institution in Texas. What surprises you about the trends in 2017 enrollment?

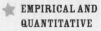 **EMPIRICAL AND QUANTITATIVE**

Directing Policy

Higher education policy in Texas is overseen by the Texas Higher Education Coordinating Board (THECB), which is made up of nine citizens appointed by the governor for six-year terms. The governor also appoints the chair and vice chair. No board member may be employed in education or be engaged in business with the THECB. Thus, while some agencies draw largely on expertise from within related fields, the law forbids such a background in higher education policy for members of the THECB. As with other state boards, these citizens serve without pay but may be reimbursed for travel expenses incurred as part of their duties as board members. The board meets quarterly and is responsible for setting the broad direction of education policy—within the boundaries established by Texas law.

Texas Higher Education Coordinating Board (THECB)
a group of nine people appointed by the governor for six-year terms to oversee higher education policy in Texas

Governor James Ferguson and the University of Texas

James E. "Pa" Ferguson came to office after the 1914 election as a champion of the small farmer. Sometimes called "Farmer Jim" (although he had been practicing law since 1897 and added insurance, real estate, and banking to his interests), he had never held office before he won the support of farmers by promising laws that limited the rent they could be charged. He also managed to win the support of anti-prohibition forces.

Ferguson's battle with the University of Texas (UT) began in 1915 when he confronted the university's president, William Battle, because Ferguson saw no reason that the university's hiring of faculty needed to be any different than his patronage hires for other state positions. Battle refused to fire six faculty members who had angered the governor. Ferguson demanded that Battle be replaced, and, when asked his reason for wanting Battle's removal, Ferguson proclaimed, "I don't have to give any reason. I am Governor of the State of Texas."[i] To make matters worse, the next year the UT Board of Regents failed to consult Ferguson before picking Robert Vinson as the university's new president, and Vinson, like Battle, then also refused to fire faculty members who irritated the governor. Ferguson warned Vinson that unless the faculty members were fired he would face "the biggest bear fight that

has ever taken place in the history of the State of Texas."[ii]

Ferguson warned the legislature when it opened the 1917 session that he opposed higher education when it "bec[a]me either autocratic or aristocratic in its ways or customs." That year Ferguson vetoed virtually the entire appropriations for UT and warned the regents, "If the University cannot be maintained as a democratic university then we ought to have no University."[iii]

Ferguson's battle with the University of Texas cemented a coalition of UT alumni, prohibitionists, and supporters of women's suffrage. Ferguson had treated others the way he treated UT, once explaining his stand on women's suffrage by saying, "If those women want to suffer, I say let 'em suffer."[iv]

The Texas Senate eventually convicted Ferguson of ten charges/articles; five were related to misapplication of public funds, three dealt with his quarrel with the university, one dealt with enforcement of the state's banking laws, and one found that he had received $156,500 in currency from a source that he refused to reveal.

Ferguson resigned from office a day before his removal by the Senate and contended that, because he had resigned, his impeachment and the ban from office that accompanied it were not

valid. Impeachment would have ended the careers of most politicians, but not Ferguson, who claimed that his family motto was "Never say 'die,' say 'damn!'"[v] Despite the ban from elective office that came with impeachment, Ferguson ran and lost in the 1918 Democratic primary for governor, and in 1920 he ran for U.S. president on the ticket of the "American Party" that he created. In 1924, "Pa" Ferguson ran his wife, Miriam A. Ferguson, for governor, and she won a term but failed to win reelection after questions about an exceptionally large number of pardons she issued undermined her campaign. The Fergusons, however, were not done, and Miriam was elected again in 1932. When Ferguson ran Miriam again for office in 1940, however, the Ferguson magic was long gone and the voters turned her away.

---

i.   Randolph B. Campbell, *Gone to Texas: A History of the Lone Star State* (New York: Oxford University Press, 2003), 350–51.

ii. Ibid., 351.

iii. Ibid., 351.

iv. James L. Haley, *Passionate Nation: The Epic History of Texas* (New York: Free Press, 2006), 468.

v.   Norman D. Brown, *Hood, Bonnet, and Little Brown Jug: Texas Politics, 1921–1928* (College Station: Texas A&M University Press, 1984), 97.

One of the most important functions of the board is the selection of a full-time commissioner of higher education to run the agency between the quarterly meetings of the THECB. Raymund A. Paredes, the current commissioner, was initially appointed in 2004, and he has played a visible role in reforms to higher education that are related to costs and accountability.

While statewide policy is set by the coordinating board, each university or university system is overseen by a board of regents. Each institution has nine regents appointed to staggered, six-year terms by the governor with the consent of the Texas Senate. Regents are volunteers who serve without pay, although they may be reimbursed for travel and other expenses. There is some disagreement about exactly what the role of regents should be. Former governor Bill Hobby has suggested that the current system ties regents more closely to politics than higher education. He points out that board members at private schools are called trustees and see themselves as representatives and advocates of the university. In contrast, the "regents" label implies that the boards of state universities rule over the schools as agents of the politician who appointed them.[38] In practice, regents seem to do some of both. Governor Perry's appointees to university boards often carried with them many of the governor's ideas about priorities in higher education. However, university regents have often been champions of their universities and strong advocates of the schools' interests.

In 2007, the legislature added a student regent to each board of regents. The law provides that the student regent is not an official member of the board of regents, but it gives him or her all the same powers and duties as the members of the board of regents of the system, except the student regent is not able to vote on any matter before the board or make or second any motion before the board. The selection of a student regent begins with the student government selecting five applicants from among the student body to recommend to the chancellor. The chancellor then selects two or more applicants as recommendations to the governor, who has the final choice. There has been some debate over whether the student regent should be able to vote on board matters. For some, the idea of giving the student regent a voice amounts to turning over control to a potentially untested and unreliable young person.[39] Representative Patrick Rose, who was one of the original supporters of a student regent and favors giving them a vote, notes, "We've met the same opposition that I think has always defeated this idea—that only middle-aged people and senior citizens ought to be making the decisions for college students."[40] Lost in the argument is the fact that, if allowed, the student vote would only be one vote. If nothing else, student regents bring a unique perspective and an up-to-date understanding of student needs and concerns to board meetings.

Expectations and Realities

Universities are under increasing pressure to meet state goals. One such initiative defines success by graduation rates. However, a four-year graduation rate may be an outdated relic of a time when more students were full-time students. Today's students are less likely to be the full-time, unmarried, and unemployed students straight out of high school that are known as traditional students. Changing demographics, a dynamic job market, and rising tuitions have all altered who attends college and what else they do while there. Further, when a study based on ACT scores indicated that only 38 percent of the class of 2015 was ready for college, it may be unrealistic to believe that universities can turn many of these underprepared students into college graduates in four years.[41] The state's universities find themselves caught between conflicting demands. In 2010, the state's colleges and universities had to return 5 percent of their current budget and then start mapping out 10 percent in budget cuts for the coming years in case the state's budget woes continued. During the 2018–2019 biennium, state support for higher education was set by the legislature at $15.6 billion, an increase of $465.5 million over the 2016–2017 budget cycle. This represented a 3.1 percent increase for 2018–2019 and accounted for 7.2 percent of the overall state budget. The level of higher education's share of state spending remained constant, so the 3.1 percent increase mostly kept spending the same when adjusted for inflation.[42] About 37 percent of the high education budget is allocated to general academic activities, health related institutions account for about 16 percent of the budget, with an additional 14.6 percent allocated to other higher education activities. Community and technical colleges received about 10 percent of the budget, while Texas A&M related agencies like agricultural extension received the remainder of the budget.[43]

Beyond the regular budget allocation for higher education in Texas, the legislature funds activities through a budget item called special item funding. Special items consume about $1 billion in higher education spending, and these funds are spent as special requests by universities for items outside the normal appropriation formulas. During the 2017 legislation session, however, an effort was made to curb special item funding in higher education. The special items budget was originally designed as short-term funding for new programs and initiatives until such activities become self-sustaining. Consistent with that intent, the University of Texas–Rio Grande Valley received $61 million in 2016–2017 to start a new medical school. However, some special items have a long-term and enduring presence in the state budget. For example, the Bureau of Economic Geology at UT Austin has existed since 1909. Other longer-term items include funding for the law enforcement management institute at Sam Houston State and the art museum at Texas A&M–Corpus Christi. Threats to eliminate all special item funding in 2016–2017 led to significant pushback from public universities, including Texas A&M–Texarkana, claiming that without special funding, the university would have to close.[44] Clearly some institutions have become dependent on special funding items as a permanent, not temporary, source of money

Access to Higher Education

With Texas's population rapidly expanding and its economy increasingly global and high tech, it becomes important to look at who has access to higher education in the state. Expanding access to higher education has been an important goal since 2000, when the state's Closing the Gap initiative was announced with the goal of adding 630,000 students to the ranks of higher education by 2015. The state fell just 25,000 short of that goal.[45]

While Texas has seen progress, it has been uneven at times, and the growth in higher education enrollment has leveled off in recent years. Texas, like other states, has a gender gap in education. In the fall of 2017, a significantly higher percentage of Texas's higher education students were women (56.8 percent) than men (43.2 percent). This is consistent with recent nationwide trends. Further, the coordinating board's analysis revealed Hispanic participation lagged behind the state's goals and that enrollment growth of white students fell well below the state's goal.[46] In 2015, Texas launched "60x30TX," a strategic plan with the goal of 60 percent of young Texans (ages 25–34) having some type of postsecondary certificate or degree by 2030. The plan also includes the goals that graduates will have completed programs with "identified marketable skills" and that undergraduate student loan debt will not exceed 60 percent of first-year wages.

Inequality in higher education has been an issue throughout the state's history. In fact, a landmark civil rights case, *Sweatt v. Painter* (1950), dealt with higher education in Texas. In that case, Heman Marion Sweatt was refused admission to the School of Law of UT on the grounds that the Texas Constitution prohibited integrated schools. Initially, the state responded to Sweatt's suit against UT president Theophilus Painter by creating a separate law school only for black students known as the Texas State University for Negroes (today the Thurgood Marshall School of Law at Texas Southern University). Sweatt continued to press his case, insisting that the school for black students was far from equal. Ultimately, the U.S. Supreme Court agreed with Sweatt that the two facilities were not equal (although the court would continue to recognize the doctrine of "separate but equal" until *Brown v. Board of Education* in 1954).

Today, legal cases deal with accusations of reverse discrimination. The Texas appellate courts specifically addressed the issue of minorities in higher education in 1996 in *Hopwood v. Texas*;[47] the courts ruled that race-based admission violated the U.S. Constitution. That standard has been loosened by subsequent U.S. Supreme Court cases, which have ruled that although race can't be the sole deciding factor, it can be used as a factor in university admissions decisions. The use of race in university admissions remains a complicated matter.

Heman Marion Sweatt walks across the campus in 1950 after winning the right to attend the University of Texas (UT) School of Law.

In October 2012, the U.S. Supreme Court heard oral arguments over the UT use of race in admissions. In the case of *Fisher v. the University of Texas*, Abigail Fisher alleged that she had been denied admission because she is white. The university uses race as part of its consideration of applicants who are not automatically admitted under the state's top 10 percent rule. The breadth of concerns behind the issue were revealed by a brief supporting the university that was filed by Tom Izzo, "Tubby" Smith, Johnny Dawkins, and other NCAA Division I basketball coaches, as well as the National Association of Basketball Coaches and the Women's Basketball Coaches Association, all of whom want to ensure that diversity at universities is not isolated within the athletic department or other corners of the campus. The brief stated, "Our student-athletes, and all of the students who attend our institutions, receive the best education when they are able to interact with others within a university community that is broadly diverse across its entire scope."[48] The coaches' brief was one of over fifty such briefs filed. The Obama administration, seventeen U.S. senators, sixty-six U.S. representatives, fifteen state governments, and about 100 colleges, as well as relatives of the late Heman Marion Sweatt, have filed such similar briefs in support of the university.[49] In 2013, the U.S. Supreme Court sent the case back to the federal circuit court with the instructions to review the school's policy with a somewhat higher standard and signaling that a university's use of affirmative action in admissions is constitutional only if it is "narrowly tailored." In

June 2016, the Supreme Court sided with UT and concluded "consideration of race has had a meaningful, if still limited, effect on the diversity" and that "the fact that race consciousness played a role in only a small portion of admissions decisions should be a hallmark of narrow tailoring, not evidence of unconstitutionality."[50]

The battle over college admissions reflects issues of representation on many dimensions. The coalition that stood behind the 10 percent rule included not just representatives of minority and border districts whose populations were the initial focus of the legislation but also legislators from rural districts who also saw it as a means of ensuring that their students had an equal opportunity to be admitted to the universities they chose. However, while this coalition of interests was winning the right for its students to gain admission to the university of their choice, the cost of a university education in the state was climbing, creating another barrier to getting the education needed to find a place in the new Texas economy.

Costs of Higher Education

The cost of higher education has become a major access issue as rising tuition and fees pose a barrier to college for many students. In 2003, the Texas Legislature deregulated tuition at state schools, allowing each campus to raise its tuition as it saw fit. Since then, colleges have responded to declining state funds for schools by turning to their students to make ends meet. Tuition and fees have more than doubled on average in Texas. (See Figure 14.1.) While some state leaders have complained about universities increasing tuition, these universities are controlled by boards of regents appointed by

FIGURE 14.1 Higher Education Average Tuition Cost, Semester of Fall 2003–Fall 2017

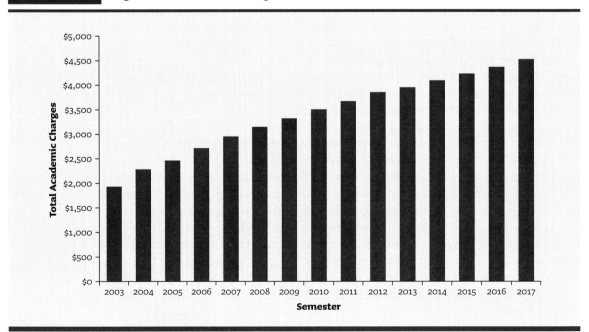

Source: Texas Higher Education Coordinating Board, "Overview: Tuition Deregulation and Tuition Set Asides, July 2018," accessed August 9, 2018, http://www.thecb.state.tx.us/reports/PDF/11328.PDF?CFID=83150185%CFTOKEN=17127910.

the governor and confirmed by the Senate.[51] These increases in tuition and fees do not count the myriad of student service fees, student athletic fees, housing and meal plan fees, and other charges. These costs, often associated with lifestyle choices like luxury residence halls, demands from students for country club-like recreation centers to attract students.

Texas has about fifty community college districts that support about eighty-five campuses. Texas public community colleges are two-year institutions that serve their communities by offering vocational, technical, and academic courses and certifications. Their tuition fees are slightly more complicated than state universities because each community district is supported by a local taxing district that supplements state funding. People living within these districts pay less in tuition and fees because their tax dollars support the college in general.

Former lieutenant governor Bill Hobby has argued that the relationship between the state and its universities has changed. "The perception that state universities are highly subsidized by tax dollars is no longer true," he said. "Such universities used to be called 'state supported.' Today, 'state-assisted' or 'public mission' might be a better term."[52] There has even been some discussion of schools such as UT "going private" by shunning state revenue. This would save some money from the state budget, but the state would also lose control over an important component in education in the state.

The challenges to families trying to put their children through college have been compounded because the state's budget cuts to its schools were accompanied by cuts to many of the state's financial aid programs for college students. For example, the THECB major financial aid programs were cut by 15 percent, and the TEXAS Grant Program was cut by 10 percent. Similarly, the Tuition Equalization Grant program was cut by 20 percent, and the B-On-Time program, which provides zero-interest loans that turn into grants for students who meet certain standards, faced a 29 percent cut. Funding for work-study programs and the Texas Educational Opportunity Grants that serve students in community colleges survived without cuts, but they saw no growth to match the rise in enrollment. Thus, the state's students and schools are facing a host of challenges as more and more students pursue the limited funding available for higher education. At the same time, the state's employers are seeing a growing demand for a workforce that needs higher levels of education. With more students needing more education than ever before, the state faces the daunting task of meeting the growing needs of students and employers with a stagnant or shrinking budget.

Accountability in Higher Education

As is the case with public schools, accountability has become a major issue in higher education. While the state's demand for accountability in higher education lags behind the systems in place in the public schools, assessment of courses and programs has become an increasingly prominent part of what universities and their faculties must do. Support for the general idea of accountability might be high, but defining what that means and how it is measured generates tremendous disagreement. For example, the state has begun to develop a system of success-based funding for schools that would allocate state funds to schools partially based on how many students graduate or meet some other standard of academic success. Even if academic success were easy to define, basing funding on such success is difficult given the different missions of the state's schools. Some institutions, such as UT, are encouraged to focus on educating the state and nation's top students; other schools open their doors to students who are less likely to graduate. There have also been initiatives aimed at making the use of funds, quality of teaching, and value of scholarly research more transparent to the community at large.

Concerns over the state of general education led the THECB to impose an assessment processes in general education core curriculum classes beginning in 2007. Initially, assessment was content based, focusing on what knowledge was mastered in courses including biology, college algebra, and political science. However, a major overhaul of the core curriculum and general education assessment process, prompted by feedback from private business and industry, led to a shift from content-based assessment to a skills-based approach in 2014. Six key skills were identified: communication skills (oral, visual, and written), critical thinking, personal responsibility, social responsibility, quantitative reasoning, and teamwork. Every broad area of the core curriculum was assigned four of these key skills that employers seek in college graduates, and individual institutions or university systems could opt to assess six in every core class. Political science, for example, is assigned communication, critical thinking, personal responsibility, and social responsibility. Each institution or system develops a plan for assessing these skills. The goal is to provide data that show Texas college students are mastering key skills for the future, and that the core curriculum and general education is valuable and essential. Objectors note that this requirement is imparting central control over universities by the THECB and is a step toward a No Child Left Behind–type approach to Texas higher education.

Universities' Other Contributions

While teaching is a primary function of universities, the state looks to universities for other reasons as well. Universities are an important resource for knowledge. As anyone who has watched a 1950s science fiction movie knows, the first place a community turns to when it encounters the unknown is a professor at the local university. Whether the nation needs Indiana Jones to find a lost relic or a small town has to confront giant ants, the knowledge developed at universities should be a helpful resource for the community. In a subtler way, higher education helps the state economy by developing the knowledge behind innovative ideas that can fuel new businesses or industries. In 2015, the Texas Legislature launched the Governor's University Research Initiative, a plan that Governor Abbott created to bring talented faculty to Texas who will encourage "new breakthroughs in the fields of science, technology, engineering, mathematics and medicine, all of which are crucial to the long-term success of the Texas economy."[53] Texas's colleges and universities have always been important players in the state's economic development program. UT has played an important role in making Austin a high-tech center, and Texas A&M hopes to have a similar impact on the state after winning a federal biosecurity contract worth $286 million to develop a center for researching and manufacturing drugs to respond to bioterrorism or pandemics. A&M system chancellor John Sharp called the award "one of the biggest federal grants to come to Texas since NASA was placed here some years ago."[54]

WINNERS AND LOSERS

The value of higher education seems clear, but so do the challenges it faces. Studies continue to show that college graduates earn higher salaries. Perhaps the most compelling evidence for the state's need for higher education is the interest that business leaders in Texas have demonstrated through their support for the state's universities. While the value of education's contribution to the state's future is clear, exactly what must be done to prepare Texans for the future is not.

Texas must continue to invest wisely in education as its students prepare to compete for jobs globally. Thomas Friedman's bestselling book, *The World Is Flat*, describes how American firms and workers need to prepare for competition from global sources. Today, the competition for jobs is arriving electronically. Thanks to the Internet, citizens of faraway countries, such as India and China, are in a position to compete for work as effectively as if they were living next door. These "digital immigrants" provide services for some Texas firms, ranging from technical assistance in call centers to outsourced accounting services. As the rest of the world provides college degrees for more and more of its citizens, higher education institutions in Texas need to help students prepare to compete with these digital immigrants from all over the globe. The state's leaders will need to decide if that learning will occur in person in traditional classrooms or in massive open online courses (MOOCs) delivered on handheld devices.

> Should Texas colleges and universities be held to standards like those used in K–12 schools? Why or why not?
>
>  **CRITICAL THINKING**

HEALTH AND HUMAN SERVICES

Health and human services encompasses programs that help provide food, shelter, and health care to millions of Texans. In fact, Texas spends over $42 billion a year through 68 different health and human services agencies.[55] This fact may directly contradict one of the state's legends: the image of the rich Texan. This image has emerged because the families that run sizable ranches or manage large oil fields make for good storytelling. The real lives of most Texans are much less glamorous than those that were seen on shows such as *Dallas* or the reality program *Big Rich Texas*. Many Texans in the real world live a modest, hardscrabble life. In 2017, the per capita income in Texas was $27,828, well below the national average of $29,829, with 15.6 percent of Texans living in poverty compared to 12.7 percent nationwide.[56]

American federalism has increasingly entwined state government with national policy related to health and human services through federal-state partnerships in programs such as Temporary Assistance for Needy Families (TANF), Supplemental Nutrition Assistance Program (SNAP), Medicare, and Medicaid. Generally, Americans think of such policies as coming from Washington, DC. In fact, the states play an important role in delivering many of the benefits, working in partnership with the federal government. Moreover, each state faces a unique set of challenges. For example, Texas has one of the highest rates of poverty in the nation, ranking twelfth in the country, with only eleven states, mostly in the south, with higher rates of poverty. However, while many Texans live in serious need of health care or other social services, the Texas tradition of individualism means that the state has only grudgingly provided these services on a limited basis.

Social Welfare Programs

Social welfare programs include a wide range of ways in which the government takes a role in providing for the needs of people who cannot or will not provide for themselves. These include programs that help with shelter, food, clothing, jobs, medical aid, or assistance in old age. Sometimes these programs partner charitable organizations with government agencies. Frequently, the state finds itself working—sometimes reluctantly—with the federal government.

Texans are often confused about the nature of social welfare programs and misunderstand the source of funding for most programs. Some are redistributive programs. These programs take resources from wealthier citizens through taxes and give to impoverished citizens. Such programs attempt to provide a minimum level of income support for low-income families. Redistributive programs are often heavily funded by the U.S. government, with states adding funds to increase the pool of available money. Some states with moralistic political cultures, like Wisconsin or Minnesota, have often dedicated significant state funds to supplement federal funds. More individualistic political cultures, like Texas and other southern states, often add little or no additional funding. Temporary Assistance for Needy Families (TANF) and the Supplemental Nutritional Assistance Program (SNAP) are examples of redistributive programs.

On the other hands, entitlement programs like Social Security and Medicare, are funded differently. Funding for these programs comes directly from citizens through taxes taken from their income. These funds go into a trust fund to help fund current recipients. To qualify for Medicare or Social Security, you must pay into the program for a set time period. Once you retire, you receive income based on what you pay into the system, plus a cost-of-living adjustment to account for inflation over time. The term "entitlement" comes from the fact that the taxpayer is receiving back what he or she is entitled to because they paid their own money into the program.

Texas aids some families with children under eighteen through Temporary Assistance for Needy Families (TANF). Under this program, eligible households receive monthly cash payments and Medicaid benefits. TANF provides cash payments through an electronic debit card known as the Lone Star Card. Cash benefit programs are those programs in which individuals receive funds that they spend themselves.

Recipients must accept the terms of a personal responsibility agreement that requires them to stay free from alcohol or drug abuse, seek and maintain employment, ensure that children are attending school, and take part in parenting and other programs if asked. In May 2018, there were 20,173 Texas families that were receiving TANF, including 42,300 children and 6,299 adults, with the average recipient receiving about $75 a month.[57] Families may also qualify for the Supplemental Nutrition Assistance Program (SNAP), which is designed to help low-income seniors and single people, people with disabilities, and families in need buy food from local retailers. (SNAP was formerly known as food stamps.) In Texas the program is overseen by the Texas Health and Human Services Commission (HHSC), and SNAP benefits are distributed using the Lone Star Card, allowing individuals to purchase food directly from retailers. These benefits cannot be used for hot, ready-to-eat foods; cigarettes; alcoholic beverages; cosmetics; or paper goods. In May 2018 about 1.6 million Texas families, including 3.7 million individual Texans, were receiving an average of $264 per family a month in benefits. The majority of recipients were children under eighteen

redistributive programs
programs funded by the U.S. government that transfer income from one group to another; states may add additional funding to these programs

entitlement programs
programs funded by taxpayers who contribute to it for a set amount of time; at retirement, the payer receives back their contributions plus a cost-of-living adjustment

Explain the differences between entitlement programs and redistributive programs.

★ **CRITICAL THINKING**

Temporary Assistance for Needy Families (TANF)
federal program that provides eligible households with monthly cash payments and Medicaid benefits

Supplemental Nutrition Assistance Program (SNAP)
program that helps low-income seniors, people with disabilities, single people, and families in need buy food from local retailers

FIGURE 14.2 Poverty: Texas versus the United States, 1980–2016

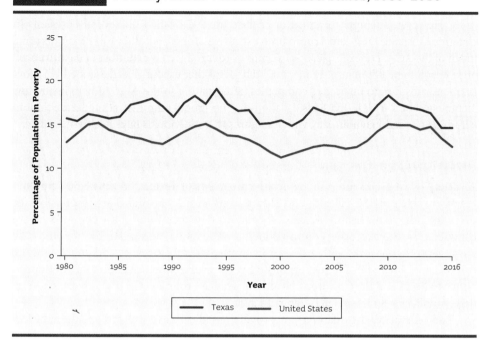

Source: U.S. Census Bureau, Historical Poverty Tables, "Table 21. Number of Poor and Poverty Rate, by State: 1980 to 2015," http://www2.census.gov/programs-surveys/cps/tables/time-series/historical-poverty-people/hstpov21.xls (accessed August 9, 2018).

(2 million) and seniors 65 or older (259,485).[58] While the benefits are available to adults with no children, they must work at least twenty hours a week or meet other work requirements in order to qualify. Adults without dependent children that do not meet work requirements are limited to three months of benefits in a thirty-six-month period. The benefit period can be longer for adults in a job training program working at least twenty hours a week.

Health Care

Health care has become an important issue for the state and the federal government. The state of Texas faces the challenges of rising health care costs as it deals with those who cannot afford health care and as it struggles to pay for the health insurance of its state employees. The state is also concerned with making sure that health care costs are as low as possible in Texas so that employers see the state as an affordable place to set up business. Recently, Texas has become a central battleground in the national health care debate. On one hand, former governor Perry was among the leading opponents of the Patient Protection and Affordable Care Act, or simply the Affordable Care Act (ACA), championed by President Obama, which attempted to extend health care coverage to all Americans. On the other hand, the U.S. Census Bureau found that Texas led the nation in 2016 in uninsured people with 16.6 percent uninsured—two points higher than second-place Alaska, where only 14.0 percent of people lack health insurance, and much higher than the national average of 8.6 percent[59] (see Map 14.1). As the state of Texas continues to resist federal programs related to the health care costs, it must consider what alternatives it can promote.

True to his promises on the campaign trail, President Donald Trump worked with the Republican majorities in both houses of the U.S. Congress to enact changes to the ACA. However, attempts to repeal or replace the ACA failed on several occasions in Congress. Instead, President Trump used executive orders and other tools to undermine much of the ACA. For example, one executive order reduced the number of days to enroll or re-enroll in health insurance in some states. Another executive order ended U.S. government subsidies to insurance companies participating in the ACA to help insure low income and high-risk individuals. In addition, the Trump administration decided not to enforce the individual mandate, which requires that individuals have health insurance.

Federal and State Programs

A variety of programs address the health care needs of Texans, and the 8,500 employees of the Texas HHSC (Health and Human Services Department) are responsible for overseeing the state's health policies. The day-to-day operations of the commission are conducted by the executive commissioner, a professional administrator appointed by the governor who works with an executive council to develop rules and policies for the commission. The HHSC holds responsibility for overseeing the state's contributions to both Medicaid and the Children's Health Insurance Program (CHIP), as well as several other smaller programs related to health care.

The federal Medicaid program provides medical coverage for people with low incomes and some elderly or disabled people. Congress created the Medicaid program in 1965, and Texas began participating in it in September 1967. Federal law requires states to cover certain groups and gives states the flexibility to cover additional groups. States share the cost of Medicaid with the federal government. In March 2018, there were almost 4 million Texans covered by Medicaid, about 3.2 million (79 percent) under twenty years of age, about 137,000 who were pregnant women, 371,000 who were aged, and another 417,000 classified as blind or disabled.[60]

Although part of the ACA encourages states to extend Medicaid coverage to nearly all nonelderly adults with incomes at or below 138 percent of the poverty level (about $39,500 for a family of four in 2016) by offering to pay the cost of this coverage, Texas has declined to participate in this expansion. The state's fear is that while the federal government would initially pay the full cost of expanded coverage, the costs of the program might shift back to the state at some point in the future.

For those families making too much to qualify for Medicaid but not enough to afford private health insurance, the Children's Health Insurance Program (CHIP), a federal-state program, offers the children in these families health care, including regular checkups, immunizations, prescription drugs, hospital visits, and many other health care services. In March 2018 that program covered about 421,000 Texas children beyond the 3.2 million children covered by Medicaid.[61]

Medicare is a federal health insurance program that in July 2018 served about 58.5 million Americans, including 4.1 million Texans.[62] Medicare is available to senior citizens who have worked and paid into the system for ten or more years. Citizens may also qualify for Medicare because of disability. There are actually several components to Medicare. Part A covers inpatient hospital care, while Part B covers doctors' fees and other outpatient costs. In 2003, President George W. Bush signed legislation adding Part D, which extended Medicare coverage to provide prescription drugs.

Based upon the "How Texas Government Works" box on the next page, how does Texas pay for social welfare policy? What does this say about our political culture?

★ SOCIAL RESPONSIBILITY

Medicaid
a federal program providing medical coverage for low-income people and some elderly and disabled people

Children's Health Insurance Program (CHIP)
a federal-state program that offers health insurance and medical care to the children of families that make too much to qualify for Medicaid but not enough to afford private health insurance

Medicare
a federal health insurance program available to senior citizens who have worked and paid into the Medicare system for ten or more years

HOW TEXAS GOVERNMENT WORKS

Who Pays for Human Services

The state and federal governments both provide benefits to Texas residents in need.
Who pays what share of the costs for these programs?

Temporary Assistance for Needy Families

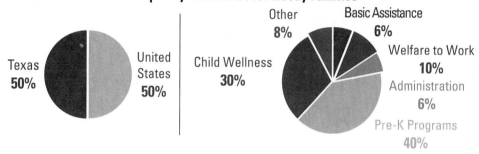

Texas **50%**

United States **50%**

Other **8%**

Basic Assistance **6%**

Child Wellness **30%**

Welfare to Work **10%**

Administration **6%**

Pre-K Programs **40%**

Source: Center on Budget and Policy Priorities, 2017, "Texas and TANF Spending," www.cbpp.org/sites/default/files/atoms/files/tanf-spending-tx.pdf (accessed July 27, 2018)

Note: This is the source for both sets of data on TANF

Medicaid

Texas **42%**

United States **58%**

Source: Kaiser Family Foundation, Federal Medical Assistance Percentage for Medicaid and Multiplier, FY 2017 http://kff.org/medicaid/state-indicator/federal-matching-rate-and-multiplier/

Medicare

Texas **0%**

United States **100%**

Source: Kaiser Family Foundation, Federal Medical Assistance Percentage for Medicaid and Multiplier, FY 2017 http://kff.org/medicaid/state-indicator/federal-matching-rate-and-multiplier/

Children's Health Insurance Program State Children's Health Insurance Program

Texas **7%**

United States **93%**

Source: Legislative Budget Board, "Top 100 Federal Funding Sources in the Texas State Budget, January 2016," http://www.lbb.state.tx.us/Documents/Publications/Primer/3149_Top_100_Federal_Funding_Sources_2017.pdf

Supplemental Nutrition Action Plan*

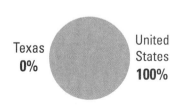

Texas **0%**

United States **100%**

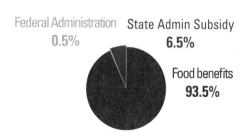

Federal Administration **0.5%**

State Admin Subsidy **6.5%**

Food benefits **93.5%**

* Percentages are approximate and may vary slightly due to rounding.

Source: Center on Budget and Policy Priorities, 2017, "Policy Basics: The Supplemental Nutrition Action Program (SNAP)," www.cbpp.org/research/policy-basics-the-supplemental-nutrition-action-program/

MAP 14.1 The Uninsured in America

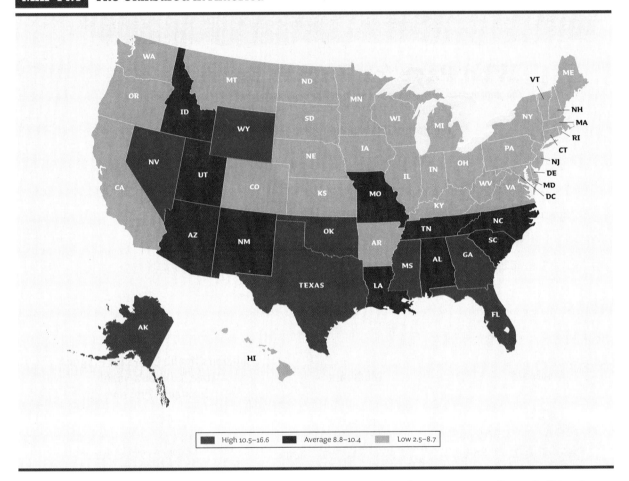

| High 10.5–16.6 | Average 8.8–10.4 | Low 2.5–8.7 |

Source: Data from Dan Witters, "Arkansas, Kentucky Set Pace in Reducing Uninsured Rate," Gallup, February 4, 2016, www.gallup.com/poll/189023/arkansas-kentucky-set-pace-reducing-uninsured-rate.aspx.

The Politics of Health Care

The controversy over the ACA continues to be a highly contentious issue that involves both partisan differences and debates about the power of the federal government. While there are many legitimate differences between the different sides, the political conflict has taken us away from fundamental issues of health care and the burdens that health care costs put on individual Texans, their employers, and the facilities that must often care for the poor and uninsured.

How does the sharing of funds between the national government and state governments to fund social welfare benefit Texas taxpayers?

 CRITICAL THINKING

WINNERS AND LOSERS

While turning down the federal money contained in the ACA might seem like a simple answer in a conservative state such as Texas, the implications of declining the federal funds associated with expanding Medicaid under the ACA are complex. State accounts may come out ahead by not accepting the burdens

TEXAS VS ILLINOIS

The Patient Protection and Affordable Care Act, also known as the Affordable Care Act (ACA) or Obamacare, remains a controversial piece of legislation enacted by the U.S. Congress in 2010 and signed into law by President Barack Obama. It attempts to change the way health care works in the United States through incentives for providers and insurers to control costs and extend access to health care to all Americans. The two goals are interrelated. By increasing the number of people with health insurance, costs theoretically decline because they are spread among all Americans, not just those who have health insurance to start. The mandate that individuals purchase health care insurance is one of the most controversial provisions of the act. College-age students were among the largest groups lacking health insurance and were among those most affected by the mandate.

One of the goals of the ACA is to encourage Americans to obtain health care from private insurance providers like Blue Cross Blue Shield if their employer does not offer health insurance. States were encouraged to set up health care exchanges—online websites on which the uninsured could purchase insurance from private companies. In addition, individuals would be able to select from several companies and many levels of coverage, choosing from various options, and buying only the types of coverage beyond the minimum that the individual wants. To help pay for health insurance, the U.S. government provided subsidies to individuals and families based on income. If a state refused to set up an exchange, individuals can buy coverage through the federal health care exchange. Those who refused to purchase insurance from a state and federal exchange might be covered by Medicare or Medicaid. To help states with possible expansion of these programs, the U.S. government offered them a limited, three-year subsidy.

Texas and Illinois offer interesting contrasts under this federal health care mandate. Illinois quickly worked to set up a state exchange, investing resources to establish the website and working with health insurance companies to develop plans that meet at least the federal and state minimum for coverage, with options for additional coverage. In contrast, Texas instead assumed that the ACA was unconstitutional, joined a lawsuit filed by the state of Florida challenging the ACA in court, and refused to establish a state exchange. When the U.S. Supreme Court ruled in 2012 that the ACA was constitutional, Texas was left without a state exchange. Residents had to rely on the federal government's exchange, and the state remained enmeshed in an ongoing fight against Medicare and Medicaid expansion. Since the enactment of the ACA in 2010, Illinois has seen about 334,107 new Medicare/Medicaid patients, a 30 percent increase. In Texas, an

Per Capita Costs of Medicare/Medicaid Spending, 2010 and 2016

Item	Texas			Illinois[1]		
	2010	2016	Percentage Change	2010	2016	Percentage Change
Total Care	**$10,737**	**$11,214**	**4.4%**	**$9,411**	**$9,894**	**+5.1%**
Inpatient	$2,781	$2,689	−3.3%	$2,978	$2827	−5.1%
Post-Acute Care	$2,930	$2729	−6.7%	$2,005	$1,664	−17.0%
Hospice	$383	$467	+21.9%	$232	$262	+12.9%
Testing and Imaging	$3,377	$3785	+12.1%	$3,162	$3723	+17.7%
Prescription Drugs	$315	$501	+59.0%	$310	$466	+50.3%
Ambulance	$175	$155	−11.4%	$130	$139	+6.9%

Source: U.S. Center for Medicare Studies, "Geographic Variation in Standardized Medicare Spending," accessed July 26, 2018, https://www.cms.gov/Research-Statistics-Data-and-Systems/Statistics-Trends-and-Reports/Medicare-Geographic-Variation/GV_Dashboard.html.

(Continued)

(Continued)

additional 193,854 people have signed up for these programs, a 5 percent increase.[i]

Is the ACA achieving its goal of helping to control the cost of health care? The table on p. 481 shows the spending per person in Texas and Illinois on Medicare/Medicaid for 2010, the year the ACA was signed into law, and 2016, the most recent year available at the time of this writing. The results are mixed. Texas contains and reduces costs better in some categories while Illinois does better in others. Some

areas of spending increased over time in both states, but the rates of increase on items such as ambulance cost vary widely, with significantly lower costs in 2016 for Texas and a slight increase in Illinois.

What responsibility do you have to ensure everyone has access to health care?

 PERSONAL RESPONSIBILITY

Why do you think Illinois does better than Texas in some categories over time?

 CRITICAL THINKING

i. Henry J. Kaiser Family Foundation, "Total Number of Medicaid and CHIP Enrollment," https://www.kff.org/health-reform/state-indicator/total-monthly-medicaid-and-chip-enrollment/?current Timeframe=0&sortModel=%7B%22colId%22:%22Location%22,%22sort%22:%22asc%22%7D.

that come with these funds, but county and private hospitals could come out losers because they will see patients without Medicaid or other insurance showing up in emergency rooms or experiencing stays in the hospital they cannot afford. Thus, county hospitals will see patients that they cannot turn away, but those poor patients will leave county taxpayers to pay their tab.

IMMIGRATION POLICY

Texas has always been an immigrant state. Early Texas attracted immigrants from Spain and France. Mexican Texas attracted Anglos from America as well as continued European immigration. Even as Stephen F. Austin established a legal colony, other Anglos flooded into Texas illegally. For Spain, Mexico, and eventually the United States, governing early Texas depended in part on populating the vast frontier. Beginning in the early 1800s, Texas attracted a significant immigrant population of Germans, along with Poles, Czechs, Swedes, and others. In 1871, the state legislature created the Texas Bureau of Immigration in order to attract immigrants. Although that bureau did not last more than a few years, the waves of immigrants continued. Recent Texas immigrants are more likely to come from Latino or Asian countries. The state's identity has always been entrenched in the immigrant's story—the story of risking everything to come to a strange and rough land and making a life from nothing. Immigration was critical to Spain's inability to control the frontier, it was central to Texans declaring independence from Mexico, and it remains crucial to the state's current economy.

While Texans feel a kinship to the immigrant story, they are less tolerant of undocumented immigrants, especially as the economy contracted in recent years. Increases in unemployment lead to worries that undocumented immigrants are taking jobs. It remains unclear, however, to what extent those jobs would be filled by native Texans. For example, when the national government cracked down on the use of illegal immigrants, the Pilgrim's Pride plants in East Texas had a hard time replacing that workforce. In 2006, chicken mogul Bo Pilgrim, along with thirty other Texas business leaders, including Texas homebuilders, hotel managers, and automobile dealers, signed

Texas unveiled the new Tejano Monument on the grounds of the capitol in Austin in 2012. The monument celebrates the contributions of Mexican and Spanish settlers to Texas.

an op-ed piece that argued that undocumented laborers were critical to their industries. Locals complained that the hours were long and the pay low at the chicken plant. Bo Pilgrim testified that the country depends on the labor of illegal immigrants. After years of having a Help Wanted sign outside and being unable to fill jobs with local workers, Pilgrim's Pride in Nacogdoches eventually hired hundreds of refugees from Burma to debone chicken in its factory there. In 2015, the state legislature passed a law that requires state agencies and public universities to use the national E-Verify. E-Verify is a national database used to verify employment eligibility when hiring. The new law cannot be applied to current employees and charges the Texas Workforce Commission with overseeing its enforcement.

In some ways, the debate over illegal immigrants tells us more about Texas politics than immigration itself. In reality, immigration is a federal issue, and the U.S. Citizenship and Immigration Services is taking the lead in sealing the country's borders and managing the flow of legal immigrants into the country. Despite this, many state and local officials continue to make public proclamations and pass new rules.

Costs and Benefits of Undocumented Workers

Some of this conflict results from differences among Texans over the costs and benefits of immigration. Other debates emerge because the costs and benefits of immigration policy fall unevenly. A 2006 study of the impact of immigration estimated that while undocumented immigrants cost the state of Texas $1.16 billion, they pay $1.58 billion

Immigration

Top States for Immigration into the U.S.

Percent of population that is foreign born

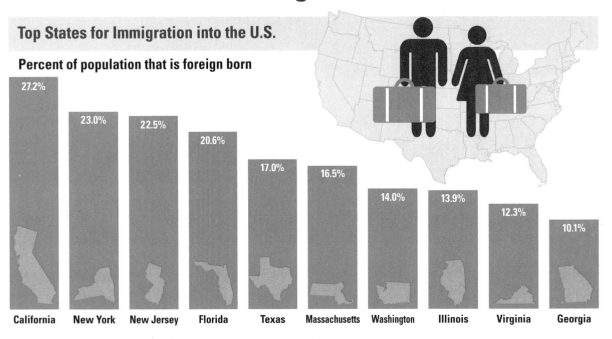

California	New York	New Jersey	Florida	Texas	Massachusetts	Washington	Illinois	Virginia	Georgia
27.2%	23.0%	22.5%	20.6%	17.0%	16.5%	14.0%	13.9%	12.3%	10.1%

Non-Citizen Immigrants

KEY

Region of Origin:

- Latin America
- Asia (including Middle East)
- Europe
- Africa
- North America
- Oceania

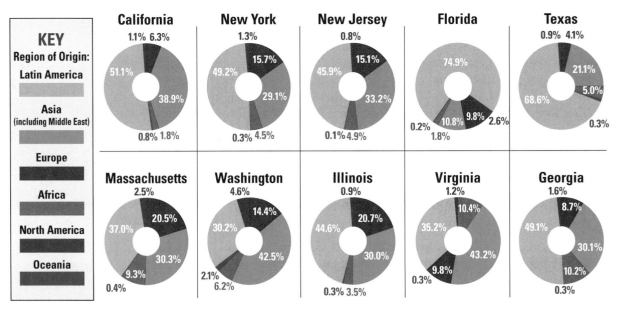

California — 1.1% 6.3% 15.7% 38.9% 1.8% 0.8% 51.1%

New York — 1.3% 15.7% 29.1% 4.5% 0.3% 49.2%

New Jersey — 0.8% 15.1% 33.2% 4.9% 0.1% 45.9%

Florida — 74.9% 9.8% 2.6% 10.8% 1.8% 0.2%

Texas — 0.9% 4.1% 21.1% 5.0% 0.3% 68.6%

Massachusetts — 2.5% 20.5% 30.3% 9.3% 0.4% 37.0%

Washington — 4.6% 14.4% 42.5% 6.2% 2.1% 30.2%

Illinois — 0.9% 20.7% 30.0% 3.5% 0.3% 44.6%

Virginia — 1.2% 10.4% 43.2% 9.8% 0.3% 35.2%

Georgia — 1.6% 8.7% 30.1% 10.2% 0.3% 49.1%

Source: U.S. Census Bureau, "American Community Survey, 2016: One Year Estimates," Table DP02, "Selected Social Characteristics in the United States" https://factfinder.census.gov/faces/tableservices/jsf/pages/productview.xhtml?pid=ACS_16_1YR_DP02&prodType=table (accessed August 10, 2018).

in state taxes and fees. While the state enjoys a net benefit from undocumented immigrants, however, local governments often feel the pinch, paying the lion's share of costs for services such as indigent care, law enforcement, and other services that result from the presence of immigrants while bringing in only a small fraction in taxes.

An increase in government taxing and spending is not the only impact of an estimated 1.4 million undocumented immigrants in Texas. A study by the Migration Policy Institute estimates that the loss of Texas's undocumented workers would cost the state $69.3 billion in economic activity, $30.8 billion in gross state product (GSP), and just over 400,000 jobs.[63] Clearly, many Texas cities and school districts bear a disproportionate burden from undocumented immigrants. At the same time, these workers were drawn to Texas by the promise of wages from businesses that then benefited from their labors. The forces of the free market drew these immigrants into the U.S. economy, if not into citizenship.

The fate of Cactus, Texas, after immigration raids illustrates the degree to which some businesses and local economies rely on immigrant labor. On December 12, 2006, U.S. Immigration and Customs Enforcement (ICE) officers raided the Swift meatpacking plants in Cactus, a small town of 2,639 in the Texas Panhandle, arresting 292 workers. Some of those arrested had lived and worked in Cactus for over fifteen years, and their arrests left behind upset families and large numbers of job openings that Swift scrambled to fill. As these families and the community tried to patch themselves together, the plant, now woefully shorthanded, found itself offering employees who referred good job candidates a bonus of $650 for unskilled candidates and $1,500 for experienced ones.[64] As other industries that rely on immigrant labor have also found, it is often difficult to fill jobs that immigrants do.

While the influx of people into the United States remains a federal issue, border states such as Texas bear the burden of delivering the promises made in the U.S. Constitution. One of the most important legal cases in the dispute over illegal immigration occurred in Tyler, Texas. In the 1982 case *Plyler v. Doe*,[65] the U.S. Supreme Court ruled that School Superintendent Jim Plyler could not charge undocumented immigrants residing in Tyler $1,000 in tuition to attend public schools. In the majority opinion written by Justice William Brennan, himself the son of Irish immigrants, the Court pointed out that the Fourteenth Amendment required that states provide equal protection of the law to "any person within its jurisdiction" and that the language of that amendment had been intentionally designed to protect the rights of aliens living in the United States.[66] Reflecting on the decision twenty-five years later, in 2007, Plyler remarked, "It would have been one of the worst things to happen in education—they'd cost more not being educated."[67]

The realization that Texas benefits from educating its immigrant population was one of the driving forces behind the 2001 Texas Dream Act. That act allows undocumented immigrants to pay in-state tuition rates at Texas state universities if they graduated from a Texas high school, have lived in the state at least three years, and are in the process of seeking legal residence. Texas was the first state to pass a dream act, and another twenty states have since adopted their own versions. According to the Texas Higher Education Coordinating Board (THECB), in 2016 students benefiting from the state's Dream Act constituted 1.8 percent of all students enrolled in Texas in public colleges and universities.[68]

It became clear in the spring of 2014 that Texas and other border states were facing a larger than usual number of immigrants attempting to cross the border. The number of

Which states are most similar in the region of origin of their immigrant population? Why do you think the patterns differ across states?

CRITICAL THINKING

Joe Raedle/Getty Images

The border wall between the United States and Mexico cuts across a hillside. The Trump administration demanded expansion of border walls, including new types of walls that were deemed more secure.

unaccompanied minors arriving had been steady since 2011, with a marked increase beginning in late 2013. These children are typically fleeing violence in Honduras, Guatemala, or El Salvador. Their families, who may pay $6,000 to $10,000 to so-called coyotes to transport the children to the United States, are often told their children will be allowed to stay once in the country. Texas cities scrambled to deal with the large influx of children, which reached record numbers in June 2014. Then-governor Perry ordered a surge on the border, authorizing the Texas Department of Public Safety to spend an additional $1.3 million a week and in July authorizing the deployment of up to 1,000 Texas National Guard troops to stop the flow of children across the border. The 84th legislature authorized $310 million in addition to the border security budget to keep Texas National Guard troops at the border until the Department of Public Safety hired and trained additional workforce. Texas towns pulled together resources to feed, house, and educate the immigrants as they waited to be processed by national immigration. Two years later, the 85th legislature in 2017 authorized another $800 million to continue these border security programs.[69]

As the Trump administration enacted "zero tolerance" for illegal immigration into the United States, the Texas border crossing and communities found themselves in the national news. The decision to continue to divide children from their parents at the border was a policy first enacted during the Obama and Bush administrations.[70] However, the size and scope of such separations were significantly less than the Trump administration policy. Under pressure from civil rights groups, media attention, and public backlash even among Republicans, the Trump administration began moving away from "zero tolerance," but reuniting families proved to be a significant challenge. The Trump administration was then criticized for not acting quickly enough in reuniting families. In addition, Texas was left with a significant number of children, in the tens of thousands, in public or private facilities, awaiting reunification with parents. These children needed access to health care, food, clothing, and other basic necessities, straining local charities and state social services agencies.

In 2013, in response to the influx of immigrants, Texas quit accepting consular identification cards, one of the most common forms of identification, as a valid form of identification for birth certificates. The result was hundreds of children born in Texas to undocumented workers were not issued birth certificates, a violation of the Fourteenth Amendment to the U.S. Constitution, which grants citizenship to anyone born on U.S. soil. When lawyers representing the undocumented families sued the Texas Department of State Health Services, Texas entered mediation with the families. After more than a year of refusing to issue birth certificates, Texas once again began issuing them in 2016. The state still does not accept consular identification cards as a form of ID, but it did expand its list of acceptable identification to include Mexican voter registration cards issued by mail, copies of utility bills, and other documents.[71]

The issue of immigration captures the state's ongoing struggle with change and the two political parties' attempts to balance the new versus the old. The political dynamic behind one side of the immigration debate was illustrated by former Republican congressman Dick Armey, for years one of the state's leading conservatives, who complained that after years of Republicans courting Hispanic voters in Texas, his party was throwing away its future on the immigration issue. As Armey articulated the issue, "Who is the genius that said, 'Now that we've identified that [the Hispanic community] is the fastest growing demographic in America, let's do everything we can to make sure we offend them?' Who is the genius that came up with that bright idea?"[72] The state's Republican Party continues to grapple with how it will reconcile immigration issues in the state. On the one hand, conservative elements within the party, who are more likely to vote in primary contests, favor stricter immigration laws. On the other hand, Hispanics remain the fastest-growing demographic in the state. Hispanics in Texas are also more likely to support the Republican Party than Hispanics in other parts of the country.[73] In the summer of 2018, Texas Attorney General sued the U.S. government in an attempt to end the Deferred Action for Childhood Arrivals (DACA) program. DACA allows undocumented immigrant who came to the United States as children, to remain in the United States by granting them amnesty from deportation.[74] This action plays to a growing anti-immigrant segment within the Republican party. Again, the 85th session of the legislature largely avoided the immigration issue, but it did reauthorize additional spending from prior sessions on border security and social services at the border. How Republicans address immigration in the near future will directly impact their future viability as the dominant party in the state.

As discussed in Chapter 11, several Texas cities and counties passed ordinances instructing their police and sheriff's departments not to comply with federal requests to check immigration status of suspected illegals when the police arrest or interview suspects or witnesses. When Senate Bill 4 was signed into law, Texas effectively required cities and counties to comply. The law went into effect immediately, but several civil rights groups have filed challenges to it. While the case is working its way through U.S. district courts, the U.S. Fifth Circuit Court of Appeals in New Orleans ruled that the law could go into effect while the lower courts are deciding its fate.[75]

Another issue is the impact of U.S. government policies on communities in and around the U.S.-Mexico border in southern Texas. From the zero-tolerance policies that led to the separation of parents from their children while immigration status could be determined,[76] to the use of private immigrant jails,[77] to the reliance on private facilities across Texas to house immigrants or their children,[78] the state government and local governments were often overwhelmed by the scope of the problem. However, because immigration policy is almost exclusively the domain of the U.S. government, the state and local governments had little recourse but to work through the issues as best as possible.

WINNERS AND LOSERS

Texans worry that immigration from Mexico will transform state politics. Yet, Texas has little control over immigration policy as that is the exclusive domain of the U.S. government. However, immigration policy has an impact on much of the state's politics. Issues surrounding immigrants and their status determine in part the activities of the state and local governments. Providing for social services, health care, and education for immigrants may strain local and state budgets. As a state built on immigration, new immigrants add to the diversity and richness of our state's culture and society. Immigration also enhances the size of the Texas economy; new Texans contribute economically to our state and pay taxes to support the public services we all enjoy. Immigrants also provide a source of labor for jobs many often do not want. In these ways, immigration makes Texans winners. This winner status extends to employers who seek workers in areas of the economy where there is difficulty filling positions. Yet, the impact on the state budget in providing services may come at the cost of funding for other needed programs. In that way, Texans may lose.

A broader view of history shows that Texas has always been in transition. Texas saw Native Americans challenged by Spanish settlers, and later Anglos. Mexican independence gave way to an Anglo-led Republic of Texas and then statehood. Less than a generation later, in its aborted attempt to leave the union during the U.S. Civil War, Texas added to its act of secession the issue of border security with Mexico alongside the need to preserve slavery. The end of the Civil War saw Texas's return to the United States but under very different terms imposed by the Radical Republicans, whose Reconstruction government was rooted in the North. Eventually, Reconstruction ended, leaving Texas to find its way through a century that saw tremendous demographic but not political change. During the past 125 years, Texas has seen its population explode as immigrants from all over the United States and the world converged on our state seeking the opportunity promised by Texas.

What are the benefits of Texas's high rate of immigration?

⭐ **CRITICAL THINKING**

CONCLUSION

Texas is experiencing dramatic changes in both its education and health care policies. Texas schools struggle to keep up with educating a growing population and meeting the demands of a rapidly changing economy. With regard to health care, the state has a population that is growing and a health care system that is becoming dramatically more expensive. While both problems seem difficult to solve, neither can be ignored. Texas businesses need an educated and healthy workforce. In addition to the thorny issue of health care for those who cannot currently afford it, businesses in Texas and the rest of the country (as well as the state government itself) are also seeing the costs of insuring their employees skyrocketing. Immigration enriches us with additional diversity and renews our population with new Texans. Yet, issues of who should be allowed into Texas, and how, remain important to our politics.

Texas has never stayed the same, and it remains in the enviable position of being a place where people can find numerous opportunities to better their lives. This promise of opportunity draws people to Texas today and will draw others in the future.

Immigrants from Central and South America are only the latest chapter in the changes that define Texas.

Occasionally, we become so engrossed in recounting our colorful and larger-than-life traditions that we don't notice that dramatic events such as the battle of the Alamo may have been the markers of great change, but that change has always been with us. Texas's myths and legends are often stories of change. Stephen F. Austin became the "Father of Texas" by bringing new settlers to the state before he played a key role in the revolutionary movement that those settlers then brought about. The Battle of the Alamo was a pivotal point in the transition from Mexican to American rule, and it immediately served as a powerful symbol that motivated the Texas army to defeat Santa Anna's army at San Jacinto.

What is especially appealing about many of Texas's legends is the degree to which we Texans all share them. Standing in the line to visit the Alamo, you will encounter people of every race. These people are drawn to the Alamo not because the battle there was between the Anglo and Mexican forces but because the battle defines a dynamic state that draws people of every race and nationality. The defenders of the Alamo took their stand *for* change rather than against it, and future generations of Texans will—each in their own way—do the same.

for CQ Press

Want a better grade?

Get the tools you need to sharpen your study skills. Access practice quizzes, eFlashcards, video, and multimedia at **edge.sagepub.com/collier6e**.

KEY TERMS

Children's Health Insurance Program (CHIP) (p. 478)

Education Reform Act (p. 458)

entitlement programs (p. 476)

Every Student Succeeds Act (ESSA) (p. 456)

Medicaid (p. 478)

Medicare (p. 478)

Permanent University Fund (PUF) (p. 466)

redistributive programs (p. 476)

Supplemental Nutrition Assistance Program (SNAP) (p. 476)

Temporary Assistance for Needy Families (TANF) (p. 476)

Texas Higher Education Coordinating Board (THECB) (p. 467)

- In a small group, discuss how much Texas should do to ensure all its citizens have the opportunity for a quality education. How much responsibility for public schools should be left to local school boards?
  Teamwork

- Take a look at what you pay to your college or university. Then develop a brief PowerPoint or other presentation addressing the following: How much of what you pay directly relates to your academic experience? How much is associated with student activities and affairs? How much is associated with what you would describe as a lifestyle choice?
  Communication

CHAPTER REVIEW

1. The Texas State Board of Education is _____.

   a. appointed by the governor and confirmed by the Texas Senate

   b. selected by the Texas Senate, with one member for each senate district

   c. elected by the voters of Texas from election districts across the state

   d. chosen by the Texas Education Agency

2. The state's system of public school financing was declared unconstitutional in which Supreme Court case?

   a. *Plessy v. Ferguson* (1896)

   b. *Englewood Independent School District et al. v. Kirby* (1989)

   c. *Brown v. Board of Education* (1954; 1955)

   d. *Plyler v. Doe* (1982)

3. The U.S. government's role in K–12 education grew tremendously due to the _____.

   a. No Child Left Behind Act

   b. Education Reform Act

   c. *Englewood Independent School District et al. v. Kirby* (1989) decision

   d. *Brown v. Board of Education* (1954; 1955) decision

4. The _____ case outlawed segregation in Texas higher education institutions.

   a. *Sweatt v. Painter* (1950)

   b. *Brown v. Board of Education* (1954; 1955)

   c. *Englewood Independent School District et al. v. Kirby* (1989)

   d. *Fisher v. University of Texas* (2013)

5. A government program in which resources are taken from one group and given to another is called _____.

   a. a distributive policy

   b. a redistributive policy

   c. an entitlement

   d. regulatory

6. A government program in which people pay into the program now and receive their contributions back in the future is called _____.

   a. a distributive policy

   b. a redistributive policy

   c. an entitlement

   d. regulatory

7. Which of the following is *not* a redistributive program?

   a. TANF

   b. SNAP

   c. Medicare

   d. Medicaid

8. Which of the following is an entitlement program?

   a. TANF

   b. SNAP

   c. Social Security

   d. Medicaid

9. The _____ case prohibited Texas public school districts from charging tuition to undocumented immigrants.

   a. *Sweatt v. Painter* (1950)

   b. *Brown v. Board of Education* (1954; 1955)

   c. *Plyler v. Doe* (1982)

   d. *Englewood Independent School District et al. v. Kirby* (1989)

10. Undocumented immigrants who graduate from a Texas high school receive in-state tuition rates for Texas public universities and colleges based on _____.

    a. the *Plyler v. Doe* (1982) case

    b. the Texas Dream Act

    c. Deferred Action for Childhood Arrivals

    d. Immigration and Customs Enforcement

APPENDIX

Declaration of Independence of the Republic of Texas

Unanimous Declaration of Independence, by the Delegates of the People of Texas, in General Convention, at the Town of Washington, on the Second Day of March, 1836

When a government has ceased to protect the lives, liberty and property of the people from whom its legitimate powers are derived, and for the advancement of whose happiness it was instituted; and so far from being a guarantee for the enjoyment of those inestimable and inalienable rights, becomes an instrument in the hands of evil rulers for their oppression; when the Federal Republican Constitution of their country, which they have sworn to support, no longer has a substantial existence, and the whole nature of their government has been forcibly changed without their consent, from a restricted federative republic, composed of sovereign states, to a consolidated central military despotism, in which every interest is disregarded but that of the army and the priesthood—both the eternal enemies of civil liberty, and the ever-ready minions of power, and the usual instruments of tyrants; When long after the spirit of the Constitution has departed, moderation is at length, so far lost, by those in power that even the semblance of freedom is removed, and the forms, themselves, of the constitution discontinued; and so far from their petitions and remonstrances being regarded, the agents who bear them are thrown into dungeons; and mercenary armies sent forth to force a new government upon them at the point of the bayonet. When in consequence of such acts of malfeasance and abdication, on the part of the government, anarchy prevails, and civil society is dissolved into its original elements: In such a crisis, the first law of nature, the right of self-preservation—the inherent and inalienable right of the people to appeal to first principles and take their political affairs into their own hands in extreme cases—enjoins it as a right towards themselves and a sacred obligation to their posterity, to abolish such government and create another in its stead, calculated to rescue them from impending dangers, and to secure their future welfare and happiness. Nations, as well as individuals, are amenable for their acts to the public opinion of mankind. A statement of a part of our grievances is, therefore, submitted to an impartial world, in justification of the hazardous but unavoidable step now taken of severing our political connection with the Mexican people, and assuming an independent attitude among the nations of the earth.

The Mexican government, by its colonization laws, invited and induced the Anglo-American population of Texas to colonize its wilderness under the pledged faith of a written constitution, that they should continue to enjoy that constitutional liberty and republican government to which they had been habituated in the land of their birth, the United States of America. In this expectation they have been cruelly disappointed, inasmuch as the Mexican nation has acquiesced in the late changes made in the government by General Antonio Lopez de Santa Anna, who, having overturned the constitution of his country, now offers us the cruel alternative either to abandon our homes, acquired by so many privations, or submit to the most intolerable of all tyranny, the combined despotism of the sword and the priesthood.

It has sacrificed our welfare to the state of Coahuila, by which our interests have been continually depressed, through a jealous and partial course of legislation carried on at a far distant seat of government, by a hostile majority, in an unknown tongue; and this too, notwithstanding we have petitioned in the humblest terms, for the establishment of a separate state government, and have, in accordance with the provisions of the national constitution, presented the general Congress, a republican constitution which was without just cause contemptuously rejected.

It incarcerated in a dungeon, for a long time, one of our citizens, for no other cause but a zealous endeavor to procure the acceptance of our constitution and the establishment of a state government.

It has failed and refused to secure on a firm basis, the right of trial by jury; that palladium of civil liberty, and only safe guarantee for the life, liberty, and property of the citizen.

It has failed to establish any public system of education, although possessed of almost boundless resources (the public domain) and, although, it is an axiom, in political science, that unless a people are educated and enlightened it is idle to expect the continuance of civil liberty, or the capacity for self-government.

It has suffered the military commandants stationed among us to exercise arbitrary acts of oppression and tyranny; thus trampling upon the most sacred rights of the citizen and rendering the military superior to the civil power.

It has dissolved by force of arms, the state Congress of Coahuila and Texas, and obliged our representatives to fly for their lives from the seat of government; thus depriving us of the fundamental political right of representation.

It has demanded the surrender of a number of our citizens, and ordered military detachments to seize and carry them into the Interior for trial; in contempt of the civil authorities, and in defiance of the laws and constitution.

It has made piratical attacks upon our commerce; by commissioning foreign desperadoes, and authorizing them to seize our vessels, and convey the property of our citizens to far distant ports of confiscation.

It denies us the right of worshipping the Almighty according to the dictates of our own consciences, by the support of a national religion calculated to promote the temporal interests of its human functionaries rather than the glory of the true and living God.

It has demanded us to deliver up our arms; which are essential to our defense, the rightful property of freemen, and formidable only to tyrannical governments.

It has invaded our country, both by sea and by land, with intent to lay waste our territory and drive us from our homes; and has now a large mercenary army advancing to carry on against us a war of extermination.

It has, through its emissaries, incited the merciless savage, with the tomahawk and scalping knife, to massacre the inhabitants of our defenseless frontiers.

It hath been, during the whole time of our connection with it, the contemptible sport and victim of successive military revolutions and hath continually exhibited every characteristic of a weak, corrupt and tyrannical government.

These, and other grievances, were patiently borne by the people of Texas until they reached that point at which forbearance ceases to be a virtue. We then took up arms in defense of the national constitution. We appealed to our Mexican brethren for assistance. Our appeal has been made in vain. Though months have elapsed, no sympathetic response has yet been heard from the Interior. We are, therefore, forced to the melancholy conclusion that the Mexican people have acquiesced in the destruction of their liberty, and the substitution therefor of a military government—that they are unfit to be free and incapable of self-government.

The necessity of self-preservation, therefore, now decrees our eternal political separation.

We, therefore, the delegates, with plenary powers, of the people of Texas, in solemn convention assembled, appealing to a candid world for the necessities of our condition, do hereby resolve and DECLARE that our political connection with the Mexican nation has forever ended; and that the people of Texas do now constitute a FREE, SOVEREIGN and INDEPENDENT REPUBLIC, and are fully invested with all the rights and attributes which properly belong to the independent nations; and, conscious of the rectitude of our intentions, we fearlessly and confidently commit the issue to the decision of the Supreme Arbiter of the destinies of nations.

RICHARD ELLIS, president of the convention and Delegate from Red River.

Charles B. Stewart	M. B. Menard	Sam P. Carson	Sam Houston
Thos Barnett	A. B. Hardin	A. Briscoe	David Thomas
John S. D. Byrom	J. W. Bunton	J. B. Woods	Edwd Conrad
Franco Ruiz	Thos J. Gasley	Jas Collinsworth	Martin Parmer
J. Antonio Navarro	R. M. Coleman	Edwin Waller	Edwin O. LeGrand
Jesse B. Badgett	Sterling C.	Asa Brigham	Stephen W. Blount
Wm D. Lacey	Robertson	Geo. C. Childress	Jas Gaines
William Menefee	Benj. Briggs	Bailey Hardeman	Wm Clark, Jr.
Jno Fisher	Goodrich	Rob. Potter	Sydney O. Penington
Mathew Caldwell	G. W. Barnett	Thomas Jefferson	Wm Carrol
William Mottley	James G. Swisher	Rusk	Crawford
Lorenzo de Zavala	Jesse Grimes	Chas. S. Taylor	Jno Turner
Stephen H. Everitt	S. Rhoads Fisher	John S. Roberts	Test. H. S. Kimble,
Geo W. Smyth	John W. Moore	Robert Hamilton	Secretary
Elijah Stapp	John W. Bower	Collin McKinney	
Claiborne West	Saml A. Maverick	Albert H. Latimer	
Wm B. Scates	from Bejar	James Power	

NOTES

CHAPTER 1

1. Clint Skinner, *Six Flags Over Texas: Fifty Years of Entertainment* (Clint Skinner, 2011), 43.
2. V. O. Key, *Southern Politics in State and Nation* (Knoxville: University of Tennessee Press, 1984), 267.
3. Ben Barnes with Lisa Dickey, *Barn Burning Barn Building: Tales of a Political Life, from LBJ to George W. Bush and Beyond* (Albany, TX: Bright Sky Press, 2006), 168.
4. John Steinbeck, *Travels with Charley: In Search of America* (New York: Bantam Books, 1961), 231.
5. Randolph B. Campbell, *Gone to Texas* (New York: Oxford University Press, 2004), 15.
6. James L. Haley, *Passionate Nation: The Epic History of Texas* (New York: Free Press, 2006), 6.
7. Campbell, *Gone to Texas*, 41.
8. Ibid., 85.
9. Ibid., 88.
10. Ibid., 80.
11. Ibid., 186.
12. Haley, *Passionate Nation*, 272.
13. Campbell, *Gone to Texas*, 207.
14. Ibid., 299.
15. Ibid., 350–51.
16. Ibid., 366.
17. Christine Barbour and Gerald C. Wright, *Keeping the Republic*, 4th brief ed. (Washington, DC: CQ Press, 2011), 23.
18. Daniel J. Elazar, *American Federalism: A View from the State* (New York: Thomas Y. Crowell, 1966), 86.
19. Ibid.
20. Colin Woodard, *American Nations: A History of the Eleven Rival Regional Cultures of North America* (New York: Viking, 2011).
21. "In Texas, 31% Say State Has Right to Secede from U.S., but 75% Opt to Stay," Rasmussen Reports, April 17, 2009, www.rasmussenreports.com/public_content/politics/general_state_surveys/texas/in_texas_31_say_state_has_right_to_secede_from_u_s_but_75_opt_to_stay.
22. Randolph B. Campbell, "History and Collective Memory in Texas: The Entangled Stories of the Lone Star State," in *Lone Star Pasts: Memory and History in Texas*, ed. Greg Cantrell and Elizabeth Hayes Turner (College Station: Texas A&M University Press, 2007), 278–79.
23. Campbell, *Gone to Texas*, 15.
24. T. R. Fehrenbach, *Lone Star: A History of Texas and the Texans* (Cambridge, MA: Da Capo Press, 2000), 24.
25. Lloyd Potter, *How the Population of Texas Is Dynamically Changing*, Leadership Women, March 4, 2018, http://demographics.texas.gov/Resources/Presentations/OSD/2018/2018_03_04_LeadershipWomen.pdf.
26. Lloyd B. Potter and Nazrul Hoque, "Texas Population Projections, 2010 to 2050," Office of the Texas State Demographer, November 2014, http://demographics.texas.gov/Resources/Publications/2014/2014-11_ProjectionBrief.pdf.
27. Steve White, Lloyd B. Potter, Helen You, Lila Valencia, Jeffrey A. Jordan, and Beverly Pecotte, "Introduction to Texas Domestic Migration," Office of the State Demographer, April 2016, 3, http://demographics.texas.gov/Resources/Publications/2016/2016_04-13_DomesticMigration.pdf.
28. U.S. Census Bureau, "Quick Facts: Texas," accessed June 21, 2018, https://www.census.gov/quickfacts/TX.

29. Lloyd Potter, "How the Population of Texas Is Dynamically Changing," Leadership Women, March 4, 2018, http://demographics.texas.gov/Resources/Presentations/OSD/2018/2018_03_04_LeadershipWomen.pdf.

30. "Fox News Exit Polls," FoxNews.com, accessed March 12, 2018, http://www.foxnews.com/politics/elections/2016/exit-polls.

31. Paul Taylor, Wendy Wang, Kim Parker, Jeffrey S. Passel, Eileen Patten, and Seth Motel, "The Rise of Intermarriage Rates, Characteristics Vary by Race and Gender, Pew Social & Demographic Trends," February 16, 2012, http://www.pewsocialtrends.org/files/2012/02/SDT-Intermarriage-II.pdf.

32. Potter, "How the Population of Texas Is Dynamically Changing."

33. U.S. Census Bureau, Population Division, "Annual Estimates of the Resident Population for Incorporated Places of 50,000 or More, Ranked by July 1, 2017 Population: April 1, 2010 to July 1, 2017, May 2018," accessed August 26, 2018, https://factfinder.census.gov/faces/tableservices/jsf/pages/productview.xhtml?src=bkmk.

34. U.S. Census Bureau, "The South Is Home to 10 of the 15 Fastest-Growing Large Cities," Census Bureau Reports, May 25, 2017, https://www.census.gov/newsroom/press-releases/2017/cb17-81-population-estimates-subcounty.html.

35. Michael Lipka and Benjamin Wormald, "How Religious Is Your State?" Pew Research Center, February 29, 2016, http://www.pewresearch.org/fact-tank/2016/02/29/how-religious-is-your-state/.

36. University of Texas and *Texas Tribune*, "Texas Statewide Survey," June 2014, http://s3.amazonaws.com/static.texastribune.org/media/documents/uttt-jun2014-summary-all.pdf.

37. "The State of Texas Agriculture," *Texas Almanac*, accessed March 13, 2018, http://texasalmanac.com/topics/agriculture/state-texas-agriculture.

38. U.S. Census Bureau, "Quick Facts: Texas," July 1, 2017, https://www.census.gov/quickfacts/TX.

39. Elizabeth McNichol, Douglas Hall, David Cooper, and Vincent Palacios, "Pulling Apart: A State-by-State Analysis of Income Trends," Center on Budget and Policy Priorities, November 15, 2012, https://www.cbpp.org/research/poverty-and-inequality/pulling-apart-a-state-by-state-analysis-of-income-trends.

40. James E. Crisp, *Sleuthing the Alamo: Davy Crockett's Last Stand and Other Mysteries of the Texas Revolution* (New York: Oxford University Press, 2004), 59.

41. Anna J. Hardwicke Pennybacker, *A New History of Texas for Schools* (Palestine, TX: P. V. Pennybacker, 1888), 49.

42. Eric S. Blake and David A. Belinsky, "Tropical Cyclone Report: Hurricane Harvey," National Hurricane Center, January 23, 2018, https://www.documentcloud.org/documents/4359965-AL092017-Harvey.html#document/p3.

43. Amy B Wang, "Flooding Trapped Workers at a Mexican Bakery for Two Days. They Spent It Baking for Harvey Victims," *Washington Post*, August 31, 2017, https://www.washingtonpost.com/news/inspired-life/wp/2017/08/31/flooding-trapped-these-mexican-bakers-for-two-days-they-spent-it-baking-for-harvey-victims/.

44. Justin J. Watt Foundation, "Hurricane Harvey Relief Effort," accessed June 30, 2018, http://jjwfoundation.org/the-foundation/harvey/.

45. Brandon Forby, "How Much Damage Did Harvey Do to Texas Homes? There May Never Be an Exact Answer," *Texas Tribune*, November 22, 2017, https://www.texastribune.org/2017/11/22/texas-may-never-know-extent-damage-harvey-did-peoples-homes/.

CHAPTER 2

1. Rick Perry, *Fed Up* (New York: Little, Brown, 2010), 23–33.

2. Edgar Walters, "Straus Condemns 'Bathroom Bill,' Talks Local Control," *Texas Tribune*, March 24, 2017, https://www.texastribune.org/2017/03/24/straus-fiercely-condemns-bathroom-bill-talks-local-control/.

3. R. G. Ratcliffe, "Abbott's War on Local Government," *Texas Monthly*, June 16, 2017, https://www.texasmonthly.com/burka-blog/abbotts-war-local-government/.

4. David Schmudde, "Constitutional Limitations on State Taxation of Nonresident Citizens," *Law Review of Michigan State*

University–Detroit College of Law (Spring 1999): 95–169.

5. Ibid., 125.

6. Henry Kaiser Foundation. "Federal and State Share of Medicaid Spending, FY 2016," accessed April 16, 2018, https://www.kff.org/medicaid/state-indicator/federalstate-share-of-spending/?currentTimeframe=0&sortModel=%7B%22colId%22:%22Location%22,%22sort%22:%22asc%22%7D.

7. South Dakota v. Dole, 483 U.S. 203 (1987).

8. Thomas Dye, American Federalism: Competition among Governments (Lexington, MA: Lexington Books, 1989).

9. Rick Perry, press release, March 21, 2010, http://governor.state.tx.us/news/press-release/14396.

10. Newt Gingrich and Rick Perry, "Let the States Lead the Way," Washington Post, November 6, 2009, http://www.washingtonpost.com/wp-dyn/content/article/2009/11/05/AR2009110504328.html?noredirect=on.

11. "Attorney General Abbott: Texas and Other States Will Challenge Federal Health Care Legislation," Attorney General of Texas, March 21, 2010, www.oag.state.tx.us/oagNews/release.php?id=3269.

12. "Statement by Gov. Perry on Supreme Court Ruling Regarding Obamacare," Office of the Governor Rick Perry, June 28, 2012, http://governor.state.tx.us/news/press-release/17385.

13. Ross Ramsey, "UT/TT Poll: Texans Want a Health Care Program That's Not Called Obamacare," Texas Tribune, February 21, 2017, https://www.texastribune.org/2017/02/21/uttt-poll-texans-want-health-care-programs-not-called-obamacare/.

14. Randolph B. Campbell, Gone to Texas (New York: Oxford University Press, 2004).

15. Ibid.

16. Ibid.

17. Ibid.

18. Ibid.

19. John Cornyn, "The Roots of the Texas Constitution: Settlement to Statehood," Texas Tech Law Review, 1995, 26.

20. Campbell, Gone to Texas.

21. Texas Constitution (1836), General Provisions, sec. 10.

22. Texas Constitution (1836), General Provisions, sec. 6.

23. Texas Constitution (1876), art. 6, sec. 2.

24. Cornyn, "The Roots of the Texas Constitution."

25. Roy R. Barkley and Mark F. Odintz, eds., The Portable Handbook of Texas (Austin: Texas State Historical Association, 2000).

26. Campbell, Gone to Texas.

27. Cornyn, "The Roots of the Texas Constitution."

28. Texas Constitution (1845), art. 3, sec. 1.

29. Joe Ericson, "An Inquiry into the Sources of the Texas Constitution" (PhD diss., Texas Tech University, 1957). See also Janice C. May, The Texas State Constitution: A Reference Guide (Westport, CT: Greenwood Press, 1996).

30. Texas State Library and Archives Commission, "Declaration of Causes: February 2, 1861: A Declaration of the Causes Which Impel the State of Texas to Secede from the Union," accessed June 10, 2016, https://www.tsl.texas.gov/ref/abouttx/secession/2feb1861.html.

31. Campbell, Gone to Texas.

32. Texas Constitution (1866), art. 8, sec. 1.

33. Ericson, "An Inquiry into the Sources of the Texas Constitution."

34. May, The Texas State Constitution.

35. Ibid.

36. Texas Constitution (1876), art. 1, sec. 1.

37. Originally a state treasurer was also included in the plural executive, but this office was eventually dissolved.

38. Oklahoma is the only other state to have two high courts.

39. James M. Smallwood and Barry A. Crouch, "Texas Freedwomen During Reconstruction, 1865–1874," in Black Women in Texas History, ed. Bruce A. Glasrud and Merline Petrie (College Station: Texas A&M University Press, 2008).

40. David Montejano, Anglos and Mexicans in the Making of Texas 1836–1986 (Austin: University of Texas Press, 1987).

41. Dick Smith, "Texas and the Poll Tax," Southwestern Social Science Quarterly 45, no. 2: 167–73.

42. V. O. Key Jr., Southern Politics (New York: Random House, 1949).

43. Robert Calvert, Arnoldo De León, and Gregg Cantrell, The History of Texas (Wheeling, IL: Harlan Davidson Press, 2002).

44. Texas Constitution (1876), art. 7, sec. 1.

45. Texas Constitution (1876), art. 7, sec. 7.

46. Caitlin Perrone and Bryce Bencivengo, "Texas Leaders, Educators, and Courts Grapple with Segregated Public Schools," Dallas Morning News, May 3, 2013, https://www.dallasnews.com/news/education/2013/05/03/texas-leaders-educators-and-courts-grapple-with-segregated-public-schools.

47. Alexa Ura, Edgar Walters, and Jolie McCullough, "Comparing

Nondiscrimination Protections in Texas Cities," *Texas Tribune*, June 9, 2016, https://www.texastribune .org/2016/06/09/comparing-nondiscrimination-ordinances-texas/.

48. Only the constitutions of South Carolina, California, and Alabama have been amended more times.
49. Texas Secretary of State, "Turnout and Voter Registration Figures (1970–Current)," accessed June 3, 2018, www.sos .state.tx.us/elections/historical/70-92.shtml.
50. May, *The Texas State Constitution*.
51. Campbell, *Gone to Texas*, 371.
52. Bill Ratliff, quoted in Juan B. Elizondo Jr., "Time to Rewrite Constitution," *Austin American-Statesman*, October 28, 1999, B6.
53. Bill Stouffer, chair of Common Cause Texas, quoted in Elizondo, "Time to Rewrite Constitution."

CHAPTER 3

1. James Madison, *Federalist No. 51*, in *The Federalist Papers*, ed. Clinton Rossiter (New York: Penguin Putnam, 1999), 288–93.
2. *Baker v. Carr*, 369 U.S. 186 (1962).
3. Audrey S. Wall, ed., *Book of the States*, vol. 44 (Lexington, KY: Council of State Governments, 2012), table 3.2.
4. National Conference of State Legislatures, "Legislative Session Length," accessed June 5, 2018, http://www .ncsl.org/research/about-state-legislatures/legislative-session-length.aspx.
5. Clifton McCleskey, T. C. Sinclair, and Pauline Yelderman, *The Government and Politics of Texas* (Boston: Little, Brown, 1966), 140.

6. National Council of State Legislatures, "Full- and Part-Time Legislatures," accessed June 6, 2018, http://www .ncsl.org/research/about-state-legislatures/full-and-part-time-legislatures.aspx.
7. Ibid.
8. Ibid.
9. Texas Ethics Commission, "Commission Rules," chap. 501, para. 50.1, accessed August 25, 2018, https:// www.ethics.state.tx.us/legal/ch50.html.
10. Senate of Texas, "Facts about the Senate of the 85th Legislature," accessed August 24, 2018, https:// senate.texas.gov/facts.php.
11. Texas Constitution (1876), art. 3, sec. 8.
12. Thomas M. Spencer, *The Legislative Process, Texas Style* (Pasadena, TX: San Jacinto College Press, 1981), 20–21.
13. National Conference of State Legislatures, "The Term Limited States," March 13, 2015, www.ncsl .org/legislatures-elections/legisdata/chart-of-term-limits-states.aspx.
14. Steven Smith, Jason M. Roberts, and Ryan J. Vander Wielen, *The American Congress*, 4th ed. (New York: Cambridge University Press, 2006), 26.
15. Ibid.
16. Quoted in Iain McLean, "Forms of Representation and Systems of Voting," in *Political Theory Today*, ed. David Held (Cambridge, UK: Polity Press, 1991), 173.
17. David M. Farrell, *Electoral Systems: A Comparative Introduction* (New York: Palgrave, 2001), 11.
18. Nancy Baker Jones and Ruthe Winegarten, *Capitol Women: Texas Female Legislators, 1923–1999* (Austin: University of Texas Press, 2000), 32.
19. Center for American Women and Politics,

"Women in State Legislatures 2018, Rutgers Eagleton Institute of Politics," accessed August 24, 2018, http://www .cawp.rutgers.edu/women-state-legislature-2018.
20. Jones and Winegarten, *Capitol Women*, 153.
21. Ibid., 23.
22. *Fortson v. Dorsey*, 379 U.S. 433 (1965).
23. *White v. Register*, 412 U.S. 755 (1973).
24. 369 U.S. 186 (1962).
25. 377 U.S. 533 (1964).
26. Sam Attlesey, "Panel OKs Map Favoring GOP," *Dallas Morning News*, November 29, 2001.
27. 548 U.S. 204.
28. Kate Alexander, "U.S. Supreme Court Blocks Texas Redistricting Maps," *Austin American-Statesman*, December 9, 2011, www .statesman.com/news/news/local/us-supreme-court-blocks-texas-redistricting-maps/nRhs3.
29. Ross Ramsey, "Redistricting Exposes a Split in the Minority Ranks," *Texas Tribune*, March 9, 2012, www.texastribune. org/2012/03/09/redistricting-exposes-split-minority-ranks.
30. Patrick L. Cox and Michael Phillips, *The House Will Come to Order* (Austin: University of Texas Press, 2010), 2.
31. Nancy Martorano, "Distributing Power: Exploring the Relative Powers of Presiding Officers and Committees in the State Legislative Process" (paper presented at the 2004 annual meeting of the American Political Science Association, Chicago, September 2–5), reported in Keith Hamm and Gary Moncrief, "Legislative Politics in the States," in *Politics in the American States: A Comparative*

Analysis, 10th ed., ed. Virginia Gray, Russell Hanson, and Thad Kousser (Washington, DC: CQ Press, 2012).

32. Keith Hamm and Robert Harmel, "Legislative Party Development and the Speaker System: The Case of the Texas House," *Journal of Politics* 55, no. 4 (1993): 1140–51.

33. S. C. Gwynne, "Tom Craddick," *Texas Monthly*, February 2005, http://www.texasmonthly.com/politics/1-tom-craddick.

34. Jeremy Warren, political communications director for Senator Rodney Ellis, telephone interview with the author, July 13, 2012.

35. Hamm and Harmel, "Legislative Party Development."

36. Jessica Farrar, Texas House of Representatives, interview with the author, August 1, 2012.

37. Ibid.

38. Speaker Joe Straus, "Interim Committee Charges Texas House of Representatives 84th Legislature," November 2015, http://www.house.state.tx.us/_media/pdf/interim-charges-84th.pdf.

39. Ross Ramsey, "Analysis: Votes Count, but the Rules Can Count More," *Texas Tribune*, May 2, 2015, https://www.texastribune.org/2015/05/27/analysis-votes-count-so-do-rules.

40. Nancy Baker Jones and Ruthe Winegarten, *Capitol Women: Texas Female Legislators, 1923–1999* (Austin: University of Texas Press, 2000), 154.

41. Aliyya Swaby, "School Finance Legislation Is Pronounced Dead," *Texas Tribune*, May 24, 2017, https://www.texastribune.org/2017/05/24/texas-house-author-school-finance-bill/.

42. Aman Batheja, "House, Senate Negotiators Reach Deal on Budget," *Texas Tribune*, May 21, 2015, https://www.texastribune.org/2015/05/21/house-senate-negotiators-reach-deal-budget.

43. Wall, *Book of the States*, 151, table 3.14.

44. Anthony Champaign et al., *The Austin Boston Connection: Five Decades of House Democratic Leadership, 1937–1989* (College Station: Texas A&M University Press, 2009).

CHAPTER 4

1. Daniel Murph, *Texas Giant: The Life of Price Daniel* (Austin, TX: Eakin Press, 2002).

2. Texas Constitution (1876), art. 4, sec. 4.

3. Texas Constitution (1876), art. 4, sec. 6.

4. Alan Rosenthal, *The Best Job in Politics: Exploring How Governors Succeed as Policy Leaders* (Washington, DC: CQ Press, 2012).

5. University of Texas, Texas Politics Project, "Governors of Texas," accessed August 30, 2014, www.laits.utexas.edu/txp_media/html/exec/governors/24.html.

6. Peter Boyer, "The Right Aims at Texas," *Newsweek*, May 29, 2011, https://www.newsweek.com/right-aims-texas-67783.

7. Kenneth E. Hendrickson, *The Chief Executives of Texas* (College Station: Texas A&M University Press, 1995).

8. Ibid.

9. Jim Yardley, "The 2002 Elections: Races for Governor: In Texas, Republican Who Inherited Top Job Is the Winner Outright," *New York Times*, November 6, 2002, B00006.

10. Jim Yardley, "In First, Texas Hispanic Seeks to Be Governor," *New York Times*, September 5, 2001, A00014.

11. Audrey S. Wall, ed., *The Book of the States*, vol. 49 (Lexington, KY: Council of State Governments, 2017).

12. Ibid.

13. "Report: Nick Saban Is College Football's Highest-Paid Coach," *ESPN*, October 25, 2017, http://www.espn.com/college-football/story/_/id/21154931/alabama-crimson-tide-coach-nick-saban-tops-college-football-coaching-salaries-11-million. See also Leigh Steinberg, "Are College Football Head Coaches Worth Their Massive Salaries?," Forbes, December 26, 2017, https://www.forbes.com/sites/leighsteinberg/2017/12/06/are-college-football-head-coaches-worth-their-massive-salaries/#90fc0935acdc.

14. Jay Root, "Perry 'Retires' to Boost Pay," *Texas Tribune*, December 16, 2011, https://www.texastribune.org/2011/12/16/perry-retires-boost-pension-pay/.

15. Wall, *Book of the States*.

16. Ibid.

17. Jay Root, "Rick Perry's Taxpayer-Funded Security Costs Rise," *Texas Tribune*, December 25, 2011, https://www.texastribune.org/2011/12/25/perry-security-costs-rise/; see also Associated Press, "Gov. Rick Perry's Security Bill for Presidential Run Grows," KHOU, July 6, 2012, https://www.khou.com/article/news/local/texas/perrys-security-bill-for-presidential-run-grows/285-339692167.

18. Frederic A. Ogg, "Impeachment of Governor Ferguson," *American*

Political Science Review
12, no. 1 (February 1918):
111–15.

19. Cortez A. M. Ewing, "The Impeachment of James E. Ferguson," *Political Science Quarterly* 48, no. 2 (June 1933): 184–210.

20. Texas Constitution (1876), art. 4, sec. 10.

21. Letter from Governor Greg Abbott to "Agency Head," June 22, 2018, accessed through *Tulsa Tribune* website: https://static .texastribune.org/media/ files/f7992dccff71636e6334 a1d69d9e4863/Abbott_ letter_to_state_agencies. pdf?_ga=2.220650779 .2050436732.1530886018- 291205256.1521206784.

22. Christian McDonald, "The Rick Perry Legacy: Government Overseers Who Think Like He Does," *Austin American Statesman*, September 22, 2017, https:// www.mystatesman.com/ news/the-rick-perry-legacy- government-overseers-who- think-like-does/mbVM77p7a MTVC2OzWqnpNP/.

23. Texans for Public Justice, "Governor Perry's Patronage," April 2006, http://info.tpj .org/reports/pdf/Perry%20 Patronage2010.pdf.

24. Matt Stiles and Brian Thevenot, "Perry's Appointed Regents Are Big Donors," *Texas Tribune*, August 24, 2010, https://www .texastribune.org/2010/08/24/ perrys-appointed-regents- are-big-donors/.

25. Brittany Pieper, "Another Former Tech Regent Says the Governor Pressured Their Resignation," KCBD News Channel 11, September 12, 2009, www .kcbd.com/Global/story .asp?S=11120348.

26. Alan C. Miller, "Texas Corporate Interests Financed Bulk of Bush Races," *Los Angeles Times*, July 14, 1999.

27. Peggy Fikac and Annie Millerbernd, "Analysis: Abbott Favors Donors, White Men for Appointments," *Houston Chronicle*, January 7, 2018, https://www .houstonchronicle.com/ news/houston-texas/ houston/article/Analysis- Abbott-favors-donors-white- men-for-12480587.php.

28. R. G. Ratcliffe, "Court Limits Perry's Power over Agencies," *Houston Chronicle*, February 21, 2007, https://www.chron .com/news/article/Court- limits-Perry-s-power-over- agencies-1530170.php.

29. Audrey S. Wall, ed., *The Book of the States*, vol. 49 (Lexington, KY: Council of State Governments, 2017).

30. Ibid.

31. Margaret R. Ferguson, "Roles, Functions, and Powers of the Governors," in *The Executive Branch of State Government,* ed. Margaret R. Ferguson (Santa Barbara, CA: ABC-CLIO, 2006).

32. Robert T. Garrett, "Abbott Wins Last-Minute Money for Recruiting Business after Threatening to Veto Texas Budget," *Dallas Morning News*, May 21, 2017, https://www .dallasnews.com/news/texas- legislature/2017/05/20/ texas-budget-negotiators- reach-consensus-austere- spending-plan.

33. Texas Constitution (1876), art. 4, sec. 11.

34. Thad Beyle and Margaret Ferguson, "Governors and the Executive Branch," in *Politics in the American States: A Comparative Analysis*, 9th ed., ed. Virginia Gray and Russell L. Hanson (Washington, DC: CQ Press, 2008).

35. Kavan Peterson, "Governors Lose in Power Struggle over National Guard," *American City and County*,

January 16, 2007, http:// americancityandcounty. com/emergency-response/ governors-lose-power- struggle-over-national-guard.

36. Ibid.

37. Paul Burka, "Guv Story: Rick Perry's Most Important Legacy Is That He Accomplished Something That No Other Governor Was Able to Do: Completely Change How Government Works," *Texas Monthly*, July 2014, www.texasmonthly .com/story/how-rick-perry- completely-changed-texas- government.

38. Ken Collier, Julie Harrelson- Stephens, and Rachel Clink, "Reevaluating the Texas Governor" (paper presented at the Southwestern Political Science Association Annual Meeting, Austin, Texas, April 2017).

39. Paul Burka, quoted in Brian McCall, *The Power of the Texas Governor: Connally to Bush* (Austin: University of Texas Press, 2009).

40. Beyle and Ferguson, "Governors and the Executive Branch," 203–4.

41. Ibid.

42. Ibid.

43. Ibid.

CHAPTER 5

1. Scott Huddleston, "DRT Blasted on Alamo," *San Antonio Express- News* (online edition), November 21, 2012, www .mysanantonio.com/news/ local_news/article/DRT- Blasted-on-Alamo-4055164. php.

2. Greg Toppo, "UNESCO Designates the Alamo 'World Heritage Site,'" *USA Today*, July 6, 2015, https://www.usatoday.com/ story/news/2015/07/05/ alamo-unesco-heritage- site/29741191/.

3. Vianna Davila, "Protestors Gather to Oppose Influence of U.N. at the Alamo," July 11, 2015, http://www.mysanantonio.com/news/local/article/Alamo-protestors-decry-U-N-s-creeping-influence-6379396.php.

4. Eva Hershaw, "Sen. Campbell Wants to Ban Foreign Control of Alamo," *Texas Tribune*, January 20, 2015, www.texastribune.org/2015/01/30/donna-campbell-looks-ban-foreign-ownership-alamo.

5. Alex Samuels, "Hey, Texplainer: Is the United Nations Going to Take over the Alamo? No, It Isn't," *Texas Tribune*, November 2, 2017, https://www.texastribune.org/2017/11/02/hey-texplainer-united-nations-going-take-over-alamo-no-it-isnt/.

6. Claire Allbright, "Land Commissioner George P. Bush's Primary Opponents Are Making Their Last Stand at the Alamo," March 1, 2018, *Texas Tribune*, https://www.texastribune.org/2018/03/01/texas-george-p-bush-land-commissioners-alamo/.

7. Alexa Arriaga, "Texas Lawmakers Battle with Land Office over Transparency in Alamo Restoration," *Texas Tribune*, December 5, 2018, https://www.texastribune.org/2017/12/05/lawmakers-battle-transparency-alamo-plan/.

8. Ross Ramsey, "Analysis: When George P. Bush Says Something Is Fake News, Remember the Alamo," *Texas Tribune*, June 4, 2018, https://www.texastribune.org/2018/06/04/analysis-when-george-p-bush-says-something-fake-news-remember-alamo/.

9. Barry Harrell, "Perry Vetoes Online Sales Bill, but Measure May Not Be Dead Yet," *Austin American-Statesman*, May 31, 2011, www.statesman.com/news/news/state-regional-govt-politics/perry-vetoes-online-sales-tax-bill-but-measure-may/nRbTh.

10. Audrey S. Wall, ed., *The Book of the States,* vol. 47 (Lexington, KY: Council of State Governments, 2017), 180–81, table 4.6.

11. Ibid., 195–200, table 4.11.

12. Morgan Smith and Patrick Svitek, "Texas Legislature Ends Special Session without Passing Property Tax Measure," *Texas Tribune*, August 15, 2017, https://www.texastribune.org/2017/08/15/texas-house-adjourns-sine-die/.

13. Texas Constitution (1876), art. 4, sec. 22.

14. Wall, *Book of the States*, vol. 47, 195–200, table 4.11.

15. Jonathan W. Singer, *Broken Trusts: The Texas Attorney General Versus the Oil Industry, 1889–1909* (College Station: Texas A&M Press, 2002).

16. Texas Attorney General, "About Attorney General Opinions," accessed June 9, 2016, www.oag.state.tx.us/opin.

17. Patrick Svitek and Morgan Smith, "SEC Charges Ken Paxton with Securities Fraud," *Texas Tribune*, April 11, 2016, www.texastribune.org/2016/04/11/sec-charges-paxton-securities-fraud.

18. Ross Ramsey, "Analysis: Is Attorney General Ken Paxton Feeling Lucky?" *Texas Tribune,* February 3, 2016, https://www.texastribune.org/2016/02/03/analysis-attorney-general-ken-paxton-feeling-lucky/.

19. Morgan Smith, "Former Paxton Aide: I Didn't Ask for Departure Deal," *Texas Tribune*, April 26, 2016, https://www.texastribune.org/2016/04/29/former-paxton-aide-i-didnt-ask-departure-deal/.

20. Brian Rosenthal, "Official Move to End De Facto Severance Pay for State Workers," *Houston Chronicle*, July 1, 2016, https://www.houstonchronicle.com/news/politics/texas/article/Officials-move-to-end-de-facto-severance-pay-for-7958044.php.

21. Ross Ramsey, "Legislature Questions Abbott's Budget Vetoes," *Texas Tribune*, July 21, 2016, www.texastribune.org/2015/07/21/abbotts-budget-vetoes-questioned-lbb.

22. Aman Batheja, "Attorney General's Office: Abbott's Budget Vetoes Should Stand," *Texas Tribune*, December 21, 2015, www.texastribune.org/2015/12/21/attorney-generals-office-abbotts-budget-vetoes-sho.

23. Wall, *The Book of the States*, vol. 46, 221–22, tables 4.24 and 4.25.

24. Ibid., vol. 47, 195–200, table 4.11.

25. Ibid., vol. 47, 230–34, tables 4.30, 4.31, and 4.32.

26. HB 7 transferred the Texas Performance Review and the Texas School Performance Review to the Legislative Budget Board.

27. Ryan McCrimmon, "Rainy Day Fund Could Be Invested More Aggressively," *Texas Tribune*, May 12, 2015, www.texastribune.org/2015/05/12/senate-oks-expansion-rainy-day-fund-investments.

28. Jim Malewitz, "Texas Comptroller Glenn Hegar Pitches Rainy Day Fund Overhaul," *Texas Tribune*, April 13, 2017, https://www.texastribune.org/2017/04/13/texas-comptroller-glenn-hegar-pitches-rainy-day-fund-overhaul/.

29. Aman Batheja, "Hegar Lets Abbott Vetoes Stand, Asks AG to Decide," *Texas*

Tribune, August 26, 2015, www.texastribune .org/2015/08/26/hegar-punts-abbott-vetoes-asks-ag-decide.

30. Jim Malewitz, "Hegar: Harvey Response Will Strain Texas Budget, Shouldn't Slow Economy," *Texas Tribune,* October 10, 2017, https://www.texastribune .org/2017/10/10/hegar-harvey-response-will-strain-texas-budget-shouldnt-slow-its-econo/.

31. Wall, *The Book of the States,* vol. 47, 195–200, table 4.11.

32. Texas Department of Agriculture, "What Does the Texas Department of Agriculture Do?," accessed June 7, 2018, www .texasagriculture.gov/About/ WhatdoesTDAdo.apx.

33. Jim Malewitz, "Miller Insists He's Fighting, Not Boosting, Childhood Obesity," *Texas Tribune,* March 10, 2016, www.texastribune .org?2016/03/10/fryers-or-not-ag-commissioner-says-hes-fighting-childhood-obesity.

34. Ibid.

35. Jay Root and Neena Satija, "Ag Commissioner Say Consumers Being 'Screwed,'" *Texas Tribune,* February 27, 2015, www.texastribune .org/2016/02/2015/consumers-getting-screwed-says-new-ag-commissioner.

36. Jay Root and Todd Wiseman, "Audio: Fiscal Hawk Sid Miller on His Need for Cash," *Texas Tribune,* March 18, 2015.

37. Jim Malewitz, "Lawmaker's Grill Miller on Ag Fee Hikes," *Texas Tribune,* December 8, 2016, www .texastribune.org/12/05/2016/ lawmakers-grill-miller-proposed-ag-fee-hike.

38. Jim Malewitz, "Ex Texas Agriculture Commission Worker Alleges Discrimination," *Texas Tribune,* January 29,

2016, www.texastribune .org/2016/01/29/former-texas-employee-sues-sid-miller-over-hiring.

39. Terri Langford, "Sid Miller Says Campaign Finance Probes Going Nowhere," *Texas Tribune,* June 5, 2016, www.texastribune. org/2016/06/05/sid-miller-expects-campaign-finance-probes-be-dismissed.

40. Jim Malewitz, "Texas Agriculture Chief Won't Face Charges for 'Jesus Shot' Trip," September 20, 2015, www.texastribune .org/2016/09/20/texas-agriculture-chief-wont-face-charges-jesus-sh.

41. Alex Samuels, "Attorney General Ken Paxton Sides With Restaurants, Retailers on Enforcement of 'Barbecue Bill,'" *Texas Tribune,* https:// www.texastribune.org/ 2018/04/23/sid-miller-ken-paxton-beef-regulations-texas-barbecue/.

42. General Land Office, "Overview," accessed June 7, 2018, http://www.glo.texas .gov/the-glo/about/ overview/index.html.

43. Texas Education Agency, "Texas Permanent School Fund Annual Report— Fiscal Year Ending August 31, 2017," accessed June 5, 2018, http://tea.texas.gov/ Finance_and_Grants/Texas_ Permanent_School_Fund/ Texas_Permanent_School_ Fund_-_Annual_Report.

44. Ryan Maye Handy, "How Texas Blew to the Top in Wind Power," *Houston Chronicle,* January 27, 2018, https://www.houston chronicle.com/business/ article/How-Texas-blew-to-the-top-in-wind-power-12529917.php.

45. "Texas Awards Rights for Offshore Wind Farm," MSN, October 3, 2007, www.msnbc.msn.com/ id/21113169.

46. Brian M. Rosenthal, "George P. Bush 'Reboot' of Land Office Has Campaign, Family Ties," *Houston Chronicle,* September 18, 2015, https:// www.houstonchronicle. com/news/politics/texas/ article/Bush-reboot-of-land-office-has-campaign-family-6515179.php; Jim Malewitz and Neena Satija, "George P. Bush: Land Office Faces Internal 'Threat,'" *Texas Tribune,* August 14, 2015, www.texastribune .org/2015/08/14/george-p-bush-land-office-faces-internal-threat.

47. Wall, *Book of the States,* vol. 47, 189, table 4.16.

48. Ibid., 195–200, table 4.11.

49. Texas Secretary of State, "History of the Office," accessed June 6, 2018, www .sos.state.tx.us/about/ history.shtml.

50. Texas Secretary of State, "Constitutional Duties," accessed June 6, 2018, www .sos.state.tx.us/about/duties .shtml.

51. Texas Department of Transportation, "TxDOT 2017–2021 Strategic Plan," accessed June 6, 2018, https://www.txdot.gov/ inside-txdot/division/state-affairs/strategic-plan.html.

52. Texas Department of State Health Services, "Commissioner," accessed June 7, 2018, https:// www.dshs.texas.gov/ commissioner/biography. shtm.

53. Jim Malewitz, "Sunset Review Suggests Changes, New Name at Railroad Commission," April 29, 2015, *Texas Tribune,* www .texastribune.org/2016/04/29/ panel-suggests-new-name-better-oversight-texas-rai.

54. Kiah Collier, "Legislature Passes Much-Criticized Bill Reforming Oil and Gas Regulatory Agency," *Texas Tribune,* https://www

.texastribune.org/2017/05/09/
long-last-railroad-
commission-reform-bill-
passes-legislature/.

55. Texas Government Code, title
6, subtitle B, chapter 655.

56. Texas Sunset Advisory
Commission, "Impact of
Sunset Reviews," accessed
June 7, 2018, https://www
.sunset.texas.gov/impact-
sunset-reviews.

CHAPTER 6

1. Morgan Smith, "Chief Justice
Delivers State of the Judiciary,"
Texas Tribune, February 23,
2011, https://www
.texastribune.org/2011/02/23/
chief-justice-delivers-state-of-
the-judiciary/.

2. Wallace B. Jefferson, "The
State of the Judiciary in
Texas," February 11, 2009,
Texas Judicial Branch
website, https://www
.sll.texas.gov/assets/pdf/
judiciary/state-of-the-
judiciary-2009.pdf.

3. Wallace B. Jefferson, "Make
Merit Matter by Adopting
New System of Selecting
Judges," *Houston Chronicle*,
March 21, 2009, https://
www.chron.com/opinion/
outlook/article/Wallace-
B-Jefferson-Make-merit-
matter-by-1544078.php.

4. Smith, "Chief Justice
Delivers State of the
Judiciary."

5. Nathan L. Hecht, "The State
of the Judiciary in Texas,"
February 1, 2017, Texas
Judicial Branch website,
http://www.txcourts.gov/
media/1437289/soj-2017.pdf.

6. Texas Constitution (1876),
art. 5, sec. 1.

7. Office of Court
Administration, "Annual
Statistical Report for the Texas
Judiciary, Fiscal Year 2017,"
accessed July 2, 2018, http://
www.txcourts.gov/media/
1441398/ar-fy-17-final.pdf.

8. Compiled from data from
the Texas Judicial Branch
website: www.txcourts.gov
(accessed June 5, 2018).

9. "Profile of Appellate and Trial
Court Judges" (as of May
2018), Texas Judicial Branch
website, accessed June 5,
2018, http://www.txcourts
.gov/statistics/information-
on-texas-judges/.

10. Texas Constitution (1876),
art. 4, sec. 19.

11. Office of Court
Administration, "Annual
Statistical Report for the Texas
Judiciary, Fiscal Year 2017."

12. Ibid.

13. Texas Constitution (1876),
art. 5, sec. 15.

14. Office of Court
Administration, "*Annual
Statistical Report for the Texas
Judiciary*, Fiscal Year 2017."

15. Ibid.

16. Texas Constitution (1876),
art. 5, sec. 8.

17. Audrey S. Wall, ed., *The
Book of the States*, vol. 49
(Lexington, KY: Council of
State Governments, 2017).

18. Tom Abrahams, "What's the
Deal with the Long Ballot?,"
ABC News, October 21,
2010, http://abc13.com/
archive/7736817.

19. Ibid.

20. Al Ortiz, "A Very High
Turnout and A Long Ballot
Were Factors for the Long
Lines on Super Tuesday,"
Houston Public Media,
March 2, 2016, https://www
.houstonpublicmedia.org/
articles/news/2016/03
/02/139941/a-very-high-
turnout-and-a-long-ballot-
were-factors-for-the-long-
lines-on-super-tuesday/.

21. "Editorial: Shot in the Dark:
Electing Judges Yet Again
Allows Name Recognition to
Trump Experience," *Houston
Chronicle,* March 4, 2016,
http://www.houstonchronicle
.com/opinion/editorials/
article/Shot-in-the-
dark-6871385.php.

22. Anna Whitney, "Consumer
Group: Supreme Court
Favors Business," *Texas
Tribune*, January 26, 2012,
https://www.texastribune
.org/2012/01/26/texas-
watch-claims-supreme-
court-favors-businesses/.

23. Honorable Thomas Phillips,
quoted in "The Texas
Judiciary: Is Justice for
Sale?" (League of Women
Voters panel discussion,
Tyler, Texas, broadcast
as part of a PBS *Frontline*
special, September 25,
2007).

24. "Judicial Salaries &
Turnover: Fiscal Years 2014
& 2015," Texas Judicial
Branch website, accessed
June 9, 2018, http://www
.txcourts.gov/statistics/
judicial-salaries-turnover/.

25. Ibid.

26. Texas Constitution (1876),
art. 5, sec. 1A.

27. State Commission on
Judicial Conduct, "Annual
Report for Fiscal Year
2015," accessed July 5, 2016,
http://www.scjc.texas.gov/
media/34163/ar-fy15.pdf.

28. Eric Dexheimer, "Texas
Judges' Misdeeds Often
Kept Secret by Oversight
Commission," *Austin
American-Statesman*, April
14, 2012, www.statesman
.com/news/statesman-
investigates/texas-judges-
misdeeds-often-kept-secret-
by-oversight-2305404.html.

29. Alexa Ura, "Trial Begins
in Case Targeting Texas'
Statewide Elections of
Judges," *Texas Tribune*,
February 12, 2018, https://
www.texastribune
.org/2018/02/12/lawsuit-
puts-texas-statewide-
elections-judges-trial.

30. Texas Research League, "The
Texas Judiciary: A Proposal
for Structural-Functional
Reform," in *Texas Courts:
Report 2* (Austin: Texas
Research League, 1991), 25.

31. Citizens' Commission on the Texas Judicial System, "Report and Recommendations," 1993, www.courts.state.tx.us/tjc/publications/cc_tjs.pdf.

32. Morgan Smith, "Odor in the Court," *Texas Tribune*, February 2010, https://www.texastribune.org/2010/02/02/lawyers-biggest-donors-to-judicial-elections/.

33. Ibid.

34. Ibid.

35. Malia Reddick, Michael J. Nelson, and Rachel Paine Caufield, "Racial and Gender Diversity on State Courts," *Judges' Journal* 48 (2009): 28–32.

36. Ibid.

CHAPTER 7

1. *In re Gault*, 387 U.S. 1 (1967).

2. U.S. Legal, "Death Penalty for Minors," 2016, accessed July 17, 2016, www.deathpenalty.uslegal.com/minors/death-penalty-for-minors.

3. Brandi Grissom, "Young Killers in Texas Await Change in Mandatory Life Sentences," *New York Times*, July 4, 2013, www.nytimes.com/2013/07/05/us/young-killers-in-texas-await-change-in-mandatory-life-sentences.html.

4. Brandi Grissom, "Case of Texas Killer Puts Spotlight on Executing the Mentally Ill," *Dallas Morning News*, September 23, 2015, https://www.dallasnews.com/news/texas/2015/09/22/case-of-texas-killer-puts-spotlight-on-executing-the-mentally-ill.

5. *Panetti v. Quarterman*, 551 U.S. 930 (2007).

6. Jolie McCullough and Ben Hansson, "Faces of Death Row," *Texas Tribune*, June 6, 2018, https://apps.texastribune.org/death-row/.

7. Jolie McCullough, "Texas Executes Man Court Recognized as Mentally Ill," *Texas Tribune*, March 22, 2016, www.texastribune.org/2016/03/22/execution-set-man-courts-recognize-menally-ill.

8. Jonathan Silver, "Issue of Mental Health Assessment a Focus as Three Fight Death Sentences," *Texas Tribune*, May 28, 2016, www.texastribune.org/2016/05/28/mentally-ill-killers-cases-create-due-process-ques.

9. Nathan Thornburgh, "Looking Kindly on Vigilante Justice," *Time*, July 3, 2008, www.time.com/time/nation/article/0,8599,1820028,00.html.

10. Philip Bean, *Punishment: A Philosophical and Criminological Inquiry* (Oxford, UK: Martin Robinson, 1981), 14–15.

11. Cindy Banks, *Criminal Justice Ethics: Theory and Practice* (Thousand Oaks, CA: Sage, 2004), 111–12.

12. Ibid., 113.

13. Herbert Morris, "A Paternalistic Theory of Punishment," in *A Reader on Punishment*, ed. Anthony Duff and David Garland (Oxford, UK: Oxford University Press, 1994), 92–111.

14. Bean, *Punishment*, 54.

15. Banks, *Criminal Justice Ethics*, 117–18.

16. International Center for Prison Studies, "Highest to Lowest Prison Population Rate," accessed June 9, 2018, http://www.prisonstudies.org/highest-to-lowest/prison-population-total?field_region_taxonomy_tid=All.

17. Ibid.

18. The Sentencing Project, "The Facts: State-by-State Data," accessed June 9, 2018, https://www.sentencingproject.org/the-facts/#map.

19. International Center for Prison Studies, "Highest to Lowest Prison Population Rate."

20. Danielle Kaeble, "Probation and Parole in the United States, 2016," Bureau of Justice Statistics, April 2018, https://www.bjs.gov/content/pub/pdf/ppus16.pdf.

21. Cal Jillson, *Lone Star Tarnished: A Critical Look at Texas Politics and Public Policy* (New York: Routledge, 2012).

22. Ross Ramey, "UT/TT Poll: Support for Marijuana Growing like a Weed in Texas," accessed June 9, 2018, https://www.texastribune.org/2017/02/21/uttt-poll-support-marijuana-growing-weed-texas/.

23. "Criminal Justice: Tough on Crime? Check. Smart on Crime? Not So Much," *Austin American-Statesman*, December 31, 2009, 23.

24. David Boeri, "Prison Overcrowding, Rising Costs Prompt Surprising Reform," NPR, March 30, 2011, www.wbur.org/2011/03/30/tough-on-crime.

25. Ibid.

26. Frauzeya Rahman, "Texas Spends More Per Inmate than Public School Student, Democrat Leeder Says," *Texas Tribune*, November 21, 2016, https://www.expressnews.com/news/local/article/Texas-spends-more-per-inmate-than-public-school-10629083.php.

27. Legislative Budget Board, "Juvenile Justice System and Adult Community Supervision Funding," April 2018, http://www.lbb.state.tx.us/Documents/Publications/Presentation/5209_Juvenile_Justice_System_Adult_Supervision.pdf.

28. Renee Lee, "Elderly Inmates Are Putting a Burden on Texas Taxpayers," *Houston Chronicle*, May 16, 2011, https://www.chron.com/news/houston-texas/

article/Elderly-inmates-are-putting-a-burden-on-Texas-1693376.php.

29. Brandi Grissom, "More Than 70% of Texas Prisons Don't Have AC, and Why That Won't Change Anytime Soon," *Dallas Morning News*, July 4, 2016, https://www.dallasnews.com/news/crime/2016/06/29/70-texas-prisons-ac-change-anytime-soon.

30. Jolie McCullogh, "Judge Approves Settlement Mandating Air Conditioning at Hot Texas Prison," *Texas Tribune*, May 8, 2018, https://www.texastribune.org/2018/05/08/settlement-air-condition-hot-texas-prison-gets-final-judicial-approval/.

31. Ramona R. Rantala, Jessica Rexroat, and Allen J. Beck, "Survey of Sexual Assault in Adult Correctional Facilities, 2009–2011, Statistical Tables," U.S. Department of Justice, January 2014, 2018, https://www.bjs.gov/content/pub/pdf/ssvacf0911st.pdf.

32. E. Ann Carson, "Prisoners in 2016," January 2018, U.S. Department of Justice, Bureau of Justice Statistics, https://www.bjs.gov/content/pub/pdf/p16.pdf.

33. Gregory Hooks, Clayton Mosher, Thomas Rotolo, and Linda Lobao, "The Prison Industry: Carceral Expansion and Employment in U.S. Counties, 1969–1994," *Social Science Quarterly* 85 (March 2004): 1.

34. Mike Ward, "Privately Run Prisons Come under Fire at Capitol," *Austin American-Statesman*, October 13, 2007.

35. Holly Becka and Jennifer LaFleur, "Texas's Youth Jail Operators Have Troubled Histories," *Dallas Morning News*, July 30, 2007.

36. Erik Kain, "Texas and the Prison-Industrial-Complex," *Forbes*, September 1, 2011, https://www.forbes.com/sites/erikkain/2011/09/01/texas-and-the-prison-industrial-complex/#78deeec01841.

37. Jonathan Silver, "Feds Ending Five Private Prison Contracts in Texas," *Texas Tribune*, August 18, 2016, https://www.texastribune.org/2016/08/18/justice-department-wants-phase-out-private-prison-/.

38. John Burnett, "Private Prison Promises Leave Texas Towns in Trouble," NPR, March 28, 2011, www.npr.org/2011/03/28/134855801/private-prison-promises-leave-texas-towns-in-trouble.

39. Josie Musico, "Littlefield Getting Sex Offender Facility," *Lubbock Avalanche-Journal*, August 1, 2015. http://lubbockonline.com/local-news/2015-07-31/littlefield-getting-sex-offender-facility.

40. Michael K. Moore and Allan K. Butcher, "Giving Timbre to Gideon's Trumpet: Evaluating the Administration and Effectiveness of Legal Representation for Texas' Indigent Criminal Defendants" (a report to the State Bar of Texas), accessed June 15, 2018, http://tidc.texas.gov/media/31123/moorebutcherevaleffectivenessreportmay2007.pdf.

41. Texas Indigent Defense Commissions, "List of Public Defender and Managed Assigned Counsel Offices," 2018, http://www.tidc.texas.gov/media/46142/direct-client-services-chart-2018.pdf.

42. Bill Hanna, "Two Dead Bikers Have Tarrant County Ties," May 15, 2015, *Fort Worth Star Telegram*, http://www.star-telegram.com/news/state/texas/article21396951.html.

43. Tommy Witherspoon, "Four Twin Peaks Bikers Seek $1 Billion in Civil Lawsuit," May 8, 2017, *The Eagle* (Bryan–College Station), http://www.theeagle.com/news/waco_shooting/four-twin-peaks-bikers-seek-billion-in-civil-lawsuit/article_d665f23d-bd4e-5716-8dc9-e4545a323299.html.

44. Nathan Hecht, "The State of the Judiciary in Texas," February 1, 2017, Texas Judicial Branch website, http://www.txcourts.gov/media/1437101/soj-2017.pdf.

45. Association of American Medical Colleges, "State Physician Workforce Data Book," 2017, https://www.aamc.org/download/484596/data/texasprofile.pdf.

46. Sanya Mansoor, "Over Opposition, Latest Tort Reform Bill Advancing through Legislature," *Texas Tribune*, May 4, 2017, https://www.texastribune.org/2017/05/04/texas-legislature-tort-reform/.

47. John Tedesco, "Damage Claims Hit City One a Day," *San Antonio Express News*, April 1, 2012, www.mysanantonio.com/news/local_news/article/Damage-claims-hit-city-one-a-day-3450565.php.

48. Charles M. Silver, "Soapbox: No Better Care, Thanks to Tort Reform," *Texas Weekly*, October 20, 2011, https://texasweekly.texastribune.org/texas-weekly/vol-28/no-40/soapbox-no-better-care-thanks-tort-reform/.

49. Greg Roslund, "The Medical Malpractice Rundown: A State-by-State Report Card," *Emergency Physicians Monthly*, 2014, www.epmonthly.com/article/the-medical-malpractice-rundown-a-state-by-state-report-card.

50. Patrick Michels, "Joe Horn and Five Years with the

Texas Castle Doctrine," *Texas Observer*, May 8, 2012, https://www.texasobserver.org/joe-horn-and-castle-doctrine-shootings-in-texas/.

51. *Furman v. Georgia*, 408 U.S. 153 (1972).

52. Texas Department of Criminal Justice, "Death Row Information," accessed August 6, 2018, https://www.tdcj.state.tx.us/death_row/dr_offenders_on_dr.html. Some calculations by author.

53. 536 U.S. 304 (2002).

54. 135 S.W.3d 1.8-9 (Tex. Crim. App. 2004).

55. Renee Feltz, "Is Texas' Death Penalty Machine Executing the Mentally Disabled?" *Texas Observer*, August 8, 2012, https://www.texasobserver.org/did-texas-execute-a-mentally-disabled-man/.

56. 543 U.S. 551 (2005).

57. 550 U.S. 930 (2007).

58. 572 U.S. ___ (2014).

59. 581 U.S. ___ (2017).

60. David Dobbs, quoted in "The Texas Judiciary: Is Justice for Sale?" (League of Women Voters panel discussion, Tyler, Texas, broadcast as part of a PBS *Frontline* special, September 25, 2007).

61. University of Texas and *Texas Tribune*, "Texas Statewide Survey," June 2014, http://s3.amazonaws.com/static.texastribune.org/media/documents/uttt-jun2014-summary-all.pdf; Gallup, "Death Penalty," accessed July 15, 2018, http://www.gallup.com/poll/1606/death-penalty.aspx.

62. Chuck Lindale, "Judge Rebuked but Avoids Ouster," *Austin American-Statesman*, July 16, 2010, https://www.statesman.com/news/local/judge-rebuked-but-avoids-ouster/ndb5149YboKk9si8PmWDBK/.

63. Texas Department of Criminal Justice, "Gender and Racial Statistics of Death Row Offenders," 2018, https://www.tdcj.state.tx.us/death_row/dr_gender_racial_stats.htm.

64. Christy Hoppe, "Executions Cost Texas Millions: Study Finds It's Cheaper to Jail Killers for Life," *Dallas Morning News*, March 8, 1992.

CHAPTER 8

1. Lloyd B. Potter and Nazrul Hoque, "Texas Population Projections, 2010–2050," Office of the State Demographer, November 2014, http://demographics.texas.gov/Resources/Publications/2014/2014-11_ProjectionBrief.pdf.

2. Ibid.

3. Gustavo López and Renee Stepler, "Latinos in the 2016 Election: Texas," Pew Research Center, January 19, 2016, http://www.pewhispanic.org/fact-sheets/2016-state-election-fact-sheets/latinos-in-the-2016-election-texas.

4. Andrew Dugan, "Texan Hispanics Tilt Democratic, but State Likely to Stay Red," Gallup, February 7, 2014, http://www.gallup.com/poll/167339/texan-hispanics-tilt-democratic-state-likely-stay-red.aspx.

5. Alexa Ura and Annie Daniel, "See Demographics Shift by Texas County," *Texas Tribune*, June 25, 2015, www.texastribune.org/2015/06/25/see-demographic-shift-tx-counties-2010-2014.

6. See, for example, Dante Chinni, "Can Texas Democrats Turn the Lone Star State Blue? NBC News, March 4, 2018, https://www.nbcnews.com/politics/first-read/can-texas-democrats-turn-lone-star-state-blue-n853006; Lomi Kriel, "Report: Shifting Demographics Favor Democrats in 2016 Unless GOP Gains Many White Voters," *Houston Chronicle*, February 26, 2016, http://www.chron.com/about/article/Report-Shifting-demographics-favor-Democrats-in-6854768.php.

7. Pew Center for Religion and Public Life, "The Shifting Religious Identity of Latinos in the United States," May 7, 2014, http://www.pewforum.org/2014/05/07/the-shifting-religious-identity-of-latinos-in-the-united-states.

8. Texas Election Code, chap. 11, sec. 002.

9. Maria L. La Ganaga, "Under New Oregon Law, All Eligible Voters Are Registered Unless They Opt Out," *Los Angeles Times*, March 17, 2015, http://www.latimes.com/nation/la-na-oregon-automatic-voter-registration-20150317-story.html.

10. Texas Election Code, chap. 16, secs. 002–003.

11. Texas Constitution (1876), art. 7, sec. 3.

12. Ricky F. Dobbs, *Yellow Dogs and Republicans: Allan Shivers and Texas Two-Party Politics* (College Station: Texas A&M University Press, 2005), 80.

13. Michael J. Klarman, "The Supreme Court and Black Disenfranchisement," in *The Voting Rights Act: Securing the Ballot*, ed. Richard M. Valelly (Washington, DC: CQ Press, 2006).

14. 383 U.S. 663 (1966).

15. 273 U.S. 534 (1924).

16. 321 U.S. 649 (1944).

17. 345 U.S. 461 (1953).

18. Klarman, "The Supreme Court and Black Disenfranchisement," 154.

19. 557 U.S. 193 (2009).

20. 570 U.S. ___ (2013).

21. Abigail M. Thernstrom, *Whose Votes Count?*

(Cambridge, MA: Harvard University Press, 1987), 55.

22. Teresa Palomo Acosta, "In Re Ricardo Rodriguez," *Handbook of Texas Online*, Texas State Historical Association, accessed July 17, 2018, www.tshaonline.org/handbook/online/articles/pqitw.

23. Chandler Davidson, "The Voting Rights Act: A Brief History," in *Controversies in Minority Voting*, ed. Bernard Grofman and Chandler Davidson (Washington, DC: Brookings Institution, 1992).

24. Thernstrom, *Whose Votes Count?*, 52.

25. Voting Rights Act Amendments of 206, Determinants under Section 203, 81 Federal Register 233, *Federal Register: The Daily Journal of the United States*, December 5, 2016, https://www.justice.gov/crt/file/927231/download.

26. Ruth P. Morgan, *Governance by Decree: The Impact of the Voting Rights Act in Dallas* (Lawrence: University of Kansas Press, 2004), 50–51.

27. Thernstrom, *Whose Votes Count?*, 56–57.

28. Christopher Smith Gonzalez, "Voter ID Gets Tense Hearing," *Texas Tribune*, March 1, 2011, www.texastribune.org/texaspolitics/voter-id/voter-id-gets-hearing.

29. Ibid.

30. Julian Aguilar, "Day 24: Stringent Voter ID Law Means Changes at Texas Polls," *Texas Tribune*, August 24, 2011, https://www.texastribune.org/2011/08/24/day-24-voter-id-law-means-changes-ballot-box/.

31. Terry Frieden, "Federal Court Strikes Downs Texas Voter ID Law," August 30, 2012, www.cnn.com/2012/08/30/politics/texas-voter-id-law.

32. Sari Horwitz, "Texas Voter-ID Law Is Blocked," *Washington Post*, August 30, 2012, www.washingtonpost.com/world/national-security/texas-voter-id-law-struck-down/2012/08/30/4a07e270-f2ad-11e1-adc6-87dfa8eff430_story.html.

33. 380 U.S. 775 (1965).

34. Texas Secretary of State, "Students," accessed August 8, 2016, http://votetexas.gov/students.

35. Texas Constitution (1876), art. 6, sec. 5.

36. John F. Bibby and Thomas M. Holbrook, "Parties and Elections," in *Politics in the American States: A Comparative Analysis*, 8th ed., ed. Virginia Gray and Russell Hanson (Washington, DC: CQ Press, 2004), 63.

37. Dobbs, *Yellow Dogs and Republicans*, 70.

38. Ibid., 88.

39. Alexander Heard, *A Two-Party South?* (Chapel Hill: University of North Carolina Press, 1952), 104–5.

40. Audrey S. Wall (ed.), *The Book of the States*, vol. 48 (Lexington, KY: Council of State Governments, 2016), 313–14, table 6.9.

41. Ibid.

42. In some rare cases, voters do mark local and state races and leave "higher" offices, such as U.S. senator or U.S. representative, unmarked. However, this pattern is much, much rarer than roll off. As a result, political scientists do not really have a term to describe this phenomenon—*roll on* seems a bit silly.

43. Samuel L. Popkin, "Information Shortcuts and the Reasoning Voter," in *Information, Participation, and Choice*, ed. Bernard Grofman (Ann Arbor: University of Michigan Press, 1993), 19.

44. Ibid., 22–27; Anthony Downs, *An Economic Theory of Democracy* (New York: Harper & Row, 1957), 85.

45. Jolie McCullough and Ross Ramsey, "See the Straight-Ticket Breakdown in Texas' 10 Most-Populous Counties," *Texas Tribune*, November 11, 2016, https://www.texastribune.org/2016/11/11/texas-2016-straight-ticket-ballots/.

46. Ibid.

47. Donald P. Moynihan, "Building Secure Elections: E-Voting, Security, and Systems Theory," *Public Administration Review* 64 (2007): 515–28.

48. Ibid., 518.

49. Paul S. Herrnson et al., "Early Appraisals of Electronic Voting," *Social Science Computer Review* 23 (2005): 274–92.

50. Jeffrey S. Connor, *Amended Texas State Plan Pursuant to the Help America Vote Act of 2002* (Austin, TX: Office of the Secretary of State, Elections Division, 2005), 3.

51. Ibid., 15.

52. Texas Secretary of State, "Election Night Returns," 2018, accessed November 26, 2018, https://enrpages.sos.state.tx.us/public/nov06_331.htm; Texas Secretary of State, "Voter Registration Figures 1991–Present," 2018, accessed November 26, 2018, https://www.sos.state.tx.us/elections/historical/nov2018.shtml.

53. Karlheinz Reif and Hermann Schmitt, "Nine Second-Order Elections: A Conceptual Framework for the Analysis of European Election Results," *European Journal of Political Research* 8 (1980): 3–44.

54. William H. Riker, *Liberalism against Populism* (Prospect Heights, IL:

Waveland Press, 1982), 5; Robert A. Dahl, *A Preface to Democratic Theory* (Chicago: University of Chicago Press, 1956), 132.

55. James Endersby, Steven Galatas, and Chapman Rackaway, "Closeness Counts in Canada," *Journal of Politics* 64, no. 2 (2002): 610–31. Specific cases finding a link in the United States at the state level include Harvey J. Tucker, "Contextual Models of Participation in U.S. State Legislative Elections," *Western Political Quarterly* 39, no. 1 (1986): 67–78; Gregory A. Caldeira and Samuel C. Patterson, "Contextual Influences on Participation in U.S. State Legislative Election," *Legislative Studies Quarterly* 7, no. 3 (1989): 359–81; and Samuel C. Patterson and Gregory A. Caldeira, "Getting Out the Vote: Participation in Gubernatorial Elections," *American Political Science Review* 77, no. 3 (1983): 675–89.

56. Randolph B. Campbell, *Gone to Texas* (New York: Oxford University Press, 2004), 175.

57. Ibid.

58. James L. Haley, *Passionate Nation: The Epic History of Texas* (New York: Free Press, 2006).

59. Ibid.

60. National Institute for Money in State Politics, "Election Overview: Texas," accessed July 13, 2018, http://www.followthemoney.org/election-overview?s=TX&y=2014.

61. Ibid.

62. *Buckley v. Valeo*, 424 U.S. 1 (1976).

63. Ibid.

64. 558 U.S. 50 (2010).

65. Morgan Smith and Zoë Gioia, "Local Court Runoff Tests Judicial Campaign Fairness Act," *Texas Tribune*, July 26, 2012, www.texastribune.org/texas-courts/texas-judicial-system/local-court-runoff-tests-judicial-campaign-fairnes.

CHAPTER 9

1. Jeremy Wallace, "Texas Republican Party Convention Begins amid a GOP Filled with Tension," *Houston Chronicle*, June 13, 2018, https://www.houstonchronicle.com/news/politics/texas/article/Texas-Republican-Party-convention-begins-amid-a-12991942.php.

2. Todd J. Gillman (@toddgillman), "Meltdown at @TexasGOP convention amid pushback on majority report on state chair nominations," Twitter, June 15, 2018, 1:24 p.m., https://twitter.com/toddgillman/status/1007720457498439680.

3. Jonathan Tilove, "Texas Republicans Pen Staunchly Conservative Platform, Call for Unity," *Austin American-Statesman*, June 16, 2018, https://www.mystatesman.com/news/state--regional-govt--politics/texas-republicans-pen-staunchly-conservative-platform-call-for-unity/VlxaYOfFbLizxfLraiThlN/.

4. Julia Azari, "Weak Parties and Strong Partisanship Are a Bad Combination," Vox, November 3, 2016, https://www.vox.com/mischiefs-of-faction/2016/11/3/13512362/weak-parties-strong-partisanship-bad-combination.

5. Carroll Doherty, Jocelyn Kiley, and Bridget Jameson, "Partisanship and Political Animosity," Pew Research Center, June 22, 2016, http://assets.pewresearch.org/wp-content/uploads/sites/5/2016/06/06-22-16-Partisanship-and-animosity-release.pdf.

6. Alwyn Barr, *Reconstruction to Reform: Texas Politics, 1876–1906* (Dallas: Southern Methodist University Press, 2000), 5.

7. T. R. Fehrenbach, *Lone Star: A History of Texas and the Texans* (Cambridge, MA: Da Capo Press, 2000), 618.

8. Ibid., 624.

9. Lewis L. Gould, *Progressives and Prohibitionists* (Austin: University of Texas Press, 1973), 39.

10. Ibid., 39.

11. Fehrenbach, *Lone Star*, 415.

12. Randolph B. Campbell, *Gone to Texas* (New York: Oxford University Press, 2004), 350.

13. Exit Polls, CNN, https://www.cnn.com/election/2018/exit-polls/texas (accessed November 14, 2018).

14. Earl Black and Merle Black, *The Rise of the Southern Republicans* (Cambridge, MA: Belknap Press, 2002), 88.

15. Ibid., 23–24.

16. James Endersby, Steven Galatas, and Chapman Rackaway, "Closeness Counts in Canada," *Journal of Politics* 64, no. 2 (2002): 610–31. Specific cases finding a link in the United States at the state level include Harvey J. Tucker, "Contextual Models of Participation in U.S. State Legislative Elections," *Western Political Quarterly* 39, no. 1 (1986): 67–78; Gregory A. Caldeira and Samuel C. Patterson, "Contextual Influences on Participation in U.S. State Legislative Election," *Legislative Studies Quarterly* 7, no. 3 (1989): 359–81; and Samuel C. Patterson and Gregory A.

Caldeira, "Getting Out the Vote: Participation in Gubernatorial Elections," *American Political Science Review* 77, no. 3 (1983): 675–89.

17. Edmund Burke, *Works*, vol. I (London: G. Bell and Sons, 1897), 375.

18. Leon Epstein, *Political Parties in Western Democracies* (New York: Praeger, 1967), 9.

19. Wayne Thorburn, "In Defense of Straight-Ticket Voting," *Texas Tribune*, https://www.tribtalk .org/2015/03/15/in-defense- of-straight-ticket-voting/.

20. Angus Campbell, Philip E. Converse, Warren E. Miller, and Donald E. Stokes, *The American Voter* (New York: Wiley), 1960.

21. Drew Westin, *The Political Brain: The Role of Emotion in Deciding the Fate of the Nation* (New York: Public Affairs, 2008).

22. Quoted in A. James Reichley, *The Life of the Parties* (Boulder, CO: Rowman & Littlefield, 2000), 316.

23. National Institute on Money in State Politics, "Texans for Lawsuit Reform," accessed October 4, 2016, www .followthemoney.org/entity- details?eid=4675&default=c ontributor.

24. *Eu v. San Francisco County Democratic Central Comm.*, 489 U.S. 214 (1989).

25. Paul Allen Beck, *Political Parties in America*, 8th ed. (New York: Longman, 1997), 67–68.

26. Republican Party of Texas, "General Rules for All Conventions and Meetings," 33, April 7, 2018, https: //www.texasgop.org/ wp-content/uploads/ 2018/04/2016-Rules- with-April-7-2018-SREC- Updates-2.pdf.

27. Marc J. Hetherington and William J. Keefe, *Parties,* *Politics, and Public Policy in America*, 10th ed. (Washington, DC: CQ Press, 2007), 21.

28. Bobby Blanchard and Brittney Martin, "How Will the Texas Delegates Be Allocated?" *Dallas Morning News*, February 16, 2016, http://interactives.dallasnews .com/2016/texas-delegates.

29. Ibid.

30. John Kenneth White and Daniel M. Shea, *New Party Politics: From Jefferson and Hamilton to the Information Age* (Boston: St. Martin's Press, 2000), 174.

31. V. O. Key, *Southern Politics in State and Nation* (New York: Knopf, 1949), 307.

32. Ibid., 11.

CHAPTER 10

1. Molly Ivins, *Molly Ivins Can't Say That, Can She?* (New York: Random House, 1991), 60.

2. Anthony J. Nownes, *Pressure and Power: Organized Interests in American Politics* (Boston: Houghton Mifflin, 2001).

3. Ibid., 8.

4. Randolph Campbell, *Gone to Texas: A History of the Lone Star State* (Oxford, NY: Oxford University Press, 2003).

5. David Truman, *The Governmental Process: Political Interests and Public Opinion*, 2nd ed. (New York: Knopf, 1971).

6. Texas Ethics Commission, "Political Committee Lists," accessed July 28, 2018, https://www.ethics.state .tx.us/dfs/paclists.htm.

7. Kevin McNellis and Robin Parkinson, "Independent Spending's Role in State Elections, 2006–2010," National Institute on Money in State Politics, March 15, 2012, www.followthemoney .org/press/ReportView .phtml?r=481.

8. Dave Mann, "A Governor's Race Full of Pettiness," *Texas Observer*, August 27, 2010, www.texasobserver.org/ contrarian/a-governors- race-full-of-pettiness.

9. 558 U.S. 50 (2010).

10. Pew Research Center, "Little Public Awareness of Outside Campaign Spending Boom," August 2, 2012, www.people-press .org/2012/08/02/little-public- awareness-of-outside- campaign-spending-boom.

11. Texans for Public Justice, "Texas PACs: 2014 Election Cycle Spending," February 2016, http://info.tpj.org/ reports/pdf/PACs2014.pdf.

12. Adam Crowther, "Citizens United Fuels Negative Spending," *Public Citizen*, November 2, 2012, www .citizen.org/documents/ outside-groups-fuel- negative-spending-in-2012- race-report.pdf.

13. 548 U.S. 204 (2006).

14. Jim Clancy, "In the Matter of Michael Quinn Sullivan before the Texas Ethics Commission," SC-3120487 and SC-3120488, Texas Ethics Commission, July 21, 2014, www.ethics.state.tx.us/ sworncomp/2012/3120488. pdf.

15. Richard West, "Inside the Lobby," *Texas Monthly*, July 1973, www.texasmonthly. com/content/inside-lobby.

16. Laylan Copelin, "Wined, Dined and Rubbed the Right Way," *Austin American- Statesman*, January 30, 2007, A1.

17. West, "Inside the Lobby."

18. Edward T. Walker, *Grassroots for Hire: Public Affairs Consultants in American Democracy* (Cambridge, MA: Cambridge University Press, 2014), 6.

19. Ibid., 22, 38.

20. Stuart A. MacCorkle and Dick Smith, *Texas Government*, 5th ed. (New York: McGraw-Hill, 1964), 92.

21. Kevin Bogardus, "Statehouse Revolvers: Study Finds More Than 1,300 Ex-Legislators among 2005 State Lobbying Ranks," Center for Public Integrity, October 12, 2006, www.publicintegrity .org/2006/10/12/5900/ statehouse-revolvers.

22. National Conference of State Legislatures, "Revolving Door Prohibitions," December 15, 2017, http://www.ncsl .org/research/ethics/50- state-table-revolving-door- prohibitions.aspx.

23. Pete Slover and Robert T. Garrett, "'Kinfolk' Lobbyists Prospering," *Dallas Morning News*, May 5, 2005, 1A.

24. Robert A. Dahl, *Who Governs?* (New Haven, CT: Yale University Press, 1961).

25. C. Wright Mills, *The Power Elite* (New York: Oxford University Press, 1956).

26. E. E. Schattschneider, *The Semisovereign People* (New York: Holt, Rinehart and Winston, 1960), 34–35.

27. Jonathan Rauch, *Government's End: Why Washington Stopped Working* (New York: Public Affairs, 1999).

CHAPTER 11

1. Hoe Yen, "Abbott Praises Harvey Response; Trump Meets and Tweets," *Houston Chronicle*, August 27, 2017, https://www.chron.com/ news/nation-world/nation/ article/Abbott-praises- Harvey-response-Trump- meets-and-12026929.php.

2. Brandon Formby, "Abbott and FEMA Are Using Harvey to Reinvent Disaster Response. Some Say That Makes Displaced Texans 'Guinea Pigs,'" *Texas Tribune*, February 27, 2018, www.texastribune .org/2018/02/27/texans-left- limbo-gov-abbott-fema-use- harvey-reinvent-disaster- response/.

3. R. G. Ratcliffe, "The Political Storm of Hurricane Harvey," *Texas Monthly*, September 15, 2017, www.texasmontly .com/burke-blog/political- storm-hurricane-harvey.

4. Mike Ward, "Hurricane Harvey Could Leave Texas $1 Billion Short," *Houston Chronicle*, December 6, 2017, https://www.chron .com/news/houston-texas/ houston/article/Harvey- could-gut-state-budget-by- 1-billion-12408699.php.

5. Mike Ward, "$90 Million Approved to Expedite Debris Removal from Hurricane Harvey," *Houston Chronicle*, November 10, 2017, www .chron.com/news/politics/ texas/article/90M-approved- to-expedite-debris-removal- from-12344582.php.

6. Ibid.

7. Mihir Zaveri, "Texas to Change Harvey Grant Spending Amid Criticism from Harris County," *Houston Chronicle*, January 31, 2018, https://www.chron .com/news/politics/houston/ article/Harris-County- officials-decry-GLO-plan- to-use-8-12536869.php.

8. Mike Morris, "Mayor Turner Letter Details Concerns about GLOs Harvey Response," *Houston Chronicle*, March 8, 2018, https://www.chron.com/ news/politics/houston/ article/Mayor-Turner-letter- details-concerns-about- state-12739118.php.

9. Data from the 2012 Census of Governments from the U.S. Census Bureau are the most recent available. This survey is conducted once every five years, but the 2017 data have not yet been released to the public.

10. *Clinton v. Cedar Rapids and Missouri River Railroad Co.*, 24 Iowa 455 (1868).

11. *Hunter v. Pittsburgh*, 207 U.S. 161 (1907).

12. Texas Constitution (1876), art. 9, sec. 1.

13. Paul Ciotti, "Money and School Performance: Lessons Learned from the Kansas City Desegregation Experiment," *Policy Analysis*, no. 298 (Washington, DC: CATO Institute, 1998).

14. Elizabeth Cruce-Alvarez, *Texas Almanac, 2018–2019* (College Station, TX: TAMU Press Texas State Historical Society), p. 355.

15. Texas Constitution (1876), art. 9, sec. 1(1).

16. Texas Association of Counties, "Chapter 1: Framework and Function of County Government," accessed May 31, 2018, www.county.org/texas- county-government/ resources/Documents/ Chap1.pdf.

17. Cruce-Alvarez, *Texas Almanac*, p. 388.

18. Texas Constitution (1876), art. 9, sec. 14.

19. Texas Local Government Code, chap. 158, sec. 158.001.

20. Texas Local Government Code, chap. 118.

21. Texas Local Government Code, chap. 6, sec. 6.001, and chap. 22, secs. 22.031– 22.042.

22. Texas Local Government Code, chap. 6, sec. 6.001, and chap. 23.

23. Texas Local Government Code, chap. 6, sec. 6.001; chaps. 24 and 25.

24. Texas Local Government Code, chap. 26.

25. Robert Brischetto, "Cumulative Voting at Work in Texas," in *Voting and Democracy Report: 1995* (Takoma Park, MD: FairVote–Center for Voting and Democracy, 1995).

26. Emily Ramshaw, "State Law Would Usurp City Control of Zoning, Neighborhood Control," *Dallas Morning News*, March 2, 2007.

27. Mihir Zaveri, "Harris County Toughens Regulations on Construction after Hurricane Harvey, Including Higher Builds," *Houston Chronicle*, December 5, 2017, https://www.chron.com/news/houston-texas/article/Harris-County-leaders-to-vote-on-post-Harvey-12403862.php.

28. Mike Morris, "More Houstonians May Be Forced to Raise Their Harvey-damaged Homes," *Houston Chronicle*, February 2, 2018, https://www.chron.com/news/politics/houston/article/More-Houstonians-may-be-forced-to-raise-their-12547588.php.

29. Melanie Feuk, "After Harvey, Houston, Harris County Propose Changes Development Regulation," *Houston Chronicle*, February 27, 2018, https://www.chron.com/neighborhood/kingwood/news/article/After-Harvey-Houston-Harris-County-propose-12713982.php.

30. Texas Local Government Code, chap. 43, sec. 43.055.

31. Peggy Heinkel-Wolfe, "Fracking Foes Turn to Cities," *Denton Record-Chronicle*, June 21, 2014, http://www.dentonrc.com/local-news/local-news-headlines/20140621-fracking-foes-turn-to-cities.ece.

32. Max B. Baker, "Denton City Council Repeals Fracking Ban," *Fort Worth Star-Telegram*, June 16, 2015, www.star-telegram.com/news/business/barnett-shale/article24627469.html.

33. David Spense, "Resolving the State vs. Local Fracking Conflict," *Texas Enterprise*, March 20, 2014, www.texasenterprise.utexas.edu/2014/03/20/policy/resolving-state-vs-local-fracking-conflict.

34. Luqman Adeniyi, "Lawmakers Support Abbott against 'Sanctuary Cities,'" *Texas Tribune*, November 6, 2015, https://www.texastribune.org/2015/11/06/both-houses-support-abbott-against-sanctuary-citie.

35. Julian Aguilar, "'Sanctuary Cities' Bill Clears Latest Hurdle, Heads to Abbott for Signature," *Texas Tribune*, May 2, 2017, https://www.texastribune.org/2017/05/03/sanctuary-cities-bill-clears-latest-hurdle-heads-abbott-signature/.

36. Julian Aguilar, "Judge Dismisses Paxton Lawsuit over 'Sanctuary Cities' Law," *Texas Tribune*, August 9, 2017, https://www.texastribune.org/2017/08/09/judge-dismisses-paxton-sb4-lawsuit/.

37. Julian Aguilar, "Critics of Texas' 'Sanctuary Cities' Law Ask Federal Appeals Court to Reconsider Case," *Texas Tribune*, March 28, 2018, https://www.texastribune.org/2018/03/28/critics-texas-sanctuary-cities-law-ask-federal-appeals-court-reconside/.

38. Jazmine Ulloa, "Legislature Declares California Will Be a 'Sanctuary State,'" *Los Angeles Times,* September 16, 2017, http://www.latimes.com/politics/essential/la-pol-ca-essential-politics-updates-california-lawmakers-take-final-action-1505534909-htmlstory.html.

39. Tatiana Sanchez, "California Cities Are Rebelling against State Sanctuary Law, but How Far Can They Go?," *Mercury News* (San Jose), April 23, 2018, https://www.mercurynews.com/2018/04/23/california-cities-are-rebelling-against-state-sanctuary-law-but-how-far-can-they-go/.

40. Susan McFarland, "Keller Homeowners Say They've Been Shut Out of Association Despite New State Law," Moss Report, July 14, 2012, http://themossreport.org/texas-keller-homeowners-say-theyve-been-shut-out-of-association-despite-new-state-law.

41. Arezow Doost, "New Laws Aimed at Curbing HOA Abuse," CBS DFW, December 28, 2011, http://dfw.cbslocal.com/2011/12/28/new-laws-aimed-at-curbing-hoa-abuse.

42. McFarland, "Keller Homeowners Say They've Been Shut Out of Association Despite New State Law."

43. Texas Constitution (1876), art. 7.

44. Texas Education Code, chap. 11, secs. 11.301 and 11.303.

45. Ibid., chap. 11, secs. 11.051–11.058.

46. Ibid., chap. 11, secs. 11.151.

47. Texas Education Agency, "SBOE: State Board of Education," accessed March 14, 2017, www.tea.texas.gov/sboe/.

48. Texas Constitution, art. 7, sec. 8.

CHAPTER 12

1. Derek Thompson, "The Texas Miracle: How Stellar Is the Lone Star State's Jobs Record, Really?," *Atlantic*, January 26, 2015, https://www.theatlantic.com/business/archive/2015/01/the-texas-miracle/384818/.

2. James L. Haley, *Passionate Nation: The Epic History of Texas* (New York: Free Press, 2006), 81.

3. Quoted in Dave McNeely and Jim Henderson, *Bob*

Bullock: God Bless Texas (Austin: University of Texas Press, 2008), 174.

4. Jared Walczak and Scott Drenkard, "State and Local Sales Taxes, Midyear 2016," Tax Foundation, July 5, 2016, http://taxfoundation.org/article/state-and-local-sales-tax-rates-midyear-2016.

5. Lori L. Taylor, "Stop Playing Favorites with the Tax Code," Mosbacher Institute for Trade, Economics, and Public Policy, *The Takeaway* 2, no. 1 (2011), http://bush.tamu.edu/mosbacher/takeaway/TakeAwayVol2Iss1.pdf.

6. Scott Drenkard, "The Margin Tax Holds Texas Business Back," *Texas Tribune*, October 23, 2013, http://www.texastribune.org/2013/10/23/guest-column-margin-tax-holds-texas-business-back.

7. Haley, *Passionate Nation*, 421.

8. Laurie Fox, "School Districts Opt for Extra Tax," *Dallas Morning News*, September 22, 2006.

9. Terrence Henry, "While South Texas Sees Dollar Signs, Roads See Damage and Accidents," NPR, State Impact: Texas Energy and Environment Reporting, March 27, 2013, https://stateimpact.npr.org/texas/2013/03/27/while-south-texas-sees-dollar-signs-roads-see-damage-and-accidents.

10. Ibid.

11. Legislative Budget Board, "Fiscal Size-Up: 2018–2019 Biennium," accessed November 1, 2018 http://www.lbb.state.tx.us/Documents/Publications/Fiscal_SizeUp/Fiscal_SizeUp.pdf.

12. Jimmy Maas, "Here's Why Property Taxes Are Higher in Texas," KUT, August 17, 2017, http://www.kut.org/post/heres-why-property-taxes-are-higher-texas.

13. Quoted in Ignacio Garcia, "Homeowners Say They Might Be Getting Overtaxed," KXAN, May 30, 2014, http://kxan.com/2014/05/30/home-owners-say-they-might-be-getting-overtaxed.

14. Robert T. Garrett, "Texas Governor Signs Tax Cuts Worth $3.8 Billion," *Dallas Morning News*, June 15, 2015, http://www.dallasnews.com/news/politics/headlines/20150615-abbott-signs-tax-cut-measures-worth-3.8-billion.ece.

15. Jack Cross, "Texas Needs to Reform Property Tax Laws—and Lay Off Local Governments," March 8, 2018, Trib Talk, https://www.tribtalk.org/2018/03/08/texas-needs-to-reform-property-tax-laws-and-lay-off-local-governments/.

16. Brenda Bell, "How an Obscure Amendment to the State's Property Tax Code Helps Corporations Leave Counties—and Citizens—Stretched Thin," January 14, 2015, *Texas Observer*, https://www.texasobserver.org/property-taxes-texas-corporations-citizen-stretched-thin/.

17. Steve Jansen, "Texas Is Losing Out on Millions of Dollars Thanks to Its Defective Property-Tax System," *Houston Press*, April 30, 2014, https://www.houstonpress.com/news/texas-is-losing-out-on-millions-of-dollars-thanks-to-its-defective-property-tax-system-6601492.

18. Institute on Taxation and Economic Policy, *Who Pays? A Distributional Analysis of the Tax Systems in All 50 States*, 5th ed., January 2015, http://www.itep.org/pdf/whopaysreport.pdf.

19. Legislative Budget Board, "Fiscal Size-Up: 2018–2019 Biennium," figure 44, accessed November 1, 2018 http://www.lbb.state.tx.us/Documents/Publications/Fiscal_SizeUp/Fiscal_SizeUp.pdf.

20. Haley, *Passionate Nation*, 231.

21. Rick Perry, "Message," May 26, 2007, www.governor.state.tx.us/divisions/press/bills/letters/letter3-052607.

22. Texas Constitution (1876), art. 3, sec. 49.

23. Evan Smith, "One Ticked-Off Grandma," *Texas Monthly*, December 2003, 163.

24. Legislative Budget Board, "Texas State Bond Debt," accessed July 31, 2018, http://www.lbb.state.tx.us/Documents/Publications/Presentation/2214_Debt_Summary.pdf.

25. Texas Bond Review Board, "2015 Local Government Annual Report Fiscal Year Ended," August 31, 2015, http://www.brb.state.tx.us/pub/lgs/fy2015/2015LocalARFinal.pdf.

26. Texas Comptroller of Public Accounts, "Your Money and Local Debt," September 2012, www.texastransparency.org/Special_Features/Your_Money/pdf/TexasItsYourMoney-LocalDebt.pdf.

27. Glenn Hegar, "Tax Exemptions and Tax Incidence: A Report to the Governor and the 85th Texas Legislature," February 2017, https://comptroller.texas.gov/transparency/reports/tax-exemptions-and-incidence/.

28. Joseph Bishop-Henchman and Scott Drenkard, "Sales Tax Holidays: Politically Expedient but Poor Tax Policy, 2017," Tax Foundation, July 25, 2017, https://taxfoundation.org/sales-tax-holidays-2017/.

29. Sandra Baker, "Helicopter Maker Seeks $13.5 Million Tax Break," *Fort Worth Star-Telegram*, November 2, 2011, www.star-telegram.com/2011/11/01/3492198/helicopter-maker-seeks-135-million.html.

30. Mitchell Schnurman, "Bell Seeks Tax Breaks

but Can Afford to Pay Wall Street," *Fort Worth Star-Telegram*, November 5, 2011, www.star-telegram.com/2011/11/05/3501816/bell-seeks-tax-breaks-but-can.html.

31. Darrell Preston, "Texas Cities Bear Financial Burden of Rapid Growth," *Fort Worth Star-Telegram*, June 7, 2014, www.star-telegram.com/2014/06/06/5880209/texas-cities-bear-financial-burden.html.

32. Office of the Governor, "Gov. Perry Announces Toyota Moving North American Headquarters to Plano, Generating 4,000 Jobs," April 28, 2014, http://governor.state.tx.us/news/press-release/19633.

33. Lauren McGaughy, "Scathing Audit Rakes Governor's Office over Texas Enterprise Fund," *Houston Chronicle*, September 25, 2014, http://www.houstonchronicle.com/news/politics/texas/article/Scathing-audit-rakes-governor-s-office-over-Texas-5781567.php.

34. Workers Defense Project, "The Failed Promise of the Texas Miracle," Lyndon B. Johnson School of Public Affairs, Ray Marshall Center for the Study of Human Resources, December 2015, http://www.workersdefense.org/wp-content/uploads/2016/02/The-Failed-Promise-of-the-Texas-Miracle-compressed-file.pdf.

35. Ibid.

36. Darrell Preston and Aaron Kuriloff, "Texas Taxpayers Finance Formula One Auto Races as Schools Dismiss Teachers," Bloomberg.com, May 11, 2011, www.bloomberg.com/news/2011-05-11/texas-taxpayers-finance-formula-one-auto-races-as-schools-dismiss-teachers.html.

37. Office of the Governor, "Gov. Perry Signs $22 Million Film Incentive Bill," June 7, 2007, http://governor.state.tx.us/news/press-release/2222.

38. Office of the Governor, "Gov. Perry Signs HB 873 to Provide Incentives for Entertainment Industries," April 23, 2009, http://governor.state.tx.us/news/press-release/12277.

39. Matt Brian, "Apple Closes Deal to Expand Austin Campus, Moves Ahead with $304 Million Texas Investment," The Next Web, July 18, 2012, http://thenextweb.com/apple/2012/07/18/apple-closes-deal-to-expand-austin-campus-moves-ahead-with-304-million-texas-investment.

40. Ross Ramsey, "UT/TT Poll: How Texas Voters Rank the State Legislature's Priorities," *Texas Tribune*, February 23, 2017, https://www.texastribune.org/2017/02/23/uttt-poll-how-texas-voters-rank-state-legislatures-priorities/.

CHAPTER 13

1. Ari Shapiro, "Texas City Leads the Way on Renewable Energy," NPR, *All Things Considered*, March 7, 2017, https://www.npr.org/2017/03/07/519064002/texas-city-leads-the-way-on-renewable-energy.

2. Bureau of Labor Statistics, "Fastest Growing Occupations," accessed August 6, 2018, https://www.bls.gov/ooh/fastest-growing.htm.

3. Randolph B. Campbell, *Gone to Texas* (New York: Oxford University Press, 2004).

4. Bryan Burrough, *The Rise and Fall of the Greatest Texas Oil Fortunes* (New York: Penguin Press, 2009).

5. Robert Calvert, Arnoldo De León, and Gregg Cantrell, *The History of Texas* (Wheeling, IL: Harlan Davidson Press, 2002).

6. Glenn Hegar, "Transparency: Revenue by Source for Fiscal Year 2017," accessed July 3, 2018, https://comptroller.texas.gov/transparency/reports/revenue-by-source/.

7. Texas Comptroller of Public Accounts, "The Energy Report," May 2008, www.window.state.tx.us/specialrpt/energy/pdf/96-1266EnergyReport.pdf.

8. Data on the PUF annual contribution and total fund value are from the UTIMCO Annual Audited Financial Statements found at https://www.utimco.org/scripts/internet/archivedetail.asp?fnd=2 (accessed July 10, 2018).

9. Mine K. Yücel and Jackson Thies, "Oil and Gas Rises Again in a Diversified Texas," Federal Reserve Bank of Dallas, *Southwest Economy*, First Quarter 2011, https://www.dallasfed.org/-/media/documents/research/swe/2011/swe1101g.pdf.

10. Texas Comptroller of Public Accounts, "Industry Report," accessed September 12, 2014, www.window.state.tx.us/specialrpt/tif/gulf/indProfiles.php#oil.

11. Office of the Governor, "Texas Oil and Gas Overview 2015" at Texas Wide Open for Business, accessed July 14, 2016, http://gov.texas.gov/files/ecodev/TXOil.pdf.

12. Lydia DePillis, "Oil Bust Even Worse Than Thought, According to New Data," *Houston Chronicle*, March 13. 2017, https://www.houstonchronicle.com/

business/article/Oil-bust-even-worse-than-thought-new-data-shows-10999265.php.

13. David Wethe, Alex Nussbaum, and Ryan Collins, "Oil Boom Bottleneck Costs Permian Investors $1 Billion a Day," *Bloomberg*, June 6, 2018, https://www.bloomberg.com/news/articles/2018-06-06/oil-boom-bottlenecks-are-costing-u-s-investors-1-billion-a-day.

14. Nick Cunningham, "Trump Tariffs Could Delay Permian Relief," OilPrice, July 19, 2018, https://oilprice.com/Energy/Energy-General/Trump-Tariffs-Could-Delay-Permian-Relief.html.

15. Zacariah Louis Hildenbrand et al., "A Comprehensive Analysis of Groundwater Quality in the Barnett Shale Region," *Environmental Science and Technology* 49, no.13 (2015).

16. Forrest Wilder, "Study: In the Midst of Drought Fracking, Industry Does Little to Recycle Water," *Texas Observer*, February 4, 2014, www.texasobserver.org/study-little-progress-made-recycling-water-fracking.

17. Academy of Medicine, Engineering, and Science of Texas, "Environmental and Community Impacts of Shale Development in Texas," 2017, http://tamest.org/wp-content/uploads/2017/07/Final-Shale-Task-Force-Report.pdf.

18. Anna Kuchment, "UT Study: Fracking-Related Activities Have Caused Majority of Recent Texas Earthquakes," *Dallas Morning News*, May 17, 2016, http://thescoopblog.dallasnews.com/2016/05/ut-study-long-before-fracking-oil-and-gas-activities-caused-texas-earthquakes.html.

19. Jin-Woo Kim and Zhong Lu, "Association between Localized Geohazards in West Texas and Human Activities, Recognized by Sentinel-1A/B Satellite Radar Imagery," *Scientific Reports* 8 (2018), https://www.nature.com/articles/s41598-018-23143-6.

20. ERCOT, "2017 State of the Grid Report," April 10, 2018, http://www.ercot.com/content/wcm/lists/144926/ERCOT_2017_State_of_the_Grid_Report.pdf.

21. American Wind Energy Association, "U.S. Wind Industry First Quarter 2018 Market Report," April 26, 2018, http://awea.files.cms-plus.com/FileDownloads/pdfs/1Q2018%20AWEA%20Market%20Report%20Public%20Version.pdf.

22. Clifford Krauss, "Move Over Oil, There's Money in Texas Wind," *New York Times*, February 23, 2008, https://www.nytimes.com/2008/02/23/business/23wind.html.

23. ERCOT, "2017 State of the Grid Report," accessed July 9, 2018, http://www.ercot.com/content/wcm/lists/144926/ERCOT_2017_State_of_the_Grid_Report.pdf.

24. Robert Fares, "Texas Sets New All-Time Wind Energy Record," *Scientific American*, January 14, 2016, http://blogs.scientificamerican.com/plugged-in/texas-sets-new-all-time-wind-energy-record.

25. Bloomberg New Energy Finance, "Tumbling Costs for Wind, Solar, Batteries Are Squeezing Fossil Fuels," Bloomberg News, March 28, 2018, https://about.bnef.com/blog/tumbling-costs-wind-solar-batteries-squeezing-fossil-fuels/.

26. Sweetwater and Nolan County Chamber of Commerce, "West Texas Wind Power," accessed August 4, 2016, http://sweetwatertexas.org/west-texas-wind-power.

27. Ben Block, "In Windy West Texas, an Economic Boom," accessed August 4, 2016, Worldwatch Institution, http://www.worldwatch.org/node/5829.

28. West Texas Wind Energy Consortium, "Nolan County: Case Study of Wind Energy Economic Impacts in Texas," July 10, 2008, http://www.moakcasey.com/articles/viewarticledoc.aspx/Nolan%20County%20Case%20Study.pdf?AID=168&DID=288.

29. Denise Marquez, "Wind Energy Technology Booms, Increases Role in Texas Electricity Power," *Lubbock Avalanche Journal*, March 5, 2016, http://www.lubbockonline.com/article/20160305/NEWS/303059900.

30. Patrick Graves and Bruce Wright, "Fiscal Notes: Solar Power in Texas: The Next Big Renewable?," Fiscal Notes, April 2018, https://comptroller.texas.gov/economy/fiscal-notes/2018/april/solar.php.

31. Ibid.

32. John Broder and Kate Galbraith, "EPA Is Longtime Favorite Target for Perry," *New York Times*, September 30, 2011, https://www.nytimes.com/2011/09/30/us/politics/epa-is-perrys-favorite-target.html.

33. U.S. Environmental Protection Agency, "Energy-Related Carbon Dioxide Emissions by State, 2000–2015," accessed July 20, 2018, https://www.eia.gov/environment/emissions/state/analysis/pdf/stateanalysis.pdf.

34. Asher Price, "Texas Sues to Stop EPA from Regulating Greenhouse Gases," *Austin*

American-Statesman, February 16, 2010, https:// www.statesman.com/news/ state--regional-govt--politics/ texas-sues-stop-epa-from- regulating-greenhouse-gases/ BJLrcoUYgVZRavKPqoIJbL/.

35. American Lung Association, "State of the Air," accessed July 20, 2018, http://www .lung.org/our-initiatives/ healthy-air/sota/city- rankings/most-polluted- cities.html.

36. Kate Galbraith, "Drought Caused Big Drop in Texas Portion of Ogallala," *Texas Tribune*, July 3, 2012, https://www.texastribune .org/2012/07/03/drought- caused-huge-drop-texas- portion-ogallala/.

37. John D. Harden, "For Years, the Houston Area Has Been Losing Ground," *Houston Chronicle*, May 28, 2016, https://www .houstonchronicle.com/ news/houston-texas/ houston/article/For-years- the-Houston-area-has-been- losing-ground-7951625.php.

38. Jim Malewitz, "Texas' Nuclear Waste Dump Gets Wiggle Room," *Texas Tribune*, August 20, 2014, https://www.texastribune .org/2014/08/20/texas- nuclear-waste-dump- poised-get-wiggle-room.

39. Calvert et al., *The History of Texas*.

40. T. R. Fehrenbach, *Lone Star: A History of Texas and the Texans* (Cambridge, MA: Da Capo Press, 2000), 319.

41. Ibid., 604.

42. Campbell, *Gone to Texas*, 306.

43. Cal Jillson, *Lone Star Tarnished: A Critical Look at Texas Politics and Public Policy* (New York: Routledge Press, 2012); Karl Wallace, "Texas and the Good Roads Movement: 1895 to 1948" (master's thesis at the University of Texas at Arlington, 2008).

44. Fehrenbach, *Lone Star: A History of Texas and the Texans*, 319.

45. Wallace, "Texas and the Good Roads Movement: 1895 to 1948."

46. Campbell, *Gone to Texas*, 351.

47. Texas Department of Transportation, "TXDOT History: 1930 to 1917," accessed September 13, 2014, http://archive.today/vHHB.

48. Fehrenbach, *Lone Star*, 649.

49. Calvert et al., *The History of Texas*.

50. Legislative Budget Board, "Texas Highway Funding: Legislative Primer," March 2011, www.lbb.state.tx.us/ Transportation/2011%20 Texas%20Highway%20 Funding%20Primer%20 0311.pdf.

51. David Ellis, "Testimony before the Texas House of Representatives Appropriations Sub- Committee on Articles VI, VII and VIII," Texas A&M Transportation Institute, February 12, 2013, http://tti.tamu. edu/policy/wp-content/ uploads/2014/01/David- Ellis-testimony-2-12-13.pdf.

52. American Petroleum Institute, "State Motor Fuel Taxes Report," July 2018, https:// www.api.org/~/media/Files/ Statistics/State-Motor-Fuel- Taxes-Report-July-18.pdf.

53. Legislative Budget Board, "Texas Highway Funding: Legislative Primer," April 2016, http://www.lbb .state.tx.us/Documents/ Publications/Primer/3143_ HighwayFundingPrimer _2016.pdf.

54. Patricia Kilday Hart, "Perry's Texas: Transportation Needs Left Unmet," *Houston Chronicle*, August 16, 2011, https://www.chron .com/news/houston-texas/ article/Perry-s-Texas- Transportation-needs-left- unmet-2132773.php.

55. Ibid.

56. Ibid.

57. Ibid.

58. Ben Wear and Jeremy Schwartz, "Toll Rates Going Up on Three Area Roads; Disabled Vets to See Tolls Waived," *Austin American- Statesman*, August 30, 2012, https://www.statesman.com/ news/local/toll-rates-going- three-area-roads-disabled- vets-see-tolls-waived-txdot- tollways/8csQ7o90b9KGQO xmnM5L5N/.

59. Dug Begley, "Eliminating Tolls Would Cost State Billions, Lawmakers Told," *Houston Chronicle*, March 30, 2016, http://www .houstonchronicle.com/ news/transportation/article/ Eliminating-tolls-would- cost-state-billions-7218979. php.

60. Fehrenbach, *Lone Star*, 319.

61. William S. Lind and Glen D. Bottoms, "The Conservative Case for More Rail Transit in Texas," *TribTalk: A Publication of the Texas Tribune*, July 19, 2015, https://www.tribtalk .org/2015/07/19/the- conservative-case-for-more- rail-transit-in-texas.

62. Jillson, *Lone Star Tarnished*.

63. TRIP National Transportation Research Group, "Key Facts about Texas' Surface Transportation System and Federal Funding," April 2018, at http://www.tripnet .org/docs/Fact_Sheet_ TX.pdf.

64. Ibid.

65. Julian Aguilar, "Abbott Urges Trump Administration to Protect Two Key NAFTA Provisions," *Texas Tribune*, April 4, 2018, https://www.texastribune .org/2018/04/04/texas-gov- greg-abbott-urges-trump- official-protect-2-key-nafta- provisi/.

66. Ibid.

67. U.S. Census Bureau, "State Exports from Texas," accessed July 23, 2018, https://www.census.gov/foreign-trade/statistics/state/data/tx.html#ctry.

68. U.S. Census Bureau, "State Imports for Texas," accessed July 23, 2018, https://www.census.gov/foreign-trade/statistics/state/data/imports/tx.html.

69. Office of the Governor, "Texas Trade and Foreign Direct Investment, 2016," accessed July 23, 2018, https://gov.texas.gov/uploads/files/business/fdi_report.pdf.

70. Ibid.

CHAPTER 14

1. Matthew Watkins and Neena Satija, "The Price of Admission," *Texas Tribune*, March 29, 2016, https://apps.texastribune.org/price-of-admission.

2. Neena Satija and Juan Torres, "Race and UT-Austin Admissions: A Snapshot of the Past Five Years," *Texas Tribune*, June 23, 2016, https://www.texastribune.org/2016/06/23/race-and-admissions-ut-austin-last-five-years.

3. James L. Haley, *Passionate Nation: The Epic History of Texas* (New York: Free Press, 2006), 232.

4. Dolph Briscoe, as quoted in Don Carleton, *Dolph Briscoe: My Life in Texas Ranching and Politics* (Austin, TX: Center for American History), 100.

5. Texas Education Agency, "Pocket Edition, 2016–2017: Texas Public School Statistics," January 2018, https://tea.texas.gov/communications/pocket-edition/.

6. Brian Thevenot, "Colbert Report Satirizes Texas History Textbooks," *Texas Tribune*, March 17, 2010, https://www.texastribune.org/2010/03/17/colbert-report-satirizes-texas-history-textbooks/.

7. Texas Education Agency, "Texas Permanent School Fund, Comprehensive Annual Financial Report," August 31, 2017, 5, http://tea.texas.gov/Finance_and_Grants/Texas_Permanent_School_Fund/Texas_Permanent_School_Fund_-_Annual_Report.

8. 163 U.S. 537 (1896).

9. 347 U.S. 483 (1954).

10. 349 U.S. 294 (1955).

11. Judge Justice's order in the *United States v. Texas* case is generally referred to as Civil Order 5821.

12. Amended Complaint, *LULAC v State of Texas*, Civil Action No. 6:14-CV-138, accessed July 22, 2018, 11, www.expressnews.com/file/825/825-130-Amended-Complaint-filed-by-LULAC.pdf.

13. Morgan Smith, "Lawsuit: Texas' English Language Programs Fall Short," *Texas Tribune*, June 10, 2014, www.texastribune.org/2014/06/10/lawsuit-texas-failing-english-language-students.

14. 777 S.W. 2d 391 (Tex. 1989).

15. Ross Ramsey, "Sales Tax Plan Would Redefine School District Wealth," *Texas Tribune*, April 7, 2014, www.texastribune.org/2014/04/07/sales-tax-plan-would-redefine-school-district-weal.

16. Kiah Collier, "Texas Supreme Court Upholds School Funding System," *Texas Tribune*, May 13, 2016, https://www.texastribune.org/2016/05/13/texas-supreme-court-issues-school-finance-ruling.

17. Aliyya Swaby, "Texas School Districts Cut Costs to Avoid Closure as State Funding Cuts Loom," *Texas Tribune*, June 2, 2017, https://www.texastribune.org/2017/06/02/school-finance-dead-cash-strapped-districts-prepare-worst/.

18. Aliyya Swaby, "'Disappointed' House Accepts Senate's Changes to School Finance Bill," August 16, 2017, https://www.texastribune.org/2017/08/15/house-school-finance/ce.

19. Aliyya Swaby, "Will Texas School Finance Panel Tell Schools to Do More with Less? Some Members Think It's Predetermined," March 16, 2018, https://www.texastribune.org/2018/03/16/school-finance-efficiency/.

20. Aliyya Swaby, "Feds Approve Texas School Accountability Plan That Includes Parts of A-F Rating System," *Texas Tribune*, March 26, 2018, https://www.texastribune.org/2018/03/26/texas-makes-accountability-decisions-federal-deadline/.

21. Aliyya Swaby, "More Standardized Testing Woes in Texas? A High-Performing School Says Over 100 Students Got Zeros on Essays," June 7, 2018, https://www.texastribune.org/2018/03/16/school-finance-efficiency/; David Yaffe-Bellany, "STAAR Glitches Affected More Than 100,000 Texas Students, Education Commissioner Says," June 13, 2018, https://www.texastribune.org/2018/03/16/school-finance-efficiency/.

22. Sydney Green, "Harvey-Affected Texas Schools May Not Have STAAR Scores Count Against Their Annual Rating," *Texas Tribune*, April 11, 2018, https://www.texastribune.org/2018/04/11/scores-harvey-impacted-schools-will-not-count-against-school-districts/.

23. Terrence Stutz, "Quirk in Texas Testing Law Could Cost High Schoolers a Shot at State Universities," *Dallas Morning News*, July 10, 2012, https://www.dallasnews.com/news/texas/2012/07/10/quirk-in-texas-testing-law-could-cost-high-schoolers-a-shot-at-state-universities.

24. Joshua Benton and Holly Hacker, "Analysis Shows TAKS Cheating Rampant," *Dallas Morning News*, June 3, 2007.

25. Joshua Benton, "TAKS Analysis Suggests Many Graduates Cheated," *Dallas Morning News*, June 11, 2006, 1A.

26. National Center for Educational Statistics, "Public High School 4-Year Adjusted Cohort Graduation Rate (ACGR), by Selected Student Characteristics and State: 2010–11 through 2014–15," accessed July 24, 2018, https://nces.ed.gov/programs/digest/d16/tables/dt16_219.46.asp.

27. College Board, "SAT Suite of Annual Assessments: Total Report, 2017," accessed July 24, 2018, https://reports.collegeboard.org/pdf/2017-total-group-sat-suite-assessments-annual-report.pdf; College Board, "SAT Suite of Annual Assessments: Texas, 2017," accessed July 24, 2018, https://reports.collegeboard.org/pdf/2017-texas-sat-suite-assessments-annual-report.pdf.

28. ACT, "Average ACT Score by State Graduating Class of 2017," accessed July 24, 2018, https://www.act.org/content/dam/act/unsecured/documents/cccr2017/ACT_2017-Average_Scores_by_State.pdf.

29. National Education Association, "Rankings & Estimates: Rankings of the States 2015 and Estimates of School Statistics 2016,"

May 2016, table C-11: "Average Salaries of Public School Teachers, 2014–15," http://www.nea.org/assets/docs/2016_NEA_Rankings_And_Estimates.pdf.

30. Bill Hobby and Saralee Tiede, *How Things Really Work: Lessons from a Life in Politics* (Austin, TX: Dolph Briscoe Center for American History, 2010), 97.

31. Ross Ramsey, "UT/TT Poll: Few Texas Voters Believe State Education Spending Is Too High," *Texas Tribune*, June 20, 2017, https://www.texastribune.org/2017/06/20/uttt-poll-few-texas-voters-believe-education-spending-too-high/.

32. Lyndsey Layton, "In New Orleans, Major School District Closes Traditional Public Schools for Good," *Washington Post*, May 28, 2014, https://www.washingtonpost.com/local/education/in-new-orleans-traditional-public-schools-close-for-good/2014/05/28/ae4f5724-e5de-11e3-8f90-73e071f3d637_story.html?noredirect=on&utm_term=.5c331cce40ff.

33. Brandon Formby, "Texas Lt. Governor Dan Patrick Wants to Change School Architecture to Prevent Mass Shootings. Experts Say That's Already Happened," *Texas Tribune*, May 24, 2018, https://www.texastribune.org/2018/05/24/mass-shootings-influenced-school-architecture-long-lt-gov-dan-patrick-/.

34. Emma Platoff and Brandon Formby, "Gov. Greg Abbott Announces School Safety Plan and Proposed Changes to Gun Laws after Santa Fe Shooting," *Texas Tribune*, May 30, 2018, https://www.texastribune.org/2018/05/30/texas-gov-greg-abbott-santa-fe-

shooting-school-safety-plan-gun-laws/.

35. Emma Platoff, "After Santa Fe, 54 percent of Texas Parents Support Arming Teachers, Poll Says," *Texas Tribune*, May 31, 2018, https://www.texastribune.org/2018/05/31/santa-fe-texas-voters-gun-control-armed-teachers/.

36. Jay Mathews, "Caveat Lector: Unexamined Assumptions about Quality in Higher Education," in *Declining by Degrees: Higher Education at Risk*, ed. Richard H. Hersh and John Merrow (New York: MacMillan/Palgrave, 2005), 48.

37. Financial Statements and Independent Auditors' Reports, "Permanent University Funds, Years Ended August 31, 2017 and 2016," accessed July 25, 2018, https://www.utimco.org/Funds/Endowment/PUF/PUF2017AuditedFinancials.pdf.

38. Hobby and Tiede, *How Things Really Work*, 124.

39. Charles Miller, "Why Student Regents Shouldn't Vote," *Texas Tribune*, May 13, 2010, www.texastribune.org/texas-education/higher-education/why-student-regents-shouldnt-vote.

40. Alexa Garcia-Ditta, "Student Regents Have a Voice but No Vote," *Texas Tribune*, May 12, 2010, www.texastribune.org/texas-education/higher-education/student-regents-have-a-voice-but-no-vote.

41. ACT, "The Condition of College and Career Readiness, 2017," accessed July 25, 2018, https://www.act.org/content/dam/act/unsecured/documents/cccr2017/CCCR_National_2017.pdf.

42. Legislative Budget Board, "State Budget by Program: 85th Regular Session," accessed July 31, 2018, http://sbp.lbb.state.tx.us/.

43. Legislative Budget Board, "Financing Public Higher Education in Texas: Legislative Primer," August 2016, http://www.lbb.state.tx.us/Documents/Publications/Primer/3148_Financing_Public_Higher_Ed_Texas_Aug_2016.pdf.

44. Matthew Watkins, "Texas Colleges Fret about $1 Billion in Expected Funding Missing from Budget Plan," accessed July 31, 2018, https://www.texastribune.org/2017/01/24/universities-worry-about-1-billion-worth-funds-exc/.

45. Texas Higher Education Coordinating Board, "Closing the Gaps Final Progress Report," June 2015, http://www.thecb.state.tx.us/reports/PDF/7980.PDF?CFID=50802435%26CFTOKEN=83831896.

46. Texas Higher Education Coordinating Board, "Texas Public Higher Education Almanac, 2018," Spring 2018. http://www.thecb.state.tx.us/reports/PDF/10900.PDF?CFID=76876980&CFTOKEN=67679196.

47. 78 F.3d 932 (5th Cir. 1996).

48. *Fisher v. University of Texas at Austin*, amicus brief, accessed July 25, 2017, http://chronicle.com/blogs/players/files/2012/08/coaches-amicus.pdf.

49. Peter Schmidt, "Supreme Court Is Flooded with Briefs Defending Race-Conscious Admissions," *Chronicle of Higher Education*, August 14, 2012, https://chronicle.com/article/Supreme-Court-Is-Flooded-With/133625.

50. 579 U.S. ___ (2016).

51. Matthew Watkins, "Lt. Gov. Patrick Slams Universities for Tuition Increases," *Texas Tribune*, April 26, 2016, https://www.texastribune.org/2016/04/26/lt-gov-patrick-excoriates-universities-tuition-inc/.

52. Hobby and Tiede, *How Things Really Work*.

53. Patrick Svitek, "Abbott Initiative Lures 10 Top Researchers to Texas," *Texas Tribune*, July 14, 2016, https://www.texastribune.org/2016/07/14/abbott-initiative-lures-10-top-researchers-texas.

54. David Muto, "The Brief: Top Texas News for June 19, 2012," *Texas Tribune*, June 19, 2012, www.texastribune.org/texas-newspaper/texas-news/brief-top-texas-news-june-19-2012/.

55. Texas Comptroller of Public Accounts, "Texas Comptroller's Office Releases Health Care Spending Report," January 31, 2017, https://comptroller.texas.gov/about/media-center/news/2017/170131-health-care-spending.php.

56. U.S. Census Bureau, "QuickFacts: Texas; United States," https://www.census.gov/quickfacts/fact/table/tx,US/PST045217.

57. Texas Health and Human Services Commission, "TANF Statistics," accessed July 26, 2018, https://hhs.texas.gov/about-hhs/records-statistics/data-statistics/temporary-assistance-needy-families-tanf-statistics.

58. Texas Department of Health and Human Services, "SNAP Statistics," accessed July 26, 2018, https://hhs.texas.gov/about-hhs/records-statistics/data-statistics/supplemental-nutritional-assistance-program-snap-statistics.

59. U.S. Census Bureau, "Table 6. Percentage of People Without Health Insurance Coverage by State: 2013–2016," accessed July 26, 2018, https://www.census.gov/library/publications/2017/demo/p60-260.html.

60. Texas Health and Human Services Commission, "Texas Medicaid and CHIP Monthly Full Benefit Caseload by Risk Group," accessed July 26, 2018, https://hhs.texas.gov/about-hhs/records-statistics/data-statistics/healthcare-statistics.

61. Ibid.

62. Center for Medicare and Medicaid Services, "Monthly Enrollment by State: 2018-07," accessed July 26, 2018, https://www.cms.gov/Research-Statistics-Data-and-Systems/Statistics-Trends-and-Reports/MCRAdvPartDEnrolData/Monthly-Enrollment-by-State.html.

63. Julian Aguilar, "Lawmaker Wants to Know Immigration Impact," *Texas Tribune*, March 6, 2015, https://www.texastribune.org/2015/03/06/bill-would-require-annual-report-immigration.

64. Isabel C. Morales and Al Dia, "Swift Plant Raid Devastated Cactus," *Dallas Morning News*, February 11, 2007.

65. 457 U.S. 202 (1982).

66. Ibid.

67. Katherine Leal Unmuth, "Tyler Case Opened Schools to Illegal Migrants," *Dallas Morning News*, June 11, 2007.

68. Texas Higher Education Coordinating Board, "Overview: Eligibility for In-State Tuition and State Financial Aid Programs," June 2018, http://www.thecb.state.tx.us/reports/PDF/9054.PDF?CFID=75314517&CFTOKEN=13839274.

69. Matthew Watkins, "The Winners and Losers of the 85th Session of the Texas Legislature," *Texas Tribune*, May 31, 2017, https://www.texastribune.org/2017/05/31/winners-and-losers-85th-session-texas-legislature/.

70. Lori Robertson, "Fact Check: Did the Obama Administration Separate Families?," *USA Today*, June 23, 2018, https://www.usatoday.com/story/news/politics/2018/06/23/trump-obama-administration-separate-families-immigration/728060002/.

71. Alexa Ura, "Texas Reaches Agreement with Families in Birth Certificate Case," *Texas Tribune*, July 25, 2016, https://www.texastribune.org/2016/07/25/texas-agrees-to-resolve-birth-certificate-case.

72. "Texas Monday Talks: Dick Armey," *Texas Monthly*, January 2007, 66.

73. Chris Tomlinson, "Poll: Hispanics in Texas More Likely to Favor GOP than the Rest of the Nation," *Austin American-Statesman*, February 7, 2014, www.statesman.com/news/news/state-regional-govt-politics/poll-hispanics-in-texas-more-likely-to-favor-gop-t/ndHM2.

74. Emma Platoff, "At Prison Reform Meeting, Trump Praises Texas' 'Very Successful' DACA Challenge, *Texas Tribune*, August 9, 2018, https://www.texastribune.org/2018/08/09/trump-praise-texas-daca-lawsuit-dreamers/.

75. Julian Aguilar, "Critics of Texas's 'Sanctuary Cities' Law Ask Federal Appeals Court to Reconsider Case," *Texas Tribune*, March 28, 2018, https://www.texastribune.org/2018/03/28/critics-texas-sanctuary-cities-law-ask-federal-appeals-court-reconside/.

76. Michael Miller, "'They Just Took Them?' Frantic Parents Separated from Their Kids Fill Courts on the Border," *Washington Post*, June 10, 2018, https://www.washingtonpost.com/local/they-just-took-them-frantic-parents-separated-from-their-kids-fill-courts-on-the-border/2018/06/09/e3f5170c-6aa9-11e8-bea7-c8eb28bc52b1_story.html?noredirect=on&utm_term=.4520a9e9f396.

77. John Burnett, "Big Money as Private Immigrant Jail Booms," NPR, *Morning Edition*, November 21, 2017, https://www.npr.org/2017/11/21/565318778/big-money-as-private-immigrant-jails-boom.

78. Emma Platoff, "A Facility to House Immigrant Children Is Planned for Houston, City Officials Don't Want It," *Texas Tribune*, June 19, 2018, https://www.texastribune.org/2018/06/19/houston-southwest-key-undocumented-separated-children-immigration/.

GLOSSARY

ad valorem tax: a tax based on property value, which is subject to periodic appraisals

administrative federalism: the process whereby the national government sets policy guidelines then expects state governments to pay for the programs they engender without the aid of federal monies

advanced or early voting: a voting system that allows a voter to cast a ballot before an election without giving a specific reason, thus making voting more convenient for the voter

affirm: appellate court upholds the lower court's decision

agenda setting: the stage in which various actors attempt to prioritize the problems facing the state

allocation: the process by which party rules designate how many of the state's delegates to the national party convention will be pledged to vote for a specific candidate or will attend as undecided

amendment: a formal change to a bill made during the committee process or during floor debate in front of the whole chamber

annexation: a process whereby areas adjacent to a city are added to the city, thereby extending the city limits

appellate jurisdiction: the authority to hear an appeal from a lower court that has already rendered a decision; an appellate court reviews the court record

from the original trial and does not hear new evidence

appointed regulatory commission: an agency of the state government whose members oversee a specific department of state government, are appointed by the governor, and are confirmed by the Texas Senate

appointment power: the ability to determine who will occupy key positions within the bureaucracy

appraisal: the official estimate of a property's value

apprenticeship laws: laws that allowed minors to be forced into contracts with unpaid labor

Astroturf lobbying: a simulation of grassroots support, usually conducted by specialized lobbying firms

at-large election: an election in which a city or county is treated as a single district and candidates are elected from the entire district as a whole

attorney general: chief legal adviser for the state who represents the state in courts and issues advisory opinions on legal matters to the governor, legislature, and other state agencies

auditor: a county officer appointed by the district judge to oversee county finances

beyond a reasonable doubt: the standard burden of proof

necessary to find a defendant guilty in a criminal trial; the defendant is presumed innocent

bicameral: a legislature that consists of two separate chambers or houses

bill: a proposed new law or change to existing law brought before a legislative chamber by a legislative member

black codes: laws passed by southern states to limit the freedom of African Americans after the Civil War; these laws affected every part of the lives of African Americans, regulating everything from whom they could marry to the conditions under which they could work, attend school, and even vote

blanket or wide-open primary: a primary in which voters do not register party affiliations and receive ballot papers containing the names of all candidates from all political parties running for office; usually voters may choose only one candidate per office rather than one candidate per political party

block grant: national funds given to state and local governments for a broad purpose; comes with fewer restrictions on how the money is spent

blocking bill: a bill regularly introduced in the Texas Senate to serve as a placeholder at the top of the Senate calendar; sometimes called a stopper

budget power: the executive's ability to exert influence on the state's budget process

bureaucracy: a method of organizing any large public or private organization that includes hierarchical structure, division of labor, standard operating procedures, and advancement by merit

calendar: list of bills and resolutions that are eligible for consideration by the chamber

capital punishment: also known as the death penalty; refers to when the state puts an individual to death for certain crimes

casework: the process of solving problems for constituents

castle doctrine: Texas law that allows the use of deadly force to defend your home, or "castle"

categorical grant: national money given to states and local governments that must be spent for specific activities

ceremonial duties: appearances made by the governor as the most visible state officeholder that can function as a source of power; includes appearances at events and the participation in formal functions

Children's Health Insurance Program (CHIP): a federal-state program that offers health insurance and medical care to the children of families that make too much to qualify for Medicaid but not enough to afford private health insurance

chronic minority: a group that rarely wins elections or achieves majority status and thus sees few reasons to become actively engaged in politics

chubbing: the act of delaying action on the current bill before the Texas House of Representatives to prevent action on an upcoming bill

citizen legislature: a legislature that attempts to keep the role of a state legislator to a part-time function so that many or most citizens can perform it; normally, a citizen legislator is provided

minimal compensation, offered few staffing resources, and has short or infrequent legislative sessions

city charter: a plan of government that details the structure and function of the city government; similar to a constitution

civil case: a case in which an aggrieved party sues for damages claiming that he or she has been wronged by another individual

civil defendant: the party alleged to have committed the wrong at issue in a civil suit

closed primary: an electoral contest restricted to party loyalists that excludes supporters of other political parties and independent voters

collective goods: benefits that, once provided, go to everyone and cannot be effectively denied to others, even those who did not contribute to the effort

commissioner of the General Land Office: this office administers state-owned lands, controls the Permanent School Fund (PSF), and controls leases for the development of mineral and other resources on public lands; the office is sometimes called the land commissioner

commissioners court: the governing body for Texas counties, consisting of four elected commissioners and the judge from the county constitutional court

committee: a formally organized group of legislators that assists the legislature in accomplishing its work, allowing a division of labor and an in-depth review of an issue or a bill before review by the entire chamber

compensatory damages: monetary damages designed to compensate the injured party

comptroller of public accounts: collects fees and taxes, invests state funds, estimates revenue,

and oversees payments by the state for goods and services

concurrent jurisdiction: a system in which different levels of courts have overlapping jurisdiction or authority to try the same type of case

concurrent powers: powers that are shared by the national government and the state governments

concurrent resolution: a legislative act that expresses an opinion of the legislature; must pass in both houses

concurring opinion: an opinion written by a justice who agrees with the decision but not with the reasoning of the court

confederal system: a type of government in which the lower units of government retain decision-making authority

conference committee: an official legislative work group that meets on a limited basis to reconcile the different versions of a bill that has passed in the Texas House and Senate

constable: an elected county officer who acts as a judicial officer for minor criminal and civil cases; assists the justice of the peace (JP) with his or her duties

constitution: a written document that outlines the powers of government and the limitations on those powers

contract outsourcing: a process whereby a government entity contracts with a private company to perform a service that governments traditionally provide, such as a contract to collect trash and garbage

conventions (caucuses): meetings at which party members participate in a range of party business

cooperative federalism: the theory of federalism that suggests that both levels of government cooperate within specific policy areas rather than maintaining distinct policy arenas

county attorney: the county official who represents the county in legal activities and offers legal advice to the county government

county civil service commission: the agency administering the county's civil service system; develops job definitions, qualification processes, employee classifications, and other aspects of the system

county clerk: the elected county official who maintains county records and in some counties oversees elections

county or senatorial district convention: a convention in which delegates to the statewide convention are selected; held on the third Saturday after the primary election

credit claiming: the advantage derived from incumbents' ability to point to positive outcomes for which they are responsible

criminal case: a case in which an individual is charged by the state with violating the law and the state brings the suit

criminal defendant: a person charged with committing a crime

crisis manager: the responsibility to act as a policymaker, coordinator of resources, and point person in the wake of natural and man-made disaster

cross-filing: a system that allows a candidate to run simultaneously as a Democratic and a Republican candidate, essentially competing in both parties' primaries

cumulative voting: a system that allows voters to take the total number of positions to be selected in a district and concentrate their votes among one or a few candidates

dark money: money spent on political activities by a nonprofit organization that does not have to report its sources of funding

de novo: to hear an appeal with a new trial in the absence of an official case record

delegate: an elected official who acts as an agent of the majority that elected her or him to office and carries out, to the extent possible, the wishes of that majority

devolution: returning power to state governments

Dillon's Rule: the principle that, regardless of the type of local government, all local governments are creatures of the state government and have only those powers specifically granted to them by the state

direct primary: a primary election in which the winning candidate directly receives the party nomination

disclosure: the reporting of who contributes money to a campaign and how much is contributed by an individual or corporation

dissenting opinion: an opinion written by a justice who disagrees with the decision of the court

distributive policy: moves benefits to meet the needs of citizens but does so without targeting any one group as the source of money

disturbance theory: a theory of group formation that states that as societies become more complex and more diverse, new interests emerge to voice their concerns, prompting established interests to mobilize to protect the status quo

dual federalism: the theory of federalism that suggests that state governments and the national government have separate spheres of policy influence and restrict their involvement to policies in their areas

Education Reform Act: a 1984 statute that requires teachers and school administrators to take a test to assure basic competency before being recertified; students are also tested periodically to monitor progress and are required to pass an exam before being allowed to graduate

elected board: a directly elected board, such as the Railroad Commission of Texas, that oversees a specific department of Texas government

electioneering: method used by organized interests to try to shape public policy by influencing who is elected to office, especially by serving as sources of campaign funding

electoral competition model: the view that parties make a pragmatic move to the center of the political spectrum as they attempt to win votes, sacrificing the more purely ideological positions

emergency clause: language that makes a bill effective immediately upon being signed into law rather than subject to the customary ninety-day waiting period

emergency legislation: a designation by the governor that allows the governor to prioritize legislation; legislation designated as an emergency can be voted on during the first sixty days of the session

eminent domain: the power of the government to take private property for public use, generally for public functions, such as roads

empresario: an entrepreneur who made money colonizing areas of the Mexican territories

en banc: an appeal that is heard by the entire court of appeals rather than by a select panel of judges

enhanced penalties: a penal code provision that specifies conditions under which the accused can be charged with a higher-degree offense

entitlement programs: programs funded by taxpayers who contribute to it for a set amount of time; at retirement, the payer receives back their contributions plus a cost-of-living adjustment

enumerated powers: the powers such as those listed in Article 1, Section 8 of the U.S. Constitution that are expressly granted to the national government

equal protection clause: clause of the Fourteenth Amendment to the U.S. Constitution requiring that state laws and state constitutions treat all citizens the same

Every Student Succeeds Act (ESSA): the federal education act that replaced No Child Left Behind and reduced federal government emphasis on mandatory testing to track student progress and evaluate schools based on that progress; states have more freedom under ESSA to develop assessment plans unique to their state

excise tax: a tax paid at the time of purchase, with the cost of the tax included in the price of the product

exclusive jurisdiction: a particular court given the sole right to hear a specific type of case

executive committee: this group, selected at the state party convention, carries on the activities of the party between party conventions; by law, the committee consists of sixty-two members—one man and one woman from each of the state's thirty-one senatorial districts

executive order: an order issued by the governor to direct existing agencies or create new committees or task forces in order to address a particular policy area

expressive benefits: benefits that arise from taking action to express one's views; motivates group membership

extradition: the constitutional requirement that a state deliver someone suspected or convicted of a crime in another state back to the state where the crime allegedly occurred so the accused can face trial or sentencing

federalism: a form of government based on the sharing of powers between the levels of government; in the United States, between the national and state governments

filibuster: an effort to kill a bill by engaging in unlimited debate and refusing to yield the floor to another member, ultimately preventing a vote on the bill

fiscal federalism: use of national financial incentives to encourage policies at the state or local level

fiscal note: a required document outlining the probable costs of the legislation

fiscal policy: how government seeks to influence the economy through taxing and spending

floor debate: period during which a bill is brought up before the entire chamber for debate

floor leader: a party member who reminds legislators of the party's position on a bill and encourages members to vote with the rest of the party caucus; the floor leader is assisted by one or more deputy floor leaders

foreign direct investment (FDI): a measure of businesses' commitment to invest in or own businesses in another country

fracking: fracturing underground rock formations and using high-pressure injections of chemicals and water to cause natural gas to rise to the surface

franchise tax: the primary tax on businesses in Texas, which is based on the taxable margin of each company

free-rider problem: occurs when citizens who do not contribute to the efforts of a group nevertheless enjoy the results of those efforts

full faith and credit clause: the constitutional requirement that court judgments or legal contracts entered into in one state will be honored by all other states

general election: an interparty election in which candidates from two or more political parties and independent candidates compete for actual political office

general law city: the default organization for Texas cities, with the exact forms of government, ordinance powers, and other aspects of city government specified in the Texas Local Government Code

general sales tax: an across-the-board tax imposed on goods and services sold within a jurisdiction

gerrymandering: the practice of politicians creating oddly shaped electoral districts to maximize their political advantage in an upcoming election

Good Roads Amendment: state constitutional requirement that 75 percent of road-user fees be spent on building and maintaining roads and the remaining 25 percent be used for education

grand jury: a panel of twelve jurors that reviews evidence, determines whether there is sufficient evidence to bring a trial, and either issues an indictment or returns no bill

grandfather clause: the granting of voting rights only to those citizens whose grandfathers had the right to vote; used to bar African Americans from voting in the South after the end of Reconstruction; used in other southern states but not used in Texas

grassroots lobbying: attempts by organized interests to influence legislators through public opinion; extension of democratic principles in which groups of citizens spontaneously mobilize to build support for a cause

grassroots organization: a group in which power and decision making reside with average citizens; the participation of average citizens is the foundation upon which these groups' legitimacy rests

grasstop lobbying: the attempt to influence legislators through key constituents or friends

Help America Vote Act (HAVA): a federal statute enacted after the 2000 presidential election to effectively standardize election procedures

home rule city: a city that has been granted greater freedom in the organization and functioning of city government; it can make structural and administrative changes without seeking permission from the state

horizontal federalism: refers to the relationship between the states

hyperpluralism: a view that the system today has evolved beyond simple pluralism and is now one in which many narrow interests are represented, often at the expense of the broader public interest

ideological caucus: a special legislative caucus in the state legislature that promotes an ideological agenda

impeachment: formal procedure to indict and remove an elected official from office for misdeeds

implied powers: powers beyond those enumerated in the Constitution; implied powers are powers deemed "necessary and proper" to execute the enumerated powers of the national government

incapacitation: an approach to criminal justice that emphasizes removing the guilty from society to prevent new or additional crime

incarceration rate: a calculation of how many prisoners a state has per 100,000 people, which controls for population size

income tax: a tax calculated as a percentage of income earned in a year

incumbency advantage: the advantage enjoyed by the incumbent candidate, or current officeholder, in elections; the advantage is based on greater visibility, a proven record of public service, and often better access to resources

incumbent: the current officeholder

independent candidate: a candidate running for office

without a political party affiliation

independent political expenditures: spending on behalf of a candidate that is done without coordination with the candidate or his or her campaign

indictment: a document (in the form of a true bill) issued by a grand jury that indicates there is enough evidence to warrant a trial

indigent defense: the requirement that governments provide legal counsel to those charged with serious crimes who cannot afford representation

individualistic political culture: the idea that individuals are best left largely free of the intervention of community forces such as government and that government should attempt only those things demanded by the people it is created to serve

informal powers: powers based on factors other than those enumerated in the constitution

initiative: a mechanism that allows voters to gather signatures on a petition in order to place statutes or constitutional amendments on a ballot

instant runoff: a type of election in which second-place votes are considered in instances where no candidate has received a majority of the vote; a winner is determined by adding together the first- and second-place votes

intergovernmental lobby: the lobbying that occurs between different levels of government, such as between the state and national government or between local governments and the state government

introduce (a bill): to officially bring a bill before a legislative chamber for the first time; this first official step in the formal legislative process is reserved for members of the legislature

issue caucus: a special legislative caucus in the state legislature that

promotes bipartisan and cross-chamber support for policies and bills advocating positions inside a relatively narrow range of policy areas or political issues

joint resolution: a legislative act whose approval by both chambers results in amendment to the Texas Constitution; an amendment must be approved by voters at the next election

judicial federalism: a system in which judicial authority is shared between levels of government

jurisdiction: the court's sphere of authority

just deserts: an approach to criminal justice in which the purpose of the criminal justice system is to enact punishment fitting for the crime

justice of the peace (JP): an elected county officer who acts as a judicial officer for minor criminal and civil cases

killer amendment: language added to a bill on an unrelated or controversial topic in order to make the bill unacceptable to the majority of the legislature, which will then be more likely to vote against it

labor unions: organizations that represent the interests of working people seeking better pay and better working conditions

Legislative Budget Board (LBB): the group that develops a proposed state budget for legislative consideration

legislative immunity: the protection from arrest that legislators receive to ensure that state and local officials cannot interfere with a legislator's efforts to represent their constituents

Legislative Redistricting Board (LRB): created by a 1948 amendment to the Texas Constitution, this group steps in if the state legislature is unable to pass a redistricting plan or when a state or federal court invalidates a plan submitted by the legislature; the LRB is active only with respect to redistricting of the state legislature

lieutenant governor: the presiding officer of the Texas Senate, elected directly by the voters; also serves as a member of the Texas executive branch and assumes the duties of the governor when the governor is out of state, dies in office, resigns from office, or is impeached

line-item veto: the ability of the executive to selectively veto only some parts of a bill; in Texas, available only on spending bills

literacy test: a test of a prospective voter's ability to read and understand aspects of American government; used to bar African Americans from voting in many parts of the post-Reconstruction South but not used in Texas

lobbying: direct contact with members of the legislative or executive branch to influence legislation or administrative action

long ballot: the result of a system in which almost all the positions in a state are elected rather than appointed

loser pay law: Texas law that requires litigants to pay those they sued if they lose their lawsuits in certain cases

machine politics: a system of patronage whereby political organizations, led by a local party boss, disperse city jobs, government contracts, and other benefits to maintain control of city governance; power, once acquired, is typically used for personal gain

magistrate functions: the authority to conduct the preliminary procedures in criminal cases, including issuing search and arrest warrants, conducting preliminary hearings, and setting bail for more serious crimes

majority election: a type of election in which a candidate must receive 50 percent of the vote plus one additional vote to be declared the winner; simply

winning the most votes is not sufficient

majority opinion: the official decision and reasoning of the appellate court

majority-minority district: an election district in which the majority of the population comes from a racial or ethnic minority

Manifest Destiny: the belief that U.S. expansion across the North American continent was inevitable

markup: process whereby a committee goes line by line through a bill to make changes without formal amendments

Medicaid: a federal program providing medical coverage for low-income people and some elderly and disabled people

Medicare: a federal health insurance program available to senior citizens who have worked and paid into the Medicare system for ten or more years

merit-based civil service system: a system in which people receive government jobs based on a set of qualifications and formal training; job promotion and pay raises are based on job performance

minority and women's caucuses: special legislative caucuses in the state legislature that represent the unique concerns and beliefs of women and ethnic groups across a broad range of policy issues

moralistic political culture: rare in Texas, the view that the exercise of community pressure is sometimes necessary to advance the public good; it also holds that government can be a positive force and citizens have a duty to participate

Motor Voter Act: the National Voter Registration Act, which allows citizens to register to vote when applying for or renewing their driver's license

multimember district (MMD): an election system in which the state is divided into many

election districts but each district elects more than one person to the state legislature

municipal bond: a certificate of indebtedness issued by a city that serves as a pledge by the city to pay back the loan over time with interest; used to raise money for services and infrastructure; may also be issued by other forms of local government, such as counties, school districts, and special districts

municipal utility district (MUD): a special district that provides water, sewer, or similar services to individuals and businesses outside city limits

NAFTA: a trade agreement between the United States, Canada, and Mexico designed to eliminate barriers to trade and investment and decrease overall tariffs

name recognition: making a voting choice based on familiarity with or previous recognition of a candidate's name

negative externality: an unintended cost imposed on someone who did not participate in the economic transaction

nonpartisan or bipartisan independent commission: a system of drawing electoral district lines that attempts to remove politics from the process of redistricting

one person, one vote: shorthand term for the requirement of the U.S. Supreme Court that election districts be roughly equal in population

open primary: an electoral contest in which voters are not required to declare a party affiliation to participate but must request a specific party's ballot at the primary; voters are subsequently barred from participating in the other party's primary

ordinance: a law enacted by a city government

organized interest: an individual, group of people, or group of businesses that organizes its efforts to influence public policy

original jurisdiction: the authority to hear the initial case; the evidence and the case record are established in this court

oversight: the process whereby the legislature reviews policies and decisions of the executive branch to make sure the executive branch is following the intentions of the legislature

pardon: an executive grant of release from a sentence or punishment in a criminal case; in Texas, the governor can grant a pardon only upon the recommendation of the state's Board of Pardons and Paroles

partisan election: a type of election in which candidates' names and party affiliations appear on the ballot

party caucus chair: a party leader whose main job is to organize party members to vote for legislation on the floor

party legislative caucus: the organization of the members of a specific legislative chamber who belong to the same political party; normally shortened to *party caucus*

party machines: state or local party organizations that sustain their control over government by providing jobs, government contracts, and other favors to citizens in return for votes

party platform: the document that officially spells out the issue stands of a party; written and approved at the party conventions

party primary: an electoral contest to win a political party's nomination for the right to appear as its candidate on the ballot in the general election

party-line voting: process in which voters select candidates by their party affiliation

patronage: when an elected official rewards supporters with public jobs, appointments, and government contracts

patronage system: when individuals who supported a candidate for public office are rewarded with public jobs, appointments, and government contracts

"pay-as-you-go" system: a fiscal discipline, adopted by Texas and many other states, that requires a balanced budget and permits borrowing only under very few circumstances

peonage: laws that allowed debts to be paid with labor; debts were often "created" by arresting individuals for vagrancy

per curiam opinion: an opinion issued by the court as a whole; these opinions are not signed by individual justices

permanent party organizations: the party officials selected by the temporary organizations to conduct party business between the primaries, caucuses, and conventions

Permanent School Fund (PSF): a fund set aside to finance education in Texas; the state's largest source of investment income

Permanent University Fund (PUF): an endowment funded by mineral rights and other revenue generated by 2.1 million acres of land set aside by the state; investment returns support schools in the University of Texas (UT) and Texas A&M systems

petit jury: a trial jury; jurors attend a trial, listen to evidence, and determine whether a defendant is innocent or guilty

plaintiff: the party who is bringing a civil suit and claiming to have been wronged

plank: an individual issue position of the party platform

plural executive: an executive branch in which the functions have been divided among several, mostly elected, officeholders rather than residing in a single person, the governor

pluralist perspective: a view of politics that argues that democracy is best practiced when citizens participate through groups; a greater number of organized interests means wider participation and a healthier democracy

plurality election: a type of election in which the candidate with the most votes wins the election

policy: the actions and activities of government

policy adoption: the stage in which formal government action takes place

policy evaluation: the stage in which the implementation of a policy is examined to see if policy goals are being met

policy formation: the stage in which possible solutions are developed and debated

policy implementation: the stage in which the policy is carried out in state agencies

political action committee (PAC): the fund-raising arm of an interest group that has been organized to raise and spend money under state and federal campaign finance rules

political ambition ladder: the manner in which a political figure has come up through the ranks, working through various levels of state governmental offices and positions on the way to the top position; climbing several levels on the ladder can increase a politician's contacts, allies, and political savvy

political culture: the shared values and beliefs of citizens about the nature of the political world that give the public a common language as a foundation to discuss and debate ideas

political party: any group, however loosely

organized, seeking to elect governmental officeholders under a given label

politico: an elected official who is expected to follow the wishes of the electorate on some issues but on others is permitted more decision-making leeway; a hybrid of the trustee and delegate

poll tax: an annual tax that had to be paid before one was allowed to vote; used in Texas

popular mandate: the claim that an elected official's legislative agenda is the will of the people based on a high margin of victory in a general election

popular sovereignty: a government in which the power to govern is derived from the will of the people

position taking: an incumbent's advantage in having an existing record of positions on issues, both from previous elections and in the context of decisions made while in office

post-adjournment veto: a veto that occurs after the legislature has adjourned, leaving the legislature unable to overturn it

precinct chair; county chair: a precinct chair is selected by party members in each voting precinct by majority vote; a county chair is selected by countywide vote; these party officials are responsible for managing the local affairs of their party for the next two years

preference primary: a primary election in which voters indicate their choice to hold office but the actual selection is left to the political party elites

preponderance of evidence: the burden of proof in a civil case, which is lower than that in a criminal case; the plaintiff must show merely that the defendant is likely to have committed the wrong

president pro tempore: a presiding officer elected by the members of the Texas Senate; takes over when the lieutenant governor is unavailable

presidential republicanism: the practice in the South of voting for Republicans in presidential elections but voting for conservative Democrats in other races; this practice continued until animosity over Reconstruction faded and the Republicans demonstrated their electability in the South

primary election: intraparty election in which candidates compete to determine who will win the party's nomination in the general election

private financing: a system of campaign financing in which citizens, interest groups, labor unions, and corporations donate funds to cover the cost of elections for political parties or candidates

private prison: a private, for-profit prison corporation that staffs and runs prison facilities in a state

privatization: a process whereby a government entity sells off assets or services to a private company that is then responsible for providing a service; for example, a school district sells its buses to a private company and then allows the company to provide transportation to schools

privileges and immunities: the constitutional requirement that states may not fundamentally treat citizens of other states differently than their own citizens

probate: the process by which a deceased person's will is validated by the court, and can be legally executed

procedural standing committee: a type of standing committee that controls how the legislature functions

professional associations: organizations that represent the needs of professionals not represented by unions

professional legislature: a legislature that meets annually, often for nine months of the year

or more; a professional legislator is provided a professional-level salary and generous allowances to hire and keep support and research staffs

progressive tax: a graduated tax, such as an income tax, which taxes people with higher incomes at higher rates

property tax: a tax on the value of real estate that is paid by the property owner; used by county and local governments to fund such programs as public schools

prosecutor: a lawyer who represents the government and brings a case in criminal trials

public financing: a system of campaign financing in which the government covers the cost of elections for political parties or candidates

public interest groups: organizations that pursue noneconomic policies on behalf of the general public, even if all members of the general public do not agree on these issues or policies

public-private partnerships (PPPs): government infrastructure built by private companies for profit

punitive damages: larger monetary awards designed to punish the defendant and, perhaps, send a message to the larger society

quorum: the minimum number of members in a legislative body who need to be present for the body to conduct business: in the Texas Senate, a quorum is twenty-one members; in the Texas House of Representatives, a quorum is 100 members

recess appointment: a gubernatorial appointment made while the Texas Senate is not in session; requires Texas Senate approval within ten days of the next legislative session

recidivism: a former inmate's resumption of criminal activity after his or her release from prison

redistributive policy: moves benefits, usually in the form of money, from one group to another in an attempt to make society more equal

redistributive programs: programs funded by the U.S. government that transfer income from one group to another; states may add additional funding to these programs

redistricting: the periodic adjustment of the lines of electoral district boundaries

referendum: a mechanism that allows voters to cast a popular vote on statutes passed by the state legislature; the legislature can place measures on the ballot for voter consideration

regressive tax: a tax that takes a higher proportion of income from people with lower incomes than from people with higher incomes

regular session: meetings of a legislature that are required by a constitution or law; the Texas Legislature meets every other year for 140 days

regulation: government rulemaking and enforcement intended to protect citizens from being harmed by private firms

regulatory policy: attempts to limit or control the actions of individuals or corporations

rehabilitation: an approach to criminal justice that focuses on therapy or education to reform criminal behavior, including efforts addressing why the behavior was wrong and how to prevent recidivism

remand: appellate court sends the case back to the lower court to be reexamined

removal power: the power of the governor, with consent of the Texas Senate, to remove their appointees

representation: the relationship between an elected official and the electorate

reserved powers: the Tenth Amendment provision that all powers not delegated to the national government belong to the states

resolution: a legislative act that expresses the opinion of the legislature on an issue or changes the organizational structure of the legislature

responsible party model: the view that each party should hold firmly to a clear and consistent set of policies with a coherent ideology distinct from that of other parties in order to present voters with clear choices

restorative justice: an approach to criminal justice that sees crime as a break in society between the community, the perpetrator, and the victim and focuses on healing this break

retribution: an approach to criminal justice that emphasizes punishment because the guilty violated societal rules

reverse: appellate court rejects the lower court's decision

revolving door: the phenomenon of legislators and members of the executive branch moving easily from government office to lucrative positions with lobbying firms

rider: an addition to a bill that deals with an unrelated subject, such as changing some aspect of law or public policy or spending money or creating programs in a specific member's district

roll call vote: a form of voting for which a permanent record of each member's vote is created; used for more important votes

roll off: process in which voters mark off only the "more important" offices on a lengthy ballot—usually national or statewide offices—and leave the county or local office choices blank

rule of capture: Texas law that says property owners own the water below their property

runoff election: a type of election in a SMDM that is held when an election fails to yield a clear majority winner in the initial

balloting; the runoff is limited to the top two vote-getters from the initial election, ensuring a majority win

runoff primary: a primary that occurs if no nominee receives the required majority of the votes in the primary; the top two finishers face off in a second primary to determine the nominee for the general election

second-order elections: elections for offices below the national executive level in countries with presidential systems like the United States' or the national legislature level in parliamentary countries like Great Britain; generally viewed as less important in scope and impact on a country

secretary of state: this position is responsible for business licensing and regulation and also administrates and supervises elections; also serves as the chief protocol officer of Texas

select or special committee: a legislative work group created by the lieutenant governor or Speaker of the Texas House of Representatives for a specific purpose; called a joint committee when the lieutenant governor and Speaker create a select committee with members from both chambers

selective incentives: benefits exclusively available to members of an organization

senatorial courtesy: the informal requirement that a gubernatorial appointee have approval of her or his own state senator in order to obtain support within the Texas Senate

severance tax: a tax on natural resources charged when the resources are produced or "severed" from the earth

sheriff: the elected county official who oversees county law enforcement

simple resolution: a legislative act that addresses organizational issues; may be limited to a single house

sin tax: a tax on products or activities such as cigarettes or gambling that some legislators would like to discourage

single-issue interest groups: groups usually organized around one side of a single issue, such as pro-choice or anti-abortion groups

single-member district (SMD): an election system in which the state is divided into many election districts and each district elects just one person to the state legislature

solidarity benefits: the social interactions that individuals enjoy from joining a group and from working together for a common cause

Speaker of the House: the presiding officer of the Texas House of Representatives

special legislative caucus: an organization of members of the state legislature who share a common interest or have constituencies with a common interest

special session: meetings of a legislature that occur outside the regular legislative session; in Texas, special sessions are called by the governor and last for up to thirty days

standing committee: a permanent, chamber-specific formal work group that typically exists across sessions and across elections

state of the state address: the constitutional requirement that the governor address the state legislature about the condition of the state; the state of the state address occurs at the beginning of each legislative session and at the end of the governor's term

state party chair: individual selected at the state party convention to head the state executive committee; state law mandates that if the chair is a

man, a woman must be the vice chair, or vice versa

straight-ticket voting: the practice of selecting all the candidates for office who are running under a party label simply by checking off a single box marked with the party label

subsidence: loss of elevation over time that results when water districts pump groundwater and the affected area sinks

subsidies: incentives designed to encourage the production or purchase of certain goods to stimulate or support some businesses

substantive standing committee: a type of standing committee that is authorized to review and revise proposed policy bills and resolutions before action by the legislature

succession: a set order, usually spelled out in the constitution, denoting which officeholder takes over when the sitting governor resigns, dies, or is impeached

suffrage: the legal right to vote

sunset review process: a formal assessment of the effectiveness of all statutory boards, commissions, and state agencies

sunshine laws: laws designed to make government transparent and accessible

super PAC: an organized group that can raise and spend unlimited amounts of money as long as it does not coordinate with candidate campaigns

supermajority: a majority that is larger than a simple majority of 50 percent plus one; supermajorities include requirements of 60 percent, two-thirds, three-fourths, or 80 percent to make a decision

Supplemental Nutrition Assistance Program (SNAP): program that helps low-income seniors, people with disabilities,

single people, and families in need buy food from local retailers

supremacy clause: the section in the U.S. Constitution that guarantees that the national government is the supreme law of the land and that national laws and the national constitution supersede state laws and state constitutions

tax assessor: the elected county officer who collects county taxes and user fees

tax expenditures: any reductions in tax liabilities that result from tax benefits to particular taxpayers rather than taxpayers in general

Temporary Assistance for Needy Families (TANF): federal program that provides eligible households with monthly cash payments and Medicaid benefits

temporary party organizations: gatherings of ordinary party members, such as primaries, caucuses, and conventions

term limit: a legal limitation on the number of terms an elected official may serve in office

Texas Commission on Environmental Quality (TCEQ): the agency that oversees state environmental policy, including air and water quality

Texas Higher Education Coordinating Board (THECB): a group of nine people appointed by the governor for six-year terms to oversee higher education policy in Texas

tort: a wrongful act by a person that results in injury to another person or property in civil law

trade associations: organizations of similar businesses that work together to advance shared goals

traditionalistic political culture: the idea, most prevalent in the parts of Texas most like the Old South, that government has a limited role concerned with the preservation of the existing social order

Treaty of Guadalupe Hidalgo: signed February 2, 1848; this agreement between the United States and Mexico ended the Mexican-American War and recognized the Rio Grande as the boundary between Texas, now part of the United States, and Mexico

trustee: an elected official who is entrusted to act in the best interests of the electorate based on his or her knowledge; he or she is understood to be generally better informed than the broader electorate

turnover: when current officeholders step down from office and are replaced by new officeholders; turnover may result from retirement, defeat in an election, or term limits

unfunded mandate: legislation passed by the national government imposing requirements on state and local governments without providing the funds required to enact the legislation

unitary system: a type of government in which a central government holds all the power

vertical federalism: the distribution of power between the national government and state governments

veto power: the formal power of the executive to reject bills that have been passed by the legislature; in Texas, a veto can be overridden only by a two-thirds vote in both houses

voter turnout: the number of people casting ballots in a given election

Voting Rights Act of 1965: a federal statute that eliminated literacy tests as a qualification to vote, greatly increasing African Americans' access to the ballot box

white primary: the attempt by the Democratic Party in Texas and other southern states to limit the voting in party primaries only to party members; in Texas, this practice was codified in state law

zoning policy: policy whereby the city restricts what individuals and entities may do with their property, usually by designating certain areas of the city for industrial, commercial, or residential uses

INDEX

organized interests,
    324–325, 328–329
political parties, 295
reform era, 17, 18
transportation policy, 435–436
Agriculture commissioner,
    168–171
Aikin, A. M., 453
Air quality, 432–433
Alabama, 146, 166, 175
Alamo, battle of the, 51, 489
Alamo controversy, 154–156,
    172, 293
Alamo Hall of Honor, 32
Alamo Heights, 457
Alamo Trust, 155
Alaska
    gasoline tax, 394
    lack of secretary of state
        position, 173
    legislature type, 86
    lobbying regulations, 342
    redistricting commissions, 97
    sales tax, 394
    special legislative sessions, 85
    taxes, 395
    uninsured people, 477
Alcala, Elsa, 209
Alcoholic beverages, 360, 397
Alcohol prohibition, 18, 19, 295
Alice, 251, 296
Allen, Oscar K., 149
Allocation, delegate, 312,
    314–315
Allwright, Smith v. (1944), 254
Alternative energy. *See*
    Renewable energy
Alternative program provision, 329
Alvarado, 221
Amazon Prime, 283
Amendments, bill, 109–110,
    117, 120
Amendments, constitutional.
    See Constitutional
    amendments, Texas;
    Constitutional
    amendments, United States
American Association of Retired
    Persons (AARP), 326
American Cancer Society, 397
American Civil Liberties Union
    (ACLU), 325
American Family Association of
    Texas, 325
American Lung Association, 433
American nations, 24,
    25 (map), 26
American Party, 468

American Wind Energy
    Association, 430
Amusement parks, 3, 381
Andrews County, 434, 435
Angelina County, 55,
    310, 360
Anglos
    immigration, 51–52, 482
    myth of Anglo primacy, 34
    population, 28
    Republic of Texas population
        statistics, 11
    Texas Revolution, 9
    voter demographics, 246
Angola Prison, 228
Annexation by cities, 365, 374
Annexation of Texas, 53–54. *See
    also* Statehood
Ann Richards School for Young
    Women Leaders, 134
Antidrug policy, 224–225, 229
Anti-immigrant sentiment, 487
Antitrust law, 161, 424
Apaches, 6
Appeals and appellate courts
    constitutional county
        courts, 199
    courts of appeals, 203–204
    judicial federalism, 195
    municipal courts, 196
    See also specific courts
Apple, 417
Appointments and appointment
    power
    commissioners of
        education, 182
    committees, 114
    Constitution of 1845, 55
    Constitution of 1869, 58
    Constitution of 1876, 62
    executive power, 147
    governorship, 139, 141–143
    judges, 206–207, 212
    municipal judges, 196
    patronage system, 183–184
    Public Utility Commission
        of Texas, 182
    regulatory commissions, 182
    secretaries of state, 173
    standing committees, 108
    Texas Highway
        Commission, 440
    Texas Sunset Advisory
        Commission, 186
    university boards of
        regents, 469
Appraisal, property, 399–400
Apprenticeship laws, 63

Appropriations Committee,
    107, 111
Arizona, 95, 97–98, 100
Arizona Independent
    Redistricting
    Commission, 100
Arkansas, 97, 281, 382
Arkansas Democrat-Gazette, 281
Arlington, 381, 428, 442
Arlington State College, 381
Armey, Dick, 381, 487
Article 8, Texas Constitution, 408
Articles of Confederation, 41–42
Asche, Cindy, 292
Asian Americans, 29, 92,
    246, 257
Assessments, tax, 401
Assistant attorneys general, 162
Astroturf lobbying, 337
Atkins v. Virginia (2002),
    237, 238
At-large elections, 94, 209–210,
    365, 370, 371, 372
AT&T, 339, 452
Attorneys general
    Legislative Redistricting
        Board, 97
    plural executive, 161–163, 165
    succession, line of, 137
    Tejanos, 34
Auditors, 112, 361
Austin
    LGBT employment rights, 377
    mass transit, 442
    minimum wage, 399
    population, 29
    property taxes, 401
    sanctuary cities, 376
    subsidies for businesses, 417
    toll roads, 441
    wind energy, 430
Austin, Moses, 8
Austin, Stephen F.
    colonization plan, 8–9
    election campaigns, 10, 11
    history of change in
        Texas, 489
    immigration policy, 482
    lack of secretary of state
        position, 173
    language issues, 52
    personal debt, 55
    Seguín, Juan Nepomuceno,
        relationship with, 32
    taxes, 393
    Texas Rangers, 227
Australia, 259, 447
Austria, 83

Colorado, 97, 185, 229, 259, 263
Colquitt, Oscar B., 18, 280
Columbia, 11
Columbus, Christopher, 6
Comanches, 222
Combs, Susan, 157, 169
Commerce, 222
Commercial property valuation, 400, 401–402
Commercial use zoning, 373
Commissioner of the General Land Office, 154–156, 171–172, 282
Commissioners courts, 358–360, 384
Commission on Judicial Conduct, 207–208
Commissions. *See* Boards and commissions
Committee on Calendars, 107, 116–117
Committees
    conference committees, 112–113
    legislative process, 116–117, 123
    select and special committees, 113
    standing committees, 107–111
    statutory committees, 111–112
    tax-related bills, 121
Common Core standards, 463
Communitarian philosophy, 235
Community college districts, 384, 385, 466, 473
Community colleges, 473
Comparisons. *See* International comparisons; States and state comparisons
Compensation (salaries). *See* Salaries and compensation
Compensation for takings, 439
Compensatory damages, 216, 233–234
Comptroller of public accounts, 97, 166–168, 408, 410–411, 440
Compulsory education, 58, 65, 66
Concurrent jurisdiction, 196
Concurrent powers, 42
Concurrent resolutions, 116
Concurring opinion, 203
Confederacy, 13, 15, 41–42, 55–57, 356
Confederal system, 41–42
Conference committees, 105, 112–113, 113–114, 121
Connally, John, 22, 130, 132, 322

Connecticut, 64, 97, 394, 395
Conquistadores. *See* Spanish exploration and colonization
Conroe, 29
Conservation programs, 172
Conservatism and conservatives
    of governors, 135
    lotteries, 405, 406
    media, 283
    organized interests, 325
    special legislative caucuses, 106
    voter demographics, 248
Conservative Party, 297
Constitutional amendments, Texas
    direct democracy, 265
    governorship terms, 136
    lobbying, regulation of, 338
    Massachusetts *vs.* Texas, 72–73
    Permanent University Fund, 467
    process, 71, 74
    prohibitionism, 18, 19
    proposed and adopted, 1879–2017, 70 (figure)
    roads funding, 438, 439
    taxes, 401
    voter turnout, 76 (figure)
Constitutional amendments, United States, 15, 21. *See also* specific amendments
Constitutional conventions (national), 249
Constitutional conventions (state)
    Abbott's call for, 146
    Constitution of 1836, 53
    Constitution of 1866, 57
    Constitution of 1869, 58
    Constitution of 1876, 65
    Reconstruction era, 15–16
    Texas Revolution, 9–10
Constitutional county courts, 198–199, 202
Constitution, Connecticut, 64
Constitution, Massachusetts, 72–73
Constitution of 1836, 10, 52, 53–54
Constitution of 1845, 55–57, 393
Constitution of 1861, 57, 356
Constitution of 1866, 15–16
Constitution of 1869, 16, 58, 60, 252–253

Constitution of 1876. *See* Texas Constitution
Constitution of Coahuila y Tejas, 51
Constitution, Republic of Texas, 10, 11
Constitutions, state, 64, 72–73
Consular identification cards, 486, 487
Consultation (1832), 52
Consultation (1835), 9–10
Consumer issues, 15, 169, 170
Continental Airlines, 452
Contract labor, 63–64
Contract law, 216
Contract outsourcing, 362
Contributions, campaign. *See* Campaign finance
Controversies
    Affordable Care Act, 477–478, 480
    city government *vs.* state laws, 374–375
    curriculum guidelines, 454
    hazardous waste, 434
    land commissioner, 172
    oil and gas industry, 426–427
    Rainy Day Fund, 414
    subsidies to businesses, 416
    textbook language, 82
    zoning and planning policies, 372–373
Conventions, constitutional. *See* Constitutional conventions
Conventions, party
    local party organization, 311
    national conventions, 94, 134, 314–315
    state party conventions, 292–293, 311–312
Cook County, Illinois, 356
Cooperative federalism, 43, 353
Coppell, 441
Cornyn, John, 98
Coronado, Francisco Vázquez de, 27
Coroners, 198
Corporations. *See* Business
Corpus Christi, 34, 68, 332, 348, 442
Correct Care Solutions of California, 230
Corrections and correctional facilities
    death row, 241
    incarceration rate, 223–224

House of Commons (Canada), 113
House of Representatives,
  Texas. *See* Texas House of
  Representatives
House of Representatives,
  U.S. *See* U.S. House of
  Representatives
House Research
  Organization, 111
Housing, 350, 379–380, 382
Houston
  city government election
    system, 372
  Galveston Plan, 366
  Hurricane Harvey, 35,
    349, 350
  LGBT rights, 69, 378
  population, 29
  sanctuary cities, 376
  trade, 443–444
  transportation projects,
    175, 437, 442
  wind energy, 430
  zoning and planning
    policies, 373, 374
Houston Astros, 381
Houston City Council, 69
Houston Club, 280
Houston Community College, 385
Houston County, 365
Houston Equal Rights Ordinance
  (HERO), 377, 378
Houston Professional Fire
  Fighters Local, 327
Houston, Sam
  annexation of Texas, 54
  anti-slavery stance, 13,
    15, 56
  Austin, Stephen F.,
    appointment of, 173
  background, 2
  biography, 14
  elections, 11, 280
  Native American tribes,
    cooperation with, 406
  personality, 149
  political parties, 294
  Texas Revolution, 10–11, 32
  as U.S. senator, 12
Houston shipping channel,
  443–444
Hudson ISD, 386
HUF. *See* Higher Education
  Fund
Human services. *See* Social
  welfare
Humble Oil, 425
Humble, Texas, 374

Hunter-gatherers, 5, 6
Hurricane Harvey
  comptroller of public
    accounts, 168
  floods, 34–35, 433
  governor as crisis
    manager, 146
  land commissioner, role
    of the, 172
  local government, 348–350
  military mobilization after, 147
  nuclear power plants, 431
  Patrick, Dan, 161
  schools, impact on, 460
  Texas City ISD, 384
  zoning and planning
    policies, 373–374
  See also Natural and
    manmade disasters
Hurricane Katrina, 147
Hutchison, Kay Bailey, 193, 442
Hybrid city election systems, 372
Hybrid legislatures, 86, 87
Hydraulic fracturing. *See*
  Fracking
Hyperpluralism, 341, 343

ICE. *See* U.S. Immigration and
  Customs Enforcement
Idaho, 86, 95, 97, 230
Identification, immigrant,
  486, 487
Identification, party, 304, 305
  (figure), 319
Ideological caucuses, 106
Illegal immigrants. *See*
  Undocumented immigrants
Illinois, 86, 137, 481–482, 484
Immigrants and immigration
  policy
  birthright citizenship, 486–487
  border security programs, 486
  city ordinances, 376–377
  history, 2–3, 8–9, 482
  Paxton, Ken, 165
  population, 28, 32–33,
    34, 484
  Texas constitutions, 51–53
  undocumented immigrants,
    482–483, 485
  western Texas settlement, 17
Impeachment
  Ferguson, James E. "Pa," 18,
    135, 280, 466, 468
  governors, 138
  judges, 207
  Nixon, Richard, 94
  Smith, Henry, 10

succession, 137, 157
  Texas Constitution, 138
Implied powers, 42
Imports. *See* Trade
Incapacitation theory of justice, 223
Incarceration rates, 223–224, 224
  (map)
Income, per capita, 31, 475
Income tax, 62, 393, 395, 403
Incumbency advantage, 206, 207,
  279–280
Incumbents, 88, 89 (figure), 282
Independence movement. *See*
  Texas Revolution
Independent candidates, 276, 277
Independent Colleges and
  Universities of Texas, 328
Independent political
  expenditures, 331
Independent school districts,
  383–384, 386
Independent Texas. *See* Republic
  of Texas
India, 445, 447, 475
Indianola, 366
Indictments, 215
Indigent defense, 231
Indirect primaries, 261
Individualistic political culture,
  22, 39, 431, 465, 476
Individual responsibility, 232
Individual rights. *See* Civil rights
Industrial use zoning, 373
Informal gubernatorial powers,
  130, 148
Information technology, 175
Initiatives, ballot, 75, 265
In-N-Out Burger, 415
In re Gault (1967), 220
Instagram, 32
Instant runoffs, 264
Institute of Taxation and
  Economic Policy, 402
Institutional memory, 148
Insurance industry, 18
Integration, school. *See*
  Desegregation, school
Intellectual disability and the
  death penalty, 237
Interest groups. *See* Organized
  interests
Interest income, 405
Intergovernmental Affairs
  Committee, 108
Intergovernmental lobby, 328
Interim charges, 111, 113
Intermediate appellate courts,
  203–204

State constitutions, 64, 72–73
State Democratic Executive
Committee, 251
State government
K-12 education funding,
456–458
vs. local government, 39, 160,
355, 374–375, 386, 429
sanctuary cities, 376
See also States and state
comparisons;
specific entities
State Highway Fund, 414
Statehood, 11–12, 12–13,
55–57
State-level trial courts, 202–203
State lottery, 404–406
State of Texas Assessments
of Academic Readiness
(STAAR), 383–384,
459, 460
State of Texas, Hernandez v.
(1954), 68
State of the state address, 128, 143
State parties, 311–312, 316
State party chairs, 312
State Preservation Board, 339
State sales tax. *See* Sales tax
States and state comparisons
administrative federalism, 354
bicameral *vs.* unicameral
legislatures, 82
budget power, 142
cabinets, 159
charter schools, 464
comptroller of public
accounts, 166
constitutions, 64, 72–73
counties, numbers of, 356
court systems, 197
criminal justice
philosophy, 235
death penalty, 238, 240
diversity, 33
education, 383
expenditures, per capita, 418
fiscal federalism, 44, 46,
48, 353–354
government employees in
key sectors, 185
governors' salaries, 137
health care, 481–482
incarceration rates, 224
judicial selection, 212, 214
legislative session lengths, 84
legislatures, size of, 83–84
legislature typologies, 86–87
lobbying, 342

local governments, number
of, 353 (table)
marijuana policy, 229
minimum wage, 399
personality politics, 149
personal property taxes,
362–363
plural executive, 156
political party competition,
302–303 (figure)
poverty rates, 475
prefiling of bills, 115
presidential primaries, 314
primaries and caucuses,
317–318
privatization of prisons, 228
redistricting, 97, 100
sales tax, 396 (map)
same-sex marriage, 48–49
secretaries of state, 173
special sessions, 144
taxes, 394, 395, 403 (map)
trade, 444
transportation boards and
commissions, 178
unicameral *vs.* bicameral
legislatures, 105
uninsured people, 480 (map)
voter registration, 249–250
voting methods, 262
women in legislatures,
96 (figure)
State spending, 412–413, 412
(figure), 414, 418
States' rights, 38–39, 146. *See also*
Federalism
States *vs.* nations, 24, 25 (map)
State taxes, 393–398, 400 (table),
403 (map)
State treasurers, 166
Statutory boards and
commissions. *See* Boards
and commissions
Statutory committees, 111–112
Statutory courts, 202
Steinbeck, John, 5, 22
Sterling, Ross, 21, 227
Stevenson, Coke, 251, 296
Stimulus program, federal, 48,
404, 442
Stopper bills. *See* Blocking bills
Straight-ticket voting, 193, 205,
266, 304
Straus, Joe
"bathroom bill," 81
censureship of, 312
interim charges, 111
interim committees, 113

standing committee
assignments, 108
Texas Republican convention,
2018, 292
transgender bathroom
issue, 160
Strayhorn, Carole, 167, 281,
408, 410
Strong mayor city governments,
365, 366–367, 368 (figure)
Structure
county government,
358–361, 359 (figure)
legislature, 51, 80, 82–83, 105
local courts, 200, 201
Student financial aid, 470, 473
Student regents, 469
Students for Academic Choice
(SAC), 335
Suazo, Miguel, 155, 172
Subcommittees, 111, 116
Subsidence, 433
Subsidies
for businesses, 415–417, 419
fiscal policy, 393
health insurance, 481
oil and gas industry, 424
tax expenditures, 414–415
Substantive standing
committees, 107
Succession, 137
Suffrage. *See* Voting rights
Sugar Land, 98, 451
Suicide, inmate, 230
Sullivan, Michael Quinn,
335, 342
Sunset Advisory Commission,
180, 186, 207
Sunset review process, 186, 187
(figure), 188
Sunshine laws, 186
Super Bowl, 416
Superdelegates, 314
Supermajority of legislators, 85
Super PACs, 333
"Super Tuesday," 314, 315
Supplemental Nutrition
Assistance Program
(SNAP), 475, 476–477
Supremacy clause, 43, 44
Supreme Court. *See* Iowa
Supreme Court; Kansas
Supreme Court; Texas
Supreme Court; U.S.
Supreme Court
Sweatt, Heman Marion, 471
Sweatt v. Painter (1950), 66, 471
Sweden, 447

rights of the accused, 231
takings, 439
voting rights, 252, 254, 260
women's suffrage, 259
U.S. Department of Education,
160, 354, 461
U.S. Department of Energy, 427
U.S. Department of Housing
and Urban Development,
348, 350
U.S. Department of Justice, 160,
230, 256, 259
U.S. Department of Labor, 163
U.S. Department of the
Treasury, 213
U.S. District Court for the Eastern
District in Tyler, 456
U.S. District Court for the Western
District of Texas, 376
U.S. District Court, Tyler, 67
U.S. Drug Enforcement Agency, 224
U.S. Environmental Protection
Agency, 429, 432
Use tax. *See* Sales tax
U.S. Fifth Circuit Court of
Appeals
abortion, 47
death penalty, 221–222, 240
prison conditions, 228
sanctuary cities, 376, 487
voting rights, 258, 259
U.S. Geological Survey, 433
U.S. government
cabinets, 157
disaster response and
relief, 348, 350
sanctuary cities, 376, 377
state government
lobbying of, 328
Texas Department of
Transportation,
relationship with
the, 177–178
See also Federalism
U.S. House of Representatives
first Texas delegation,
12–13
former Texas legislators, 123
Jordan, Barbara C., 94
redistricting for seats in
the, 98, 99–100
Tejanos in the, 34
U.S. Immigration and Customs
Enforcement (ICE), 376
U.S. Senate, 21, 251, 297
U.S. Supreme Court
abortion rights, 47
Affordable Care Act, 481

campaign finance cases,
284–285, 308
death penalty, 236,
237, 238, 240
education of immigrants, 485
elections, oversight of, 249
fiscal federalism, 46
higher education diversity,
471, 472
implied powers, 42
judicial federalism, 194
juvenile offenders treated
as adults, 220
LGBT rights, 68–69
mental capacity cases, 221
nonpartisan blanket
primaries, 262
race/ethnicity of jury
members, 68
redistricting cases,
98–99, 100–101
representation cases,
83, 94, 96–97
same-sex marriage, 48
school desegregation,
66–67, 353
vertical federalism, 43
voting rights, 256, 257
Utah, 86
Utilities. *See* Energy

Valdez, Lupe, 376
Valeo, Buckley v. (1976), 284
Valero, 401–402
Validity of elections, 283
Value added taxes, 395
Van de Putte, Leticia, 158,
247, 281
Vandergriff, Tommy Joe, 381
Vehicle registration tax, 438
Velocity television network, 283
Verdicts, 216
Vermont, 33, 48, 86, 95, 97
Vertical federalism, 43
Veterans courts, 195, 225
Veterans Land Board, 171
Veto power
Abbott, Greg, 148
advisory opinions, 165
budgets, 407
comptroller of public
accounts, 168
Constitution of 1866, 57
Constitution of 1869, 58
governors, 121, 142–143,
144–145, 150
Victims of crime, 231, 232
Victoria, 348

Vinson, Robert, 468
Violence, 225, 228, 253, 255–256
Virginia, 82, 238, 254, 484
Virginia, Atkins v. (2002), 237, 238
*Virginia State Board of Elections,
Virginia v.* (1966), 254
Vitter, David, 268
Voice votes, 120–121
Volatile organic compounds, 427
Voluntary spending limits, 287
Volunteers, 35, 334
Voter identification laws, 257–259
Voters
demographics, 246–248,
275, 278, 300–301
party affiliation and primary
elections, 309–310
qualifications, 42, 250,
259–260, 272
registration of, 249–252,
271–274, 272
(figure), 360
Voter turnout
constitutional amendments,
71, 74, 76 (figure)
Hispanics, 247
minorities, 288
national and state
comparisons, 276 (table)
Oregon *vs.* Texas, 263
overview, 272–274
party functions, 306
political parties and electoral
competition, 298, 299
presidential primaries
and caucuses, 318
primaries, 300 (figure)
special interests, 343
Voting by mail, 263
Voting equipment, 269–271, 289
Voting on legislation, 120–121
Voting rights
African Americans, 252–256
Constitution of 1836, 52
Constitution of 1845, 55
Constitution of 1866, 57
Constitution of 1876, 65
freed slaves, 16
Hispanics, 256–259
history of, 260–261
horizontal federalism, 43
institutional barriers
to voting, 287
League of United Latin
American Citizens, 332
military, 259–260
NAACP, 66
organized interests, 334